Detroit Studies in Music Bibliography, No. 69

Editor
J. Bunker Clark
University of Kansas

American Operas: A Checklist

by

EDITH BORROFF

edited by

J. Bunker Clark

HARMONIE PARK PRESS   1992

Frontispiece:
Crosby's Opera House (1865), Chicago. Lithograph after a drawing by Louis Kurtz,
published in James W. Sheahan, *Chicago Illustrated,* part 3 (Chicago: Jevne & Almini, March 1866).
Courtesy of Chicago Historical Society.

Printed and bound in the United States of America
Published by
Harmonie Park Press
23630 Pinewood
Warren, Michigan 48091

Library of Congress Cataloging in Publication Data

Borroff, Edith, 1925-
    American operas : a checklist / Edith Borroff ; edited by J.
Bunker Clark.
        p.   c.m. — (Detroit studies in music bibliography; no. 69)
    Includes bibliographical references and index.
    ISBN 0-89990-063-1
    1. Opera—United States—Bibliography.   I. Clark, J. Bunker.
II. Title.   III. Series.
ML128.04B58   1992
782.1′0973 — dc20   92-35617

for my friends

Lyn and Bunker Clark

Contents

Introduction

This study comprises a preliminary listing of operas by composers of the United States. What I have attempted in this study is to make available the knowledge that American opera, far from being simply a short list of works to be classified as exceptions within an essentially European tradition, indeed consists of a vast repertory well worth consideration in its own right.

Essentially, then, this bibliography is simply a list of works, a checklist of operas by composers of the United States, works that I have been able to learn about in eight years of looking for them. It contains well over four thousand titles by over two thousand composers—numbers far in excess of any estimate I have heard. The list itself is vital, for anyone who would be aware of—and proud of—the American heritage in opera.

I call it preliminary because it represents only the works I have been able to learn about in my search. The list is *ipso facto* incomplete, yet it can serve those who would complete it. In that sense it is also exploratory, since it can provide an initial survey that others will be able to continue and emend. It will take a great deal of work by a great many people before anything like a complete bibliography can result.

The list is essentially of works of music: that is, the name of the composer and the title of the opera. All other information is supernumerary, addressed either to the producer or to the scholar.

For the producer I have included the date of the work, its length, the identity of the librettist, and the type of work or type of subject matter when this is not suggested by the title. For the scholar I have included the place of performance of the work, along with the opening date, in order to suggest specific lines of further inquiry. (Actually, both producer and scholar may be interested in all of the data.) But information is extremely spotty, and most entries do not provide all of these data; the information is furnished here if I was able to find it. Not finding a date of performance does not mean the work was not performed. (It is extremely difficult to obtain information about unperformed operas.)

In cases where two performances are listed, it is likely that some revision—even a rewrite—has taken place. Some of these are documented—watch Mira Spektor's *The Housewives' Cantata* evolve before your very eyes: a "revue" in 1973, a "short opera" in 1979, a "full-length opera" in 1980!

Further, if two performances are listed close together in time, perhaps only the second one was staged. But readings can be as important for a composer as staged performances (and many readings are in fact staged).

Of course, the process is frustrating, since it is possible to obtain the fullest information only on those composers and works for whom scholars don't need it. Some 90% of these composers are undocumented in standard sources.

So the study is tantalizing. Operas have been performed in virtually every large city in the United States. According to the *Central Opera Service Bulletin* of 1990,[1] there were 1285 opera companies in the United States in 1989. *Opera Companies and American Opera: A Directory*, issued by the American Music Center, has 66 companies, including one Canadian, "that have shown an interest in performing twentieth century American operas and musical theater works."[2] American opera has grown steadily since the 1954-55 season; the figures show production of 210 operas in that season, none of them American. In the 1988-89 season, 731 operas were produced, 400 of them American. These figures, by the Central Opera Service, are limited to those by composers of the United States—it has a separate list of works by Canadians. The list does not include musicals; these are separately counted, "exclusive of commercial theatres," and, in the 1988-89 season, they amounted to 279 works in addition to the 731 classified as operas. (The criteria of the Central Opera Service are not stated, however.)

The number of cities in which American operas have been produced is well over two hundred, and I have been able to visit only a handful of them. Other scholars will discover many more works produced in other cities.

Problems invade every aspect of this academic adventure. Deciding exactly what comprises an opera is one of them; deciding who qualifies as American is another. Defining opera is possibly only in general terms. For one, I am quite ready to agree that a work designated by its composer as an opera is indeed an opera. For another, I feel strongly that works produced by opera companies as operas should be considered to be operas. Over the years, many works that began outside the operatic genre have entered it. The productions of Jerome Kern's *Showboat* by several opera companies for the 1988-89 season indicates that this work is undergoing such a transformation (there is much evidence that both Kern and his librettist Oscar Hammerstein II thought of this work as an opera).[3] And it is being sung now by singers with operatic rather than show-business training, which will validate and reinforce the transformation.

I have included both pantomime and melodrama (spoken drama with synchronized music), because these works must be offered by opera companies rather than playhouses. They are rare in the United States, but they do exist. In the same spirit I have included a half-dozen dramatic cantatas and oratorios, such as R. Nathaniel Dett's 1937 oratorio *The Ordering of Moses*. The composer, in fact, designated this work as a "Biblical folk scene," and although it was first performed as a cantata (in Cincinnati, Ohio, in 1937), it has indeed been produced as an opera (at the Manhattan School of Music, New York City, in 1976). Undine Smith Moore's *Scenes from the Life of a Martyr* could very well be staged. When I attended a performance of that work in Ann Arbor in 1985, I assumed it to be a concert performance of an opera, and I visualized its staging

---

1. *Central Opera Service Directory/Bulletin* 30, nos. 2-4 (Summer 1990): 323.

2. Compiled by Li-Chen Hwang, edited by Eero Richmond, 1st edition, April 1990.

3. See, for example, the interesting article by Ethan Morddern, "'Show Boat' Crosses Over," *New Yorker*, 3 July 1989, 79-94. He considers (p. 88) the difference between opera and show business singing, stating that the former has the aim of beauty and the latter of personality.

(it could be enormously effective). There is, I believe, an essential difference between a "cantata" and a "dramatic cantata." According to the *Amerigrove* article on George F. Root, by Dena J. Epstein, his *Flower Queen* (1852) "was intended to be staged and is an opera in everything but name."

But no matter what criteria one sets up, individual works will raise questions, and on the fringes I found no certitude. And I imagine that I would make some different decisions now than I did then, both for inclusion and exclusion.

The toughest call is between opera and musical comedy, and that call is getting tougher. It is clear that popular and traditional theater are closer than they used to be. *Exhalations* by Al Carmines, designated as a "musical" in the *Central Opera Service Bulletin* listing operas and music theater works composed by Americans from 1980 to 1989,[4] is described as dealing with "people coping with the 1980s." It is educative and was performed at the Madison Avenue Baptist Church, New York City, in 1984. Such a work seems to me to reside outside the typical view of "musicals," and it is included in my list. But the entire concept of musicals "exclusive of commercial theatres" raises questions; the Central Opera Service drew that line but didn't speak to the issues it raises.

In addition, its survey adds a third category, "music theater works" that bridges "opera" and "musical." I here follow the general policy of including "opera" and "music theater work," but list a "musical" only if its place of performance and its intended audience indicated that it would be appropriate. In all, this involves perhaps a half-dozen works.

The decisions are further complicated by the fact that a number of composers are credited with works from both sides of that spectrum. The breadth of musical vision of American composers is worth noting. Early in the century, Carl Venth composed a "musical play," a "musical extravaganza," a "short music drama," and an "oriental opera." More recently, Stewart Wallace composed a "musical," an "opera," a "musical comedy on the New Testament," and a "rock opera." It is dangerous to categorize such works arbitrarily; I might misrepresent a composer by my own incompleteness. There are no easy answers.

I was most generous with the category of "children's musical," which I confess I find confusing. Dozens of works for children have been presented in the United States in the past few years; these must certainly be of vital importance in tilling the soil so that young people will become adult opera *aficionados*. Such a work as Bonnie Wilder's *The Music Dreaming Man*, about the composer Lowell Mason, contains the seeds of such fruition—it is designated as a "children's musical."[5]

But more than that, I became convinced as I proceeded, seeing works on the same subject variously designated, that producers found the word "musical" more enticing to a prospective young audience than the word "opera," and advertised their productions accordingly. I doubt that a valid distinction exists between a "children's opera" and a "children's musical." One can calibrate the relative time allotted to speech and song, propose a percentage that will be viewed as acceptable for the designation "opera," and enforce a strict obedience from composer and producer. But certainly such a rigid test is made from the

---

4. *Central Opera Service Directory/Bulletin* 30, nos. 2-4 (Summer 1990): 22.

5. Ibid., 143.

wrong direction, a judgment inward rather than an artistic statement outward. It is exclusionary and revives a distinction that bore poor fruit when it was embraced two centuries ago.[6] The heart of the matter would seem to be a simple question: "Is this work *about music*?" If it is, then I welcome it into this bibliography no matter what it is called.

The issue of whether a composer is or was American is, strangely, easier to decide, probably because that kind of decision is essentially arbitrary and the process can be more easily defined. A composer born and educated in the United States, is, of course, ideal for such purposes. And a composer such as Baldwin Bergersen, born in Vienna to American parents and brought home to the United States at the age of six months, is so clear-cut as to need no justification; he too is an American composer. So are most composers who arrived in the United States at the age of six years. But at sixteen, twenty-six, thirty-six, and forty-six—the decision becomes increasingly problematic.

My criterion, though not easily arrived at, proved relatively easy to administer. A composer who arrived as a fully trained adult, such as Kurt Weill, who immigrated to the United States at 35, who turned consciously to American idiom and composed *Knickerbocker Holiday* and *Down in the Valley* (a Kentucky enterprise in which he used folk materials of that area), is to be considered American. Works composed before his arrival in the United States will not be included, unless they have been adapted and produced here—this includes both *Mahagonny* (produced in Baden-Baden in 1927, then in Los Angeles in 1989) and *The Threepenny Opera* (produced in Berlin in 1928, Americanized with the help of Marc Blitzstein and produced in Waltham, Massachusetts, in 1952, then in New York City for over 2500 performances, 1954-61).

Actually, composers coming to the United States generally leave a fairly clear indication of their attitude on this point. Some live in the past and think of themselves as temporary transplants to this country, remaining spiritual aliens here. I honor that choice.

Canadian opera is another kind of problem. It is a large repertory, but I am not knowledgeable in it, and I rather think that the United States should define itself before reaching out either to the north or to the south. With the large representation of Mexican-Americans in the United States (much larger than the representation of Canadian-Americans), it would seem necessary to include Mexicans if one includes Canadians. And what about Central and South Americans? At that point I would face a project that would expand into the unmanageable. These studies, like the surveys of all operatic cities in the United States, await future scholars.

It should be made clear, then, that no decision made on the fringes of such attempts to categorize can ever be entirely satisfactory. And I doubt that any two people would make the same decisions on all of the problem works. But happily the area of doubt is minimal—I estimate it as well under 1% of the total.

In fact, the joys of this list far outweigh its problems, however thorny. It implies an American creative energy and joy that is the very nutmeat of our art and our nation. I found myself singing organa as I typed, troping the implied

---

6. Such works as Weber's *Der Freischütz* and Bizet's *Carmen*, both important in history as well as musical literature, were initially blackballed from production as operas. It is bizarre to think of *Carmen*'s première, before the spoken portions were set to music as recitatives (by an American!) as a comic opera, considering its emotional seriousness.

treasures and probable future studies of American opera. The incomplete data turned into strands of glowing question marks, strings of pearls.

One could produce a cadenza of fascinating bits: short titles such as David Hollister's *TF. . .*, Mirta T. Mulhare's *O.T.*, or Brian Morgan's *s*; long titles such as *The Legend of Etheldethe/wethelberga* by William Pommer, *Chewin' the Blues with Bowling Green John and Harmonica Phil* by Phil Wiggins and John Cephas, or *No Plays No Poetry But Philosophical Reflections Practical Instructions Provocative Prescriptions Opinions and Pointers from a Noted Critic and Playwright* by Neal Kirkwood.

The lengths of the works themselves provide enjoyment: Alan Blank's *Finale: Melange* runs four minutes, David Snow's *Spa Lady from Hell* runs five, Paul Nahay's *Minute Opera/Minute Soap Opera* runs two minutes (one minute for each), and Charles Shere's opera *Ladies Voices*, although five acts, lasts only seven minutes. If nothing else, such whimsies illustrate the difficulties of showing the length in acts or scenes rather than overall time (Roger Zahab's one-act *Hegemony* runs 100 minutes—fourteen times longer than Shere's five-act *Ladies Voices*). Most operas listed by the Central Opera Service are "full length," but that is not defined. I have given overall time when I could; otherwise, the number of acts or scenes. There are many inconsistencies, however: many works are presented by one source as one act and by another source as three acts, for example—in such cases I omitted the information altogether. Some operas are indeed very long: for example, Bob Telson's *The Warrior Ant* lasts twelve hours, and Alan Lloyd's *The Life and Times of Joseph Stalin* lasts thirteen.

I was endlessly fascinated with titles of imagination and suggestiveness: from the last century Benjamin Edward Woolf's *Lawn Tennis: or, Djakh and Djill*; or, more recently, Louis Krohl's *Madame Butterfly Recovers*, or (my own favorite) Alec Wilder's *The Truth about Windmills*.

There are also fascinating details. William Franke Harling, for example, composed jazz operas in 1925 and 1926; Isaac van Grove composed operas fifty years apart (1926 and 1976); Menotti composed *Death of Pierrot* when he was eleven (I too composed an opera at eleven: *Au jardin*, a tale of unrequited love for which I wrote my own libretto, in French, and in which corpse piled upon corpse in the garden in the final scene); and Wendy Fang Chen (born in 1971) composed an opera that was performed at the Metropolitan Opera Guild in New York City in 1986. William Howland's *Sarrona*, composed in 1901, was performed in Italian in Bruges in 1903, in English in New York City in 1910, and in German in Philadelphia in 1911. Tom Johnson turned out a musicological work called *Riemannoper*.

I was personally very much interested in the composers who sang in their own operas—Mabel Daniels, John Jones, Mary Carr Moore, and Mikas Petrauskas—and also in those who conducted their own works: Ethel Leginska, Otto Luening, Marc Blitzstein, Henry Hadley, Jules Jordan, E. Bruce Knowlton, Aldo Franchetti, Everett Helm, Wassili Leps, and Silas Gamaliel Pratt, myself, and Mary Carr Moore (the last being the only composer who both sang and conducted, though not at the same performance!).

But serious questions are raised as well by these works. A substantial number were composed by black composers, and not only those well-known such as William Grant Still, Hale Smith, Dorothy Rudd Moore, T. J. Anderson, and Clarence Cameron White. There have been many operas by lesser-known composers well worth investigating, such as J. Willard Roosevelt, Shirley Graham, Mark Oakland Fax (whose 1967 opera *The Victory Is Won* was performed in

Washington, Baltimore, and New York City, and also in Bermuda), Clarence Bernard Jackson, Betty Jackson King, Penman Lovingood, Normal Lavelle Mennifield, Lena McLin, Sam Rivers, Alvin Singleton, and many others, some of whom, of course, I have not been able to identify. Harry Lawrence Freeman (1869-1954), of Cleveland, who is better known than most American opera composers, most likely composed the greatest number of operas by any American of his generation; I believe that when discussions of Americanism are sufficiently developed, his work should be looked at again. He composed two tetralogies, and also dealt with general American issues, African issues, Jewish issues, native American issues, and jazz. His works were performed in Cleveland, Denver, New York City, and in Mexico. Or Evelyn Pittman (born in Oklahoma in 1910), whose third opera *Cousin Esther* (1954) was performed in Paris and New York City (twice) and broadcast in 1963 as part of the American Music Festival.

Pittman also represents well the many women composers whose operas are listed in this study. I cannot claim to have an accurate number of women: is "R. Graf" a man or woman? Or R. R. Rescia, H. G. Tregillus, N. Winter, M. Witni, S. Frankenpohl, R. Valenti? And there are foreign names that do not suggest the gender of the bearer to me, such as Noa Ain, Shellen Lubin, or Bright Sheng, and the unisex names of Kim or Pat. The number of identifiably women composers runs about 11% until World War II and then goes up to about 15%. Their presence raises questions. In my count at about the half-way mark, women were at 12% of the total, in composition and performance, but under 1% in publication. My recent work has drawn the conclusion that the practical, apprenticeship venues did not discriminate against women, but that the university-controlled venues did—and, since composing and production were apprenticeship matters and publication a university matter, I am confirmed in these earlier conclusions by the history of the treatment of women in opera. Women such as Eusebia Hunkins, Emma R. Steiner (a conductor who led performances of over six thousand operas and composed nine), Lucille Crews March (who won a Pulitzer Prize), and Rosalie Balmer Cale (operas in 1897 and 1907) are waiting to be studied.

So, of course, are many men. Edward Maryon (1867-1965), for example, composed seventeen operas, including a heptalogy; Richard Winslow composed four operas that were performed in four different cities; S. Woodward's *The Deed of Gift* dates from 1822. And of many others only the names are known: Irving M. Wilson's *King Zim of Zniba* (lovely title!), John Wilson's *Baker's Dozen*, Winifred Wolf's *The Happy Ending*.

Many works are undated in my sources, and the details of these must come to light through regional and local studies. Perhaps my work will encourage such studies. I hope so. I can be of little help, even though the titles themselves frequently suggest a period. Conrad Bryant Schaeffer's *Bridges of Stars: or, The Impressment* suggests a nineteenth-century ambiance, both because of the double title and because of the use of the word "impressment," which is now obsolete. Of course, more is likely to be known about a new work than an old one.

But the overall consideration of such a vast repertory and so broad a scope of interests and types must lead to the single most important question: is there a tradition of American opera? My answer is affirmative. But its most important characteristic (unfortunately) is negative; that is, American opera is not European opera and should not be held to the European template for analysis and discussion. We have finally reached the point of considering American cuisine, American dance, American literature, and American painting as rich arts not dependent upon foreign definitions or seals of approval. Unhappily, music has not—and this is passing strange, since the United States is now in a position of world leadership in the international musical scene.

The problems here, too, are thorny, for it is the line of least resistance to compare American works against the ideal we all know best, and to consider them wanting to the extent that they do not conform to the European ideal. Martin Bookspan skirted this in a recent article, but the headline writer zoomed in on operatic considerations of an exclusionary nature by giving the title "Is There a Great American Opera?,"[7]—"great" by European standards, that is. But the title did pick up on Bookspan's statement that "while none may eventually be regarded as the Great American Opera, all have their points of musical or archival interest." Bookspan may skirt the question, but he did limit the article to works that are closest to the European ideal. This was forced upon him through the subject itself, which was, in fact, a review of the recent release of operas by Copland, Moore, Barber, and Ward on CDs. These releases, remastered reissues of earlier performances, were selected by the same university types who have restricted the publication of works by blacks and by women, and who most fervently work to maintain the European ideals of music in the minds and hearts of the American public. Reviewers deal with American operas in European terms. The marvelous energy and directness of American works, their rhythmic excitement, is ignored in favor of discussions of harmony and grandeur; the virtues of the small orchestra are ignored and the standard of the symphony orchestra is waved like a pennant. This is not the place either to preach or to fight. I prefer not to be contentious, but simply to state that when American music is reviewed on its own terms it comes off very well indeed. Any work of art must be examined on its own terms if we are to understand or appreciate it. I will further note that American opera has suffered also from European-ideal-infused performances. In a recent lecture I discussed Scott Joplin's *Treemonisha* in this regard.[8]

American composers as a whole prefer chamber opera to grand opera, and they are marvelous orchestrators who prefer a pit orchestra to a symphony orchestra—the pungency of the small group more than the grandness of the larger one. The stunning scoring in Lee Hoiby's *Summer and Smoke*, for example, is pithy and vitalizing.

The average American opera is fairly short (any estimate is guesswork, but if you want an estimate it is 45 minutes). The American opera composer strives to create a work not yet heard, a work very much itself and not poured into some European mold. (I speak for myself, of course, in my latest work, produced in 1977, but I know I speak also for others.) The average recent American opera is on an American subject (many earlier ones were too, but now American subjects comprise the majority), fewer and fewer on dark subjects. It has a male composer and a female librettist. And it was performed anywhere but

---

7. *New York Times*, 16 December 1990.

8. I compared it with Richard Strauss's *Salome* (chosen for its closeness in time). Critics have put down *Treemonisha* for lacking the size, the "operatic" voices, and the grandeur of *Salome*, but that regards what is not there, rather than what is. Why not reverse the critical direction and discuss what is not there in *Salome*: lean clean sound, interesting rhythm, clarity? And Strauss called for an orchestra of 108 in *Salome*, and surely no soprano in her right mind would choose that losing battle.

in the "big" houses, which are the houses most firmly stamped with European concepts. In fact, American operas have been presented in well over two hundred American cities and towns, all over the map.

Perhaps the most America-conscious of American operatic cities is Chicago, where American works have been given a marvelous consideration. It was the city of the David Bispham Medal, established by Eleanor Freer and Edith Rockefeller McCormick in 1924, and presented to many composers through the early forties. The medal was an ideal way to foster American opera, since, once the master was made, it was relatively cheap to produce, and since the attendant publicity (in Chicago, in the home town of the composer, and the city of the opera's production) was something splendid. Chicago has been a fascinating opera center for over a hundred years, but of course it has centered in European opera rather than American. St. Louis is another important center for American opera. I could name others: Waterford, Connecticut; Omaha, Nebraska; Glens Falls, New York; Des Moines, Iowa; Houston, Texas; and of course the many houses in New York City, from the 92nd Street Y (Young Men's Hebrew Association) to Golden Fleece and OPERA America Showcase.

It seems to me that an excellent project for those who would learn (and teach) our American operatic tradition would be to seek out operas on the same source composed a generation or more apart and perform them as a double or triple bill: *Robin Hood* by Hewitt (1800) and De Koven (1890); *Rip Van Winkle* by Bristow (1855), Jordan (1897), and Manning (1932); *The Scarlet Letter* by Damrosch (1896), Giannini ((1938), and Kaufmann (1961).

I have a sense of the vigor of American opera through the works I have examined, from Eleanor Freer's *The Brownings in Italy* (at the Newberry Library in Chicago—a fine repository, in fact, for American music in general and opera in particular) to Ross Lee Finney's *Weep Torn Land* (about the American West) and *The Computer Marriage* (soon to be finished—a marvelous theatrical romp), and T. J. Anderson's *Thomas Jefferson's Orbiting Minstrels and Contraband* (a multimedia work of wonderful exhilaration and joy). These operas, in fact, can bracket the concept of opera in the United States: Freer's, not on an American subject but exploring harmonic juxtapositions in a manner worth looking at as we scan the scope of style in the last century; Finney's, so marvelous a combining of musical, poetic, and theatrical elements in a new and newly American style; and Anderson's, as energetic and as American as one could ask, with its huge scope of musical types (from jazz to electronic, and much between) and its exciting stage presence. It is not the point to ask how closely these works fit the European ideal, and it is not the point to burden them with vain wondering if any of them is a "great" opera (which is, of course, a subtle—or not so subtle—way of putting them into a European box). The valid questions are not arbitrary; they do not deal with European suitability, or with a scorecard of points for methodology on some theoretical basis. The valid questions deal with *responses*—of audiences. Many opera companies are financing productions of European operas with their American offerings.

Two summers ago I was treated on my birthday to attendance at a production of Sousa's *El Capitan* offered by the Skylight Opera Theater in Milwaukee, Wisconsin. It was a marvelous evening of marvelous music. I attended that performance as a human being, a birthday honoree, not as a "highly educated woggle-bug," and I loved it. Why should I question that?

Edith Borroff
State University of New York at Binghamton
January 1992

Editor's note

Out of a sense of respect and admiration for Edith Borroff and enthusiasm for her project, I decided to invest more time than is usual for an in-house editor. After converting the draft from her computer program to mine, I first began to doublecheck it through *Amerigrove*; and eventually we both used that work with an exchange of my copy through the mails. Subsequently I went through the following for more information (see pp. xxi-xxiii, below, for abbreviations): new edition of *Baker's*; Kornick; Anderson; *Annals*; *Who's Who*; Cohen; Porter; *WhoAm*; Hipsher; Morton/Collins; Schoep. Finally I laid out the individual pages, obtained a few appropriate illustrations, and made the final computer printout.

J. Bunker Clark
University of Kansas
September 1992

Sources

Several organizations have been helpful in this study. Listing ACA after a composer's name indicates that the composer is a member of the American Composers Alliance; AMC means that scores are housed at the American Music Center; ASCAP means that the composer is a member of the American Society of Composers, Authors, and Publishers. Listing *COS* after an opera indicates that it is listed in the *Central Opera Service Bulletin*. Rebecca Hodell Kornick's *Recent American Opera: A Production Guide* (1991) was consulted for amplifying information in the editing stage of this study.

I recommend that studies of any composer begin with these sources, double-checking the information here and looking for more. I did not mention theaters in all cities, for example, since there is little choice of performance place in most small towns, and often my sources gave cities only. I recommend further that when a city is given, both theaters and universities be checked, since colleges and universities sponsor many opera productions. Older operas can be checked in the books and articles listed after the organizations.

Organizations

ACA   American Composers Alliance
170 West 74th St.
New York, NY 10023
212/362-8900

ACA provides brochures listing works of their composers by type of work; this includes a brochure on operas.

ACE/CFE American Composers Edition/Composers Facsimile Edition

These are part of ACA; composers' scores are ordered from ACE (same address and phone).

AMC   American Music Center
30 W. 26th St., Suite 1001
New York, NY 10010-2011
212/366-5260

ASCAP   American Society of Composers, Authors, and Publishers
         One Lincoln Plaza
         New York, NY 10023
         212/595-3050

AMRC   American Music Research Center
         College of Music, Campus Box 301
         University of Colorado
         Boulder, C0 80309-0301
         303/492-7540

         AMRC houses many interesting opera scores. The collection
         was founded by Sister Dominic Ray, O.P., at Dominican
         College in San Raphael, California.

COS   Central Opera Service
         Lincoln Center Plaza
         Metropolitan Opera
         New York, NY 10023
         212/957-9871

         COS has gone out of business, but I imagine that their Bulletins
         will be available for some time to come. COS published four
         directories that include lists of all American operas dating from
         specific years:

         COS-1: *Directory of American Contemporary Operas*, vol. 10,
         no. 1 (December 1967), containing works from 1930 to 1966.

         COS-2: *Directory of American and Foreign Contemporary
         Operas and American Opera Premières, 1967-1975*, vol. 17, no.
         2 (Winter 1975).

         COS-3: *Directory of American and Foreign Contemporary
         Operas and American Opera Premières, 1975-1980*, vol. 22, no.
         2 (1980).

         COS-4: *Directory of Contemporary Operas & Music Theater
         Works and North American Premieres, 1980-1989*, vol. 30, nos.
         2-4 (Summer 1990).

Opera America
777 14th St., N.W., Suite 520
Washington, DC 20005
202/347-9262

         OA brings out a yearly list of all productions planned by
         American opera companies for the following season.

Publications

Amerigrove	*The New Grove Dictionary of American Music.* 4 vols. London: Macmillan, 1986.
Anderson	E. Ruth Anderson, comp. *Contemporary American Composers: A Biographical Dictionary.* 2nd ed. Boston: G. K. Hall, 1982.
Annals	*Annals of the Metropolitan Opera: The Complete Chronicle of Performances and Artists . . . 1883-1985.* 2 vols. Boston: G. K. Hall, 1989.
ASCAP	*ASCAP Biographical Dictionary.* 4th ed. New York: R. R. Bowker, 1980.
Baker's	*Baker's Biographical Dictionary of Musicians.* 8th ed., rev. Nicolas Slonimsky. New York: Schirmer Books, 1992. 5th ed., 1958; 6th ed., 1978; 7th ed., 1984.
Cohen	Cohen, Aaron I. *International Encyclopedia of Women Composers.* 2nd ed. 2 vols. New York: Books & Music, 1987.
	Cohen, Frederic. "A Manifesto for Opera in the United States." *Juilliard Review* 4 (Fall 1957): 17-35.
	Croissant, Charles R. *Opera Performances in Video Format: A Checklist of Commercially Released Recordings.* MLA Index and Bibliography Series, 26. Canton, MA: Music Library Association, 1991.
	Fleckten, Twila Kathryn. *A Survey of Contemporary American Opera.* B.S. thesis, Department of Music, Skidmore College, 1962.
	Gillis, Don, and Barre Hill. *A List of American Operas Compiled for the American Opera Workshop of the National Music Camp.* Interlochen, Mich.: Interlochen Press, ca. 1959.
Hipsher	Hipsher, Edward Ellsworth. *American Opera and Its Composers.* Philadelphia: Theodore Presser, 1927; reprint of 2nd ed. of 1934, with introduction by H. Earle Johnson, New York: Da Capo, 1978.
Morton/Collins	Morton, Brian, and Pamela Collins, eds. *Contemporary Composers.* Chicago and London: St. James Press, 1992.
	Johnson, Carl. "American Opera at the Met: 1883-1983." *American Music Teacher,* February/March 1984.
	Johnson, Edward. "The Future of Opera in America." *Proceedings of the National Federation of Music Clubs* 1 (1935): 29-32.
Johnson	Johnson, H. Earle. *Operas on American Subjects.* New York: Coleman-Ross, 1964.
Kornick	Kornick, Rebecca Hodell. *Recent American Opera: A Production Guide.* New York: Columbia University Press, 1991.
Krohn	Krohn, Ernst. *A Century of Missouri Music.* St. Louis: privately printed, 1924; reprint, New York: Da Capo, 1970.
	Laufer, Beatrice. "Problems in Writing an Opera." *Bulletin of American Composers Alliance* 6 (Autumn 1956): 11-12.

Mattfeld, Julius. *A Handbook of American Operatic Premières, 1731-1962*. Detroit Studies in Music Bibliography, 5. Detroit: Information Coordinators, 1963.

Pan Pipes, quarterly of Sigma Alpha Iota. Mendota, IL: Wayside Press.

Parsons, Charles H., comp. *The Mellen Opera Reference Index*. Lewiston/Queenston: Edwin Mellen Press, 1986-89. Vols. 1-4: *Opera Composers and Their Works*; vols. 7-8: *Opera Premières: A Geographical Index*; vol. 9: *Opera Subjects*.

Peltz, Mary Ellis. "American Schoolroom Opera." *Opera* 9 (February 1958): 88-92.

Porter   Porter, Susan L. *With an Air Debonair: Musical Theatre in America, 1785-1815*. Washington: Smithsonian Institution Press, 1991. Appendix A: "A Preliminary Checklist of Musical Entertainments Performed in the United States, 1785-1815."

Rodríguez   Rodríguez, José, ed. *Music and Dance in California*. Hollywood, CA: Bureau of Musical Research, 1940.

Ross, Anne, ed. *The Opera Dictionary*. New York, 1961.

Schleifer   Schleifer, Martha Furman, ed. *American Opera and Music for the Stage: Eighteenth and Nineteenth Centuries* and *American Opera and Music for the Stage: Early Twentieth Century*. Three Centuries of American Music, 5-6. Boston: G. K. Hall, 1990.

Schoep   Schoep, Arthur, ed., and Brenda Lualdi, assistant ed. *The National Opera Association Catalog of Contemporary American Operas*. Denton, TX: North Texas State University, 1976.

Schonberg, Harold. "Chicago Lyric." *New York Times*, 3 December 1961.

"Settings for American Opera." *Modern Music* 20 (March-April 1943): 180-81.

Sonneck-Upton   Sonneck, Oscar George Theodore, rev. William Treat Upton. *A Bibliography of Early Secular American Music (18th Century)*. Washington: Library of Congress Music Division, 1945; reprint, New York: Da Capo, 1964.

Southern   Southern, Eileen. *Biographical Dictionary of Afro-American and African Musicians*. Westport, Conn.: Greenwood Press, 1982.

"The Story of American Opera." *The Triangle of Mu Phi Epsilon*, January 1964.

Teasdale, May Silva. *Handbook of Twentieth-Century Opera*, 1938.

Thompson's   *The International Cyclopedia of Music and Musicians*, ed. Oscar Thompson. 11th ed., ed. Bruce Bohle. New York: Dodd, Mead & Co, 1985.

Virga, Patricia H. *The American Opera to 1790*. Ann Arbor: UMI Research Press, 1082.

WhoAm   *Who's Who in American Music: Classical*. 2nd ed. New York: R. R. Bowker, 1985.

Who's Who   *International Who's Who in Music and Musicians' Directory*. 12th ed., 1990-91. Cambridge, England: International Who's Who in Music, 1990.

Wolfe Wolfe, Richard J. *Secular Music in America, 1801-1825: A Bibliography.* 3 vols. New York Public Library, 1964.

Publishers

(Information mainly from *Music Publishers Sales Agency List, 1992*, by
Music Publishers' Assocation of the United States,
National Music Publishers' Association,
and Church Music Publishers' Association)

(see also the listing in Kornick)

Aquarius Music, Long Eddy, NY 12760
Boosey & Hawkes, 24 East 21st St., New York, NY 10010
Broude Brothers, 141 White Oaks Rd., Williamstown, MA 01267
CCP/Belwin Music, 15800 N.W. 48th Ave., Miami, FL 33014
Chappell & Co., distributed by Hal Leonard
Choudens, distributed by C. F. Peters
John Church, distributed by Theodore Presser
I. E. Clark, St. John's Rd., Schulenburg, TX 78956
Franko Columbo, distributed by CCP/Belwin
Concord, distributed by Henri Elkan Music Publishing Co., Box 7720, FDR
    Station, New York, NY 10150-1914
Da Capo Press, 233 Spring St., New York, NY 10013; ordering address: 150 Bay
    St., 7th floor, Bay City, NJ 07302
Departed Feathers Music, 245 Chestnut St., Cambridge, MA 02139
Oliver Ditson, distributed by Theodore Presser
Faber Music, London, distributed Hal Leonard
Carl Fischer, 62 Cooper Square, New York, NY 10003
H. T. FitzSimons, distributed by Antara Music Group, Box 210, Alexandria, IN
    46001-0201
Harold Flammer, distributed by Shawnee Press, Waring Dr., Delaware Water Gap,
    PA 18327
Sam Fox, distributed by Plymouth Music Co., 170 Northeast 33rd St., Fort
    Lauderdale, FL 33334
Frank, distributed by Hal Leonard
Jane Ferry Associates, 20 Kingsley Place, St. Louis, MO 63112
General Music Publishing Co., 53 West 54th St., New York, NY 10019
H. W. Gray Co., distributed by CCP/Belwin
Highgate Press, distributed by E. C. Schirmer Music Co., 138 Ipswich St., Boston,
    MA 02215
Huntzinger, distributed by Willis
Interlochen Press, distributed by FEMA Music Publications, Box 395, Naperville,
    IL 60566
Jerona Music Corp., P.O. Box 5010, South Hackensack, NJ 07606-4210
Lance Productions, 353 West 57th St., New York, NY 10019
Hal Leonard Publishing Corp., 7777 West Bluemound Rd., Milwaukee, WI 53213
Leeds, distributed by Hal Leonard
E. B. Marks, distributed by Hal Leonard

MMB Music Inc. (formerly Magna Music-Baton), 10370 Industrial Page Blvd., St. Louis, MO 63121

Music Corporation of America, distributed by Hal Leonard

Mills Music, distributed by CCP/Belwin

Not Nice Music, 720 Greenwich St, 5C, New York, NY 10014

Novello Publications, distributed by Theodore Presser

Oxford University Press, 200 Madison Ave., New York, NY 10016

C. F. Peters Corp., 373 Park Ave. South, New York, NY 10016

Theodore Presser Co., Presser Place, Bryn Mawr, PA 19010

G. Ricordi & Co., distributed by Boosey & Hawkes

G. Schirmer, distributed by Hal Leonard

Schotts Sohne, distributed by European American Music Distributors Corp., 2480 Industrial Blvd., Paoli, PA 19301

Seesaw Music Corp., 2067 Broadway, New York, NY 10023

Shawnee Press, Waring Dr., Delaware Water Gap, PA 18327

Southern Music Co., Box 329, San Antonio, TX 78292

Southern Music Publishing Co., distributed by Theodore Presser

STEORRA, 243 West End Ave., Suite 907, New York, NY 10023

Tams-Witmark Music, 757 Third Ave., New York, NY 10017

Tams-Witmark Music Library, 560 Lexington Ave., New York, NY 10022

Walker Publications, 409 S. Delaware Ave., Tampa, FL 33606

Waterloo Music Co. 3 Regina St North, Waterloo, Ontario N2J 4A5, Canada

Weintraub Music Co., distributed by Music Sales Corp., 5 Bellvale Rd., Chester, NY 10918

Willis Music Co., 7380 Industrial Blvd., Florence, KY 41042

American Operas:

A Checklist

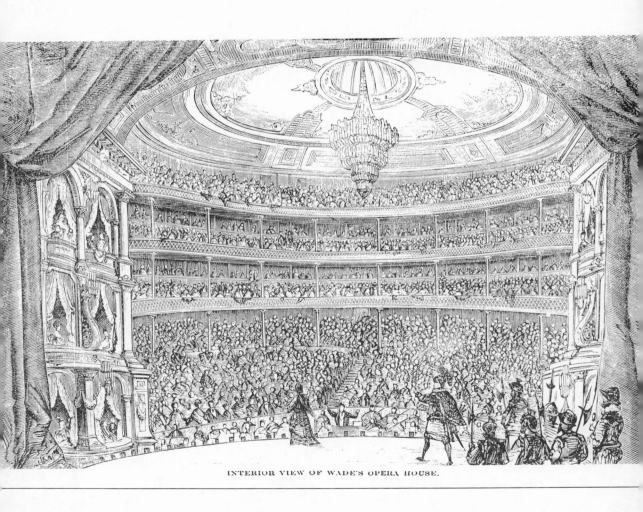

INTERIOR VIEW OF WADE'S OPERA HOUSE.

Wade's Opera House, San Francisco, 1876.
Published in B. E. Lloyd, *Lights and Shades in San Francisco* (San Francisco, 1876).
Courtesy of the California State Library.

American Operas

Hyphen indicates unknown date

Anonymous

1798   *Americania and Elutheria: or, A New Tale of the Genii.* Performed Charleston, SC, ?February 1798.

1789   *The Better Sort: or, The Girl of Spirit* (an "operatical, comical farce"). Published in Boston in 1789.

1783   *Columbus: or, The Discovery of America.* Performed Baltimore, 21 March 1783.

c 1801   *Federation Triumphant in the Steady Hearts of Connecticut Alone: or, The Turnpike Road to a Fortune.* Performed Hartford, CT.

1787   *May Day in Town: or, New York in an Uproar.* Performed New York, 18 May 1787.

1794   *Slave in Algiers: or, A Struggle for Freedom.* Performed Philadelphia, 22 December 1794.

1803   *The Story of Columbus.* Published in 1803 by D. Longworth, New York.

1812   *Yankee Chronology: or, Huzza for the Constitution* (1 act). Performed New York.

Abbott, Michael

1983   *The All American Girls* (libretto by Ellen Fitzhugh and Tom Cone). NEA grant.

Aborn, Lora

1975   *The Gift of the Magi* (1 act; after O. Henry). Performed Oak Park, IL, December 1975.

1976   *The Secret Life of Walter Mitty* (1 act; after James Thurber). Performed October 1976.

Achter, Morton (b. 1937; on faculty of Otterbein College in Ohio)

1957   *Il Principessa Ronzoni* (comedy-burlesque; 18 minutes). First performed at the Massachusetts Institute of Technology, Cambridge, when the composer was an undergraduate there. Later published by Interlochen Press, MI.

Ackerman, Jean

1989   *Compound Interest.* Performed Monterey, CA, 10 March 1989.

Acosta, Jaime
  1987   *Remote Control*, with José Garcia and Tomas Rodriguez (libretto, in
        English and Spanish, by Rosalba Rolan). Performed by Pregones
        Puerto Rican Theater Collective, New York, 30 December 1987.

Adair, James (b. Quincy, IL, 21 September 1909; *Who's Who*)
  -   *Isolde and the Shortstop* (also listed as *Isolde of the Shortstop*) (1
      act—28 minutes; libretto by Thomas K. Baker). Listed in *COS*-1.
  -   *Jean Marie* (1 act—8 minutes; radio opera).
  -   *The Scarlet Letter*.

Adams, John (b. Worcester, MA, 15 February 1947; *Amerigrove*)
  1987   *Nixon in China* (145 minutes; libretto by Alice Goodman).
        Commission by Houston Grand Opera, Brooklyn Academy,
        Kennedy Center, and Netherlands Opera. Excerpts performed at
        the Guggenheim Museum, New York, 2 November 1986.
        Performed San Francisco, 21 May 1987, and Houston, 22 October
        1987. Recording: Nonesuch 79177-2. Kornick.
  1991   *The Death of Klinghoffer* (libretto by Alice Goodman; on the
        hijacking of the Achille Lauro in 1985). Performed at Théâtre
        Royal de la Monnaie, Brussels, Belgium, 19 March 1991, then at
        Brooklyn Academy of Music, 5 September 1991. See Nancy
        Malitz, "Front Page to Opera Stage," *New York Times Magazine*,
        25 August 1991, 34.

Adams, John Luther (b. Meridian, MS, 23 January 1953; Anderson)
  1987   *Giving Birth to Thunder*; *Sleeping with His Daughter*; *Coyote Builds
        North America* (American Indian stories compiled and written for
        the stage by Barry Lopez). *Coyote Builds North America* was
        performed Juneau, AK, 29 October 1987; all three of them there
        on 1 November 1987.
  -   *Suisitna, Sleeping Lady* (on a Te'naina legend). Projected for
      Anchorage Opera, 1994-95.

Adams, Leslie (b. Cleveland, 30 December 1932; Anderson)
  1986   *Blake* (libretto by Daniel Mayers after Martin R. Daleny's novel
        Blake: or, The Huts of America, 1859, about slavery). Excerpts
        performed Hudson, Cleveland, and Oberlin, OH, in the period
        1983-85. See Yvonne C. Williams, "Leslie Adams and the Making
        of the Opera *Blake*: An Interview with the Composer," in *New
        Perspectives on Music: Essays in Honor of Eileen Southern*, ed.
        Josephine Wright with Samuel A. Floyd, Jr., Detroit Monographs
        in Musicology/Studies in Music, 10 (this publisher, 1992).

Addison, George
  1982   *Sodom* (an opera about moral choices). Reading, OPERA America
        Showcase, 1982.

Addiss, Stephen (b. New York, 2 April 1935; Anderson; *WhoAm*; *Who's Who*)
  1960   *Love Is a Science* (chamber opera). Reading, Living Theatre, New
        York. Listed in *COS*-4. Former title: *A Tree, a Rock, a Cloud*.

Adlam, Basil
- *Trilby*, with Roy Benowitz and John Bowden (libretto by John Tratmer and Robert Day after George Du Maurier).

Adler, Marvin Stanley (b. Bronx, NY, 25 February 1938; *WhoAm*)
1967   *Brock's Place*, with Charles Levy. Performed Lincoln Center, New York, 6 February 1967.

Adler, Samuel H. (b. Mannheim, Germany, 4 March 1928; to U.S. in 1939; *Amerigrove*; *Who's Who*)
1959   *The Outcast of Poker Flat* (1 act; after Bret Harte). Performed Denton, TX, 8 June 1962, and University of Alabama, 1977.
1971   *The Wrestler* (1 act; libretto by Judith Stampfer after the biblical story of Jacob). Performed Dallas, TX.
1973   *The Lodge of Shadows* ("music drama" for baritone, dancers, orchestra; 1 act—40 minutes; libretto by Jarold Ramsey). NEA grant. Performed Fort Worth, TX, 3 May 1988.
1976   *The Disappointment*. New music to Andrew Barton's opera of 1767, with Jerry Graue. Published as Recent Researches in American Music, 3-4 (Madison: A-R Editions, 1976). Recorded by Turnabout. *See* Barton, Andrew.

Adolphe, Bruce (b. New York, 31 May 1955; *WhoAm*)
1982   *The Tell-Tale Heart* (1 act—50 or 60 minutes; libretto by composer after Poe). Performed by Opera Theatre of Boston, 22 January 1982, and New York Chamber Opera Co., 4 November 1988. Kornick.
1982   *Mikhoels the Wise* (2 acts—150 minutes; libretto by Mel Gordon, based on the life of Solomon Mikhailovich Mikhoels). Performed at the 92nd Street Y, New York, 8 May 1982. Kornick. Published by Galaxy.
1983   *The False Messiah* (2 acts—150 minutes; libretto by Mel Gordon, based on the life of Shabtai Zvi). Performed at the 92nd Street Y, New York, 9 April 1983. Kornick.
1989   *Sharehi (Dancing Stories)* ("chamber music dance theatre piece" on five American Indian stories).

Aglinskas, Peter
1989   *Steel Grin* (libretto by Dan Sutherland). One act performed by Chicago Lyric Theater Showcase, Chicago, 1 November 1989.

Ahlin, Lee
1988   *Charlotte's Web* (children's opera after E. B. White). Performed by American Stage, St. Petersburg, FL, 20 October 1988.

Ahlstrom, David (b. Lancaster, NY, 22 February 1927; Anderson; Schoep; *WhoAm*; *Who's Who*)
1953   *The Open Window* (1 act; libretto by composer). Performed Cincinnati, 1 March 1953.
1953   *Three Sisters Who Are Not Sisters* (1 act [Schoep: 3 acts]; melodrama; text by Gertrude Stein based on her play of the same name), revised 1962. Performed Cincinnati, 1 March 1953; *Baker's*: San Francisco, 17 September 1982.

1954   *Charlie's Uncle* (libretto by composer; 1 act). Performed Cincinnati, and Columbus, IN, April 1954.

1975   *Wicked Was He That Took Away the Flowers* (1 act—10 minutes; libretto by composer after Boccaccio's *Decameron*). Performed at National Opera Association convention, Detroit, MI, December 1962, and at National Association of Teachers of Singing convention, Indianapolis, December 1975.

1982   *Doctor Faustus Lights the Light* (1 act—45 minutes; libretto after Gertrude Stein's play of the same name). Performed San Francisco, 29 October 1982.

1982   *America, I Love You* (3 acts; libretto by e. e. cummings after his poems). Performed San Francisco, 12 December 1982. (*Baker's* indicates first performance was in San Francisco, 25 June 1983.)

1983   *The Secret Box with the Big Brass Combination Lock.*

1983   *The Tumbler of Notre Dame* (chamber opera).

1984   *The Bishop's Horse.* Performed San Francisco, 19 May 1984.

1985   *Aesop's Fables* (children's opera). Performed San Francisco, April 1986.

1986   *The Song of the Golden Fish.* Performed San Francisco, May 1986.

1986   *On Tepeyac Hill* (on the story of Our Lady of Guadalupe). Performed San Francisco, November 1986.

1990   *The Birds.* Performed San Francisco, May 1990.

-    *My Heart's in the Highlands* (2 acts; libretto after William Saroyan's play of the same name).

Ahrold, Frank (b. Long Beach, CA, 12 December 1931; ASCAP; Anderson)

-    *The Spider and the Fly* (1 act—35 minutes; madrigal opera after poem by Mary Howitt; Anderson: ballet). Published by Belwin-Mills.

-    *The Tour Guide* (1 act; monodrama; libretto by R. L. Diggers). Published by Belwin-Mills.

-    *The View* (1 act; dramatic allegory; libretto by R. L. Diggers). Published by Belwin-Mills.

Ain, Noa (b. 1941; ASCAP; Cohen)

(She writes her own librettos.)

1982   *Bring on the Bears.* Performed at Lenox Art Center, Stockbridge, MA, summer 1982.

1984   *Trio* (1 act—60-70 minutes; jazz/gospel chamber opera; libretto by composer). Performed Philadelphia, 28 June 1984 (Kornick: American Music Theatre Festival, Philadelphia, July 1984).

1988   *The Outcast* (on the story of Ruth and Naomi). Reading at Opera Ebony, New York, 11 December 1988; staged at Opera Ebony, 19 June 1990.

Aitken, Hugh (b. New York, 7 September 1924; *Amerigrove*; *Who's Who*)

1975   *Fables* (chamber opera; 2 acts—90 minutes; libretto by composer on the La Fontaine/Aesop poems). Commissioned by the Elizabeth Sprague Coolidge Foundation. Performed at Library of Congress, 1 November 1975. Recording available. Kornick.

1981   *Felipe* (3 acts; libretto by composer after Cervantes).

Albert, Thomas (b. Lebanon, PA, 14 December 1948; Anderson)
1976   '*Lizbeth* (also listed as *Elizabeth*; 1 act—60 minutes; on the story of Lizzie Borden). Performed at Shenandoah Conservatory, Winchester, VA, 18 November 1976.

Albright, Lois (b. 1904; Cohen)
1955   *Hopitu* (*Hopi People*; *Hopity*) (1 act; libretto by M. W. Billingsley). Performed New York.
\-   *Saul and the Medium*. Listed in *COS*-3.

Albright, William (b. Gary, IN, 20 October 1944; ASCAP; *Amerigrove*; *Who's Who*)
1978   *The Magic City* (libretto by G. Garrett). Guggenheim Fellowship.

Alderman, Pauline (b. 16 January 1893 in Oregon; d. Los Angeles, 11 November [Cohen: 22 June] 1983)
1930   *Bombastes Furioso* (after a play by William Barnes Rhodes, a farce). Performed Los Angeles, 30 April 1930, and Frankfurt, Germany, 1938.
1941   *Come on Over*.

Aldrich, David (b. Covington, KY, 1951; ASCAP)
1982   *Gorey Stories* (libretto by Stephen Currens after stories by Edmond Gorey). Performed WPA Theatre, New York, 1982.

Aleksis, Aleksandras
1919   *Uz Tevyne* (*For the Native Land*) (2 acts). Premièred, in Lithuanian, Waterbury, CT.

Alexander, Connie, with Elizabeth Swados, et al.
1988   *Mythos Oedipus* (dance opera). *See* Swados, Elizabeth.

Alexander, Roland, with Sam Rivers and Emory Taylor
1978   *Hodges & Co.* (2 acts; on black cowboys in the American West). Performed by Harlem Opera Co., Houston, TX, June 1978.

Alexander, William (b. Lompoc, CA, 8 November 1927; AMC; *WhoAm*)
1972   *The Monkey's Paw* (libretto by composer). Performed at Edinboro State College, PA, 13 November 1972.
1980   *Samson at Gaza*. Performed at Edinboro State College, PA, 1980.

Allen, Gilbert
1934   *Steal Away* (1 act). Performed at 138th Street Y, New York, 26 July 1934.

Allen, John
1971   *Young Abe Lincoln*, with Victor Ziskin, Richard Bernstein, and Joan Javits. Performed New York, February 1971.

Allen, Judith. *See* Shatin, Judith

Allen, Paul Hastings (b. Hyde Park, MA, 28 November 1883; d. Boston, 28
September 1952; *Amerigrove*; Hipsher)
(N.B.: *Baker's*, 7th ed., and *Amerigrove* indicate that Allen
composed 12 operas; *Thompson's*, 13.)

1911   *O munasterio* (2 parts, 1 hour). Performed Florence, Italy.

1912   *Il filtro* (1 act). Performed Genoa, Italy, 26 October 1913 (*Baker's*:
26 October 1912).

1916   *L'ultimo dei Moicani* (3 acts; libretto by Zangarini from James
Fenimore Cooper's *The Last of the Mohicans*). Performed at
Politeamo Fiorentino, Florence, Italy, 24 February 1916.
Published by Ricordi.

1913   *Milda* (1 act). Performed Venice, Italy, 14 June 1913. Published
by Sonzogno.

1921   *Cleopatra* (libretto after the melodrama by Sardou). Commission
from its publisher, Sonzogno, of Milan.

1931   *La piccola Figaro* (*Little Miss Figaro* (opera buffa; libretto by
Golisciani). Perhaps the same as *Mamzelle Figaro* (1 hour),
performed Lindenhurst, NY, 20 March 1948.

  -    *I fiori* (*The Flowers* (based on a Spanish melodrama by the Quintero
brothers).

  -    *The Love Potion*. Published by Sonzogno.

Allen, Terry

1988   *The Mormon Project*. NEA grant. Performed at the Guthrie
Theatre, Minneapolis, 1990-91 season.

Allgood, Dexter

1987   *Brown Alice* (libretto by Marie Thomas after Lewis Carroll).
Performed at New York College, January 1987.

Alper, Steven M.

1987   *Minute by Minute* (libretto by Sarah Knapp). Performed by Musical
Theatre Works, New York, 28 October 1987.

Alspach, Addison

1958   *Calvario* (1 act; after a play by Marcus Beach). Performed at
University of Minnesota, Duluth, May 1958.

Altman, Adella C.

1937?   *Souvenir, or Grief's Music Box*. Published by Willis Music.

1948   *Behind Castle Walls*. Published by Willis Music.

1971   *A Treasured Jewell* (musical play). Performed Miami Shores, FL,
27 May 1971.

  -    *The First King of Israel* (musical play).

  -    *Rebecca at the Well* (musical play).

Amadek, Steve

1981   *Illuminatus!*, with John Engerman, Ken Campbell, and Chris
Langham (after novels by Robert Shea and Robert A. Wilson).
Performed at Equinox Theatre, Houston, TX, July 1981.

Amend, Richard

1985   *Sleeping Beauty* (50 minutes; libretto by Steven Otfinoski).
Performed at Club Bene Dinner Theatre, NJ, 1985.

Ames, Roger (b. Cooperstown, NY, 2 December 1944; Anderson)
    1980   *Amarantha* (2 acts; after Wilbur D. Steele's short story "How Beautiful with Shoes"). Performed New London, CT, 19 July 1980; by Lake George Opera, NY, 15 August 1984; and in College Park, MD, 29 November 1989.
    1988   *Angel Face* (1 act; libretto by Laura Harrington). Performed St. Paul, MN, 1988, and Omaha, NE, 15 June 1989.
    1989   *Martin Guerre* (libretto by Laura Harrington). Performed New York, September 1989.
    -    *Amistad* (45 minutes; about the 1839 revolt on the slave ship Amistad; libretto by Virginia Artist). NEA grant, 1976.

Amram, David (b. Philadelphia, 17 November 1930; *Amerigrove*; *Who's Who*)
    1965   *The Final Ingredient* (libretto by Arnold Weinstein). Televised 11 April 1965.
    1968   *Twelfth Night* (libretto by Joseph Papp after Shakespeare). Performed by Lake George Opera, NY, 20 July 1968. Published by Peters.

Anders, Emile
    1948   *King Harald*. Performed at Hunter College, New York, 7 January 1948.

Anderson, Beth (b. Lexington, KY, 3 January 1950; *Amerigrove*)
    1973   *Queen Christina*. Performed at Mills College, 1973.

Anderson, Garland (b. Union City, OH, 10 June 1933; Anderson)
    1979   *Soyazhe* (1 act—70 minutes; libretto by Jamie Lee Cooper; set in a Navaho village). Première by Central City Opera, CO, 28 July 1979. Kornick.

Anderson, Laurie (b. Chicago, 5 June 1947; *Amerigrove*; *Who's Who*)
    1982   *United States: Parts I-IV* (multimedia work). Performed at Holland Festival, Amsterdam, Holland, 21 April 1982, and Next Wave Festival, Brooklyn, NY, 3 February 1982, and, with *Americans on the Move* (1979), as a complete four-part work at the Brooklyn Academy of Music, 1983. Recorded in part as *United States Live*, by Warner Bros.
    1989   *Empty Places*. Performed Spoleto Festival USA, Charleston, SC, 8 June 1989. Recorded in part by Warner Bros.

Anderson, Leroy (b. Cambridge, MA, 29 June 1908; d. Woodbury, CT, 18 May 1975; *Amerigrove*)
    1958   *Goldilocks* (musical; libretto by Jean and Walter Kerr). Performed New York, 11 October 1958.

Anderson, T. J. (b. Coatesville, PA, 17 August 1928; *Amerigrove*; *Who's Who*; Southern)
    1977   *The Shell Fairy* (operetta).
    1982   *Soldier Boy, Soldier* (libretto by Leon Forrest). Performed at Indiana University, 1982.
    1983   *Thomas Jefferson's Minstrels*. Performed Medford, MA, 1983.

1984   *Thomas Jefferson's Orbiting Minstrels and Contraband.* Performed at Northern Illinois University, 12 February 1986.

Andrews, Mrs. Alfred Burritt. *See* Etten, Jane Van

Angelo, Judy Hart
1983   *Preppies,* with Gary Portnoy. Performed at the Promenade Theatre, New York, 9 August 1983. Recorded by Alchemy.

Angles, Langston
1962   *Black Nativity* (1 act; gospel play). Performed by the New York Philharmonic on a European tour.

Antheil, George (b. Trenton, NJ, 8 July 1900; d. New York, 12 February 1959; *Amerigrove*; Hipsher)
1928   *Transatlantic: or, The People's Choice* (3 acts; 35 scenes; libretto by composer). Performed Frankfurt-am-Main, Germany, 25 May 1930. Published by Universal Edition.
1930   *Flight (Ivan the Terrible)* (chamber opera-ballet for marionettes; 1 act; libretto by composer and B. Antheil).
1931   *Helen Retires* (3 acts; libretto by John Erskine). Bispham Medal, 1932. Première by Juilliard School, New York, 28 February 1934.
1952   *Volpone* (3 acts; libretto by A. Perry after Jonson). Performed at University of Southern California, Los Angeles, 9 January 1953.
1954   *The Brothers* (1 act; libretto by composer). Performed at University of Denver, CO, 28 July 1954.
1954   *The Wish* (1 act, 4 scenes; libretto by composer). Performed Louisville, KY, 2 November 1955. Recorded by Louisville series.
1954   *Venus in Africa* (3 scenes—1 hour; libretto by M. Dyne). Performed at University of Denver, CO, 24 May 1957.

Antoniou, Theodore (b. Athens, Greece, 10 February 1935; to U.S. in 1969; *Amerigrove*; *Who's Who*)
1979   *Periander* (prologue and 2 acts—100 minutes; libretto by George Christodoulakis on the historic figure Periander). Performed Munich, Germany, 11 February 1983 (Kornick: 6 February 1983).

Applebaum, Edward (b. Los Angeles, 28 September 1937; Anderson)
1983   *The Frieze of Life* (1 act; libretto by Julia Garza after paintings by Edvard Munch). Performed Newport Beach, CA, 29 January 1983.

Appleton, Adeline Carola (b. Waverley, IA, 29 November 1886; Cohen; Hipsher)
1926   *The Witches' Well* (prologue and 1 act of 2 scenes; libretto by composer with Percy Davis). Performed at Tacoma Hotel, Tacoma, WA, May 1928.

Appleton, Jon (b. Los Angeles, 4 January 1939; *Amerigrove*; *Who's Who*)
1983   *The Lament of Kamuela* (1 hour; multimedia science fiction; libretto by composer). Performed Hanover, NH, 10 August 1983.

Argento, Dominick (b. York, PA, 27 October 1927; *Amerigrove*; *Who's Who*; also
see *New Yorker*, 12 December 1985, 136, and *Newsweek*, 28
November 1988)

1954 *Sicilian Limes*. Performed at School for Social Research, New
York, October 1954.

1957 *The Boor* (1 act; opera buffa; libretto by John Olon-Scrymgeour).
Performed Rochester, NY, 6 May 1957, and Lake George, NY,
1985. Published by Boosey & Hawkes.

1963 *Christopher Sly* (comic opera; 1 act—70 minutes; libretto by John
Manlove after Shakespeare's *The Taming of the Shrew*).
Performed at University of Minnesota, Minneapolis, 31 May 1963.
Published by Boosey & Hawkes.

1963 *Colonel Jonathan and the Saint* (comic opera; libretto by John Olon-
Scrymgeour). Performed Denver, CO, 31 December 1971.
Published by Boosey & Hawkes.

1963 *The Masque of Angels* (1 act—70 minutes; libretto by John Olon-
Scrymgeour). Performed Minneapolis, 9 January 1964. Published
by Boosey & Hawkes.

1967 *Shoemaker's Holiday* (libretto by John Olon-Scrymgeour after T.
Dekker). Performed at Tyrone Guthrie Theatre, Minneapolis, 1
June 1967. Published by Boosey & Hawkes.

1971 *Postcard from Morocco* (1 act—90 minutes; libretto by John
Donahue). Performed by Center Opera, Minneapolis, 14 October
1971, with other performances in Chicago and cities in Illinois,
Indiana, and Wisconsin, New York (according to *New Yorker* of 11
March 1985), and Houston, 1990.

1974 *Jonah and the Whale* (libretto after an anonymous medieval English
text). Performed Minneapolis, 9 March 1974. Published by
Boosey & Hawkes.

1974 *A Waterbird Talk* (monodrama; 1 act—45 minutes; libretto by
composer after Chekhov's *On the Harmful Effects of Tobacco* and
J. J. Audubon's *The Birds of America*). Performed by Minnesota
Opera, Minneapolis, 19 May 1977 (Kornick: at Brooklyn Academy
of Music, New York).

1974 *Krapp's Last Tape*. NEA grant.

1976 *The Voyage of Edgar Allan Poe* (2 acts; libretto by Charles Nolte
using words by Poe). Performed by Minnesota Opera,
Minneapolis, 24 April 1976. Published by Boosey & Hawkes.
Recording available. Kornick.

1978 *Miss Havisham's Fire* (2 acts; libretto by John Olon-Scrymgeour
after Charles Dickins's *Great Expectations*). Commissioned by
New York Opera and performed by them 22 March 1979.
Published by Boosey & Hawkes. Kornick.

1980 *Miss Havisham's Wedding Night* (melodrama; libretto by John Olon-
Scrymgeour after Charles Dickins's *Great Expectations*).
Performed by Minnesota Opera, Minneapolis, 1 May 1981, and
New York Lyric Opera, 7 April 1983. Kornick.

1984 *Casanova's Homecoming* (opera buffa; 3 acts—134 minutes; libretto
by composer). Commissioned by the Minnesota Opera. Performed
New York, 2 December 1985 (Kornick: by New York Opera, 2
November 1985 and 20 September 1987). Published by Boosey &
Hawkes.

1988   *The Aspern Papers* (2 acts, two prologues—116 minutes; libretto by composer). Performed by Dallas Opera, TX, 19 November 1988, and Kassel, Germany, 9 June 1990. On public television, 9 June 1989 in the Great Performances series. Kornick.

-    *Sebastian's Dream.*

Aria, Pietro

1968   *Jericho Road* (2 acts; biblical story). Performed by Philadelphia Grand Opera, 12 March 1968.

Arlan, Dennis (b. 1945)

1976   *Meanwhile, Back at Cinderella's* (1 act—65 minutes; satire; libretto by James Billings). Performed by New York Lyric Opera, New York, 5 May 1976. Published by Jerona. Kornick.

1977   *The Ballad of the Bremen Band* (1 act—45 minutes; libretto by James Billings after the Grimm Brothers's *The Brementown Musicians*). Performed Katonah, NY, 25 June 1977. Published by European-American. Kornick.

1978   *The Daughter of the Double Duke of Dingle* (1 act—45 minutes; libretto by James Billings). Performed Katonah, NY, 17 June 1978. Published by Jerona.

Arlington, Donald

1978   *I Love My Voice: The First Neurotic Opera* (1 act; monodrama; libretto by Stephen Holt). Performed at Riverside Church, New York, 18 May 1978.

Armitage-Carnes, C. W. (AMC)

1985   *Stanislaus and Clare* (150 minutes; libretto by the composer; set in Florida during World War II).

Armour, Eugene (AMC)

1981   *We're Back* (1 act—20 minutes). Gertrude Stein and Alice B. Toklas are characters. Performed New York, 1 May 1981.

Armstrong, William Dawson (b. Alton, IL, 11 February 1868; d. there, 9 July 1936; *Amerigrove*)

1899   *The Spectre Bridegroom* (libretto after Washington Irving). Performed St. Louis.

Arnatt, Ronald (b. London, England, 16 January 1930; to U.S. 1947, citizen 1953; Anderson)

1968   *The Boy with a Cart.* Commissioned by the Danforth Foundation. Performed St. Louis, 8 May 1968.

Arnold, Maurice (real name Maurice Arnold Strothotte; b. St. Louis, 19 January 1865; d. New York, 23 October 1937; *Baker's*; Hipsher)

1896   *The Merry Benedicts* (comic opera). Performed Brooklyn, NY (Hipsher: at Criterion Theater, 1894, composer conducting).

-    *Cleopatra* (grand opera).

-    *The Last King* (grand opera; libretto by composer).

Arnstein, Ira B.
    1925   *The Song of David* (2 acts). Performed in a concert version,
            Aeolian Hall, New York, 17 May 1925, composer conducting.

Artau, Estrella
    1988   *Marine Tiger* (in Spanish and English). Performed by Puerto Rican
            Traveling Theater, New York, 10 August 1988.

Arthur, Alfred (b. Pittsburgh, PA., 8 October 1884; d. Lakewood, OH, 20
            November 1918)
            (All 3 operas unproduced, according to *Baker's*, 5th ed.)
    1876   *The Water-Carrier.*
    1878   *The Roundheads and Cavaliers.*
    1879   *Adaline.*

Aschaffenburg, Walter (b. Essen, Germany, 20 May 1927; in U.S. from 1938;
            Anderson; *Who's Who*)
    1964   *Bartelby* (libretto by Jay Leyda after Herman Melville). Performed
            Oberlin, OH, 12 November 1964. Published by Presser.

Ashley, Robert (b. Ann Arbor, MI, 28 March 1930; *Amerigrove*; *Who's Who*)
    1967   *That Morning Thing.* Performed Ann Arbor, 8 February 1968, and
            by Center for Contemporary Music, Oakland, CA, 8 December
            1970.
    1967   *In Memoriam Kit Carson.* Performed at Mills College, Oakland,
            CA, 10 December 1971.
    1976   *Music with Roots in the Aether.* Performed Paris, 1976.
    1976   *Title Withdrawn.* Performed Paris, 1976.
    1978   *Perfect Lives (Private Parts)* (4 hours; takes place in a small
            American town). Excerpts performed by New York Dance
            Theatre Workshop, NY, 26 December, 1978; complete version at
            The Kitchen, New York, 1980. Recorded by Lovely Music.
    1981   *The Lessons.* Performed New York, 1981.
    1982   *Atalanta (Acts of God)* (90 minutes; multimedia work). Performed
            Paris, November 1982, and New York, 18 January 1990.
            Recorded by Lovely Music Sound and Video.
    1984   *Atalanta Strategy.*

Atherton, Percy Lee (b. Roxbury, MA, 1871; d. Atlantic City, NJ, 1944;
            Anderson)
    1890   *The Heir Apparent.*
    1900   *Maharajah.*

Atwell, Shirl Jae
    1986   *Sagegrass* (80 minutes; folk opera; libretto by Delmas W. Abbott).
            Excerpts performed New York, 13 January 1986.

Austin, John (b. Mt. Vernon, NY, 8 June 1934; *WhoAm*)
    1967   *Orpheus* (1 act; rock opera; libretto by composer). Performed
            Chicago, 10 March 1967.

Austin, Larry (b. Duncan, OK, 12 September 1930; *Amerigrove*; *Who's Who*)
    1966   *The Maze: A Theater Piece in Open Style.*
    1970   *Agape* ("a celebration for priests, musicians, dancers, a rock band, actors and poets"; text from the Bible). Performed Buffalo, NY, 25 February 1970.
    1979   *Catalogo voce* (mini-opera).
    1982   *Euphonia* (2 acts; libretto by T. Holliday after Berlioz). Performed Potsdam, NY, 1 May 1984.

Averill, Louise
    -    *A Christmas Carol* (libretto by Robert Odle after Dickens). Published by Waterloo.

Avril, Lloyd
    1968   *Heads or Tails* (1 act). Performed at Glassboro State College, NJ, 23 February 1968.

Avshalom, Aaron (formerly Avshalomov; b. Nikolayevsk, Siberia, 11 November 1894; d. New York, 26 April 1965; to U.S. in 1947; Anderson)
    1924   *Kuan Yin* (*Goddess of Mercy*) (1 act—50 minutes; a Chinese opera). Première, Peking, 1925; performed Portland, OR, 1926, and New York, 16 March 1927.
    1945   *The Great Wall* (1 act). Performed Shanghai, 1945, and at Columbia University, New York, 21 April 1956.
    -    *The Twilight Hour of Yang-Kuei-Fei* (libretto by A. E. Grantham).

Babbitt, Milton (b. Philadelphia, 10 May 1916; *Amerigrove*; *Who's Who*)
    1946   *Fabulous Voyage* (musical theater; libretto after *The Odyssey*). Performed at Juilliard School, New York, 27 January 1989.

Babcock, Jeffrey
    1972   *Mirrors* (multimedia). Performed at University of California, Santa Barbara, 6 April 1972.

Baber, Joseph W. (b. Richmond, VA, 11 September 1937; AMC; Anderson; ASCAP)
    1978   *Frankenstein* (libretto by John Gardner). "In progress," according to *COS*-3.
    1978   *Rumpelstiltskin* (2 acts; satire; after Grimm). Anderson: "called a satire on practically everything." Performed by Opera Company of Philadelphia, 26 December 1978.
    -    *The Cave* (passion play; libretto by Jascha Kessler). Listed in *COS*-3.

Bach, Jan Morris (b. Forrest, IL, 11 December 1937; ASCAP; *Who's Who*)
    1973   *The System* ("black comedy"; 1 act—50 minutes; libretto by composer after Poe). Performed at Mannes School of Music, New York, 5 March 1974 (Kornick: March 7).

1978   *The Happy Prince* (after Oscar Wilde). First prize, Omaha
        Symphony, 1979. Performed in Omaha, NE, April 1980.
1979   *The Student from Salamanca* (opera buffa; 1 act—50 minutes;
        libretto by composer after Cervantes). Winner, New York Opera
        Competition, 1980. Performed by New York Opera, 9 October
        1980. Kornick.

Bacon, Ernst (b. Chicago, 26 May 1898; d. Orinda, CA, 16 March 1990;
        Amerigrove; Anderson; ASCAP; *Who's Who*)
1942   *A Tree on the Plains* ("musical play"; libretto by P. Horgan).
        Performed Spartanburg, SC, 4 February 1942; at St. Bartholomew's
        Church, New York, 5 May 1945; and Stanford, CA, 1947-48
        season. Bispham Medal, 1946. Published by Schirmer.
1949   *A Drumlin Legend* (libretto by Helen Carus). Performed New York,
        4 or 9 May 1949.
1976   *Dr. Franklin* ("musical play"; libretto by C. Lenyel).
-       *Take Your Choice* (105 minutes).

Badale, Andy (pseudonym for Angelo Daniel Badalumenti; b. Brooklyn, NY,
        1937; ASCAP)
1984   *The Bachelor's Wife* (2 acts; libretto by Barbara Friend and Anthony
        Stimac). Performed by Musical Theatre Works, New York,
        October 1984.

Bagneris, Vernel
1990   *Further 'Mo* (jazz work set in New Orleans in the twenties).
        Performed by Norzar Productions, New York, 16 May 1990.

Baker, Larry (b. Ft. Smith, AR, 7 September 1948; ASCAP; *WhoAm*)
1987   *Haydn's Head* (1 act). Ohio Arts Council Grant. Performed
        Cleveland, 30 July 1987.

Baksa, Robert (Frank) (b. New York, 7 February 1938; *Amerigrove*; Anderson;
        ASCAP; *Who's Who*)
1966   *Aria da capo* (30 minutes; after Edna St. Vincent Millay), revised
        1978. Reading, Philadelphia, 10 March 1981; première by
        Academy of Vocal Arts, Philadelphia, 11 May 1981.
1969   *Red Carnations* (1 act—35 minutes; after play by Glenn Hughes).
        Composed for the Metropolitan Opera Studio. Performed in St.
        Luke's Chapel, New York, 24 October 1974.

Balada, Leonardo (b. Barcelona, Spain, 12 September 1933; to U.S. 1956;
        Amerigrove; ASCAP; *Who's Who*)
1982   *Hangman, Hangman!* (chamber opera; 50 minutes; libretto by
        composer on a cowboy theme). Performed Barcelona, Spain, 13
        October 1982, and at Carnegie Mellon University, Pittsburgh, 8
        October 1983.
1984   *Zapata!* (2 hours; libretto by Tito Capobianco and Gabriela
        Roebke). Commissioned by the San Diego Opera. Performed
        Pittsburgh, 1985.
1987   *Cristobal Colón* (130 minutes; libretto by Tito Capobianco).
        Commissioned by the Society for the 500th Anniversary of the

Discovery of America. Performed Pittsburgh, 1988, and Barcelona, Spain, 24 September 1989.

Baldwin, Anita
   1932   *California.* Score in AMRC.

Baldwin, Philip
   1988   *Frottage.* Performed at Knickerbocker Theater Festival, New York, 23 July 1988.

Bales, Ginny
   1989   *Stanton Women's Chorus.* Performed by Ensemble Theatre Company of New Haven, Hamden, CT, 30 March 1989.

Balin, Marty
   1979   *Rock Justice* (rock opera; libretto by Robert Heyman). Performed San Francisco, December 1979.

Balk, Wesley
   1974   *The Newest Opera in the World* (optional development of the plot; libretto by Philip Brunelle). Performed Minneapolis, May 1974.
   1974   *Gallimaufry* ("seasoned party for singers and guests"; collage of Banchière, Corwin, Joplin, and "traditional" sources. Performed by Minneapolis Opera, St. Paul, MN, 13 December 1974.

Balkin, Al(fred) (b. Boston, 12 August 1931; *WhoAm*)
   1972   *The Musicians of Bremen* (libretto by composer; 2 acts—90 minutes). Published by New View Music.

Ballantine, Edward (b. Oberlin, OH, 6 August 1886; d. Oak Bluffs, MA, 2 July 1971; *Amerigrove*)
   1907   *The Lotos Eaters* "musical play").

Bampton, Ruth (b. Boston, 7 March 1902; Anderson; Cohen)
   1976? *Stars over Christmas* (musical play). Cited in *Panpipes*, May 1978.

Banfield, Raffaello de
   1955   *Lord Byron's Love Letter* (after Tennessee Williams). Performed at Tulane University, New Orleans, 17 January 1955.
   1965   *Alissa* (a fantasy, libretto by Richard Miller). Performed Geneva, Switzerland, 15 May 1965.
   -   *Orpheus Descending.* "In preparation," *COS*-1.

Barab, Seymour (b. Chicago, 9 January 1921; *Amerigrove*; Anderson; ASCAP)
   1954   *The Rajah's Ruby* (1 act—45 minutes; farce). Performed New York, 1956. Published by Boosey & Hawkes.
   1954   *Chanticleer* (1 act—40 minutes; comic opera; libretto by M. C. Richards after Chaucer). Performed Aspen, CO, 4 August 1956, and Des Moines, IA, 1984. Published by Boosey & Hawkes.
   1956   *A Game of Chance* (1 act—35 minutes; libretto by E. Manacher). Performed Rock Island, IL, 11 January 1957. Published by Boosey & Hawkes.

1958 *Little Red Riding Hood* (children's opera; libretto by composer after the Grimm brothers). Performed San Francisco, 1958, and New York, 1962.

1959 *Pink Siamese* (1 act—45 minutes; libretto by Susan Otto). Performed Detroit, MI, April 1959.

1960 *The Malatroit Door, or Sire de Malatroit* (1 act—30 minutes). Performed New York, 28 January 1960. Published by Boosey & Hawkes.

1964 *The Ransom of Red Chief* (1 act; after O. Henry). Performed Newark, NJ.

1971 *Who Am I?.* Performed Tempe, AZ, 5 February 1971, and Arlington, VA, 5 December 1987. Published by G. Schirmer.

1974 *Philip Marshall, or Tender Mercies* (libretto after Dostoevski's *The Idiot*). Performed Chautauqua, NY, 12 July 1974.

1977 *Not a Spanish Kiss* (opera buffa; 1 act—30 minutes; libretto by composer). Première for New York Singing Teachers Association, 1977; also performed by Golden Fleece, New York, May 1981, and Association for Opera Awareness, New York, November 1982. Kornick.

1978 *The Toy Shop* (children's opera; 1 act—45 minutes; libretto by composer). Commissioned by New York Opera. Performed New York, 3 June 1978 and 29 November 1989. Kornick.

1979 *Little Stories in Tomorrow's Papers* (1 act). Commissioned by the Lighthouse Music School. Performed New York, 14 June 1979.

1981 *The Ruined Maid* (on a poem by Hardy). Performed at Abraham Goodman Hall, New York, 3 June 1981.

1982 *A Kiss from Alice* (pantomime). Performed Ruston, LA, 24 March 1982.

1982 *Fortune's Favorites* (comedy; 1 act—45 minutes; libretto by composer after the short story "Baker's Dozen" by H. H. Munro [Saki]). Première by After Dinner Opera, New York, 19 June 1982. Published by Galaxy. Kornick.

1984 *A Piece of String* (3 acts; after Guy de Maupassant). Performed Dallas, TX, November 1984, and Greeley, CO, 23 May 1985.

1985 *Out the Window* (45 minutes). Performed by After Dinner Opera, New York, March 1985.

1985 *Predators* (70 minutes). Reading by After Dinner Opera, New York, 15 April 1985; première by the same company, 11 May 1985. Published by G. Schirmer.

1985 *The Maker of Illusions* (libretto by composer). Performed New York, 21 April 1985.

1985 *Father of the Child* (1 act—75 minutes). Performed by After Dinner Opera, New York, 7 October 1985.

1986 *I Can't Stand Wagner* (40 minutes; after Evelyn E. Smith's story "Floyd and the Eumedides"). Performed at Singer's Forum, New York, 12 December 1986.

1987 *Passion in the Principal's Office* (20 minutes). Performed by After Dinner Opera, New York, 1 November, 1987. Published by G. Schirmer.

1988 *Snow White.* Performed Norman, OK, 30 September 1988.

1989 *Let's Not Talk about Lenny Any More.* Performed Charlemont, MA, 18 August 1989.

1989   *La pizza con funghi* (*Pizza with Mushrooms*). Performed by After Dinner Opera, New York, 6 November 1989.

-   *Death in December* (after a story by Stanley Ellin). Published by Boosey & Hawkes.

-   *Everything Must Be Perfect* (20 minutes). Published by G. Schirmer. Listed in *COS-4*.

-   *How Far to Bethlehem* (1 act—30 minutes). Published by Boosey & Hawkes.

-   *Jonah* (1 act; libretto by Paul Goodman).

-   *Public Defender* (1 hour). Published by G. Schirmer.

-   *Reba* (1 act—60 minutes; libretto by Martha England after William March's story "The Funeral"). Published by Boosey & Hawkes.

Barber, Samuel (b. West Chester, PA, 9 March 1910; d. New York, 23 January 1981; *Amerigrove*)

1920   *The Rose Tree* (libretto by A. S. Brosius), incomplete.

1957   *Vanessa*. Performed by Metropolitan Opera, New York, 15 January 1958, and Opera Theatre of St. Louis, 26 May 1989. Pulitzer Prize, 1958. Published by G. Schirmer. Recorded by RCA Victor. Video by Lyric Distribution, 1978.

1960   *A Hand of Bridge* (1 act—9 minutes). Performed at Spoleto Festival, Italy, 17 June 1959, and in New York, 6 April 1960. Published by G. Schirmer.

1966   *Antony and Cleopatra* (3 acts; libretto by composer and F. Zeffirelli after Shakespeare). Commissioned for opening of Lincoln Center and premièred by Metropolitan Opera, New York, 16 September 1966; revised version by Juilliard School, New York, 6 February 1975. Lyric Opera of Chicago performance broadcast on Great Performances series, PBS, 16 December 1991. Recording: New World NW 322-324. Kornick.

Barbie, Richard A.

-   *Good King Hal* (2 acts; libretto by composer after Shakespeare's *Henry IV* and *Henry V*). Published by Dramatic Publishing Co.

Barclay, Paris

1985   *Almo: A Man* (2 acts; libretto after Richard Wright story). Performed by Solo Repertory Theater, New York, April 1985.

Barkin, Elaine (b. Bronx, NY, 15 December 1932; ACA; *Amerigrove*; Cohen)

1980   *De amore* (*On Love*) (chamber mini-opera; 50 minutes; libretto by composer after A. Capellanus; in Latin, Provençal, and English). Performed Oberlin, OH, 14 February 1982.

1981   *Media Speak* (15 minutes).

Barlow, Samuel L. M. (b. New York, 1 June 1892; d. Wyndmoor, PA, 19 September 1982; *Amerigrove*)

1935   *Mon ami Pierrot* (1 act; libretto by Sacha Guitry concerning the life of Lully, aiming to tell the origin of the children's song "Au clair de la lune"). Performed by Opéra-Comique, Paris, 11 January 1935 (first American work to be performed there, according to *Baker's*). Bispham Medal.

1936   *Amanda* (2 scenes—75 minutes; libretto by composer). Published by Choudens.

\-   *Eugenie.*

Barnard, Francis
1969   *The Masque of Maska.* Performed at Cubiculo Theatre, New York, 26 April 1969.
1982   *The Glory Coach* (3 acts; libretto by composer after the Wakefield Mystery Plays). Performed at First Presbyterian Church, New York, 28 March 1982.

Barnes, Edward
1980   *Feathertop* ("fantasy parable"; 2 acts—100 minutes; libretto by Maurice Valency after Hawthorne). Premièred at Juilliard School, New York, 7 February 1980. Kornick.
1983   *Nezha* (libretto by composer after an old Chinese story). NEA grant). Workshop performance, Waterford, CT, summer 1983; reading, New York, 3 October 1984; première, St. Paul, MN, spring 1986.
1989   *The Vagabond Queen.* Performed at McPherson College, KS, 22 April 1989.

Barnett, David (b. New York, 1 December 1907; d. Weston, CN, 7 December 1985; Anderson)
1972   *Inner Voices*, with Josephine Barnett (1 act). Performed New York, 17 December 1972.

Baron, Maurice (b. Lille, France, 1 January 1889; d. Oyster Bay, NY, 5 September 1964; to U.S. early; he used pseudonyms Francis Delille, Morris Aborn, Alice Tremblay [his wife]; ASCAP; *Baker's*)
1940   *François Villon* (3 acts). Performed on NBC radio, 14 April 1940.

Barr, Albert Earl (b. Preakness, NJ, 1912; ASCAP)
\-   *The Coat of Many Colors* (libretto by the composer after the biblical story). *COS*-2.

Barri, Richard
\-   *Wuthering Heights* (3 acts; after Brontë). *COS*-1.

Barrie, S. James
1988   *The Magical Kingdom of Demos* (90 minutes). Published by Everest Cultural Enrichments, 1988.

Barry, Daniel
1989   *Face the Music*, with John Kelly (90 minutes; on the social roles of composers in different eras of history). Performed Santa Barbara, CA, July 1989.

Barsha, Debra
1987   *Sophie* (libretto by Rose Leiman Goldenberg after the life of Sophie Tucker). Performed by Jewish Repertory Theater, New York, October 1987.

Barth, Hans (b. Leipzig, Germany, 25 June 1897; d. Jacksonville, FL, 8
December 1956; to U.S. in 1907; Anderson; ASCAP; *Amerigrove*)
1938   *Miragia*, op. 2 (operetta).

Barthelson, Joyce (also Helen Joyce Holloway, Mrs. B. M. Steigman; b. Yakima,
WA, 18 May 1908; Anderson; ASCAP; Cohen; Schoep)
1967   *Chanticleer* (45 minutes; fairy tale/comic fantasy after Chaucer's
"The Nun's Priest's Tale"). Won National Federation of Music
Clubs award, 1967. Performed by Metropolitan Opera Studio, 15
April 1967. Staged for National Federation of Music Clubs, in
Rhode Island, 18 February 1968. Published by Carl Fischer, 1967.
1969   *Greenwich Village, 1910* (1 act). Performed Scarsdale, NY, 20
December 1970.
1973   *The King's Breakfast* (1 act; libretto by composer, about Catherine
Parr). Performed by Community Opera, New York, 26 February
1973. Published by Carl Fischer, 1973.
1977   *The Devil's Disciple* (melodrama; 2 acts—135 minutes; libretto by
composer after the play by George Bernard Shaw). Première at
Highlands School, White Plains, NY, 4 November 1977. Published
by Carl Fischer. Kornick.
1981   *Lysistrata* (comic satire; 1 act—60 minutes; libretto by composer
after Aristophanes play). Performed at New York University, 27
March 1981. Kornick.
-       *Feathertop* (opera buffa, with overture; 2 acts—113 minutes; libretto
by composer). Published by Carl Fischer.

Barthol, Bruce
1985?   *The Dragon Lady's Revenge*. Performed by San Francisco Mime
Troupe.
1985   *Steeltown* (2 acts). Performed by San Francisco Mime Troupe.
1986   *Spain/36* (libretto by the composer, about the Spanish Civil War).
Performed by San Francisco Mime Troupe, June 1986.
1987   *The Mozangola Caper* (libretto by John O'Neal and Joan Holden).
Performed by San Francisco Mime Troupe, 10 February 1987.

Bartlett, Homer Newton (b. Olive, NY, 28 December 1846; d. Hoboken, NJ, 3
April 1920; *Amerigrove*; Hipsher)
1887   *La Vallière* (3 acts).
1910   *Magic Hours* (operetta).
-       *Hinotito* (Japanese subject). Unfinished, according to *Baker's* and
Hipsher.

Barton, Andrew (librettist; perhaps pseudonym for Thomas Forrest, d. 1828, or
Joseph and John Leacock)
1767   *The Disappointment: or, The Force of Credulity*. Libretto published
in New York, 1767, but performance suppressed. Performed 3
March 1937 at Majestic Theatre, Brooklyn NY, under the name
Treasure Hunt. With "musical accompaniments and an original
overture" by Samuel Adler (q.v.), it was performed at the Library
of Congress, Washington, 29-30 October 1986. This version is
published as Recent Researches in American Music, 3-4 (Madison:
A-R Editions, 1976), and recorded on Turnabout TV-S 34650.

See Carolyn Rabson, "*Disappointment* Revisited: Unweaving the Tangled Web," *American Music* 1 (1983): 12-35, and 2 (1984): 1-28.

Bass, Claude L. (b. Gainesville, TX, 31 October 1935; Anderson)
1979   *The Father's Love.* Performed Fort Worth, TX, 10 April 1979.

Battista, Ned
1980   *Shah* (libretto by Jim Bernhard). Performed Houston, TX, 1980.

Bauer, Harold Gene (ASCAP)
1965   *Lazarus.* Performed Lake Forest, IL, 1965.

Bauer, John (b. National, TN, 6 August 1933; *WhoAm*)
1990?   *Macbeth.* Scheduled performance by Portland Opera, OR.

Bauman, Jon Ward (b. Big Rapids, MI, 7 June 1939; Anderson; *Who's Who*)
1987   *Dialogues* (1 hour; chamber opera; Christmas opera; libretto by Sister Maura). Performed Frostburg, MD, December 1987.

Baylor, H. Murray (b. What Cheer, IA, 8 April 1913; Anderson; *Who's Who*)
1949   *By Gemini* (prolog and 2 acts; comic opera). Performed Galesburg, IL, 2 March 1949.

Beach, Amy Cheney (Mrs. H. H. A. Beach; b. Henniker, NH, 5 September 1867; d. New York, 27 December 1944; wrote and performed under the name Mrs. H. H. A. Beach; *Amerigrove*; ASCAP)
1932   *Cabildo* (1 act; chamber opera; libretto by Nan Bagby Stephens). Performed at University of Georgia, Athens, 27 February 1945; and Conservatory of Music, University of Missouri-Kansas City, March 1982. Cassette by UMKC available.

Beach, John Parsons (b. Gloversville, NY, 11 October 1877; d. Pasadena, CA, 6 November 1953; *Amerigrove*)
1915   *Pippa's Holiday* (1 act; libretto after Browning's "Pippa Passes"). Performed at Théâtre Rejane, Paris, 1915. Hipsher.
-    *Jornida and Jornidel* (2 acts).

Beach, Lazarus (1760-1816)
1807   *Jonathan Postfree: or, The Honest Yankee* (musical farce; 3 acts; libretto by composer). Performed New York. Published there by David Longworth, ca. 1807.

Beadell, Robert Morton (b. Chicago, 18 June 1925; Anderson; ASCAP)
1957   *The Kingdom of Caraway* (operetta).
1960   *The Sweetwater Affair* (2 acts). Performed Lincoln, NE, October 1961.
1966   *The Number of Fools* (libretto by Stanley Peters), revised 1976. Performed by Northwestern University, Evanston, IL, 14 May 1966, and University of Nebraska, Lincoln, October 1976, and a portion for the National Opera Association, Seattle, WA, 4 November 1976.

1973   *Napoleon* (libretto by Dean Tschetter and William Wallace).
        Performed Lincoln, NE, February 1973.
1978   *Out to the Wind* (music drama; after Willa Cather; about Nebraska in
        the 1880s). Performed Lincoln, NE, 2 February 1979.

Beale, Frederic Fleming (b. Troy, KS, 13 July 1876; d. Caldwell, ID, 16 February
        1948; Anderson)
1915?   *The Magic Wheel*, with Jessie L. Gaynor (2 acts; libretto by Alice C.
        D. Riley). Published by John Church, 1915?.
-       *Fatima*.
-       *Poor Richard*.

Beall, Mark
1982   *The Going*. Performed Cincinnati, 7 November 1982.

Beaton, Isabella (b. Grinnell, IA, 20 May 1870; d. Mt. Pleasant, IA, 19 January
        1929; Anderson; Cohen)
-       *Anacoana*.

Bechtel, Frederick
1880   *Alfred the Great*

Beck, Jeremy (b. Painesville, OH, 15 January 1960; *WhoAm*)
1984   *Anne Boleyn* (15 minutes; libretto by the composer). Concert
        version performed at Mannes School, New York, 27 January 1984;
        staged by Golden Fleece, New York, 27 June 1985.
1985   *Once a Year of Christmas Eve*. Performed New York, 27 December
        1985.

Beck, Johann Heinrich (b. Cleveland, OH, 12 September 1856; d. there, 26 May
        1924; *Amerigrove*; Hipsher)
1887   *Salammbô* (music drama; libretto by composer after the novel by
        Flaubert), begun 1887, unfinished.

Becker, Chris
1990   *Satie*. Performed Columbus, OH, February 1990.

Becker, John J. (b. Henderson, KY, 22 January 1886; d. Wilmette, IL, 21
        January 1961; ACA; *Amerigrove*)
1939   *Privilege and Privation* (1 act; satire; libretto by Alfred Kroymborg).
        Performed Amsterdam, 22 June 1982.
1956   *The Queen of Cornwall* (after Hardy), incomplete.
1945   *Dierdre of the Sorrows* (after Synge). Performed by National
        Association of Teachers, Chicago, 1956-57 season.

Beckett, (William) Wheeler (b. San Francisco, 7 March 1898; d. Philadelphia, 25
        January 1986; Anderson; ASCAP; *Baker's*)
1955   *The Magic Mirror* (3 acts). Performed Newark, NJ, 27 April 1955.
-       *The Queen's Mirror*. Listed in Anderson.
-       *Snow White and the Seven Dwarfs*.

Beckler, Stanworth R. (b. Escondido, CA, 26 December 1923; Anderson; AMC)
1945   *Faust* (chamber opera).
1960   *The Outcasts of Poker Flat* (1 act; libretto by Jon Pearce after Bret
        Harte). Won Pi Kappa Lambda Composition contest. Performed
        Stockton, CA, 16 December 1960.
1973   *The Catbird Seat* (1 act—40 minutes; after Thurber).

Beckley, Connie
1989   *The Score Keeper.* Performed by American Opera Projects, New
        York, 8 November 1989.

Becktel, F. (b. ca. 1864; Hipsher)
-       *Alfred the Great.*

Beeson, Jack (b. Muncie, IN, 15 July 1921; *Amerigrove*; ASCAP; *Who's Who*)
1950   *Jonah* (2 or 3 acts; libretto by composer after P. Goodman).
1954   *Hello Out There* (chamber opera; 1 act—50 minutes; libretto by
        Kenward Elmslie after William Saroyan.) Performed at Columbia
        University, New York, 27 May 1954, and Houston, TX, 1980.
        Published by Mills Music. Recorded by Columbia.
1956   *The Sweet Bye and Bye* (libretto by Kenward Elmslie). Performed
        at Juilliard School, New York, 21 November 1957. Published by
        Mills Music.
1965   *Lizzie Borden* (3 acts; libretto by Kenward Elmslie). Commission
        from the Ford Foundation. Performed by New York Opera, 25
        March 1965. Published by Boosey & Hawkes. Recorded by
        Desto.
1969   *My Heart's in the Highlands* (chamber opera; 2 acts; libretto by
        composer after William Saroyan). Performed New York, on
        National Educational Television, 18 March 1970. Published by
        Boosey & Hawkes. (See *New Yorker*, 12 December 1988, 112.)
1975   *Captain Jinks of the Horse Marines* (romantic comedy; 3 acts—120
        minutes; libretto by Sheldon Harnick after a play by Clyde Fitch;
        about New York in the 1870s). NEA grant. Premièred by Lyric
        Opera of Kansas City, MO, 26 September 1975. Published by
        Belwin-Mills. Recording: CMS Desto DC7222/3L (discs) and
        DCX47222/3L (cassette). Kornick.
1978   *Dr. Heidegger's Fountain of Youth* (satirical tale; 1 act—40 minutes;
        libretto by Sheldon Harnick after Nathaniel Hawthorne's "Dr.
        Heidegger's Experiment"). Commissioned and premièred for
        National Arts Club, New York, 17 November 1978 (Kornick:
        November 19); additional performances by Bel Canto Opera, New
        York, May 1981; New York, 16 February 1990. Published by
        Belwin-Mills. Recording: Composers Recordings, CRI SD 406.
        Kornick.

Beglarian, Eve
1987   *Maiden Songs—Sappho and Elkman: A Theater Piece* (1 hour; in
        classical Greek). Performed by Greek Drama Company, New
        York, 14 May 1987.

Behrens, Jack (b. Lancaster, PA, 25 March 1935; ASCAP; Anderson; *Baker's*)
    1968   *The Lay of Thrym* (2 acts; libretto by Keith Cockburn). Performed
           at University of Saskatchewan, Canada, 13 April 1968.

Belcher, Mary Williams
    1918   *The Legend of Ronsard and Madelon* (2 acts). Performed
           Cleveland.
    -      *Madelaine* (1 act).

Belich, Sam Michael
    1982   *The Trojan Women* (2 acts; libretto after Euripides). Performed at
           Grace and St. Paul's Lutheran Church, New York, 8 January 1982.
    1986   *Laius and Chrysippus* (2 acts; libretto by the composer and Sam
           Shirakawa). Performed at Jesse Isador Strauss School, New York,
           4 December 1986.

Bellardo, Samuel John (AMC)
    -      *Trilby* (1 act; after George Du Maurier).

Beni, Gimi (James J.) (b. Philadelphia; ASCAP; *WhoAm*)
    1978   *Forever Figaro* (libretto after Rossini, using some of Rossini's
           music). Performed by Opera Theatre of Saint Louis, 20 May
           1978.
    -      *Bricktop.* Première projected by AMAS Repertory Theater, New
           York in *COS*-4.

Benjamin, Thomas Edward (b. Bennington, VT, 17 February 1940; Anderson;
           ASCAP; *Who's Who*)
    1980   *The Rehearsal* (romantic drama; 1 act—45 minutes; libretto by
           Cynthia MacDonald; about a rehearsal of Mozart's *Der
           Schauspiedirektor*). Reading by Lake George Opera, Lake George,
           NY, 7 August 1980; performed at University of Mississippi, 12
           November 1980. Kornick.
    1985   *Chicken Little.* Performed Houston, TX, 6 June 1985.
    1987   *What A Night!* (2 hours; libretto by Elaine Gerdine after Feydeau's
           Hotel de la libre échange). Performed Houston, TX, 1987.
    1988   *Vayero* (1 act—25 minutes; libretto by Sarah Schlesinger after a
           medieval Jewish story). Won Jewish Music Commission contest,
           1988. Performed Los Angeles, September 1989.
    -      *Hammer in His Hand* (operetta).

Bennett, Lawrence (Edward) (b. Rock Island, IL, 27 September 1940; *WhoAm*)
    1986   *The Divine Orlando* (2 acts; libretto by William Luce after Orlando
           Lassus's life, and incorporating some of his music). Performed
           New York, 12 May 1986.

Bennett, Robert Russell (b. Kansas City, MO, 15 June 1894; d. New York, 18
           August 1981; *Amerigrove*; ASCAP)
    1927   *Endymion* (ballet-operetta).
    1935   *Maria Malibran* (3 acts—90 minutes). Performed New York, 8 April
           1935.
    1944   *The Enchanted Kiss* (1 act—90 minutes). Performed New York, 30
           December 1945; also on WOR radio, New York, 1945.

1961   *The Ledge.* Performed at Sadler's Wells, London, England, 12 September 1961.

1963   *The Mines of Sulphur.* Performed London, England, 1965.

1967   *Penny for a Song* (comic opera). Performed London, England, 31 October 1967.

1968   *All the King's Men* (children's opera in 1 scene).

1970   *Victory* (after Conrad). Performed at Covent Garden, London, England, 18 April 1970.

-    *An Hour of Delusion* (1 act—30 minutes).

Benowitz, Roy, with Basil Adam and John Bowden
-    *Trilby* (libretto by Joan Tratner and Robert Dey after George Du Maurier). *COS*-4.

Benson, Philip
1988   *The Journey of Charles Cello* (libretto by Ilsa Gilbert). Performed by Downtown Music Productions, New York, 13 November 1988.

Bentley, John (fl. 1780s; Porter; Sonneck-Upton)
1785   *Genii of the Rock* (pantomime). Première, New York, 20 August 1785.

1785   *Cave of Enchantment: or, The Stockwell Wonder* (pantomime), music selected and composed by Bentley. Première, New York, 26 August 1785.

1785   *The Touchstone: or, Harlequin Traveller* (operatical pantomime), music by Charles Dibdin and Bentley. American première, New York, 1 September 1785.

Benton, Lynne and **Robert**
-    *Jason and the Golden Fleece. COS*-4. Published by Presser.

Bentz, Cecil William (b. Platte Center, NE, 1915; ASCAP; Anderson)
1967   *Window Games* (1 act; opera-ballet; after Guy de Maupassant's "Playing with Fire"). Performed Clark Center, NY, 18 November 1967.

Berezowsky, Nicolai (b. St. Petersburg, Russia, 17 May 1900; d. New York, 27 August 1953; to New York in 1922; AMC; *Amerigrove*; ASCAP)
1953   *Babar the Elephant*, op. 40 (children's opera; 1 act—60 minutes; libretto by D. Heyward-Randa). Performed New York, 21 February 1953.

-    *Prince Batrik.*

Berg, Chris(topher Paul) (b. Detroit, MI, 30 June 1949; *WhoAm*)
1988   *Tidworth.* Performed by Music Theater Works, New York, 23 May 1988.

Berge, Irenee Marius
1910   *Corsica* (1 act). Performed Kingston, NY.

Berger, Jean (b. Hamm, Germany, 27 September 1909; to New York in 1941;
    Amerigrove; ASCAP)

1968   *The Pied Piper* (1 act; after Browning). Published by G. Schirmer.

1972   *Yiphth and His Daughter* (libretto by composer in Hebrew, Latin,
    Spanish, and English). Performed Montclair, NJ, 11 May 1972.

1974   *Birds of a Feather* (1 act; music dance piece). Performed
    Carbondale, IL, 20 December 1974.

1975   *The Cherry Tree Carol* (liturgical drama).

Bergersen, Baldwin (b. Vienna, Austria, 20 February 1914, of American parents;
    to U.S. as a baby; ASCAP)

1945   *Carib Song* ("lyric drama" in 2 acts; libretto by William Archibald).
    Performed New York, 27 September 1945.

1948   *Far Harbour* (libretto by William Archibald). Commission from
    Lincoln Kirstein. Performed at Hunter College Playhouse, New
    York, 30 January 1948.

Bergh, Arthur (b. St. Paul, MN, 24 March 1882; d. on ship *S. S. President
    Cleveland* en route to Honolulu, 11 February 1962; Anderson;
    ASCAP; *Baker's*)

-    *The Goblin Fair* (operetta).

-    *In Arcady* (operetta).

-    *Niorada* (romantic opera).

-    *The Pied Piper of Hamelin* (melodrama).

-    *The Raven* (melodrama).

Bergsma, William (b. Oakland, CA, 1 April 1921; *Amerigrove*; ASCAP)

1956   *The Wife of Martin Guerre* (3 acts; libretto by William Archibald).
    Performed at Juilliard School, New York, 15 February 1956.
    Recorded by CRI.

1973   *The Murder of Comrade Sharik* (comic satire; prologue and two
    acts—89 minutes; libretto by composer after Mikhail Bulgakov's
    novel *Heart of Dog*). Performed Seattle, WA, 1973, and Brooklyn,
    NY, 10 April 1986. Kornick.

Berkeley, Edward

1982   *Dear Friends and Gentle Hearts* (on the life of Stephen Foster).
    Performed Aspen, CO, 21 June 1982.

Berkeley, F. H. F.

1830   *Rokeby*. Performed New York.

Berkowitz, Ralph (b. New York, 5 September 1910; Anderson)

1955   *A Telephone Call*. Première, Rio de Janeiro, Brazil, 15 December
    1955.

Berkowitz, Sol (b. Warren, OH, 27 April 1922; Anderson; ASCAP)

1956   *Fat Tuesday* (jazz opera; 2 acts). Performed Tamiment, PA, 11
    August 1956.

Berkson, Jeff

1989   *Pastel Refugees*. Performed Evanston, IL, 4 April 1989.

Berl, Paul
> 1951   *Judgment Day* (1 act—70 minutes). Performed at Hunter College, New York, 28 May 1951.

Berman, Norman (b. Detroit, MI, 1949; ASCAP)
> 1986   *Mandragola* (libretto by Peter Maloney after Machiavelli). Performed at Folger Shakespeare Theater, Washington, DC, 9 December 1986.

Bernardo, José Paul (or Raoul) (b. Havana, Cuba, 3 October 1938; *WhoAm*)
> 1974   *The Child* (*La niña*) (after 1878 poem by José Marti; set in Guatemala). Performed at St. George Opera Festival, Albany, NY, 8 August 1974.
> 1980   *Something for the Palace* (libretto by Bob Joyner; about a vaudeville performer). Performed by Central City Opera, CO, August 1980.
> 1983   *The Unavoidable Consequences of Getting Caught in a Farce.* Published by Belwin-Mills.

Berney, William
> 1967   *Dark of the Moon* (libretto by Howard Richardson; a folk-drama set in the Great Smokies). Performed Gatlinburg, TN, 1967.

Bernstein, D. J.
> 1986   *Aladdin and Company.* Performed by Heights Players, Brooklyn, NY, 27 September 1986.

Bernstein, Doug
> 1988   *Artistic License* (1 act; libretto by Denis Markel). Performed by Musical Theater Works, New York, 13 April 1988.

Bernstein, Leonard (b. Lawrence, MA, 25 August 1918; d. New York, 14 October 1990; *Amerigrove*; Anderson; ASCAP)
> 1952   *Trouble in Tahiti* (1 act, 7 scenes; libretto by composer). Performed Waltham, MA, 12 June 1952. Recorded by MGM. Used in 1984 as the second act of an expanded version of *A Quiet Place* (3 acts); performed in full at Teatro alla Scala, Milan, Italy, 19 June 1984, and Kennedy Center, Washington, 20 July 1984.
> 1956   *Candide* (comic operetta—commedia dell'arte vignettes; 1 act; libretto by composer, Lillian Hellman, Richard Wilbur, John Latouche, D. Parker after Voltaire). Performed Boston, 29 October 1956; New York, 1 December 1956; by New York Opera, 13 October 1982; Pennsylvania Opera, 3 March 1989; New York Opera, 18 July 1989; in Berlin, Germany, May 1989; and by Lyric Opera, Dallas, TX, 11 June 1990. Recordings: Random House (1957), Columbia (1973), New World (1973 and 1982). Kornick.
> 1957   *West Side Story* (tragedy; prologue and 2 acts; libretto by Stephen Sondheim. Premièred at Winter Garden Theatre, New York, 26 September 1957. Recordings: Random House (1958), Chilton (1973), Columbia (1985). Kornick.
> 1971   *Mass* (multimedia work; libretto from the Roman Mass and by composer and Stephen Schwartz). Performed for the opening of

Kennedy Center, Washington, 8 September 1971. Recording: Columbia. Kornick.

1983   *A Quiet Place* (domestic tragedy; 1 act; libretto by Stephen Wadsworth). Commissioned by Houston Grand Opera, Teatro alla Scala, Milan, and Kennedy Center. Premièred in Houston, 17 June 1983; performed Milan, June 1984, and Washington, DC, 22 July 1984. Revised 1987 to 3 acts, including *Trouble in Tahiti*. (See *New Yorker*, 20 November 1989, 114.) Kornick.

-    *Lolita* (after Nabokov). Was in progress for performance by Vienna Staatsoper and Houston Opera (*COS*-3).

Bernstein, Richard

1971   *Young Abe Lincoln*, with Victor Ziskin, Joan Javits, and John Allen (1 act). Performed New York, February 1971.

1987   *Israel, Oh Israel*, with Morris Bernstein.

Berry, Wallace (b. La Crosse, WI, 10 January 1928; d. 1991; *Amerigrove*; ASCAP; *Who's Who*)

1954   *The Admirable Bashville* (1 act—65 minutes; after Shaw).

Besoyan, Rick (b. Reedley, CA, 2 July 1924; d. Sayville, NY, 13 March 1970; *Amerigrove*)

1959   *Little Mary Sunshine*. Performed off Broadway, New York, 1959.

Beveridge, Thomas (ASCAP)

1958   *Dido and Aeneas* (1 act). Performed Boston, 14 February 1958.

Beversdorf, (Samuel) **Thomas** (b. Yoakum, TX, 8 August 1924; Anderson)

1969   *The Hooligan* (1 act; after Chekhov's *The Boor*).

Beynon, Jared

1984   *Iphigenia* (1 act; libretto by R. Radin after Euripides). Performed by New Opera, New York, 21 February 1984.

Bezanson, Philip (b. Athol, MA, 6 January 1916; d. Hadley, MA, 11 March 1975; ACA; *Amerigrove*)

1959   *Western Child* (3 acts; libretto by P. Engle). Performed at University of Iowa, Iowa City, 28 July 1959. Revised as *Golden Child* for Hall of Fame, NBC television, 1 act only, 16 December 1960.

1963   *Stranger in Eden* (3 acts; libretto by John Reardon).

Biales, Albert (AMC)

1985   *Belisa* (after Federico García Lorca). Performed St. Paul, MN, 29 January 1985.

Bielawa, Herbert Walker (b. Chicago, 3 February 1930; AMC; Anderson; ASCAP; *Baker's*)

1962   *A Bird in the Bush* (1 act; chamber opera).

Bilota, John George (AMC)

-    *Aria da capo* (1 act; libretto after Edna St. Vincent Millay play).

Bilunas, Michael (AMC)

1982   *You Were Perfectly Fine* (15 minutes; libretto after Dorothy Parker).

Bimboni, Alberto (b. Florence, Italy, 24 August 1882; d. New York, 18 June 1960; in U.S. from 1912; Anderson; ASCAP; *Baker's*)

1926   *Winona* (3 acts; libretto by Perry Williams after a Sioux legend). Première by American Grand Opera Co., Portland, OR, 11 November 1926; also performed Minneapolis, MN, 27 January 1928, with an audience of 9,000. Bispham Medal, 1927-28. Hipsher.

1928   *Karina.* Performed Minneapolis, 1928. (Title in *Baker's*: *Karin.*)

1936   *There Was a Little Gate* (*Il cancelleto d'oro*) (1 act). Performed New York, 11 March 1936.

1949   *In the Name of Culture* (1 act—70 minutes). Performed at Eastman School, Rochester, NY, 9 May 1949.

-    *Calandrino* (*The Fire Worshipers*) (1 act).

-    *I fiaschi* (*The Flask*).

Binder, Abraham Wolfe (b. New York, 13 January 1895; d. there, 10 October 1966; Anderson; *Baker's*)

1960   *A Goat in Chelm* (Hassidic for "Gotham"; 1 act). Performed New York, 20 March 1960.

Bingham, Seth (b. Bloomfield, NJ, 16 April 1882; d. New York, 21 June 1972; *Amerigrove*; ASCAP)

1917   *La Charelzenn* (150 minutes).

Bingham, Susan (b. Waltham, MA, 31 May 1944; AMC; *Who's Who*)

(N.B.: all operas were written to librettos by the composer, and performed New Haven, CT, unless otherwise specified.)

1980   *The Awakening* (25 minutes; libretto by Neil Olsen; set in Jesus's time). Performed at Trinity Church-on-the-Green, 1980.

1980   *The Sacrifice of Isaac* (28 minutes). Performed by Chancel Opera, 1980.

1980   *Simeon* (30 minutes). Performed by Chancel Opera Company of Connecticut, 1980.

1981   *On the Road to Emmaus* (20 minutes). Performed by Chancel Opera, 1981.

1982   *The Emperor and the Nightingale* (70 minutes). Performed at Worthington Hooker School, June 1982.

1983   *Ruth* (20 minutes). Performed by Chancel Opera, 1983.

1984   *Eli W* (on the life of Eli Whitney). Performed at Shubert Center for the Performing Arts, 18 May 1984.

1984   *The Gift of the Magi* (20 minutes; after O. Henry). Performed by Chancel Opera, 1 December 1984.

1984   *The Last Leaf* (23 minutes; after O. Henry). Performed by Chancel Opera, 1 December 1984.

1984   *Tiny Operas* (a trilogy of short operas after O. Henry). Performed by Chancel Opera, 1984.

1985   *Tales of a Magic Monastery* (40 minutes). Performed by Chancel Opera, 1985.

1986   *By the Pool of Siloam* (25 minutes).

1986   *Isis and Osiris* (50 minutes).

1987   *The Fisherman and His Wife* (25 minutes).

1987   *Magdalene* (30 minutes).

1987   *Makes the Whole World Kin* (1 act). Reading by After Dinner Opera, New York, 27 March 1987.

1987   *Piece Together* (25 minutes). Performed by Chancel Opera on tour, 1987.

1988   *Alice Meets Mock Turtle* (after Carroll). Performed by After Dinner Opera, New York, 28 March 1988.

1988   *The Wild Swans* (1 hour; after Andersen). Performed at Worthington Hooker School and Chancel Opera, April 1988.

1988   *The Twelve Dancing Princesses* (40 minutes; libretto by composer with Michael Lerner and Jennifer Schulsberg). Performed by Chancel Opera, 8 July 1988.

1988   *The Musicians of Bremen* (50 minutes; libretto by the composer with Michael Lerner and Jennifer Schulsberg). Performed by Chancel Opera, 29 July 1988.

-   *The Conversation Between Mary and the Angel Gabriel* (10 minutes).

-   *The Raising of Lazarus*. Performed by Chancel Opera.

Bird, Arthur (b. Belmont, MA, 23 July 1856; d. Berlin, Germany, 22 December 1923; *Amerigrove*; Hipsher, 428)

1895   *Daphne: or, The Pipes of Arcady* (operetta; 3 acts; libretto by Marguerite Merington). Concert version, 1895; private staged performance at Waldorf-Astoria Hotel, New York, 13 December 1897. *New York Times*: "a pretty and clever little opera with good choruses." The libretto won 1st prize by the National Conservatory of Music.

Bird, Hubert C. (b. Joplin, MO, 12 October 1939; Anderson)

1971   *The Powerful Potion of Dr. Dee*. Performed Palm Desert, CA, 24 October 1971.

Birkenhead, Susan (b. New York, 1935; ASCAP)

1979   *A Long Way to Boston*, with Michael Lohman and Donald Siegal. Performed East Haddam, CT, 7 September 1979.

1986   *212* (on the House Un-American Committee in the 1950s). Performed by Musical Theatre Works, New York, 10 November 1986.

Biscardi, Chester (b. Kenosha, WI, 19 October 1948; *Amerigrove*; *Who's Who*)

1985   *Tight-Rope* (chamber opera; 9 uninterrupted scenes—89 minutes; libretto by Henry Butler). Performed at Musicians's Club, New York, 16 February 1985, and at University of Wisconsin, Madison, 5 October 1985. Published by Presser. Kornick.

Bixel, James

1978   *The Annuity* (2 acts; libretto by Lawrence Templin after Pirandello). Performed at Bluffton College, OH, 26 May 1978.

1989   *Dance of the Kobzar: Scenes from the Life of John Peter Klassen; Artist as Peacemaker* (2 acts). Performed at Bluffton College, OH, 25 May 1989.

Black, Arnold (ASCAP)
- 1955 *The Prince and the Pauper* (after Mark Twain). Performed Duxbury, MA, 26 August 1955.
- 1983 *The Beautiful Dream of Ilya Ilyich Oblomov*. Performed Waterford, CT, May 1983.

Blackman, Gary
- 1988 *The Life and Times of Bobby Bloom*. Performed by National Musical Theater Network, 21 November 1988. Published by that company.
- 1988 *Journey into Jazz*. Performed by National Musical Theater Network, 28 November 1988.

Blackwood, Easley (b. Indianapolis, IN, 21 April 1933; ASCAP; *Amerigrove*; Anderson; *Baker's*; *Who's Who*)
- 1975 *Gulliver: A Spatialoperadramafilmevent*. Composed with Elliot Kaplan, Frank Lewin, Robert Karmon, and Louis Phillips. Performed by Minnesota Opera, Minneapolis, 22 February 1975.

Blakely, Kent
- 1987 *Mask* (27 minutes; libretto by composer). Performed at Peabody Conservatory, Baltimore, 1 November 1987.

Blakeslee, Samuel Earle (native of Colorado; Hipsher, 428: E. Earle Blakeslee)
- 1924 *The Legend of Wiwaste* (on a Dakota legend). Performed Ontario, Canada, 25 April 1924, and also 1927. Bispham Medal.
- 1927 *Red Cloud*. Performed Ontario, Canada, 1927, and at University of California, Los Angeles, July 1967.

Blanchard, Frederick W.
- 1898 *Cosita: or, The Daughter of a Don*. Reading, San Francisco, for the Boston Opera on tour, March 1898. See *Los Angeles Capital*, 27 May 1899.

Blank, Allan (b. New York, 27 December 1925; AMC; *Amerigrove*; Anderson; *Who's Who*)
- 1960 *Aria da capo* (1 act; chamber opera; libretto by composer after Edna St. Vincent Millay).
- 1980 *Finale: Melange* (4 minutes).
- 1980 *Zuluz Live in a Land Without a Square* (5 minutes).
- 1983 *The Magic Bonbons* (8 scenes—45 minutes; libretto by composer after L. G. Baum). NEA grant.
- 1986 *The Noise* (90 minutes; libretto after Boris Vian's *Les Batisseurs d'empire*). Performed Richmond, VA, April 1986.
- 1986 *Excitement at the Circus* (children's play; 1 act; piano accompaniment; libretto by Irving Leitner). Published by Seesaw Music.

Blatt, Josef (b. Vienna, Austria, 20 October 1906; to U.S. 1937; longtime director of orchestra at University of Michigan; information from composer)
- c 1940 *Moses* (1 hour—3 acts; libretto by composer after the biblical story of the exodus to the Golden Calf), for 7 men, 1 woman, chorus,

ballet, and an orchestra of 14 players. Act 2 (20 minutes; for one singer—Moses—and offstage chorus, set on Mount Sinai) performed at University of Michigan, Ann Arbor, 22 January 1964.

Blau, Eric
1986 *Dori* (libretto by Elliot Weiss). Performed at Cathedral of St. John the Divine, New York, 4 November 1986.

Bledsoe, Robert
1984 *The Stranger* (1 hour; after Kotzebue, Menschenhass, and Reue). Performed at University of Texas, El Paso, 17 April 1984.

Bley, Carla Borg (b. Claremont, CA, 11 May 1938; *Amerigrove*; Anderson)
1985 *For Under the Volcano* (1 act; about Malcolm Lowry). Performed by New Music America, Los Angeles, 1 November 1985.

Blisa, Alica
1966 *The Music Club* (1 act). Performed Atlanta, GA, 22 April 1966.
- *The School Board* (1 act).

Bliss, P. Paul (b. Chicago, 25 November 1872; d. Oswego, NY, 2 February 1933; Anderson; *Baker's*)
- *Feast of Little Lanterns.*
- *Feast of Red Corn.*
- *In India.*

Blitzstein, Marc (b. Philadelphia, 2 March 1905; d. Fort de France, Martinique, 22 January 1964; *Amerigrove*; ASCAP)
1928 *Triple Sec* (opera-farce; 1 act—18 minutes). Performed Philadelphia, 6 May 1929, and by After Dinner Opera, New York, 6 June 1950. Published by Schott.
1929 *Parabola and Circula* (opera-ballet; 1 act—"full evening").
1931 *The Harpies* (1 act—50 minutes; libretto by composer). Performed New York, 25 May 1953, and 5 May 1954. Recorded by Premier.
1932 *The Condemned* (choral opera; 1 act; libretto by composer).
1937 *The Cradle Will Rock* (1 act, 10 scenes; libretto by composer). Composer conducted first performance, New York, 16 June 1937 and 26 December 1947, and by New York Opera, 1960. (The first performance had an advance ticket sale of 14,000).
1937 *I've Got the Tune* (radio song-play; libretto by composer. Performed on CBS radio, New York, 24 October 1937.
1940 *No for an Answer* (2 acts; libretto by composer). Performed New York, 5 January 1941.
1945 *Goloopchik* (musical play; libretto by composer); incomplete.
1949 *Regina* (3 acts; libretto by composer after Lillian Hellman's *The Little Foxes*), revised 1953 and 1958. Performed New Haven (Gilbert Chase: Boston), 6 October 1949, and New York, 31 October 1949; by New York Opera, April 1953, and Lyric Opera of Kansas City, MO, 16 September 1989. Published by TAMS-Whitmark.
1955 *Reuben, Reuben* (musical play; 2 acts—2 hours; libretto by composer). Performed Boston, 10 October 1955. Published by Chappell.

1959   *Juno* (musical; 2 acts; libretto by composer and J. Stein after O'Casey). Performed New York, 9 March 1959.

1963   *The Magic Barrel* (1 act; libretto by composer and Bernard Malamud), completed by Leonard J. Lehrman. Performed Ithaca, NY, August 1964.

1964   *Sacco and Vanzetti* (libretto by composer), incomplete.

1973   *Idiots First* (fable; 1 act—60 minutes; libretto by composer after Bernard Malamud), completed by Leonard J. Lehrman. Performed with Leonard Lehrman's *Karla* as *Tales of Malamud*. Première by Marc Blitzstein Opera Co., Bloomington, IN, 14 March 1976; also performed by Bel Canto Opera, New York, 11 January 1978. Kornick.

Bloch, Ernest (b. Geneva, Switzerland, 24 July 1880; d. Portland, OR, 15 July 1959; in U.S. from 1909; *Amerigrove*; ASCAP)

1909   *Macbeth* (lyric drama; libretto by E. Fleg after Shakespeare). Performed at Opéra-Comique, Paris, France, 30 November 1910.

Block, Steven (b. Bronx, NY, 5 November 1952; ACA/AMC; *Who's Who*)

1981   *The Tumbler of God* (2 hours; libretto by Stephanie Block after a medieval legend). Mellon Fellowship.

-   *Canterbury Tales of Marriage* (puppet opera; after Chaucer).

Blumenfeld, Aaron Joel (b. Newark, NJ, 18 April 1932; *WhoAm*)

1988   *Hashiur* (*The Lesson*) (20 minutes; on spiritual issues in Judaism). Performed in Trinity Chamber Series, Berkeley, CA, 7 February 1988.

Blumenfeld, Harold (b. Seattle, WA, 15 October 1923; *Amerigrove*; Anderson; ASCAP; *Who's Who*)

1962   *Amphitryon 4* (3 acts; libretto by the composer after Molière).

1968   *Gentle Boy* (after Hawthorne). Commission by St. Louis New Music Circle.

1969   *The Road to Salem* (TV opera).

1979   *Fritzi* (1 act; libretto by Charles Konchek after Molnar's *The Witch*). Reading by OPERA America Showcase, January 1981; performed by Chicago Opera Theater, 30 November 1988. *COS*-1 and 4.

1985   *Fourscore: An Opera of Opposites* (2 acts; libretto by Charles Kondek after Nestroy's *Haus der Temperamente*). Performed Cincinnati, 3 March 1989.

Boatner, Edward H. (b. New Orleans, 13 November 1898; d. New York, 16 June 1981; AMC; ASCAP; Southern)

1963   *Julius Sees Her in Rome, Georgia* (libretto by composer).

-   *Troubled in Mind: Forbidden Love* (Afro-American slave opera).

Boaz, Norman

-   *Wee Pals* (45 minutes; libretto by Ole Kittleson and Morrie Turner after Turner's comic strip).

Bobrow, Morrie
1990 *Love and Money* (10 minutes; after O. Henry's "The Hypo-Thesis of Failure"). Performed at Climat Theatre, San Francisco, 15 February 1990.

Bobrow, Sanchie (b. Brooklyn, NY, 3 October 1960; *WhoAm*)
1981 *Life Song—A Stage Piece for Passover* (1 act; libretto by composer). Performed at Rutgers University, New Brunswick, NJ, 9 April 1981.

Bock, Jerry (b. New Haven, CN, 23 November 1928)
1964 *Fiddler on the Roof* (musical comedy; 2 acts; libretto by Sheldon Harnick based on stories by Sholem Aleichem). Première at Imperial Theatre, New York, 22 September 1964. Recordings: RCA (1964), Chilton (1973). Kornick.

Boehnlein, Frank Clifford (b. Bedford, OH, 2 February 1945; Anderson; ASCAP)
1976 *The Last Best Hope of Earth* (multimedia work). Performed Denton, TX, 1977.

Boessing, Paul and **Martha**
1970 *The Wanderer: A Ballad of Now* (folk opera). Performed by Center Opera, Minneapolis, 28 February 1970.

Bohlen, Donald
1969 *Ismene* (2 acts; libretto by Robert Jones). Performed at Central Missouri State College, Warrensburg, 17 February 1969.

Bohmler, Craig
1985 *The Harlot and the Monk* (libretto by James Howley after an 8th-century Indian play). Performed Banff, Canada, February 1985.
1991? *The Achilles Heel* (libretto by Mary Carol Warwick). Performed by Texas Opera Theater, Houston, February 1992.

Bohrnstedt, Wayne R. (b. Onalaska, WI, 19 January 1923; Anderson; ASCAP)
1956 *The Necklace* (1 act; chamber opera; libretto by Lucile March). Performed Redlands, CA, 12 March 1956.

Bokser, Zelmar
1984 *The Woman Who Dared: A Fine Agitation* (75 minutes; libretto by Cynthia Fuller, about Susan B. Anthony). Performed Rochester, NY, 17 November 1984.

Bolcom, William (b. Seattle, WA, 26 May 1938; *Amerigrove*; *Who's Who*)
1963 *Dynamite Tonite* (cabaret opera; 2 acts; libretto by Arnold Weinstein; 2 actors). Performed New York, February 1964.
1966 *Greatshot* (cabaret opera; 2 acts; libretto by Arnold Weinstein; 2 actors).
1987 *Casino Paradise* (libretto by Arnold Weinstein). Performed at American Music Theater Festival, Philadelphia, 10 October 1987, and 8 April 1990.
- *Gold* (after Norris's *McTeague*). Commissioned for performance by Chicago Lyric Opera, 1992-93 season.

Bolossy, Kiralfy (Krohn)
1904   *Louisiana Purchase.* Composed for performance at the St. Louis
Fair.

Bonawitz, Johann Heinrich (1839-1917; in the U.S. 1852-76)
1874   *The Bride of Messina.* Performed Philadelphia.
1875   *Ostrolenka* (4 acts). Performed Philadelphia.

Bond, Victoria (b. Los Angeles, 6 May 1945; *Amerigrove*; *Who's Who*)
1986   *Everyone Is Good for Something* (45 minutes; after a Slavic tale).
Performed Louisville, KY, 8 March 1986.
1988   *Gulliver* (after Swift). Reading, Louisville, KY, 17 February 1988;
was scheduled for première there, 1990.

Bonds, Margaret Allison (b. Chicago, 3 March 1913; d. Los Angeles, 26 April
1972; *Amerigrove*; ASCAP; Southern)
-   *Burlesque Is Alive.* Performed Los Angeles, 1970.
-   *Romey and Julie* (comic opera or musical; libretto by R. Dunmore).
-   *Shakespeare in Harlem: U.S.A.*
-   *Tropics After Dark.*
-   *Troubled Island.*
-   *U.S.A.* (after Dos Passos).
-   *Winter Night's Dream.*

Bonner, Eugene MacDonald (b. Washington, NC, 1889; *Amerigrove*; Anderson)
1917   *Barbara Frietchie* (3 hours; based on Clyde Fitch's play of that
title). Hipsher.
1927   *He Who Marries a Dumb Wife* (also given as *La Comédie de celui
qui épousa une femme muette*; libretto after the play with that title
by Anatole France). Hipsher
c 1928   *The Venetian Glass Nephew* (2 hours; libretto after E. Wylie).
Performed New York.
1936   *The Gods of the Mountain.*
-   *Frankie and Johnnie.*

Bonsignore, Camillo
1925   *I miserabili* (4 acts). Performed at Brooklyn Academy of Music,
1925.

Boren, Murray
1976   *Abraham and Isaac* (libretto by Orson Scott Card). Performed at
Brigham Young University, Provo, UT, 3 March 1976. Videotape
available.

Bornschein, Franz Carl (b. Baltimore, MD, 10 February 1879; d. Baltimore, 8
June 1948; *Amerigrove*; ASCAP)
1918   *Mother Goose's Goslings* (children's operetta; libretto by composer).
1932   *The Willow Plate* (operetta; libretto by D. Rose).
1934   *Song of Songs* (lyric opera; libretto by composer and F. Coutts).

Borowski, Felix (b. Burton in Kendal, England, 10 March 1872; d. Chicago, 6
September 1956; in Chicago from 1897; *Amerigrove*; Anderson;
ASCAP)
1935　*Fernando del nonsensico* (1 hour).
-　*Boudoir* (pantomime).

Borroff, Edith (b. New York, 2 August 1925; ACA/AMC; *Amerigrove*; Anderson;
Baker's; Cohen; *Who's Who*)
1977　*The Sun and the Wind* (1 act—43 minutes; libretto by composer).
Performed Binghamton, NY, 29 April 1977, composer conducting.

Boshkoff, Ruth
-　*Little Red Riding Hood* (25 minutes; libretto by composer). *COS*-4.
Published by MMB Music.

Boswell, William (b. Cynthiana, KY, 18 June 1948; *WhoAm*)
1980　*Memories* (1 act; libretto by J. Fowles, D. Lalley, K. Breverman,
and R. Bryan). Performed New York, 22 June 1980.
1980　*A Thousand Words* (libretto by Joyce Hill Stonor). Performed by
Encompass Musical Theater, New York, 23 June 1980.
1981　*Unguided Tour* (1 act). Performed by New Workshop Theater, New
York, 6 February 1981.
1982　*Frog-Hopping* (25 minutes; libretto by Robert Solomon). Performed
at Brooklyn College, NY, 5 February 1982.
1984　*Scene Changes* (interludes between the acts of operas). Performed
at Brooklyn College, NY, 3 February 1984.

Bottje, Will Gay (b. Grand Rapids, MI, 30 June 1925; *Amerigrove*; Anderson)
1968　*Altgeld* (3 acts; libretto by composer). Performed Carbondale, IL, 7
March 1969.
1972　*Root!* (2 acts; comic chamber opera; libretto by J. Maloon).
Performed by Pro Musica Opera of New Jersey, 1978.
1977　*From the Winds and Farthest Spaces* (multi-media; texts by Loren
Eiseley). Performed at Grand Valley State College.
1987　*The Village That Voted the Earth Is Flat* (2 acts—150 minutes;
libretto by Christian Moe after Kipling). Performed by New
Tuners Workshop, Chicago, 1987-88 season.

Bouchard, Linda (b. Val d'Or, Québec, Canada, 21 May 1957; Cohen; *WhoAm*)
1982　*Triskelion* (concert-drama; 1 act—42 minutes; libretto by Amme
Tierney on interactions of imagination, love, and reason).
Workshop performance by Manhattan Contemporary Ensemble,
New York, December 1982; première by Open Circle, New York,
March 1983.

Boutte, Duane
1987　*Bottoms Up: The Musicommedi* (3 acts; libretto by Luke Han, Ron
Marasco, Dwight Smith, and Paul Svendsen). ASCAP Foundation
award, 1988. Performed at University of California, Los Angeles,
1987-88 season.

Bowden, John
- *Trilby*, with Basil Adlam and Roy Benowitz (libretto by Joan Tratner and Robert Day). Published by Janco Music.

Bowers, Clarence W.
1915 *The Mendicant.* Performed San Diego, CA, 1915.

Bowers, Robert Hood (b. Chambersburg, PA, 24 May 1877; d. New York, 29 December 1941; Anderson; ASCAP)
1911 *The Red Rose* (musical comedy or operetta; 3 acts; libretto by Harry B. and Robert B. Smith). Performed New York. Vocal score published in New York by Remick, 1911.
1924 *Old English* (operetta).
1927 *Oh, Ernest* (operetta).
1929 *Listen In* (operetta).
- *The Anniversary* (1 act).

Bowles, Anthony
1981 *Mandrake!* (90 minutes; after Machiavelli's *Mandragola*). Performed by Solo Repertory Theatre, New York, September 1981.

Bowles, Paul Frederic (b. Jamaica, NY, 30 December 1910; *Amerigrove*; Anderson; ASCAP; *Baker's*)
1937 *Denmark Vesey.*
1943 *The Wind Remains* (libretto after Federico García Lorca).
1955 *Yerma.*

Boylan, Mary
1980 *Alias Jimmy Valentine* (libretto by Robert Dahdah after O. Henry). Performed by Theatre for the New City, New York, 25 September 1980.

Boyle, George F. (b. Sydney, Australia, 29 June 1886; d. Philadelphia, 20 June 1948; to U.S. in 1910; Anderson)
- *The Black Rose* (operetta).

Boyle, Harrison Robert (b. Philadelphia, 9 January 1953; Anderson)
1984 *Crazy Nora* (3 acts; libretto by Robert Barnett on a Philadelphia incident of 1820). Reading by the Muse (WHYY-TV), Philadelphia, 28 December 1984.

Braden, John Stuart (b. Ashboro, NC, 1946; ASCAP)
- *Downriver* (libretto by the composer and Jeff Tanborino after Mark Twain's *Huckleberry Finn*). *COS*-4.

Bradley, Ruth (b. 1894 in New Jersey; Anderson; Cohen)
1961 *The Barren Pines* (1 act; libretto by Dorothy Dix Lawrence). Performed New York, 12 February 1961.

Bradbury, William Batchelder (b. York County, ME, 6 October 1816; d. Montclair, NJ, 7 January 1868; *Amerigrove*; Hipsher)
1856 *Esther, the Beautiful Queen* (dramatic cantata; libretto by C. M. Cady after the biblical story), for solo voices, chorus, piano.

Braine, Robert (b. Springfield, OH, 27 May 1896; d. New York, 26 August 1940; Anderson)
- 1924 *The Eternal Light.*
- 1926 *Virginia.*
- 1927 *The Wandering Jew* (libretto by E. Temple Thurston). Private audition, New York, 4 May 1927. Hipsher, 428.
- 1929 *Diana.*

Bramberg, Joyce
- 1990 *The Hook* (after John Collier's "The Chaser"). Ten Minute Musicals Project winner. Performed San Francisco, 15 February 1990.

Branca, Glenn (b. Harrisburg, PA, 6 October 1948; *Amerigrove*)
- 1975 *Anthropophagoi* (music-theater work). Performed Boston, 1975.
- 1986 *Woyzeck* (after Büchner). Reading by Minnesota Opera, St. Paul, MN, 11 April 1986.
- 1989 *The Tower* (multimedia work). Reading by New Dramatists, New York, 13 April 1989; première by Creation Production Co., New York, summer 1989.

Brand, Max (b. Lemberg, Germany [Lvov, USSR; Lwòw, Poland], 26 April 1896; d. Langenzersdorf, near Vienna, Austria, 5 April 1980; in U.S. in 1940-75, citizen 1945; Anderson; *Baker's*)
- 1928 *Maschinist Hopkins* (3 acts).
- 1944 *The Gate* (scenic oratorio), with narrator. Performed by Metropolitan Opera, New York, 23 May 1944.
- 1955 *Stormy Interlude* (1 act; libretto by composer).

Brandon, Johnny
- 1982 *Shim Sham* (2 acts; libretto by the composer and Eric Blau on the life of Buddy Bradley). Performed by Pennsylvania Stage Co., Allentown, PA, 3 November 1982.
- 1987 *Prime Time* (libretto by composer and Ra Shiomi).

Brandorff, Carl (b. Newark, NJ, 17 December 1892; Hipsher)
- - *The Gypsy Queen* (light opera).
- - *Noah* (religious music drama).
- - *Jesus Christ* (religious music drama).

Brandt, Noah (b. New York, 8 April 1858; d. San Francisco, 11 November 1925; Hipsher)
- 1892 *Captain Cook* (light opera, on the subject of Cook landing on Hawaii in 1778). Performed at Bush Street Theater, San Francisco, week beginning 2 September 1895; also at Madison Square Garden, New York, 12 July 1897, composer conducting.
- - *Daniel* (biblical opera; 5 acts).
- - *Leona.*
- - *Wing Wong* or *A Chinese New Year*. Neither the original, nor its revision, was produced at Tivoli Opera House, San Francisco, as originally planned.

Brandt, William Edward (b. Butte, MT, 14 January 1920; Anderson; Schoep; *WhoAm*)

1961   *No Neutral Ground: An Incident in the Civil War* (1 act—45 minutes; about the Civil War). Performed at Washington State University Pullman, December 1961.

\-   *Beaumarchais* (3 acts). "In preparation," *COS*-1.

Branscombe, Gena (Mrs. John Ferguson Tenney; b. Picton, Ontario, 4 November 1881; d. New York, 26 July 1977; studied at Chicago Musical College; Anderson; ASCAP; *Baker's*)

1920   *Pilgrims of Destiny* (choral drama). Performed for National Federation of Music Clubs, Plymouth, MA, 1920.

1930   *Bells of Circumstance* (about Quebec; unfinished, but a substantial amount performed). Published by Ditson.

Brant, Henry (Dreyfus) (b. Montreal, Québec, 15 September 1913; *Amerigrove*; Anderson; ASCAP)

1956   *Grand Universal Circus* (1 act)

1978   *Everybody, Inc.* (2 acts; libretto by Patricia Brant). NEA grant. Performed by Santa Fe Opera, NM, summer 1981.

\-   *Alisaunde.*

\-   *Dischord* (2 hours).

\-   *Entente cordiale* (40 minutes).

\-   *Miss O'Grady* (90 minutes).

Brantley, Royal

1978   *Samuel* (2 acts; libretto by composer). Performed at West Texas State University, Canyon, 16 November 1978.

Braswell, John

1973   *Interior Castle* (about St. Theresa of Avila). Performed at Lenox Arts Center, MA, 19 July 1973.

Bratt, C. Griffith (b. Baltimore, MD, 21 November 1914; Anderson)

1962   *A Season for Sorrow* (libretto by Hazel Weston; about Idaho in 1905; for the state centennial). Performed Boise, ID, 13 September 1962, and 19 January 1990.

1972   *Rachel* (5 acts; libretto by Hazel Weston). Performed by Boise Opera Guild with the Boise Philharmonic, ID, 1972.

\-   *Year of the One Reed.* Commission by the Boise Civic Opera, ID.

Bray, John (b. England, 19 June 1782; d. Leeds, England, 19 June 1822; in U.S. 1805-22; *Amerigrove*; Porter)

1808   *The Indian Princess: or, La Belle Sauvage, an Operatic Melo-drame in Three Acts* (libretto by James Nelson Barker; about Pocahontas). Performed Philadelphia, 6 April 1808; and, as *Pocahontas*, at the Drury Lane Theatre, London, 15 December 1820. Published by G. E. Blake in Philadelphia, 1808; reprint, New York: Da Capo, 1972.

1809   *Who Pays the Piper?: or, My Lord Knows Who* (comic opera; 1 act; libretto by composer). Première, Philadelphia, 25 March 1809.

1809   *Whitsuntide Frolics: or, Harlequin Hurry Scurry* (interlude; 1 act). Première, Baltimore, 22 May 1809.

1811   *Alberto Albertini: or, The Robber King* (dramatic romance; 5 acts; libretto by William Dunlap). Première, New York, 25 January 1811.

1814   *The Miller and His Men* ("grand melodrama"; 2 acts; libretto by Isaac Pocock), vocal music by Bray, music for action compiled and adapted by Dupuy. Performed in London, 21 October 1813; in New York, 4 July 1814.

Bray, M.

1975   *Memoirs from a Holocaust* (1 act). Performed at Barry College, Miami Shores, FL, 27 December 1975.

Bredemann, Dan

-    *Homespun*. Performed Cincinnati. *COS*-2.

Breedon, Daniel

-    *The Frog Prince* (2 acts; libretto by Catherine Breedon). *COS*-4.

Breil, Joseph Carl (b. Pittsburgh, PA, 29 June 1870; d. Los Angeles, 23 January 1926; *Amerigrove*; Anderson; Hipsher.)
(Breil wrote most of his own librettos.)

1898   *Orlando of Milan*. Written before his 18th birthday, it was given an amateur performance in Pittsburgh.

1910   *Love Laughs at Locksmiths*. Performed Portland, ME, 27 October 1910; Kingston, OH; and New York.

1913   *Professor Tattle*. Performed Chicago.

1913   *The Seventh Chord* (comic opera). Performed New York.

1917   *The Legend* (libretto by Jacques Byrne). Performed by Metropolitan Opera, New York, 12 March 1919.

1925   *Der Asra* (miniature opera; 1 act; libretto after Heinrich Heine). Performed at Gamut Club Theater, Los Angeles, 24 November 1925.

-    *Old Harvard* (opera buffa; 1 act).

-    *Orlando of Milan*.
(In 1912 Breil composed a score to the film *Queen Elizabeth* for showing in Chicago.)

Bremers, Beverly (ASCAP)

1987   *Have a Jewish Christmas. . . !?*. Performed by Burbank Theatre Guild, CA, December 1987.

Bresnick, Martin (b. New York, 13 November 1946; *Amerigrove*; ASCAP)

1976   *Ants* (theater piece; libretto by composer and R. Myslewski).

1982   *The Signal* (1 act—15 minutes; libretto by the composer after a Yiddish tale; in Yiddish and English). Performed by Musical Elements, New York, 28 January 1982.

Briggs, Donald

1986   *Least of My Children* (libretto by Loren Linnard; about AIDS). Reading, San Francisco School of Dramatic Arts, 22 June 1986; concert première, First Church Concerts, 12 May, 1989.

Brisman, Heskel (Burt Haskell, Ben Britt; b. New York, 12 May 1923; Anderson; ASCAP; *Who's Who*)

1977   *Whirligig* (satirical comedy; 1 act—35 minutes; libretto by Jerome Greenfield after O. Henry). Première at Ball State University, Muncie, IN, 25 October 1977. Kornick.

\-   *The Strangers* (1 act).

Bristow, George Frederick (b. Brooklyn, NY, 19 December 1825; d. New York, 13 December 1898; *Amerigrove*)

1855   *Rip Van Winkle*, op. 22 (3 acts; libretto by Jonathan Howard Wainwright after Washington Irving). Performed at Niblo's Gardens, New York, 27 September 1855, with a run of 17 by the end of October; and at Academy of Music, Philadelphia, 21 November 1870. Vocal score published by G. Schirmer, 1882; reprint, New York: Da Capo, 1991. Hipsher.

1894   *King of the Mountains*, op. 80 (libretto by M. A. Coioney), unfinished.

Britain, Radie (Mrs. Ted Morton; b. Silverton, TX, 17 March 1903; *Amerigrove*; Anderson; ASCAP; see Walter B. and Nancy Gisbrecht Bailey, *Radie Britain: A Bio-Bibliography* [Westport, Conn.: Greenwood, 1990])

1937   *Ubiquity* (musical drama, solo voices and piano; 1 hour; libretto by Lester Luther). Score available from Heroico Music Publications.

1946   *Happyland* (children's operetta, voices and piano; 2 acts—1 hour; libretto by A. Greenfield). Score available from Heroico Music Publications.

1952   *Carillon* (grand opera, voices and piano; 3 acts—135 minutes). Piano-vocal score available from Heroico Music Publications.

1953   *The Spider and the Butterfly* (children's operetta, voices and piano; 3 acts—45 minutes; libretto by Lena Priscilla Hesselberg). Score available from Heroico Music Publications.

1960   *Kuthara* (*The Scythe*) (chamber opera; 3 acts; libretto by Lester Luther). Performed Santa Barbara, CA, 24 June 1961. Piano-vocal score at American Music Center, and available from Heroico Music Publications.

Brockington, Frances

1985   *The Opera Time Machine* (45 minutes; traces history of opera).

Broekhoven, John Van. *See* Van Broekhoven, John

Brody, Martin

1992   *Heart of a Dog* (satirical fable with political overtones; 1 act; libretto by Fred Pfeil based on Mikhail Bulgakov's 1925 novella). Première by Boston Musica Viva, Boston University, 29 May 1992.

Broekman, David (b. Leiden, Holland, 13 May 1899; d. New York, 1 April 1958 [Anderson: b. 13 May 1902; d. 1 January 1958]; in U.S. from 1924; Anderson; ASCAP; *Baker's*)

1954   *Barbara Allen* (1 act—30 minutes). Performed New York, 26 December 1954.

1956   *The Toledo War*. Broadcast on CBS radio, New York, 4 May 1956.

Brookmeyer, Bob (b. Kansas City, MO, 19 December 1929; *Amerigrove*)
   1991   *Gott in Wuppertal* (German libretto by Gerold Theobalt after a book by Liza Kristwalst). Performed by Wuppertal Opera, Germany, 14 April 1991.

Brooks, Richard James (b. Syracuse, 26 December NY, 1942; ACA/AMC; Anderson; *Who's Who*)
   1969   *Rapunzel* (1 act—45 minutes; for young audiences; libretto by Harold Mason after Grimm). *COS-3*.
   1977   *The Wishing Well* [*The Wishing Tree*?] (3 acts; operetta for children).
   1987   *Moby Dick* (2 acts—150 minutes; libretto by John Richards after Herman Melville). *COS-4*.

Brotons, Salvador (b. Barcelona, Spain, 17 July 1959; to U.S. in 1985; *Who's Who*)
   1990   *Everyman* (after Hofmannsthal's modernization of the medieval morality play; for stage or TV). Performed Tallahassee, FL, summer 1990.

Brounoff, Platon B. (1863-1924; born in Russia; in the U.S. from 1891)
   -   *Ramona* (opera).
   -   *Titanic* (music drama).
   -   *Xilona* (music drama).

Brown, Allyson
   1985   *Miranda* (1 act). Performed Houston, TX, 6 June 1985.

Brown, Buck
   1984   *Jericho* (on the 1979 murder of five civil rights workers in Greensboro, NC). Performed for Greensboro Civil Rights Fund, Symphony Space, New York, 9 November 1984.

Brown, J. Harold (b. Shellman, GA, 28 September 1902; *Southern*)
   1951   *King Solomon* (1 act). Performed Cleveland, 28 September 1951.

Brown, Nacio Herb (b. Deming, NM, 22 February 1986; d. San Francisco, 28 September 1964; *Amerigrove*)
   1983   *Singin' in the Rain* (2 acts; libretto by Arthur Freed and Tommy Steele after the 1952 movie by Betty Comden and Adolph Green). Performed London, England, 30 June 1983, and New York, 20 June 1985.
   1984   *A Broadway Baby* (libretto by Arthur Freed, Carl Kleinschmitt, and Marty Krofft). Performed Chester, PA, 4 December 1984.

Brown, Richard Earl (b. Gloversville, NY, 21 February 1947; Anderson; *Who's Who*)
   1985   *The Gift of the Magi* (1 act—25 minutes; libretto by Nancy Grobe after O. Henry). *COS-4*.

Brown, Theodore
   1937   *The Natural Man*. Performed Seattle, 1937, and New York, 1941.

Brown, William Hill (librettist)
> 1789   *The Better Sort: or, The Girl of Spirit* ("an operatical, comical farce"). Libretto published Boston: Isaiah Thomas, 1789; in AMRC. Sonneck-Upton, 42; Porter, 8. Performed at American Antiquarian Society, Worcester, MA, 8 November 1985.

Browne, John Lewis (b. London, England, 18 May 1866; d. Chicago, 23 October 1933; in the U.S. from 1875; ASCAP; Hipsher)
> 1902   *The Corsican Girl* (*La Corsicana*) (1 act; libretto by Stuart Maclean, translated to Italian by H. Ringler). 7th among 256 operas submitted for Sonzogno Prize, Milan, 1902. Published 1905. Première at Playhouse of Chicago, 4 January 1923. Bispham Medal, 1925.

Bruce, Charlotte
> 1990   *The Eagle among Ravens* (165 minutes; libretto by composer, about Robert the Bruce of Scotland). Performed Tenafly, NJ, 7 June 1990.

Bruce, (Frank) Neely (b. Memphis, TN, 21 January 1944; *Amerigrove*; *Baker's*)
> 1965   *Pyramus and Thisbe* (chamber opera; 1 act; after Shakespeare). Performed at University of Alabama, 14 November 1967.
> 1971   *The Trials of Psyche* (1 act; libretto by J. Orr after Apuleius).
> 1980   *Americana: or, A New Tale of the Genii* (4 acts; libretto by Tony Connor). Performed Middletown, CT, April 1980.

Brumit, J. Scott (b. Kansas City, MO, 7 September 1949; *WhoAm*)
> 1989   *Friends and Dinosaurs* (1 act; libretto by Helen O'Keefe). Performed Needham, MA, 20 May 1989, and Lake George Festival, NY, summer 1990.

Brunswick, Mark (b. New York, 6 January 1902; d. London, England, 26 May 1971; *Amerigrove*; Anderson)
> 1966   *The Master Builder* (3 acts; libretto after Ibsen). Performed New York, 16 December 1966.

Brush, Bob
> -   *The First* (libretto by Martin Charmin and Joel Siegel about Jackie Robinson).

Brush, Ruth Damaris (b. Fairfax, OK, 7 February 1910; Anderson; ASCAP; Cohen)
> (The composer writes her own librettos.)
> 1965   *The Fair.* Performed Bartlesville, OK, February 1965.
> 1965   *The Street Singers of Market Street* (folk opera; 1 act). Performed Borger, TX, 16 February 1965.
> 1982   *Sing a New Song to the Lord* (1 act—40 minutes; libretto after the Book of Exodus).
> -   *The Courtesan and the Scholar* (1 act; libretto after an old Chinese legend). "In progress," *COS*-4.

Bryan, Charles Faulkner (b. McMinnville, TN, 26 July 1911; d. Helena, AL, 7 July 1955; Anderson; ASCAP)

1952   *Singin' Billy* (2 acts; libretto by Donald Davidson). Performed Nashville, TN, 23 April 1952. Published by J. Fischer, 1952.

- *Strangers in This World* ("a musical folk play in 2 acts"—2 hours).
- *Shooting the Stars* ("A Gay Musical").

Bucci, Mark (b. New York, 26 February 1924; MCA; *Amerigrove*; Anderson; *Who's Who*)

1948   *The Caucasian Chalk Circle* (musical; after the Brecht play).

1949   *The Boor* (1 act; libretto by E. Haun after Chekhov). Performed New York, 28 (or 29) December 1953.

1950   *The Beggar's Opera*, after John Gay. Performed New York, June-October 1950.

1952   *The Adamses* (3 acts—135 minutes; after play by Paula Jacobi). Published by Leeds.

1953   *The Thirteen Clocks* (musical; libretto by composer after J. Thurber).

1953   *Sweet Betsy from Pike* (1 act; libretto by composer). Performed New York, 8 December 1953.

1953   *The Dress* (1 act; libretto by composer). Performed New York, 19 (or 29) December 1953. Published by Frank.

1957   *Tale for a Deaf Ear* (1 act; libretto after E. Enright's "Moment before the Rain"). Performed Tanglewood, MA, 5 August 1957. Published by Frank.

1965   *The Hero* (1 act; libretto by David Rogers after Gilfrey's "Far Rockaway"). Performed on National Educational Television, 24 September 1965.

1970   *Triad*. Performed Ogden, UT, 1970–71 season.

1981   *Midas: or, The Golden Touch*.

- *Elmer and Lily* (60 minutes; "fantasy").
- *Myron It's Deep Down Here* (pop opera; libretto by composer).
- *The Square One* (jazz opera; libretto by T. Brown).
- *Summer Afternoon* (1 act).

Bucharoff, Simon (formerly Buchhalter; b. Berdichev, Russia, 20 April 1881; d. Chicago, 24 November 1955; to the U.S. at age 11; Anderson; *Baker's*; Hipsher)

1915   *A Lover's Knot* (libretto by Cora Bennett-Stephenson concerning post-Civil War America). Performed in concert version in Evanston, IL, 1915; staged at the Auditorium, Chicago, 15 January 1916.

1919   *Sakahra* (libretto by Isabel Buckingham, translated to German by Rudolph Lothar; set in Algiers after 1830), revised 1953. Première, Frankfurt-am-Main, Germany, 8 November 1924. Bispham Medal, 1925.

- *Addio*.
- *The Jewel*.
- *The Marble Statue*. In progress, according to Hipsher (1927).
- *The Wastrel*.

Buck, Dudley (b. Hartford, CT, 10 March 1839; d. West Orange, NJ, 6 October 1909; *Amerigrove*; Hipsher)

1880   *Deseret: or, A Saint's Affliction* (comic opera; 3 acts; libretto by William Augustus Croffut). Score lost; selections published in 1880. Première at Haverly's Fourteenth Street Theater, New York, 11 October 1880; also performed at Academy of Music, Baltimore, and Pike's Opera House, Cincinnati.

1889   *Serapis* (grand opera; 3 acts; libretto by composer). Vocal score published in 1891.

Buckman, David

1990   *The Waves* (libretto by Lisa Peterson after Virginia Woolf). Performance by New York Theater Workshop, New York, 27 April 1990.

Budenholzer, Joe

1984   *Astro-Bride*, with Jerry Kazakevicius and John J. Sheehan (1 act; science-fiction satire; libretto by Jo Ann Schmidman). Performed Omaha, NE, 22 December 1985.

1985   *The Rip-It-Up Hate Aggregate Rape Tapes* (libretto by John J. Sheehan and James Larsen). Performed Omaha, NE, 22 February 1985.

1986   *Disko Ranch* (libretto by Megan Terry). NEA grant, 1985-86.

1986   *Sea of Forms* (libretto by John J. Sheehan and Jo Ann Schmidman). Performed Omaha, NE, 5 September 1986.

1987   *One Beat—One Vote* (libretto by Jo Ann Schmidman).

Bugg, G. William (b. Memphis, TN, 27 October 1943; *WhoAm*)

1986   *Bartolo* (music from Rossini's *The Barber of Seville* and Mozart's *The Marriage of Figaro*). Performed Birmingham, AL, 13 September 1986.

Buhrman, Bert

1968   *The Bald Knobbers* (1 act; libretto by Karl Bratton after an Ozark folk story). Performed at School of the Ozarks, Point Lookout, MO, 12 May 1968.

Bulgarelli, Diane

1980   [untitled work]. Performed by Music Theatre, New York, 20 June 1980.

Burge, David (b. Evanston, IL, 25 March 1930; *Amerigrove*; *Who's Who*)

1962   *Intervals* (1 act). Performed Evanston, IL, 11 November 1962.

Burgess, Brio (b. San Francisco, 27 April 1943; *Who's Who*)

1982   *Rooftops* (4 acts—90 minutes; libretto by composer). Broadcast in Melbourne, Australia, 4 October 1987; reading, Saratoga Springs, NY, 14 February 1988.

Burgstahler, Elton E. (b. Orland, CA, 16 September 1924; Anderson; ASCAP)

1965   *Hat Spat*. Performed Springfield, MO, 2 May 1965.

Burnand, N. Solomon
1956   *Pickwick*. Performed Eureka Springs, AR, August 1956.

Burnham, Cardon Vern (b. Kewanee, IL, 1927; ASCAP; *Who's Who*)
1955   *Aria da capo* (1 act). Performed New Orleans, 17 April 1955.
1956   *The Nitecap* (1 act). Performed New Orleans, 14 March 1956.
1972   *Ceremony of Strangers*. Performed Minot, ND, 14 December 1972.

Burton, Robert L., Jr.
1972   *Suddenly Last Summer*.

Burton, Stephen Douglas (b. Whittier, CA, 24 February 1943; Anderson; ASCAP)
1974? *Bell Tower* (after Melville). NEA grant.
1974? *Dr. Heidegger's Experiment* (after Hawthorne). NEA grant.
1974? *Maggie* (after Crane). NEA grant.
1974   *Benito Cereno* (1 act—37 minutes; libretto by the composer after
          Melville). Reading by OPERA America Showcase, January 1981.
1975   *Americana* (3 1-act operas).
1975   *The Duchess of Malfi* (3 acts; libretto by Christopher Keane after
          John Webster). Commissioned by National Opera Institute.
          Premièred at Wolf Trap, Vienna, VA, 18 August 1978. Published
          by Belwin-Mills. Kornick.

Busby, Gerald (b. Abilene, TX, 1935; AMC; ASCAP)
1979   *The Lady and Her Lovers* (1 act; libretto by Carl Laanes after *The
          Arabian Nights*).
1985   *Sleepsong* (1 act; libretto by Craig Lucas). Performed Houston, TX,
          6 June 1985.
1985   *Viola* (1 act; libretto by Craig Lucas). Performed Houston, TX, 6
          June 1985.

Busch, Richard
1985   *Das Wiederherstellungsmittel* (*The Restorative*) (1 act—40 minutes;
          libretto by composer). Performed by Dinosaur Annex, Boston,
          May 1985.

Bush, Gordon (b. Detroit, MI, 4 May 1943; Anderson)
1973   *The Hermit* (1 act—30 minutes; chamber opera; libretto by Robert
          Lallamant). Performed Brooklyn, NY, 12 May 1973.
-        *The Visitation* (chamber opera; 1 act).
-        *Revival* (short music drama).

Buskirk, Carl Van
1956   *The Land Between the Rivers* (2 acts). Performed Bloomington, IN
          (Johnson: St. Louis), 18 May 1956.
1966   *Christmas Doll* (on a Noh play). Performed Bloomington, IN
          (sponsored by the National Federation of Music Clubs), March
          1966.

Butler, Blaine
1980   *Pocahontas* (libretto by Marty Martin after Mossiker). Performed
          New York.

Butler, Martin
> 1986   *The Sirens' Song* (2 scenes; libretto by the composer after *The Odyssey*). Performed at Heraklion Summer Festival, Crete, Greece, 25 August 1986. Published by Oxford University Press, 1988.

Byrd, William Clifton, Jr.
> 1949   *Lyneia* (2 acts). Performed Cincinnati, 20 January 1949.
> 1953   *The Scandal at Mulford Inn* (1 act—35 minutes). Performed Cincinnati, 1 April 1953.
> 1954   *Hold That Note* (1 act; satirizes voice teachers). Performed Philadelphia, 10 December 1954.

Byrne, David
> 1984   *The CIVIL warS: The Knee Plays* (or *The American/Minneapolis*) (13 parts). *See* Glass, Philip. Performed Minneapolis, 26 April 1984.
> 1988   *The Forest* (libretto by Heiner Mueller and Darryl Pinckney after the Epic of Gilamesh). Conceived and developed by Robert Wilson. Commission by City of West Berlin, Germany; performed there, October 1988. American première, Brooklyn, NY, 2 December 1988.

Cabanis, Thomas
> 1987   *Denmark Vesey* (libretto by composer; on a slave revolt in South Carolina). Performed Waterford, CT, August 1987; and by American Opera Projects, New York, 8 November 1989.
> 1988   *Earhart* (libretto by Steven Scott Smith, about Amelia Earhart). Performed Waterford, CT, summer 1988.

Cabena, Barrie
> 1970   *The Selfish Giant* (1 act; libretto by composer). Performed London, Ontario, April 1970.

Cadman, Charles Wakefield (b. Johnstown, PA, 24 December 1881; d. Los Angeles, 30 December 1946; *Amerigrove*; Hipsher)
> 1912   *Drasoma: or, Land of Misty Water*) (4 acts; "Indian Idyll"; based on an Indian story by Francis La Flesche of the Omahas).
> 1918   *Shanewis: or, The Robin Woman* (2 acts—90 minutes; libretto by Eberhart). Première by Metropolitan Opera, New York, 23 March 1918, with 4 additional performances; also performed there 3 times beginning 12 March 1919, "thus becoming the first American opera to achieve a second season on the Metropolitan stage"—Hipsher; also: ". . . as given in Chicago, on November 9, 1922, was the first completely American production of an American opera," and it was also performed there 5 April 1923. Bispham Medal, 1924.

1920   *The Sunset Trail* (operatic cantata; 2 scenes). Performed San Diego, CA, 23 August 1920; Denver, CO, 5 December 1922; 4 performances at Kilbourn Hall, Rochester, NY, conducted by Howard Hanson, week of 13 November 1926; and Los Angeles, 1936. Published by Presser.

1925   *The Garden of Mystery* (or *The Enchanted Garden*; 1 act; libretto by Eberhart after Hawthorne's *Rappaccini's Daughter*). Première at Carnegie Hall, New York, 20 March 1925.

1925   *A Witch of Salem.* Première by Chicago Civic Opera, 8 December 1926; revived there 24 January 1928, and by that company at Shrine Auditorium, Los Angeles, 9 March 1928. Published by Mercury.

1926   *The Ghost of Lollypop Bay* (operetta; 2 acts; libretto by C. and J. Roos).

1926   *Lelawala, or The Maiden of Niao* (operetta; 3 acts; libretto by G. M. Brown). Published by Willis, 1926. Score at AMRC.

1928   *The Belle of Havana* (operetta; libretto by G. M. Brown).

1932   *South in Sonora* (operetta; 3 acts; libretto by C. and J. Roos). Published by Ditson, 1932.

1932   *The Willow Tree* (1 act—23 minutes). Performed on NBC radio, 4 August 1932 and 3 October 1932.

Cage, John (b. Los Angeles, 5 September 1912; d. New York, 12 August 1992; *Amerigrove*; *Who's Who*)

1972   *Theatre Piece.* Performed Kiel, Germany, December 1972.

1986   *The Bus to Stockport and Other Stories*; with Eric Valinsky and Peter Schubert. Performed by Opera Uptown, New York, 20 February 1986.

1987   *Europas 1 & 2* (135 minutes; prepared with Andrew Culver from 70 operas). Performed Frankfurt, Germany, 12 December 1987, and at State University of New York at Purchase, 14 July 1988. *See also* Culver, Andrew

Caggiano, Philip (b. New York, 11 August 1949; *WhoAm*)

1979   *The Ring of the Niebelung* (90 minutes; a children's version of Wagner's operas). Performed Somers, NY, 5 March 1979.

Cain, Thomas

1979   *The Lesson* (1 act). Performed Prince George's Civic Opera, 30 December 1979.

1981   *Jack and Roberta* (2 acts; libretto by composer after Ionesco). Performed Largo, MD, January 1981, and Riverdale, MD, 16 January 1981.

1982   *The Price of Eggs* (a revised version of *Jack and Roberta*). Performed Riverdale, MD, 24 January 1982.

Calabro, Louis (b. Brooklyn, NY, 1 November 1926; Anderson; *Baker's*)

1984   *The Paradise Bird.* Performed by Downtown Opera Players, New York, 6 May 1984.

Calderwood, Michael

1988   *The Nutcracker in the Land of the Nuts* (Christmas extravaganza). Performed at Wings Theatre, New York, 27 November 1988.

Caldwell, Mary Elizabeth Glockler (b. Tacoma, WA, 1 August 1909; ASCAP; Anderson; Cohen)

1955   *Pepito's Golden Flower* (1 act). Performed Pasadena, CA, 13 March 1955.

1961   *A Gift of Song* ("Christmas opera"; 1 act—60 minutes). Performed Pasadena, CA, 3 December 1961.

1965   *The Night of the Star* ("Christmas opera"; 60 minutes). Performed Pasadena, CA, 5 December 1965.

1978   *In the Fullness of Time.* Performed Pasadena, CA, 3 December 1978.

Cale, Rosalie Balmer

1897   *Love, Powder, and Patches.* Krohn (1924) called this opera "fascinating." Performed St. Louis, 1897.

1907   *Four Pecks or a Bushel of Fun.* Performed St. Louis, 1907, and in New York as *Cupid's Halloween.*

Callner, Jan

1988   *Noah* (libretto by Bill Wheeler). Performed at Wings Theatre, New York, 17 December 1988.

Campbell, Ken

1981   *Illuninatus!*, with Steve Amadek, John Engerman, and Chris Langham (on novels by Robert Shea and Robert A. Wilson). Performed Houston, TX, July 1981.

Campbell, Marion

1944   *Osceola* (1 act). Performed at National American Indian League, Los Angeles, 1944.

Canning, Thomas Gratwick (b. 1911; AMC; Anderson)

1956   *Beyond Belief* (75 minutes). Performed Rochester, NY, 14 May 1956.

1956   *Albert and Tiberius* (1 act—20 minutes). Performed Williamsport, PA, May 1956.

\-   *Krazy Kat* (1 act).

Cansino, Edward (AMC)

1978   *Ubi Roi: A Musical Tragedy* (libretto by Everett C. Frost). NEA grant, 1978.

Capers, Virginia

1985   *Sojourner* (1 act; on the life of Sojourner Truth). Performed by Opera Ebony, New York, 24 February 1985, and 15 October 1989.

1988   *Paul Laurence Dunbar.* Performed by Opera Ebony, New York, 12 February 1988.

Carbon, John (b. 1951 in Chicago)

1983   *Marie Laveau* (libretto by composer, about voodoo in New Orleans).

1987   *Franklin: An Opera of Our Own Invention* (2 acts; libretto by Sarah White, about the life of Benjamin Franklin). Performed Lancaster, PA, 23 April 1987.

Carbonara, Gerald (b. New York, 8 December 1896; d. Sherman Oaks, CA, 11
January 1959; ASCAP; Anderson)
-    *Armand*. Completed by 1925. Hipsher.
-    *Nanal*.

Cardillo, Salvatore Napoleone
1913   *Romilda* (1 act). Performed New York.

Carlsen, Philip
1982   *Implications of Melissa* (1 act—15 minutes; libretto by composer).
Performed Brooklyn, NY, 5 February 1982. Published by MMB
Music.

Carlson, Charles Frederick (b. Denver, CO, 24 October 1875; Hipsher)
1912   *Phelias*. Bispham Medal, 1926. Published 1912.
1913   *Hester: or, The Scarlet Letter* (libretto by composer after
Hawthorne).
-    *The Courtship of Miles Standish* (grand opera; 2 acts; libretto by
composer after Longfellow).
-    *The Merchant of Venice* (libretto by composer after *The Bard of
Avon*).
-    *Enoch Arden* ("concert music drama"; libretto after Tennyson), for
4 solo voices, chorus, piano, with narrator.

Carlson, Roberta
1984   *The Nightingale*. Performed by Children's Theatre Co.,
Minneapolis, 16 March 1984.
1986   *The Legend of Sleepy Hollow* (1 act; libretto by Fred Gaines after
Washington Irving). Performed Louisville, KY, 26 October 1986.
1987   *African Tales* (1 act; libretto by Timothy Mason). Performed by
Children's Theatre Co., Minneapolis, 17 January 1987.
1987   *Dreamers of the Day* (2 acts; libretto by Gary Gisselman, Michael
Grady, and John Donahue). Performed by Arizona Theatre Co.,
Tucson, 1987-88 season.

Carmines, Alvin A. (b. Hampton, VA, 1938; Anderson)
(The composer writes his own librettos.)
1971   *Joan* (1 act). Performed New York, 21 November 1971.
1974   *The Duel* (1 act). Performed by Metropolitan Opera Studio,
Brooklyn, NY, 22 April 1974.
1977   *A Memoir* (libretto after Gertrude Stein). Performed at Judson
Memorial Church, New York, 22 April 1977.
1978   *In Praise of Death*. Performed at Judson Memorial Church, New
York, 11 November 1978.
1979   *Dr. Faustus Lights the Lights*. Performed at Judson Memorial
Church, New York, October 1979.
1979   *Christmas Rappings*. Performed at Judson Memorial Church, New
York, 14 December 1979.
1982   *The Evangelist*. Performed by TRG Repertory Company, New
York, 6 April 1982.
1984   *Exhalations*. Performed at Madison Avenue Baptist Church, New
York, 24 May 1984.

1985   *The Making of Americans* (90 minutes; libretto by Leon Katz, about
        Gertrude Stein). Performed at Lenox Art Center, New York, 5
        March 1985.

Carnelia, Craig
1977   *Is There Life after High School* (libretto by composer with Jeffrey
        Kindley). NEA grant, 1977. Performed New York, 7 May 1982.
1987   *Three Postcards* (libretto by composer with Craig Lucas).
        Performed by Workshop South Coast Repertory Theater, Costa
        Mesa, CA, 6 January 1987, and by Playwrights Horizons, New
        York, 14 May 1987.

Carr, Arthur (b. 1908 in Pontiac, MI)
1939   *Captain Jupiter.*

Carr, Benjamin (b. London, England, 12 September 1768; d. Philadelphia, 24
        May 1831; to U.S. in 1793; *Amerigrove*; Porter)
1795   *Poor Jack: or, The Sailors' Return* (pantomime; 1 act). Performed
        New York, 7 April 1795.
1796   *The Archers: or, Mountaineers of Switzerland*, with additions by
        Victor Pelissier (libretto by William Dunlap, based on the story of
        William Tell). Performed at John Street Theater, New York, 18
        April 1796. Most of the music is lost. The aria "Why, huntress,
        why?" was published in an edition by Philip Weston (New York:
        Concord, 1941; and in W. Thomas Marrocco and Harold Gleason,
        Music in America (New York: Norton, 1964), no. 76; "Rondo from
        the Overture to the Opera of the Archers or Mountaineers of
        Switzerland" was published by Carr, ca. 1813, as no. 7 of his
        series *Musical Miscellany in Occasional Numbers* (reprint, New
        York: Da Capo, 1982). Sonneck-Upton, 31.
1796   *The Patriot: or, Liberty Obtained* (play; 3 acts), with original medley
        overture, and other music compiled and selected by Carr.
        Performed Philadelphia, 16 May 1796, and Baltimore, 3 September
        1796. Sonneck-Upton, 326.
1797   *Bourville Castle: or, The Gallic Orphan* (comic opera; music to a
        play by John Blair Linn), with pastiche by Victor Pelissier.
        Performed New York, 16 January 1797. Sonneck-Upton, 48.

Carrier, Loran
1969   *Game Opera* (1 act). Performed at Smithsonian Institution,
        Washington, 12 December 1969.

Carrier, Naomi
1989   *I Am Annie Mae* (libretto by Ruth Weingarten, about early civil
        rights advocacy in Texas). Performed Houston, TX, 8 June 1989.

Carroll, Baikida (b. St. Louis, 15 January 1947; Anderson)
1989   *Betsey Brown* (libretto by Ntozake Shange and Emily Mann, about
        civil rights in St. Louis in the 1950s). Performed at American
        Music Theater Festival, Philadelphia, 25 March 1989.

Carroll, Frank Morris (b. Norfolk, VA, 19 March 1928; Anderson; *Who's Who*)
   1983   *The Old Woman and the Pig*. Performed by Shreveport Opera, LA, 20 October 1983.

Carroll, Peter
   1955   *Margaret in Fairyland* (1 act—20 minutes). Performed by Children's Opera, Milwaukee, WI, 1955. Published by Boosey & Hawkes.

Carroll, Vinette
   1988   *At Our Age We Don't Buy Green Bananas* (libretto by composer, about senior citizens). Performed Fort Lauderdale, FL, 1988-89 season.

Carter, ?
   1988   *Little Red Riding Hood* (libretto by Jane Stanton). Performed by Penny Bridge Players, Brooklyn, NY, 2 February 1988.

Carter, Elliott (b. New York, 11 December 1908; *Amerigrove*)
   1934   *Tom and Lily* (1 act—30 minutes). Destroyed in 1957.

Carter, Ernest Trow (b. Orange, NJ, 3 September 1866; d. 1953; student of William Mason; Hipsher)
   1917   *The White Bird* (libretto by Brian Hooker). Concert performance at Carnegie Chamber Music Hall, New York, 23 May 1922, composer conducting; also performed Chicago, 17 February 1924; New York (*COS*-1 and Hipsher: Chicago), 6 March 1924; and Osnabrück, Germany, 15 November 1927. Rated 2nd among 18 operas in 1916-17 Hinshaw contest. First recipient of the Bispham Medal, 1924.
   1931   *The Blonde Donna: or, The Fiesta of Santa Barbara* (comic opera in 3 acts; libretto by Brian Hooker [Hipsher: libretto by composer]). Concert performance at Century Theater, New York; first full performance at Brooklyn Little Theater, NY, 8 December 1931; official première the following night when the National Federation of Music Clubs presented him a laurel wreath; performed December 14-19 at Heckscher Theater, New York. Published by Composers Press, ca. 1936.

Cascarino, Romeo (b. Philadelphia, 28 September 1922; Anderson)
   1976   *William Penn* (3 acts; libretto by Peggy Oppenlander after Penn's "Holy Experiment"). Performed at Drexel University, Philadelphia, 14 November 1976, and by Concerto Soloists of Philadelphia, 24 October 1982.

Case, Henry Lincoln
   1922?   *Hinotito: A Romance of Love and Politics* (libretto by Frederic W. Pangborn). Hipsher.
   1922   *Camaralzaman*. Hipsher.

Catalano, Joe
   1985   *Yesterday Foretold* (over five hours; multimedia work using the Codex Fiorentino, about the conquest of Mexico). Grants from

NEA and Missouri Arts Council. Performed St. Louis, 16 February 1985.

Cave, Michael (b. Springfield, MO, 17 May 1944; Anderson)
1971   *Pandora's Box* (children's opera).
1989   *Canto.* Performed at Merkin Hall, 11 November 1989.
1989   *Renascence* (40 minutes; libretto by composer after Edna St. Vincent Millay). Performed at Merkin Hall, 11 November 1989; also in Jackson, MI.

Caviani, Ronald Joseph (b. Iron Mountain, MI, 12 March 1931; Anderson; *Who's Who*)
1985   *The New Step* (1 act). Performed Stockton, CA, 5 May 1985.

Cearley, Buster
1980   *Airport 1904* (90 minutes; libretto by composer and Eddie Cope). Performed Houston, TX, 1980-81 season.

Cephas, John
1989   *Chewin' the Blues with Bowling Green John and Harmonica Phil*, with Phil Wiggins (libretto by Jeff Church). Performed at Ethnic Diversity Festival, Washington, 17 February 1989.

Cessana, Otto (ASCAP)
-    *Ali Baba and the Forty Thieves.*

Chadabe, Joel (b. New York, 12 December 1938; *Amerigrove*; *Who's Who*)
1967   *Street Scene* (multimedia work, with Moog synthesizer). Performed at Kaufmann Hall, New York, 25 March 1969. Published by Carl Fischer. Recorded by Opus One.

Chadwick, George Whitefield (b. Lowell, MA, 13 November 1854; d. Boston, 4 April 1931; *Amerigrove*; Hipsher)
1884   *The Peer and the Pauper* (comic operetta; 2 acts; libretto by R. Grant).
1892   *A Quiet Lodging* (operetta; 2 acts; libretto by A. Bates). Performed Boston, 1 April 1892.
1894   *Tabasco* (burlesque opera; 2 acts; libretto by R. A. Barnet). Performed Boston, 29 January 1894; professional production, 9 April 1894; also January 1929.
1901   *Judith* (lyric drama; 3 acts; libretto by W. C. Langdon, after scenario by composer after *Book of Judith*). Concert performance at Worcester Festival, MA, 23 September 1901. Piano-vocal score published by G. Schirmer, 1901; reprinted by Da Capo, 1972.
1913   *The Padrone* (2 acts; libretto by D. Stevens after scenario by composer; about Italian immigrants in the United States).
1917   *Love's Sacrifice* (pastoral opera; 1 act—45 minutes; libretto by D. Stevens). Performed at Playhouse, Chicago, 1 February 1923, with patronage of Opera in Our Language Foundation..
     (N.B.: Chadwick also composed incidental music for *Everywoman: Her Pilgrimage in Quest of Love*, 1910, performed in New York and London, 1911.)

Chaffin, Lon
>1989   *Daystar* (rock opera on the Gospel according to St. John). Performed Paris, TX, 27 April 1989.

Chaikin, Jack W. (b. Brooklyn, 24 August 1918; Anderson)
>1983   *The Woman with the Eggs* (children's opera; libretto after Hans Christian Andersen). Performed by Brooklyn Center Children's Opera, NY, 9 May 1983.
>\-   *An Anteater Named Arthur* (children's opera).
>\-   *Mr. Tall and Mr. Small* (children's opera).
>\-   *Robert the Rose Horse* (children's opera).
>\-   *You Look Ridiculous* (children's opera).

Chajes, Julius (b. Lwow, Poland, 21 December 1910; to U.S. in 1950; AMC; *WhoAm*)
>1966   *Out of the Desert* (90 minutes). Commission by Temple Israel, Detroit, MI; performed there, 18 April 1966. Published by Transcontinental Music.

Chance, Fred
>1985   *Stiff* (1 act; libretto by composer). Performed Houston, TX, 6 June 1985.

Chaney, Charles Ross
>\-   *The Belle of Barcelona.*
>\-   *Melinka of Astrakhan.*
>\-   *Sailor Maids.*

Chang, Du-Yee
>1989   *The Song of Shim Chung* (libretto by composer and Terence Cranendonk after a Korean story; it includes original and traditional music). Performed by Pan Asian Repertory Theatre, New York, 14 November 1989.

Chanler, Theodore Ward (b. Newport, RI, 29 April 1902; d. Boston, 27 July 1961; *Amerigrove*)
>1955   *The Pot of Fat* (chamber opera, 6 scenes; after Grimm). Concert performance Cambridge, MA, 8 May 1955; staged in New York, 1956. Published by Associated Music.

Chapin, Tom
>1987   *The Magic Fishbone.* Reading, New York, 10 October 1987; staged by On Stage Productions, New York, 8 October 1988.

Chapman, Alan
>1983   *The Lady That's Known as Lou* (libretto by Gordon Duffey after Robert Service). Reading by Lehman Engel Musical Theatre Workshop, Los Angeles, 1983-84 season; staged Douglas, AK, 12 November 1985. Shorter version (1 hour) performed Anchorage, AK, 15 May 1987.

Chapman, Charles Wayne (b. Ardmore, OK, 7 October 1936; *Who's Who*; *WhoAm*)

1978   *Peter Gray* (folk opera; 1 act; libretto by composer). Master's degree project. Performed at Southwestern Oklahoma State University, Weatherford, 11 October 1979.

1983   *High Dollar Woman in a Low Dollar Town* (libretto by Claude Kezer, after a story from Oklahoma history). Performed Weatherford, OK, 5 October 1983.

Chapman, Harold (1909-74)

1956   *The Rose and the Ring* (libretto by Harold and Elizabeth Chapman). Performed at Wilshire Avell Theater (Los Angeles?), CA.

1971   *Crosses of Tears: or, The Fairy Stones* (libretto by Alexander Crosby Brown). Bound copy in the library of Christopher Newport College, Newport News, VA, along with other manuscripts by Chapman.

-   *The Pied Piper of Hamelin* (1 act; libretto by Margaret A. Tucker).

-   *Simple Simon* (3 acts).

Chauls, Robert (b. Port Chester, NY, 18 July 1942; Anderson; *Who's Who*)

1976   *Alice in Wonderland* (comic fantasy; 90 minutes—also a 38-minute version available for school audiences; libretto by composer after the story by Lewis Carroll). Première by Valley Opera, Los Angeles Valley College, Van Nuys, CA, 16 January 1976; also performed Lake George, NY, 8 August 1980. Kornick.

1983   *The Thirteen Clocks* (1 act; libretto by Rhoda Levine, after Thurber). Performed Waterford, CT, May 1983.

1986   *The Magic Rhyme* (20 minutes; libretto by composer with Barbara Azriely). Published by Belwin Mills.

1988   *The Trial for Goldilocks* (1 act—40 minutes; libretto by Joseph Robinette). Reading, Columbus, OH, 16 November 1988; staged at Glassboro State College, NJ, 31 October 1989.

Chavez, Carlos (b. Mexico City, 13 June 1899; d. there, 2 August 1978; *Baker's*; Schoep)

1957   *Panfilo and Loretta* (3 acts). Commission by Rockefeller Foundation. Performed New York, 9 May 1957.

1963   *The Visitors* (*Love Propitiated*) (3 acts—135 minutes; libretto by Chester Kallman, set in 14th-century Florence). Performed Mexico City, 21 May 1963. Published by Carl Fischer.

Chen, Wendy Fang (b. 1971)

(All operas commissioned by Metropolitan Opera Guild.)

1986   *Fighting Problems* (35 minutes). Performed at P.S. 314K, New York, 1986.

1987   *Hello, Diary* (35 minutes). Performed at P.S. 179K, New York, 1987.

1988   *The Teasers* (25 minutes). Performed at P.S. 208M, New York, 1988.

1989   *And the Bell Cracked* (40 minutes). Performed at P.S. 145M, New York, 28 February 1989.

Chenette, Jonathan Lee (b. Libertyville, IL, 8 May 1954; *Who's Who*; *WhoAm*)
  1987 *Eric Hermannson's Soul* (chamber opera; 2 acts—85 minutes).
      Commission by Grinnell College. Performed at Iowa Composers
      Forum, Grinnell, 16 September 1988.

Cherney, Chris
  1988 *The Coney Island Kid* (libretto by Crystal Field and George
      Bartenieff). Performed at Theater for the New City, New York, 6
      August 1988.

Cherry, Don (b. Oklahoma City, 18 November 1936; *Amerigrove*)
  1987 *Sim Sallah Bim* (1 act—75 minutes; libretto by John Benedict after
      Arabian Nights). Performed by Penny Bridge Players, Brooklyn,
      NY, 1987.

Cheslock, Louis (b. London, England, 25 September 1899; d. Baltimore, MD, 19
      July 1981; to the U.S. as an infant; *Amerigrove*)
  1930 *The Jewel Merchants* (75 minutes; libretto by J. B. Cabell).
      Performed Baltimore, MD, 26 February 1940.

Chew, Shiy Ji
  1985 *The Censorship Project* (libretto by Carolyn Forche, Valerie
      Wasilieweski, and Ruth Maleczech). NEA grant. Performed
      Waterford, CT, August 1985, and New York, 1985-86 season.

Chihara, Paul (b. Seattle, WA, 9 July 1938; *Amerigrove*)
  1990 *Shogun* (libretto by John Driver after Clavell). Performed at
      Kennedy Center, Washington, DC, 25 April 1990.

Child, Peter (b. Great Yarmouth, England, 6 May 1953; to U.S. in 1973; AMC;
      Anderson)
  1985 *Embers* (1 act—1 hour; libretto after Samuel Beckett's radio play).
      Performed by Alea III, Boston, 1 May 1985.

Ching, Michael (ASCAP)
  1980 *Levees.* Performed Durham, NC, summer 1980.
  1985 *Leo* (1 act—15 minutes; libretto by Fernando Fonseca after Massey's
      "Leo Spat"). Performed Houston, TX, 6 June 1985.
  1985 *Cocks Must Crow* (1 act; libretto by composer after Rawlings).
      Performed by Greater Miami Opera, FL, 12 December 1985.

Chitty, Botie
  1980 *Baze* (libretto by Albert Pendleton). Performed by Opera
      Southwest, Valdosta, GA, 20 June 1980.

Chlarson, Linder (AMC)
      (The composer writes his own librettos.)
  1980 *Montezuma's Death* (1 act).
  1982 *Mr. Lion* (1 act). Performed by Golden Fleece, New York, 7 May
      1982.
  1982 *Maximilian's Dream* (1 act; about Mexico in 1865). Performed at
      Dumbarton United Methodist Church, Washington, DC, 31 May
      1983.

1985   *Trio Sonata* (1 act). Performed by Golden Fleece, New York, 26 June 1985.

Chodosh, Richard
1984   *Molière* (libretto by Barry Grail, Robert Gerlach, and James McDonald). Performed Shreveport, LA, 8 March 1984.

Christiansen, Arne
1989   *Robin Hood* (libretto by Ole Kittleson and Tim Kelly). Performed Moorpark, CA, 13 January 1989.

Chudacoff, Edward (b. 22 October 1925; on faculty of University of Michigan))
1952   *Circus* (chamber opera; 20 minutes; libretto by Daniel Waldron). Performed at National Music Camp, Interlochen, MI, 26 July 1952.

Chumley, Robert
1990   *Ordinary People* (libretto by Dugg McDonough after J. Guest). OPERA America grant. Workshop performance, Winston-Salem, NC, April 1990; scheduled for stage performance there, spring 1993.

Claassen, Kalina
1986   *There Was a Man from the Land of UZ* (1 act; libretto by composer). Performed Seattle, WA, 10 October 1986.

Claflin, Avery (b. Keene, NH, 21 June 1898; d. Greenwich, CT, 9 January 1979; *Amerigrove*)
1921   *The Fall of Usher* (3 scenes; libretto by composer after Poe).
1933   *Hester Prynne* (150 minutes; libretto by D. Claflin after Hawthorne). Performed Hartford, CT, 15 December 1934 (*COS*-1 says 15 December 1935).
1948   *La Grande Bretèche* (libretto by G. R. Mills after Balzac). On CBS Radio, New York, 3 February 1957. Recorded by CRI.
1964   *Uncle Tom's Cabin* (libretto by D. Claflin after Stowe). Performed by Metropolitan Opera Studio, New York, 1964.

Clapp, Philip Greeley (b. Boston, 4 August 1888; d. Iowa City, 9 April 1954; *Amerigrove*)
1948   *The Taming of the Shrew* (libretto by composer after Shakespeare).
1953   *The Flaming Brand* (libretto by composer; on John Brown). Performed Iowa City, summer 1975.

Clark, Edgar Rogie (b. 1914; ASCAP)
1963   *Ti Yette, the Stranger* (on John Matheus). Performed Detroit, MI, 28 December 1963.

Clark, Philip
1970   *No Game for Kids.* Performed at Tougaloo College, MS, 1970-71 season.

Clarke, Gerry E. (b. Moline, IL, 19 March 1943; Anderson)
   1973   *Westchester Limited* (1 act; libretto by Norman James). Performed
        Chestertown, MD, 23 March 1973.

Clarke, Henry Leland (b. Dover, NH, 9 March 1907; ACA/AMC; *Amerigrove*;
        Who's Who)
   1954   *The Loafer and the Loaf* (1 act—45 minutes; libretto by Evelyn
        Sharp). Performed New York, 1 May 1954, and Stockbridge, MA,
        July 1954.
   1984   *Lysistrata* (2 acts—2 hours; libretto by Janet Stevenson after
        Aristophanes). Performed Marlboro, CT, 9 November 1984.

Clarke, Hugh Archibald (b. Toronto, Ontario, 15 August 1839; d. Philadelphia,
        16 December 1927; *Amerigrove*)
   1886   *Acharnians* (incidental music on text by Aristophanes)
    –   *Iphigenia in Tauris* (incidental music on text by Euripides).

Clarke, Rosemary (b. Daytona Beach, FL, 23 June 1921; ACA; Anderson; Cohen)
    –   *Agamemnon. COS*-1: "in preparation."
    –   *The Cat and the Moon.*

Clausen, Alf
   1986   *Men Are Like That.* Performed by Harlequin Opera, Los Angeles,
        18 January 1986.

Clausen, Bruce E.
   1982   *Whims and Oddities* (monodrama for soprano). Performed Los
        Angeles, 1982.

Clay, Carleton (AMC)
   1982   *Howcum, Oklahoma?.* Performed Syracuse, NY, 12 May 1982;
        Oneonta, NY, 1 October 1990; and Syracuse, NY, 3 October 1990.

Cleary, Margaret
   1938   *Jeanne d'Arc.* Performed at St. Bernard Auditorium, Chicago, 2
        June 1938.

Clemens, John
   1830   *Justina.* Performed Philadelphia.

Clenny, David
   1986   *La Contessa Dei Vampiri* (90 minutes; libretto by composer, on the
        story of Dracula; a parody of bel canto opera; in Italian).
        Performed by West Side Opera, New York, June 1986.

Clifton, Arthur (b. Philip Antony Corri, Edinburgh, Scotland, ?1794; d.
        Baltimore, 19 February 1832; to U.S. and assumed new name
        1812-17; *Amerigrove*; Porter)
   1812   *M.P.: or, The Bluestocking* (comic opera; libretto by Thomas
        Moore), music by Moore with additions by Clifton. Première,
        London, 9 September 1811; performed New York, 12 June 1812.

1822   *The Enterprise: or, Love and Pleasure* (libretto by Col. W. H.
        Hamilton). Première, Baltimore, 27 May 1822. Eighteen numbers
        printed separately in 1823; reprint, Schleifer, 5:51-102.

Clokey, Joseph Wadell (b. New Albany, IN, 28 August 1890; d. Covina, CA, 14
        September 1961; ASCAP/AMC; Anderson; *Baker's*; Hipsher)
1919   *The Pied Piper of Hamelin* (libretto by Anna J. Beiswenger after
        Robert Browning). Première at Miami University, OH, 14 May
        1920, conducted by the composer. Published by H. W. Gray.
1924   *The Emperor's Clothes* (comic opera; 3 acts; libretto by Frances
        Gibson Richard).
1925   *The Nightingale* (comic opera; 3 acts; libretto by Willis Knapp Jones
        after Hans Christian Andersen). Première at Miami University,
        OH, 12 December 1925.
1931   *Our American Cousin* (libretto by Willis Knapp Jones after the
        English comedy by Tom Taylor). Performed at Claremont
        College, CA, 2 March 1931.
   -    *Builders* (Easter pageant).

Closson, David M.
   -    *The Twelve Dancing Princesses* (3 acts). Published by J. Fischer.

Cobert, Robert
   -    *Frankie and Johnnie.* Recorded by MGM.

Coe, Kenton (b. 12 November 1932 in Tennessee, where he has been named
        composer laureate; Anderson)
1965   *South* (libretto about the Civil War, after Julien Green). Performed
        Marseilles, France, 14 October 1965, and Paris, France, 1972.
1972   *Le Grand Siècle* (1 act; after Ionesco). Performed by Opera of
        Nantes, France, 1972.
1981   *Rachel* (135 minutes; libretto by Anne Howard Bailey, about Rachel
        and Andrew Jackson). Performed by Knoxville Opera, TN, 1981,
        6 June 1988, and 7 April 1989. (Anderson: commission by
        Tennessee Arts Commission and Tennessee Performing Arts
        Foundation for the U.S. bicentennial and opening of the Tennessee
        Cultural Center Opera House, Nashville.)
   -    *The River* (libretto by Mary H. Johnson).
   -    *The White Devil* (2 acts; after play by John Webster).

Coerne, Louis Adolphe (b. Newark, NJ, 27 February 1870; d. Boston, 11
        September 1922; *Amerigrove*)
        (Most Coerne manuscripts are in the Boston Public Library.)
1894   *A Woman of Marblehead*, op. 40 (Johnson gives 1897).
1902   *Zenobia* (3 acts). Performed Bremen, Germany, 1 December 1905.
        Baker's and Hipsher state that this was the first American opera
        staged in Europe.
1904   *Sakuntala*, op. 67 (melodrama; libretto after Kalidasa).
   -    *The Bells of Beaujolais.*
   -    *The Maiden Queen*, op. 69.

Cohen, David (b. Pulaski, TN, 14 October 1927; Anderson)
    1977   *Beauty Is Fled* (children's opera). Performed Phoenix, AZ, 7
           August 1977.

Cohen, Douglas (ASCAP)
    1987   *No Way to Treat a Lady* (libretto by composer after William
           Goldman). Performed Hudson Guild Theater, New York, 11 June
           1987.

Cohen, Joel (b. Providence, RI, 23 May 1942; *Amerigrove*; *Who's Who*)
    1988   *Tristan and Iseult* (90 minutes; libretto by composer, on medieval
           songs). Performed by Boston Camerata, New York, February
           1988. Recorded by Erato.

Cohen, Joseph (b. New York, 3 August 1917; Anderson)
    1970   *A Christmas Carol.* Performed West de Pere, WI, 5 December 1970.

Cohen, Mae (b. Chicago, 30 June 1929; *Who's Who*)
    1989   *Significant Lives.* Performed at Northeastern Illinois University, 20
           September 1989.
    1989   *Variations on a Theme.* Performed at Northeastern Illinois
           University, 20 September 1989.

Cohen, Michael
    1981   *Rappaccini's Daughter* (1 act; libretto by Linsey Abrams after
           Hawthorne). Performed Waterford, CT, 12 August 1981, and St.
           Paul, MN, 2 September 1983.
    1984   *Yours, Anne* (libretto by Enid Futterman after the diary of Anne
           Frank). Performed by Minnesota Opera Workshop, November
           1984, and Playhouse 91, New York, 10 October 1985.

Cohen, Scott (b. 1968 in Mt. Vernon, NY)
    1990   *Before Breakfast* (1 act; libretto by composer after O'Neill).
           Performed Binghamton, NY, 10 May 1990.

Cohen, Sol B. (pen name of André Vaneuf; b. Urbana, IL, 11 January 1891;
           Anderson)
    1932   1-act opera at the MacDowell Colony "based on a Spanish-Jewish
           theme."

Cohen, Steve (Stephen B.) (b. New York, 3 September 1954?; AMC; Anderson)
    1979   *La Pizza del destino* (10 minutes; libretto by Joseph Renard).
    1980   *The Cop and the Anthem* (1 act; libretto by Alison Hubbard).
           Performed Lake George, NY, 7 August 1980.

Cohn, James Myron (b. Newark, NJ, 28 February 1928; Anderson; *Baker's*; *Who's
           Who*)
    1955   *The Fall of the City* (30 minutes; libretto after Archibald
           MacLeish). Performed Athens, OH, 8 July 1955.

Colburn, George (b. Colton, NY, 25 June 1878; d. Chicago, 18 April 1921;
    Anderson)
  1912   *Masque of Montezuma* (Johnson gives 1913).
  1913   *Masque of Demeter and Persephone.*
  1914   *Anthony and Cleopatra.*

Cole, Rosseter Gleason (b. near Clyde, MI, 5 February 1866; d. Lake Bluff, IL,
    18 May 1952; *Amerigrove*)
  1931   *The Maypole Lovers* (2 hours; libretto by C. Ranck). Bispham
      Medal.

Colgrass, Michael (b. Chicago, 22 April 1932; AMC; *Amerigrove*; *Who's Who*)
  1967   *Virgil's Dream* (35 minutes; libretto by composer). Commission by
      Brighton Festival, England, April 1967. Performance at Xavier
      University, New Orleans, October 1972.
  1971   *Nightingale, Inc.* (comic opera; 1 act; libretto by composer).
      Commission by Corporation for Public Broadcasting. Performance
      Urbana, IL, 13 March 1975.
  1978   *Something's Gonna Happen* (children's musical; 1 act). Performed
      Toronto, Ontario, 1978

Collins, Anthony Vincent
  1953   *Caterina Parr* (comedy; libretto by Maurice Baring). Performance
      by Opera Futures, New York, February 1953.
   -    *Perseus and Andromeda.*

Collins, Edward (1887-1951)
   -    *Daughter of the South.* Bispham Medal, 1945.

Combs, Ronald (b. War Creek, NY, 2 July 1938; Anderson)
  1968   *The Three Wishes.* Performed Evanston, IL, 30 April 1968.
  1974   *The Monkey's Paw* (libretto after Jacobs), with wind instruments.
      Performed Stevens Point, WI, February 1974.
   -    *A Christmas Carol* (libretto after Dickens).
   -    *The Legend of the Christmas Rose.*
   -    *The Rider on the Bare Horse: The Three Wishes* (children's opera
      with woodwind quintet).
   -    *The Visitor* (1 act; science fiction opera).

Conde, Emilia
  1984   *The Magical Forest* (*El conejito*) (1 hour; libretto by the composer
      and Toni Muletti, available in English or Spanish). Performed by
      Puerto Rican Traveling Theatre, New York, 7 August 1984.

Condon, Elmore
  1922   *Once Upon a Time* (3 acts). Performed St. Louis, 19 May 1922.
   -    *The Village Master* (3 acts).

Connell, Gordon
  1985   *Bertha, the Sewing Machine Girl* (libretto by Robert Emmett after a
      19th-century melodrama). Grand prize, Seagram's New Music
      Theater Awards, 1986. Readings, New York, 16 February 1985,
      and Minneapolis, 21 February 1987; performed Lowell, MA, 1988.

Constantinides, Constantine Dinos (b. Ioannina, Greece, 10 May 1929; U.S. citizen, 1967; AMC; Anderson)

1975 *Fugue for Two Voices* (expanded in 1981; libretto by David Madden). Performed Baton Rouge, LA, 23 February 1981.

1977 *Antigone: Scene IV* (20 minutes; libretto by Fitts and Fitzgerald after Sophocles). (Anderson dates the opera 1973.) Performed Baton Rouge, LA, 20 April 1989.

1981 *Intimations* (1 act; libretto by David Madden). Performed at Brooklyn College, NY, 5 February 1982.

Converse, Frederick S. (b. Newton, MA, 5 January 1871; d. Westwood, MA, 8 June 1940; *Amerigrove*; Hipsher)

1905 *Iolan: or, The Pipe of Desire*, op. 21 ("romantic opera in one act"; libretto by George Edward Barton, German translation by Charles Henry Meltzer). Performed at New England Conservatory of Music, Boston, 31 January, 2 February, 6 March 1906. First American opera to be performed at the Metropolitan Opera, New York, 18 March 1910. Bispham medal, 1926. Full score published New York: H. W. Gray/Novello & Co., 1908; reprint, Schleifer, 6:103-326.

1910 *The Sacrifice* (libretto by composer and John A. Macy after story by Henry Augustus Wise). Performed at Boston Opera House, 3 March 1911.

1913 *Beauty and the Beast* (*Sinbad the Sailor*) (libretto by Percy Mackaye). Unperformed.

1914 *The Immigrants* (libretto by Percy MacKaye). Unperformed.

Convey, Robert

1972 *Quince's Dream* (libretto by composer after Shakespeare's *A Midsummer Night's Dream*). Performed Waterford, CT, 29 May 1982.

1982 *Pyramus and Thisbe* (45 minutes; libretto by composer after Shakespeare's *A Midsummer Night's Dream*). Workshop performance, Waterford, CT, May 1982, and staged at Glens Falls, NY, July 1982.

1989 *The Blanket* (16 minutes). Performed at Spoleto Festival, Charleston, SC, 31 May 1989.

Cook, Gerald

1980 *Daddy, Daddy*, with Hamilton Grandison and Tad Truesdale (2 acts; blues drama). Performed by LaMama, New York, 3 December 1980.

Cook, Will Marion (b. Washington, DC, 27 January 1869; d. New York, 19 July 1944; *Amerigrove*; Southern)

(These works, except the last, have also been considered musicals.)

1898 *Clorindy: or, The Origin of the Cakewalk* (*Amerigrove*: "first Negro musical-comedy sketch"; libretto by P. Dunbar). Performed New York.

1899 *Jes' lak White Fo'ks* (libretto by P. Dunbar).

1900 *The Sons of Ham.*

1901 *The Cannibal King* (libretto by P. Dunbar and J. R. Johnson).

1902 *In Dahomey.*
1904 *The Southerners* (libretto by W. Mercer and R. Grant).
1906 *In Abyssinia.*
1906 *The Shoo-Fly Regiment.*
1908 *In Bandanna Land.*
1908 *The Red Moon.*
1913 *The Traitor* (libretto by A. Creamer).
1915 *Darkeydom* (libretto by H. Troy and L. Walton).
1929 *Swing Along*, with W. Vodery.
1929 *St. Louis 'ooman* (grand opera).

Cooper, Harry E.
- *La señora de los rosas.* In Krohn.

Cooper, John Craig (b. Kansas City, MO, 14 May 1925; Anderson)
1976 A work with a colonial American setting was commissioned by the Performing Arts Society, New York, for performance in White Plains, NY, 1976.

Cooper, Rose Marie (b. Cairo, IL, 21 February 1937; Anderson; Cohen)
1976 *Oh, Penelope* ("bicentennial play"; libretto by Susan Graham Williamson). Performed Charlotte, NC, April 1976.

Cooper, Seth
1985 *Echoes of the Shining Prince* (1 act; libretto by Elizabeth Aldridge after Lady Murasaki's *The Tale of Genji*). Performed at Merkin Hall, New York, 25 April 1985.

Copeland, Stewart
1986 *Holy Blood and Crescent Moon* (2 acts; libretto by Susan Shirwen, about Palestine during the Crusades). Commission by Cleveland Opera for 1987-88 season; performed there 10 October 1988 (Kornick: 12 October 1989), and Fort Worth, TX, 17 November 1989.

Copland, Aaron (b. Brooklyn, NY, 14 November 1900; d. Westchester, NY, 2 December 1990; *Amerigrove*)
1936 *The Second Hurricane* (school play-opera; 2 acts—90 minutes; libretto by E. Denby). Performed New York, 21 April 1937.
1954 *The Tender Land* (2 acts—95 minutes libretto by H. Everett after E. Johns); revised to 3 acts, 1955. Performed by New York Opera, New York, 1 April 1954; revised version performed Oberlin, OH, 20 May 1955. Published by Boosey & Hawkes.

Coppola, Carmine (b. New York, 11 June 1910; AMC; Anderson)
- *Escorial* (libretto by Fred M. Swenson after Michel de Ghelderode).

Corcoran, William (listed in Anderson but with no biographical information)
1973 *Games of Cards* (30 minutes). Performed by Baby Grand Opera Co., Cincinnati, 6 December 1973.
- *Trilogy on the Quality of Life* (three 1-act operas). 1976 Bicentennial work commissioned by the Baby Grand Opera Co. Performed Cincinnati.

Corigliano, John (b. New York, 16 February 1938; *Amerigrove*; *Who's Who*)
  1975   *Gulliver* (1 act; libretto by William M. Hoffman). NEA grant, 1975.
  1975   *The Frog Prince* (1 act). NEA grant, 1975.
  1985   *The Naked Carmen* ("Bizet for singers, rock and pop groups, Moog synthesizer, and instruments").
  1987   *The Ghosts of Versailles* ("grand opera buffa"; 2 acts; libretto by William Hoffman, loosely based on Beaumarchais's *La Mère coupable*). Commission and première by Metropolitan Opera, New York, 19 December 1991—the first since Marvin David Levy's *Mourning Becomes Electra*, 1967. See *New Yorker*, 13 January 1992, 69-72.

Corina, John (b. Cleveland, 21 April 1928; Anderson)
  1983   *The Telling of the North Star* (45 minutes; libretto by Vincent Ferrini). Performed Athens, GA, 29 March 1983.

Cornett, Ewel (ASCAP)
  1981   *The Hatfields and the McCoys* (libretto by Billy Edd Wheeler). Performed Beckley, WV, 20 June 1981.
  1981   *Honey in the Rock* (libretto by Jack Kilpatrick and Kermit Hunter). Performed Beckley, WV, 21 June 1981.

Corse, Larry
  1982   *The Open Window* (1 act; libretto after Saki). Performed Morrow, GA, 2 May 1982 and 26 May 1989.

Costinescu, George (b. Bucharest, Romania, 12 December 1934; to U.S. in 1969; Anderson)
  1971   *The Musical Seminar* (1 act—90 minutes; libretto by composer). Performed by New and Newer Music Festival, New York, 1971, and Tanglewood, Lenox, MA, 3 August 1982.

Cotel, Morris Moshe (b. Baltimore, MD, 20 February 1943; Anderson)
  1985   *Dreyfus* (1 act—135 minutes; libretto by Mordecai Newman). Performed Brooklyn, NY, 17 January 1985.
  1988   *Deronda* (3 acts; after George Eliot).

Coughlin, Bruce
  1984   *Silas* (libretto by Michael Korie and Anthony Stein). Performed by All Children's Theatre, New York, 4 November 1984.

Cowell, Henry (b. Menlo Park, CA, 11 March 1897; d. Shady, NY, 10 December 1965; *Amerigrove*)
  1949   *O'Higgins of Chile* (3 acts—95 minutes; libretto by Elizabeth Harald Lomax on the story of Gen. Bernardo O'Higgins; not orchestrated). Commission from the Alice M. Ditson Fund. Not performed. William Lichtenwanger, *The Music of Henry Cowell: A Descriptive Catalog* (New York: Institute for Studies in American Music, Brooklyn College, 1986), no. 743.

Crabtree, Ray
  1970   *The Fool*. Performed New York, 29 March 1970.

Cramer, ?
1988   *8½ x 11.* Performed New York, 29 September 1988.

Crane, Lor (ASCAP)
1984   *Adam and Eve III* (1 act; libretto by Seymour Reiter).   Performed
by Golden Fleece, New York, 7 June 1984.

Crawford, Dawn Constance (b. Ellington Field, TX, 19 December 1919;
Anderson; Cohen; *Who's Who*)
1971   *The Pearl* (chamber opera; 3 acts; libretto by composer after
Steinbeck).   (Cohen: 1954.)   Performed at Dominican College,
Houston, TX, April 1972.

Crawford, John Charlton (b. Philadelphia, 19 January 1931; ASCAP; Anderson;
Who's Who)
1970   *The Tragicomedy of Don Cristóbal and Rosita* (chamber opera; 1
act—75 minutes; libretto by James Graham-Lujan and Richard L.
O'Connell based on Federico García Lorca's play "The Billy-Club
Puppets").   Performed at Wellesley College, MA, 22 March 1970.

Creatore, Luigi (*see also* Peretti, Hugo)
1986   *Jokers.*   Begun by Hugo Peretti and completed after Peretti's death
by Creatore with David Weiss.   Performed Chester, CT, 14
October 1986.

Crews, Lucille (Mrs. Marsh; b. Pueblo, CO, 23 August 1888; d. San Diego, CA, 3
November 1972; Anderson; *Baker's*; Cohen; Hipsher)
1923   *The Call of Jeanne d'Arc* (1 act; adapted from act 1 of Percy
Mackay's *Joan of Arc*).   Prize of $250 from Mrs. Cecil Frankel,
1926, according to Hipsher; perhaps this is the award of the
California Federation of Music Clubs.
1926   *Eight Hundred Rubles* (grand opera; 1 act; libretto by John G.
Neidhardt).
1935   *Ariadne and Dionysus* (miniature opera).   NBC music guild.
1958   *The Concert.*

Crist, Bainbridge (b. Lawrenceburg, IN, 13 February 1883; d. Barnstable, MA, 7
February 1969; *Amerigrove*)
1913   *Le Pied de la Momie* ("choreographic drama").   Performed
Bournemouth, England, 1915.
1926   *The Sorceress* ("choreographic drama").

Cross, James A. (AMC)
1980   *Knossos.*

Crowell, Joan (AMC)
1985   *The Bell Witch of Tennessee* (45 minutes; libretto by composer after
a 19th-century legend).   Performed Suffolk Music Guild, Stony
Brook, NY, 2 November 1985.
1988   *The Heights* (5 acts; libretto by composer after Shakespeare's *The
Tempest*).   Reading, Quogue, NY, 22 May 1988.

Crozier, Daniel
    1985   *The Reunion* (1 act; libretto by Roger Brunyate). Reading, Peabody Conservatory, Baltimore, MD, 29 April 1985; staged there, 14 October 1989.

Crystal, Raphael (ASCAP)
    1983   *My Heart Is in the East* (libretto by Richard Engquist and Linda Kline, on the life of the 12th-century poet Judah Halevy). Performed at Jewish Repertory Theatre, New York, 28 May 1983.
    1984   *Kuni-Leml* (3 acts; libretto by Richard Engquist and Linda Kline after Goldfaden). Performed at Jewish Repertory Theatre, New York, June 1984.
    1987   *Half a World Away* (libretto by Richard Engquist and Linda Kline after Aleichem). Performed at Jewish Repertory Theatre, New York, 2 July 1987.
    1989   *The Land of Dreams* (in Yiddish; libretto by Nahum Stutchkoff and Miriam Kressyn). Performed New York, 28 October 1989.

Csonka, Paul
    1981   *Storm at Sea* (40 minutes; libretto by Herman Geiger-Torel). Performed by OPERA America Showcase, New York, January 1981. Telecast on CMQ-TV, Havana, Cuba.

Cuckson, Robert (*WhoAm*: no birth place or date)
    1988   *Adrian and Jusemina.* Performed at Mannes College of Music, New York, May 1988.

Culver, Andrew
    1987   *Europas 1 & 2*, with John Cage (135 minutes; prepared from 70 operas). Performed Frankfurt, Germany, 12 December 1987, and State University of New York at Purchase, 14 July 1988.

Cumberworth, Starling A. (b. Medina County, OH, 25 July 1915; *WhoAm*)
    1955   *Home Burial* (20 minutes).

Cumming, Richard Jackson (b. Shanghai, China, 9 June 1928, of American parents; Anderson; *Who's Who*)
    1976   *The Picnic* (2 acts—100 minutes; libretto by Henry Butler). NEA grant, 1976 (Anderson dates the opera 1964-74). Performed by Central City Opera, CO, 10 May 1979, and New York, 11 November 1985.

Cummings, Conrad (b. San Francisco, 10 February 1948; Anderson)
    1983   *Eros and Psyche* (3 acts—150 minutes; libretto by composer after Apuleius; music in the Baroque style). Performed Oberlin, OH, 16 November 1983.

Cummins, Rick (Anderson has Richard Cummins; b. Petersburg, VA, 30 September 1936)
    1987   *Sherlock Holmes and the Red-Headed League* (libretto by composer with John Forster and Greer Woodward after Doyle). Performed by Theatreworks/USA, New York, 24 January 1987.

1987   *Right in Your Own Back Yard* (libretto by John Forster). Performed
by Theatreworks/USA, New York, 14 February 1987.

Cunningham, Arthur (b. Piermont, NY, 11 November 1928; *Amerigrove*; *Who's
Who*; Southern)
1969   *His Natural Grace* (rock opera; libretto by Louey and Louey).
1972   *Slave Song.* Performed at Howard University, Washington, DC,
and Malcolm X College, Chicago.
-      *Ostrich Feathers* (rock opera). Performed "in the New York area."

Cunningham, Michael (b. Warren, MI, 5 August 1937; AMC; Anderson)
1975   *Figg and Bean* (55 minutes; libretto by composer after John
Madison Morton). Performed Eau Claire, WI, 7 March 1975.
1978   *Catherine Sloper of Washington Square* (3 acts; libretto by composer
after Henry James). Performed Eau Claire, WI, 31 March 1978.
1985   *Dorian Gray* (2 acts; libretto by composer after Wilde). Performed
Eau Claire, WI, 25 January 1985.

Cuppett, Charles Harold (b. Coquimbo, Chile, 25 June 1894; studied at Ohio
Wesleyan University; Anderson)
-      *Le Baiser.*

Currie, Russell (b. North Arlington, NJ, 3 April 1954; *WhoAm*)
1982   *The Cask of Amontillado* (horror story; 1 act—30 minutes; libretto by
Carl Laanes after Edgar Allan Poe). Commission by Bronx
Historical Society and Bronx Arts Ensemble. Première by Bronx
Arts Ensemble, Bronx, NY, 3 April 1982. Kornick.
1983   *The System of Dr. Tarr and Prof. Fether.*
1984   *A Dream within a Dream* (1 act—60 minutes; libretto by Robert
Kornfield after Poe's *The Fall of the House of Usher*).
Commissioned and performed by Bronx Arts Ensemble, New
York, 29 April 1984 and 15 June 1985.
1987   *Ligeia* (2 acts; libretto by Robert Kornfield after Poe). Performed
by Bronx Arts Ensemble, New York, 5 April 1987.
1989   *Rimshot* (libretto by Ron Singer). Reading by ORRA, New York,
16 October 1989; staged by the same, 10 May 1990.

Curtis, Elyse
1986   *The Perils of Paul* (2 acts; libretto by composer, about the Apostle
Paul). Workshop performance, 1986; staged by Broadway
Tomorrow Musical Theatre, New York, 20 July 1989.

Curtis, Louis Woodson
(Rodríguez states that Curtis composed six operas.)

Curty, Gene
1975   *The Lieutenant*, with Nitra Scharfman and Chuck Strand (rock
opera). Performed at Lyceum Theater, New York, 11 March
1975.

Cusenza, Frank J. (b. San Vito, Italy, 25 December 1899; U.S. citizen in 1923; Anderson)
-     *The Creation.*

Cutler, R. J.
    1989   *Sitting on the Edge of the Future* (with James Youmans and others). Performed by American Musical Theater Festival, fall 1989.

Czerny-Hydzik, Thomas
    1979   *The Tell-Tale Heart* (1 act; libretto after Poe). Performed by Prince George's Civic Opera, Largo, MD, 27 December 1979.

Dabney, Sheila
    1985   *Mythos Oedipus*, with Elizabeth Swados, Connie Alexander, Genji Ito, David Sawyer, and Michael Sirotta (90 minutes; libretto by Ellen Stewart after Sophocles; in Greek). Performed Delphi, Greece, summer 1985, and by LaMama, New York, 6 February 1988.

Dabrusin, Ross
    1977?   *The Night Harry Stopped Smoking* (15 minutes; libretto by John Davies). Performed Syracuse, NY, 28 April 1983. Published by Jane Ferry Associates.

Daccash, Leslie
    1988   *Della's Palace* (libretto by Morgan Taylor). Performed by AMAS Repertory Theatre, New York, 17 June 1988.

Da Costa, Noel (b. Lagos, Nigeria, 24 December 1929; to U.S. at age 11; *Amerigrove*; Southern)
    1958   *The Cocktail Sip* (libretto by T. Brewster).
    1971   *Tortoise* (theater piece for children).
    1974   *Babu's Juju.* Performed Flint, MI.
-     *The Singing Tortoise.*

Dafore Horton, Asadata (b. Freetown, Sierra Leone, Africa, 1889; d. New York, 4 March 1965; Southern)
    1934   *Kykuntor (The Witch Woman)* (folk opera). Performed May 1934 with cast of Africans and black Americans.
    1940   *Zunguru* (dance opera).
    1944   *Africa* (tribal opera).

D'Agostino, Joseph
    1982   *Winds of Change* (libretto by Gary Romero and Franklin Tramutola). Performance by AMAS Repertory Theatre, New York, 4 February 1982.

Dalton, Jane
- *Once Upon a Time* (3 acts; libretto by composer after *Rumpelstiltskin*). *COS-1*. Published by H. T. FitzSimmons.

Damashek, Barbara (Cohen)
1982 *Quilters* (2 acts; libretto by composer and Molly Newman after Cooper & Allen). Performed Denver, CO, 8 November 1982.
1986 *Olympian Games* (libretto by composer with Kenneth Cavander after Ovid). Performed Cambridge, MA, 9 May 1986.

Damrosch, Walter (b. Breslau, Germany, 30 January 1862; d. New York, 22 December 1950; to U.S. in 1874; *Amerigrove*; Hipsher)
1895 *The Scarlet Letter* (3 acts; libretto by George P. Lathrop after Nathaniel Hawthorne). Première by Damrosch Opera Co., Boston, 10 February 1896; also in New York and Philadelphia for a total of six performances.
1912 *The Dove of Peace* (comic opera; 3 acts; libretto by Wallace Irvin). Performed New York, 14 March 1912 (*Amerigrove*: Philadelphia, 15 October 1912).
1913 *Cyrano de Bergerac* (romantic opera; 4 acts; libretto by William J. Henderson after Edmond Rostand). Première by Metropolitan Opera, New York, 27 February 1913. Bispham Medal, 1929. Published by G. Schirmer.
1937 *The Man Without a Country* (2 acts; libretto by Arthur Guiterman after E. E. Hale). Performed by Metropolitan Opera, New York, 12 May 1937. Published by G. Schirmer.
1942 *The Opera Cloak*. Performed at Broadway Theatre, New York, 3 November 1942.
- *Congress and the Two Elephants*.

Daniels, David (b. Penn Yan, NY, 20 December 1933; *Who's Who*)
- *The Tribunal* ("a short opera").

Daniels, Mabel Wheeler (b. Swampscott, MA, 27 November 1878; d. Boston, 10 March 1971; *Amerigrove*)
1900 *A Copper Complication* (operetta; libretto by R. L. Hooper).
1900 *The Court of Hearts* (operetta; libretto by R. L. Hooper). Performed Cambridge, MA, 2 January 1901 (the composer sang the role of the Jack of Hearts).
1902 *The Show Girl* (operetta; libretto by R. A. Barnett), in collaboration with D. K. Stevens.
1904 *Alice in Wonderland Continued* (opera sketch). Performed Brookline, MA, May 1920 (*Amerigrove* says 1904).

Daniels, Melvin L. (b. Cleburne, TX, 11 January 1931; Anderson; *Who's Who*)
1989 *Lazarus* (39 minutes; libretto by Jack Welch). Commission by Abilene Christian University. Performed at Episcopal Church of the Heavenly Rest, Abilene, TX, spring 1989.

Danks, Hart Pease (b. New Haven, CT, 6 April 1834; d. Philadelphia, 20 November 1903; *Amerigrove*)
1872 *Pauline: or, The Belle of Saratoga*.

1881   *Conquered by Kindness.*

D'Anna, Tony
1983   *Parrot Island—The Nuclear Opera* (1 act—1 hour; libretto by Fred Curchak). Contains improvisation and audience participation. Performed Petuluma, CA, 20 May 1983.

Dansicker, Michael Edward (AMC)
1980   *Epilogue* (1 act; libretto by Sarah Marie Schlesinger).
1990   *Twenty, Fingers, Twenty Toes* (libretto by composer with Bob Nigro, about Siamese Twins). Performed at WPA Theatre, New York, 7 January 1990.

D'Antalffy, Dezso
1934   *Onteora's Bride.* Performed at Radio City Music Hall, New York.

Dara, Olu
1986   *The Tale of Madame Zora* (libretto by Aishah Rahman, about black novelist Zora Neale Hurston). Performed by Ensemble Studio Theater, New York, February 1986.

Darnell, August
1989   *In a Pig's Valise* (libretto by Eric Overmyer; a satire of detective stories). Performed by Second Stage, New York, 13 February 1989.

Davidson, Charles (b. Pittsburgh, 8 September 1929; ASCAP; Anderson)
-   *Gimpel the Fool* (1 act—60 minutes; libretto by Paul Kresh after Isaac Singer).

Davidson, Jerry F. (b. in Arkansas, 26 July 1942; Anderson)
-   *The Fall of Man.* Bingham prize, 1969.

Davidson, Wayne
1979   *Scrooge* (1 act; libretto by composer after Dickens). Performed Memphis, TN, 30 November 1979.
1980   *Aladdin and His Magic Lamp* (1 act; libretto by composer). Performed Memphis, TN, 1980.

Davies, John
1825   *The Forest Rose: or, The American Farmers.* Performed New York, 1949 and 1955.

Davis, Allan Gerald (b. Watertown, NY, 29 August 1922; ASCAP; Anderson; Schoep)
1945   *The Sailing of the Nancy Bell* (chamber opera; 1 act—25 minutes). Performed Duxbury, MA, 3 August 1955. Published by Boosey & Hawkes.
1949   *The Ordeal of Osbert* (1 act—40 minutes; libretto after Wodehouse). Performed Duxbury, MA, summer 1949. Published by Boosey & Hawkes.
1958   *Otherwise Engaged* (1 act). Performed at Sullivan Street Playhouse, New York, 23 April 1958.

1975   *The Departure* (tragedy; 3 acts—180 minutes; libretto by composer).
        Premièred at University of Montevallo, AL, 24-25 April 1975.
        Kornick; see also *NOA Opera Journal* 8/3 (1975): 22-28.
        Published by E. C. Kerby, 198 Davenport Rd., Toronto 5,
        Ontario, Canada.

Davis, Anthony (b. Paterson, NJ, 20 February 1951; *Amerigrove*)
1983   *X (The Life and Times of Malcolm X)* (3 acts—150 minutes; story
        by Christopher Davis; libretto by Thulani Davis). Performed
        Philadelphia, 27 June 1984; Springfield, MA, April 1985; operatic
        première by New York Opera, October 1986. See *Third Stream
        Music*, 28 October 1985, 85; and *People*, 6 October 1986, 129f.
        Published by G. Schirmer. Kornick: première of revised version
        by New York City Opera, New York, 28 September 1986.
1989   *Under the Double Moon* (science fiction; story and libretto by
        Deborah Atherton). Commission by Opera Theatre of Saint Louis;
        OPERA America grant. Performed Waterford, CT, 9 August
        1988, and St. Louis, 15 June 1989 (Kornick: première in St. Louis
        this date).
1992   *Tania* (libretto by Michael John LaChiusa; about Patty Hearst).
        Première at American Music Theater Festival, Philadelphia, 17
        June 1992. See *New York Times*, 7 June 1992, sec. 2, pp. 1, 30.

Davis, Bob (b. Philadelphia, 17 July 1947; ASCAP; Anderson)
1988   *Poison Hotel*, with John Raskin and Allan Finneran (involves
        audience participation). Performed by Soon 3, San Francisco,
        October 1988.

Davis, Carl
1962   *Pubcrawl* (1 act). Performed at Yale Summer School, New Haven,
        CT, August 1962.

Davis, John S. (b. Evanston, IL, 1 October 1935; Anderson)
1967   *The Pardoner's Tale* (1 act; libretto after Chaucer). Performed at
        University of Arizona, 23 May 1967.

Davis, Katherine K. (b. St. Joseph, MO, 25 June 1892; d. Concord, MA, 20 April
        1980 [Cohen: 1981]; Anderson)
1955   *The Disappointed Impresario* (1 act; libretto by Heddie Ruth Kent).
        Performed Duxbury, MA, 15 July 1955. Published by G.
        Schirmer, 1956, as *The Unmusical Impresario*.
 -      *Cinderella.*

Davis, Mary
1973   *Columbine* (3 acts; libretto Joanna Sampson). Performed by Boulder
        Civic Opera, CO, 12 April 1973.

Davis, Ralph
1976   *How a Fish Swam in the Air and a Hare in the Water.* Performed at
        University of Arizona, Tucson, 1 July 1976.

Day, Kingsley
>   1988   *Aztec Human Sacrifice* (libretto by Phillip LeZebnik). Performed at
>   Columbia College, Chicago, 18 April 1988.

Deak, Jon (b. Hammond, IN, 27 April 1943; Anderson)
>   1986   *Lady Chatterley's Dream* (1 act; libretto by composer). Performed
>   by Apple Hill Chamber Players at Symphony Space, New York, 18
>   April 1986.
>   1986   *Owl in Love* (libretto by composer). Performed together with the
>   above.

Deal, William Albert (b. Dayton, OH, 29 February 1874; Hipsher)
>   1929   *The Rings of Chaunto* (lyric drama; 2 acts; libretto by Mrs. William
>   McQuisto Sykes after a story by the composer). Première,
>   Greenwood, MS, 7 March 1929; also performed Asheville, NC,
>   June 1930, and broadcast Jackson, MS, 25 November 1932.

De Banfield, Raffaello
>   1955   *Lord Byron's Love Letter* (1 act). Performed New Orleans.

Debbins, ?
>   1988   *The Scheme.* Performed by Delaware Valley Arts, Narrowsburg,
>   NY, 19 November 1988.

DeBenedictus, Dick
>   1987   *Soufflé* (libretto by Herb Martin and Lou Firimonte). Performed at
>   California Institute of the Arts, Valencia, 8 December 1987.

De Berry, David
>   1988   *A Christmas Carol* (libretto by Richard Hellesen after Dickens).
>   Performed Sacramento, CA, 1988.

Debusman, Emil (ACA)
>   -   *Capriccio Boyesca* (35 minutes). Published by American Music
>   Edition.
>   -   *Dilemma* (1 act).
>   -   *Magic Square* (1 act—1 hour). Published by American Music
>   Edition.

DeCarmillis, Lisa
>   1983   *Mother Goose.* Performed Louisville, KY, 1 February 1983.

Dede, Edmund (1829-1903; b. in New Orleans)
>   -   *Sultan d'Ispaha.*

Deems, James (b. Baltimore, MD, 9 January 1818; Hipsher)
>   -   *Esther* (grand opera; libretto after the Bible).

De Filippi, Amadeo (b. Ariano, Italy, 20 February 1900; to U.S. 1905; Anderson;
>   *Who's Who*)
>   1927   *The Green Cuckatoo* (1 act).
>   1937   *Malvolio* (2 acts).

DeForest, Charles

1989   *Prizes* (libretto by Raffi Pehlivanian). Performed by AMAS Repertory Theatre, New York, 26 April 1989.

DeKnight, René

1987   *Lady Sweets* (libretto by Maggie Monahan). Performed by Long Beach Civic Light Opera, CA, 17 January 1987.

De Koven, Reginald (b. Middletown, CT, 3 April 1859; d. Chicago, 16 January 1920; ASCAP; *Amerigrove*; Hipsher)

1889   *The Begum.* Performed 21 November 1887.

1889   *Don Quixote.* Performed Boston, 1889.

1890   *Robin Hood* ("comic opera in 3 acts"; libretto by Harry B. Smith). Première at Chicago Opera House, 9 June 1890. It ran for more than 3,000 successive performances after the Chicago run, including a Boston run of 20 years. Performance run at Prince of Wales Theatre, London, beginning 5 January 1891, with title *Maid Marian*. Piano-vocal score, New York: G. Schirmer, 1891; reprinted in Schleifer, 5:105-330. *Amerigrove*: ". . . began the era when American operetta dominated the musical stage in the USA, was perennially in the repertory of the Bostonians, the first important operetta troupe after the introduction of Gilbert and Sullivan to America; and a song from it, 'Oh promise me,' has remained a popular wedding ballad."

1892   *The Fencing Master.* Performed Boston, 1892.

1893   *The Algerian.* Performed Philadelphia, 1893.

1893   *The Knickerbockers.* Performed Boston, 1893.

1894   *Rob Roy* ("romantic opera"; 3 acts). Performed New York, October 1894.

1895   *The Tzigane.* Performed 16 May 1895.

1896   *The Mandarin.* Performed Cleveland, 1896.

1897   *The Paris Doll.* Performed Hartford, CT, 1897.

1897   *The Highwayman.* Performed 13 December 1897.

1899   *The Three Dragoons.* Performed 30 June 1899.

1899   *The Man in the Moon* (libretto by L. Harrison and S. Strange), in collaboration with L. Englander and G. Keller. Performed 24 April 1899.

1899   *Papa's Wife.* Performed 13 November 1899.

1900   *Broadway to Tokyo* (libretto by L. Harrison and G. V. Hobart), in collaboration with A. B. Sloane. Performed 23 January 1900.

1900   *Foxy Quiller.* Performed 5 November 1900.

1901   *The Little Duchess.* Performed 14 October 1901.

1901   *Maid Marian* ("comic opera"; 3 acts; after the story of Robin Hood). Performed Philadelphia, 1902 (*Amerigrove*: 4 November 1901).

1903   *The Canterbury Pilgrims* ("dramatic opera"; 4 acts; libretto by Percy Mackaye). Published by John Church, 1903. Première by Metropolitan Opera, New York, 8 March 1917; five performances its first season.

1903   *The Jersey Lily* (libretto by G. V. Hobart), in collaboration with W. Jerome and J. Schwartz. Performed 14 September 1903.

1903   *Red Feather* (book by C. Klein; lyrics by C. E. Cook). Performed 11 November 1903.

1905   *Happyland* (libretto by F. Rancken). Performed 2 October 1905.

1906   *The Student King* (libretto by F. Rancken and S. Strange). Performed 25 December 1906.

1907   *The Girls of Holland* (libretto by S. Strange). Performed 18 November 1907.

1908   *The Golden Butterfly.* Performed 12 October 1908.

1909   *The Beauty Spot* (libretto by J. W. Herbert). Performed 10 April 1909.

1911   *The Wedding Trip.* Performed 25 December 1911.

1913   *Her Little Highness.* Performed 13 October 1913.

1920   *Rip Van Winkle* (libretto by Percy Mackaye). Première by Chicago Opera Company, at the Auditorium, 2 January 1920, and this company also performed it at Lexington Theatre, New York, 30 January 1920.

Delaney, Charles Oliver (b. Winston-Salem, NC, 21 May 1925; *WhoAm*)

-    *A Very Special Date* (20 minutes).

Del Borgo, Elliot Anthony (b. Port Chester, NY, 27 October 1938; Anderson)

1982   *Drum Taps* (12 minutes; about the Civil War; libretto after Whitman).

DeLeone, Francesco Bartolomeo (b. Ravenna, OH, 28 July 1887; d. Akron, OH, 10 December 1948; Anderson; Hipsher)

1910   *A Millionaire's Caprice.* Performed as *Capriccio di miliario* by Gravina-Fournier Opera Co. at Teatro Eldorado, Naples, Italy, 26 July 1910.

1924   *Alglala: A Romance of the Mesa* ("Buckeye opera"; 2 acts; libretto by Cecil Fanning). Performed at the Akron Armory, OH, 23 May 1924, Cleveland, 14-15 November 1924, and Chicago, 10 March 1936. Published by G. Schirmer, 1924. Bispham Medal, 1924. In AMRC.

-    *Cave-Man Stuff* (operetta).

-    *David* (sacred music drama).

-    *The Golden Calf* (sacred music drama).

-    *Pergolesi.*

-    *Princess Ting-Ah-Ling* (operetta).

-    *The Prodigal Son* (sacred music drama).

-    *Ruth* (sacred music drama).

Delinger, Lawrence Ross (b. Hyannis, NE, 11 November 1937; Anderson)

1986   *Two Dopes on a Rope* (libretto by John Fletcher). Performed at PCPA Theaterfest, Solvang, CA, September 1986.

-    *Photograph* (on text of Gertrude Stein).

Delli Ponti, R.

1911   *Haschisch*, with Else Gregori. Performed Torino, Italy.

Dello Joio, Norman (b. New York, 24 January 1913; *Amerigrove*; *Baker's*)

1950   *The Triumph of St. Joan* (55 minutes; libretto by Joseph Machlis), withdrawn. Performed Bronxville, NY, 9 May 1950. Performed, as *The Trial at Rouen* (2 hours), NBC-TV, 8 April 1956. New version of *The Triumph of St. Joan* (libretto by composer) performed by New York City Opera, 16 April 1959; it received a New York Music Critics' Circle Award, and was published by Franco Columbo.

1953   *The Tall Kentuckian* (incidental music; 17 minutes). Published by Carl Fischer. Perhaps the same as *Tall K* (libretto by Barbara Anderson).

1953   *The Ruby* (1 act; libretto by William Mass after Lord Dunsany's *Night at the Inn*). Performed Bloomington, IN, 13 May 1955. Published by Franco Columbo.

1961   *Blood Moon* (3 acts; libretto by composer and Gale Hoffman). Performed San Francisco, 8 September 1961.

1979   *As of a Dream* ("a modern masque"; libretto after Whitman). Performed Midland, MI, 18 May 1979. Published by Associated Music.

1987   *Nativity: A Canticle for the Child* ("Christmas opera-oratorio"). Commission by Music Society of the Midland Center for the Arts, MI; performed there, 4 December 1987.

De Marque, Mr. (late 18th-century bassist and arranger; Porter)

1795   *Rural Revels: or, The Easter Holiday* (pantomime; libretto arr. William Francis). Première, Philadelphia, 6 April 1795.

1796   *Rural Merriment: or, The Humors of a Country Wake* (pantomime; libretto arr. William Francis). Première, Philadelphia, 4 January 1796.

Dembo, Royce (b. Troy, NY; *WhoAm*)

1982   *The Audience* (comedy; 1 act—30 minutes; libretto by Glen Miller). Commission by Meet the Composer. Performed by Golden Fleece, New York, 7 May 1982. Kornick.

1988   *Metamorphosis*. Performed by Golden Fleece, New York, March 1988.

Dembska, Anna

1985   *The Juniper Tree* (1 hour; libretto by composer after Grimm). Performed by Carrying Place, Salisbury, ME, September 1985 and, by the same group, New York, 25 March 1988.

1988   *Enough Is Enough* (90 minutes; libretto by composer and Andrea Hawks after Grimm's "Godfather Death"). Performed by Theater International, Leysin, Switzerland, July 1988, and Carrying Place, Portland, ME, summer 1989.

Dembski, Stephen Michael (b. Boston, 13 December 1949; ACA; Anderson; *Who's Who*)

1982   *Elsaveta* (video opera; libretto by Laurence J. Davies). NEA grant, 1982.

1986   *The Show* (14 minutes; libretto by Donald Barthelme after his story; uses printed or projected illustrations). Commission by 20th Century Consort of Hirschhorn Museum, Washington, DC; performed there, 22 February 1986.

DeMerchant, John
   1976   *Thin Rain.* Performed Ellensburg, WA, 3 March 1976.

"Demi" (AMC)
   1978   *Pearl Girl* (libretto by composer).

Denhard, David
   1987   *Waiting Forever* (30 minutes; libretto by composer, about a historical
         incident in New York State). Commission by Friends of Music,
         Guilford, VT. Performed by Vermont Academy of Arts and
         Sciences, Bennington, October 1987.

Denni, Lucien (b. in St. Louis)
   1907   *Margy the College Girl.* Performed St. Louis.
   1908   *Don't Tell My Wife.* Performed St. Louis, and also on tour.
   1912   *The Skylarks.* Performed Kansas City, KS.
   1913   *The Spartans.* Performed Kansas City, KS.
   1914   *Mlle. Juliette.* Performed Kansas City, KS.
   1915   *Petticoat Lane.* Performed Kansas City, KS.
   1915   *The Girl from Frisco.* Performed Kansas City, KS.
   1916   *The Chase.*
   1916   *Fame.*
   1916   *The Carnival.*
   1917   *Marzie Came Back.*
   1922   *De Molay Revels of 1922* (cast of 1000). Performed Kansas City,
         KS, St. Louis, and Los Angeles.
   1922   *We Wonder Why.* Performed Kansas City, KS, spring 1922.
   1922   *Hello Dearie.* Performed Kansas City, KS, 8 November 1922.

Dennis, Robert (b. St. Louis, 5 May 1933; ASCAP; Anderson)
   1984   *Bound to Rise* (libretto by Karen Campbell, a spoof of Horatio
         Alger). NEA grant. Performed by Medicine Show Theatre
         Ensemble, New York, 1 December 1984.

Dennison, Sam (b. Geary, OK, 26 September 1926; Anderson)
   1952   *The Last Man on Earth* (1 act).
   1973   *Conrad Crispin's Broom* (1 act).
   1984   *Rappaccini's Daughter* (55 minutes; libretto by Karen Campbell
         after Hawthorne). Performed Philadelphia, and Groton, CT, 1984,
         and by Minikin Opera, Washington, DC, 22 March 1985.

Densmore, John Hopkins (b. Somerville, MA, 7 August 1880; d. Boston, 21
         September 1943; Anderson; *Baker's*, 5th ed., says he wrote
         "operettas" for the Hasty Pudding Club at Harvard)

DePoy, Philip
   1987   *Hamlet: The Musical* (libretto by Levi Lee and Rebecca Wackler;
         updated version of Shakespeare). Performed Atlanta, GA, summer
         1987.

DePue, Wallace Earl (b. Columbus, OH, 1 October 1932; Anderson; Schoep)
   1974   *Dr. Jekyll and Mr. Hyde* (3 acts; libretto by composer based on
         story by Robert Louis Stevenson). NEA grant. Performed at

Bowling Green University, OH, April 1974. Recorded by Ocean Records.

1976 *Something Special* (1 act—1 hour; libretto by composer), "for barbershop chorus." Performed by Maumee Chapter, SPEBSQSA, Toledo, OH, 22 May 1976, and on TV, 10 and 26 September 1976.

1977 *The Three Little Pigs.*

De Pury, Marianne (b. St. Gall, Switzerland, 3 April 1935; Cohen)

1981 *Running Gag*, with Joe Budenholzer and Megan Terry (about jogging). Performed Omaha, NE, July 1981.

1982 *Kegger* (1 hour; about teen drinking).

1990 *Body Leaks*, with Luigi Wates (libretto by Megan Terry). Performed Omaha, NE, 27 April 1990.

DeSergei, Michael

1986 *Where Panthers Feasted* (1 act; libretto by composer on the life of Oscar Wilde). Performed Philadelphia, 16 September 1986 and 9 April 1988.

DeTurk, Scott

1987 *The Ghost and Mrs. Muir* (libretto by composer with Arthur Marx and Robert Fisher after Josephine Lesie's novel). Performed at PCPA Theaterfest, Santa Maria, CA, 4 March 1987.

Dett, R. Nathaniel (b. Drummondsville [now Niagara Falls], Ontario, 11 October 1882; d. Battle Creek, MI, 2 October 1943; *Amerigrove*; Southern)

1937 *The Ordering of Moses* (oratorio; 1 act; libretto by composer; "Biblical Folk Scene"). Performed as oratorio, Cincinnati, 7 May 1937; by National Negro Opera Co., 1951; staged by Manhattan School of Music, New York, 1976. Published by J. Fischer (#7230). Recorded by Talladega College Choir and the Mobile Symphony Orchestra.

Deyo, Ruth Lynda (Mrs. Charles Dalton; b. Poughkeepsie, NY, 21 April 1884; d. Cairo, Egypt, 4 March 1960; Anderson; Cohen)

1930 *The Diadem of Stars* (on Egyptian themes). The Prelude performed by Philadelphia Orchestra, Leopold Stokowski conducting, 4 April 1931.

Diamond, David (b. Rochester, NY, 9 July 1915; *Amerigrove*; Morton/Collins; *Who's Who*)

1935 *David* (libretto by D. H. Lawrence).

1940 *Twisting of the Rope* (libretto by W. B. Yeats).

1958 *Mirandolina* (musical comedy; 4 acts; libretto by P. Brown after Goldoni).

1965 *The Golden Slippers* (musical folk play; 2 acts; libretto by S. Citron after Pérez Galdós).

1975 *The Noblest Game* (2 acts—150 minutes; libretto by Katie Louchheim).

Diamond, Stuart Samuel (b. New York, 15 January 1950; Anderson)

1982 *Instillations: Master of the Astral Plane* (1 act). Performed at Brooklyn College, NY, 2 February 1982.

Dias, Susan. *See* Namanworth, Philip

Di Chiera, David (b. McKeesport, PA, 8 April 1937; *Who's Who*)
    1976   *Vigilance* (1 act). Performed by Michigan Opera Theatre, Detroit,
            spring 1976.

Di Chiera, Karen Vander Kloot
    1973   *Rumpelstiltskin*, with David Di Chiera (50 minutes; libretto by Joan
            Hill). Performed Detroit, MI, January 1973.
    1979   *Look to the Land* (50 minutes; libretto by Joan Hill; about the
            American gold rush; guide available). Performed by Luddington
            Magnet Middle School, Detroit, MI, March 1979.
    1987   *Nanabush* (1 act; libretto by William Kirk, based on Michigan
            Indian legends; for Michigan sesquicentennial). Performed by
            Michigan Opera, Detroit, 1987.
    1988   *All About Our Voices* (libretto by Henry Holt, designed for opera
            appreciation courses). Performed by Opera Pacific, Costa Mesa,
            CA, May 1988.

Dickerson, Roger Donald (b. New Orleans, 24 August 1934; *Amerigrove*)
    1986   *Preacher Man! Preacher Man!.* NEA grant, 1985-86.

Dickinson, Clarence (b. Lafayette, IN, 7 May 1873; d. New York, 2 August 1969;
            Amerigrove)
    1895   *The Medicine Man* (comic opera).
     -     *Priscilla.*

Dickman, Stephen (b. Chicago, 2 March 1943; *Amerigrove*)
    1971   *Real Magic in New York* (libretto by R. Foreman).
    1988   *Tibetan Dreams* (libretto by Gary Glickman). Performed East
            Hampton, NY, 16 April 1988.

Di Domenica, Robert Anthony (b. New York, 4 March 1927; *Amerigrove*; *Who's
            Who*)
    1972   *The Balcony* (2 acts—100 minutes; libretto by composer after Genet).
            Performed by New England Conservatory, Boston, 9 May 1975,
            and Opera Company of Boston, 14 June 1990.
    1986   *The Scarlet Letter* (2 hours; libretto by Katie Louchheim after
            Hawthorne).

Diehl, Paula Jespersen (Cohen)
     -     *Waiting Room* (20 minutes; libretto by composer after Frederick
            Meyer Diehl's story). In *COS*-4.

DiGiacomo, Frank
    1974   *The Beauty and the Beast* (1 act). Performed Syracuse, NY, 24 May
            1974.
    1978   *Dybbuk* (on Anski). Performed Syracuse, NY, 19 May 1978.

DiGiovanni, Rocco
    1955   *Medea* (2 acts). Performed at Brooklyn Museum, NY, 13 February
            1955.

DiJulio, Max (b. Philadelphia, 10 October 1919; Anderson; *WhoAm*)
1956   *Baby Doe* (2 acts). Performed Loretto, CO, 24 May 1956.

Dillon, Robert (b. Downs, KS, 29 September 1922; Anderson)
1976   *Oklahoma, USA!* ("pageant"). Performed at Wantland Stadium,
        England, 24 June 1976.
1978? *Prof. Tremont and His Guardian Angel* (libretto by Elizabeth
        Dillon).

Dilthey, Michael
1987   *Pinderblock* (libretto by composer). Performed by Chicago Opera
        Theater, 2 May 1987. Philip Hagemann Prize, 1988.

DiPalma, Mark (b. Brooklyn, NY, 2 October 1959; *WhoAm*)
1983   *Courting* (1 act). Performed Brooklyn College, NY, 4 February
        1983.

Dixon, Ed
1983   *Oliver Quade* (2 acts; libretto by composer). Performed by
        American Jewish Repertory Theatre, New York, 1983.
1987   *Shylock* (on Shakespeare's *The Merchant of Venice*). Performed by
        York Theatre Co., New York, 23 April 1987.

Dodds, Malcolm
1987   *Lucinda* (libretto by Hanna Fox, on interracial and interfaith
        themes). Performed New York, 1987, and at Jewish Center of
        Princeton, NY, 13 February 1988. New Jersey State Council on
        the Arts grant, 1987.

Dodge, Charles (b. Ames, IA, 5 June 1942; *Amerigrove*; *Who's Who*)
1974   *Story of Our Lives*. NEA grant, 1974.
1978   *Cascando* (radio drama with actor and tape; 1 act; libretto after
        Samuel Beckett). Performed Chicago, 2 November 1978, and at
        Brooklyn College, NY, 4 February 1983.

Doellner, Robert
1948   *Escape from Liberty*. Performed Hartford, CT.

Donato, Anthony (b. Prague, NE, 8 March 1909; ASCAP; *Amerigrove*; *Who's Who*)
1964   *The Walker-through-Walls* (2 acts; libretto by composer after Marcel
        Aymé). Performed at Northwestern University, Evanston, IL, 26
        February 1965.

Donenfeld, James
-      *New York Town*. Published by Carl Fischer.
-      *Three Little Pigs*.

Doran, Matt (b. Covington, KY, 1 September 1921; *Amerigrove*; *Who's Who*)
1953   *The Committee* (1 act). Performed Corpus Christi, TX, 25 May
        1955, and New York, 1958. Published by Franco Colombo.
1969   *The Little Hand So Obstinate* (grand opera; 3 acts; libretto by Sonia
        Brown).

1977   *The Marriage Counselor* (1 act; libretto by composer). Performed Los Angeles, 12 March 1977 and 1 May 1982.

Dorff, Daniel (b. New Rochelle, NY, 7 March 1956; *Who's Who*)
1983   *Stone Soup: An Operatic Fable* (40 minutes; libretto by Frank McQuilkin).

Doub, Patrice
1979   *The Trojan Woman* (1 act; libretto by composer after Euripides). Performed at University of Minnesota, Minneapolis, 1 June 1979.

Dougherty, Celius (b. Glenwood, MN, 27 May 1902; *Amerigrove*)
1962   *Many Moons* (1 act; libretto by composer after Thurber). Performed Santa Fe, NM, and at Vassar College, NY, 6 December 1962. Published by G. Schirmer.

Douglas, David
1984   *A Winter's Tale* (libretto by Kelli James and Dana Axelrod). Performed by New Burbank Theatre Guild, CA, 7 December 1984.

Douglass, John Thomas (b. New York, 1847; d. there, 12 April 1886; Southern)
1868   *Virginia's Ball* (3 acts). Copyrighted and performed at Stuyvesant Institute, New York, 1868. Southern, *The Music of Black Americans: A History*, 2nd ed. (New York: Norton, 1983), 248: "Douglass is notable as the first black composer to write an opera."

Dove, Neville (b. Johannesburg, South Africa, 29 January 1952; *WhoAm*)
1985   *Babes in the Woods: or, Hansel and Gretel and Percy and the Prune* (50 minutes; libretto by James Billings after *Hansel and Gretel*).

Downard, Bob
1980   *Celebration of the Angels* (1 hour; libretto by composer with John Spindler, about the history of Los Angeles). Performed Los Angeles, 7 September 1980.
1985   *Martin Avdeich: A Christmas Miracle* (1 hour; libretto by the composer after Tolstoy's "Martin the Cobbler"). Performed Denver, CO, 15 December 1985.
1988   *One Little Acre* (2 acts; libretto by composer, about the southeast in the 1950s). Performed at Loretto Heights College, Denver, CO, 3 May 1988.

Downing, Lulu Jones
1909? *An Amateur Gamble* (libretto by Helen Bagg, Mary Cameroc, Theodora Sturkow-Ryder, and Marie Bergersen, with additional dances by John Alden Carpenter). Performed at Orchestra Hall, Chicago, 29 November ?1909.

Drake, Earl R. (b. Aurora, IL, 26 November 1865; d. Chicago, 6 May 1916; *Amerigrove*)

1914   *The Blind Girl of Castel-Cuilé* (3 acts; libretto by Jacques Jasmin, translated by Longfellow). Performed at Globe Theater, Chicago, 19 February 1914. Hipsher.

1915   *The Mite and the Mighty* (3 acts). Performed Chicago, 1915.

Dresher, Paul Joseph (b. Los Angeles, 8 January 1951; *Amerigrove*; *Baker's*; *Who's Who*)

The How Trilogy:

1980   *The Way of How* (80 minutes; libretto by George Coates). Performed at Cornish Institute, Seattle, WA, 8 August 1980.

1983   *are/are* (music theater). Performed at New Wave Festival, Brooklyn, NY, 1984.

1984   *Seehear* (music theater; 80 minutes; no text, but uses melodies from arias of *I Pagliacci* and *Tosca*). Performed at American Music Theater Festival, Philadelphia, 12 July 1984.

American Trilogy:

1985   *Slow Fire* (music theater/opera; 90 minutes; libretto by Rinde Eckert). Performed by New Music America, Los Angeles, 1 November 1985, Philadelphia, 25 September 1986, Spoleto Festival USA, Charleston, SC, 24 May 1990, and Binghamton, NY, 1990. Kornick: première at Theatre Artaud, San Francisco, February 1988.

1989   *Power Failure* (music theater/opera; science fiction; 105 minutes; libretto by Rinde Eckert). Commissioned by Walker Art Center, Musical Traditions, American Music Theatre Festival, University of Iowa, and Robin Kirck. Performed Miami, FL, March 1989, and Philadelphia, 29 April 1989. Kornick: première at American Music Theatre Festival, 4 May 1989, with additional performances by Paul Dresher Ensemble, University of Iowa, Iowa City, 27 October 1989, and in Minneapolis, 4 November 1989.

1990   *Pioneers* (music theater/opera). Performed at Spoleto Festival USA, Charleston, SC, 26 May 1990.

1987   *Floating Opera: A Treading of Steps* (all day long; libretto by composer and others; designed for performance on a floating stage). The work uses music by Norman Durkee, Janice Giteck, Philip Glass, Bun-Ching Lam, and Jarrad Powell. Performed on waterways around Seattle, WA, 20 September 1987.

1988   *In the Jungle of Cities* (libretto by James Yoshimura after Brecht). NEA grant; developed by Wisdom Bridge Theatre, Chicago.

Drew, James (b. St. Paul, MN, 9 February 1929; *Amerigrove*; *Baker's*; Morton/Collins; *Who's Who*)

1975   *Mysterium* (television opera; libretto by composer).

1975   *Crucifixus Domini Christi*. Performed Baton Rouge, LA.

1975   *Surprise Opera* ("open-form"—improvised). Performed by MMT Theater, 1982. Revised version performed by MMT Theater, 1983. (*Amerigrove* and Morton/Collins give title as *Suspense Opera*.)

1977   *Dr. Cincinnati*.

1980   *Five O'Clock Ladies* (1 hour). Performed by MMT Theater, 1980.

1987   *"Live" from the Black Eagle* (30-60 minutes). Performed by MMT Theater, 1987.

1989   *Rats Teeth.* Performed by MMT Theater, 1989.

-    *Cantolobosolo* (variable length).

Drexler, Rosalyn
1983   *Dear.* Performed by Musical Theatre Works, New York, October 1983.

Dreyfuss, Randy
1989   *Symmes' Hole.* Performed by Odyssey Theatre Ensemble, Los Angeles, February 1989.

Driver, John
1988   *Ducks.* Performed by Musical Theatre Works, New York, 30 March 1988, 16 May 1988, and 8 June 1988.

Drobny, Christopher (ASCAP)
1985   *Koch's Postulate.* Performed by New Dramatists, New York, 2 October 1985.

1987   *Fire in the Future: The Heroic Life and Tragic Death of Joan the Maid* (libretto by Joan Schenkar). Performed by Minnesota Opera, St. Paul, MN, 2 April 1987, and New Dramatists, New York, 25 February 1988.

1987   *Lucy's Lapses* (1 hour; libretto by Laura Harrington, about old age). OPERA America grant. Performed Waterford, CT, 20 August 1987, by Playwrights Horizons, New York, June 1989 and 19 July 1989, and by Portland Opera, OR, 27 April 1990.

-    *Touch and Go.* Performed Memphis, TN.

Drogin, Barry J.
1984   *Love and Idols/A Jewish Opera* (52 minutes; libretto by composer after Matthew Paris's "All in Good Time"). Private reading, Queens, New York, July 1984. Published by Not Nice Music.

1988   *Typhoid Mary* (45 minutes; libretto by composer on medical reports about Mary Mallon). Performed by Bicycle Shop, New York, 30 September 1988.

Drossin, Julius (b. Philadelphia, 17 May 1918; Anderson)
1981   *Spinoza* (150 minutes; libretto by Leonard M. Trawick after Spinoza's life). Performed by OPERA America Showcase, January 1981.

Druckman, Jacob (b. Philadelphia, 26 June 1928; *Amerigrove*)
1982-   *Medea* (libretto by Tony Harrison after Euripides). The commission by Metropolitan Opera, New York in 1981 was cancelled in 1986. Recommissioned by Bonn Opera for performances in the 1996-97 season. See K. Robert Schwarz, "The Met Proposes . . . and Disposes," *New York Times*, 2 August 1992, sec. 2, pp. 1, 14.

Dubbiosi, Stelio (b. Naples, Italy, 25 August 1929; U.S. citizen, 1947; Anderson)
1936   *Romance with Double Bass* (comic opera).

1965   *The Pied Piper.* Performed by Amato Opera, New York, December
        1965.

Dubensky, Arcady (b. Viatka, Russia, 15 October 1890; d. Tenafly, NJ, 14
        October 1966; in U.S. from 1921; ASCAP; *Amerigrove*; *Baker's*)
1916   *Romance with Double Bass* ("opera miniature"; libretto after
        Chekhov). Performed New York, 31 October 1936.
1930   *Down Town.*
1936   *On the Highway.*
1944   *Two Yankees in Italy.*

Dubois, Shirley. *See* Graham, Shirley

Duffalo, Richard John (b. East Chicago, IN, 30 January 1933; *Amerigrove*; *Who's
        Who*)
1975   *Meeting Mr. Ives* (2 parts; Charles Ives's music "arranged by
        Dufallo"; libretto by Brendan Gill). Performed at Lenox Arts
        Center, MA, August 1975, and San Francisco, CA, 27 February
        1976.

Duffy, John (b. New York, 29 June 1928; Anderson; *Who's Who*)
1955   *The Eve of Adam* (1 act). Performed Interlochen, MI, 1955.
-       *Everyman Absurd* (music drama). For ABC-TV.

Dugger, Edwin (b. Poplar Bluff, MO, 21 March 1940; Anderson)
1980   *Matsukaze* (38 minutes; libretto by composer after a Kan'ami Noh
        play). Commission by Koussevitzky Music Foundation.
        Performed at University of California, Berkeley, 14 November
        1980.

Duisberg, Rob
1986   *Dulcimer Boy.* Performed Seattle, WA, 1986-87 season.

Duke, John (b. Cumberland, MD, 30 July 1899; d. Northampton, MA, 26
        October 1984; ASCAP; *Amerigrove*)
1944   *The Cat That Walked by Itself* (children's musical; libretto by
        Dorothy Duke).
1953   *Captain Lovelock* (chamber opera; 1 act—35 minutes; libretto by
        Dorothy Duke after Holberg's *Changed Bridegroom*). Performed
        Schroon Lake, NY (*COS-1*), Hudson Falls, NY, 18 August 1953,
        and in 1956. Published by Carl Fischer.
1958   *The Sire de Maladroit* (chamber opera; 1 act; libretto by Dorothy
        Duke). Performed Schroon Lake, NY, 15 August 1958.
1962   *The Yankee Pedlar* (operetta; 2 acts; libretto by Dorothy Duke).
        Performed Schroon Lake, NY, 17 August 1962. Published by Carl
        Fischer.

Duke, Vernon [Vladimir Dukelsky] (b. Parfianovka near Pskov, Russia, 10
        October 1903; d. Santa Monica, CA, 16 January 1969; in U.S.
        from 1920; ASCAP; *Amerigrove*)
1925   *Zephyr et Flore.* Performed Paris, France, January 1931.
1928   *Demoiselle Paysanne* (2 acts).
1958   *Mistress into Maid* (2 acts; libretto by composer after Pushkin).
        Performed Santa Barbara, CA, 1958.

84

1963   *Zenda.* Performed San Francisco, August 1963.

Dun, Tad
1989   *The Silk Road.* Performed 8 November 1989.

Duncan, John (b. Lee County, AL, 25 November 1913; d. Montgomery, AL, 15
        September 1975; Anderson; Southern)
1972   *Gideon and Eliza* (1 act). Performed at Xavier College, New
       Orleans, 22 March 1972.
1977   *Hellish Bandetti.* (Anderson dates it 1974.)

Dundee, A. McLauren
1784   *Coup de Main: or, American Adventures.* Performed 1784.

Dungan, Olive (b. Pittsburgh, 19 July 1903; Anderson)
1976? *The Mysterious Forest* ("school opera"; libretto by Irene Archer).
       Cited in *SAI Panpipes*, May 1978, 29.

Dunn, James Philip (b. New York, 10 January 1884; d. Jersey City, NJ, 24 July
        1936; Anderson)
  -   *The Galleon.* On Freer's 1924 list.

Du Page, Florence Elizabeth (née Anderson; Mrs. Richard Du Page; b.
        Vandergrift, PA, 20 September 1910; ASCAP; Anderson; Cohen)
1963   *Trial universelle* (sacred chamber opera; 4 acts; libretto by Sister
       Jean, T.C.G.). Performed at Advent Tuller School, Westbury, NY,
       17 May 1963.
1964   *Whither* (sacred drama; 3 acts; libretto by Sister Jean, T.C.G.).
       Performed Westbury, NY, 12 December 1959.
1965   *New World for Nellie* (ballad opera; 1 act; libretto by composer
       after R. Emett). Performed Westbury, NY, 11 June 1965.
  -   *Alice in Wonderland* (operetta).
  -   *Contemporary Mass.*
  -   *Whither* (allegorical music drama; libretto by Sister Jean).

Durkee, Norman
1984   *Oxymora.* Performed Seattle, WA, 1984–85 season.
1987   Some of Durkee's music was used in Paul Dresher's *Floating Opera*,
       performed Seattle, WA, 20 September 1987.

Dusman, Linda J.
1989   *Fustina* (75 minutes; libretto by Susan McCully after *Faust*,
       mythology, and the history of flight). Performed Washington,
       October 1988, and at American College Theater Festival Regional
       Conference, Binghamton, NY, January 1989.

Dutton, Daniel
1989   *The Stone Man* (80 minutes; libretto by composer after an
       Appalachian legend). Performed Louisville, KY, 10 January 1989
       and 6 January 1990.

Dvorkin, Judith (b. New York, 1930; Cohen)
1955   *The Crescent Eyebrow* (legend).
1956   *Crescent Eyebrows* (1 act). Performed at Town Hall, New York, 8 January 1956.
1983   *Blue Star* (libretto by composer).
1985   *What's in a Name?* (40 minutes; libretto by composer after *Rumpelstiltskin*). Commission by Singing Theater, New Rochelle, NY. Performed Binghamton, NY, 23 September 1985, and New Rochelle, NY, 19 October 1985.
1988   *Humpty and Alice* (15-minute "curtain raiser"; libretto by composer after Carroll's *Through the Looking Glass*, chapter 6). Performed by After Dinner Opera, New York, March 1988.
1989   *The Emperor's New Clothes* (45 minutes; libretto by composer). Performed by Singing Theater, New York, September 1989.

Dweir, Leslie Scott
1981   *The Raft* (libretto by Bill Thompson after Twain's *Adventures of Huckleberry Finn*). Performed Huntington Station, NY, 19 October 1985.

Dyville, Jack
1981   *A Country Christmas Carol* (90 minutes; libretto by composer after Dickens). Performed North Richland Hills, TX, December 1981.

Eakin, Charles G. (b. Pittsburgh, 24 February 1927; Anderson; Schoep)
1966   *The Box* (1 act; libretto by composer). Performed at University of Oklahoma, 15 April 1966; and Boulder, CO, 3 or 13 March 1972, where it ran for six weeks.
1972   *Being of Sound Mind* (1 act [Schoep: 2 acts—60-65 minutes]; libretto by composer). Performed Boulder, CO, 3 or 13 March 1972, where it ran for six weeks. Review: *Opera Journal* 5/2 (1972).
1977   *Pasticcio* (theater of the absurd). Performed Denver, CO, July 1977; it too ran for six weeks.

Eakin, Thomas
1974   *Pasticcio.* Performed Cedar Falls, IA, 2 May 1974.

Eames, Henry Purmont (b. Chicago, 12 September 1872; d. Claremont, CA, 25 November 1950; *Baker's*; Hipsher)
1916   *The Sacred Tree of the Omaha* (1 act). Performed Lincoln, NE, five times, June 1916.
1920   *Priscilla and John Alden* (comic opera; libretto by Hartley Burr Alexander after Longfellow). Bispham Medal, 1926. Performed Chicago, 1942.

Earle, Henry Edmund
-   *The Crypt of Old San Gabriel.* Performed Los Angeles and Pasadena, CA.

-    *Zuna, Queen of the Inca.* Performed Los Angeles and Pasadena, CA.

Earls, Paul (b. Springfield, MO, 9 June 1934; AMC; Anderson; *Who's Who*)
1964   *Flight* (chamber opera).
1975   *The Death of King Phillip* (1 act—70 minutes; libretto by Romulus Linley, on New England history—King Phillip was an American Indian at the time of the Puritans). NEA grant, 1974. Premièred by New England Chamber Opera, Brookline, MA, 26 March 1976.
1976   *A Grimm Duo* (*Dog and Sparrow* and *Bremen Town Musicians*) (two 1-act operas). Performed by New England Chamber Opera, Boston, 31 December 1976.
1981   *Der Struwwelpeter* (30 minutes; after Heinrich Hoffman poems; in German with English translation spoken during performance).
1982   *Icarus* (or *Itkarus*; "a sky opera"; 50 minutes; after Greek myths, to be sung by men and boys). Performed Linz, Austria, 25 September 1982 (in German), and by Boston Musica Viva and M.I.T. Center for Advanced Visual Studies, Cambridge, MA, 30 May 1984.

Earnest, John David (AMC/ASCAP)
1980   *Howard* (50 minutes; libretto by Troy Christopher, about Howard Hughes). Performed by Golden Fleece, New York, 26 March 1987.
1983   *The Opera of the Worms* (1 act; libretto by R. Richard, about a garden). Performed at New York University, 30 June 1983, and by Golden Fleece, New York, March 1987.
1988   *The Mummy* (libretto by Mervyn Goldstein). Performed by Golden Fleece, New York, 13 December 1988.
1988   *Murder in the Kitchen* (after Alice B. Toklas). Performed by Golden Fleece, New York, 13 December 1988.

Eastman, Donna Kelly
1984   *The Mirror* (19 minutes; libretto by composer after Japanese folk tales). Performed Bangkok, Thailand, 11 February 1984.

Eaton, John (b. Bryn Mawr, PA, 30 March 1935; *Amerigrove*; *Who's Who*)
1957   *Ma Barker* (1 act; libretto by A. Gold).
1964   *Heracles* (grand opera; 3 acts; libretto by Michael Fried). Performed Turin, Italy, 10 October 1968; Rome, Italy (*COS*-1); and at Indiana University, Bloomington, 15 May 1971. Published by Shawnee Press.
1973   *Myshkin* (1 hour; libretto by Patrick Creagh after Dostoevsky's *The Idiot*). Performed Bloomington, IN, 23 April 1973. Telecast on PBS.
1973   *The Lion and Androcles* (children's opera; 1 act; libretto by E. Walter and Anderson). Performed Indianapolis, 1 May 1974, and at Cincinnati, summer 1983.
1978   *Danton and Robespierre* (grand opera, 3 acts—120 minutes; libretto by Patrick Creagh). Première at Indiana University, Bloomington, 21 April 1978. Published by Shawnee Press. Kornick.
1979   *The Cry of Clytemnestra* (1 act—75 minutes; libretto by Patrick Creagh after the Greek tragedy by Aeschylus). Première by

Indiana University Opera, Bloomington, 1 March 1980; also performed by Brooklyn Philharmonia, November 1980. Recording available. Kornick.

1985　*The Tempest* (3 acts—150 minutes; libretto by Andrew Porter after Shakespeare). Commission by Santa Fe Opera, NM; performed there, 27 July 1985. Kornick.

1988　*The Reverend Jim Jones* (150 minutes; libretto by James Reston Jr., on the Guyana suicides). NEA grant.

Ebel-Sabo, Victoria

-　*King John's Christmas* (1 act; libretto by composer after A. A. Milne's *Now We Are Six*). COS-4.

Echols, Paul Clinton (b. Santa Monica, CA, 13 February 1944; *Who's Who*)

1986　*The City of Ladies* (1 act; libretto by composer after Christine de Pisan, 15th century; includes music by Binchois, Ciconias, Dufay, and Fontaine). Performed at Mannes College of Music, New York, 10 January 1986.

1988　*Romance of the Rose* (1 hour; libretto by composer after the medieval poem; with music by Binchois, Brumel, Busnois, Dufay, and van Ghizeghem; in Old French). Performed at Mannes College of Music, New York, 7 October 1988.

Eddleman, G. David (b. Winston-Salem, NC, 20 August 1936; Anderson; *Who's Who*)

1964　*The Cure* (1 act). Performed Lexington, MA, 17 April 1964.

Edminster, David

1985　*The Green Automobile* (monodrama; setting of Allen Ginsberg). Tour of the U.S., 1985.

Edwards, Julian (b. Manchester, England, 11 December 1855; d. Yonkers, NY, 5 September 1910; in U.S. from 1888; *Amerigrove*; Hipsher)

1892　*Jupiter: or, The Cobbler and the King* (comic opera, 2 acts; libretto by H. B. Smith). Performed New York, 14 April 1892.

1893　*Friend Fritz* (libretto after Erckmann-Chatrian). Performed New York, 26 January, 1893.

1893　*King René's Daughter* (lyric drama; libretto by I. J. Edwards after H. Hertz). Performed New York, 22 November 1893.

1894　*Madeleine: or, The Magic Kiss* (comic opera; 3 acts; libretto by S. Strangé). Performed New York, 31 July 1894.

1896　*The Goddess of Truth.* Performed New York, 26 February 1896.

1896　*Brian Boru* ("romantic Irish opera"; 3 acts; libretto by S. Strangé). Performed New York, 19 October 1896.

1897　*The Wedding Day* (comic opera, 2 acts; libretto by S. Strangé). Performed New York, 8 April 1897.

1901　*Dolly Varden* (comic opera; 2 acts; libretto by S. Strangé after Dickens's *Barnaby Rudge*). Performed London, England, 1901. Published by Witmark, 1901.

1902　*When Johnny Comes Marching Home.*

1907　*The Patriot* (1 act; libretto by S. Strangé; tragic opera about an attempted assassination of George Washington). Performed

Boston, 1907; New York, 23 November 1908; Boston and Newport, RI, 1975. Published by Witmark, 1907.

- *Corinne.*

Edwards, Leo (b. Cincinnati, OH, 31 January 1937; Anderson)
1986 *Harriet Tubman* (1 hour). Performed by Opera Ebony, New York, 9 November 1986, and at Mannes College of Music, New York, May 1988.

Edwards, Robert
- *Tennessee.*

Effinger, Cecil (b. Colorado Springs, Colorado, 22 July 1914; ASCAP; *Amerigrove*; *Who's Who*; scores in AMRC)
1961 *Pandora's Box* (children's opera; 1 act, 15 minutes; libretto by Sally Monsour). Performed Boulder, CO. Published by G. Schirmer, 1962.
1965 *Cyrano de Bergerac* (3 acts; libretto by Donald Sutherland after E. Rostand). Performed Boulder, CO, 21 July 1965.
1976 *Let Your Mind Wander Over America.* Performed Nashville, TN, 7 February 1976.
1976 *The Gentleman Desperado (and Miss Bird)* (2 acts; libretto by Donald Sutherland). For the centennial of the University of Colorado. Performed Boulder, 6 October 1976.

Eggers, Anton C.
1906 *Nina* (2 acts). Performed New York.

Ehrman, Michael
1988 *Alice Through the Opera Glass* (libretto by Paul Dorgan after Carroll). Performed Norfolk, VA, October 1988.

Eichberg, Julius (b. Düsseldorf, Germany, 13 June 1824; d. Boston, 19 January 1893; in U.S. from 1856; *Amerigrove*)
1862 *The Doctor of Alcantara*, in collaboration with Benjamin Edward Woolf. Performed Boston, and widely elsewhere.
1864 *A Night in Rome.* Performed Boston
1865 *The Rose of Tyrol.* Performed Boston.
1868 *The Two Cadis.* Performed Boston.

Eisenstein, Linda
1987 *The Last Red Wagon Tent Show in the Land* (libretto by Teddi Davis). Performed Cleveland, 1987.
1988 *The Touch of an Angel* (1 act; libretto by Migdalia Cruz). Performed by New Dramatists Composer-Librettist Studio, New York, 1988, and DUO Theatre/Teatro DUO, New York, 20 April 1989.

Ekstrom, Peter
1980 *The Gift of the Magi* (2 acts; libretto by composer after O. Henry). Performed Louisville, KY, 1980.
1988 *Kiss Me Quick Before the Lava Reaches the Village* (2 acts; libretto by composer and Steve Hayes, about Hollywood in the 1940s).

Performed by Musical Theatre Works, New York, 12 April 1988
and 26 October 1988.

El-Dabh, Halim (b. Cairo, Egypt, 4 March 1921; U.S. citizen, 1961; *Amerigrove*;
Baker's; Southern)
1968   *Black Epic* (opera-pageant).
1971   *Opera Flies* (3 acts; libretto by composer about Kent State
University in 1970). Performed Washington, DC, May 1971.
   Ptahmose and the Magic Spell (opera trilogy, 1972-73; librettos by
composer):
1972   *The Osiris Ritual.*
1973   *Aton, the Ankh, and the World.*
1973   *The Twelve Hours Trip.*
1981   *Drink of Eternity* (opera-pageant).

Elisha, Haim (b. Jerusalem, Israel, 27 September 1935; U.S. citizen, 1969;
Anderson)
1988   *The Big Winner* (libretto by Miriam Kressyn after Aleichem; in
Yiddish). Performed by Folksbiene Theatre, New York, 22
October 1988.

Elkus, Jonathan (b. San Francisco, CA, 8 August 1931; ASCAP; *Amerigrove*;
Schoep; *Who's Who*)
1953   *Tom Sawyer* (1 act—1 hour; libretto by composer after Mark Twain).
Performed by San Francisco Boys Chorus, 22 May 1953, and 1956;
by Sacramento Civic Repertory Theatre, 1954, and at New York
College of Music, 1956. Published by Novello.
1959   *The Outcasts of Poker Flat* (1 act—65 minutes; libretto by Robert
Gene Bander after Bret Harte). Performed at Lehigh University,
Bethlehem, PA, 16 April 1960, and by West Bay Opera Co., Palo
Alto, CA, 1961. Published by Southern.
1961   *Treasure Island* (2 acts; libretto by Robert Gene Bander [Schoep:
Bruce M. Snyder] after Robert Louis Stevenson). Performed by
San Francisco Boys Chorus, 1967. Published by H. W. Gray
[Schoep: Novello].
1963   *Medea* (1 act; libretto by composer after Euripides). Performed by
Opera Theatre, University of Wisconsin, Milwaukee, 13 November
1970.
1967   *The Mandarin* (3 acts; libretto by Richard Franko Goldman after
Eça de Queiroz). Performed New York, 26 October 1967.
Published by Carl Fischer.
1970   *Helen in Egypt* (1 act; libretto by Jere Knight after the epic poem
by Hilda Doolittle). Performed by Opera Theatre, University of
Wisconsin, Milwaukee, 13 November 1970.

Ellington, Edward Kennedy ("Duke") (b. Washington, DC, 29 April 1899; d. New
York, 13 May 1974; *Amerigrove*)
1941   *Jump for Joy.*
1946   *Beggar's Holiday.* Performed New York, 1947.
1965   *Sugar City.* Performed Detroit.
1974   *Queenie Pie* ("street opera or opera buffa"; 2 acts). Unfinished at
Ellington's death, the work was completed by his son Mercer, and
expanded by Maurice Peress. NEA grant. WNET opera program.
Performed Philadelphia, 18 September 1986. Kornick.

Elliot, Clinton (AMC)
- *Pope Joan* (*COS*-2).

Elliot, Marc
1985 *One-Man Band*, with Larry Hochman (libretto by composer with James Lecesne). Performed at South Street Theater, New York, June 1985.

Elliott, Janice Overmiller (b. Atchison, KS, 5 February 1921; Cohen)
1988 *A Hero Goes to Heaven*. Performed Leavenworth, KS, fall 1989.

Elliott, Marjorie Reeve (b. Syracuse, NY, 7 August 1890; Cohen)
- *Big Sister's Wedding* (operetta).
- *Gypsy Moon* (opera).
- *The Happy Scarecrow* (operetta).
- *Medics and Merriman* (operetta).
- *A Strange Adventure* (operetta; for elementary students).

Elliott, William F.
1967 *Daniel Boone* (1 act). Performed at Bracken Storyland, New York, 6 May 1967.
1975 *Between the War* (multimedia). NEA grant. *COS*-2.

Ellis, David
1987 *The Hunting of the Snark* (1 hour; libretto by Eugene R. Jackson after Carroll). Performed Mobile, AL, 1987.
- *Song of Hiawatha* (90 minutes; libretto by Eugene R. Jackson after Longfellow). Performed Mobile, AL. *COS*-4.

Ellis, Merrill (b. Cleburne, TX, 9 December 1916; Anderson)
1976 *The Queen is Dead*. Performed Denton, TX.
1977 *The Sorcerer*. Performed Marshall, TX, 22 February 1977.
1977 *The Choice is Ours* (multimedia). Performed Denton, TX, 12 September 1977.
1977 *Nostalgia*. Performed Fort Worth, TX.
1977 *Trains Used to Run Late*. Performed Denton, TX.

Ellstein, Abraham (b. New York, 9 July 1907; d. there, 22 March 1963; Anderson)
1959 *The Thief and the Hangman* (1 hour). Performed Athens, OH, 17 January 1959, and Salzburg, Austria, 26 November 1965. Published by Mills Music.
1961 *The Golem* (4 acts; libretto by Sylvia Regan). Commission by Ford Foundation. Preview, Boston, November 1961; performed by New York Opera, 22 March 1962.

Elmore, Robert Hall (b. Ramaputnam, India, 2 January 1913, of American parents; d. Ardmore, PA, 22 September 1985; ASCAP/AMC; Anderson; *Baker's*)
1941 *It Began at Breakfast* (1 act). Performed Philadelphia, 18 February 1941. *Baker's*: the first televised opera by an American.
- *The Incarnate Word* (1 act). Published by J. Fischer.

Elson, Steve
1989   *Dangerous Glee Club* (libretto by Charles Moulton). Performed by Music-Theatre Group, New York, 14 February 1989.

Enenbach, Frederic (b. Des Moines, IA, 1 December 1945; Anderson)
1979   *The Crimson Bird* (55 minutes; libretto by Richard R. Strawn after Marie de France, 12th-century poet). Performed Crawfordsville, IN, 19 April 1979.

Engel, Lehman (b. Jackson, MS, 14 September 1910; d. New York, 29 August 1982; *Amerigrove*)
1927   *Pierrot of the Minute* (1 act; 1 hour). Performed Cincinnati, 3 April 1928 (*COS*-1 says 1929).
1935   *Medea.*
1953   *Brother Joe* (2 acts). Performed Cleveland, 28 May 1953.
1953   *Golden Ladder* (1 scene; collaborated with W. A. King, J. Ross, Lewis Allan). Performed Cleveland, 28 May 1953.
1954   *The Malady of Love* (1 act; 27 minutes; libretto by Lewis Allan). Performed New York, 27 April or 27 May 1954. Published by Harold Flammer.
1955   *The Soldier* (55 minutes; libretto by Lewis Allen after a "psycho drama" by Roald Dahl). Performed New York, 25 November 1956, and Jackson, MI, 1958.
1956   *Serena* (libretto after S. N. Behrman)

Engels, Peter Joseph (b. Cologne, Germany, 5 June 1867; to U.S. at age of 20; listed as deceased in 1945; Hipsher)
1922   *Adelgunde* (romantic opera; introduction and 3 acts; libretto by composer, transl. Anna L. von Raven; based on 11th-century legend of the Rhinegold).
1924   *King Solomon* (introductory scene and 3 acts—2½ hours; libretto by composer). Performed first in German, then translated to English by Anna L. von Raven. Prelude and act 3 given concert performance at New Madison Sqaure Garden, New York, 23 May 1926.
1935   *Minnehaha.* Bispham Medal.

Engerman, John
1981   *Illuminatus!*, with Steve Amadek, Ken Campbell, and Chris Langham (after novels by Robert Shea and Robert A. Wilson). Performed Houston, TX, July 1981.

Englander, Ludwig (b. Vienna, Austria, 1859; d. New York, 13 September 1914; in U.S. from 1882; *Amerigrove*)
1884   *1776* (comic opera; libretto by L. Goldmark). Performed New York, 1884.
1895   *The 20th Century Girl* (comic opera; libretto by Rosenfeld). Performed New York, 25 January 1895.
1895   *A Daughter of the Revolution* (comic opera; libretto by J. C. Goodwin). Performed New York, 27 May 1895.
1896   *The Caliph* (comic opera; libretto by H. B. Smith). Performed New York, 3 September 1896.

1896 *Half a King* (comic opera; libretto by H. B. Smith). Performed New York, 14 September 1896.

1898 *The Little Corporal* (comic opera; libretto by H. B. Smith). Performed New York, 19 September 1898.

1899 *In Gay Paree* (comic opera; libretto by G. Stewart). Performed New York, 20 March 1899.

1899 *The Man in the Moon* (comic opera; libretto by L. Harrison, and S. Strange; in collaboration with Reginald De Koven and G. Keller). Performed New York, 24 April 1899.

1899 *The Rounders* (comic opera; libretto by H. B. Smith). Performed New York, 12 July 1899

1900 *The Casino Girl* (comic opera; libretto by H. B. Smith). Performed New York, 19 March 1900.

1900 *The Cadet Girl* (comic opera; libretto by H. B. Smith and Goodwin). Performed New York, 25 July 1900.

1900 *The Monks of Malabar* (comic opera; libretto by Goodwin). Performed New York, 14 September 1900.

1900 *The Belle of Bohemia* (comic opera; libretto by H. B. Smith). Performed New York, 24 September 1900.

1901 *The Strollers* (comic opera; libretto by H. B. Smith). Performed New York, 24 June 1901.

1901 *The New Yorkers* (comic opera; libretto by G. V. Hobart). Performed New York, 7 October 1901.

1902 *The Jewel of Asia* (comic opera; libretto by H. B. Smith). Performed New York, 16 February 1902.

1902 *The Wild Rose* (comic opera; libretto by H. B. Smith and G. V. Hobart). Performed New York, 5 May 1902.

1902 *Sally in our Alley* (comic opera; libretto by G. V. Hobart). Performed New York, 29 August 1902.

1903 *The Office Boy* (comic opera; libretto by H. B. Smith). Performed New York, 2 November 1903.

1904 *A Madcap Princess* (comic opera; libretto by H. B. Smith). Performed New York, 5 September 1904.

1904 *The Two Roses* (comic opera; libretto by S. Strange after O. Goldsmith's *She Stoops to Conquer*). Performed New York, 21 November 1904.

1905 *The White Cat* (comic opera; libretto by H. B. Smith). Performed New York, 2 November 1905.

1906 *The Rich Mr. Hoggenheimer* (comic opera; libretto by H. B. Smith). Performed New York, 22 October 1906.

1908 *Miss Innocence* (comic opera; libretto by H. B. Smith). Performed New York, 30 November 1908.

1914 *Madam Moselle* (comic opera; libretto by E. Paulton). Performed New York, 23 May 1914.

English, Granville (b. Louisville, KY, 27 January 1895; d. New York, 1 September 1968; Anderson)
- *Wide, Wide River* (folk opera).

Enna, Emil (1877-1951)
1915 *The Dawn of the West* (4 acts). Performed Portland, OR.

Eppert, Carl E. (b. Carbon, IN, 5 November 1882; d. Milwaukee, WI, 1 October 1961; Anderson)
 1916 *Kaintuckee.*

Epstein, Solomon
 1986 *The Wild Boy* (1 act; libretto by composer, about the "wild boy of Aveyron"). Performed Philadelphia, 1986.

Erickson, Elaine May (b. Des Moines, IA, 22 April 1941; *Who's Who*)
 1985 *The Upstairs Bedroom* (22 minutes; libretto by composer). Performed at Peabody Conservatory of Music, Baltimore, 13 May 1985.
 1987 *From Winter Darkness* (1 act; libretto by composer). Performed at Peabody Conservatory, Baltimore, 1 November 1987.

Ernest, David John (b. Chicago, 16 May 1929; Anderson; *Who's Who*)
  - *Ten Year Thunder.*

Errolle, Ralph (b. Chicago, 20 September 1890; d. 1973; Hipsher)
 1912 *Bondri* (short opera; 4 acts).
 1916- *Prince Elmar* (3 acts; libretto by composer), begun in 1916. Bispham Medal, 1932.

Esile, Joseph
 1960 *Still Dark Clouds* (1 act; libretto by Frank Langer). Performed Scottsdale, AZ, November 1960.
 1963 *Sara* (1 act; libretto by Frank Langer). Performed Scottsdale, AZ, March 1963.

Espinosa, Felipe
 1971 *Macias.* Performed by Puerto Rico Opera Festival, New York, September 1971.

Etten, Jane Van. *See* Van Etten, Jane

Evans, ?
 1989 *Avon Calling* (1 act). Performed Birmingham, AL, 26 January 1989. (No infomation on this performance, however, could be found in the Birmingham newspapers around this date; thanks to Donald C. Sanders for investigating.)

Evans, David
 1987 *Birds of Paradise* (libretto by composer with Winnie Holzman). Performed Promenade Theater, New York, 25 October 1987.

Evans, Gil (Ian Ernest Gilmore Green) (b. Toronto, Canada, 1912; d. Cuernavaca, Mexico, 20 March 1988; to U.S. in 1933; Anderson; *Baker's*)
 1976? *A Concert Opera* (?). Commission by New York Jazz Repertory Company, with New York State Council on the Arts grant, for the U.S. Bicentennial.

Everitt, Margaret
    1976   *The Tunesmith of Boston* (1 act). Massachusetts State Arts Council grant.

Eversole, James (b. Lexington, KY, 1 August 1929; Anderson)
    1976   *Bessie* (1 act). Performed at Montclair State College, NJ, 4 May 1976.

Eyerly, Scott
    1986   *Confidence Game*, with William Holab (135 minutes; libretto by Andrew Kurtzman and Scott Eyerly after Jonson's *The Alchemist*). Performed by National Music Theater Network, New York, 13 January 1986; ASCAP workshop, 1986. Published by National Music Theater Network.
    1986   *On Blue Mountain* (105 minutes; libretto by composer, about Appalachia during the 1930s). Commission by Philip Morris, Inc. Performed Town Hall, New York, 16 October 1986.

Faetkenhauer, Max (ca. 1870-1940)
    1901   *Amelia Mora*. Performed Cleveland.

Fagin, Gary
    1987   *Punch and Judy/Judy and Punch* (libretto by composer). Performed Waterford, CT, 20 August 1987.

Fairchild, Blair (b. Belmont, MA, 23 June 1877; d. Paris, France, 23 April 1933; *Amerigrove*)
    -   *Lady Dragonfly* (*Dame Libellule*). (*Amerigrove* lists this, dated 1921, as a ballet-pantomime, and that it became the first work by an American composer to be presented at the Paris Opéra.)

Fairlamb, James Remington (b. Philadelphia, 23 January 1838; d. Ingleside, NY, 16 April 1908 [Hipsher: d. New York, 26 March 1908]; *Baker's*)
    1869   *Valérie: or, Treasured Tokens* (grand opera; 4 acts). Performed Philadelphia, 15 December 1869.
    -   *The Interrupted Marriage* (light opera).
    -   *Lionello* (grand opera).
    -   *Love's Stratagem* (light opera).

Faith, Richard Bruce (b. Evansville, IN, 20 March 1926; Anderson)
    1971   *Sleeping Beauty* (2 acts). Performed at University of Arizona, Tucson, 21 April 1971 and/or December 1971.

Fagin, Gary
    1987   *Punch and Judy/Judy and Punch* (libretto by composer). Performed Waterford, CT, 20 August 1987.

Fairchild, Blair (b. Belmont, MA, 23 June 1877; d. Paris, France, 23 April 1933; *Amerigrove*)

- *Lady Dragonfly* (*Dame Libellule*). (*Amerigrove* lists this, dated 1921, as a ballet-pantomime, and that it became the first work by an American composer to be presented at the Paris Opéra.)

Fairlamb, James Remington (b. Philadelphia, 23 January 1838; d. Ingleside, NY, 16 April 1908; *Baker's*)

1869 *Valérie: or, Treasured Tokens* (grand opera; 4 acts). Performed Philadelphia, 15 December 1869. Hipsher: he was in Washington, DC, for 3 years, "where he organized a company and produced his grand opera in four acts, 'Valerie'."

- *The Interrupted Marriage* (light opera).
- *Lionello* (grand opera; 5 acts).
- *Love's Stratagem* (light opera).

Faith, Richard Bruce (b. Evansville, IN, 20 March 1926; Anderson)

1971 *Sleeping Beauty* (2 acts). Performed at University of Arizona, Tucson, 21 April 1971 and/or December 1971.

Fanciulli, Francesco (b. Porto San Stefano near Orbetello, Italy, 29 May 1853; d. New York, 17 July 1915; in U.S. from 1876; *Amerigrove*; Hipsher)

1901 *Priscilla, The Maid of Plymouth* (libretto after Longfellow's *Courtship of Miles Standish*). Première, Norfolk, VA, 1 November 1901, then on tour as far north as Brooklyn.

- *Gabriel di Montgomery* (Italian text).
- *The Interpreter* (comic opera).
- *The Maid of Paradise* (comic opera).
- *Malinche* (after Lew Wallace's *The Fair God*, Mexican plot).

Fanidi, Theo

1982 *The Little Match Girl* (1 hour; libretto by Sidney L. Berger after Andersen). Performed Houston, TX, December 1982.

Farber, Bill

1987 *Future Soap* (libretto by Megan Terry). Performed by Omaha Magic Theatre, NE, 30 January 1987.

1987 *Walking through Walls*, with Mark Nelson and John J. Sheehan (libretto by Megan Terry and Jo Ann Schmidman). Nebraska Arts Council grant. Performed by Omaha Magic Theatre, NE, 20 November 1987.

Farberman, Harold (b. New York, 2 November 1929; Anderson; *Baker's*; *Who's Who*)

1961 *Medea.* Performed Boston, 26 March 1961. Published by General Music.

1971 *The Losers* (2 acts—120 minutes; libretto by Barbara Fried). Commissioned by Juilliard American Opera Theatre, New York; première there, 26 March 1971. Published by Belwin-Mills. Kornick.

- *If Music Be . . .* (multimedia; needs four conductors). Published by Belwin-Mills.

Farner, Eugene Adrian (or Grubb-Farners; b. Brooklyn, NY, 20 May 1888;
        Hipsher)
-    *The White Buffalo Maiden* ("Western Indian Music-Play"; 1 act;
        libretto by Alfred Grubb; uses Sioux melodies). Second of an
        intended trilogy of 1-act operas or music dramas. Première at
        High School Auditorium, Boise, ID, 26-27 April 1923.

Farwell, Arthur (b. St. Paul, MN, 23 April 1872; d. New York, 20 January 1952;
        AMC; *Amerigrove*)
1915   *Caliban by the Yellow Sands* (masque; libretto by P. MacKaye after
        Shakespeare). Performed New York, May 1916.
1917   *The Evergreen Tree* (Christmas masque; 1 act; libretto by P.
        MacKaye). Published by Presser.
1921   *Pilgrimage Play* (incidental music from masque; libretto by C. W.
        Stevenson).
1925   *Grail Song Masque.*
1948   *Cartoon, or Once Upon a Time Recently* (operatic fantasy; libretto
        by composer and E. K. Wallace).

Fax, Mark Oakland (1911-74; b. in Maryland; Southern)
1956   *Merry-Go-Round* ("liturgical opera"). Performed Washington, DC,
        1969.
1958   *A Christmas Miracle* (1 act).
1967   *Till Victory is Won* (4 episodes with prologue). Separate episodes
        performed Bermuda, 1967, Washington, DC, 1969, and Baltimore,
        MD, 1970. The whole performed in New York in 1974 (two
        months after the composer's death) and in 1979.

Feigin, Joel
1986   *Mysteries of Eleusis* (75 minutes; libretto by composer with Jaime
        Manrique after Homer's "Hymn to Demeter"). Performed Ithaca,
        NY, 23 April 1986.

Feinblum, Joel
1986   *Neon Frontier.* Performed San Francisco, 30 June 1986.

Fejko, Paul
1987   *Matteo Falcone* (1 act; libretto by Dino Yannopoulos after
        Merimee). Workshop performance, Philadelphia, May 1987; staged
        27 October 1987.

Felciano, Richard (James) (b. Santa Rosa, CA, 7 December 1930; *Amerigrove*)
1964   *Sir Gawain and the Green Knight* (chamber opera; 100 minutes;
        libretto by Robert Fahrner after an anonymous Englishman).
        Performed at Lone Mountain College, San Francisco, CA, 4 April
        1964. Published by Belwin-Mills.

Feldman, Jack
1984   *Miami* (2 acts; libretto by composer with Bruce Sussman and Wendy
        Kesselman). Performed by Playwrights Horizons, New York,
        December 1987, and Philadelphia, 27 October 1987.

Feldman, James
> 1984   *The Intruder* (45 minutes; libretto by Gary Stolcals after Maeterlinck). Performed Berea, OH, 10 February 1984.

Feldman, Joann E. (b. New York, 19 October 1941; Anderson; Cohen)
> 1986   *The Computer Kid's Magic Night* (50 minutes; libretto by composer). Performed Robnert Park, CA, 30 October 1986.

Feldman, Morton (b. New York, 12 January 1926; d. Buffalo, NY, 3 September 1987; *Amerigrove*; *Who's Who*)
> 1976   *Neither* (50 minutes; monodrama after Beckett). Performed by Rome Opera, Italy, 1976, and Manhattan School of Music, New York, November 1978.

Felix, Hugo (b. Vienna, Austria, 19 November 1866; d. Los Angeles, 24 August 1934; in U.S. from 1914; *Baker's*)
> 1920   *The Sweetheart Shop.* Performed Chicago, 1920.
>   -   *Resurrection.*
> (Felix also composed incidental music to Otis Skinner's *Sancho Panza*, and other plays.)

Fennimore, Joseph (b. New York, 16 April 1940; ASCAP; Anderson)
> 1975   *Apache Dance* (1 act; libretto by composer after James Purdy). Performed at Lincoln Center, New York, 1 April 1975.
> 1975   *Don't Call Me By My Right Name.* Performed at Carnegie Recital Hall, 1 October 1975.
> 1975   *Eventide* (1 act; libretto by composer after James Purdy). Performed at Carnegie Recital Hall, New York, 1 October 1975, and by After Dinner Opera, New York, 3 October 1983.
> 1978   *Isadora* (1 act; libretto by composer, about the life of Isadora Duncan). Performed at Carnegie Recital Hall, New York, 11 March 1978.

Ferlauto, Leo
> 1987   *The Monkey and Mrs. Little* (libretto by Ivo Bender, on a Brazilian story; in Portuguese, with English translation by Maria Cesnik). Performed Indianapolis, IN, 18 June 1987.

Ferris, William Edward (b. Chicago, 26 February 1937; AMC; Anderson; *Baker's*; *Who's Who*)
> 1978   *Little Moon of Alban* (1 hour; after James Costigan's play about Ireland in 1918).
> 1980   *The Diva* (1 act—1 hour; libretto by John Vorrasi). Premièred by New Works Showcase, Chicago Opera Theatre (workshop performance with 2 pianos), Chicago, 13 June 1987. Kornick.

Fetler, Paul (b. Philadelphia, 17 February 1920; Anderson; *Baker's*)
> 1965   *Sturge Maclean* (opera for youth; 3 acts; libretto by Joyce Houlton). Performed St. Paul, MN, 11 October 1965.

Fewell, Marvin
> 1976   *Light Horse Harry Lee.* Commission by Arlington Historical Society. Performed Arlington, VA, 18 June 1976.

Fickenscher, Arthur (b. Aurora, IL, 9 March 1871; d. San Francisco, 15 March
        1954; *Amerigrove*)
    1909   *The Chamber Blue* ("minidrama for orchestra, soli, women's chorus,
        and dancers"; libretto by W. Morris). Performed at University of
        Virginia, 5 April 1938.

Filippi, Amandeo de
    -    *The Green Cockatoo* (50 minutes).
    -    *Malvolio.*

Fine, Vivian (b. Chicago, 28 September 1913; AMC; *Amerigrove*; *Who's Who*)
    1977   *The Women in the Garden* (chamber opera; 1 act—1 hour; libretto by
        the composer). NEA grant. Performed by Port Costa Players, San
        Francisco, 2 December 1978, and at San Francisco Opera Center,
        April 1982. Kornick.
    -    *Finnegan's Wake* (after Joyce). 1974 NEA grant. (Not listed in
        Amerigrove or Cohen.)

Fink, Harold
    1966   *The Bridegroom* (1 act). Performed Cleveland, 26 November 1966.

Fink, Myron S. (b. Chicago, 19 April 1932; AMC; Anderson)
    1952   *Jeremiah* (4 acts; libretto by P. Fink and E. Hawley). Performed
        Binghamton, NY, 25 April (or May), 1962.
    1955   *The Boor* (1 act). Performed St. Louis, 14 February 1955.
    1955   *Susanna and the Elders.* Performed Vienna, Austria.
    1977   *Judith and Holofernes* (3 acts; libretto by Donald Moreland after
        Giraudoux). Performed Binghamton, NY, January 1982.
    1981   *Chinchilla* (light operetta; 3 acts—140 minutes; libretto by Donald
        Moreland; comedy about the 1920s). Performed Binghamton, NY,
        1981; OPERA America Showcase, New York, 14 December 1982;
        and Binghamton, NY, 18 January 1986. Kornick.
    1986   *The Island of Tomorrow* (1 act; libretto by Lou Rodgers, about Ellis
        Island). Performed by Golden Fleece, New York, July 1988.
    1988   *The Trojan Women.* Performed by Golden Fleece, New York, July
        1988.

Finkelstein, David
    1987   *Self-Reference* (1 act). Downtown Opera Players, New York, 25
        April 1987.

Finko, David Rafael (b. Leningrad, Russia, 15 May 1936; *WhoAm*)
    1965   *Polinka* (35 minutes; libretto by composer after Chekhov), revised
        1982. Performed El Paso, TX, 26 February 1983.

Finn, Ben
    1967   *Little Women.* Performed at Bracken Storyland Theatre, New York,
        12 October 1967.

Finn, William
> *Falsetto Trilogy* (librettos by composer; all performed by Playwrights Horizons, New York):
1978 *In Trousers*. Performed fall 1978.
1981 *March of the Falsettos* (70 minutes). Performed 1 April 1981.
1990 *Falsettoland* (70 minutes). Performed 28 June 1990.
1982 *Romance in Hard Times* (1 hour; about a soup kitchen in the 1930s). Performed by Playwrights Horizon, New York, 1982; also at New York Shakespeare Festival, 30 May 1989 and December 1990.

Finnerman, Allan
1988 *Poison Hotel*, with Bob Davis and John Raskin (involves audience participation). Performed San Francisco, October 1988.

Finney, Doug
- *The Song of the Gypsy Princess* (1 hour). Published by Dramatic Publishing.

Finney, Ross Lee (b. Wells, MN, 23 December 1906; *Amerigrove*; *Who's Who*) (Finney writes his own librettos.)
1965 *The Nun's Priest's Tale* (18 minutes; libretto after Chaucer). Performed Hanover, NH, 1965.
1984 *Weep Torn Land* (2 acts; about the American West). See Kenneth Peacock, "Ross Lee Finney at Eighty-Five: *Weep Torn Land*," *American Music* 9/1 (Spring 1991): 1-19.
1991 *Computer Marriage* (a farce, about computer problems).

Fiore, Roland (or Ronald) **Michael**
1961 *Linda* (1 act). Performed Philadelphia, 13 March 1961.

Fischer, William S. (b. Shelby, MS, 5 March 1935; Anderson; Southern)
1966 *Jesse* (3 acts). Performed Buffalo, NY, 1966.
- *About Indians*.
- *Jack Jack*.
- *Simone Wilde*.

Fischoff, George (ASCAP)
1985 *Bingo!* (libretto by Hy Gilbert and Ossie Davis after Brashler's baseball novel *The Bingo Long Traveling All-Stars and Motor Kings*). Performed by AMAS Repertory Theatre, New York, 24 October 1985.
1987 *Sayonara* (2 acts; libretto by Hy Gilbert and William Luce after Michener). Performed Milburn, NJ, 8 December 1986, 10 February 1987, and 16 September 1987.

Fisher, Truman Rex (b. Taft, CA, 10 November 1940; Anderson)
1965 *The Wasps* (1 act). Performed at Occidental College, Los Angeles, 21 May 1965.
- *Lysistrata* (2 acts).

Fisher, Van Dirk
   1985   *No Name in the Street* (on Book of Job). Performed by Black
         Experimental Theater, Brooklyn, NY, April 1985.

Fisher, William J.
   1962   *The Happy Prince* (1 act; libretto by John Gutman after Wilde).
         Performed Iowa City, IA, 10 March 1962.

Fishman, Jack
   1976? *Bim! Bam! Bim!* A New Jersey Bicentennial project. Commission
         by New Theatre, Inc.

Fitelberg, Jerzy (b. Warsaw, Poland, 20 May 1903; d. New York, 25 April 1951;
         in U.S. from 1940; AMC; *Amerigrove*)
   1949   *Henny Penny* (children's opera; 1 act—30 minutes; libretto by N.
         Brant). Published by Marks.

Flagello, Nicholas (b. New York, 15 March 1928; Anderson; *Baker's*; *Who's Who*)
   1953   *Mirra* (3 acts; libretto by composer after V. Alfieri). Published by
         Belwin-Mills. *COS*-2.
   1953   *The Wig* (comic opera in 1 act; libretto by composer after
         Pirandello). *COS*-2.
   1957   *Rip van Winkle* (children's operetta; libretto by C. Fiore).
   1958   *The Sisters* (1 act; libretto by Dean Mundy). Performed at
         Manhattan School of Music, New York, 23 February 1961.
         Published by Franco Colombo.
   1959   *The Judgment of St. Francis* (1 act—80 minutes; libretto by Armand
         Aulleino). Performed New York, 18 March 1966. Published by
         Franco Colombo.
   1970   *The Piper of Hamelin* (children's opera; 1 hour; libretto by
         composer after Browning). Performed New York, 18 April 1970.
   1983   *Beyond the Horizon* (libretto by composer after O'Neill).

Flagg, Mary Houts
   -      *The Land of Manana*. In Krohn.

Flaherty, Stephen
   1986   *The Emperor's New Clothes* (libretto by Lynn Ahrens). Performed
         Theatreworks/USA, New York, 21 December 1986.
   1987   *Lucky Stiff* (2 acts; libretto by Lynn Ahrens after Butterworth's
         The Man Who Broke the Bank at Monte Carlo). Richard Rogers
         Development Award, 1987; National Institute of Music Theatre
         grant, 1987. Performed Playwrights Horizons, New York, fall
         1987 and 26 April 1988.
   1990   *Once on This Island* (libretto by Lynn Ahrens after Rosa Guy's *My
         Dove, My Dove*). Performed by Playwrights Horizons, 6 April
         1990.
   -      *Destiny*. *COS*-4.

Flanagan, Thomas J., Jr. (b. New Haven, CN, 30 November 1927; Anderson)
   1980   *I Rise in Flame, Cried the Phoenix* (1 act; libretto after Tennessee
         Williams). Performed by Golden Fleece, New York, 7 February
         1980.

1982   *Statues on a Lawn* (50 minutes; libretto by Matthew Calhoun based on his own short story). Performed by Golden Fleece, New York, 24 March 1982. Kornick.

Flanagan, William (b. Detroit, MI, 14 August 1923; d. New York, 31 August or 1 September 1969; *Amerigrove*)

1957   *Bartleby* (60 minutes; libretto by I. J. Hinton and Edward Albee after Melville). Performed at York Playhouse, New York, 24 January 1961.

1967   *The Ice Age* (libretto by Edward Albee). Commission by Ford Foundation and New York Opera. Incomplete.

(Flanagan also composed incidental music for Albee's *The Sandbox*, 1961, and *The Ballad of the Sad Cafe*, 1963.)

Flanders, William

1981   *Strether* (2 hours; libretto by composer after James's *The Ambassadors*). Performed Washington, DC, ca. 1981.

Fletcher, Grant (b. Hartsburg, IL, 25 October 1913; ASCAP; *Amerigrove*; *Baker's*; *Who's Who*)

1948   *The Carrion Crow* (folk, or buffa-fantasy, opera; 1 act—44 minutes; libretto by composer after John Jacob Niles). Performed at Illinois Wesleyan University, Bloomington, 20 March 1953.

1966   *The Sack of Calabasas* (3 acts; libretto by composer after J. M. Myers). Arizona State University Creative Research award. Performed Phoenix, 6 April 1964.

Fletcher, Stanley

1982   *The Five Dollar Opera* (libretto by composer and Frank Fletcher after O. Henry's "Whirligig"). Performed El Paso, TX, 5 March 1982.

Flick-Steger, Carl L. (b. Vienna, Austria, 13 December 1889; to U.S. at about age 4; Hipsher)

1930   *Dorian Gray* (libretto by Olaf Pedersen after Oscar Wilde's novel). Performed (in German) Aussig, Bohemia, 1, 10, 15 March 1930.

1936   *Leon and Edrita*. Performed Krefeld, Germany (in German).

Floridia-Napolina, Pietro (also Pietro Floridia, Baron Napolino di San Silvestro; b. Modica, Sicily, Italy, 5 May 1860; d. New York, 16 August 1932; in U.S. from 1904, citizen 1917; Hipsher)

1899   *La Colonia* (after Bret Harte's *M'Liss*). Première, Rome, 1899.

1902   *The Scarlet Letter*. Submitted to the Metropolitan Opera, New York, which rejected it.

1910   *Paoletta* (4 acts; libretto by Paul Jones from his story "The Sacred Mirror"). Performed at Music Hall, Cincinnati, 29 August 1910, with 48 curtain calls; and in a run of 29 times in 1915 alone. Bispham Medal, 1930.

1932   *Malia*. Not produced.

Florio, Caryl (professional name of William James Robjohn; b. Tavistock, Devon, England, 2 November 1843; d. Morganton, NC, 21 November 1920; in U.S. from 1857; *Amerigrove*; Hipsher)

1869   *Les Tours de Mercure* (*Tours of Mercury*; operetta). (Hipsher: 1872.)

1871   *Inferno* (comic opera).

1879   *Suzanne* (operetta). Incomplete and lost. (Hipsher: 1876.)

1879   *Gulda* (grand opera; libretto by composer). Incomplete.

1882   *Uncle Tom's Cabin* (serious opera; libretto by composer after Harriet Beecher Stowe). Performed Philadelphia, 1882.

Flower, Edward John Fordham (b. Stratford on Avon, England, 23 June 1948; *COS-4*; *WhoAm*)

1985   *Alliances* (libretto by composer). Performed Stockbridge, MA, 7 August 1985.

1986   *Chacona* (2 acts; libretto by Susan Landau after Mistral poems). Performed Stockbridge, MA, 26 February 1986.

Floyd, Carlisle (b. Latta, SC, 11 June 1926; ASCAP; *Amerigrove*; *Who's Who*)

1949   *Slow Dusk* (1 act). Performed Syracuse, NY, 2 February 1949, and Houston, TX, 1977. Published by Boosey & Hawkes.

1951   *The Fugitives* (3 acts). Performed Tallahassee, FL, 17 April 1951.

1954   *Susannah* (music-drama; 2 acts). Performed Tallahassee, FL, 24 February 1955; by New York Opera, 27 September 1956; by Metropolitan Opera, 20 September 1965; Tulsa, OK, 21 January 1989; Cincinnati, 30 June 1989; and Chautauqua, NY, 12 August 1989.

1958   *Wuthering Heights* (3 acts; libretto by composer after Brönte). Performed Santa Fe, NM, 16 July 1958, and New York, 1959. The work has also been performed in Seattle. Published by Belwin-Mills.

1962   *The Passion of Jonathan Wade* (3 acts; about the Civil War). Performed New York, 11 October 1962. Commission to revise this opera by Houston Grand Opera, TX; workshop performance by Houston Grand Opera Studio, 13 May 1989; full performance by Houston Grand Opera, 18 January 1991.

1963   *The Sojourner and Mollie Sinclair* (1 act—75 minutes). Performed Raleigh, NC, 2 December 1963. Televised 2 December 1963.

1966   *Markheim* (1 act, 60 minutes; libretto by composer after Stevenson). Performed New Orleans, 31 March 1966. Published by Boosey & Hawkes.

1969   *Of Mice and Men* (music drama, 3 acts; libretto by composer after Steinbeck). Commission by San Francisco Opera 1965. Performed Seattle, WA, 22 January 1970. Published by Belwin-Mills.

1972   *Flower and Hawk* (monodrama, about Eleanor of Aquitaine). Performed Jacksonville, FL, 16 May 1972.

1976   *Bilby's Doll* (romantic tragedy; 3 acts—210 minutes; libretto by composer after Esther Forbes's *A Mirror for Witches*). Premièred by Houston Grand Opera, 27 February 1976. Kornick.

1981   *Willie Stark* (3 acts; libretto by composer after William Penn Warren's *All the King's Men*). Commission by Kennedy Center, Washington, DC, 1976. Premièred by Houston Grand Opera, 24 April 1981. Telecast on PBS, 3 September 1984. Kornick.

Fong, Frank
1989   *Headlights*, with Rex Gray, Rick Hiatt, Lori Loree, Mark Nelson, and Luigi Waites. Performed Omaha, NE, 28 April 1989.

Ford, Nancy (see Cohen)
1985   *The Game of Love* (80 minutes; libretto by Tom Jones after Schnitzler's *Anatole*; uses music by Offenbach). Performed Cleveland, 5 September 1985. Published by Music Theatre International.
-    *Shelter.*

Fore, Burdette
1951   *Aria da capo* (45 minutes). Performed Stockton, CA, 19 May 1951.

Foreman, Richard
1983   *Egyptology (My Head Was a Sledgehammer)* (surrealistic work; 80 minutes; libretto by composer). Performed by Ontological-Hysterical Theater, New York, May 1983.
-    *The Blind Man.*
-    *Polly Barker.*

Forman, Joanne (b. Chicago, 26 June 1934; AMC; Anderson; Cohen)
1977   *Polly Baker* (chamber opera).
1978   *The Blind Men* (chamber opera). Performed, with *Polly Baker*, Portland, ME, 6 May 1978.
1981   *Icarus* (50 minutes; after Bruegel's painting and Auden's *Musée des Beaux Arts*). Performed Albuquerque, NM, 17 May 1981.
-    *The Little Tin Soldier* (libretto after Hans Christian Andersen).
-    *My Heart Lies South* (operetta).
-    *North Star* (music drama; libretto by composer and Avis Worthington).

Forrest, Hamilton (b. Chicago, 8 January 1901; d. London, England, 26 December 1963; Anderson; *Baker's*; Hipsher)
1925   *Yzdra* (3 acts; libretto by composer after Louis V. Ledoux's *Alexander the Great*). Dedicated to Mary Garden. Bispham Medal, 1926.
1927   *Camille* (prologue and 3 acts; libretto by composer after Dumas's novel *The Lady of the Carmelites*). Première by Chicago Civic Opera, 10 December 1930, starring Mary Garden, plus five other performances; also by the same company, Boston, 6 February 1931.
1952   *Don Fortunio* (40 minutes). Performed Interlochen, MI, 22 July 1952.
1954   *Daelia* (1 act). Performed Interlochen, MI, 21 July 1954.
1954   *A Matinee Idyll* (1 act). Performed Interlochen, MI, 17 August 1954.
-    *Kismet* (lyric drama).
-    *Marie Odile* (after Edward Knoblock's play).

Forrest, Robert
    1984   *Paradise!* (2 acts; libretto by George Wolfe). Performed by
            Playwrights Horizons, New York, June 1984, and Cincinnati, OH,
            20 February 1985.

Forster, John
    1980   *Grownups.* Performed New York, April 1980.
    1987   *How to Eat like a Child (and Other Lessons in Not Being a Grown-*
            up) (1 act; libretto by Judith Kahane and Della Ephron).
            Performed by TADA!, New York, 10 July 1987. Published by
            Samuel French.

Forsyth, Cecil (b. London, England, 30 November 1870; d. New York, 7
            December 1941; to U.S. in 1914; Anderson)
    -    *Cinderella* (comic opera).
    -    *Westward Ho!* (comic opera).

Foss, Lukas (b. Berlin, Germany, 15 August 1922; in U.S. from 1937;
            Amerigrove; *Who's Who*)
    1949   *The Jumping Frog of Calaveras County* (2 acts, 45 minutes; libretto
            by J. Karsavina after Twain). Performed Bloomington, IN, 18
            May 1950, and New York. Recorded by Lyrichord.
    1955   *Griffelkin* (3 acts, 150 minutes; libretto by Alistair Reed after H.
            Foss). Telecast on NBC, New York, 6 November 1956.
            Performed Tanglewood, MA, 6 August 1956. Published by Carl
            Fischer.
    1959   *Introductions and Goodbyes* (1 act, 9-minute "mini-opera"; libretto
            by Carlo Menotti). Performed New York 5 May 1960 and at
            Spoleto Festival, June 1960. Published by Carl Fischer.
    1970? *MAP (Men at Play)* ("a musical play for five instrumentalists").

Foster, Arnold
    -    *Lord Bateman. COS*-2. Published by Novello.

Foster, Fay (b. Leavenworth, KS, 8 November 1886; d. Bayport, NY, 17 April
            1960; Anderson; *Baker's*; Cohen)
    -    *Blue Beard* (operetta).
    -    *The Castaways* (operetta).
    -    *The Honorable Mme. Yen* (opera).
    -    *Land of Chance* (operetta).
    -    *The Moon Lady* (opera).
    (*Baker's* says she composed 3 operettas, but mentions no operas.)

Foster, Owen
    1899   *La Fiesta de San Xavier.* Performed Los Angeles, 16 December
            1899. Review in *Los Angeles Times* called him "young."

Fox, Malcolm
    1977   *Sid the Serpent Who Wanted to Sing* (50 minutes; libretto by James
            and Susal Vile). Performed Des Moines, IA, 1988. Published by
            Associated Music Publishers.

Frackenpohl, Arthur (b. Irvington, NJ, 23 April 1924; Anderson; *Baker's*; Schoep; *Who's Who*)

    1964   *Domestic Relations ("To Beat or Not to Beat")* (chamber opera; 1 act; libretto by composer after O. Henry's "A Harlem Tragedy"). Performed Potsdam, NY, 17 December 1972.

Fragale, Frank D.

    1953   *Dr. Jekyll and Mr. Hyde* (2 acts). Performed Berkeley, CA, 28 August 1953.

Franceschina, John

    1986   *Kingfish!* (libretto by Jeff Eric Frankel about the life of Huey Long). Festival of Southern Theater Playwriting Competition winner, 1988. Performed Millburn, NJ, 17 November 1986; and University, MS, 1988-89 season.

Franchetti, Aldo (b. Mantua, Italy, 1883; spent 25 years in U.S.; Hipsher)

    1925   *Namiko-San* (1 act; libretto by Leo Duran after his play *The Daymio*). Performed at Chicago Auditorium, 11 December 1925, composer conducting; also on tour by the Manhattan Opera Co., 1926-27. Bispham Medal, 1925.

Franchetti, Arnold (b. Lucca, Italy, 18 August 1906; AMC; Anderson; *Who's Who*)

    1950   *The Lion* (1 hour). Performed New London, CT, 16 December 1950.

    1952   *The Princess* (20 minutes). Performed at Hartt College of Music, Hartford, CT, 16 March 1952. Published by Composers Press.

    1952   *The Maypole* (22 minutes). Performed Westport, CT, 6 July 1952.

    1955   *The Game of Cards* (27 minutes). Concert version performed Hartford, CT, 20 March 1955, and staged 19 May 1956.

    1956   *The Anachronism* (40 minutes). Performed Hartford, CT, 4 March 1956.

    1959   *Prelude and Fugue* (1 act). Performed Elmwood, CT, 21 April 1959.

    1966   *As a Conductor Dreams: or, Nocturne* [Notturno] *in La* (2 acts). Performed Hartford, CT, 20 October 1966.

    1973   *The Sunsnatcher* (1 act; libretto by Barbara Sargent). Performed at University of Hartford, CT, 8 February 1973.

    1976   *Soap Opera* ("in the style of the commedia dell'arte"; 1 act). Performed Hartford, CT, 13 February 1976.

    1975   *Married Men Go to Hell* (prologue and 3 acts; libretto by Emanuel Willheim after Machiavelli). NEA grant, 1975.

Franco, Johan (b. Zaandam, Netherlands, 12 July 1908; d. 14 April 1988; *WhoAm*)

    -    *The Prince and the Prophecy.*

Frank, Charles (AMC)

    -    *The Captain and the Cowboy* (1 act). *COS*-1.

Frank, René (b. Mulhouse, Alsace-Lorraine [now France], 16 February 1910; d.
Fort Wayne, IN, 21 March 1965; to U.S. in 1947; Anderson)
- *Call of Gideon* (1 act).

Frawley, Mark
1990 *Goose: Beyond the Nursery* (libretto by Austin Tichenor and Scott
Evans). Performed New York, 24 January 1990.

Frederick, Robin
- *My Sister Makes Me Sick*, with Elaine Heilveil (45 minutes; libretto
by composers).

Freed, Arnold (b. New York, 29 September 1926; Anderson)
1965 *Zodiac* (masque; 40 minutes). Performed Rochester, MN, 19 May
1965. Published by Boosey & Hawkes.

Freed, Isadore (b. Brest-Litovsk [now Brest, Belarus], 26 March 1900; d. New
York, 10 November 1960; to U.S. 1903; ASCAP; *Amerigrove*;
Baker's)
1930 *Homo sum* (1 act; libretto after J. D. Townsend).
1946 *The Princess and the Vagabond* (2 acts—150 minutes; libretto by R.
Sawyer). Performed Hartford, CT, 13 May 1948.

Freeman, Anthony
1984 *Carmencita y el Soldado* (on Bizet; takes place during the Spanish
Civil War, with added scenes; in Spanish and English). Performed
Tucson, AZ, 14 October 1984.

Freeman, Harry Lawrence (b. Cleveland, OH, 9 October 1869; d. New York, 21
March 1954; *Amerigrove*; *Baker's*; Hipsher; Southern)
(All librettos by the composer except *Uzziah*.)
1892 *Epthelia*. Performed Denver, CO, 1893.
1893 *The Martyr* (2 acts; libretto by composer). Performed by Freeman
Grand Opera Co. at Deutsches Theater, Denver, CO, September
1893, composer conducting, and Chicago, October 1893;
Cleveland, 1897 and 1900; at Wilberforce University, Xenia, OH,
1904; and at Carnegie Hall, New York, 1947.
1895 *Valdo* (1 act). (Hipsher: 1905.) Performed by Freeman Grand
Opera Co. at Weisgerber's Hall, Cleveland, May 1906 (Johnson and
Amerigrove: 1905), composer conducting.
1898 *Zuluki* (3 acts; originally entitled *Nada*). Performed New York,
1930; scenes performed by Cleveland Symphony, March 1900.
1903 *African Kraal* (libretto by composer). Performed at Wilberforce
University, Xenia, OH.
1904 *The Octaroon* (prelude and 4 acts; libretto after story by M. E.
Braddon). Performed on CBS radio, 1931.
1909 *The Tryst* (1 act; libretto by composer, on an American Indian
subject). Première by Freeman Operatic Duo at Crescent Theater,
New York, May 1911.
1911 *The Prophecy* (1 act; libretto by composer). Performed at 125th
Street Y, New York, 1912.

1914   *Voodoo* (3 acts; libretto by composer; set in Louisiana). Performed by Negro Grand Opera Co. at Fifty-Second Street Theater, New York, 10-11 September 1928. Revised 1934.

1915   *The Plantation* (3 acts; libretto by composer). Performed New York, 1930.

1914?   *The Confederate* (prologue and 3 acts).

1916   *Athalia* (prologue and 3 acts; libretto by composer). Performed New York, 1923.

1923   *Vendetta* (3 acts; libretto by composer; about Mexico). Performed by Negro Grand Opera Co. at Lafayette Theater, New York, composer conducting, for one week beginning 12 November 1923.

1927   *American Romance* ("Jazz Grand Opera").

1929   *The Flapper* (jazz opera; 4 acts).

1930   *Leah Kleschna* (grand opera in 4 acts).

1931   *Uzziah* (2 acts; libretto by Florence Lewis Soare; "on a Jewish subject").

   Zululand: A Tetrology of Music Dramas:

1941 *Nada.*

1933 *The Lily.*

1947 *Allah.*

1934 *The Zulu King.* (*Amerigrove* lists this as a ballet.)

   The Destiny: A Tetrology of American Operas:

1941   *Chaka.*

1941   *The Ghost-Wolves.*

1942   *The Storm Witch.*

1944   *Umslopagaas and Nada.*

  -    *Dark Canyon* ("American Grand Opera" in 5 acts).

  -    *Yazoo River.*

Freeman, Thomas Frederick (b. in California; works listed in *Pacific Coast Musical Review*, 1 February and 3 April 1915).

  -    *The Island of Cocoteros.*

  -    *Slumberland.*

Freer, Eleanor Warner Everest (b. Philadelphia, 14 May 1864; d. Chicago, 13 December 1942; *Amerigrove*; *Baker's*; Cohen; Hipsher; Sylvia M. Eversole, "Eleanor Everest Freer: Her Life and Music" [Ph.D. diss., City University of New York, 1992])

(Freer's operas were published in Milwaukee by William A. Kaun.)

1921   *The Legend of the Piper.* op. 28 (1 act; setting of a portion of the poetic drama *The Piper* by Josephine Preston Peabody). Performed Boston, 1922; South Bend, IN, 28 February 1928 (*COS-1* says 24 February 1925; Cohen, 1924); and by American Opera Co., Chicago in October, Boston, 5 December, and Brooklyn, NY, 12 December 1928. Bispham Medal, 1926.

1925   *Massimilliano (the Court Jester): or, The Love of a Calibran*, op. 30 (1 act; libretto by Elia W. Peattie). Performed Lincoln, NE, 19 January 1926; Philadelphia, 18 February 1926; and Chicago, 1932. Published privately, 1925. In AMRC.

1926   *The Chilkoot Maiden*, op. 32 (1 act; libretto by J. J. Underwood after an Alaskan legend). Performed 2 April 1932 (Johnson says 1927; *Amerigrove*, 1926). Published by Kaun, 1926.

1928   *A Christmas Tale*, op. 33 (1 act; libretto after the play by Maurice Boucher, transl. Barrett H. Clark). Première, Houston, TX, 27 December 1929; performed by Chicago Arts Club, 19 December 1936.

1927   *A Legend of Spain*, op. 35 (1 act; libretto by composer after Washington Irving's *Tales of the Alhambra*). Performed in concert form, Milwaukee, 19 June 1931 (Hipsher: September), and in Chicago, 24 October 1933.

1928   *The Masque of Pandora*, op. 36 (1 act; libretto by composer after Henry Wadsworth Longfellow). Published by Kaun, 1930.

1928   *Preciosa: or, The Spanish Student*, op. 37 (1 act; libretto by copmoser after Henry Wadsworth Longfellow).

1929   *Joan of Arc*, op. 38 (1 act; libretto by composer). Concert performance by Junior Friends of Art, Chicago, 3 December 1929.

1929   *Frithiof*, op. 40 (2 acts; libretto by composer after poem *Prithiof's Saga* by Esias Tegner, transl. Clement B. Shaw). Performed in concert form, Chicago, 11 April 1929 and 1 February 1931. Published by Kaun, 1929.

1934   *Scenes from Little Women*, op. 42 (2 acts; libretto by composer after Louisa May Alcott). Performance for Musician's Club of Women, Chicago, 2 April 1934.

1936   *The Brownings Go to Italy*, op. 43 (1 act; libretto by G. A. Hawkins-Ambler; about Robert Browning and Elizabeth Barrett Browning). Performed by Chicago Arts Club, 11 May 1938. In the Newberry Library, Chicago.

Fremont, Rob
-    *Piano Bar* (libretto by composer and Doris Willens). Published by Samuel French.

Freund, Donald Wayne (b. Pittsburgh, 15 November 1947; Anderson)
1974   *The Bishop's Ghost* (1 act; libretto by Hall Peyton). Performed Memphis, TN, 31 October 1974.

Frey, Matthew
1922   *The Violin Maker of Cremona* (1 act). Performed Pittsburgh, PA.

Friedman, Gary William
1979   *Mordecai* (90 minutes). Performed by Kosciuszko Foundation, New York, 30 November 1979.

1980   *Taking My Turn* (libretto by Will Holt and Robert Livingston, on the elderly). Performed New York, 1980, and at Entermedia Theatre, New York, 9 June 1983.

1986   *Waning Powers* (libretto by Gerald Walker). Performed by Vineyard Theatre, New York, 11 January 1986.

Friedman, Joel
1989   *A Vindictive Poem for a Hot Summer's Evening* (libretto by Bela Lisa Friedman).

Friml, Rudolf (b. Prague, Bohemia, 7 December 1879; d. Los Angeles, 12 November 1972; in U.S. after 1906; *Amerigrove*)

1912   *The Firefly* ("Comic Opera in 3 acts"; libretto by O. Harbach). Performed New York, 2 December 1912. Issued as a movie, MGM, 1937.

1913   *High Jinks* (operetta). Performed New York, 10 December 1913.

1915   *The Peasant Girl* (operetta; libretto by E. Smith, H. Reynolds, H. Atteridge; collaboration with O. Nedbal). Performed New York, 2 March 1915.

1915   *Katinka* (operetta; libretto by Harbach). Performed New York, 23 December 1915.

1917   *You're in Love* (operetta; libretto by Harbach and E. Clark). Performed New York, 6 February 1917.

1917   *Kitty Darlin'* (operetta; libretto by Harbach, and P. G. Wodehouse after D. Belasco). Performed New York, 7 November 1917.

1918   *Sometime* (operetta; libretto by R. J. Young). Performed New York, 4 October 1918.

1918   *Glorianna* (operetta; libretto by C. C. Cushing). Performed New York, 28 October 1918.

1919   *Tumble In* (operetta; libretto by Harbach after M. R. Rinehart and A. Hopwood). Performed New York, 24 March 1919.

1919   *The Little Whopper* (operetta; libretto by Harbach and B. Dudley). Performed New York, 13 October 1919.

1921   *June Love* (operetta; libretto by Harbach, W. H. Post, and B. Hooker). Performed New York, 25 April 1921.

1922   *The Blue Kitten* (operetta; libretto by Harbach and W. C. Duncan after Y. Miranda and G. Quinson). Performed New York, 13 January 1922.

1923   *Cinders* (operetta; libretto by Clark). Performed New York, 3 April 1923.

1924   *Rose Marie* ("Musical Play in 2 acts"; libretto by Harbach and Oscar Hammerstein II; collaboration with H. Stothart). Performed New York, 2 September 1924. Issued as a movie, 1954.

1925   *The Vagabond King* ("Musical Play in 2 acts"; libretto by Hooker, Post, and R. Janney after J. H. McCarthy). Performed New York, 21 September 1925. Issued as a movie, 1956.

1926   *The Wild Rose* (operetta; libretto by Harbach and Hammerstein). Performed New York, 20 October 1926.

1927   *The White Eagle* (operetta; libretto by Hooker and Post after E. M. Royle). Performed New York, 26 December 1927.

1928   *The Three Musketeers* (operetta; libretto by W. A. McGuire, Wodehouse, and C. Grey after Alexander Dumas). Performed New York, 13 March 1928.

1930   *Luana* (operetta; libretto by H. E. Rogers and J. K. Brennan after R. W. Tully). Performed New York, 17 September 1930.

1934   *Music Hath Charms, or Annina* (operetta; libretto by R. Leigh, G. Rosener, and J. Shubert). Performed New York, 29 December 1934.

Frith, Fred

1987   *Propaganda* (libretto by Matthew Maguire). Performed by La Mama, New York, 8 May 1987.

Fry, William Henry (b. Philadelphia, PA, 19 August 1813; d. Santa Cruz, Virgin
          Islands, 21 December 1864; *Amerigrove*; Hipsher)
1838? *I cristiani ed i pagani.* Overture and a duet used in:
1841   *Aurelia the Vestal* (3 acts; libretto by Joseph R. Fry).
          Unperformed? Excerpts possibly performed as *Cristiani*, above.
1845   *Leonora* (3 acts; libretto by Joseph R. Fry after E. G. Bulwer-
          Lytton's *The Lady of Lyons*). Performed at the Chestnut Street
          Theatre, Philadelphia, 4 June 1845, and, revised and translated to
          Italian, in New York, 1858. This is the first grand opera by an
          American-born composer to be performed. Libretto in AMRC.
1863   *Notre Dame de Paris* (grand opera; 4 acts; libretto by Joseph R. Fry
          after Victor Hugo). Performed at the American Academy of
          Music, Philadelphia, 4 May 1864.
-      *The Bridal of Dunure.* Early work; a chorus used in *Notre Dame.*

Fuchs, Peter Paul (b. Vienna, Austria, 30 October 1916; U.S. citizen, 1943;
          Anderson)
1965   *Serenade at Noon* (1 act). Performed at Louisiana State University,
          Baton Rouge, 22 March 1965. Published by Presser.
1989   *Die weisse Krankheit* (*The White Agony*) (libretto by composer after
          Capek). Performed by Komische Oper, East Berlin, Germany, 12
          June 1989; scheduled by Greensboro Opera, NC, 1992-93 season.
-      *The Heretic* (3 acts; libretto by composer and Morris West, about
          Giordano Bruno, 1600). *COS*-3.

Fuleihan, Anis (b. Kyrenia, Cyprus, 2 April 1900; d. Stanford, CA, 11 October
          1970; in U.S. from 1915; *Amerigrove*)
1958   *Vasco.*

Fullam, Victoria
1986   *Mermaid* (1 act; libretto by composer after Andersen). Performed
          Minneapolis, 10 May 1986.

Funk, Eric (b. Deer Lodge, MT, 28 September 1949; Anderson)
1980   *Sanctuary* (3 acts—90 minutes; a short version is also available, 1
          act—27 minutes; about 16th-century monastic life).
1986   *Pamelia* (3 acts; libretto by Linda Peavy and Ursula Smith, on
          American pioneers). Composed for the centennials of Idaho,
          Montana, North Dakota, South Dakota, Washington, and Wyoming.
          Performed Portland, OR, 15 April 1986; and Billings, MT, 25
          August 1989.

Furgeri, Vittorio
1985   *Tough Kids* (2 acts; libretto by Janet Harvey-Rowe). Workshop
          performance by J. Harvey-Rowe Community Theatre, Brooklyn,
          NY, 1985; performed by the same company at Lincoln Square
          Theater, New York, 21 October 1988.

Fussell, Charles C. (b. Winston-Salem, NC, 14 February 1938; Anderson; *Who's
          Who*)
1962   *Caligula.*
1972   *Julian* (drama for soloists, chorus, orchestra; 5 scenes; after
          Flaubert). Performed Winston-Salem, NC, 15 April 1972.

- *Eurydice* (drama for soprano and 9 players; text of Edith Sitwell).

Futterman, Enid
1990   *The Open Window* (libretto by Sarah Ackerman after Saki). Ten Minute Musical Project winner. Performed at Climat Theater, San Francisco, 15 February 1990.
-    *Coemeterium* ("choreo-music drama" in 14 scenes—100 minutes; libretto by composer; text includes part of the Requiem Mass).

Gabriel, Charles Hutchinson (b. Wilton, IA, 18 August 1856; d. Hollywood, CA, 14 September 1932; *Amerigrove*)
1890?   *The Merry Milkmaids: An Amateur Operetta* (2 acts; libretto by composer). Published by Fillmore Bros.; 2nd ed., 1891.
1893   *The Merry Cyclers: or, Love the Golden Key* (2 acts; libretto by Palmer Hartsough). Published by Fillmore Bros., 1896.
1899   *Paulin: or, An Eventful Day* (2 acts). Published by Fillmore Bros., 1899.
1904   *Crowning of the Fairy Queen* (the Fairy Queen speaks, all others sing). Published by A. Bierly, 1904.

Gaburo, Kenneth Louis (b. Somerville, NJ, 5 July 1926; ASCAP; *Amerigrove*; *Who's Who*)
1952   *The Snow Queen* (3 acts; libretto by Marjorie Wilson). Performed Lake Charles, LA, 5 May 1952.
1957   *Bodies* ("abstract theater piece"—*Baker's*).
1961   *The Widow* (1 act; libretto by composer after Herman Melville). Performed Urbana, IL, 26 February 1961 (*Amerigrove* has première in Saratoga Springs, NY, 1961).

Gaines, Samuel Richards (1869-1945; b. Detroit, MI)
-    *Daniel Boone.*

Galasso, W.
1975   *The $ Value of Man.* Performed Brooklyn, NY, 8 May 1975.

Gallagher, C. W.
1975   *The Strange Case of Margie-Nancy* (1 act; libretto by Patrick Mahony). Performed Bemidji, MN, 2 February 1975.

Gallagher, Dick
1985   *Have I Got a Girl for You* (2 acts; libretto by composer with Joel Greenhouse and Penny Rockwell; a spoof of *The Bride of Frankenstein*). Performed by Inroads, New York, February 1985.

Gallico, Paolo (b. Trieste, 13 May 1868; d. New York, 6 July 1955; in U.S. from 1892; *Amerigrove*)
-    *Harlequin* (or *Harlekin*).

Galloway, James
　　1988　　*Pastoral* (1 act; libretto by James Morley). Performed Albuquerque, NM, 22 May 1988.

Garabedian, Paul
　　–　　*Nannie Johnson* (90 minutes).
　　–　　*Through the Story Book* (45 minutes; libretto by Greg Atkins after fairy tales). Performed by Long Beach Children's Theatre, CA.

García, José
　　1987　　*Compound Interest*, with Jaime Acosta and Thomas Rodriguez (libretto by Rosalba Rolan, in English and Spanish). Performed by Pregones Puerto Rican Theater Collective, New York, 30 December 1987.

García Marruz, Sergio
　　1988　　*Wishing You Well* (1 act; libretto by Eduardo Machado). Commission by DUO Theater/Teatro DUO, New York, and performed there 12 February 1988.
　　1989　　*Chinese Charade* (*El chino de la charada*), with Saul Spangenberg (Spanish libretto by Emilia Conde and Anita Velez; English version by Manuel Pereiras). Performed by Puerto Rican Traveling Theater, New York, 9 August 1989 (in English).

Garfein, Herschel
　　1988　　*Suenos* (*Dreams*) (2 acts; libretto by Ruth Maleczeck and George Emilio Sanchez, on Latin America in the 17th and 18th centuries, including quotations from Latin-American authors; in English and Spanish). NEA grant, 1988. Performed by Mabou Mines, Boston, 1988.

Gargarian, Gregory
　　–　　*Friar William*. NEA Producers grant, 1985-86.

Garland, Charles Raleigh (b. Potter, NE, 10 June 1917; *WhoAm*)
　　1952　　*If Men Played Cards as Women Do* (15 minutes). Performed at American Conservatory of Music, Chicago, 22 May 1952.

Garland, Kathryn
　　1952　　*Ruth* (6 scenes). Performed Fredericksburg, MD, 4 May 1952.

Garwood, Margaret (b. in New Jersey, 22 March 1927; Anderson; Cohen; *Who's Who*)
　　1967　　*The Trojan Women* (1 act—40 minutes; libretto by Howard Wiley). Commissioned and performed by Suburban Opera, Chester, PA, 22 October 1967.
　　1973　　*The Nightingale and the Rose* (fairytale; 1 act—60 minutes; libretto by composer after a story by Oscar Wilde). NEA grant, 1974. Performed by Pennsylvania Opera Co., 21 October 1973. Published by Carl Fischer. Kornick.
　　1980　　*Rappaccini's Daughter* (tragedy; 2 acts—120 minutes; libretto by composer after the story by Nathaniel Hawthorne). Performed by

Pennsylvania Opera Theater, Philadelphia, 21 November (Kornick: November 23) 1980, with piano, and 6 May 1983, with orchestra.
1987　*Joringel and the Songflowers* (1 act; libretto by composer after Grimm). Performed Roxborough, PA, 25 February 1987.

Garza, Edward
1980　*Saga of the Hidden Sun* (1 act; libretto by Elizabeth Shaw after the Finnish epic *Kalevala*). Performed Dallas, TX, 1980.
1981　*Nuestra Señora de Guadalupe* (*Our Lady of Guadalupe*) (2 acts; about the Aztecs; in Spanish with English narration). Performed San Antonio, TX, 12 December 1985.
1984　*A Marriage Proposal* (1 act; libretto by composer after Chekhov). Brooklyn College Chamber Opera Competition winner, 1984. Performed Brooklyn, NY, 3 February 1984.

Garza, W.
1973　*The Blue Angel* (1 act). Performed Tucson, AZ, 13 April 1973.

Gaston, Bruce
1977　*Chuchok* (on an ancient Buddhist story). Performed Chiangmai, Thailand, 1977.

Gates, Keith (b. Lake Charles, LA, 29 September 1949; Anderson)
1967　*Migle and the Bugs* (chamber opera).
1988　*The Hollow* (1 hour; libretto by Susan E. Kelso after Hawthorne's *The Hollow of the Three Hills*). Shearman Foundation grant. Performed Lake Charles, LA, 4 February 1988.

Gatty, Alfred
1954　*Rumpelstilzchen* (1 act). Performed Milwaukee, WI, 1954.

Gaughan, Jack
1980　*Abelard and Heloise* (libretto by Brian Wilson). Performed by Encompass Music Theatre, New York, summer 1980.

Gaul, Harvey Bartlett (b. New York, 11 April 1881; d. Pittsburgh, 1 December 1945; Anderson)
-　*Alice in Wonderland* (operetta).
-　*Pinocchio* (operetta).
-　*Storybook* (operetta).

Gaynor, Jessie Love (née Smith; b. St. Louis, 17 February 1863; d. Webster Groves, MO, 20 February 1921; Cohen)
1915?　*The Magic Wheel*, with F. F. Beale (2 acts; libretto by Alice C. D. Riley). Piano-vocal score published, Cincinnati: John Church, 1915.
-　*The First Lieutenant.*
-　*The House That Jack Built* (operetta).
-　*Pierre the Dreamer.*
-　*Princess Bo-Peep.*
-　*The Toy Shop.*

Gehlen, Michael (Schoep)

    (Gehlen wrote his own librettos; all of the operas are in *COS*-3.)

- *Brave New World*, op. 24 (3 acts—130 minutes; libretto after Huxley).
- *The Legend of Acoma* (1 act—55 minutes; libretto after a Spanish legend).
- *The Outcasts of Poker Flat*, op. 36 (3 acts—90 minutes; libretto after Bret Harte).
- *The Scarlet Letter*, op. 1 (3 acts—112 minutes; libretto after Hawthorne).

Gelpe, Joel

    1987   *A Little Moon Christmas* (1 hour; after Irene Haas's *The Little Moon Theatre*). Performed by TADA!, New York, 12 December 1987.

Gentemann, Sr. Mary Elaine (b. Fredericksburg, TX, 4 October 1909; Anderson; Cohen)

    1977   *Love Was Born at Christmas* ("A Christmas Pageant"). Performed at Our Lady of the Lake University, San Antonio, TX.

George, Earl (b. Milwaukee, WI, 1 May 1924; Anderson; *Amerigrove*; *Who's Who*)

    1976   *Another Fourth of July* (1 act; Bicentennial opera set in 1912; libretto by composer). Performed Syracuse, NY, 23 April 1976.

    1976   *Pursuing Happiness* (1 act; takes place 4 July 1777; libretto by composer). Performed Syracuse, NY, 23 April 1976. These two operas have the collected name of *Birthdays*.

Gerberg, Miriam

    1986   *The Yellow Wallpaper* (8 minutes; libretto by Judith McGuire after Charlotte Perkins Gilman). Brooklyn College Chamber Opera Competition winner. Performed there, 10 April 1986.

Gerschefski, Edwin (b. Meriden, CT, 19 June 1909; ACA; *Amerigrove*; *Who's Who*)

    1984   *Man Overboard!* ("a sea chantey for sound and light"; 14 minutes; libretto by Paul O'Neill). Performed at University of Georgia, Athens, 24 May 1984.

Gershwin, George (b. Brooklyn, NY, 26 September 1898; d. Hollywood, CA, 11 July 1937; *Amerigrove*)

    1922   *Blue Monday* ("a la Afro-American"; libretto by B. G. DeSylva). Written as an opener to *George White's Scandals of 1922*, act 2, at the Globe Theatre, New York, 28 August 1922, but withdrawn afterwards. Revised as:

    1925   *135th Street* (1 act). Concert version of *Blue Monday* performed at Carnegie Hall, New York, 29 December 1925.

    1925   *The Song of the Flame* (operetta, 1 act; with Herbert Stothart; libretto by Oscar Hammerstein II and O. Harbach).

    1927   *Strike Up the Band*, edited by Eric Salzman. Performed at American Music Theatre Festival, 1984. Kornick.

    1935   *Porgy and Bess* ("Folk Opera in Three Acts"; libretto by DuBose Heyward and Ira Gershwin after DuBose and Dorothy Heyward's play *Porgy*). Performed Boston, 30 September 1935; New York,

10 October 1935; revived 1942, 1943; European tour, 1956; Metropolitan Opera, New York, 6 February 1985 and 17 October 1989; Opera North, October 1988; Connecticut Opera, 13 April 1989; Syracuse, NY, 21 April 1989; Milwaukee, WI, 16 November 1989; and Knoxville, TN, 13 January 1990. Bispham Medal, 1937. Published by Gershwin, 1935, and Chappell.

Gerut, Rosalie
1989   *Songs of Paradise* (2 acts; libretto by Miriam Hoffman and Rena Berkowicz Borow after Itsik Manger's story of *Genesis*). Performed by Joseph Papp Yiddish Theater, New York, 22 January 1989.

Gesensway, Louis (b. Dvinsk, Latvia, 19 February 1906; d. Philadelphia, 13 March 1976; U.S. citizen, 1942; Anderson; *Baker's*)
1953   *The Great Buffo and His Talking Dog* (comic opera for children; 20 minutes; libretto by Christopher Davis). Performed Philadelphia, 7 February 1961. Published by Presser.

Gessner, Clark
1990   *Animal Fair* (on animal rights and the environment). Performed Denver, CO, 18 April 1990.

Gessner, John
1971   *Faust Counter Faust* ("a collage of operas and plays on Mefistofelian subject"; libretto by Wesley Balk). Performance Minneapolis, 30 January 1971.

Geto, Alfred D.
1953   *The Treasure* (1 act). Performed Pottersville, NY, 22 August 1953.

Getty, Gordon (Peter) (b. Los Angeles, 20 December 1933; *WhoAm*)
1985   *Plump Jack* (1 act; libretto by composer after Shakespeare's *Henry IV* and *Henry V*). Performed at Cathedral of St. John the Divine, New York, 31 December 1985; Aspen, CO, 4 July 1986; Graz, Austria, 17 July 1987; San Francisco, 26 June 1987; at Incline Village, NY, 24 July 1988; by Marin Opera, CA, 29 December 1988; Hanover, NH, May 1989; at Spoleto Festival, 4 July 1989; and Larkspur, CA, 9 March 1990. Published by Presser.

Giannini, Vittorio (b. Philadelphia, 19 October 1903; d. New York, 28 November 1966; *Amerigrove*; see also Anne Simpson and Karl Wonderly Flaster, "A Working Relationship: The Giannini-Flaster Collaboration," *American Music* 6/4 [Winter 1988]: 375-408)
1934   *Lucedia* (3 hours; libretto by Karl Flaster, transl. to Italian by G. M. Sala, and into German by Hans Redlich). Première, Munich, Germany, 20 October 1934. Published Berlin: Drei Masken Musik, 1934.
1937   *Not All Prima Donnas Are Ladies* (150 minutes).
1937   *Flora.*
1938   *The Beauty and the Beast* (1 hour; libretto by Robert A. Simon). Broadcast CBS radio, ?1938. Performed Hartford, CT, 14 February 1946. Published by Ricordi.

1938　*The Scarlet Letter* (150 minutes; libretto by Karl Flaster after Hawthorne, transl. to German by Julius Kapp). Première at Hamburg State Opera, Germany, 2 June 1938, as *Das Brandmal*. Published Hamburg: Ahn und Simrock.

1939　*Blennerhasset* (30 minutes; libretto by Roe and Corwen). Performed New York, 22 November 1939 and 12 April 1940. Broadcast on CBS radio, 2 February 1939. Published by Ricordi.

1952　*Casanova*.

1952　*The Taming of the Shrew* (150 minutes; libretto by composer and Dorothy Fee after Shakespeare). Performed Cincinnati, 31 January 1953. Published by Ricordi.

　　　Christus: Four Operas on the Life of Christ (1956); never performed:
　　　The Nativity.
　　　The Resurrection of Lazarus.
　　　The Triumph.
　　　Passion.

1960　*The Medead* (monodrama in 1 act). Performed Atlanta, GA, October 1960.

1961　*The Harvest* (3 acts; libretto by composer and Karl Flaster). Première by Chicago Lyric Opera, 25 November 1961. Published by Ricordi.

1961　*Rehearsal Call* (3 acts; libretto by Swann and Simon). Performed New York, 15 February 1962.

1966　*The Servant of Two Masters* (libretto by Stambler after Goldoni). Posthumous performance, New York, 9 March 1967. (Anderson indicates it was performed in New York in 1957.)

Gibbs, C. Armstrong
1964　*The Three Kings.* Performed at Prospect High School, New Haven, CT, 15 December 1964.

Gibbs, Geoffrey David (b. Copiague, NY, 29 March 1940; Anderson)
1965　*Dolphin Off Hippo* (5 scenes; libretto by Alonzo Gibbs). Performed Rochester, NY, 9 May 1965.

Gibson, Archer (b. Albany, NY, 5 December 1875; d. Lake Mahopac, NY, 15 July 1952; Anderson)
–　*Ysdra.*

Gibson, Jon Charles (b. Los Angeles, 11 March 1940; *Amerigrove*)
1983　*The Voyage of the Beagle* (prologue and 9 scenes; libretto by JoAnne Akalaitis, about Charles Darwin). Performed by OPERA America, New York, 12 December 1983; and in Philadelphia, 2 October 1986 and 18 April 1987. Published by Undertow Music.

Gibson, Richard
1978　*Butler's Lives of the Saints*, with G. Rickard and S. Tittle ("experimental opera"; libretto by Ann Wilson; texts from Dante, Ovid, Goethe, Shakespeare, Melville, etc.). Performed by Performing Space, New York, 13 January 1978. Videotape available.

Gideon, Miriam (b. Greeley, CO, 23 October 1906; *Amerigrove*; Cohen; *Who's Who*)

1958   *Fortunato* (3 scenes, 60 minutes; on the Quintero brothers). Recorded on CRI-128.

1960   *The Adorable Mouse* ("a French folk tale for narrator and chamber orchestra").

Giglio, Clemente (Hipsher, 429)

1926   *La monaca bianca* (*The White Sister*; libretto after Marion Crawford's novel of the same name). Performed New York (in Italian), 1927, and Patterson, NJ (in English), April 1927.

Gilbert, Charles

1988   *The Cry of Toth*. Video opera. Performed Minneapolis, 9 January 1988.

Gilbert, Henry Franklin Belknap (b. Somerville, MA, 26 September 1868; d. Cambridge, MA, 19 May 1928; *Amerigrove*; Hipsher)

c 1906   *Uncle Remus* (libretto by C. Johnston after J. C. Harris), incomplete.

1919   *Fantasy in Delft* (1 act; libretto by Thomas P. Robinson).

Gilbert, John (ACA)

1963   *A Mother's Requiem* (1 act). Performed Lubbock, TX, 30 April 1963.

1964   *If This Be Madness* (1 act). Performed Lubbock, TX, 12 April 1964.

Gilfert, Charles (b. ?Prague, Bohemia, 1787; d. New York, 30 July 1829; *Amerigrove*; Porter; Wolfe)

1813   *Rokeby*.

1815   *Freedom Ho!* ("melodramatic opera"; 2 acts; libretto by Isaac Pocock). Première, New York, 5 April 1815.

1816   *The Champions of Freedom* ("romance"; libretto by S. Woodworth).

1823   *Virgin of the Sun* "grand historical opera").

Gillespie, Marian (ASCAP)

\-   *Blue Rose*.

Gillis, Don (b. Cameron, MO, 17 June 1912; d. Columbia, SC, 10 January 1978; ASCAP; *Amerigrove*)

1957   *The Park Avenue Kids* (1 act; libretto by composer). Performed Elkhart, IN, 12 May 1957.

1957   *Pep Rally* (1 act). Performed Interlochen, MI, 15 August 1957.

1958   *The Libretto* (30 minutes). Performed Norman, OK, December 1960.

1962   *The Legend of Star Valley Junction*. Performed by Metropolitan Opera Studio, New York, 7 January 1969.

1965   *The Gift of the Magi*. Performed Fort Worth, TX, 7 December 1965.

1967   *World Première*.

1968   *The Nazarene*.

1973   *Behold the Man*.

Ginsberg, Jeremiah
    1985   *Rabboni* (libretto by composer, on the Gospels). Performed at Perry Street Theater, New York, March 1985.

Giobbi, Chambliss (BMI)
    1989   *Onement: The Self* (5 parts; libretto by composer). Performed Baltimore, MD, 3 February 1989.

Gireaud, Tiye
    1988   *Song of Lawino*, with Edwina Lee Tyler (70 minutes; libretto by Valeria Vasilevski after Okot p'Bitek). NEA grant. Performed Los Angeles, December 1988.

Giteck, Janice (b. Brooklyn, NY, 27 June 1946; Anderson; *Baker's*; Cohen)
    1973   *Messalina* (mini-opera for male voice, cello, piano).
    1976   *A'agita* (originally, *Wi'igita*) (1 hour; libretto by R. Giteck after Pima and Papago Native American stories). Ceremonial opera for 3 singing actors, 1 dancing actor, 8 instrumentalists. Performed Seattle, WA, spring 1983.
    1977   *Thunder Like a White Bear Dancin'* (libretto after Native American stories). Performed Seattle, WA, November 1983.
    1978   *Callin' Home Coyote* (burlesque; libretto after Native American stories). For tenor, steel drums, string bass. Performed Seattle, WA, November 1983.
    (Giteck's music was included in Paul Dresher's *Floating Opera*, Seattle, 20 September 1987.)

Gladstein, Richard (AMC)
    1959   *The Lookout* (or *The Lockout*; 15 minutes).

Glanville-Hicks, Peggy (b. Melbourne, Australia, 29 December 1912; d. Sydney, Australia, 25 June 1990; in U.S. from 1939 and became a citizen; BMI; *Amerigrove*; *Baker's*; Cohen)
    1953   *The Transposed Heads* (6 scenes, 75 minutes; libretto by composer after Thomas Mann). Performed (and recorded) Louisville, KY, 27 March 1954. Published by American Music.
    1959   *The Glittering Gate* (1 act, 30 minutes; libretto by Lord Dunsany). Performed New York, 14 May 1959. Published by Franco Colombo.
    1961   *Nausicaa* (3 acts; after Robert Graves's *Homer's Daughter*). Performed Athens, Greece, 19 August 1959.
    1961   *Sappho* (3 acts; libretto by Lawrence Durrell). Commission by San Francisco Opera.
    1990   *Beckett*.

Glass, Dudley (AMC)
    –   *Cerda: An Opera of the North* (1 act; libretto after a poem by Madeline Mason). *COS*-3.

Glass, Philip (b. Baltimore, MD, 31 January 1937; *Amerigrove*)
    1976   *Einstein on the Beach* (4 acts, 5 hours; libretto by composer; collaboration with Robert Wilson). Performed in Avignon,

France, 25 July, 1976; since then in Venice, Belgrade, Brussels, Paris, Hamburg, Rotterdam, Amsterdam, and New York, 21 November 1976. Recording: CMS M4 38875. Kornick. See *Akhnaten*, below.

1979   *Edison* (over 4 hours; libretto by Robert Wilson). Performed at Lion Theatre, New York, 19 June 1979.

1980   *Satyagraha* (3 acts—120 minutes; libretto by Constance de Jong after the Bhagavad-Gita; in Sanskrit). Commission by Netherlands Opera, Rotterdam. Performed Rotterdam, Netherlands, 5 September 1980; New York, 29 July 1981; Chicago, 1988; Seattle, WA, 23 July 1989; San Francisco, 3 June 1990. Kornick. See *Akhnaten*.

1980   *Attaca—A Madrigal Opera* (variable texts). Performed Amsterdam, Netherlands, 1980, Houston, TX, 25 April 1981, and at Kennedy Center, Washington, DC, June 1982.

1982   *The Photographer* (chamber opera; 90 minutes; libretto by Rob Malasch after the life and photographs of Eadweard Muybridge). Commission for Holland Festival, Amsterdam, Netherlands. Performed Amsterdam, 26 May 1982, Brooklyn, NY, 10 April 1983, and at Carnegie Hall, New York, 10 May 1983.

1983   *Akhnaten* (3 acts—150 minutes; libretto by composer and others from ancient documents). Performed Stuttgart, Germany, 24 March 1984 (as *Akhanaton and Daedalus*); at Guggenheim Museum, New York, 6 May 1984; Houston, TX, 12 October 1984. Recording: CBS Masterworks M2K 42458. Video on Video Arts International 69049, with excerpts from *Satyagraha* and *Einstein on the Beach*. *Einstein on the Beach*, *Satyagraha*, and *Akhnaten* were performed as a trilogy, Stuttgart, Germany, June 1990. Kornick.

1984   *The CIVIL WarS, a Tree is Best Measure when it is Down, Acts I and V (The Italian/Rome Section)*. Performed Rome, Italy, 22 March 1984; New York, 20 May 1983; and Brooklyn, NY, 14 December 1986. The work is still incomplete. Kornick.

1985   *The Juniper Tree*, with John Moran (2 acts; libretto by Arthur Yorinks after Grimm fairytale). Commission by American Repertory Theater, Cambridge, MA. Performed by Relanche Ensemble for Contemporary Music, New York, March 1985, and American Repertory Theater, 6 December (Kornick: December 17) 1985.

1986   *The Making of the Representative for Planet 8* (science fiction; 3 acts—180 minutes; libretto by Doris Lessing after her novel). Commission by Netherlands Opera, Houston Grand Opera, English National Opera. Performed Scheveningen, Netherlands, March 1986, and Houston, TX, 8 July 1988. Kornick.

1988   *1000 Airplanes on the Roof*, with David Henry Hwang and Jerome Serlin. Commission by Donaufestival, City of Berlin, Germany, and American Music Theater Festival. Performed at American Music Theater Festival, 21 September 1988; Montreal, Canada, November 1988; and London, England, October 1989.

1988   *The Fall of the House of Usher* (110 minutes; libretto by Arthur Yorinks after Poe). Commission by American Repertory Theatre, Cambridge, MA, and Kentucky Opera, Louisville. OPERA America Grant. Performed Cambridge, MA, 18 May 1988, by

Kentucky Opera, Louisville, May 1988, and in Bonn, Germany, 1990. Kornick.

1989   *Mattogrosso* (about the need to protect the environment). Commission by Teatro Municipal, Rio de Janeiro, Brazil. Performed there, 15 July 1989.

1989   *The Hydrogen Jukebox* (libretto by Allen Ginsberg). Performed Philadelphia, 29 April 1990, and Charleston, SC, 26 May 1990.

1990   *Orphée* (libretto after Cocteau). Performed Montreal, Canada, 1 November 1990.

1992   *The Voyage* (libretto by David Henry Hwang, on explorers, including Columbus). Commission by Metropolitan Opera, New York, with performance projected for October 1992.

Gleason, Frederick Grant (b. Middletown, CT, 17/18 December 1848; d. Chicago, 6 December 1903; *Amerigrove*; Hipsher)

1877   *Otho Visconti* (3 acts; libretto by composer). Performed at College Theater, Chicago, 4 June 1907.

1885   *Montezuma* (grand romantic opera; libretto by composer).

Godin, Robert (b. Springfield, MA, 14 January 1954; AMC; Anderson)

1981   *Next Step* ("sound theater work"). Performed by Eventworks, New York, 24 April 1981.

Goldbeck, Robert (b. Potsdam, Germany, 19 April 1839; d. St. Louis, 16 May 1908; in U.S. from 1857; *Amerigrove*)

1886   *The Commodore.* Published in *Philadelphia Music Journal.* At AMRC.

1889   *Newport.* Performed London, England.

–   *Saratoga.*

Goldberg, Lawrence

1988   *Dealing in Justice* (libretto by Margaret Kelso, on the civil rights movement of the 1960s). Performed at Carnegie Mellon University, Pittsburgh, PA, 9 December 1988.

Goldberg, Theo

1969   *Galatea Elettronica* (1 act; libretto by composer). Performed Bellingham, WA, 14 May 1969.

Goldenberg, Michael

1989   *Down the Stream* (libretto by composer). Performed Waterford, CT, 31 July 1989, and New York, September 1989.

Goldenthal, Elliot

1986   *The Transposed Heads* (libretto by Sidney Goldfarb and Julie Taymor after Mann). Performed Philadelphia, 11 September 1986.

1988   *Juan Darien* (formerly *Missa Carnival*; libretto by composer and Julie Taymor after Quiroga).

Goldstaub, Paul R. (AMC)

1978   *The Marriage Proposal* (1 act; libretto after Chekhov). Commission by Mankato State University, MN. Performed there, 25 May

1978, and by Golden Fleece, New York, 20 March 1986. Recording available.

1980   *The Stars Sing a Music.* Performed Mankato, MN, 30 March 1980.
1986   *The Trojan Women* (1 act; libretto by George A. Sand). Performed St. Paul, MN, 11 April 1986.

Goldstein, George (Fleckten says Richard; AMC)
-      *Lockout, A Thumbnail Opera* (23 minutes). *COS*-1.

Goldstein, Lee Scott (b. Woodbury, NJ, 16 November 1952; d. Chicago, 12 January 1990; *WhoAm*)
1976   *An Idiot Dance* (1 act). Performed at Baldwin-Wallace College, OH.
1984   *Miriam and the Angel of Death.* Performed 1984.
1988   *The Fan* (2 acts—130 minutes; libretto by Charles Kondek after Carlo Goldoni's *Il ventalio.* NIMT grant; composer-in-residence, Lyric Opera of Chicago, 1987-88. Performed by Lyric Opera workshop (act 1), 10 June 1988; full performance there, 17 June 1989. Kornick.

Goldstein, Raymond
-      *The Jewbird* (3 acts; libretto by Jacobo Kaufmann after Malamud).

Goldstein, William (b. Newark, NJ, 25 February 1942; Anderson)
1963   *Dancing, Dancing Good-By* (musical).
1964   *A Bullet for Billy the Kid* (folk opera; 45 minutes; libretto by Marvin Shofer). On CBS-TV. Published by Sam Fox.
1965   *A Total Sweet Success* (musical; 70 minutes; libretto by Marvin Shofer after Twain's "The £1,000,000 Bank Note"; incorporates texts of the Requiem Mass; in Spanish and Latin). Published by Sam Fox. Performed by Music-Theatre Group, New York, 8 March 1988.
1966   *The Peddler* (25 minutes; libretto by Marvin Shofer). Published by Sam Fox.

Goldsworthy, William Arthur (b. Cornwall, England, 8 February 1878; d. Santa Barbara, CA, 20 August 1966; to U.S. in 1887; Anderson)
-      *The Queen of Sheba.*
-      *The Return of the Star* (music drama).

Golub, Peter
-      *The Odyssey* (2 acts; libretto by Leon Katz after Homer). *COS*-4.

Gomer, Llywellyn (AMC)
-      *The Divine Mystery. COS*-1.

Gonya, Stephen
1985   *Close Encounters of the Third Grade* (libretto by composer and John and Maureen Cielinski, on space adventure movies). Performed at Center Stage Community Playhouse, Bronx, NY, 22 June 1985.

Gonzales, Manuel Benjamin (b. Arecibo, Puerto Rico, 3 January 1930; *WhoAm*)
1974   *Nela* (3 acts). Performed by Puerto Rican Opera, Bronx, MY, May 1974.

1980   *Los jibaros progresistas* (*The Progressive Country Men*) (1 hour;
        libretto by composer after Quiñones; set in Puerto Rico in 1880).
        Performed New York, 5 May 1980, and by Bronx Arts Ensemble,
        Alice Tully Hall, New York, 28 December 1981.

Gooding, David (b. Lockport, NY, 7 August 1935; Anderson)
1988   *The Legend of Sleepy Hollow* (50 minutes; libretto by Paul Lee
        after Irving). Commission by Cleveland Opera Children's Theatre.
        Performed Cleveland, 1 December 1988.

Goodman, Alfred Grant (b. Berlin, Germany, 1 March 1920; in U.S. in 1940-60;
        AMC; Anderson; *Baker's*)
1954   *The Audition* (45 minutes). Performed Athens, OH, 27 July 1954.
1968   *The Actor.* Performed Pforzheim, Germany, April 1968.
1969   *Der Läufer.*
1984   *The Lady and the Maid* (35 minutes; libretto by Elliot Arluck;
        contains blues music).
 -      *Prometheus.* Commission by Westdeutscher Rundfunk, Cologne.
 -      *The Statues of Turtle Bay* (1 act).

Goodman, J. F.
1955   *The Pizza Pusher* (1 act). Performed San Francisco, September
        1955.

Goodman, John
1987   *The Garden of Flowers* (1 act). Performed at Boston University, 1
        May 1987.

Gordon, David Alexander
1966   *Damask Drum* (1 act; libretto after 15th-century Noh dramas).
        COS-1. Performed at the Conservatory of Music, University of
        Missouri-Kansas City, where he was on the faculty at the time.

Gordon, John J.
1986   *I Just Wanna Tell Somebody* (2 acts; musical drama for children).
        Performed by Wheatley Drama Workshop, Houston, TX, August
        1986.

Gordon, Michael [the composer listed in *WhoAm* as born in Managua, Nicaragua
        in 1956?]
1989   *Ben Hur!.*

Gordon, Peter (b. New York, 20 June 1951; *Amerigrove*).
1984   *The Birth of the Poet* (surrealistic opera; 100 minutes; libretto by
        Kathy Acker, about many times and places; conceived by Kathy
        Acker and Richard Foreman). Performed Rotterdam, Netherlands,
        April 1984, and Brooklyn, NY, 3 December 1985.
1986   *The Immigrant Road* ("electronic opera for stage and television").
        NEA grant, 1985-86.

Gordon, Philip (b. Newark, NJ, 14 December 1894; d. 11 October 1983; ASCAP/AMC; Anderson)
1966　*A Tale from Chaucer* (1 act). Performed Trenton, NJ, May 1966.
-　*The Shoe of Little Noby* (1 hour).

Gordon-Borg, Richard
1988　*Jane Heir* (2 acts; parody opera; libretto by Janet Norquist and Peter Healey after Brontë). Performed by Mesopotamian Opera, Brooklyn, NY, 10 May 1988.

Gorelli, Olga (b. Bologna, Italy, 14 June 1920; U.S. citizen, 1945; Anderson; Cohen)
1972　*Between the Shadow and the Dream.* Performed Princeton, NJ, 28 May 1972.
-　*Dona Petra.*

Gosnell, Kirby
1985　*Rulers* (35 minutes; libretto by composer).
1987　*Twelve United* (1 hour; libretto by composer on the life of Jesus through the eyes of the disciples). Performance projected.
-　*Dona Petra.*

Gotanda, Kan
1985　*Dream of Kitamura* ("theater piece with music, dance, and puppets"; libretto by composer). Performed by Theater of the Open Eye, New York, March 1985.

Gottlieb, Jack S. (or Jacob; b. New Rochelle, NY, 12 October 1930; AMC; *Amerigrove*)
1955　*Tea Party, or Sonata Allegro* (1 act, 40 minutes; libretto by Horace Everett). Performed Urbana, IL, 9 March 1958, and at Donnell Library, New York, 18 April 1964. Published by Boosey & Hawkes. (*Amerigrove*: librettist is E. Johns.)
1964　*Public Dance* (1 act; libretto by E. Johns). Withdrawn.
1976　*The Song of Songs Which Is Solomon's* (90 minutes; an "operatorio"). NEA grant, 1976.
1985　*The Movie Opera (Prevue)* (1 act; libretto by composer, about a torch singer). Performed by Golden Fleece, New York, 19 June 1986.
1988　*Death of a Ghost* (libretto by composer after Wilde's "The Canterville Ghost"). Performed by Golden Fleece, New York, 13 December 1988.

Gottschalk, Louis-Moreau (b. New Orleans, 8 May 1829; d. Tijuca, Brazil, 18 December 1869; *Amerigrove*)
1856　untitled, lost.
1859　*Isaura di Salerno* (3 acts), lost.
1860　*Charles IX*, fragment.
1860　*Amalia Warden* (3 acts; libretto by A. Lorenzana). Lost except act 1.
1860　*Escenas campestres* (1 act; libretto by M. Ramirez; set in Cuba). Performed Havana, Cuba in the Teatro di Tacón, 17 February 1860 and New York, 1969.

Gottschalk, Max
        (Krohn lists "an opera" by him.)

Gould, Elizabeth Davies (b. Toledo, OH, 8 May 1904; AMC; Anderson; Cohen; *Who's Who*)
  1966   *Ray and the Gospel Singers* (comic chamber opera; 1 hour; libretto by Eugene J. Hochman).

Graf, R.
  1976   *The State of Very Good U.S.* Performed Fredonia, NY, 24 April 1976.

Graham, Jack (Harry Jerome; b. Mishawaka, IN, 14 September 1896; Hipsher)
  1926   *Lord Byron* (light lyric drama; libretto by Norbert Engels and James Lewis Cassaday). Performed at University Theater, South Bend, IN, 17 December 1926.
  -     *Aranea.* Hipsher, 1934: "near completion."

Graham, Shirley Lola (Mrs. W. E. B. Dubois; b. Indianapolis, 11 November 1906; d. Peking, China, 27 March 1977; Cohen; Southern)
  1932   *Tom-Tom* (3 acts; libretto by composer). For 500 singers, dancers, orchestra. Performed Cleveland, 30 June 1932. Excerpts broadcast on NBC, Cleveland, 26 June 1932; also on NBC, New York. Hipsher: première at Cleveland Stadium, 3 July 1933.
  1937   *Little Black Sambo* (children's opera; libretto based on the story by Helen Bannerman).
  1938   *The Swing Mikado* (based on Gilbert & Sullivan).

Grandison, Hamilton
  1977   *Godsong*, with Tad Truesdale (2 acts; libretto by Truesdale after James Weldon Johnson's poem "God's Trombones"). Performed by LaMama, New York, 1977.
  1980   *Daddy, Daddy*, with Gerald Cook and Tad Truesdale (2 acts; blues drama). Performed by LaMama, New York, 3 December 1980.

Granger, Milton Lewis (b. Kansas City, MO, 17 November 1947; *WhoAm*)
  1977   *Troy, N.Y., 1869.* Performed at Hollins College, VA, 21 November 1977.
  1986   *The Great Man's Widow* (32 minutes; libretto by composer). Performed at Hollins College, VA, November 1986.
  1986   *Sparkplugs* (34 minutes; libretto by composer). National Opera Association award, 1986. Performed at National Opera Association Convention, Los Angeles, 1986, and Hollins College, VA, 2 November 1986.
  1987   *The Queen Bee.* Performed at Hollins College, VA, November 1987.
  1988   *The Proposal.* National Opera Association Competition winner, 1988. Performed Roanoke, VA, 1 November 1988.
  1988   *O. Henry's Christmas Carol* (Christmas opera, after stories by O. Henry). Performed Roanoke, VA, 9 December 1988.

Granovetter, Matthew
  -     *The Princess and the Pauper* (1 act; libretto by composer and Patricia Sternberg after Twain).

–   *The Treasure Makers* (1 act; libretto by composer and Patricia Sternberg, about recycling).

Grant, Bruce
1973   *The Women of Troy*. Performed Bloomington, IN, 17 April 1973.

Grant, Mark
1988   *Chautauqua* (libretto by composer, about a child prodigy). Performed at Fashion Institute of Technology, New York, 13 February 1988.

Grant, Micki (Minnie Perkins McCutcheon; b. Chicago, 30 June 1941; Southern)
1977   *The Ups and Downs of Theophilus Mailand* (libretto by Vinnette Carroll). Performed Dallas, TX, September 1985.

Grant, W. Parks (b. Cleveland, OH, 4 January 1910; ACA; Anderson)
1973   *The Ballet-Master's Dream*.

Grantham, Donald (b. Duncan, OK, 9 November 1947; ASCAP; Anderson; *Baker's*)
1984   *From the Diaries of Adam and Eve*. Performed by After Dinner Opera Company, New York, 22 October 1984.
1989   *The Boor* (1 hour; comic opera after Chekhov's *The Bear*). Performed Austin, TX, 23 February 1989.

Grant-Schaefer, George Alfred (b. Williamstown, Ontario, 4 July 1872; d. Chicago, 11 May 1939; to U.S. in 1896; Anderson)
(*Baker's*, 5th ed.: he "composed operettas for schools.")

Graves, William Lester (b. Terry, MS, 26 August 1915; ASCAP; Anderson; *Who's Who*)
1959   *The Juggler* (1 act; libretto by Jean Anne Lustberg). Performed Washington, DC. Televised on WNBC-TV.

Gray, Rex
1989   *Headlights*, with Frank Fong, Rick Hiatt, Lori Loree, Mark Nelson, and Luigi Waites. Performed Omaha, NE, 28 April 1989.

Greco, José-Luis
1981   *Aria da capo* (1 act; libretto after Millay). Performed by Encompass, the Music Theatre, New York, June 1981.

Greenberg, Lionel
1976   *Masada*. Performed by Camarata of Los Angeles, March 1976.

Greenwood, John
1986   *Swan Song*, with Jonathan Levi (2 acts; libretto by composers; a spoof of detective novels, after Crispin; contains music by Rossini). Performed at Masur Theater, New York, November 1986.

Gregory, David
 1988 *Wolf* (monodrama; 1 act; libretto by Nicholas Delbanco). Performed Ann Arbor, MI, March 1988.

Griffes, Charles Tomlinson (b. Elmira, NY, 17 September 1884; d. New York, 8 April 1920; *Amerigrove*)
 1917 *Shojo* ("Japanese pantomime drama").

Griffis, Elliot (b. Boston, 28 January 1893; d. Los Angeles, 8 June 1967; ASCAP; *Amerigrove*)
 1934 *The Blue Scrab* (operetta)
 1963 *Port of Pleasure* (1 act). Performed at Immaculate Heart College, Los Angeles, 29 June 1963.

Griffith, Bobby
 1987 *The Nightingale* (1 act). Performed Denton, TX, 25 April 1987.

Griggs, Alice Maynard
 - *A Swift Engagement.*

Grigsby, Beverly Pinsky (b. Chicago, 11 January 1928; Anderson; Cohen; *WhoAm*)
 1977 *Moses.* NEA grant, 1977.
 1982 *Augustine, the Saint.* Performed at California State University at Northridge, Los Angeles, 3 April 1982.
 1983 *The Mask of Eleanor* (monodrama with electronic tape; 1 act; on the life of Eleanor of Aquitaine). Performed at California State University at Northridge, Los Angeles, 8 October 1987.

Gross, Nathan
 1985 *Pearls* (libretto by composer after Gordin's *Mirele Efros*, a Yiddish play; in English). Performed by Jewish Repertory Theater, New York, July 1985.

Gross, Robert Arthur (b. Colorado Springs, CO, 23 March 1914; d. Los Angeles, 6 November 1983; ASCAP; *Amerigrove*; Schoep)
 1962 *The Bald Soprano* (chamber opera; 1 act—85 minutes; libretto by composer and Donald Allen after Ionesco). Performed at Occidental College, Los Angeles, 13 May 1962.
 1967? *Project 1521* (science fiction satire; 3 acts—130 minutes; libretto by composer). Performed at Occidental College, Los Angeles, 1-3 November 1974. Kornick.

Grossmith, Leslie (b. Birmingham, England, 19 May 1870; Hipsher)
 1928 *Uncle Tom's Cabin* (3 acts; libretto by composer after Harriet Beecher Stowe). Bispham Medal, 1932.

Groth, Howard
 1954 *Petruchio.* Performed Conway, AR, 19 March 1954.

Grove, Isaac Van. *See* Van Grove, Isaac

Grubb-Farner. *See* Farner, Eugene Adrian

Grundahl, Nancy

1986   *'Twas the Night Before Christmas, or The Night Big Daddy Dropped In* (libretto by Dana Blanck; for children). Published by Curtis Music.

Gruenberg, Louis (b. Brest-Litovsk, Belorussia, 3 August 1884; d. Beverly Hills, CA, 10 June 1964; in U.S. from 1886; ASCAP; *Amerigrove*; Hipsher)

1910   *Signor Formica* (operetta; libretto by composer after E. T. A. Hoffmann).

1912   *The Witch of Brockten* (*Die Hesa*) (fairy operetta; 1 act; libretto by E. F. Malkowski, translated by L. Vandevere). Published by Birchard.

1913   *Piccadillymädel* (operetta).

1913   *The Bride of the Gods*, op. 2 (1 hour; libretto by Feruccio Busoni, translated by C. H. Meltzer).

1919   *Roly-Boly Eyes* (musical; libretto by E. A. Woolf), in collaboration with E. Brown.

1923   *The Dumb Wife*, op. 12 (chamber opera; libretto by composer from Anatole France's novel *Celui qui épousa une femme muette*, after Rabelais). Hipsher: "finished at the MacDowell Colony in 1919 and is said to be witty and effective; but, by a legal technicality, it may not be performed till thirty years after the death of the novelist" (d. 1924).

1920s   *Hallo! Tommy!* (operetta; libretto by L. Herzer). Written under pseudonym George Edwards.

c 1927   *Lady X* (operetta; libretto by L. Herzer). Published under pseudonym George Edwards.

1931   *Jack and the Beanstalk*, op. 35 (3 acts; 90 minutes; libretto by John Erskine). Première at Juilliard School, New York, 19 November 1931, and at the 44th Street Theatre, New York, 1932.

1931   *The Emperor Jones*, op. 36 (prologue and 2 acts, with interlude; libretto by composer and K. de Jaffa after Eugene O'Neill). Première by Metropolitan Opera, New York, 7 January 1933 (14th American work to have its première by the Met); and Berlin, Germany, 1935 (as *Kaiser Jones*). Bispham Medal. Published by Juilliard.

1936   *Queen Helena*.

1937   *Green Mansions*, op. 39 (radio opera; 1 act; libretto after W. H. Hudson). Performed on CBS radio, 17 September 1935 and 17 October 1937.

1938   *Helena's Husband*, op. 38 (libretto by P. Moeller).

1945   *Volpone*, op. 57 (1 act; libretto by composer after Ben Jonson).

-    *One Night of Cleopatra*, op. 64 (libretto by composer after T. Gautier).

1954   *The Miracle of Flanders*, op. 65, for narrator, actors, orchestra (legend with music, after Balzac).

1955   *The Delicate King*, op. 67 (libretto by composer after Dumas).

1955   *Antony and Cleopatra*, op. 68 (libretto by composer after Shakespeare). Revised in 1958 and 1961.

-    *"MS."*

Gruendler, Hermann Frederick (b. New York, March 1850; Hipsher)
    1908   *La Carouche: or, King of the Barefoots* (romantic opera; 3 acts).

Grunn, John Homer (b. West Salem, MA, 5 May 1880; d. Los Angeles, 6 June 1944; Anderson; *Baker's*)
    1936   *Barbecue Isle.* Performed Los Angeles, 1936.
    -    *The Golden Pheasant* (operetta).
    -    *In a Woman's Reign.*
    -    *The Isle of Cuckoos.*
    -    *The Mars Diamond* (operetta).

Gualillo, Nicholas
    1976   *The Phantom Princess* (three 1-act operas; libretto by composer after Basisle and Perrault). Performed Syracuse, NY, and New York, 1976.

Guerrieri, Stefano
    1917   *Evandro.* Performed New York, in Italian.

Guilmartin, Ken (ASCAP)
    1982   *The Marriage of Heaven and Hell* (1 act; libretto by Alan Brody after William Blake). Performed by Magic Circle, New York, 27 April 1982.
    1985   *City of Gypsies* (1 act; libretto after Federico García Lorca). Performed by Magic Circle, New York, 8 June 1985.

Guiraud, Ernest (b. New Orleans, 23 June 1837; d. Paris, France, 6 May 1892; *Baker's*)
    1852   *Le Roi David.* Performed in New Orleans, when the composer was 15.
    (Guiraud composed six more operas in Paris, where he lived from 1863; he also composed the recitatives for Bizet's *Carmen.*)

Gunn, Lily
    -    *David and Saul* (on the Old Testament).

Gury, L.
    1962   *Hither and Thither of Danny Dither* (1 act). Performed Cleveland, April 1962.

Gustafson, Dwight Leonard (b. Seattle, WA, 20 April 1930; Anderson; *Who's Who*)
    1954   *The Jailer* (1 act). Performed at Bob Jones University, Greenville, SC, 27 May 1954.
    1960   *The Hunted* (1 act). Performed Greenville, SC, 26 May 1960.

Guthrie, James Martin (b. Portsmouth, MA [NH?], 24 October 1953; *Who's Who*)
    1990   *The Song of Glory* (1 act). Performed Baton Rouge, LA, 4 March 1990.

Gutiérrez y Espinosa, Felipe (b. San Juan, Puerto Rico, 26 May 1825; d. there, 27 November 1899; *Amerigrove*; Southern)

1856   *La palma del Cacique.*

1877   *Macías* (3 acts; libretto by Antonio Tapia y Rivera after M. J. de Larra). DeLerma, 1984: "recently successfully revived."

\-   *El amor de un pescador* (zarzuela), lost.

\-   *El bearnés* (4 acts; libretto by D. Antonio Biaggi), lost.

\-   *Guarionex* (3 acts; libretto by Antonio Tapia y Rivera), lost.

Gwiazda, Henry

1983   *House of Cards* (1 act; libretto by Elizabeth Haley). Performed Moorhead, MN, 12 May 1983.

Gyring, Elizabeth (b. Vienna, Austria, 1906; d. in U.S. 1970; to New York 1939; ACA; Cohen)

\-   *Night at Sea and Day in Court* (2 acts; libretto by composer). *COS-1.*

Haber, John

1987   *Alias Jimmy Valentine* (libretto by Hal Hackady after O. Henry). Performed by Music Theatre Works, New York, 12 October 1987 and 25 February 1988.

Hackett, Charles F. (Hocket in *COS*-1)

1973   *Don Rosita* (3 acts; libretto by composer and William Oliver after Federico García Lorca's *Lostiteres de Catchiporra*). Performed Ithaca, NY, 6 April.

Hadley, Henry Kimball (b. Somerville, MA, 20 December 1871; d. New York, 6 September 1937; *Amerigrove*; Hipsher)

1897   *Happy Jack* (operetta; libretto by S. F. Batchelder).

1903   *Nancy Brown* (comic opera; libretto by F. Ranken). Performed New York, 1903.

1909   *Safié* (1 act; libretto by Edward Oxenford). Performed at Stadt-Theater, Mainz, Germany, 4 April 1909, where the composer was one of the staff conductors.

1912   *The Atonement of Pan* (masque). Performed for the Bohemian Club of San Francisco, 10 August 1912.

1914   *Azora, the Daughter of Montezuma* ("legendary opera"; 3 acts; libretto by D. Stevens). Première by the Chicago Opera Association at the Auditorium, Chicago, 26 December 1917, then the Chicago company performed the work at the Metropolitan Opera, New York. Bispham Medal, 1925. Published by G. Schirmer, 1917. At AMRC. Hipsher, 429.

1916?   *The Fire Prince* (operetta; libretto by D. Stevens). Published by Ditson, 1917. Performed Schenectady, NY, 1924. At AMRC.

1917   *Bianca* (1 act; libretto by G. Stewart after Goldoni). Performed New York, 18 October 1918. Hinshaw Prize, 1917. Published by H. Flammer.

1918   *Cleopatra's Night* ("romantic opera"; 2 acts, 90 minutes; libretto by Alice Leal Pollock after Théophile Gautier's *Une Nuit de Cléopatre*). Première by Metropolitan Opera, New York, 31 January 1920; also performed there, 20 January 1931. Published by Ditson, 1920.

1923   *Semper virens* (music-drama; libretto by J. Redding). Performed Sonoma County, California, 1923.

1924   *A Night in Old Paris* (libretto by F. Truesdell after G. McDonough). Performed New York, 1924 and 22 February 1933, on NBC radio.

1933   *Legend of Hani.*

-   *La locardiera* (*The Innkeeper*).

Hageman, Richard (b. Leeuwarden, Netherlands, 9 July 1882; d. Beverly Hills, CA, 6 March 1966; in U.S. from 1906; ASCAP; *Amerigrove*; Hipsher)

1932   *Caponsacchi* (prologue, 3 acts, and epilogue; libretto by Arthur Goodrich after Robert Browning's *The Ring and the Book*). Première at Stadttheater, Freiburg, Germany (as *Tragödie in Arezzo*), 18 February 1932; also performed Münster, Germany, 4 March 1932; Vienna, Austria, 1935; and by Metropolitan Opera New York, 4 February 1937. Bispham Medal. Published by Peters.

1943   *The Crucible.*

Hagemann, Philip Henry (b. Mt. Vernon, IN, 21 December 1932; *Who's Who*) (Hagemann writes his own librettos.)

1980   *The Aspern Papers* (2 acts—90 minutes; after Henry James). Performed Bloomington, IN, 4 December 1980, and at Northwestern University, Evanston, IL, 19 November 1988. Kornick.

1984   *The Music Cure* (1 act; after Shaw; uses music by other composers, including Chopin). Performed Bloomington, IN, and New Harmony, IN, August 1984.

1987   *The King Who Saved Himself from Being Saved* (20 minutes). Performed Chico, CA, 4 April 1987.

1987   *The Six of Calais* (45 minutes; after Shaw). Performed New Harmony, IN, April 1987.

1989   *Roman Fever* (1 act). Performed Santa Fe, NM, 25 November 1989.

-   *Passion, Poison and Petrifaction.*

Hagemann, Virginia (Cohen)

1976   *The Pied Piper* (1 act; libretto by composer).

-   *The Bird's Christmas Carol* (libretto by Eleanor Jones). Published by Theodore Presser, 1957.

-   *A Christmas Carol* (libretto by Eleanor Jones).

Hagen, Daron Aric (b. Milwaukee, WI, 4 November 1961; *WhoAm*)
   1985   *The Sandbox* (1 act; libretto by composer after Albee). Commission
      by Texas Opera Theatre One Aria Opera Project, 1984.
      Performed Houston, TX, 6 June 1985.

Hagen, Ernest
   1978   *Beret and Per Hansa* ("folk opera" after *Giants in the Earth*).
      Performed Little Rock, AR, 8 April 1978.

Hagen, Peter Albrecht van, Sr. (b. Netherlands, 1755; d. Boston, 20 August 1813;
      to U.S. in 1774; *Amerigrove*; Porter; Sonneck-Upton)
   1796   *The Adopted Child: or, The Baron of Milford Castle* ("musical
      drama"; 2 acts; libretto by Samuel Birch). Originally composed by
      Thomas Atwood in 1795, this version is with "the music entirely
      new and composed" by Peter van Hagen (Sonneck-Upton, 6).

Hager, George
   1922   *Pan* (1 act). Performed Seattle, 1922.

Haile, Eugen (b. Ulm, Germany, 21 February 1873; d. Woodstock, NY, 14
      August 1933; in U.S. from 1903; Anderson; *Baker's*; Hipsher, 429)
   1916   *The Happy Ending* (melodrama). Performed New York, 21 August
      1916. *Baker's*: "an interesting attempt to combine spoken words in
      the play with pitch inflections in the vocal parts, in the manner of
      Sprechstimme."
   1933   *Harold's Dream* (written to a German libretto, then translated to
      English). Private performance, Woodstock, NY, 30 June 1933.

Haines, Margaret E.
   -   *Revelation of Jesus Christ* (90 minutes; after the Book of
      Revelation).

Hall, Philip
   1984   *Sleeping Beauty* (2 acts; libretto by Brandon Garside and Robert
      Johanson; uses music by Tchaikovsky). Performed by Muni
      Opera, St. Louis, 13 August 1984.

Hall, William John (1867-1931)
   1904   *Louisiana*. Commissioned for and given over 500 performances at
      the St. Louis Exposition.
   -   *The Apple Blossoms*.
   -   *Creole Belle*.
   -   *Tactics*.

Halpern, Jeff
   1987   *Cinderella/Cendrillon*, or *Cinderella in a Mirror: Small Town/Big
      Dreams* (9 scenes; libretto by Eve Ensler; arrangement of
      Massenet's *Cendrillon* with new libretto; conceived by Halpern and
      Anne Bogart). Performed by Music-Theater Group, New York,
      12 January 1988. (An earlier version had been performed
      Stockbridge, MA, 6 August 1987.)

Halpern, Sidney (AMC)
 1965 *Macbeth* (1 act). Performed by Off-Broadway Opera, New York, 4
  April 1965.
 1965 *The Monkey's Paw* (1 act). Performed by Off-Broadway Opera,
  New York, 4 April 1965.

Halsey, Onaje
 1989 *No Laughing Matter* (libretto by Harvey S. Henderson). Performed
  by Mind Builders Creative Arts, Bronx, NY, February 1989.

Halstenson, Michael
 1981 *Red Riding Hood and the Wolf* (15 minutes; libretto by composer).
  Performed at University of Minnesota, Minneapolis, 8 June 1981.

Hamilton, Kelly
 1979 *Saga* (American folk opera). Performed by Lyric Theater of New
  York, 20 April 1979.

Hamilton, Marcia (Cohen)
 1957 *To Please Mr. Plumbjoy* ("A Christmas Eve with Music"; libretto
  by composer). Performed Pittsburgh, PA, 1957-58 season.

Hamm, Charles Edward (b. Charlottesville, VA, 21 April 1925; *Amerigrove*)
 1952 *The Monkey's Paw* (20 minutes). Performed Cincinnati, 2 May
  1952.
 1953 *The Cask of Amontillado* (1 act; libretto after Poe). Performed
  Cincinnati, 1 March 1953.
 1953 *The Secret Life of Walter Mitty* (1 act). Performed Athens, OH, 30
  July 1953.
 1954 *A Scent of Sarsaparillo* (1 act). Performed San Francisco, 5
  September 1954.
 1955 *The Salesgirl* (1 act). Performed Bristol, VA, 1 March 1955.
 1961 *The Box* (1 act). Performed New Orleans, 4 February 1961.

Hammill, Roseanne
 - *The Blessed Event* (20 minutes).

Hammond, Terrence
 1972 *The Friend* (2 acts). Performed by Interstate Opera, Lincoln
  Center, New York, 16 September 1972.

Hannan, Joseph
 1987 *Speer: A 20th Century Faust Story*. NEA grant, 1985-86.
  Performed at Kitchen Center of Video and Music, New York, 2
  February 1987.

Hannay, Roger Durham (b. Plattsburgh, NY, 22 September 1930; ASCAP;
   Amerigrove; *Who's Who*)
 1960 *Two Tickets to Omaha, or The Swindlers* (chamber opera; 1 act;
  libretto by Jerome Lamb). May be the same as:
 1960 *Two Tickets to Omaha (Perfidy Compounded)* (1 act; libretto by
  Jerome Lamb). Performed Moorehead, MN.

1964   *The Fortune of St. Macabre* (1 act). Performed Moorehead, MN, 21 March 1964.

1982   *The Journey of Edith Wharton* (2 acts; libretto after Russell Graves), for 5 voices and chamber orchestra. Performed Chapel Hill, NC, 30 March 1988.

Hannistan, Raymond
-    *Lurking on the Railroad* (2 acts; libretto by Lee Stametz and Dutton Foster). *COS*-4.

Hanson, Daryl L. (b. Belmond, IA, 17 February 1924; AMC; Anderson)
1958   *The Promise* (1 act).

1968   *Wish I Had a Nickel* (musical).

1976   *Christopher Columbus* (children's opera; libretto by Bert Stimmel). Performed Carbondale, IL, 1 May 1976.

1977   *The Happy Prince* (libretto by Bert Stimmel after Wilde).

-    *Talent, Like Murder, Will Out* (opera buffa).

-    *Toys* (2 acts; libretto by Bert Stimmel after his story "The Loves of George Sand"). *COS*-4.

-    *The Waterbabies* (musical).

Hanson, Howard Harold (b. Wahoo, NE, 28 October 1896; d. Rochester, NY, 26 February 1981; ASCAP; *Amerigrove*; Hipsher)
1933   *Merry Mount* ("dramatic opera in 3 acts"; libretto by Richard L. Stokes after Hawthorne's *Maypole Lovers of Merry Mount*). Commission by Metropolitan Opera, New York. Concert performance, Ann Arbor, MI, 20 May 1933; stage première by Metropolitan Opera, 10 February 1934 (the 15th première by the Met for an American opera). Bispham Medal.

Hanson, William Frederick (b. Vernal, UT, 23 October 1887; Hipsher)
1913   *The Sun Dance* (5 acts; libretto by composer, about the Sioux nation). Première by music department of Uintah Academy at Orpheus Hall, Vernal, UT, 20 February 1913.

1928   *Täm-Män'-Näcup'* (3 acts; about Uintah Indian life). Performed Provo, UT, 3 May 1928; and by Los Angeles Philharmonic Orchestra at University of Utah, Salt Lake City, 22 May 1929.

1937   *The Bleeding Heart of Timpanogas* (3 acts). Performed Provo, UT.

Harbach, Barbara (b. Lock Haven, PA, 14 February 1946; *Who's Who*)
(All librettos by Jonathan Yordi; all performances in Buffalo, NY.)

1987   *The Littlest Angel* (1 act).

1988   *Daniel and the Beastly Night* (1 act).

1989   *A Page from the Christmas Story* (1 act).

1990   *The Loneliest Angel* (1 act). Performed 23 December 1990.

Harbison, John (b. Orange, NJ, 20 December 1938; *Amerigrove*; *Baker's*; *Who's Who*)
1974   *The Winter's Tale* (tragedy; 2 acts—75 minutes; libretto by composer after the play by Shakespeare). NEA grant. Performed by San Francisco Opera, 20 August 1979. Kornick.

1977   *A Full Moon in March* (tragedy; 1 act—45 minutes; libretto by composer after the play by W. B. Yeats). Performed by Boston

Musica Viva, Cambridge, MA, 30 April 1979 (*Amerigrove* says New York on this date), and by American Chamber Opera, New York, 1987. Recording: Composers Recordings Inc., SD 454. Kornick.

Harder, Eleanor and **Ray**
- *Annabelle Broom, the Unhappy Witch. COS*-4.

Hardin, Louis T. ("Moondog") (b. Marysville, KS, 26 May 1916; Anderson)
- *Die Erschaffung der Weld*.

Harling, W(illiam) Franke (b. London, England, 18 [Hipsher: 17] January 1887; d. Sierra Madre, CA, 22 November 1958; to U.S. in 1888; ASCAP; Anderson; Hipsher)
1908   *Alda* (1 act). Performed Boston, 1908.
1925   *A Light from St. Agnes* (1 act; after the play with same name by Minnie Maddern Fiske; about Louisiana; includes some jazz). Première at the Auditorium, Chicago, 26 December 1925, starring Rosa Raisa; and at Théâtre Champs ÉlysÉes, Paris, France, June-July 1929; revived in 1940. Bispham Medal, 1925. Published by Huntzinger, 1925.
1926   *Deep River* ("a native opera with jazz"; about New Orleans in 1830). Première, Lancaster, PA, 18 September 1926; then at Shubert Theater, Philadelphia, 21 September 1926; and a 2-week season in New York, beginning 4 October 1926.
-    *The Sunken Bell* (1 act; to poem by Gerhart Hauptmann). World War I prevented its appearance.

Harlow, Larry
1973   *Hommy* ("Latin rock opera based on the rock opera *Tommy*"). Performed Carnegie Hall, New York, 30 March 1973.

Harman, Carter (b. Brooklyn, NY, 14 June 1918; *Amerigrove*; *Who's Who*)
1951   *Circus at the Opera* (children's opera; libretto by D. Molarsky).

Harmonic, Phil (b. Newton, MA, 10 June 1949; Anderson)
-    *Duke of Windsor* (mixed media opera for solo performer).

Harnick, Sheldon Mayer (b. Chicago, 30 April 1924; *Amerigrove*)
1989   *Dragons*. Performed Ann Arbor, MI, April 1989.
-    *Frustration* (1 act; a spoof of Debussy's *Pelleas*), for two women and piano trio. Published by Presser.

Harper, William
1987   *Snow Leopard* (90 minutes; libretto by composer and Roger Nieboer after Peter Matthieson and the Tibetan *Book of the Dead*). OPERA America grant. Performed St. Paul, MN (as *Tantracidal Mania*), 11 April 1987, and 24 October 1987; by Organic Theater, Chicago, May and June 1988; and, the official première, St. Paul, 9 November 1989. Kornick.

Harris, Donald (b. St. Paul, MN, 7 April 1931; *WhoAm*; *Who's Who*)
-     *Little Mermaid.*

Harris, Matthew (b. North Tarrytown, NY, 18 February 1956; *Who's Who*)
1985   *As You Choose* (monodrama; 32 minutes; libretto after Baudelaire, translation by Michael Hamburger). Commission by NEA, 1986. Performed Long Beach, CA, June 1985; by League-ISCM, New York, April 1987; and Minneapolis, 7 January 1988.

Harris, Russell G. (b. Graymont, IL, 3 August 1914; ACA; Anderson)
1943   *The Only Jealousy of Emer* (after Yeats).

Harris, Theodore (ASCAP)
1964   *The First President* (1 act; libretto after William Carlos Williams). Performed Rutherford, NJ, 1964.

Harrison, Lanny
1986   *Acts from Under and Above*, with Meredith Monk (90 minutes; uses ragtime by contemporaries). Performed by La Mama, New York, 3 April 1986.

Harrison, Lou (b. Portland, OR, 14 May 1917; BMI; Anderson; *Amerigrove*; *Who's Who*)
1954   *Rapunzel* (40 minutes; libretto by W. Morris). Performed in Rome 1954, and New York, 14 May 1954 (Anderson: 14 May 1959). Published by Southern Music.
1963   *Jephtha's Daughter* ("theatre kit"). Performed at Cabrillo College, 9 March 1963; Seattle, WA, 21 November 1980.
1971   *Young Caesar* (puppet opera; libretto by R. Gordon). Performed Aptos, CA, 21 August 1971.
-     *The Marriage of the Eiffel Tower.*
-     *The Only Jealousy of Elmer* (1 act; libretto after Yeats).

Hart, Frederic Patton (b. Aberdeen, WA, 5 September 1894; ACA; Anderson)
1934   *The Wheel of Fortune* (150 minutes). (*Baker's* date: 1943.)
1937   *The Romance of Robot* ("ballet-opera"; 1 act). Performed by Federal Theatre, New York, 12 April 1937.
1984   *Poison* (45 minutes) and *The Farewell Supper* (30 minutes; two chamber operas; librettos by Francis Barnard after Schnitzler's *Anatole*). Performed Brooklyn, NY, 3 February 1984 (*Baker's*, 8th ed.: posthumous).
-     *Fantastic Opera.*

Hartig, Hugo
-     *A Cask of Amontillado* (1 act; libretto after Poe). *COS*-3.

Hartway, James John (b. Detroit, MI, 24 April 1944; Anderson)
1987   *Ke-Nu and the Magic Coals* (children's opera on a Native American legend; libretto by Anca Vlasopolis and Anthony Ambrogio). Performed Detroit, MI, 27 September 1987 and February 1988.

Harwill, S. H. (from Chicago; Hipsher)
-     *Bella Donna.* Bispham Medal, 1926.

Haskins, Robert James (b. Denver, CO, 27 December 1937; Anderson)
1960   *Benjamin.*
1961   *Mr. Godfry.*
1963   *Cassandra Southwick* (1 act; libretto by John Koppenhaver after Whittier, about Quakers and Puritans). Performed Springfield, OH, 24 January 1964.
1964   *The Prisoners* (libretto by John Koppenhaver).
1968   *The Cask of Amontillado* (libretto by John Koppenhaver after Poe).
1971   *Young Goodman Brown* (libretto by John Koppenhaver).
1976   *The Bell Tower* (1 act; libretto after Melville). NEA grant, 1974.
1976   *Legend of Sleepy Hollow* (1 act; libretto after Washington Irving). NEA grant, 1974.
1976   *The Mask of the Red Death* (1 act; libretto after Edgar Allan Poe). NEA grant, 1974.
1976   *Transparent Morning* (libretto by John Koppenhaver).

Haslam, Herbert (b. Philadelphia, 23 April 1938; ASCAP; Anderson)
1960   *Postlogue* (1 act; libretto by M. Heiner). Performed Piermont, NY, August 1960.
1969   *Carnival of Eden.* Commission by and performed at University of Delhi, India, February 1969.

Hassell, Jon (b. Memphis, TN, 22 March 1937; *Amerigrove*)
1985   *The Shadow Play* (on the Indonesian tradition). NEA grant. Performed by Performing Artservices, New York, 16 October 1985.

Haubiel, Charles (b. Delta, OH, 30 January 1892; d. Los Angeles, 26 August 1978; *Amerigrove*; *Baker's*)
1929   *Brigands Preferred* (comic opera; libretto by M. Leonard). (*COS* has title as *Brigands Referred.*)
1940   *The Witch's Curse* (fairy tale opera).
1942?   *The Birthday Cake* (operetta; libretto by H. Flexner).
1947   *Sunday Costs Five Pesos* (Mexican folk opera; 1 act; libretto by Josephine Niggli after a Mexican folk story). Performed Charlotte, NC, 6 November 1950. Published by Composers Press (Southern Music).
1955?   *The Enchanted Princess.*
1971?   *Adventure on Sunbonnet Hill* (children's operetta; libretto by K. H. Bratton).
-     *Berta* (Mexican folk opera).

Haufrecht, Herbert (b. New York, 1909; ACA/AMC; Anderson)
1951   *Boney Quillen* ("pantomime opera" in 1 act). Performed Chichester, NY, 18 August 1951. Published by Broude Brothers, 1953.
1963   *A Pot of Broth* (on Yeats). Performed by After Dinner Opera, New York, 1964; broadcast on WNYC radio.
1964   *The Story of Ferdinand* (1 act). Performed Rochester, NY.
-     *We've Come from the City* (25 minutes).

Hawkins, Micah (b. Head of the Harbor, near Stony Brook, NY, 1 January 1777; d. New York, 29 July 1825; *Amerigrove*)

1824   *The Saw Mill, or a Yankee Trick* (2 acts). Performed at Chatham Garden, New York, 1824-25. (*Amerigrove*: "the first such work by a native American on an American theme.")

Hayes, Hiram

Louisiana. Performed at St. Louis Exposition, 1904? —Krohn.

Hayes, Kevin

1990?   *Larry and the Gypsy.* "New"—*COS Bulletin*, spring 1990.

Hayes, Terry

    (All works still in progress—*COS*-4.)
- *Christ in Egypt* (15 minutes; libretto by composer).
- *Hitler.*
- *A Midsummer Night's Dream* (after Shakespeare).
- *Paul Robeson: Here I Stand* (2 acts).
- *Yes, I AM a Suffragette* (libretto by Hazelita Fauntroy).

Hayman, Richard Perry (b. Sandia, NM, 29 July 1951; Anderson; *WhoAm*)

1986   *Fire Works*, with Ned Sublette (90 minutes; libretto by Valeria Vasilevski and Ruth Maleczech; a country and western Chinese opera). Performed Waterford, CT, 1986; and by Theatre for the New City, New York, September 1988.

Hays, Henry Bryan (AMC)

1973   *The Sauna* (50 minutes; libretto by composer).
1976   *The Little Match Girl* (after Hans Christian Andersen). Performed St. Joseph, MN, 24 January 1977.

Hays, Sorrel Doris (b. Memphis, TN, 6 August 1941; *Who's Who*)

1989   *The Glass Woman* (libretto by composer and Sally Ordway). Commission by Chattanooga Symphony and Opera Association. OPERA America grant. Performed by Encompass Theater workshop, New York, 1 August 1989.
- *Love in Space.* Performed on West Berlin Radio, Germany.
- *Touch of Touch* (video opera).

Head, Michael

1961   *Bachelor Mouse.* Performed Charleston, PA, April 1961. Published by Boosey & Hawkes.

Hecker, Zeke

1981   *Pericles, Prince of Tyre* (135 minutes; libretto by composer after Shakespeare). Performed Brattleboro, VT, 13 November 1981.

Heckscher, Céleste de Longpré (née Massey; b. Philadelphia, 23 February 1860; d. there, 18 February 1928; *Baker's*; Hipsher)

1918   *The Rose of Destiny* (prelude and 3 acts; libretto by composer). Performed at Metropolitan Opera House, Philadelphia, 2 May 1918, in aid of the Red Cross.
- *The Flight of Time.*

Heiden, Bernhard (b. Frankfurt am Main, Germany, 24 August 1910; in the U.S. from 1935; *Amerigrove*; *Who's Who*)
 1961   *The Darkened City* (3 acts; libretto by Robert Kelly). Performed Bloomington, IN, 23 February 1963. Published by Associated Music.

Heilveil, Elaine
 -   *My Sister Makes Me Sick*, with Robin Frederick (45 minutes).

Heink, Felix
 -   *Mirabeau.* In Krohn.

Heinrich, Anthony Philip (Anton Philipp; Antonín Filip) (b. Schönbüchel [now Krásný Buk], Bohemia, 11 March 1781; d. New York, 3 May 1861; in U.S. from 1810; *Amerigrove*)
 1821   *The Child of the Mountain: or, The Deserted Mother* (melodrama; 3 acts; libretto by Dr. H. McMurtrie). Première at Walnut Street Theatre, 10 February 1821; also performed March 7.
 -   *The Minstrel* (opera). Burned in a 1835 fire.

Helfman, Max (b. Radzin, Poland, 25 May 1901; d. Dallas, TX, 9 August 1963; in U.S. from 1909; Anderson; *Baker's*)
 1949   *New Hagadah* (dramatic cantata).

Heller, Alfred (b. New York, 8 December 1931; *Who's Who*)
 1969   *Sister Carrie.* Performed Bloomington, IN, 1969-70 season.

Hellermann, William David (b. Milwaukee, WI, 15 July 1939; ACA; *Amerigrove*; *Who's Who*)
 1972   *Parted . . .* ("for three actors and tape"). Performed 1973.
 1982   *Extraordinary Histories . . . and the Raven, of Course* (formerly *The Poe Project*; libretto by Harry Lewis, including extracts from Poe). Performed by Medicine Show, New York, 28 April 1982.
 1983   *Three Sisters Who Are Not Sisters* (after Gertrude Stein). Performed by Medicine Show, New York, 5 November 1983 and, in a revised version, 7 April 1988.
 1984   *Still Lives* (parody of minimalism). Performed by Medicine Show, New York, November 1984.

Hellum, Mark
 1985   *The Departure* (1 act; libretto by composer). Performed Houston, TX, 6 June 1985.

Helm, Everett Burton (b. Minneapolis, MN, 17 July 1913; *Amerigrove*; *Baker's*)
 1951   *Adam and Eve* (adaptation of a medieval mystery play). Performed Wiesbaden, Germany, 28 October 1951, the composer conducting.
 1956   *Die Belagerung von Tottenburg* (*The Siege of Tottenburg*) (radio opera; 3 acts). Performed on Radio Stuttgart, Germany.
 1956   *500 Dragon-Thalers* ("singspiel").

Hemphill, Julius
 1988   *Anchorman* ("blues operetta"; libretto by Paul Carter Harrison). Composed for the 20th anniversary of the Negro Ensemble

Company of New York. Performed by American Folk Theater, New York, 11 February 1988.

Henderson, Alan
-     *Truth of Truths* ("rock opera on stories from the Bible"; arrangements by Dick Hieronymus).

Henderson, Alva (b. San Luis Obispo, CA, 8 April 1940; Anderson; *Baker's*)
1972   *Medea* (3 acts; libretto by composer after Robinson Jeffers's adaptation of Euripides's play). Premièred by San Diego Opera, 29 November 1972. Kornick.
1976   *The Last of the Mohicans* (3 acts—180 minutes; libretto by Janet Lewis after James Fenimore Cooper). Commission and première by Wilmington Opera Society, DE, 12 June 1976; also performed at Lake George Opera Festival, NY, 1977. Kornick.
1979   *The Last Leaf* (libretto by composer after O. Henry). Performed San Jose, CA, 17 June 1979, and Lake George, NY, 8 August 1980.
1980?   *Mulberry Street* (45 minutes; libretto by Janet Lewis after O. Henry's "The Third Ingredient"). Performed San Jose, CA, ?1980. *COS*-4.
1988   *West of Washington Square* (libretto by composer and Janet Louis after O. Henry's short stories "The Last Leaf" and "Room Across the Hall"). Commission and première by Opera San Jose, CA, 26 November 1988. (*COS*-4 considers this opera to be the same as *The Last Leaf*.) Kornick.
-     *Achilles* ("opera based on *The Iliad*"). In progress, *COS*-4.
-     *The Tempest* (after Shakespeare). *Baker's*: his second opera.
-     *The Unforgiven* (after 1895 book by Alan LeMay, about Indians and settlers in Texas).

Hendricks, W. Newell
1986   *The Cell* (1 act; libretto by Karen S. Henry). Performed Boston by Theater Group, MA, 1986 (reading) and 3 June 1988.

Herbert, Victor August (b. Dublin, Ireland, 1 February 1859; d. New York, 26 May 1924; in U. S. from 1886; *Amerigrove*; Hipsher)
1897   *The Serenade* (3 acts; libretto by Harry B. Smith). Performed Cleveland, 17 February 1897.
1910   *Naughty Marietta* ("comic opera in two acts"; book and lyrics by Rida Johnson Young). First performances: Werting Opera House, Syracuse, NY, 24 October 1910; New York, 7 November 1910. Produced as an opera by Opera North, October 1989, New York Opera, 30 August 1989, and Gold Coast Opera, 25 March 1990. Piano-vocal score published New York: M. Witmark & Sons, 1910; reprinted in Schleifer, 6:329-521.
1911   *Natoma* ("romantic opera in 3 acts"). Première at Metropolitan Opera House, Philadelphia, 8 February 1911 (Hipsher: February 25), then in Baltimore, MD, Chicago, Los Angeles, and San Francisco, among other cities, for a total of 35 performances. The première, by the Philadelphia-Chicago Opera Company, starred Mary Garden and John McCormack. Bispham Medal, 1925, with *Madeleine*. Published by G. Schirmer, 1911. In AMRC.

1914   *Madeleine* ("lyric opera in 1 act"; libretto by Grant Stewart after the French play *Je dine chez ma mère* by Delourcelles and Thibaut). Première at Metropolitan Opera, New York, 24 January 1914.
(Herbert also composed 35 operettas.)

Herbolsheimer, Bern
1976   *Aria da capo* (libretto by William Lewis after Edna St. Vincent Millay). Performed Seattle, WA, 5 November 1976. (In *COS*-4 as *Da capo*.)

Herman, Reinhold Ludwig (1849-ca. 1920; in U.S. from 1871)
1891   *Vineta*. Performed Cassel, Germany.
1891   *Lanzelot*. Performed Braunschweig, Germany.
1894   *Spielmannsglück*. Performed Cassel, Germany.
1898   *Wulfrim*. Performed Cassel, Germany, 11 October 1898.
1911   *Sundari*. Performed Cassel, Germany.

Herman, Thomas Alan (b. Alexandria, VA, 3 June 1947; Anderson)
1975   *Objets trouvés*, for soprano, 5 actors, narrator, chamber orchestra. NEA grant, 1975.

Herrick, Lynn
1981   *Running Gag*, with Marianne de Pury (for children; libretto by Terry Megan, about jogging). Performed Omaha, NE, July 1981.

Herrmann, Bernard (b. New York, 29 June 1911; d. Los Angeles, 24 December 1975; ASCAP; *Amerigrove*)
1938   *Moby Dick* (dramatic cantata; libretto by W. C. Harrington after Herman Melville), for solo voices, male chorus, orchestra. Performed New York, 1940.
1940   *Johnny Appleseed* (dramatic cantata), for solo voices, chorus, orchestra.
1943   *Wuthering Heights* (4 acts; libretto by Lucille Fletcher after Emily Brontë). Première by Portland Opera, OR, 6 November 1982. Recorded in England for Pye. Kornick.
1954   *A Christmas Carol* (television opera; 1 act; libretto by M. Anderson after Charles Dickens). On CBS-TV, 23 December 1954.
1955   *A Child Is Born* (television opera; 1 act; after S. V. Benét).

Herst, Jerry
1987   *Sweet Man* (jazz opera, 2 acts; libretto by Jack Sharpe). Performed 1987.

Hess, Mirabell
1988   *Confession* (video opera). Performed Minneapolis, 9 January 1988.

Hess, Stephen
1976   *Muertedemonza* (libretto by James Fowler). Performed Vienna, Austria, 21 April 1976.

Hewitt, James (b. ?Dartmoor, England, 4 June 1770; d. Boston, 2 August 1827; in U.S. from 1792; *Amerigrove*; Porter)

1781   *Medea and Jason: or, The Golden Fleece* (serious pantomime; 1 act). First performed at King's Theatre, Haymarket, London, 8 August 1781; performed Boston, 6 February 1797.

1792   *Old Soldier: or, The Two Thieves* ("historical pantomime"). Première, New York, 15 February 1792.

1792   *Harlequin's Vagaries: or, The Village in an Uproar* (pantomime). Performed at Royal Saloon, London, 24 May 1792; New York, 14 May 1794.

1794   *Tammany: or, The Indian Chief* ("serious opera"; libretto by Anne Hatton). Première, New York, 3 March 1794. One song extant.

1795   *Tyranny Suppressed: or, Freedom Triumphant* (grand serious pantomime). Première, New York, 23 June 1795.

1798   *Flash in the Pan* ("musical farce"; libretto by William Milns). Première, New York, 20 April 1798.

1800   *Wild Goose Chase: or, Mad Cap of Age Tomorrow* (comic opera; 4 acts; libretto by William Dunlap after Augustus von Kotzebue's *Der Wildfang*). Première, 24 January 1800.

1800   *The Spanish Castle: or, Knight of Guadalquiver* (comic opera; libretto by William Dunlap). Première, New York, 5 December 1800.

1801   *The Cottagers* (comic opera; 2 acts). Première, New York, 6 May 1801.

1805   *Great Battle of Marengo: or, Apotheosis of General Dessaix* (heroic pantomime). Première, New York, 15 May 1805.

1805   *La Fille d'Hungerie: ou, La Père Riged* ("grand military heroic pantomime"; 3 acts; libretto by John Turnbull). First performance, Paris; first U.S. performance, New York, 24 May 1805.

1805   *Coronation of Napoleon Bonaparte, Emperor of the Gauls* (historical drama; 2 acts). Première, New York, 31 May 1805

1809   *The Wounded Hussar: or, The Rightful Heir* (comic opera; 2 acts; libretto by Joseph Hutton). Première, Philadelphia, 29 March 1809.

1813   *La Fille Hussar* (*The Female Hussar*) (heroic pantomime, with horses; libretto by James Sanderson). Première, New York, 13 1813.

Hewitt, John Hill (b. New York, 12 July 1801; d. Baltimore, MD, 7 October 1890; son of the preceding; *Amerigrove*)

1872   *The Musical Enthusiast* (operetta; libretto by composer). Performed Boston, 1872.

Hiatt, Rick

1989   *Headlights*, with Frank Fong, Rex Gray, Lor Loree, Mark Nelson, and Luigi Waites (about literacy). Performed Omaha, NE, 28 April 1989.

Hill, Edward Burlingame (b. Cambridge, MA, 9 September 1872; d. Francestown, NH, 9 July 1960; *Amerigrove*)

1908   *Jack Frost in Midsummer* (ballet/pantomime).

1914   *Pan and the Star.*

Hill, Mabel Wood
- *The Rose and the Ring.* *COS*-1.

Hillebrand, Fred (b. Brooklyn, NY, 25 December 1893; d. New York, 15
    September 1963; ASCAP; Anderson)
- *Southland.*
- *The Swing Princess* (operetta).

Hiller, Lejaren Arthur, Jr. (b. New York, 23 February 1924; *Amerigrove; Who's
    Who*)
1972   *A Rage Over the Lost Beethoven* (3 acts). Performed Buffalo, NY,
    19 February 1972.

Hines, Jerome Albert Link (b. Hollywood, CA, 8 November 1921; *Amerigrove;
    Who's Who*)
1959   *I AM the Way* (sacred music drama on the life of Christ; 150
    minutes). Performed by Christian Arts, NJ.

Hinrichs, Gustav (b. Ludwigslust, Germany, 10 December 1850; d. Mountain
    Lake, NJ, 26 March 1942; in U.S. from 1870; from 1903 to 1908
    Hinrichs was a conductor at the Metropolitan Opera in New York;
    Amerigrove)
1877   *Der vierjährige Posten* (1 act). Performed San Francisco.
1890   *Onti-Ori* (Indian name for the Catskills; 3 acts) Performed
    Philadelphia, 28 July 1890.

Hisell, Matt
1989   *A Midsummer Night's Dream* (libretto after Shakespeare).
    Performed at University of Cincinnati, 15 May and 24 May 1989.

Hively, Wells (b. San Joaquin Valley, CA, 1902; d. Palm Beach, FL, 1969;
    ACA/AMC; Anderson)
1956   *Junipero Serra* (90 minutes). Performed Palma, Majorca, 28 March
    1956.
- *Canek* (1 act).
- *The Discreet Cadiga.*
- *The River* (radio opera; 1 act).

Hoag, Charles Kelso (b. Chicago, 14 November 1931; ASCAP; *WhoAm*)
1961   *Lonely Game* (1 act; libretto by Howard Stein). Ph.D. dissertation,
    University of Iowa; performed there, 11 March 1961.

Hochman, Arthur
1913   *Fiammetta.* Performed New York.

Hochman, Larry
1985   *One-Man Band*, with Marc Elliot (libretto by Marc Elliot and James
    Lecesne). Performed at South Street Theater, New York, June
    1985.

Hodkinson, Sydney Phillip (b. Winnipeg, Canada, 17 January 1934; *Amerigrove*; *Baker's*)

1962 *Lament for Guitar and Two Lovers.*

1965 *Taiwa.* Performed Athens, OH, 28 April 1965.

1971 *Vox populous* (1 act). Performed Minnesota, 1 December 1973.

1974 *The Black Glass Butterfly* (libretto by Philip Lee Devin). NEA grant, 1974.

1975 *The Swinish Cult* (on the trials of Oppenheimer). NEA grant, 1975.

1980 *The Wall*

1981 *In the Gallery.*

1985 *Catsman.*

Hoffman, David

1988 *A Noble and Sentimental Death* (1 act). Performed at Boston University, 29 April 1988

Hoiby, Lee (b. Madison, WI, 17 February 1926; ASCAP; *Amerigrove*; *Baker's*; *Who's Who*)

1956 *The Scarf*, op. 12 (formerly *The Witch*; 1 act; 45 minutes; libretto by Harry Duncan after Anton Chekhov's *The Witch*). Performed at the Spoleto festival, 20 June 1958, and by New York City Opera, 5 April 1959.

1959 *Beatrice*, op. 18 (3 acts; libretto by Marcia Nardi after Maeterlinck). Commission by WAVE-TV, Louisville, KY. Performed Louisville, 23 October 1959; broadcast 30 October 1959. Withdrawn.

1964 *Natalia Petrovna* (2 acts; libretto by William Ball after Turgenev). Commission by Ford Foundation. Performed by New York City Opera, 8 October 1964. Revised as *A Month in the Country* (see below). Published by Boosey & Hawkes.

1970 *Summer and Smoke*, op. 27 (2 acts; libretto by Lanford Wilson after Tennessee Williams). Commission by St. Paul Opera Co., MN. Performed St. Paul, 19 June 1971; and by New York City Opera, 19 March 1982. Telecast on PBS, 1981. Published by Aquarius Music.

1979 *Something New for the Zoo*, op. 31 (revision of a work from 1954; opera buffa in 1 act—55 minutes; libretto by Dudley Huppler). Performed New London, CT, 18 July 1980, and Cheverly, MD, 17 May 1982. Published by Aquarius Music.

1980 *A Month in the Country* (2 acts; libretto by William Ball after Turgenev—a revised version of *Natalia Petrovna*). Performed Boston, 23 January 1981.

1980 *The Italian Lesson*, op. 34 (monodrama; satire; 30 minutes; libretto after Ruth Draper), for mezzo-soprano and chamber orchestra. Performed Aspen, CO, 6 July 1980; Newport, RI, July 1982; Baltimore, MD, 18 January 1985. Published by Aquarius Music. Kornick.

1985 *The Tempest* (3 acts—140 minutes; libretto by Mark Shulgasser after Shakespeare). Commission by Des Moines Metro Opera, Indianola, IA; performed there, 21 June 1986, and by Lyric Opera of Kansas City, MO, 13 April 1988. Kornick.

1987   *A Christmas Carol* ("a play with music"; libretto by Dennis Powers and Laird Williamson after Dickens). Performed San Francisco, 2 December 1987.

1988   *Bon Appetit!* (20 minutes; libretto after Julia Child; designed as a curtain-raiser for *The Italian Lesson*). Performed at Kennedy Center, Washington, DC, 8 March 1989. Published by G. Schirmer.

1991-   *Romeo and Juliet* (libretto by Mark Shulgasser after Shakespeare). In progress.

Hokanson, Dorothy Cadzow (b. Edmonton, Alberta, 5 August 1916; studied and lived in U.S.; Anderson; Cohen)

1958   *Undine* (1 act; libretto by Esther Sheppard and John Ashby Conway). Performed at University of Washington, Seattle, 2 May 1958.

Holab, William Joshua (b. Chicago, 6 May 1958; *Who's Who*; *WhoAm*)

1986   *Confidence Game*, with Scott Eyerly (150 minutes; libretto by Andrew Kurtzman and Scott Eyerly after Ben Jonson's *The Alchemist*). Performed 13 January 1986, and at ASCAP Musical Theatre Workshop, 1986.

Holcomb, Robin

1989   *Angels at the Four Corners* (2 acts; libretto by composer). Performed at Next Wave Festival workshop, New York, 12 November 1989.

Holdridge, Lee (b. Port au Prince, Haiti, 3 March 1944, of U.S. parents; AMC; Anderson; *WhoAm*)

-    *Lazarus and His Beloved* (1 act; libretto by composer after the text by Kahil Gibran).

Hollingsworth, Stanley (b. Berkeley, CA, 27 August 1924; Anderson; *Baker's*)

1954   *The Mother* (1 act; libretto after Andersen). Performed at Curtis Institute, Philadelphia, 29 March 1954.

1957   *La Grande Bretèche* (TV opera; 60 minutes; libretto after Balzac). On WNBC-TV, 20 February 1957.

1981   *The Selfish Giant* (1 act; libretto by composer and Herbert Moulton after the fairytale by Oscar Wilde). Première at Spoleto Festival, Charleston, SC, 24 May 1981, as a trilogy with *The Mother* and *Harrison Loved His Umbrella*.

1981   *Harrison Loved His Umbrella* (1 act—25 minutes; libretto by Rhoda Levine after her book of the same title). Première by students of Oakland University, Rochester, MN, at Spoleto Festival, Charleston, SC, 24 May 1981. Published by Belwin-Mills. Kornick.

Hollister, David Manship (b. New York, 1 May 1929; Anderson; *Who's Who*)

1980   *The Girl Who Ate Chicken Bones* (90 minutes; libretto by the composer and Stan Kaplan). Performed by Soho Repertory, New York, 24 November 1980 and 16 April 1982. Recorded by Rebus Music.

1984   *TF . . .* (1 hour; libretto by June Siegel and Marcia Kesselman after Molière's *Tartuffe*). Performed White Plains, NY, 9 January 1984, and by Broadway Tomorrow, New York, 30 April 1984. Recorded by Rebus Music.

1985   *A Change of Hearts* (comic opera; 45 minutes; libretto by Kenneth Koch). Performance Medicine Show, New York, 17 July and 14 November 1985. Record and video by Rebus Music.

Holsinger, David (b. Kansas City, MO, 26 December 1945; Anderson)

1976   *A Day in the Death of Stephen Voltov* (30 minutes; libretto by composer after Tolstoy's *The Death of Ivan Illyitch*). Performed Warrensburg, MO, 5 May 1976.

Holst, Edvard (b. Copenhagen, 1843; d. New York, 4 February 1899; in U.S. from 1874; *Baker's*)

1897   *Our Flats* (comic opera). Performed New York, 1897.

Holton, Bob (Robert in *COS*-1)

1958   *A Real Strange One* (1 act). Performed New York, 23 April 1958.

Honigman, Saul

1958   *The Ticket* (1 act). Performed Woodstock, NY, 11 July 1958.

Hopkins, Charles Jerome (b. Burlington, VT, 4 April 1836; d. Athenia [now a part of Clifton], NJ, 4 November 1898; *Amerigrove*; *Baker's*)

1877   *Samuel* (operatic oratorio). Performed New York.

1878   *Dumb Love.*

1880   *Taffy and Old Munch* ("musicianly and scientific Kinder-Oper"). (*Amerigrove*: 1882.)

Hopkinson, Francis (b. Philadelphia, 21 September 1737; d. there, 9 May 1791; *Amerigrove*)

1781   *America Independent* or *The Temple of Minerva* (2 scenes; on an American subject), text written, and music compiled, by Hopkinson. See Gillian B. Anderson, "'Samuel the Priest Gave Up the Ghost' and *The Temple of Minerva*," *Notes* 31/3 (March 1975): 493–516.

Horacek, Leo

1968   *The Tell-Tale Heart* (1 act; libretto by Joseph Golz after Poe). Performed Morgantown, WV, 7 August 1968.

Horn, Charles Edward (b. London, England, 21 June 1798; d. Boston, 21 October 1849; in U.S. from 1827; *Amerigrove*)

1828   *Dido* (with music of Rossini). Performed New York, 9 April 1828.

1829   *The Quartette, or Interrupted Harmony* (1 act). Performed at Bowery Theatre, New York, 27 April 1829.

1832   *Nadir and Zuleika.* Performed New York, 27 December 1832.

1840   *Ahmad al Kamel, or The Pilgrim of Love* (libretto by H. J. Finn after Washington Irving's *Alhambra*). Performed at National Theatre, New York, 12 October 1840.

1842   *The Maid of Saxony* (3 acts; libretto by G. P. Morris after M. Edgeworth). Performed New York, 23 May 1842.

Horvit, Michael Miller (b. New York, 22 June 1932; AMC; Anderson; *WhoAm*)
  1968　*Tomo* (children's opera; 1 act; libretto by composer). Performed Houston, TX, 21 November 1968.
  1976　*Adventure in Space* (chamber opera for children; 50 minutes; libretto by composer). NEA grant. Performed by Piccolo Opera Co. of Detroit, 1981.

Hoschna, Carl L.
  1910　*Madame Sherry* (3 acts). Performed Bloomington, IN.

Hosmer, Lucius (b. South Acton, MA, 14 August 1870; d. Jefferson, NH, 9 May 1935; ASCAP; Anderson; *Baker's*)
  1905　*The Rose of the Alhambra.* Performed Rochester, NY, 1905, and New York, 4 February 1907.
  -　*The Koreans* (formerly *The Walking Delegate*).

House, Marguerite (b. St. Louis; ASCAP; Cohen)
  -　*The Tourists* (chamber opera; 1 act). First prize, Michigan State Federated Music Clubs, 1973. *COS*-1.

Houseley, Henry (b. Sutton-in-Ashfield, Nottinghamshire, England, 20 September 1852; d. Denver, CO, 13 March 1925; in U.S. from 1888; *Baker's*; Hipsher)
  c 1891　*Native Silver* (operetta). Performed at Broadwood Theater, Denver, CO, about 1891.
  1895　*The Juggler* (light opera; 3 acts; libretto by Randolph Hartley). Performed at Broadway Theater, Denver, CO, 23 May 1895 and 26 October 1898.
  1912　*Pygmalion* (grand opera; 1 act; libretto by composer's wife S. Frances Houseley).
  1912　*Narcissus and Echo* (1 act; libretto by S. Frances Houseley). Performed at El Jebel Temple, Denver, CO, 30 January 1912, and at Broadway Theater, Denver, 16 February 1923.
  1912　*Pygmalion* (1 act). Performed Denver.
  -　*Love and Whist* (operetta; 1 act; libretto by Randolph Hartley). Performed Denver, Boulder, Greeley, and Colorado Springs.
  -　*Ponce de Leon* (operetta; 3 acts; libretto by Randolph Hartley). Not performed.

Houston, Mark
  1987　*Hazel Kirke* (2 acts; libretto by composer and Francis Cullinan after a 1879 melodrama by Steele MacKaye). Performed Glens Falls, NY, 7 August 1987 (Kornick: 31 July 1987 at Lake George Opera Festival).
  1989　*The Juggler.* Performed Kansas City, KS, January 1989.

Houtz, Dyrphrn
  1979　*North of Boston.* Performed Bloomington, IN, 12 April 1979.

Hovey, Serge (b. New York, 10 March 1920; d. Los Angeles, 3 May 1989; Anderson)
  1949　*Dreams in Spades* (chamber opera; 1 act). Performed Philadelphia.

Hovhaness, Alan (b. Somerville, MA, 8 March 1911; *Amerigrove*; *Who's Who*)
(All librettos by the composer; all operas published by Peters.)
1946   *Etchmiadzin*, op. 62.
1959   *Blue Flame*, op. 172 (chamber opera; 4 scenes). Performed San
    Antonio, TX, 15 December 1959.
1960   *The Burning House*, op. 185 (opera ballet/chamber opera; 1 act—126
    minutes). Performed Gatlinburg, TN, 23 August 1964.
1962   *Spirit of the Avalanche*, op. 197 (chamber opera; 1 act). *COS*-1.
1963   *Pilate*, op. 196 (chamber opera; 1 act). Performed at Pepperdine
    College, Los Angeles, 26 June 1966.
1964   *Wild Drum* (dance-drama). Performed Gatlinburg, TN, 23 August
    1964.
1965   *Travellers*, op. 215 (chamber opera; 15 minutes). Performed at
    Foothill College, CA, 22 April 1967.
1965   *The Leper King*, op. 219 (dance-drama). *COS*-1.
1969   *Lady of Light*, op. 227 (opera-oratorio).
1975   *Pericles*, op. 283. NEA grant.
1978   *Tale of the Sun Goddess Going into the Stone House*, op. 323.

Howland, William Legrand (b. Asbury Park, NJ, 1873; d. Long Island, NY, 26
    July 1915; Anderson; Hipsher: b. New Haven, CN, 1872)
1898   *Nita*. Performed at Théâtre Nouveau, Paris, France; later at Aix-
    les-Bains and Monte Carlo.
1901   *Sarrona: or, the Indian Slave* (2 acts; libretto by composer).
    Performed in New York, 1901; Bruges, Belgium (in Italian), 3
    August 1903; New York, 1910 (in English); and Philadelphia, 23
    March 1911 (in German)—200 performances in 21 opera houses of
    Italy and Austria.

Hoy, Bonnee Hendricks (b. Jenkintown, PA, 27 August 1936; AMC; Anderson;
    Cohen)
1980   *Freedom's Road* (1 act).
1983   *The Spring of Earth's Rebirth* (dramatic oratorio; libretto by
    composer). Performed Carversville, PA, winter 1983; and at
    Academy of Music Ballroom, Philadelphia, 25 April 1983.

Huckaby, William
1976   *Jesse* (libretto by Vern Sutlon, about Jesse James). Performed
    Northfield, MN, 9 September 1976.

Hufsmith, George William (b. Omaha, NE, 27 August 1924; Anderson)
1976   *Sweetwater Lynching* (*Battle of Cattle Kate*) (3 acts). Performed
    Laramie, WY, 2 March 1976.

Hugo, John Adam (b. Bridgeport, CN, 5 January 1873; d. there, 29 December
    1945; Anderson; Hipsher)
1919   *The Temple Dancer* (1 act; libretto by Jutta Bell-Ranske). Première
    by Metropolitan Opera, New York, 12 March 1919; also performed
    5 times at the Playhouse, Chicago, beginning 7 December 1922;
    Honolulu, Hawaii, 19 February 1925. Bispham Medal, 1925.
-    *The Hero of Byzanz*. Begun while a student in Germany, age 18; 3
    years spent writing it.

   –   *The Sun God* (about Pizzaro and the Incas).
(Johnson states that others were performed in Germany.)

Humel, Gerald (b. Cleveland, OH, 7 November 1931; Anderson)
   1950   *The Proposal* (17 minutes). Performed Winfield, KS. Published by
         Mills Music.
   1955   *The Triangle* (2 acts; libretto by Roger Brucker). Performed
         Oberlin, OH, 14 November 1958.
   1962   *Jochim Wessels* (150 minutes).

Humphreys-Rauscher, Henry Sigurd (b. Vienna, Austria, 27 November 1909; his
        father an American citizen; Anderson)
   1957   *Mayerling* (3 acts). Performed Cincinnati, 16 November 1957.
   1968   *Joan of Arc at Reims* (1 act). Performed Cincinnati, 17 March
         1968. *COS*-2.
   1981   *Sea-Thorn* (*An American Phaedra*) (2 acts; libretto by composer).
         Performed Covington, KY, 20 March 1981.
   1984   *Quo vadis Domine* (*Where Are You Going, Lord?*) (for performance
         in church; libretto after Sienkiewicz's *Quo vadis*).
    –   *Night of the Hunter* (12 scenes; after novel by Grubb and movie by
         Agee).

Hundley, Richard (b. Cincinnati, OH, 1 September 1931; Anderson)
   1965   *Emma Immaculata of Lies* (1 act). Performed by Metropolitan
         Opera Studio, New York, 2 April 1965.
    –   *Wedding Finger* (libretto after a play by James Purdy).

Hunkins, Eusebia Simpson (b. Troy, OH, 20 June 1902; d. 9 September 1980;
        ASCAP; Anderson; Cohen)
        (Many of these operas published by Carl Fischer, except *The Young
        Lincoln* and *Child of Promise*.)
   1954   *Smoky Mountain* (folk drama; 2 acts). Performed at Monmouth
         College, IL, February 1954.
   1955   *Wondrous Love* ("mountain choral drama of the Nativity").
   1956   *Mice in Council* (operetta; 1 act—35 minutes).
   1956   *The Reluctant Hero.*
   1956   *The Spirit Owl* (2 acts; concerns the American Indian; uses
         authentic Indian materials).
   1958   *Forest Voices* (operetta).
   1958   *Young Lincoln* (folk opera; 1 act). Performed Galesburg, IL,
         October 1959.
   1960   *Young Lincoln II* (folk opera; 1 act).
   1964   *Child of Promise* (children's choral dance opera; 1 act). Performed
         Eureka Springs, AR, 25 July 1965.
   1973   *What Have You Done to My Mountain?* (musical play or folk opera; 2
         acts).
   1974   *The Magic Laurel Trees* (operetta for children).
   1975   *Happy Land: Our American Heritage in Song and Story* (operetta; 1
         act).
    –   *The Witch's Curse* ("fairy opera").

Hunsaker, Dave
1989   *Pieces of Eight*. Performed Douglas, AL, 14 November 1989.

Hunt, Jerry E. (b. Waco, TX, 1943; Anderson)
1973   *Quaquaversal Transmission* (theater work).

Huston, Scott (b. Tacoma, WA, 10 October 1916; d. Cincinnati, 1 March 1991; Anderson; *Baker's*)
1974   *The Giggling Goblin* (1 act; libretto by Karl Bratton). Performed Cincinnati, 2 June 1974.
1974   *Tamar* (monodrama for soprano and piano).
1976   *Land Rights* (libretto by Dan Bredeman). Performed Cincinnati, 1976.
1987   *Blind Girl* (video opera; 58 minutes; libretto by Dan Bredeman). Performed Cincinnati, 15 October 1987; telecast by Warner Cable, 13 February 1988.

Hutcheson, Jere Trent (b. Marietta, GA, 16 September 1938; Anderson; *Who's Who*)
1990   *Long Live the Protagonist* (45 minutes; libretto by composer). Performed East Lansing, MI, 1990.

Hutchinson, Brenda
1956   *Maniian* (operetta).
1988   *Fly Away All* (formerly *Electricity*) (libretto by Theodore Shank, using text by Madsen in expressionist collage). Performed St. Paul, MN, January and (revised) 19 May 1988.

Hwang, David Henry
1988   *1000 Airplanes on the Roof*, with Philip Glass and Jerome Serlin. Performed at American Music Theater Festival, 21 September 1988, and in London, England, October 1989.

Hyde, Herbert
1927   *The Kitchen Clock* (40 minutes; libretto by Florence C. Comfort). Performed 1927 (*COS*-1), and by Children's Opera, Milwaukee, WI, 1955. Published by FitzSimons.

Ihara, Richard
1989   *Wiseman of Chichen-Itza* (libretto by Estela Scarlata). Performed by Bilingual Foundation of the Arts, Los Angeles, CA, February 1989.

Imbrie, Andrew (b. New York, 6 April 1921; *Amerigrove*; *Who's Who*)
1963   *Three Against Christmas: or, Christmas in Peebles Town* (comic opera; 4 scenes; libretto by Richard Wincor). Performed Berkeley, CA, 3 December 1964.

1976 *Angle of Repose* (3 acts—180 minutes; libretto by Oakley Hall after the novel by Wallace Stegner). NEA grant. Commission and première by San Francisco Opera, 6 November 1976. Kornick.

Innerarity, Memrie
1987 *Moonlight Sonata* ("music drama set in a vampire household"; 1 act; libretto by composer). Performed by National Music Theater Network, New York, 30 November 1987, and by Golden Fleece, New York, 7 April 1987.
1988 *Unruly Caucasian Female* (libretto by composer). Performed by Golden Fleece, New York, 13 December 1988.

Irwin, Pat
1989 *Empires and Appetites* (libretto by Odora Skipitares; uses puppets). Performed by Theater for the New City, New York, 11 May 1989.

Isaacs, Gregory
1973 *The Death of Tintagiles* (25 minutes; libretto by composer after a Maeterlinck puppet play). Performed Indianola, IA, 4 May 1973, and San Gabriel, CA, 25 February 1983.

Isele, David Clark (b. Harrisburg, PA, 25 April 1946; Anderson; *Who's Who*)
1989 *Opera Buffet* (comic opera; 45 minutes; libretto by Gwyneth Walker). Published by Walker, 1980.
- *Taking It Off* (comic opera). Published by Walker, 1983.

Isen, Richard
1981 *Night City Diaries* (libretto by composer after poems by Rimbaud and Apollinaire). Performed by Skyboat Road, Edinburgh Festival, Scotland, 1981, and Playwrights Horizons, New York, May 1982.
1982 *Salford Road* (libretto by Gareth Owen). Performed by Theatre of the Open Eye, New York, 14 December 1982.
1986 *Spring Awakening* (2 acts; libretto by Joel Beard and David Petrarca after Wedekind). Performed at Chelsea Theater Center, New York, 9 June 1986.
1987 *A Fine and Private Place* (libretto by Erik Haagensen after Peter Beagle). Performed Waterford, CT, 19 August 1987; and by Goodspeed Opera, Chester, CT, August 1989.

Israel, Brian M. (b. New York, 5 February 1951; Anderson)
1979 *Winnie the Pooh* (90 minutes; libretto by Joseph Y. Israel after Milne). Performed Syracuse, NY, 1 June 1979 and 27 October 1989.

Ito, Genji
1985 *Mythos Oedipus*, with Elizabeth Swados, Connie Alexander, Sheila Dabney, David Sawyer, and Michael Sirotta (90 minutes; libretto by Ellen Stewart after Sophocles; in Greek). Performed Delphi, Greece, summer 1985, and by LaMama, New York, 6 February 1988.

Ives, David
1990 *Philip Glass Buys a Loaf of Bread*. Ten Minute Musicals Project
winner. Performed at Climat Theatre, San Francisco, CA, 1990.

Ivey, Jean Eichelberger (b. Washington, DC, 3 July 1923; *Amerigrove*; Cohen;
WhoAm)
1976 *Testament of Eve* (monodrama; libretto by composer), for
mezzosoprano, tape, orchestra. Performed Baltimore, 21 April
1976; and at Columbia University, New York, 7 November 1976.
1982 *The Birthmark* (75 minutes; libretto by composer after Hawthorne).

Jackson, Clarence Bernard
1960 *Fly Blackbird*. Performed Los Angeles, 1961.
- *Departure*.

Jackson, J. David
1988 *Welcome, Jesus!* (Christmas opera; libretto by Joan Drew Ritchings).
Performed Rye, NY, 15 January 1988.

Jacobi, Frederick (b. San Francisco, 4 May 1891; d. New York, 24 October 1952;
Amerigrove)
1944 *The Prodigal Son* (3 acts; libretto by H. Voaden). Performed
Stanford, CA, 1949; London, England, 1951; and Chicago, 1945.
Bispham Medal, 1945.

Jacobi, Victor
1919 *Apple Blossoms*, with Fritz Kreisler (3 acts). Performed Baltimore,
MD, and New York. Published by Harms.
1933 *Sybil* (3 acts). Performed Washington, DC, and New York.

Jaffe, Karen
1989 *Legacy* (libretto by R. Walker after Breece). Performed
Stockbridge, MA, 9 August 1989.

Jager, Robert Edward (b. Binghamton, NY, 25 August 1939; Anderson; *Who's
Who*)
- *Lysistrata* (165 minutes; libretto by composer after Aristophanes).

James, Dorothy (b. Chicago, 1 December 1901; d. St. Petersburg, FL, 1
December 1982; *Amerigrove*)
1930 *Paolo and Francesca* (3 acts; libretto by S. Phillips). Performed
Rochester, NY, 2 April 1931.

James, Harlan
1988 *Ali Baba* (1 act; libretto by John Benedict). Performed by Penny
Bridge Players, Brooklyn, NY, 16 February 1988.

James, Philip (b. Jersey City, NJ, 17 May 1890; d. Southampton, NY, 1
November 1975; *Amerigrove*)
1927   *Judith* ("dramatic reading with ballet and small orchestra").
(James also composed incidental music for *Arms and Venus*, 1937.)

Janas, Mark
1985   *Composer's Nightmare* (1 act; libretto by Scott Heumann).
Performed Houston, TX, 6 June 1985.

Jannata (or Jannatta), Alfredo
1912?   *Alidor* (libretto by Ned Anderson). Performed in Los Angeles, 21
January 1913. The *Los Angeles Express* of that date (p. 11) noted
that this opera had already been performed "with great success in
Cincinnati, St. Paul and Chicago."

Jarrett, Jack Marius (b. Asheville, NC, 17 March 1934; Anderson; *WhoAm*)
1956   *Cinderella* (3 acts). Performed Gainesville, FL, 1956.
1972   *Cyrano de Bergerac* (3 acts). Performed Greensboro, NC, 1972.

Javits, Joan
1971   *Young Abe Lincoln*, with John Allen, Richard Bernstein, and Victor
Ziskin (1 act). Performed New York, February 1971.

Jebeles, Elizabeth Wenk (Mrs. Thomas Jebeles; AMC; Cohen)
1962   *The Audition* (folk opera; 1 act; libretto by composer), revised 1979.
Performed Birmingham, AL, 7 March 1979.

Jeffers, Grant
1983   *What Happened* (1 act; libretto after Gertrude Stein). Performed at
University of California, Los Angeles, 25 February 1983.

Jenkins, Daniel
1989   *Feast Here Tonight* (2 acts; libretto by composer and Ken Jenkins;
contains bluegrass music). Performed Vineyard Theatre, New
York, 14 June 1989.

Jenkins, Leroy (b. Chicago, 11 March 1932; *Amerigrove*)
1990   *The Mother of Three Sons*. Performed by Aachen Opera at Munich
Biennale, Germany, April and May 1990.

Jenni, Donald Martin (b. Milwaukee, WI, 4 October 1937; ACA/AMC; Anderson;
Who's Who)
1964   *The Emperor Clothed Anew* (45 minutes; after Andersen).
Performed at De Paul University, Chicago, 2 April 1965.

Jennings, Carolyn
1981   *What a Fine Day* (on an African tale). Commission by Minnesota
Composers Forum. Performed Northfield, MN, 15 May 1981.

Jennings, Richard
1979   *Space Opera One* (*As We Travel through the Stars*) (multimedia).
Performed Ann Arbor, MI, fall 1979.

Jessye, Eva (b. Coffeyville, KS, 20 January 1895; d. Ann Arbor, MI, 21
February 1992; Anderson; *Amerigrove*; Cohen)
1955   *Chronicle of Job* (folk drama with music).

Johnson, A. Paul (b. Indianapolis, IN, 27 January 1955; Anderson; *Who's Who*;
WhoAm)
1983   *Anzollo and Valeria* (1 act). Performed Sarasota, FL, 17 February
1984.

Johnson, Carl
1966   *Escorial* (1 act; tragedy by de Ghelderode). Performed Iowa City,
IA, 7 March 1966.

Johnson, Dean
1982   *Intrusions I-V* (5 parts; libretto by William Boswell; parts are
variable). Performed at Brooklyn College, NY, 5 February 1982.
1983   *East River Bridge* (1 act; composed for the centenary of the
Brooklyn Bridge). Performed at Brooklyn College, 4 February
1983.

Johnson, Dee Strickland
1968   *MacLeod O'Dunatore* (90 minutes). Performed Tucson, AZ, 21 June
1968.

Johnson, Hall (b. Athens, GA, 12 March 1888; d. New York, 30 April 1970;
Amerigrove; Southern)
1933   *Run, Littl' Children* (play with music). It ran four months, and has
had many revivals, including the Federal Theater Project, Los
Angeles, 1935-37.
  -    *Coophered* (composed before 1930).
  -    *Fi-Yer* (*Fire*).

Johnson, Harold Victor (b. Omaha, NE, 16 May 1918; Anderson)
(Performances of the first four listed here at Southern California
Conservatory of Music.)
1975   *Cinderella* (35 minutes). Performed 29 June 1975.
1976   *The Barnyard Quartette* (54 minutes; libretto after Grimm).
Performed 28 September 1976.
1977   *The Little Mermaid* (90 minutes; libretto after Andersen).
Performed 9 July 1977.
1978   *The Pied Piper* (45 minutes; libretto after Browning). Performed 19
December 1978.
1986   *Mother Goose* (libretto by Lurrine Burgess). Performed Sun Valley,
CA, 24 March 1986.
  -    *Judas.*

Johnson, Harriet
  -    *Pets of the Met* (1 act; libretto by Don and Lydia Freeman).

Johnson, Henry (Schoep)
1967   *The Mountain* (2 acts—90 minutes; libretto by David Grozier).
Performed by University of Arizona Opera Theatre, Tucson, 12
December 1967.

Johnson, James P. ("Jimmy"; b. New Brunswick, NJ, 1 February 1891; d. New
York, 17 November 1955; *Amerigrove*; Southern)
- 1940   *The Organizer* (or *De Organizer*; blues opera; 1 act). Première,
New York, 31 May 1940.
- *c* 1942   *Dreamy Kid* (1 act; libretto after E. O'Neill).
(See *Amerigrove* for other stage works.)

Johnson, James Weldon (b. Jacksonville, FL, 17 June 1871; d. Wiscasset, ME, 26
June 1938; brother of John Rosamond Johnson; *Amerigrove*;
Southern)
-    *The Czar of Zani.*
-    *Toloso.*

Johnson, John Rosamond (b. Jacksonville, FL, 11 August 1873; d. New York, 11
November 1954; brother of the preceding; *Amerigrove*; Southern)
- 1930   *Jazz Sunday (It Happened in Harlem/Blue Sunday).*

Johnson, Lockrem (b. Davenport, IA, 15 March 1924; d. Seattle, WA, 5 March
1977; *Amerigrove*)
- 1951   *A Letter to Emily*, op. 37 (chamber opera; 1 act—40 minutes; libretto
by composer after R. Hupron; about Emily Dickinson).
Performed Los Angeles, 22 April 1951; Seattle, WA, 24 April
1951; and New York 25 January 1955.
-    *The Aspen Grove.* NEA grant, 1977.

Johnson, Mary Ernestine Clark (b. West Alden, NY, 8 July 1895; Cohen)
- 1953   *The Thirteen Clocks* (operetta; 2 acts; libretto by composer, and
Maritz and Norman Morgan after Thurber). Performed at Hunter
College, New York, 18 March 1958; telecast on ABC-TV.

Johnson, Ralph
- 1986   *Canterbury Tales* (libretto by Steve Swenson after Chaucer).
Performed at Children's Theater Institute, St. Olaf College,
Northfield, MN, 9 July 1986.

Johnson, Tom (b. Greeley, CO, 18 November 1939; AMC; *Amerigrove*; *Who's
Who*)
(Johnson wrote his own librettos.)
- 1970   *411 Lines* ("a theater piece").
- 1972   *The Four-Note Opera* (1 act; for chorus, piano, and tape; libretto by
composer and R. Kushner)—only four notes used. Performed by
Cubiculo, New York, 11 May 1972, and Århus, Denmark, 1989.
Published by G. Schirmer.
- 1976   *The Masque of Clouds* (libretto by composer and R. Kushner).
Performed New York, 10 October 1976.
- 1978   *Door-Window-Drawers-Dryer-Box: Five Shaggy-Dog Operas* (each
is very short). Performed New York, 15 September 1978.
- 1984   *Sopranos Only* (originally *Reservé aux sopranes*; 35 minutes).
Performed Paris, France, March 1984, in French; Oneonta, NY, 1
October 1990; Syracuse, NY, 3 October 1990.
- 1986   *Riemannoper (An Opera after Riemann)* (90 minutes). Performed
West Berlin, Germany, February 1986, and Bremen, Germany, 3
November 1988.

1989   *200 Ans* (*200 Years*) (30 minutes). Composed for the bicentennial of the French Revolution; in French). Association Acanthes prize winner. Performed Avignon, France, January and 25 July 1989.

Johnston, Benjamin (b. Macon, GA, 15 March 1926; *Amerigrove*; *Who's Who*)
1965   *Gertrude: or, Would She Be Pleased to Receive It?* (chamber opera; 2 acts; libretto by W. Leach).
1970   *Carmilla: A Vampire Tale* (90 minutes; libretto by W. Leach after Sheridan Le Fanu). Performed Urbana, IL, 21 November 1974.

Johnston, Donald O. (b. Tracy, MN, 6 February 1929; Anderson; *Who's Who*)
1984   *The Private World of Private Dubek*. Performed Missoula, MT, April 1984.

Jolas, Betsy (b. Paris, France, 5 August 1926; to U.S. in 1940, divides her time between the two countries; *Amerigrove*; Cohen; Morton/Collins; *Who's Who*)
1975   *Le Pavillon au bord de la rivière* (Chinese chamber opera; 4 acts; libretto by Kua Han Chin). Performed Avignon, France, July 1975.
1982   *L'Un opéra de poupée*, with 11 instruments. Published Paris: Salabert, 1982.
1986   *Le Cyclope* (chamber opera; libretto by Euripides), for 3 trombones, electric guitar, bass guitar, percussion, 9 singers. Première in Avignon, July 1986.
1987   *Schliemann* (libretto by Bayen). Première in Lyon, France, 1991.

Jones, Abbie Gerrish (or Gerrish-Jones; b. Vallejo, CA, 10 September 1863; d. 5 February 1929; Hipsher)
1887   *Priscilla* (4 acts; libretto by composer).
1917   *The Snow Queen* (fairy music drama; libretto by Gerda Wismer Hofmann after Hans Christian Andersen). Première, San Francisco, 9 February 1917; then performed Oakland, CA, for a run of 2 weeks; later in Fresno, Los Angeles, Cleveland, and New York.
  -     *Abon Hassan: or, The Sleeper Awakened* (3 acts; based on Arabian Nights tale).
  -     *The Andalusians* (3 acts; libretto by Percy Friars Valentine).
  -     *The Aztec Princess* (grand opera).
  -     *The Milkmaid's Fair* (romantic opera; 1 act; libretto by composer and Pauline Turner Gregory).
  -     *Two Roses* (3 acts; libretto by composer after the Grimm fairy tale "Rose White and Rose Red").

Jones, C. Robert
  -     *Mandy Lou* (2 acts; libretto by composer).

Jones, George Thaddeus (b. Asheville, NC, 6 November 1917; ASCAP; Anderson)
1959   *The Cage* (1 act). Performed at Catholic University, Washington, DC, April 1959; telecast on NBC-TV, New York, 10 May 1959.
  -     *Break of Day*.

Jones, Jeffrey (b. Los Angeles, 11 May 1944; Anderson)
-    *Orythia* (ballet opera in 3 tableaux).

Jones, John
   1844   *The Enchanted Horse*. Performed New York; the composer sang the tenor role of the Prince.

Jones, Samuel (b. Inverness, MS, 2 June 1935; Anderson; *WhoAm*; *Who's Who*)
-    *A Christmas Memory* (1 act; after Capote). Published by MMB Music.

Jones, Stephen
   1992   *The New Son* (libretto by David Warner). To be performed Provo, UT, October 1992.

Jones, Vincent
-    *Miss Melodicus* (comic opera).

Joplin, Scott (b. near Marshall, TX, or Shreveport, LA, 24 November 1868; d. New York, 1 April 1917; *Amerigrove*; Southern)
   1903   *A Guest of Honor* (rag opera); score lost. Performed St. Louis.
   1911   *Treemonisha* (3 acts). Reading, New York. Performed Atlanta, GA (orchestration by T. J. Anderson), 1972; Houston, TX (orchestration by Gunther Schuller), 1975. Video of Houston Grand Opera performance, 1981: Sony C0427, 1982; Video Artists International; Home Vision TRE087; Kultur 1240.

Jordan, Jules (b. Willimantic, CN, 10 November 1850; d. Providence, RI, 5 March 1927; *Baker's*; Hipsher)
   1897   *Rip Van Winkle* (romantic comedy opera; 3 acts; libretto by composer after Washington Irving). Première at Providence Opera House, RI, composer conducting, 25 May 1897; many later performances.
-    *The Alphabet* (school operetta).
-    *The Buccaneers* (light opera).
-    *Cloud and Sunshine* (school operetta).
-    *An Eventful Holiday* (light opera).
-    *Her Crown of Glory* (light opera).
-    *A Leap Year Furlough* (light opera).
-    *Nisida* (grand opera; 3 acts; libretto by composer after Alexandre Dumas). Not performed.
-    *An Ounce of Gold* (1 act).
-    *Princess of the Blood* (light opera).
-    *The Rivals* (1 act).
-    *Star of the Sea* (light opera).
   (Jordan also composed "school operettas": *The Alphabet*, and *Cloud and Sunshine*.)

Jordan, Ray
   1975   *Las Rojas* (90 minutes; libretto after the legend of Our Lady of the Roses). Performed New York, 5 December 1975.

Jost, Brian
    1989   *Opera Under Glass* (parody opera). Performed by Gunther Funn Productions, New Theatre, New York, 31 March 1989.

Jump, Frank
    1988   *Hotel Martinique*, with Anne Pope (libretto by composer and Kevin Malony, about the infamous welfare hotel). Performed Irish Arts Center, New York, 15 December 1988.

Jurman, Karl
    -   *Kiddywinks!* (for children; 50 minutes; libretto by Joseph Robinette).
    -   *An Evening Holiday.*

Kabalin, Fedor (AMC; Schoep)
    1973   *A Fable* (1 act—50 minutes; libretto by Dorothy B. Abernathy).

Kagen, Sergius (b. St. Petersburg, Russia, 22 August 1909; d. New York, 1 March 1964; in U.S. from 1925; Anderson; *Baker's*)
    1962   *Hamlet* (3 acts). Performed Baltimore, 9 November 1962.

Kahn, Emil
    1952   *The Ribbon* (1 act). Performed Montclair, NJ, 8 May 1952.

Kalmanoff, Martin (b. Brooklyn, NY, 24 May 1920; ASCAP; Anderson; Schoep)
    1949   *Fit for a King* (1 act; on *The Emperor's New Clothes*). Broadcast on WNYC, New York, 13 February 1949; staged in New York, 1950.
    1951   *Noah and the Stowaway* (1 act—30 minutes; libretto by Atra Baer). Performed at New York College of Music (WNYC), 18 February 1951; New York, 12 October 1952.
    1952   *The Empty Bottle* (3 acts—150 minutes; libretto by Atra Baer based on a news event). Performed by New York College of Music on WNYC, New York, 17 February 1952; at Judson Hall by Ruffino Opera, New York, 29 February and 2 April 1966; and by Amato Opera, New York, July 1991.
    1953   *Godiva* (3 acts; libretto by Atra Baer). Excerpts performed on WNYC, 15 February 1953.
    1953   *Brandy Is My True Love's Name* (1 act—60 minutes; libretto by Atra Baer). Performed by American Lyric Theatre, summer 1953; on WNYC, New York, February 1954; New York, 17 June 1963.
    1954   *A Quiet Game of Cribbage* (1 act—35 minutes; libretto by composer). Performed New York, 8 June 1954, and Detroit, MI, 12 April 1961, etc.
    1955   *The Delinquents* (1 act—60 minutes; libretto by composer). Performed by Co-Opera, Philadelphia, 26-30 April 1955; on WNYC, New York, 1955.

1956   *Opera, Opera* (1 act—30 minutes; libretto after William Saroyan). Performed by After Dinner Opera Co., New York, 22 February 1956, etc. Published by Carl Fischer.

1958   *Videomania* (1 act; libretto by composer), accompanied by piano. Performed at Lincoln College, IL, 8 May 1958, and Denison University, Granville, OH, 18-20 February 1965, and University of Dayton, OH, 27 February 1965.

1958   *Lizzie Strotter: or, The Women War on War (A Modern Lysistrata)* (1 act—40 minutes; libretto after Aristophanes's *Lysistrata*). Performed at Drake University, Des Moines, IA, 6-7 March 1958 [Schoep: 1959], etc.

1962   *The Bald Prima Donna* (1 act—60 minutes; libretto by Eugene Ionesco based on his "Cantatrice Chauve"). Performed New York, 15 December 1962 (more performances in Schoep: by Community Opera at West Side YMCA, New York, 3 and 15-17 1963, etc.). Published by Carl Fischer.

1963   *Young Tom Edison* (1 act). Performed New York, April 1963.

1963   *Half Magic in King Arthur's Court* (1 act). Performed New York, 7 May 1963.

1966   *Huck Finn and Tom Sawyer* (1 act). Performed New York, 15 October 1966.

1966   *Mr. Scrooge* (1 act; libretto after Dickens). Performed New York, 3 December 1966.

1967   *Canterville Ghost* (1 act; libretto after Wilde). Performed New York, 11 March 1967.

1968   *The Audition* ("aleatory opera"; 1 act—10-30 minutes; libretto by composer with Sigmund Spaeth, Illica and Giacosa, and Jay S. Harrison). Performed by Chatham College Opera Workshop, Pittsburgh, PA, 21 August 1968; on WNYC, 22 September 1974.

1968   *The Victory at Masada* (2 acts). Performed Detroit, MI, 10 November 1968.

1968   *The Great Stone Face* (1 act—50 minutes; libretto by composer based on the short story by Nathaniel Hawthorne). Performed at Ball State University, Muncie, IN, 14-16 1968; on WFUV, New York, 29 February 1970. Published by Carl Fischer.

1969   *Aesop, the Fabulous Fabelist*. Performed at Camp Pemigewasset, NH, August 1969.

1969   *King David and David King*. Performed New York, 12 October 1969.

1969   *Legends Three* (1 act). Performed New York, November 1969.

1971   *Photograph—1920* (5 acts—15 minutes; libretto by Gertrude Stein based on her play of the same name). Performed by After Dinner Opera Co., Lake Placid, NY, summer 1971, etc.

1972   *Hipopera: Mod Traviata, Mod Faust, Mod Carmen, Mod Aïda* (4 acts; libretto by composer with music based on Verdi, Gounod, and Bizet). Televised on Mike Douglas Show, April 1972.

1975   *Give Me Liberty or Give Me Death* (1 act). Performed New York, 2 January 1975.

1976   *Christopher Columbus* (1 act). Performed New York, 1976; on tour.

1976   *Smart Aleck and the Talking Wire* (1 act). Performed New York, 1976; on tour.

1977   *Mod Carmen and Mod Traviata*. Performed Boise, ID, 9 April 1977.

1977   *Beautiful Beast* (1 act). Performed Monticello, NY, 13 July 1977.

1979   *The Harmfulness of Tobacco* (satirical comedy; 30 minutes; libretto by Eric Bentley after Anton Chekhov). Performed by Manhattan Opera Singers, Tully Hall, New York, 22 March 1979. Kornick.

1979   *Ralph and the Stalking Bear* (1 act). Performed Monticello, NY, 8 July 1979.

1980   *The Flatbush Football Golem* (90 minutes; libretto by composer and David Lifson). Performed at 13th Street Theatre, New York, 18 December 1980.

1980   *This Week, East Lynne* (musical; 2 acts; libretto by composer and Jack Fletcher after Wood). Performed at Trinity School, New York, 1980.

-    *The Four-Poster* (musical).
-    *The Ghost of the Mountain* (1 act).
-    *Green Mansions* (musical).
-    *The Insect Comedy* (libretto after Capek).
-    *The Mating Machine* (musical).
-    *Maestro* (musical).
-    *No Bed of Roses* (musical).

Kanitz, Ernest (b. Vienna, Austria, 9 April 1894; d. Menlo Park, CA, 7 April 1978; in U.S. from 1938; AMC; Anderson; *Baker's*)

1953   *Kumana* (2 hours).

1958   *Room No. 12* (30 minutes). Performed Los Angeles, 26 February 1958. Published by Mills Music.

1958   *Royal Auction* (1 act). Performed Los Angeles, 26 February 1958.

1958   *The Lucky Dollar* (folk opera; 45 minutes). Performed at University of California, Los Angeles, 1958.

1961   *Perpetual* (17 minutes; libretto after Ellen Terry). Performed at Antelope Valley College, Los Angeles, 26 April 1961.

1964   *Visions at Midnight* (opera-cantata). Performed at University of California, Los Angeles, 26 February 1964.

Kanouse, Monroe (b. Berkeley, CA, 11 July 1936; *WhoAm*)

1988   *Voices of Calafia* (libretto by Corinne Swall, about California history). Performed Tiburon, CA, 9 April 1988, and at Mother Lode Musical Theatre, Kentfield, CA, 4 February 1989.

Kaplan, Elliot

1975   *Gulliver* ("A Spatialoperadramafilmevent"; 3 parts).

Kassern, Tadeusz Zygfrid (b. Lwow, Poland, 19 March 1904; d. New York, 2 May 1957; in U.S. from 1945; Anderson; *Baker's*)

1951   *The Anointed*.

1952   *Sun-Up* ("an American folk opera"; 1 act). Performed New York, 10 November 1954.

1953   *Comedy of the Dumb Wife*.

1954   *Eros and Psyche*. Unfinished.

Kastle, Leonard Gregory (b. New York, 11 February 1929; ASCAP; Anderson; *Amerigrove*; *Baker's*; *Who's Who*)

1954   *The Swing* (1 act—15 minutes). Performed at Carl Fischer Hall, New York, 11 June 1956, and telecast on NBC-TV.

1960   *Deseret* (comedy; 3 acts; libretto by A. H. Bailey). Performed
       Memphis, TN, 1 January 1961, and telecast on NBC-TV.
       Published by Boosey & Hawkes.

1966   *The Pariahs* (3 acts; libretto by composer about early whaling in the
       U.S.). Commission by Deerfield Foundation (Anderson:
       commission by Seattle Opera Association for 1976).

1985   *The Calling of Mother Ann* (*Who's Who*: title is *The Journal of
       Mother Ann*). Performed at Hancock Shaker Village, MA, 21 June
       1985.

Katsaros, Doug

1984   *Just So* (90 minutes; libretto by David Zippel and Mark St.
       Germain after Kipling). Performed by Pennsylvania Stage Co.,
       Philadelphia, October 1984.

1986   *Moby Dick* (2 acts; libretto by Mark St. Germain after Herman
       Melville). Performed by York Theatre Co., New York, 21
       February 1986.

1990   *Suds and Lovers* (libretto by Jume Siegel). Winner, Ten Minute
       Musicals Project. Performed at Climat Theatre, San Francisco, 15
       February 1990.

  -    *Hearts* (libretto by Indira Stefanianne Christopherson).

Katz, David (b. Syracuse, NY, 2 June 1955; *WhoAm*; *Who's Who*)

1984   *The Light of the Eye* (1 act; libretto by composer). Performed
       Danbury, CT, 18 May 1984. Winner, Brooklyn College Chamber
       Opera competition, 1985.

Katzman, Saragail

1990   *The Furnished Room* (libretto by composer after O. Henry).
       Performed at Climat Theatre, San Francisco, CA, 15 February
       1990.

Kaufmann, Walter (b. Karlsbad [now Karlovy Vary], Bohemia, 1 April 1907; d.
       Bloomington, IN, 9 September 1984; to Canada in 1948; in U.S.
       from 1957; *Amerigrove*; see his *Selected Musical Terms of Non-
       Western Cultures: A Notebook-Glossary*, this series, no. 65, 1990)

1950   *The Cloak* (libretto after Gogol).

1951   *The Research*. Performed Tallahassee, FL, 1953.

1952   *A Parfait for Irene* (75 minutes). Performed Bloomington, IN, 21
       February 1952.

1953   *The Golden Touch* (short opera for children).

1955   *Christmas Slippers* (television opera).

1955   *Sganarelle* (1 act). Performed by Metropolitan Opera Studio,
       December 1961; and New York, 18 May 1974.

1958   *George from Paradise* (1 act).

1958   *Paraclesus*.

1961   *The Scarlet Letter* (3 acts; libretto by composer after Hawthorne).
       Performed Bloomington, IN, 6 May 1961, and Indianapolis, IN,
       1962.

1966   *A Hoosier Tale* (3 acts). Performed Bloomington, IN, 30 July 1966.

1966   *Rip van Winkle* (short opera for children).

Kavanaugh, Patrick (b. Nashville, TN, 20 October 1954; Anderson)
- 1974   *Jack and the Beanstalk* (1 act). Performed Washington, DC, 24 November 1974.
- 1983   *The Last Supper* (50 minutes; libretto by composer after the New Testament). Performed at Folger Shakespeare Theatre, Washington DC, 1983.
- 1989   *The Song of Songs* (1 hour; libretto by composer, on his own translation). Performed Washington, DC, summer 1989.

Kay, Ulysses (b. Tucson, AZ, 7 January 1917; *Amerigrove*; *Baker's*; *Who's Who*)
- 1955   *The Boor* (1 act—55 minutes; libretto by composer after Chekhov). Performed Louisville, KY, 3 April 1968. Published by Music Corporation of America.
- 1956   *The Juggler of Our Lady* (1 act—30 minutes; libretto by Alexander King). Performed New Orleans, 23 February 1962, and Jackson, MS, 1972.
- 1970   *The Capitoline Venus* (1 act; libretto by J. Dvorkin after Mark Twain). Performed Chicago, 1971, and Urbana, IL, 12 March 1971.
- 1971   *Trials of Psyche*. Performed Urbana, IL, 12 March 1971.
- 1976   *Jubilee* (3 acts—180 minutes; libretto by Donald Dorr after Margaret Walker's novel of the same name). U.S. bicentennial commission and première by Opera/South, Jackson, MS, 20 November 1976 (*Baker's*: 12 April 1976); also 19 November 1977. Kornick.
- 1983   *Frederick Douglass* (3 acts; libretto by Donald Dorr). Commission by NEA and Rockefeller Foundation. Performed Newark, NJ, 23 February 1989 and in 1990. (*Baker's* date: 1980-85, performed Newark, NJ, 14 April 1991.)
- -   *The Game*. Guggenheim grant.

Kayden, Mildred (b. New York; ASCAP/AMC; Anderson; Cohen)
- 1958   *Mardi gras* (1 act). Broadcast on WNYC radio, New York.
- 1980   *Sepia Star*. Performed New York, June 1980.
- -   *Solomon* (1 act).

Kazakevicius, Jerry
- 1984   *Astro*Bride*, with Joe Budenholzer and John J. Sheehan (libretto by Jo Ann Schmidman). Performed Oma, NE, 21 December 1984.

Kechley, Gerald (b. Seattle, WA, 18 March 1919; Anderson; *WhoAm*)
- 1954   *The Beckoning Fair One* (2 acts). Performed Seattle, 30 November 1954.
- 1959   *The Golden Lion* (2 acts; libretto Elwyn Kechley). Performed Seattle, 28 April 1959; revised version performed Seattle, 1 December 1959. Published by Presser.
- -   *Robin Goodfellow*.

Keller, Walter (b. Chicago, 23 February 1873; d. there, 7 July 1940; Anderson; *Baker's*)
- -   *Alaric's Death* (melodrama).
- -   *The Crumpled Isle* (comic opera).

Kelley, Edgar Stillman (b. Sparta, WI, 14 April 1857; d. New York, 12 November 1944; *Amerigrove*)

1887   *Pompeiian Picnic*, op. 9 (operetta; libretto by A. C. Gunter).

1892   *Puritania: or, The Earl and the Maid of Salem*, op. 11 (comic opera in 2 acts; libretto by C. M. S. McLellan). Performed Boston, 9 June 1892 (over one hundred performances). Published by John Church, 1892.

1902   *Ben-Hur*, op. 17 (incidental music; 6 acts; libretto by Lew Wallace), for solo voices, chorus, orchestra. Piano-vocal score published New York: Towers & Curran, 1902; reprint, Schleifer, 6:7-99.

1917   *The Pilgrim's Progress*, op. 37 ("musical miracle play"; libretto by Elizabeth Hodgkinson after John Bunyan). Performed Cincinnati, 10 May 1918. Vocal score published Boston: Oliver Ditson, 1917. (Kelley also composed incidental music for *Macbeth* and *The Cherub*.)

Kelly, John

1989   *Face the Music* (90 minutes). Performed Santa Barbara, CA, July 1989.

Kelly, Robert (b. Clarksburg, VW, 26 September 1916; Anderson; *Baker's*; Schoep; *Who's Who*)

1950   *Tod's Gal* (folk opera; 55 minutes). Performed Norfolk, VA, 8 January 1971. Published by Presser.

1966   *The White Gods* (3 acts—120 minutes; libretto by composer and Chester Israel about the conquest of Mexico from the Aztec view). Performed Urbana, IL, 3 July 1966.

Kemeny, C. E.

1990   *A Spinning Tale* (libretto by A. Kemeny after "Rumpelstiltskin"). Performed by Playhouse 91, New York, 22 February 1980.

Kemner, Gerald (b. Kansas City, MO, 28 September 1932)

1987   *Duse and D'Annunzio* (libretto by Felicia Londre). University of Missouri Weldon Spring grant. Performed at University of Missouri-Kansas City, 9 April 1987.

Kent, Charles Stanton (b. Minneapolis, MN, 20 January 1914; d. Baltimore, 31 May 1969; Anderson)

1954   *A Room in Time* (supernatural opera; 1 act). Telecast on WBAL-TV, Baltimore, 9 January 1966.

Kent, Richard (b. Harris, MO, 23 January 1916; AMC; Anderson)

-     *Arno* (2 acts).

Kerker, Gustave (b. Herford, Germany, 28 February 1857; d. New York, 29 June 1923; in U.S. from 1867; *Amerigrove*)

(All of the below are operettas, and performances were in New York.)

1879   *The Cadets*. Performed on a 4-month tour by the Herman Grau English Opera Company.

1888   *The Pearl of Pekin* (libretto by C. A. Byrne after A. C. Lecocq).

1890 *Castles in the Air* (libretto by C. A. Byrne), after Jacques Offenbach's *Les Bavards*. Performed 5 May 1890.

1894 *Prince Kam: or, A Trip to Venus* (libretto by C. A. Byrne and L. Harrison). Performed 29 January 1894.

1895 *Kismet* (libretto by R. F. Carroll). Performed 8 December 1895.

1896 *The Lady Slavey* (libretto by H. Morton). Performed 3 February 1896.

1896 *An American Beauty* (libretto by H. Morton). Performed 28 December 1896.

1897 *The Whirl of the Town* (libretto by H. Morton). Performed 25 May 1897.

1897 *The Belle of New York* (libretto by H. Morton). Performed in New York, 28 September 1897; also London, England (697 performances).

1897 *The Telephone Girl* (libretto by H. Morton). Performed 27 December 1897.

1901 *The Girl from Up There* (libretto by H. Morton). Performed 7 January 1901.

1902 *A Chinese Honeymoon* (libretto by G. Dance). Performed 2 June 1902.

1902 *The Billionaire* (libretto by H. B. Smith). Performed 29 December 1902.

1903 *The Blonde in Black* (libretto by H. B. Smith). Performed 8 June 1903.

1903 *Winsome Winnie* (libretto by F. Rankin). Performed 1 December 1903.

1906 *The Social Whirl* (libretto by J. W. Herbert). Performed 7 April 1906.

1906 *The Tourists* (libretto by R. H. Burnside). Performed 25 August 1906.

1907 *The White Hen: or, The Girl from Vienna* (libretto by P. West). Performed 16 February 1907.

1907 *Fascinating Flora* (libretto by R. H. Burnside and J. W. Herbert). Performed 20 May 1907.

1907 *The Lady from Lane's* (libretto by G. Broadhurst). Performed 19 August 1907.

1912 *Two Little Brides* (libretto by A. Anderson and H. Atteridge). Performed 12 April 1912.

Kern, Carl William

- *The Duke of Texas* (comic opera).

Kern, Jerome (b. New York, 27 January 1885; d. there, 11 November 1945; *Amerigrove*)

1927 *Show Boat* (2 acts; libretto by Oscar Hammerstein II after Edna Ferber). Première at Ziegfeld Theatre, New York, 27 December 1927; more recent performances by Houston Grand Opera, TX, 27 January 1989, Portland Opera, 16 June 1989, Opera Pacific, 6 July 1989, Minnesota Opera, 7 July 1989; at Omaha, NE, 14 September 1989; and by Cleveland Opera, 11 May 1990. Kornick.

1941 *Lamplight*. Performed New York; broadcast on WOR, Mutual Broadcasting System radio.

Kerr, Harrison (b. Cleveland, 13 October 1897; d. Norman, OK, 15 August 1978; *Amerigrove*)
1960   *The Tower of Kel* (4 acts; libretto by composer).

Kerr, Walter
1956   *Sing Out, Sweet Land* (1 act). Performed Los Angeles, April 1956.

Kerrison, Davenport (of Jacksonville, FL; earned Doctor of Music from University of New York; Hipsher: still active at age 84 [in 1927 or 1934?])
1914   *The Last of the Aztecs* (libretto by composer).

Kesselman, Lee R.
1988   *The Bremen Town Musicians* (40 minutes; libretto by James Tucker). Performed Madison, WI, 3 September 1988.

Kesselman, Wendy
1982   *The Juniper Tree: A Tragic Household Tale*, with William Schimmel (70 minutes; libretto by composer after Grimm). Performed Stockbridge, MA, 7 July 1982.

Kessner, Daniel Aaron (b. Los Angeles, 3 June 1946; AMC; Anderson; *Who's Who*)
1981   *The Telltale Heart* (40 minutes; libretto by composer after Poe). Holland Festival winner, 1981. Performed Utrecht, Netherlands, 12 March 1982, and The Hague, Netherlands, 12 June 1982.
1987   *Texts for Nothing* (28 minutes; libretto after Beckett). Performed at New Music Los Angeles Festival, CA, 4 March 1987.

Kievman, Carson (b. Hollywood, CA, 27 December 1949; Anderson; *Who's Who*)
1974   *California Mystery Pack* (sound drama/comedy).
1974   *The Repercussive Sojourn* (sound drama/comedy; text by Gertrude Stein), for women's voices.
1977   *New Opera* (mystery chamber opera; 1 act).
1977   *Red Light—Green Light* (mystery opera; 40 minutes). Published by Associated Music.
1978   *Wake Up—It's Time to Go to Bed* (1 act). Published by Associated Music. Performed at Tanglewood Festival, MA, 9 August 1978.
1980   *California Mystery Park*. Published by Associated Music.
1982   *Intelligent Systems* (multimedia; 2 acts; libretto by the composer; uses puppets and animated film). Commission by Southwest German Radio, 1982. NEA grant. Performed at Donaueschingen Musiktage, Germany, 20 October 1984. Published by Intelligent.
1986   *Piano Concert—Prisoners of Conscience* (75 minutes; libretto by composer). Performed Grand Cayman Island, December 1986, and Miami, FL, spring 1989. Published by Intelligent.
1987-   *Tesla* (libretto by composer and Thomas Babe, about the life of Nikola Tesla). Portions performed Waterford, CT, August 1987; to be completed 1991. Published by Intelligent.
1991   *Hamlet* (3 acts; libretto by composer). Scheduled for New York Shakespeare Festival, 1990-91 season. Published by Intelligent.

Killian, Scott
1983   *Lenny and the Heartbreakers*, with Kim Sherman (libretto by the composers and Kenneth Robins). Performed at New York Shakespeare Festival, New York, 22 December 1983.

Kilpatrick, Jack Frederick
1959   *Blessed Wilderness* (or *The Blessed Wilderness*; 3 acts, about Indians in Georgia). Performed Dallas, TX, 18 April 1959.

Kim, Earl (b. Dinuba, CA, 6 January 1920; *Amerigrove*; *Baker's*; Morton/Collins; *Who's Who*)
1971   *Exercises en route* (musical theater; libretto by Samuel Beckett), for soprano, flute/piccolo, oboe, clarinet, violin, cello, 2 percussion, dance, narrator. Première, Cambridge, MA, 1971.
1975   *Narratives*. NEA grant, 1975. Première, Cambridge, MA, 2 February 1979.
1983   *Footfalls* (1 act; libretto after Samuel Beckett), for soprano, mezzo, 2 pianos, harpsichord. NEA grant, 1982. (*Baker's*, Morton/Collins, and *Who's Who* date it 1981.) Première, Cincinnati, OH, 1985.

Kinberg, Max
1980   *Torquemada* (2 acts; libretto by Al Reynolds). Performed by Encompass Theatre, New York, 22 June 1980 and 12 May 1981. Published by National Music Theater Network.

Kindler, Andrew
1977   *Mad Dog Blues*. Performed Binghamton, NY, 1977.

King, Betty Jackson (b. Chicago, 19 February 1928; Cohen; Southern)
1952   *Saul of Tarsus* (biblical opera or oratorio). Performed Chicago.

King, Diane
1985   *The Right Self* (libretto by Jerry Patch; for children). Performed Costa Mesa, CA, 4 February 1985.

Kirchner, Leon (b. Brooklyn, NY, 24 January 1919; *Amerigrove*; *Who's Who*)
1957   *Scenes for an Opera*.
1976   *Lily* (3 acts—90 minutes; libretto by composer after Saul Bellow's *Henderson, the Rain King*). Première by New York City Opera, 10 April 1977 (*Amerigrove*: April 14). Published by Associated Music. Kornick.
-    *Rappaccini's Daughter*. Commission by Lincoln Center, New York.

Kirk, Theron (b. Alamo, TX, 26 September 1919; Anderson)
1972   *The Lib: 393 B.C.* (comic opera; 1 act; 50 minutes; libretto by composer after Aristophanes's *Lysistrata*). Performed San Antonio, TX, 5 May 1972. Published by Carl Fischer.

Kirkpatrick, Howard (b. Tiskilwa, IL, 26 February 1873; Hipsher)
1912   *Olaf* (grand opera; 2 acts; libretto after epic poem by Louise Cox, based on a Norse myth). Performed Lincoln, NE, 5 March 1912.

1924   *La Menuette* (light opera; libretto by H. B. Alexander). Performed
         at Orpheum Theater, Lincoln, NE, 8 December 1924.

Kirkwood, Neal
1988   *No Plays No Poetry But Philosophical Reflections Practical
         Instructions Provocative Prescriptions Opinions and Pointers from a
         Noted Critic and Playwright* (libretto by Harry Mann after
         Brecht). Performed by Via Theater and Otrabanda, New York, 19
         March 1988.

Kirschner, Bob
1990   *The Bohemians* (rock opera; libretto by Diane Brown and Lizzie
         Olesker after *La Bohème*). Performed by Paradise Opera, New
         York, 1 June 1990.

Kitzke, Jerome P. (b. Milwaukee, WI, 6 February 1955; Anderson)
1981   *A Thousand Names to Come* (75 minutes; libretto by James Hazard).
         Commission by Society of Fine Arts, Milwaukee, WI; performed
         by that organization, 18 September 1981.

Klaus, Kenneth Blanchard (b. Earlville, IA, 11 November 1923; d. Baton Rouge,
         LA, 4 August 1980; AMC; Anderson; *Baker's*)
1957   *Tennis Anyone?* (operatic farce).
  -     *Crimson Stones.*
  -     *Moira* (monodramatic opera), for female singer.

Klauss, Kenneth
  -     *The Fall of the House of Usher.*

Klein, Bruno Oscar (b. Osnabrück, Germany, 6 June 1858; d. New York, 22 June
         1911; in U.S. from 1878; *Baker's*; Hipsher)
1895   *Kennilworth* (grand opera; introduction and 3 acts; libretto after
         Scott). Performed Hamburg, Germany, 13 February 1895, with
         title *Ivanhoe*. Hipsher: ". . . the first serious opera by an
         American to be performed in Europe."

Klein, Manuel (b. London, England, 6 December 1876; d. there, 1 June 1919; to
         U.S. in 1900; Anderson)
         (*Baker's*, 7th ed., states that Klein composed music "for many
         productions"; Anderson has some titles of "musical shows.")
1911   *Bow Sing*. Performed at Winter Garden, New York.

Klein, Sheldon
1982   *Revolt in Flatland* (variable length; libretto by composer after
         Abbott's *Flatland*, a "geometrical fantasy"; text and music
         generated by computer). "Performed" at University of Wisconsin
         Computer Sciences Department, Madison, ca. 1982.

Kleinsinger, George (b. San Bernardino, CA, 13 February 1914; d. New York, 28
         July 1982; ASCAP; *Amerigrove*; *Baker's*)
1941   *Farewell to a Hero* (melodrama; text by Walt Whitman).
1945   *Peewee the Piccolo* (melodrama; text by P. Tripp).
1946   *Pan the Piper* (melodrama; text by P. Wing).

1947   *The Story of Celeste* (melodrama; text by P. Tripp).

1954   *archy and mehitabel* (chamber opera; 30 minutes; libretto by J.
        Darion after Marquis). Performed New York, 6 December 1954,
        and as a Broadway musical, titled *Shinbone Alley*, 13 April 1957.
        Published by Chappell.

1955   *The Tree That Found Christmas* (melodrama; 1 act; text by C.
        Darion after C. Morley). Performed New York, 17 December
        1955. Published by Chappell.

  -     *A Day in the Life of a Secretary.*

  -     *Jack and Homer the Horse.* Published by Chappell.

  -     *Tommy Pitcher* (folk opera; 1 act). Published by Chappell.

Knight, Morris (b. Charleston, SC, 25 December 1933; AMC; Anderson)

1962   *A Legend* (50 minutes; after Sieg). NEA grant.

Knodle, Walter St. Clare (little information in Hipsher)

  -     *Belshazaar* (4 acts). Performed Philadelphia?.

Knowles, Christopher

1980   *Dialog/Curious George*, with Dale Ward and Robert Wilson.
        Performed New York, 24 June 1980.

Knowlton, E. Bruce (b. Hillsboro, WI, 25 June 1875; d. 1941; Hipsher: founded
        American Grand Opera Co., Portland, OH, 1925)
        (The Knowlton scores are in the Oregon State Library, Salem.
        Bispham Medal, 1932, for *The Monk of Toledo* and *Wakuta*.)

1915   *The Monk of Toledo* (grand opera; prologue and 3 acts; libretto by
        composer), revised 1922. Première at the Auditorium, Portland,
        OR, 10 May 1926.

1928   *Wakuta* (4 acts; libretto by composer). Performed by American
        Opera Co., Portland, OR, 14 October 1928, composer conducting.

1929   *The Woodsman* (3 acts). Performed by Bruce Knowlton Opera Co.,
        Portland, OR, 4 April 1929.

1929   *Charlotte* (comic opera; 3 acts). Performed Portland, OR, 11
        December 1929.

1931   *Antonio* (serious opera; 2 acts). Performed Portland, OR, 27
        October 1931, composer conducting.

1933   *Montana* (2 acts). Performed Portland, OR.

Knudson, Paul

1976   *The Actress: or, Doll in Pink Dress* (libretto after Merritt).
        Performed Montclair, NJ, May 1976.

Knussen, Oliver (b. Glasgow, Scotland, 12 June 1952; in U.S. from 1970; *Baker's*;
        Who's Who)

1980   *Max and the Maximonsters.* Performed Brussels, Belgium, 28
        November 1980.

1981   *Where the Wild Things Are* (after Maurice Sendak). Performed at
        Glyndebourne Festival, England, 1984; New York Center, October
        or November 1987; Chicago, 17 December 1988; by Minnesota
        Opera, 16 December 1989; and Los Angeles Music Center Opera,
        7 June 1990. Recorded by Arabesque. 1985 Glyndebourne
        performance video: Home Vision 8339243 and WIL01.

1984 *Higglety, Pigglety, Pop!: or, There Must Be More to Life* (45 minutes; libretto after Maurice Sendak). Performed at Glyndebourne Festival, England, 1984 and 1985; by Los Angeles Music Center Opera, 7 June 1990. Published by Faber. 1985 performance on video: Home Vision 8339261 and HIG01; laserdisc: Pioneer Artist 88212, with *Where the Wild Things Are*.

Koch, Frederick (b. Cleveland, OH, 4 April 1924; Anderson)
1974 *Invasion.*
1976 *Music—Music—Music* (contains parts of the last three listed below). Performed at Lakewood Little Theatre, OH, 25 October 1976.
1985 *The Shepherds* (prologue and 1 act—1 hour; libretto by Seymour Reiter after the 15th-century Christmas *Second Shepherd's Play*). Performed West Shore Unitarian Church, Cleveland, 1 December 1985. Kornick.
- *Comedy of Errors.*
- *Good Woman of Setzuan.*
- *Italian Straw Hat.*

Kociolek, Ted
1983 *Babes in the Woods: or, Hansel and Gretel and Percy and the Prune* (libretto by James Billings). Performed Philadelphia, 15 December 1983.

Kohs, Ellis Bonoff (b. Chicago, 12 May 1916; ACA/BMI; *Amerigrove*; *Baker's*; *Who's Who*)
1969 *Amerika* (3 acts; libretto by composer after Kafka). Performed by Western Opera Theatre, CA, 27 May 1970 (*Baker's*: abridged concert version, Los Angeles, 19 May 1970).
- *Lord of the Ascendant* (concert narrative in 3 acts after the Sumerian legend of Gilamesh). Commission by Thor Johnson.
- *Rhinoceros* (after Ionesco).

Kondorossy, Leslie (b. Bratislava, Slovakia, 25 June 1915; in U.S. after World War II; AMC; Anderson; *Baker's*; Schoep)
1953 *A Night in the Puszta* (1 act—45 minutes; libretto by Jeno Poharnok, English book by Shawn Hall). Première, Music Hall, Cleveland, 28 June 1953, broadcast by Radio Voice of America, 4 July 1953.
1954 *The Pumpkin* (1 act—20 minutes; libretto by composer and Shawn Hall based on a comedy by Béla Pasztor). Première, concert form, Severance Chamber Music Hall, Cleveland, 15 May 1954; broadcast on WSRS, Cleveland, 13 February 1955; staged at Mayfield Temple Hall, Mayfield Heights, OH, 5 May 1956.
1954 *The Voice* (1 act—20 minutes; libretto by Steven N. Linek and Shawn Hall). Première in concert form at Severance Chamber Music Hall, Cleveland, 15 May 1954; staged at Opera and Drama Festival, Plymouth [Duxbury?], MA, 11-14 August 1954; broadcast on WSRS, Cleveland, 9 January 1955.
1955 *The Midnight Duel* (1 act—45 minutes; libretto by composer and Shawn Hall). Broadcast by WSRS radio, Cleveland, 20 March 1955; staged at Mayfield Temple Hall, Mayfield Heights, OH, 9 January 1956.

1955   *The Headsman.*
1955   *The Two Imposters* (1 act—35 minutes; libretto by Shawn Hall after
        a comedy by G. Vaszary). Broadcast on WSRS radio, Cleveland,
        10 April 1955; staged at Public Auditorium-Little Theater,
        Cleveland, 21 October 1956; broadcast by Radio Voice of
        America, New York, 23 October 1956.
1955   *The String Quartet* (1 act). Broadcast by WSRS radio, Cleveland, 8
        May 1955.
1955   *The Mystic Fortress* (1 act). Broadcast by WSRS radio, Cleveland,
        12 June 1955.
1956   *The Unexpected Visitor* (1 act—40 minutes; libretto by composer,
        Julia Kemeny, and Shawn Hall). Première at Public Auditorium-
        Little Theater, Cleveland, 21 October 1956, broadcast by Radio
        Voice of America, New York, 24 October 1956.
1957   *Alms from the Beggar.*
1961   *The Fox* (1 act—35 minutes; libretto by Shawn Hall after Kalman
        Mikszath's novel). Performed Cleveland, 28 January 1961.
1964   *The Baksheesh* (or *Baksis*).
1964   *Nathan the Wise.*
1967   *The Poorest Suitor* (children's opera-oratorio). Performed
        Cleveland, 24 May 1967. Broadcast by WBOE (NPR), Cleveland,
        25 January 1971.
1969   *Shizuka's Dance* (children's opera-oratorio). Telecast, Tokyo,
        Japan, 22 April 1969 (*Baker's*: performed Cleveland, 22 April
        1969). Broadcast by WBOE (NPR), Cleveland, 26 January 1971.
1969   *Ruth and Naomi* ("church opera"; 1 act—20 minutes; libretto by
        Shawn Hall and Richard L. Glass, after the Bible). Performed at
        Church of the Master (Baptist) Cleveland, 28 April 1974; also at
        Sophia University, Tokyo, Japan, 6 August 1974.
1971   *Kalamona and the Four Winds* (children's opera-oratorio; 1 act;
        libretto by Elizabeth Kondorossy after a Hungarian folk tale).
        Broadcast by WBOE (NPR), Cleveland, 27 January 1971.

Koppenhaver, Allen J.
1977   *A Piano Comes to Arkansas* (libretto by Robert Haskins after
        Thomas Thorpe). Performed Springfield, OH, fall 1977.

Korie, Michael
1989   *Kabbalah*, with Stewart Wallace. Performed Brooklyn, NY, 16
        November 1989.

Korn, Clara Anna (née Gerlach or Gerlack; b. Berlin, Germany, 30 January 1866;
        d. New York, 14 July 1940; to U.S. as a child; Cohen)
-       *Their Last War.*

Korn, Peter Jona (b. Berlin, Germany, 30 March 1922; left Germany 1933; in
        U.S. 1941-67; *Amerigrove*; *Baker's*)
1963   *Heidi in Frankfurt*, op. 35 (1 act; libretto by composer after
        Johanna Spyri). Performed Saarbrücken, Germany, 28 November
        1978.

Korngold, Erich Wolfgang (b. Brno, Moravia, 29 May 1897; d. Hollywood, CA,
        29 November 1957; to U.S. in 1934; *Amerigrove*)

1916   *Violanta*, op. 8 (libretto by Hans Müller). U.S. première by Metropolitan Opera, New York, 5 November 1927.

1917   *Die tote Stadt*, op. 12 (libretto by Paul Schott [composer and J. Korngold] after G. Rodenbach's *Bruges la morte*). Première in Hamburg and Cologne, Germany, 4 December 1920; performed by Metropolitan Opera, New York, 19 November 1921 and 29 November 1922; revived in New York, 1975, and by the Deutsche Opera, Berlin, 1985.

1939   *Die Kathrin*, op. 28 (libretto by E. Decsey). Performed Stockholm, Sweden, 7 October 1939.

1946   *The Wildnet Serenade*, op. 36 ("stage comedy"; libretto by composer after H. Reisfeld).

Kosakoff, E. G.
1978   *A Thread of Scarlet*, with Howard Richardson. Performed New York, 30 November 1978.

Kosakoff, Reuven (b. New Haven, CN, 8 January 1898; d. New York, 6 May 1987; Anderson; *Baker's*)
-    *The Cabalists* (1 act).

Kosch, Michael
1988   *Scotichronicon* (video opera; libretto by Jack El-Hai). Performed at Minnesota Composers Forum, 7 January 1988.

Kosteck, Gregory (b. Plainfield, NJ, 2 September 1937; Anderson)
1964   *Vengeance Is Mine*.
1966   *Maurya* (1 act; libretto after Synge's *Riders to the Sea*). Performed Greenville, SC, 24 April 1968.
1970   *The Stronger* (libretto after Strindberg). Performed Greenville, SC, 30 April 1970.

Koutzen, Boris (b. Uman, near Kiev, Ukraine, 1 April 1901; d. Mount Kisco, NY, 10 December 1966; in U.S. from 1922; ASCAP; *Amerigrove*)
1954   *The Fatal Oath* (1 act—50 minutes; libretto after Balzac's *Grand Bretèche*). Performed New York, 25 May 1955. Published by General Music.
1962   *You Never Know* (comic opera; 1 act; libretto by composer). Published by General Music.

Kowalsky, Steven
1989   *Commuter!* (1 act; libretto by composer). Performed Chicago, 1 November 1989.

Kraft, Leo (b. New York, 24 July 1922; *Amerigrove*; *Who's Who*)
-    *The Caliph's Clock* (150 minutes).

Kraft, William [not the composer/percussionist in *Amerigrove*] and **Barbara**
1976   *The Innocents* (on Salem witch trials). Performed Pasadena, CA, January 1976.

Kramer, Cathy

1986   *Love in the Third Degree* (libretto by Olan Jones). Performed by
New Dramatists, New York, 8 October 1986.

Krane, David

1982   *Adventures of Pinocchio* (100 minutes; libretto by William M.
Wauters after Collodi). Performed by OPERA America Showcase,
New York, December 1982.

-    *Peck's Bad Boy* (2 hours; libretto by composer and Bill Keaton
after Wilbur).

Krane, Sherman M. (b. New Haven, CN, 18 November 1927; Anderson)

1960   *The Giant's Garden* (or *Grant's Garden*; 30 minutes). Performed
Norfolk, VA, 12 March 1960. Published by Carl Fischer.

Kremenliev, Boris (b. Razlog, Bulgaria, 23 May 1911; in U.S. from 1929;
Amerigrove; *Who's Who*)

1966   *The Bridge* (3 acts; libretto by E. Kremenliev).

Krenek, Ernst (b. Vienna, Austria, 23 August 1900; d. Los Angeles, 22 December
1991; in U.S. from 1937; ASCAP; *Amerigrove*; *Baker's*;
Morton/Collins; *Who's Who*)

1940   *Tarquin*, op. 90 (drama with music; libretto by E. Lavery).
Première, Poughkeepsie, NY, 13 May 1941; also performed
Cologne, Germany, 1950.

1946   *What Price Confidence?*, op. 111 (comic chamber opera; libretto by
composer). Performed Saarbrücken, Germany, 22 May 1962.

1950   *Dark Waters*, op. 125 (1 act—35 minutes; libretto by composer).
Performed Los Angeles, 1950; also performed 2 May 1951.

1953   *Pallas Athene weint*, op. 144 (prologue and 3 acts; libretto by
Alistair Reid [*Amerigrove*: libretto by composer]). Performed
Hamburg, Germany, 1955.

1956   *The Belltower*, op. 153 (1 act—56 minutes; libretto by composer after
Melville). Performed at University of Illinois, Urbana, 17 March
1957. Recorded on University of Illinois CRS 5.

1962   *Ausgerechnet und verspielt*, op. 179 (television opera; 1 act; libretto
by composer). Performed Vienna, Austria, 25 July 1962.

1963   *Der goldene Bock*, op. 186 (4 acts; libretto by composer).
Performed Hamburg, Germany, 16 June 1964.

1966   *Der Zauberspiegel*, op. 206 (television opera; 1 act; libretto by
composer). Première, Munich, Germany, 6 September 1967.

1969   *Sardakai*, op. 206 (*Das kommt davon: oder Wenn Sardakai auf
Reisen geht*) (2 parts; libretto by composer). Performed Hamburg,
Germany, 27 June 1970, composer conducting.

1973   *Flaschenpost von Paradies: oder der Englischer Ausflug* (television
play), for tenor, bass, mime dancers, speakers, tape, percussion,
piano. Première, Vienna, Austria, 8 March 1974.

-    *Jonny spielt auf* (*Johnny Strikes up the Band*) (libretto by
composer). U.S. première by Metropolitan Opera, New York, 19
January 1929.

Kreutz, Arthur (b. La Crosse, WI, 25 July 1906; d. Oxford, MS, 11 March 1991; Anderson; *Baker's*)

1950   *Acres of Sky* ("ballad opera"; 135 minutes). Performed Fayetteville, AR, 16 November 1951; and at Columbia University, New York, 7 May 1952.

1954   *The University Greys* ("a ballad opera of Civil War days"; 2 hours). Performed at University of Mississippi, 15 March 1954.

1958   *Sourwood Mountain* ("folk opera"; 1 hour). Performed Oxford, MS, 1958; Clinton, MS, 8 November 1959 (composer conducting); and at 1959 Music Educators National Conference convention, Roanoke, VA (Anderson: Roanoke, 4 April 1958; *Baker's*: Clinton, 8 January 1959). Published by Franco Colombo.

\-   *Verbena* (libretto after Faulkner).

Kreutz, Robert Edward (b. La Crosse, WI, 21 March 1922; *Who's Who*)

\-   *Francesco* (based on the life of St. Francis of Assisi).

Kroeger, Ernest Richard (b. St. Louis, 10 August 1862; d. there, 7 April 1934; *Amerigrove*)

\-   *A Masque of Dead Florentines.*

Kroll, Louis

1934   *Mme. Butterfly Recovers* (1 act). Performed New York.

1935   *La Bella: or, André Goes Commercial* (1 act). Performed New York.

Krouse, Ian

1987   *Lorca, Child of the Moon* (or *Mariana Pineda*; 3 hours; libretto by Margarita Galban after Federico García Lorca). NEA grant, 1985-86. Performed by Bilingual Foundation of the Arts, Los Angeles, June 1987, and 6-11 August 1991.

Kubik, Gail (b. South Coffeyville, OK, 5 September 1914; d. Claremont, CA, 20 July 1984; *Amerigrove*; *Baker's*)

1946   *A Mirror in the Sky* (folk opera; 1 act; about Audubon). Performed Eugene, OR, 23 May 1939; and New York, 12 May 1947.

1950   *Boston Baked Beans* ("opera piccola"; 20 minutes). Performed at Museum of Modern Art, New York, 9 March 1952. Published by Chappell.

Kucharz, Larry

\-   *The Bar* (multimedia; of variable length; libretto by composer).

Kuhn, Kevin

1989   *Midsummer Nights.* Performed New York, 13 September 1989.

Kupferman, Meyer (b. New York, 3 July 1926; *Amerigrove*; *Baker's*; *Who's Who*)

1948   *In a Garden* (1 act—20 minutes; libretto after Gertrude Stein). Performed New York, 29 December 1949. Revised 1963.

1957   *The Curious Fern* (1 act). Performed New York, 5 June 1957. Published by Presser.

1957   *Voices for a Mirror* (55 minutes). Performed New York, 5 June 1957. Published by Presser.

1958   *Draagenfut Girl* (children's opera; 2 acts). Performed Bronx, NY, 8 May 1958. Published by Mercury.

1967   *The Judgement* (*Infinities 18a*) (3 acts; libretto by P. Freeman after the Bible), for a cappella voices and tape. Published by General Music.

1971   *Visions and Games* (multimedia). Performed at Sara Lawrence College, 24 May 1971.

1975   *Prometheus Condemned* (5 scenes; libretto by composer after Goethe).

-    *Dr. Faustus Lights the Lights* (comedy). Published by Mercury.

-    *In a Garden* (fantasy; 20 minutes). Published by Presser.

Kupris, Maija

1988   *Sold Out* (formerly *Robin's Band*; libretto by composer, Anthony Abeson, and Jerome Eskow). Performed by AMAS Repertory Theatre, New York, 14 April 1988.

Kurka, Robert (b. Cicero, IL, 22 December 1921; d. New York, 12 December 1957; *Amerigrove*)

1957   *The Good Soldier Schweik* (2 acts; libretto by L. Allen after J. Hašek), orchestrated by Hershy Kay. Première by New York City Opera, 23 April 1958; European première, Dresden, 10 November 1959. Published by Weintraub.

Kuss, Malena (b. Cordoba, Argentina, 11 August 1940; *WhoAm*)

1989   *My Fellow Traveler* (1 act). Performed Seattle, WA, 13 March 1989.

La Barbara, Joan (Joan Linda Lotz La Barbara Subotnick) (b. Philadelphia, 8 June 1947; Morton/Collins)

1988   *Prologue to The Book of Knowing . . . (and) of Overthrowing*. Solo aria for voice and tape, to become an opera. Aria first performed New York, 6 July 1988.

1990   *Events in the Elsewhere* (interactive media opera; inspired by Stephen Hawking). Première, Santa Fe, NM, 24-26 August 1990.

LaBruyère, Louise

1989   *Everyman* (1 act; libretto by composer after Hofmannsthal's version of a medieval morality play). Performed New Orleans, 10 June 1989.

LaChiusa, Michael John

1989   *Buzzsaw Berkeley* (spoof of horror movies; libretto by the composer; conceived by Christopher Ashley and Douglas Wright). Performed by WPA Theater, New York, 1 August 1989.

1990   *Eulogy for Mister Hamm* (1 act; libretto by composer). Performed by Ensemble Studio Theatre, New York, May 1990.

Lachmund, Carl Valentine (b. Booneville, MO, 27 March 1857; d. Yonkers, NY, 20 February 1928; *Amerigrove*)

-    *Narrowly Averted*. In Krohn.

Lackey, Lionel (Schoep)
> 1978   *Follow Me Where?* (50 minutes—there is an original and a shorter
> version; libretto by composer, based on 1959-60 murder case),
> orchestra of 11 players. Performed Madison, WI, 30 March 1978.
>
> 1979   *The Heart of Midlothian* (50 minutes; libretto after Scott).
> Performed at Edinboro State College, PA, 26 February 1979.
>
> 1979   *Osrella de Poughkeepsie* (30 minutes; bel canto parody). Performed
> Granville, OH, 20 April 1979.
>
> 1979   *Mr. Pegotty's Dream Comes True* (14 minutes; libretto after
> Dickens's *David Copperfield*). Performed Greensboro, NC, 13
> November 1979.
>
> 1981   *Le senatori* (*The Senators*) (14 minutes; libretto by the composer; a
> parody of Verdi that takes place in Yonkers, NY). Performed at
> Jacksonville University, FL, 20 May 1981 and 19 June 1981.
>
> \-   *Guy Mannering* (75 minutes; libretto after Sir Walter Scott),
> orchestra of 11 players.
>
> \-   *Ligela* (12 minutes). Performed Santa Cruz, CA, 4 May 1980.
>
> \-   *Stephen de Schenectady* (1 act; bel canto parody; companion piece
> to *Osrella de Poughkeepsie*).
>
> \-   *Willie Boy* (50 minutes; libretto by composer after Harry Lawton).

Lackman, Susan Cohn (b. Tsing Tao, China, 1 July 1948; Cohen; *WhoAm*)
> 1982   *Lisa Stratos* (40 minutes; libretto by composer after Aristophanes's
> *Lysistrata*). Performed by OPERA America Showcase, 1982.

Laderman, Ezra (b. New York, 29 June 1924; ASCAP/AMC; *Amerigrove*; *Baker's*;
> Morton/Collins; *Who's Who*)
> 1954   *Jacob and the Indians* (3 acts; libretto by E. Kinoy after Stephen
> Vincent Benét). Performed Woodstock, NY, 24 July 1957.
>
> 1956   *Goodbye to the Clowns* (1 act—45 minutes; libretto by E. Kinoy).
> Performed New York, 22 May 1960. Published by Mercury.
>
> 1958   *The Hunting of the Snark* (opera-cantata; 45 minutes; libretto after
> Lewis Carroll). Performed New York, 25 March 1961; staged
> there, 13 April 1978.
>
> 1959   *Sarah* (30 minutes; libretto by C. Roskam). Telecast on CBS-TV,
> New York, 29 November 1959. (*Baker's*: telecast, 30 November
> 1958.)
>
> 1962   *Dominique* (musical comedy; 2 acts; libretto by Joe Darion after E.
> Kinoy).
>
> 1965   *Air Raid* (1 act; libretto by Archibald MacLeish).
>
> 1967   *Shadows Among Us* (2 acts; libretto by Norman Rosten). Performed
> Philadelphia, 14 December 1979.
>
> 1970   *And David Wept* (biblical drama; 50 minutes; libretto by Joe
> Darion). Première (unstaged) on CBS-TV, 11 April 1971; also
> performed (staged) at 92nd Street YMHA, New York, 31 May
> 1980. Kornick.
>
> 1973   *The Questions of Abraham* (opera-cantata; 1 act; libretto by Joe
> Darion). On CBS-TV, 30 September 1973.
>
> 1978   *Galileo Galilei* (3 acts and epilogue—120 minutes; libretto by Joe
> Darion after *The Trials of Galileo*). Staged première by Tri-Cities
> Opera and the State University of New York, Binghamton, NY, 3
> February 1979. Telecast on CBS-TV, 14 May 1967, as opera-

oratorio *The Trials of Galileo*. Published by Oxford University Press. Kornick.

LaFlamme, Linda (ASCAP)
1987   *The Ugly Duckling*. Performed San Francisco, 8 May 1987.

La Grassa, L.
1856   *Anne of Austria*. Performed Philadelphia.

Laird, Bruce
1969   *The Partisans*. Performed Wilmington, DE, February 1969.

Lam, Bun-Ching
1987   *Floating Opera: A Treading of Steps*, with Paul Dresher, Norman Durkee, Janice Giteck, Philip Glass, and Jarrad Powell. Performed on waterways around Seattle, all day, 20 September 1987.

Lamb, Dorothy
1954   *The Nightingale* (1 act; libretto after Andersen). Performed Poughkeepsie, NY, 27 April 1954.

Lambord, Benjamin (b. Portland, ME, 10 June 1879; d. Lake Hopatcong, NJ, 7 June 1915; *Amerigrove*)
-    *Woodstock* (2 acts completed).

LaMonaca, Joseph (b. Noicattaro, Bari, Italy, 10 February 1872; to U.S. in 1900; Hipsher)
-    *The Festival of Guari* (libretto by Francesco Cubiciotti based on a Hindu story).

La Montaine, John (b. Chicago, 17 March 1920; ASCAP; *Amerigrove*; *Baker's*; *WhoAm*)
1957   *Spreaking the News*, op. 27.
    Trilogy:
1960   *Novellis, novellis*, op. 31 (Christmas pageant opera; 60 minutes; libretto by composer after medieval English). Performed at Washington Cathedral, DC, 24 December 1961. Published by G. Schirmer.
1967   *The Shephardes Playe*, op. 38 (Christmas pageant opera; 1 act; libretto by composer after medieval English; TV opera). Commission by and performed at Washington Cathedral, 24 December 1967 (*Baker's*: December 27).
1969   *Erode the Great*, op. 40 (Christmas pageant opera; libretto by composer after medieval English). Performed at Washington Cathedral, 31 December 1969.
1976   *Be Glad Then America: A Decent Entertainment from the Thirteen Colonies*, op. 43 (choral opera/oratorio; 2 acts—80 minutes; libretto by composer), for U.S. bicentennial. Première at Institute for the Arts and Humanistic Studies, Pennsylvania State University, 6 February 1976. Kornick. Published by Fredonia Press.

La Mothe, Susan
> 1965   *The Kitchen Sink* (satire; 1 act; libretto by David Posner).
> Performed Buffalo, NY, 19 February 1965.

Lancaster, Samuel
> 1987   *Tunes in His Head* (libretto by composer; for children). Performed
> Denver, CO, 1987.

Landau, Siegfried (b. Berlin, Germany, 4 September 1921; in U.S. from 1940;
> ASCAP; Anderson; *Who's Who*)
> 1959   *The Sons of Aaron* (2 acts). Performed Scarsdale, NY, 28 February
> 1959.

Langert, Jules (b. New York, 25 March 1932; Anderson)
> 1982   *Rites of Passage* (1 act; libretto by composer). Performed San
> Rafael, CA, 12 March 1982.
> -   *Sea Change* (for 4 singers and chamber ensemble).

Langham, Chris
> 1981   *Illuminatus!*, with Steve Amadek, John Engerman, and Ken
> Campbell (on novels by Robert Shea and Robert A. Wilson).
> Performed Houston, TX, July 1981.

Langston, Paul
> Commission by Stetson University Opera Program, Deland, FL, for
> a 1-act work, 1991.

Lapham, Claude
> 1933   *Sakura.* Reported as the first Japanese-language opera produced in
> the U.S. Performed at the Hollywood Bowl, CA, 1933.

Lapine, James
> 1978   *Twelve Dreams.* Performed New York, 18 February 1978.

Lapinskas, Darius (b. Kaunas, Lithuania, 9 March 1934; *Who's Who*)
> 1984   *Dux Magnus (The Great Leader)* (3 acts; libretto by Kazys
> Bradunas, about Casimir, patron saint of Lithuania; in Lithuanian,
> with quotations in other languages). Performed Toronto, Ontario,
> 1 September 1984; and by New Opera, Chicago, 31 May 1986.
> 1987   *Rex Amos* (1 act). Performed by New Opera, Chicago, 30 May
> 1987.
> 1988   *Ives of Danbury* (libretto by composer, about Charles Ives and using
> some of his music). Performed by New Opera, Chicago, 14 May
> 1988.

La Plante, Skip
> 1984   *Second Species* (2 acts; libretto by composer, about a future
> postnuclear age; contains excerpts from well-known operas).
> Performed by Keith King/Local Color, New York, 7 December
> 1984, and in Newark, NJ, February 198—revised version.

La Prade, Ernest (b. Memphis, TN, 20 December 1889; d. Sherman, CN, 20
April 1969; Anderson; *Baker's*)
1917   *Xantha* (comic opera). Performed London, England.

Larsen, Libby (b. Wilmington, DE, 24 December 1950; ASCAP; *Amerigrove*;
Cohen; Morton/Collins; *Who's Who*)
1973   *Some Pig.* Performed at University of Minnesota, Minneapolis, 6
June 1973.
1977   *The Words upon the Windowpane* (1 act; after Yeats). Performed
Minneapolis, 1 June 1978.
1979   *The Silver Fox* (children's opera; 1 act). Performed St. Paul, MN,
20 April 1979. Published by G. Schirmer.
1979   *The Emperor's New Clothes* (1 act; libretto by Timothy Mason).
Performed Minneapolis, 13 October 1979.
1980   *Tumbledown Dick* (2 acts; libretto by V. Sutton). Performed
Minneapolis [*Amerigrove*: St. Paul], 16 May 1980. Published by G.
Schirmer.
1982   *Psyche and the Pskyscraper.*
1984   *Clair de lune* (3 acts; libretto by Patricia Hampl). Première by
Arkansas Opera Theatre, Little Rock, 22 February 1985. Kornick.
1985   *Holy Ghosts* (libretto after Linney). NEA grant, 1985.
1986   *Daytime Moon* (video opera). Performed St. Paul, MN, 11 April
1986.
1986   *Four on the Floor* (film/opera). Performed St. Paul, MN, 11 April
1986.
1987   *Frankenstein: The Modern Prometheus* (libretto by composer after
Mary Shelley; calls for video projections). Commission by
Minnesota Opera. Performed St. Paul, MN, spring 1987 and 25
May 1990.
1988   *Christina Romana* (libretto by Vern Sutton). Commission by
University of Minnesota, Minneapolis; performed there, May
1988.
1989   *Beauty and the Beast.*
1992   *A Wrinkle in Time.* Commission by Opera Delaware, Wilmington,
for performance in 1992.
-       *Woman of Letters.*

Lasker, Henry (b. Hyde Park, MA, 25 October 1909; d. Newton Center, MA, 30
July 1976; ASCAP; Anderson)
1964   *Jack and the Beanstalk* (1 act). Commission by Brookline Youth
Concerts. Performed Boston, 25 April 1964.
-       *Beauty and the Beast.*

Lászlo, Alexander (b. Budapest, Hungary, 22 November 1895; d. Los Angeles, 17
November 1970; U.S. citizen, 1944; Anderson; *Baker's*)
1968   *Wanted: Sexperts and Serpents for Our Garden of Maidens*
(musical).

Latham, William Peters (b. Shreveport, LA, 4 January 1917; *Baker's*; *Who's Who*)
1980   *Orpheus in Pecan Springs* (1 act; libretto by Thomas Holliday, about
Texas in the 1830s). Performed Denton, TX, 4 December 1980.

Lauer, Elizabeth (b. Boston, 2 December 1932; Cohen)
- *Desire under the Dryer* (comic chamber opera; 1 act; libretto by Gerald Walter).

Laufer, Beatrice (b. New York, 27 April 1923; Anderson; Cohen)
1958   *Ile* (1 act; libretto after O'Neill's *The Long Voyage Home*). Première by Royal Opera Co., Sweden; also performed Brooklyn, NY, 28 April 1957. Broadcast by National Public Radio, 1978. Performed also in China; see *New Yorker*, 6 February 1989, 102.
1968   *My Brother's Keeper* (biblical opera).

Lauridsen, Cora
1965   *Job* (1 act). Performed Los Angeles, 28 February 1965.

Lauten, Elodie (ASCAP)
1985   *The Death of Don Juan* (libretto by Gregor Capodieci). NEA grant, 1985-86 season.

Lavallée, Calixa (b. Ste. Théodosie de Verchères [now Calixa-Lavallée], Québec, Canada, 28 December 1842; d. Boston, 21 January 1891; *Amerigrove*; Hipsher)
1882   *The Widow* (opéra comique; 3 acts; libretto by F. H. Nelson). Performed by C. D. Hess's Acme Opera Co., Springfield, IL, 1 April 1882. Vocal score published Boston, 1882.
1883   *Tiq: or, Settled at Last* (melodramatic musical satire; 2 acts; libretto by W. F. Sage and P. Hawley on the "Indian question"). Vocal score published Boston, 1883.

La Violette, Wesley (b. St. James, MN, 4 January 1894; d. Escondido, CA, 29 July 1978; *Amerigrove*; Hipsher)
1929   *Shylock* (2 hours; libretto by composer after Shakespeare's *Merchant of Venice*). Excerpts performed at Casino Club, Chicago, 1930. Bispham Medal, 1930. (*Baker's*: date of composition 1927.)
1935   *The Enlightened One* (prologue and 3 acts; about the life of Buddha). (*Baker's* date: 1955.)
- *Falstaff.*
(His book *The Crown of Wisdom*, 1949 [*Baker's*: Bombay, 1960], was nominated for the Nobel Prize.)

Lavry, Marc
1970   *Tamar and Judah* (libretto by Rabbi Newman after Genesis 38). Performed New York, 22 March 1970.

Lawergren, Bo (b. Sweden, 4 January 1937; to U.S. in 1967; AMC; Anderson; *Who's Who*)
1969   *Captain Cook* (chamber opera; 25 minutes). Published by Belwin-Mills.
1974   *Deep Tongue* (chamber opera).
- *Three Acts. COS-2.*

Lawrence, Charles W.
1929   *Atsumori* (1 act). Performed Seattle, WA, 11 December 1929, Tokyo, Japan, 9 February 1950, and Seattle, WA, 26 February 1954.

Leake, Damien
1981   *Child of the Sun* (libretto by composer; about twenty years of a black urban family). Richard Rodgers award, 1981. Performed by New Federal Theatre, New York, 30 November 1981.

Le Baron, Anne (b. Baton Rouge, LA, 30 May 1953; Anderson)
1987   *The E and O Line* (libretto by Edwin Honig). Performed by Musical Theater Works, New York, 23 November 1987, and CSC Repertory Theatre, New York, 20 March 1988.

Lebeau, Annie
1986   *Louis Braille* (2 acts; libretto by Jane Smuylan and Joel Vig; for children). Performed Theatreworks/USA, New York, summer 1986 and 24 October 1987.

Lee, Bill
1970   *The Depot: A Negro in Snow Hill, Ala.* (folk opera). Performed New York, 8 May 1970.

Lee, Dai-Keong (b. Honolulu, HI, 2 September 1915; ASCAP/AMC; *Amerigrove*)
1940   *The Poet's Dilemma* (1 act). Performed New York, 12 April 1940.
1951   *Open the Gates* (150 minutes; libretto by R. Payne, based on the life of Mary Magdalene). Commission and production by Blackfriars Theater Guild of New York.
1952   *Phineas and the Nightingald* (libretto by R. Healy). Withdrawn; see *Two Knickerbocker Tales*, below.
1957   *Two Knickerbocker Tales: Phineas and the Nightingale* (opera buffas; 1 act—52 minutes; libretto by composer and R. Healy).
1957   *Speakeasy* (45 minutes). Performed New York, November 1964. Withdrawn; see *Ballad of Kitty the Barkeep*, below.
1972   *Noa Noa* (musical play).
1979   *Ballad of Kitty the Barkeep* ("cabaret opera" in 1 act; libretto by composer and R. Healy, based on *Speakeasy*). *COS*-3.
1981   *Jenny Lind* (musical play; libretto after P. T. Barnam's *Recollections*).
  -     *Night People* (1 act). Published by Belwin-Mills.
  -     *The River*.

Lee, Thomas Oboe (b. Peking, China, 5 September 1945; AMC; *Who's Who*)
1981   *The Cockscomb* (monodrama; 12 minutes; libretto by Barbara Kuehn Center). Performed Lenox, MA, 4 August 1981.
1987   *Unmasked* (30 minutes; libretto by Barbara Kuehn Center). NEA grant, 1987. Performed Boston, 26 April 1989. Published by Departed Feathers.
  -     *Octopus Wrecks*.

Leeds, James
> 1989   *The Last Leaf* (libretto by William Cotter after O. Henry). Performed by Golden Fleece, New York, 27 June 1989.

Lees, Benjamin (b. Harbin, China, 8 January 1924; to U.S. as a baby; *Amerigrove*; Morton/Collins)
> 1955   *The Oracle* (60 minutes; libretto by composer). Published by Boosey & Hawkes. (*Amerigrove* and Morton/Collins date: 1956.)
> 1964   *The Gilded Cage* (1 act; libretto by A. Reid). Performed November 1964. (*Amerigrove* and Morton/Collins: 3 acts, composition date 1970-72, withdrawn.)
> 1971   *Medea in Corinth* (28 minutes). Première, London, England, 10 January 1971. Telecast on CBS-TV, May 1974. Published by Boosey & Hawkes.

Legg, James
> 1983   *Wedding Night* (20 minutes; libretto by Melvin Freedman). Performed Rochester, NY, 13 December 1983.
> 1986   *The Wife of Bath's Tale* (1 hour; libretto by composer and Melvin Freedman after Chaucer). Performed Aspen, CO, 1986.
> 1989   *The Informer* (formerly *The Tattle Tale*; 1 act; libretto by Sandra Russell). Winner, Brooklyn College Chamber Opera Competition, 1987. Performed Houston, TX, 6 June 1985.

Leginska, Ethel (real name Liggins; b. Hull, England, 13 April 1886; d. Los Angeles, 26 February 1970; to U.S. in 1917; *Amerigrove*; *Baker's*; Cohen)
> 1932   *The Rose and the Ring* (3 acts). Performed Los Angeles, 23 February 1957, composer conducting).
> 1935   *Gale* [or *Gale the Hunting* according to *COS*-2] (1 act; libretto by C. A. Dawson-Scott). Performed by Civic Opera, Chicago, 23 November 1935, composer conducting, and in Los Angeles, 19 December 1969. Bispham Medal.
> -   *The Haunting* (1 act).

Lehmer, Derrick Norman
> 1933   *The Harvest* (musical folk drama; 3 acts). Performed San Francisco, 14 October 1933 (Hipsher, 430: that date at Theater of the Legion of Honor, San Jose).
> 1934   *The Necklace of the Sun.* Performed Oakland, CA, December 1934, and San Francisco, 2 April 1935.

Lehrman, Leonard J. (b. Fort Riley, KS, 20 August 1949; ASCAP/AMC; Anderson; *Baker's*; *Who's Who*)
> 1970   *Beowulf: or, The Great Dane* ("parodic musical fantasy").
> *Tales of Malamud*, two 1-act operas with librettos after Bernard Malamud:
> 1973   *Idiots First*, completion of Marc Blitzstein's unfinished opera. *See also* Blitzstein, Marc.
> 1974   *Karla* (1 act—45 minutes; libretto by composer after Malamud's "Notes from a Lady at a Dinner Party"). Performed (concert preview) at Cornell University, Ithaca, NY, 3 August 1974;

première by Marc Blitzstein Opera Co., Bloomington, IN, 14 March 1976; also performed by Bel Canto Opera, New York, 22 January 1978. (Anderson: both performed Ithaca on 2 August 1974.) Kornick.

1976   *Sima.* Performed Ithaca, NY, 22 October 1976.

1980   *Hannah* (150 minutes; libretto by composer and Orel Odinov; Chanukah opera about Hannah, sister of the Maccabees). Performed Mannheim-Seckenheim, Germany, 22 May 1980; broadcast on WBAI-FM, New York, 26 December 1989.

1984   *The Family Man* (44 minutes; libretto by composer after Sholokhov's "Semyoniy Chelovek"; contains Russian melodies). Performed by TOMI, New York, 8 January 1984, and in Berlin, Germany, January 1985.

1988   *The Birthday of the Bank* (55 minutes; after Chekhov's *The Jubilee*, in English or Russian). Commission by Opera America for the Lake George Opera Festival. Performed Glens Falls, NY, 2 August 1988 (in English).

-   *New World* (libretto by Joel Shatzky). In progress, *COS*-4. (Lehrman has also composed the musicals *E.G.: A Musical Portrait of Emma Goldman*, *Emma Goldman in Exile* [or *Scenes from the Life of Emma Goldman*], *Growing Up Woman*, *Let's Change the World*, and *Superspy: The Secret Musical*.)

Leichtling, Alan (b. Brooklyn, NY, 1947; Anderson)

1971   *A White Butterful.* Performed New York, 18 February 1971. Published by Seesaw.

-   *The Tempest* (1 act). Published by Seesaw.

Leigh, Mitch (b. Brooklyn, NY, 30 January 1928; *Amerigrove*; *Baker's*)

1965   *Man of La Mancha* ("musical play"; 2 acts and epilogue; lyrics by Joe Darion based on life and works of Miguel de Cervantes—Don Quixote). Première, New York, 22 November 1965; performed by Indianapolis Opera Co., IN, 4 May 1990. Kornick.

1966   *Chu Chem* (musical play; lyrics by J. Haines and J. Wohl).

1970   *Cry for Us All* (musical play; lyrics by W. Alfred and P. Robinson).

1976   *Home Sweet Home* (musical play).

1978   *Savará* (musical play; lyrics by N. R. Nash).

Leighton, David

1988   *The Bacchae* (libretto by Joel Casey after Euripides). Performed by OperaWorks, New York, 1988.

LeMon, Melvin

1964   *Down, Down, Down* (1 act; about coal miners). Performed Rockville Centre, NY, 6 February 1964.

Lenel, Ludwig (b. Strasbourg, France, 20 May 1914; U.S. citizen, 1962; Anderson)

1962   *Young Goodman Brown* (1 act). Performed Allentown, PA, 25 April 1963.

1964   *The Boss* (folk-tale opera; 1 act). Performed Allentown, PA, 13 May 1965.

LeNoire, Rosetta
 1988 *Little Drops of Sugar* (1 act; libretto by composer; for children). Performed by AMAS Repertory Theatre, New York, 25 June 1988.

Lenzi, Paul
 1984 *No More Secrets: The Musical* (libretto by Geraldine Ann Snyder; for children—about child abuse). Performed Louisville, KY, 1984-85 season (tour).
 1986 *Passing in the Night* (libretto by Geraldine Ann Snyder; for children—about teen-age suicide). Performed Louisville, KY 24 February 1986.
 1986 *The Melting Pot—An American Story* (libretto by Geraldine Ann Snyder; for children). Performed Louisville, KY, 26 October 1986.
 1986 *The Three Little Pigs* (libretto by Geraldine Ann Snyder). Performed Louisville, KY, November 1986.

León, Tania (Justina) (b. Havana, Cuba, 14 May 1944; to U.S. in 1967; ASCAP; Anderson; *Baker's*; Cohen)
 1986 *I Got Ovah* (1 act). Winner, Brooklyn College Chamber Opera Competition, 1986. Performed at Brooklyn College, NY, 6 February 1987.
 1987 *Rita and Bessie* (libretto by Manuel Martin, Jr., about Rita Montaner and Bessie Smith). Performed by DUO Theater/Teatro Duo, New York, 2 June 1988.

Leoni, Eva (Cohen)
 1964 *Mr. Cupid, American Ambassador. COS*-1. Performed New York.

Leps, Wassili (b. St. Petersburg, Russia, 12 May 1870; d. Toronto, Ontario, 22 December 1943; to U.S. in 1894; Anderson; *Baker's*; Hipsher)
 1909 *Hoshi-San* (grand opera; 3 acts; libretto by John Luther Long of his poem "Andon," which had been set to music by Leps in 1905). Performed by Philadelphia Operatic Society, 21 May 1909, composer conducting.

Lerman, Richard M. (*WhoAm*)
 1981 *Incident at Three Mile Island: Perhaps an Elegy for Karen Silkwood*. Performed Brussels, Belgium, 3 October 1981.

Lessner, George (b. Budapest, Hungary, 15 December 1904; U.S. citizen, 1926; Anderson)
 1942 *The Nightingale and the Rose* (1 act; libretto after Oscar Wilde). Broadcast New York, NBC radio, 25 April 1942. Published by Lance Productions.

Lester, Thomas William (b. Leicester, England, 17 September 1889; d. Berian Springs, MI, 4 December 1956; in U.S. from 1902; Anderson; Hipsher)
 1926 *Everyman* ("choral opera"; prologue and 4 acts; libretto by composer after a medieval morality play). Première for the National

Federation of Music Clubs in Chicago, 24 April 1927, composer conducting. Bispham Medal, 1926.

Trilogy: The Wampum Belt:

1930 *Manabozo*. Performed Paris, France, and Chicago, 26 March 1930.

1931 *Hiawatha*. Performed Chicago 17 February 1931.

- ("As yet unnamed," according to an article published 28 August 1931)

Letovsky, Stanislav

1913 *Frau Anne, Die Dame am Putztisch*. Performed Posen, Germany, 1913.

Levenson, Boris (b. Ackerman, Bessarabia, 10 March 1884; d. New York, 11 March 1947; in U.S. from 1920, citizen in 1927; Anderson; *Baker's*)

- *Woman in the Window*.

Levi, Paul Alan (b. New York, 30 June 1941; *WhoAm*)

1977 *Thanksgiving* (1 act—1 hour). Performed by Juilliard Workshop, New York, 2 November 1977, and by National Music Theater Network, New York, 25 November 1985.

Levin, Gregory (b. Washington, DC, 8 March 1943; Anderson)

1957 *Crazy Horse* (libretto by composer).

1959 *Buffalo*.

1959 *A Minuet*.

1970 *Rebel and Empire* (libretto by Dan Levin, composer's father).

1970 *Son of Judah* (libretto by Dan Levin).

1974 *The Temple of Love*. Performed at Bowdoin College, ME, 28 April 1974.

- *Rebel and the Empire* (libretto by Dan Levin after his novel *Son of Judah*). Performed Alberta, Canada.

Levine, Julius

1956 *The Golden Medal* (25 minutes). Performed Fort Wayne, IN, 25 February 1956, and Boston, 10 April 1965.

Levister, Alonzo

1958 *Blues in the Subway* (jazz opera; 1 act). Performed New York, 27 September 1958.

Levy, Charles

1967 *Brock's Place*, with Marvin Adler. Performed New York, 6 February 1967.

Levy, Marvin David (b. Passaic, NJ, 2 August 1932; *Amerigrove*; *Who's Who*)

1956 *The Tower* (1 act—5 scenes; libretto by T. Brewster). Performed Santa Fe, NM, 2 August 1957. Published by Boosey & Hawkes.

1957 *Sotoba Komachi* (1 act—30 minutes; libretto by S. H. Brock after a Noh play). Performed New York, 7 April 1957.

1958 *Escorial* (60 minutes; libretto by Lionel Abel, transl. M. de Ghelderode). Performed New York, 4 May 1958. Published by Boosey & Hawkes.

1967   *Mourning Becomes Electra* (3 acts; libretto by Henry Butler after O'Neill), with sound effects by Vladimir Ussachevsky. Commission and première by Metropolitan Opera, New York, 17 March 1967. Published by Boosey & Hawkes.

1974   *Touch the Earth.* NEA grant.

1978   *The Balcony* (2 acts; libretto after J. Genet). Published by Boosey & Hawkes. *COS-2.* (*Baker's*: musical, 1981-87.)

Lewin, Frank (b. Breslau, Germany, 27 March 1925; U.S. citizen, 1946; Anderson)

1979   *Burning Bright* (3 hours; libretto by composer after Steinbeck). NEA fellowship, 1977. Performed Denver, CO, summer 1981; and by OPERA America Showcase, December 1982, and at Yale School of Music, New Haven, CT, November 1990.

Lewis, John (ASCAP)

1987   *No Time Flat* (libretto by Larry Ketron). Performance by WPA Theatre, New York, May 1987.

Lewis, Leo Rich (AMC)

-   *Old Fortunatis* (1 act). *COS-1.*

Lewis, William (AMC)

1976   *Night Must Fall* (1 act; libretto by composer after Emlyn Williams). Performed Lake Tahoe, CA, July 1985.

Lieber, Arthur

-   *Arlington Lightfoot, P.D..*
-   *The Dancing Master.*
-   *Miss Cupid of Chicago.*
(Works listed in Krohn, 1924.)

Lieber, Edvard (b. Rockville Centre, NY, 11 April 1948; Anderson; *WhoAm*; *Who's Who*)

1979   *Neither Arakawa nor Jasper Jones Are Each Other* (chamber opera). Performed by New York Arts Chorus and soloists, New York, 8 May 1979.

Lieberson, Kenneth

1982   *Birdbath* (formerly *Still Wings*; 70 minutes; libretto by composer after Melfi). Commission by Quaigh Theatre, New York; performed there, May 1982 and 1 August 1982.

Liebl, Brad

1986   *The Ransom of Red Chief* (66 minutes; libretto by composer after O. Henry). Performed Birmingham, AL, 11 January 1986.

Lieurance, Thurlow (b. Oskaloosa, IA, 21 March 1878; d. Boulder, CO, 9 October 1963; *Amerigrove*)

1919?   *Drama of the Yellowstone* (American Indian subject), lost.

Lifchitz, Max (b. Mexico City, 11 November 1948; to U.S. in 1966; Anderson; *Who's Who*)
1973   *Bluebells* (dramatic musical). Performed Boston, 26 March 1973.

Liggett, Lonnie
1964   *The Hermits* (1 act). Performed Syracuse, NY, 23 April 1964.

Lilienfeld, Harris
1980   *The Duchess* (libretto by William Rosenfeld after Browning). Performed at Hamilton College, NY, 15 February 1980.

Lind, Lanette
1982   *The Emperor and the Nightingale* (80 minutes; libretto by composer after Andersen). Performed Raleigh, NC, 1982.
1983   *Carousel of Dreams* (95 minutes; libretto by composer). Performed Raleigh, NC, October 1983.

Linden, Einar
1916   *Le Jardinier*. Performed New York.

Lindsey, Edwin S.
1936   *Elizabeth and Leicester* (1 act). Performed Chattanooga, TN, 21 April 1936.

Lipkis, Larry (b. Los Angeles, 27 July 1951; Anderson)
1989   *Peronelle* (1 act; libretto by Barry Spacks; about Machaut, using some of his music). Reading by American Chamber Opera, New York, 1988-89 season; staged 16 February 1990.

List, Kurt (b. Vienna, Austria, 21 June 1913; d. Milan, Italy, 16 November 1970; in U.S. from 1938 but returned to Europe after World War II; *Baker's*)
1951   *The Wise and the Foolish* (30 minutes). Performed New York, 2 June 1951.
−   *Mayerling*. Unperformed.
−   *Der Triumph des Todes*. Unperformed.

Livingston, Julian Richard (b. Spencer, IN, 25 August 1932; Anderson; *WhoAm*; *Who's Who*)
1977   *Twist of Treason*. Première at Battleground Arts Center, Freehold, NJ, 1977.

Lliso, Joseph M. (b. New York, 12 October 1943; *WhoAm*)
1981   *Judith* (1 act). Performed by Manhattan Opera, Brooklyn, NY, 5 April 1981.

Lloyd, Alan (b. Baltimore, MD, 10 January 1943; Anderson)
1973   *The Life and Times of Joseph Stalin* (13 hours!; libretto by Robert Wilson).
1974   *A Letter for Queen Victoria* (hours). Performed Spoleto, Italy, 15 July 1974, and New York, 22 March 1975.
1979   *Death, Destruction, and Detroit*, with Robert Wilson (5 hours). Performed Berlin, Germany, 13 February 1979.

Lloyd, Caroline Parkhurst (b. Uniontown, AL, 12 April 1924; Anderson; Cohen)
1967   *Dona Barbara*. Performed Caracas, Venezuela, 8 times, summer 1967, for 400th anniversary of that city.
1976   *Dona Rosita la Soltera* (libretto after Federico García Lorca). NEA grant. Two children's songs from the opera performed Washington, DC, 4 November 1976.

Lloyd, Timothy Cameron
1979   *Conjur Moon* (3 acts; libretto after Richardson's "The Dark of the Moon"). Performed Houston, TX, 17 May 1979, and Glens Falls, NY, 7 August 1980. Revised 1982 as *The Witch Boy*, performed Houston, TX, 1982, Glens Falls, NY, 1982, and (after Lloyd's death) by Juilliard American Opera Center, New York, 6 May 1988.

Locklair, Dan Steven (b. Charlotte, NC, 7 August 1947; AMC; Anderson; *Who's Who*)
1977   *Good Tidings from the Holy Beast* (1 act—50 minutes; libretto by composer based on the Chester miracle play *Wrightes Play*). Première at First Plymouth Congregational Church, Lincoln, NE, 21 December 1978; also performed at First Presbyterian Church, Binghamton, NY, 1981. Published by Seesaw. Kornick.

Lockwood, Normand (b. New York, 19 March 1906; AMC; *Amerigrove*)
       (Opera scores in AMRC.)
1945   *The Scarecrow* (chamber opera; 2 acts; libretto by composer after P. McKaye; about witchcraft at Salem). Performed at Columbia University, New York, 19 May 1945.
1961   *Early Dawn* (3 acts; libretto by R. Porter; for the centennial of Denver). Performed Denver, CO, 7 August 1961.
1962   *The Wizards of Balizar* (comic children's opera; 2 acts; libretto by R. Porter). Performed Denver, CO, 1 August 1962.
1964   *The Hanging Judge* (3 acts; libretto by R. Porter), originally entitled *The Inevitable Hour*. Performed Denver, CO, March 1964.
1964   *Requiem for a Rich Young Man* (1 act—28 minutes; libretto by D. Sutherland). Performed Denver, CO, 24 November 1964.

Loeffler, Alfred
1984   *Love's Labor's Lost* (3 acts; libretto by composer after Shakespeare). Performed Chico, CA, 15 November 1984.

Loeffler, Charles Martin (b. Schöneberg, near Berlin, Germany, or Mulhouse, Alsace, France, 30 January 1861; d. Medfield, MA, 19 May 1955; in U.S. from 1881; *Amerigrove*)
1913   *The Passion of Hilarion* (1 act and 2 tableaux; libretto by W. Sharp). Performed Boston, 1936.
1918   *Les Amants jaloux* (libretto by composer). Sketches in Library of Congress.
c 1919   *The Peony Lantern* (libretto by composer after Okakura-Kakuzo). Sketches in Library of Congress.
  -     *Life is But a Dream* (4 acts).

Loesser, Frank (b. New York, 29 June 1910; d. there, 26 July 1969; *Amerigrove*)
  1950   *Guys and Dolls* ("romantic comedy," according to Kornick; 2 acts; lyrics by composer; book by Jo Swerling and Abe Burrows based on Damon Runyan's short story "The Idyll of Miss Sarah Brown"). Première at 46th Street Theatre, New York, 24 November 1950.
  1956   *The Most Happy Fella* (quasi-opera, or "extended musical comedy" according to the composer; 3 acts; lyrics and libretto by composer after Sidney Howard's *They Knew What They Wanted*). Première, New York, 3 May 1956. Kornick.

Loewe, Frederick (b. Berlin, Germany, 10 June 1901; d. Palm Springs, CA, 14 February 1988; *Amerigrove*)
  1947   *Brigadoon* (musical; 2 acts; libretto by Alan Jay Lerner). Première, New York, 13 March 1947; performance by New York City Opera, 1986. Recordings: RCA (1947), Chilton (1973). Kornick.
  1956   *My Fair Lady* (musical; 2 acts; libretto and book by Alan Jay Lerner after George Bernard Shaw's play *Pygmalion*). Première at Mark Hellinger Theatre, New York, 15 March 1956; performed as an opera by Cleveland Opera, 12 May 1989, Opera Pacific, 23 June 1989, Minnesota Opera, 7 July 1990, and Knoxville Opera, 14 July 1990. Kornick.
  1960   *Camelot* (musical; 2 acts; book and lyrics by Alan Jay Lerner after T. H. White's *The Once and Future King*). Première at Majestic Theatre, New York, 3 December 1960; performed as an opera by Marin Opera, 9 May 1990. Recording: RCA, Random House (1961); film (1967). Kornick.

Logan, Richard and Gary
  1985   *The Adventures of Rhubarb, the Rock and Roll Rabbit* (1 act; libretto by Chico Kasinoir). Performed by LaMama, New York, March 1985.

Logan, Wendell (b. Thomson, GA, 24 November 1940; *Amerigrove*; *WhoAm*)
  1974   *From Hell to Breakfast*. NEA grant.

Lohman, Michael. *See also* Siegal, Donald
  1979   *A Long Way to Boston*, with Susan Birkenhead and Donald Siegal. Performed East Haddam, CT, 1979.

Lombard, Louis
  1907   *Errisinola*. Performed Lugano, Italy, 1907.

Lombardo, Robert (b. Hartford, CN, 5 March 1932; Anderson)
  1975   *The Dodo* ("chamber opera on ecology as seen through the eyes of vanishing animals"; for TV).
  1980   *The Death of Lincoln*. NEA grant 1974. Performed Glens Falls, NY, 8 August 1980.
  1981   *Metaphysical Vegas* (1 act; libretto by composer; about poet Andrew Marvell as a night-club singer in Las Vegas, using poetry by Marvell and others). Performed Milwaukee, WI, 22 October 1981.
  1987   *Tango on the Moon* (20 minutes). Performed by New Opera, Chicago, 30 May 1987.

-     *Sorrows of a Supersoul* (chamber opera). Performed Chicago. COS-2.

London, Edwin (b. Philadelphia, 16 March 1929; Anderson; *Amerigrove*)
1960   *Santa Claus* (mine opera; libretto by E. E. Cummings).
1976   *The Death of Lincoln* (libretto by Justice).
-     *Tala Obtusities.*

Long, Newell (b. Markle, IN, 12 February 1905; Anderson) and **Eleanor**
1969   *The Music Hater* (1 act). Performed Aberdeen, SD, October 1969.

Loomis, Clarence (b. Sioux Falls, SD, 13 December 1889; d. Aptos, CA, 3 July 1965; *Amerigrove*; *Baker's*; Hipsher; *Who's Who*)
1926   *Yolanda of Cyprus* (4 acts; libretto by Cale Young Rice). Première by American Opera Co., London, Ontario, September 1927; also Hamilton, Ontario; Chicago, 9 October 1929; and in New York—30 in all. Bispham Medal, 1926.
1931   *Susannah Don't You Cry* (theater piece). Performed New York.
1932   *A Night in Avignon* (1 act; libretto by Cale Young Rice, on life of Petrarch). Performed Indianapolis, IN, July 1932.
1935   *The White Cloud* (5 scenes; after Ferenc Molnar).
1941   *The Fall of the House of Usher* (1 act—6 scenes; libretto after Poe). Performed Indianapolis, IN, 11 January 1941.
1942   *Revival* (1 act). Broadcast on WFWB radio, Los Angeles, April 1942.
1953   *The Captive Woman.* (*Baker's* says 1943.)
-     *Dun an Oir* (*Castle of Gold*) (libretto by Howard McKent Barnes).
-     *David* (biblical opera; libretto by Cale Young Rice).
    (Loomis also composed incidental music for *King Lear*.)

Loomis, Harvey Worthington (b. Brooklyn, NY, 5 February 1865; d. Boston, 25 December 1930; *Amerigrove*; Hipsher)
1896   *Sandalphon* (melodrama of "musical symbolism").
1913   *The Traitor Mandolin* (grand opera; 1 act; libretto by Edwin Starr Belknap). (*Amerigrove*: performed New York, 1898.)
1913   *The Song of the Pear Tree* (dramatic recitation).
-     *The Bey of Baba* (comic opera).
-     *Blanc et noir* (pantomime).
-     *The Burglar's Bride* (burlesque opera).
-     *The Enchanted Fountain* (pantomime).
-     *Going Up?* (comic opera).
-     *Her Revenge* (pantomime).
-     *In Old New Amsterdam* (pantomime).
-     *Love and Witchcraft* (pantomime).
-     *The Maid of Athens* (burlesque opera).
-     *Put to the Test* (pantomime).
-     *The Story of a Faithful Soul* (melodrama).

Lopatnikoff, Nikolai (b. Reval [now Tallinn], Estonia, 16 March 1903; d. Pittsburgh, PA, 7 October 1976; in U.S. from 1939; *Amerigrove*)
1932   *Danton*, op. 20 (3 acts; libretto by G. Büchner). Concert excerpts performed Pittsburgh, PA, 25 March 1967.

Lo Presti, Ronald (b. Williamstown, MA, 28 October 1933; Anderson; *Baker's*)
  1962   *The Birthday.* Performed Winfield, MA, May 1962.
  1970   *Playback* (children's opera). Performed Tucson, AZ, 18 December 1970.
      (Anderson indicates he wrote a total of four 1-act operas.)

Lora, Antonio (b. in Italy, 1899; d. 1965; to U.S. in early youth; ACA/AMC; Anderson)
  1959   *Violante* (1 act; libretto after Boccaccio's "Untold Tale").
  1961   *Shoes and Ships* (60 minutes; libretto after O. Henry's "Cabbages and Kings").
  -   *Launcelot and Elaine* (3 acts). *COS*-1. (Anderson: 1-act opera based on Tennyson's *Idylls of the King*, commisioned by the Cologne State Opera.)
  -   *The Legend of Sleepy Hollow* (2 acts). *COS*-1.

Loree, Lori
  1989   *Headlights*, with Frank Fong, Rex Gray, Rick Hiatt, Mark Nelson, and Luigi Waites (about literacy). Performed Omaha, NE, 28 April 1989.

Lorenz, Ellen Jane (Mrs. James B. Porter; b. Dayton, OH, 3 May 1907; Anderson; Cohen; *WhoAm*)
  1974   *Johnny Appleseed* (for children). Published, Dayton, OH: Lorenz Publishing Co.
  -   *Up on Old Smoky* (operetta).

Lourié, Arthur Vincent (b. St. Petersburg, Russia, 14 May 1892; d. Princeton, NJ, 13 October 1966; U.S. citizen, 1947; Anderson; *Baker's*)
  1961   *The Blackamoor of Peter the Great.*

Love, Loretta
  1974   *The Stone Princess* (on a fairy tale by Bratton). Performed Phoenix, AZ, 29 April 1974.

Lovingood, Penman (b. in Texas, 25 December 1895; Anderson)
  1936   *Menelik* (3 acts). Performed by Central Opera, New York, 16 November 1936. "Staged several times." ASCAP award for performance, 1967, Long Beach, CA.
  -   *Evangeline and Gabriel.*

Low, James
  1955   *Moby Dick* (2 acts). Performed Idyllwild, CA, 2 September 1955.

Lubin, Ernest (b. New York, 2 May 1916; d. there, 15 March 1977; ASCAP; Anderson)
  1966   *The Pardoner's Tale* (50 minutes; libretto after Chaucer). Performed Denver, CO, 19 November 1966.

Lubin, Shellen
  -   *Bad News* (2 acts; libretto by Harmon Dresner).

Lucchesi, Riccardo
    1913   *Francesco da Rimini* (tragic opera).

Luce, William
    1986   *Orlando di Lasso* (about the composer, using some of his music).

Luders, Gustav (b. Bremen, Germany, 13 December 1865; d. New York, 24
                January 1913; to U.S. from 1888; *Amerigrove*)
    1899   *Little Robinson Crusoe* (libretto by H. B. Smith). Performed
           Chicago, 1899.
    1900   *The Burgomaster* (libretto by F. Pixley). Performed 31 December
           1900.
    1902   *King Dodo* (comic opera; 3 acts; libretto by F. Pixley). Performed
           New York, 12 May 1902.
    1903   *The Prince of Pilsen* (libretto by F. Pixley). Performed 17 March
           1903.
    1903   *Mam'selle Napoleon* (libretto by J. W. Herbert). Performed 8
           December 1903.
    1904   *The Sho-Gun* (comic opera; 2 acts; libretto by G. Ade). Performed
           10 October 1904.
    1904   *Woodland: A Forest Fantasy* (2 acts; libretto by F. Pixley).
           Performed 83 times in New York, beginning 21 November 1904,
           and in St. Louis, 1926.
    1907   *The Grand Mogul* (libretto by F. Pixley). Performed 25 March
           1907.
    1909   *The Fair Co-Ed* (libretto by G. Ade). Performed 1 February 1909.
    1910   *The Old Town* (libretto by G. Ade). Performed 10 January 1910.
    1912   *The Gypsy* (libretto by G. Ade). Performed 14 November 1912.
    1913   *Somewhere Else* (libretto by A. Hopwood). Performed 20 January
           1931.

Ludtke, William G.
    1977   *Atsumori at Ikuta.* Performed Oak Park, IL, 22 January 1977.

Luening, Otto (b. Milwaukee, WI, 15 June 1900; ASCAP/AMC; *Amerigrove*;
                Hipsher; *Who's Who*)
    1932   *Evangeline* (grand opera; 4 acts—150 minutes; libretto by composer
           after Longfellow). Commission by American Opera Co.
           Performed New York, 1932, composer conducting. 1947-48
           revision, performed at Columbia University, New York, 5 May
           1948, composer conducting. Bispham Medal, 1932.

Luke, Ray (b. Fort Worth, TX, 30 May 1926; Anderson; *Baker's*; *Who's Who*)
    1979   *Medea* (libretto by Carveth Osterhaus after Euripides). Performed
           by New England Conservatory Opera Theater, Boston, 3-5 May
           1979, composer conducting.

Lundenberg, Karl
    1986   *In a Pig's Valise* (libretto by Eric Overmyer; parody of detective
           novels). Performed by Playwrights '86, Baltimore, MD, 3 June
           1986.

Lustig, Leila

1986   *Deirdre of the Sorrows*. Opening scenes performed Buffalo, NY, 12
        July 1986.

Lutyens, Sally Speare (b. Syracuse, NY, 31 October 1927; Anderson; Cohen)
1976   *The Minister's Black Veil* (30 minutes; libretto by Nicolas Deutsch
        after Hawthorne). Performed Boston, 19 November 1976.
1979   *The Light Princess* (1 act). Performed Newport, RI, 5 August 1979.

Lybbert, Donald (b. Cresco, IA, 1923; d. New York, 26 July 1981; *Amerigrove*)
1952   *Monica*. Performed Amsterdam, Netherlands, 2 November 1952.
1965   *The Scarlet Letter*.

Lydon, Michael
1985   *Passion in Pigskin*, with Ellen Mandel (libretto by Michael Lydon;
        about football). Performed by Third Street Music School, New
        York, 18 October 1985.

Lyford, Ralph (b. Worcester, MA, 22 February 1882; d. Cincinnati, OH, 3
        September 1927; Anderson; *Baker's*; Hipsher)
1922   *Castle Agrazant* (2 acts). Première at Music Hall, Cincinnati, 29
        April 1926. Bispham Medal, 1925. Published by Ralph Lyford.

Lynn, Jonathan
1983   *French Follies* (libretto by Monty Norman). Performed by
        American Repertory Theatre, Cambridge, MA, May 1983.

Lyon, Laurence
1977   *Give Us Gals* (libretto by Lloyd Hansen). Performed Monmouth,
        OR, January 1977.

Macbride, David Huston (b. Oakland, CA, 3 October 1951; ACA/AMC;
        Anderson; *WhoAm*)
1983   *Pond in a Bowl* (1 act—40 minutes; from Chinese poetry, translation
        by K. Hanson). Performed by Golden Fleece, New York, 26
        March (Kornick: March 24) 1983.
1989   *Permit Me Voyage* (30 minutes; libretto by composer after Agee).
        Performed by Golden Fleece, New York, 6 April 1989.

Macero, Ted (b. Glens Falls, NY, 30 October 1925; *Amerigrove*)
1970   *The Heart* (libretto by B. Ulanov).
1978   *The Share* (libretto by R. Capra).
 -      *Twelve Years a Slave*. (*Amerigrove*: in progress.)

Macfarlane, William Charles (b. London, England, 2 October 1870; d. North
        Conway, NH, 12 May 1945; in U.S. from 1874; Anderson)

1916   *Little Almond Eyes*. Performed in Portland (?).
1917   *America First* (Boy Scout operetta).
1918   *Sword and Scissors*.

MacFeeley, P. Pullen
1976   *They Nobly Dar'd* (about the American Revolution). Performed in Boston, 1976. Published by G. Schirmer.

Machover, Tod (b. New York, 24 November 1953; *Amerigrove*; *Who's Who*)
1986   *Famine* (libretto by composer and Rose Moss; for four voices and tape). Performed by Electric Phoenix, New York, 18 March 1986.
1986   *VALIS* (Vast Active Living Intelligence System; 105 minutes; libretto by composer, Catherine Ikam, and Bill Raymond after the novel by Philip K. Dick). Commission by IRCAM, Paris, France; Massachusetts Institute of Technology; and Museum of Modern Art, New York. Performed Paris, France, 2 December 1987 (Kornick: 1 December 1988). Revised and performed Cambridge, MA, June 1989 (Kornick: première at MIT Experimental Media Facility, February 1988). Recording: Bridge Records BCD 9007 (DDD), 1988.

Mack, Gordon
1967   *Nora* (libretto by composer after Ibsen *A Doll's House*). Performed Shreveport, LA, 23 January 1967.

MacLean, John Torry (b. Jersey City, NJ, 12 April 1933; Anderson; *Who's Who*; *WhoAm*)
-   *The Bacchae* (50 minutes; libretto by Richard Larkin after Euripides). *COS*-4.

Maddow, Ellen
1988   *The Three Lives of Lucie Cabrol*, with Harry Mann (libretto by Paul Zimet after John Berger). Performed by Theatre for the New City, New York, December 1988.

Mader, Clarence Victor (1904-71; Anderson)
   (A "sacred opera" of Mader's composition is in the Mader Archive, University of California, Los Angeles.)

Madsen, Gunner and **Bob**
1988   *Cowboy Lips* (libretto by Bob and Richard Greene). Performed St. Paul, MN, 19 May 1988.

Maeder, James Gaspard (b. Dublin, Ireland, ca. 1809; d. 28 May 1876; to U.S. 1833; *Amerigrove*)
1852   *The Peri* ("grand fairy opera"; 3 acts; based on an episode from Washington Irving's *Life of Columbus*). Performed Boston, 10 February 1844, and New York, 1852. Score lost.

1855 *Po-ca-hon-tas*, by John Brougham, music "dislocated and re-set"
by Maeder, "a landmark in the history of music theater"
(*Amerigrove*).
1861? *Ponce de Leon*.

Maesch, La Vahn (b. Appleton, WI, 15 October 1904; Anderson)
1972 *The Grandmother and the Witch* (1 act). Performed Appleton, WI,
November 1972.

Maganini, Quinto (b. Fairfield, CA, 30 November 1897; d. Greenwich, CN, 10
March 1974; ASCAP; Anderson; *Amerigrove*)
1924 *Tennessee Partner* (or *Tennessee's Partner*). Broadcast on WOR
radio, New York.
1927 *The Argonauts* (195 minutes). Bispham Medal, 1940.

Magee, John Thomas
- *Shylock* (2 acts; libretto by composer). *COS*-4.
- *Twist* (musical drama; libretto after Dickens).
(Magee also composed a musical, *Problems*.)

Magnuson, Karl
1953 *Adam and Eve and the Devil* (20 minutes). Performed Cincinnati, 1
April 1953.

Mahoney, Patrick
1975 *The Strange Case of Marge-Nancy*, with C. W. Gallagher (1 act).
Performed Bemidji, MN, 7 February 1975.

Mailman, Martin (b. New York, 30 June 1932; *Amerigrove*; *WhoAm*; *Who's Who*)
1959 *The Hunted* (50 minutes; libretto after D. Friedkin and M. Fine).
Performed Rochester, NY, 27 April 1959. Published by Mills
Music.
1986 *Mirrors* (multimedia theater piece).

Maiuz, ?
1987 *Coqui (Tree Frog)* (libretto by Iufino). Performed by INTAR
Hispanic-American Music Theatre Lab, New York, 14 January
1987.

Mana Zucca (Gizella Augusta Zuckermann; b. New York, 25 December 1885; d.
Miami, FL, 8 March 1981; *Amerigrove*)
c 1920 *Hypatia* (4 acts).
c 1920 *The Queue of Ki-Lu*.

Mandel, Ellen
1985 *Passion in Pigskin*, with Michael Lydon ("cabaret opera"; libretto
by Michael Lydon, about football). Performed by Third Street
Music School, New York, 18 October 1985.

Mandel, Mel (AMC)
- *Gambler's Paradise*, with Norman Sachs. *COS*-3.

Mandelbaum, M. Joel (b. New York, 12 October 1932; *Amerigrove*; *Baker's*; *WhoAm*)
 1955   *The Man in the Man-Made Moon* (1 act; libretto by composer).
 1956   *The Four Chaplains* (1 act; libretto by M. R. Mandelbaum).
 1971   *The Dybbuk* (4 acts; libretto by composer after S. Ansky).
     Performed New York, 24 May 1972. Revised 1978.
 1983   *As You Dislike It* (libretto by L. Fichandler).

Mangold, Martin Clarence (b. Clinton, IA, 13 June 1952; *Who's Who*)
 1985   *Huckleberry Finn* (libretto after Mark Twain).
 1986   *Bleah!* (comic opera; 1 act—24 minutes; libretto by composer).
     Performed College Park, MD, 14 May 1986.

Mann, Harry
 1988   *The Three Lives of Lucie Cabrol*, with Harry Mann (libretto by Paul
     Zimet after John Berger). Performed by Theatre for the New
     City, New York, December 1988.

Mann, Peter
 1977   *Jack: A Flash Fantasy* (rock opera). Telecast on PBS, 26 July 1977.

Mann, Robert W.
 -    *The Scarlet Letter* (libretto after Hawthorne). *COS*-2.

Manning, Edward B. (b. St. John, New Brunswick, Canada, 14 December 1874; d.
     1948; Hipsher)
 1931   *Rip Van Winkle* (3 acts; libretto by composer). Première by
     Charlotte Lund Opera Co. at Town Hall, New York, 12 February
     1932.

Manning, Kathleen Lockhart (b. Hollywood, CA, 24 October 1890; d. there, 20
     March 1951; ASCAP; *Amerigrove*; Cohen; Hipsher)
 1926   *Mr. Wu* (libretto by Louise Jorden Miln).
 -    *For the Soul of Raphael* (based on book of that name by Marah
     Ellis Ryan).
 -    *Operetta in Mozartian Style*.

Manschinger, Kurt. *See* Vernon, Ashley

Mantell, Mark D. (b. Milwaukee, WI, 15 August 1961; *Who's Who*)
 1986   *Intimate Strangers*. Performed Long Beach, CA, 20 September
     1986.

Marais, Josef (b. Sir Lowry Pass, South Africa, 17 November 1905; d. Los
     Angeles, 27 April 1978; in U.S. from 1939, citizen 1945; ASCAP;
     Anderson)
 1952   *Tony Beaver* (75 minutes; libretto by Max Burton). Performed
     Idyllwild, CA, 1 August 1952. Published by G. Schirmer.
 1953   *African Heartbeat*. Performed Idyllwild, CA, 28 August 1953.

Marble, Earl
 1884   *Puritan Days*, with Richard Stahl (on the same subject as Howard
     Hanson's *Merry Mount*).

Marek, Robert (on faculty of University of South Dakota from 1957; Anderson)
    1967   *Arabesque* (1 act). Performed Vermillion, SD, 14 April 1967.

Maretzek, Max (b. Brno, Moravia, 28 June 1821; d. New York, 14 May 1897; in
    U.S. from 1848; *Amerigrove*; *Baker's*; Hipsher)
    1876   *Baba* ("musical play"). Performed New York, September 1876,
    composer conducting.
    1879   *Sleepy Hollow: or, The Headless Horseman* ("pastoral opera"; 3
    acts; libretto by Charles Gaynor after Washington Irving).
    Première at Academy of Music, New York, 25 September 1879;
    then Chicago, 19 November 1879. Review in *Dwight's Journal of
    Music*, 4 October 1879.

Margolis, Jerome N. (b. Philadelphia, 30 October 1941; Anderson)
    1982?   *Jekyll and Hyde* (2 hours; libretto by composer). Performed at
    Harvard School, North Hollywood, CA, ?1982.

Marin, Ravonna
    1986   *Peter Rabbit in the Garden* (75 minutes; libretto after Potter).
    Performed Fairbanks, AK, 1986-87 season.
    1986   *The Velveteen Rabbit* (libretto after Margery Williams). Commission
    by Alaska State Arts Council and Fairbanks Choral Society.
    Performed Fairbanks, May 1986.

Markoe, Peter
    1790   *The Reconciliation: or, The Triumph of Nature* (2 acts). Published
    in Philadelphia.

Marks, Walter
    -   *Bajour* (2 acts; libretto by Ernest Kinoy after Joseph Mitchell
    stories in *New Yorker*).

Mars, Louisa Melvin Delos
    1889   *Leoni, the Gypsy Queen* (operetta). Premièred by Ideal Dramatic
    Company, Providence, RI, 4 December 1889. See Josephine
    Wright, "Black Women in Classical Music in Boston During the
    Late Nineteenth Century: Profiles of Leadership," in Wright, ed.,
    New Perspectives on Music: Essays in Honor of Eileen Southern,
    Detroit Monographs in Musicology/Studies in Music, 11 (this
    publisher, 1992), 384-85, 388, which indicates she wrote five full-
    length musical dramas, and published the three listed here.
    -   *Fun at a Boarding School.*
    -   *Love in Disguise: or, Things Are Not What They Seem.*

Marsh, John
    1967   *Entr'acte* (1 act). Performed New York, 22 May 1967.
    1967   *Sound Studio* (1 act). Performed New York, 22 May 1967.

Marsh, Lucille Crews. *See* Crews, Lucille

Marsh, William J. (of Dallas, TX; Hipsher)
    1931   *The Flower Fair of Peking.* Première, Dallas, TX, 23 April 1931.

Marshall, Lauren
    1989   *Whadda 'Bout My Legal Rights?* (75 minutes; libretto by Andrew
           Duxbury and Suzanne Grant; for children). Performed Seattle,
           WA, spring 1989.

Marshall, Yale
    1969   *Oedipus and the Sphinx* (2 parts; libretto by Wesley Balk).
           Performed Minneapolis, 29 November 1969.
    1974   *Gallimaufry*, with Wesley Balk and Philip Brunelle (collage).
           Performed St. Paul, MN, 13 December 1974.

Marshall, Warner (b. Pomona, CA, 11 December 1947; Anderson)
    1972   *Fragment from an Unwritten Opera.*

Martel, Tom (ASCAP)
    1972   *Hard Job Being God* (rock opera). Performed New York, 14 May
           1972.

Martin, Vernon (b. Guthrie, OK, 15 December 1929; ASCAP; Anderson; *WhoAm*;
           Who's Who)
    1956   *Ladies' Voices* (chamber opera; 1 act; libretto after the Gertrude
           Stein text). Performed Norman, OK, 3 June 1956. Published by
           Carl Fischer, 1979.
    1984   *Waiting for the Barbarians* (after Cavafy). Performed by After
           Dinner Opera, New York, 6 February 1984.
    1984   *Fables for Our Times* (18 minutes; libretto after James Thurber).
           Performed by After Dinner Opera, New York, 6 February 1984
           and 6 November 1989.
    -      *Capital, Capitals* (1 act).
    -      *Dr. Faustus Lights the Lights* (1 act).

Martinelli, Rodolfo
    1951   *Alone I Stand* (2 acts). Performed Brooklyn, NY, 18 May 1951.

Martinez, Odaline de la (b. Matanzas, Cuba, 31 October 1949; to U.S. in 1961,
           citizen in 1971; *Amerigrove*; *Baker's*; Cohen; *Who's Who*)
    1983   *Sister Aimee* (formerly *Aimee Semple McPherson*; 1 hour; libretto
           by John Whiting). NEA grant, 1978. Performed at Tulane
           University, New Orleans, 12 April 1984.

Martino, Donald (b. Plainfield, NJ, 16 May 1931; *Amerigrove*; *WhoAm*; *Who's
           Who*)
    1975   *Paradiso* (1 act; libretto after Dante). Performed Boston, 7 May
           1975.

Martinů, Bohuslav (b. Polička, Bohemia, 8 December 1890; d. Liestal,
           Switzerland, 28 August 1959; in U.S. 1941–56; *Amerigrove*)
    1952   *Cim clovek zije* (*What Men Live By*) (television opera; libretto by
           composer after Tolstoy). Performed New York, 1953 (*Baker's*:
           New York, 20 May 1955).
    1952   *Zenitba* (*The Marriage*) (television opera; libretto by composer after
           Gogol). Performed New York, 1953 (*Baker's*: NBC-TV, 7
           February 1953).

1953   *La Plainte contre inconnu.* Unfinished.

1954   *Mirandolina* (comic opera). Performed Prague, 17 May 1959.

Martirano, Salvatore (b. Yonkers, NY, 12 January 1927; *Amerigrove*; *Baker's*)

1951   *The Magic Stones* (chamber opera; libretto after Boccaccio's *Decameron*). Performed at Oberlin Conservatory, OH, 25 April 1952.

1965   *Underworld*, for 4 actors, 4 percussion instruments, 2 double basses, tenor saxophone, tape. Performed by University of Illinois, in New York, 8 May 1965. Video version, 1982.

Maryon, Edward (b. London, England, 3 April 1867; d. there, 31 January 1954; in U.S. 1914-33; *Baker's*; Hipsher)

(Many of his operas were performed in the U.S.; the manuscripts are in the Boston Public Library.)

1889   *L'Odalisque.* Gold Medal, Paris Exposition of 1889 (Hipsher: 1890), but the composer destroyed the score.

1905   *The Feathered Robe* (*La Robe de plume*).

-    *Abelard and Heloise.*

-    *Chrysalis* ("lyric mystery-play"; 2 acts).

-    *Greater Love.*

-    *Helen of Troy* ("a cinema opera"), for screen, vocal quartet, symphony orchestra.

-    *A Lover's Tale* (1 act; World War I version of Dante's *Paolo and Francesca*).

-    *Paola and Francesca.*

-    *The Prodigal Son.*

-    *Rembrandt.*

-    *Rip Van Winkle.*

-    *The Smelting Pot* (3 acts; dedicated to the memory of Walt Whitman).

-    *Werewolf* (4 acts; dedicated to the memory of Edgar Allan Poe).

The Cycle of Life (an operatic heptalogy, begun 1886):

-    *Lucifer.*

-    *Cain.*

-    *Krishna.*

-    *Magdalen.*

-    *Sangraal.*

-    *Psyche.*

-    *Nirvana.*

Mason, Charles

1990   *Season's Reasons* (folk opera of the 1980s). Performed at University of California, Los Angeles, 2 March 1990.

Mason, Roger

-    *Requiem* ("experimental opera-dance"; 2 scenes).

Mason, Wilton

1953   *Kingdom Come* (1 act). Performed Boone, NC, 17 August 1953.

Mathewson, Ramona B. (AMC)

1966   *Other Years, Other Christmases* (1 act). Performed Los Angeles, December 1966.

Matthews, Harry Alexander (b. Cheltenham, England, 11 December 1879; d. Middletown, CN, 12 April 1973; U.S. citizen, 1923; brother of the following composer; Anderson)
-    *Hades, Inc.* (comic opera).
-    *Play the Game.*

Matthews, John Sebastian (b. Cheltenham, England, 11 December 1870; d. Pawtucket, RI, 23 July 1934; to U.S. in 1900; Anderson)
-    *Narragansett Pier.*

Maurice-Jacquet, H. (b. St. Mande, France, 18 March 1886; d. New York, 29 June 1954; Anderson)
-    *Romanitza.*
-    *Messaouda.*
-    *La Petite Dactylo* (operetta).
-    *Le Poilu* (operetta).

Maury, Lowndes (b. Butte, MT, 7 July 1911; d. Encino, CA, 11 December 1975; Anderson; *Baker's*)
-    *The Celebration* (30 minutes). Published by Boosey & Hawkes.

Mautner, Michael
>   1988   *Cartazan: An Original Musical Fantasy* (libretto by Diane Bostick). Performed Syracuse, NY, 17 May 1988.

Maves, David W. (b. Salem, OR, 3 April 1937; Anderson; *WhoAm*)
-    *Bodas de sangre* (*Blood Wedding*) (3 hours; libretto after Federico García Lorca).

Mavseth, ?
>   1987   *Shoot the Buffalo* (about the history of Oregon). Performed Seattle, WA, 4 December 1987.

Maxfield, Richard Vance (b. Seattle, WA, 2 February 1927; d. Los Angeles, 27 June 1969; *Amerigrove*)
>   1960   *The Stacked Deck* ("electronic opera" with tape; 22 minutes; libretto by Dick Higgins). Performed New York, 3 April 1960.

Maxwell, Charles
-    *Passions in Purgatory* (1 act; with two pianos for an orchestra).

Mayer, Carl
>   1887   *The Conspiracy of Pontiac.* Performed Detroit, MI, 1887.

Mayer, Lutz Leo (b. Hamburg, Germany, 14 December 1934; *WhoAm*)
>   1965   *Refuge* (60 minutes; libretto by Edward Devany). Performed at State University of New York at Cortland, 20 July 1965.
>   1968   *The Paranoid Parakeet.* Performed at the same place.

Mayer, Robert
>   1954   *The Porter at the Door* (2 acts). Performed Winston-Salem, NC, 26 February 1954.

Mayer, William (b. New York, 18 November 1925; *Amerigrove*; *Baker's*; Schoep; see *New Yorker*, 14 July 1986)

1950 *The Greatest Sound Around* (short children's opera). (*Baker's*: 1954.)

1956 *Hello World!* ("a musical trip around the world"; 1 act), for narrator, orchestra, and audience participation. Performed New York, 10 November 1956 and January 1960.

1962 *One Christmas Long Ago* (1 act—1 hour; libretto by composer after "Why the Chimes Rang"). Performed at Ball State University, Muncie, IN, 9 November 1962; by Philadelphia Orchestra, 1963 and 12 February 1964; Pullman, WA, 1977; New York, 30 December 1989.

1964 *Brief Candle* ("micro-opera"; 3 acts—6 minutes ["shortest 3 acts in existence"]; libretto by Milton Feist). Performed New York, 22 May 1967; by After Dinner Opera Co., New York, 1968, etc. Published by Presser.

1981 *A Death in the Family* (80 minutes; libretto by composer after the novel by James Agee and Tad Mosel's play *All the Way Home*). NEA grant, 1978; commission by Minnesota Opera, St. Paul. Performed St. Paul, 29 May 1981 and 11 March 1983, and St. Louis, 1986. "The outstanding new America opera or music theater work of 1983 by the National Institute for Musical Theater" (*Amerigrove*). Kornick.

Mazzucato, Eliza (Mrs. Bicknell Young)

- *The Maid and the Reaper* (1 act). Performed Chicago.

- (Also: "a comic opera in Salt Lake City.")

McAnuff, Des

1987 *Silent Edward* (for children). Performed at La Jolla Playhouse, CA, fall 1987.

McAuliffe, Jason

1985 *A Womansong* (2 hours; libretto by John Paul Hudson). Missouri Arts Council grant. Performed by National Music Theater Network, New York, December 1985; and in Tarkio, MO, 1986. Published by National Music Theater Network.

McClain, Floyd A. (b. Alva, OK, 30 April 1917; Anderson)

1958 *The Snack Shop* (1 act). Performed Yankton, SD, 12 June 1958.

1959 *The Princess and the Frog* (musical; 1 act). Performed Yankton, SD, 13 June 1959.

1961 *Dakota Dakota Dakota* (full-length musical).

- *Arrow of Love* (based on novel by F. Manfred).

- *Hangin'* (after the story of the murderer of Wild Bill Hickok).

McClenahan, Andrew

1980 *A Comedy of Errors* (1 act; libretto after Shakespeare). Performed Sun Valley, CA, 15 December 1980.

McClure, Lee

1990 *Mother and Child* (45 minutes; libretto by Ron Whyte; about birth defects). Performed at Cathedral of St. John the Divine, New York, 23 May 1990.

McCollin, Frances (b. Philadelphia, 24 October 1892; d. there, 25 February 1960;
    ASCAP; Anderson; Cohen; see also Annette Maria DiMedio,
    Frances McCollin: Her Life and Music [Metuchen, NJ: Scarecrow,
    1990])
-   *King Christmas: or, King of the Holidays* (children's opera; 1 act;
    libretto by Charles I. Junkin). Published by G. Schirmer, 1926.

McCord, Emily
  1913 *The Mojave Maid*, with A. E. Stearn. Performed in San Diego,
    CA?.

McCoy, William J. (b. Crestline, OH, 15 March 1848; d. Oakland, CA, 15
    October 1926; *Baker's*; Hipsher)
  1904 *Hamadryads* ("a masque of Apollo"). "Grove-play" composed for
    the Bohemian Club of California; produced at their Sequoia
    Grove, summer 1904.
  1910 *The Cave Man* (libretto by Charles K. Field). Composed for the
    Bohemian Club, 1910.
  1921 *Egypt* (2 acts; libretto after the Antony and Cleopatra story).
    Concert performance of 2 acts at Greek Theater for Berkeley
    Music Festival, University of California, Berkeley, 17 September
    1921; also at Auditorium, San Francisco, 29 September 1921.
    Bispham Medal, 1926.

McCraw, Charles
  1966 *The Annunciation* ("opera-choral-ballet"). Performed New York, 21
    June 1966.
  1966 *Trista* (folk opera). Performed New York, 21 June 1966.

McDaniel, William J. (b. Jellico, TN, 4 March 1918; Anderson)
  1974 *The Green Tint* (chamber opera; 1 act). Performed Eureka Springs,
    AR, 7 July 1974 (Anderson: July 18).
-   *Waterhole* (chamber opera).

McDermott, Vincent (b. Atlantic City, NJ, 5 September 1933; *Amerigrove*;
    Baker's; *Who's Who*)
  1978 *A Perpetual Dream* (chamber opera).
  1987 *Spirits among the Spires* (chamber opera).
  1989 *The King of Bali* (75 minutes; libretto by composer), for singers,
    puppets, gamelan. Commission by NEA Opera Program.
    Performed Portland, OR, 20 April 1990.

McDowell, John Herbert (b. Washington, DC, 21 December 1926; d. Scarsdale,
    NY, 3 September 1985; *Amerigrove*)
  1965 *Oklahoma Danger Remark* (1 act; libretto by A. Williams and J.
    Waring). Performed at Bridge Theater [city unknown], 25 May
    1965.
  1971 *A Dog's Life* (1 act; libretto by M. Smith). Performed New York, 9
    May 1971.
  1973 *After the Ball*. Performed New York, 19 July 1973.

McFarland, Ronald George (b. San Bernardino, CA, 20 April 1928; *Who's Who*)

1979   *The Dinner Party* (130 minutes; libretto by Maria Woodward after Keithley). Performed Chico, CA, 14 November 1979; revised version performed Squaw Valley, CA, 1982. Published by STEORRA.

1983   *Song of Pegasus* (fantasy opera for children; 90 minutes; libretto by Maria Woodward after Godden's "In Noah's Ark"). Performed at Ebenezer Lutheran Church, San Francisco, 24 September 1983; by Voices/SF, San Francisco, 21 January 1984; and in San Rafael, CA, 28 June 1985.

1986   *The Audition of Molly Bloom* (opera buffa; 12 minutes; after Joyce's *Ulysses*). Commission by Playwrights United, 1985. Performed at Marin Community Theater, Forest Meadows, CA, May 1986.

1989   *King Lear* (2 acts; libretto by composer after Shakespeare). Performed Mill Valley, CA, 18 January 1989.

-   *Lear and Cordelia* (30 minutes; libretto by composer after Shakespeare). Commission by William Lewis. Published by STEORRA.

McGlowen, Loomis

1987   *Lazar and the Castle of the Peers* (for children; 1 act; libretto by Charleen Swansee). Commission by Opera Carolina. Performed Charlotte, NC (and on tour), January 1987.

McIntosh, Ladd (b. Akron, OH, 14 July 1941; Anderson)

1972   *Today Is a Good Day to Die* (rock opera). Performed Salt Lake City, ID, 20 March 1972.

McKay, David (b. Athens, GA, 1927)

(Scores or cassettes available from Robinson Music Co., 108 Milk St., Westborough, MA 01581. The following information from the composer.)

1988   *As I Lay Dying* (libretto by Laura Jehn Menides after Faulkner). Excerpts performed in a concert performance by New England Concert Opera Ensemble at University of Mississippi, Oxford, MS, 28 July 1991. For details, see *WPI Journal* (Worcester Polytechnic Institute, Massachusetts), spring 1991.

1989   *The Yellow Wallpaper* ("monologue opera"; 45 minutes; libretto by Kent Ljungquist after Charlotte Perkins Gilman's 19th-century novel), for soprano and keyboard. Performed by Golden Fleece, New York, 27 June 1989.

-   *The Arbitrator: or, You Are One and Your Husband's One Too* ("farcical musical spoof"; concerning Nancy Reagan being insulted over an order of stationery; 22 minutes), for soprano, 2 tenors, baritone, keyboard.

-   *Birds Beaks and Beautification: or, How the Nightingale Got Its Voice* (25 minutes), for SA chorus, 7 soloists, keyboard, flute, bassoon.

-   *The Devil in the Belfry* ("operatic extravaganza"; 35 minutes; libretto after Edgar Allan Poe), for 2-voiced chorus, 3 high soloists, keyboard or winds. Performed for Modern Language Association.

- *Golly Moses* (story of Moses and the Ten Commandments), for solo voices, chorus, keyboard, violin.
- *Little Johnnie Boy* ("a jazz chancel opera"; 24 minutes; texts from Luke 1:5-79), accompanied by keyboard and optional percussion.
- *Nicodemus* (comic opera dealing with the biblical character), accompanied by string quartet or keyboard.
- *Susannah and the Elders* (the story of how Daniel saves Susannah, from the Old Testament Apocrypha), accompanied by string quartet or keyboard.

McKay, Neil (b. Ashcroft, BC, Canada, 16 June 1924; U.S. citizen, 1962; ASCAP; Anderson; *Who's Who*)

1967 *Ring Around Harlequin* (1 act). Performed Honolulu, HI, 24 April 1967.

1970 *Planting a Pear Tree* (1 act). Performed Honolulu, HI, 17 May 1970.

McKee, Jeanellen

(All operas in *COS*-1.)

1958 *Collector's Piece* (or *Collector's Pieces*; 1 act). Performed Chicago, 2 May 1958.

1959 *Dream of an Empire* (20 minutes). Performed Chicago, March 1959.

- *The Depot* (15 minutes).
- *The Fire Warden* (12 minutes).
- *Monette* (20 minutes).
- *Reunion* (10 minutes).

McKeel, James, Jr.

1989 *The Constant Cannibal Maiden* (1 hour; libretto by composer after Wallace Irwin). Performed Minneapolis, 28 January 1989.

McKelvy, Lori

1983 *The Captain's Wife* (Irish folk opera; 40 minutes; libretto by composer after Eugene O'Neill).

1984 *The Golden Island* (Irish folk opera; 40 minutes; libretto by composer after Eugene O'Neill). Performed by Musical Theater Project, New York, September 1984; Pennsylvania Opera Theater, Philadelphia, November 1984; and National Music Theater Network, New York, 25 April 1988.

McKenna, Edward J.

1988 *The Magic Cup* (150 minutes; libretto after a novel by Andrew M. Greeley). Performed by Opera Factory, Chicago, 12 March 1988.

McLean, Edwin (b. Bastrop, LA, 3 April 1951; *WhoAm*)

1979 *Apollinaire, Poker . . . and Other Diversions* (30 minutes).

McLin, Lena (née Johnson; b. Atlanta, GA, 5 September 1929; Cohen; Southern)

(McLin's music is published by Neil Kjos.)

- *Bancrof, Inc.*
- *Comment* (rock opera).

- *Humpty Dumpty* (operetta).
- *Jack and the Beanstalk* (operetta).
- *The Party.*
- *Rumplestiltskin* (operetta).
- *You Better Rise Women, Face the Challenge* (for Women's Day program).

Mead, George (b. New York, 21 May 1902; Anderson)
1969   *The Broker's Opera* (1 act). Performed New York, 8 May 1969.

Meade, Glenn
1981   *My Son the Doctor* (comic opera; 150 minutes; libretto by the composer). Performed at Roosevelt University, Chicago, 15 January 1981.

Meader, J. G. (Hipsher)
1852   *Peri: or, The Enchanted Fountain* (3 acts; libretto by S. J. Burr). Première at Broadway Theater, New York, 13 December 1852.

Mechem, Kirke Lewis (b. Wichita, KS, 16 August 1925; Anderson; *WhoAm*; *Who's Who*)
1978   *Tartuffe* (comic opera; 3 acts—140 minutes; libretto by composer after the comedy by Molière). Première by San Francisco Opera, 27 May 1980; performed by Arizona State University Lyric Opera Theatre, 14 November 1986, Lyric Opera Theatre of Baton Rouge, LA, 9 January 1987, and Northwestern University Opera, 13 November 1987. One hundred performances by October 1989. Piano-vocal score published by G. Schirmer, 1980. Kornick.
-    *John Brown.*
-    *The King's Contest* (dramatic cantata; 26 minutes; after the Apocryphal). Published by G. Schirmer, 1974. *COS*-4.

Medema, Ken (ASCAP)
1983   *Sunday Eyes, Opus #1.* Performed Phoenix, AZ, 16 April 1983.

Megan, Thomas F. (ASCAP)
1986   *A Vision* (libretto by composer, on the life and works of Yeats). Performed Waterford, CT, 21 August 1986 and 9 August 1988, and by Boston Music Project, MA, 1 February 1988.

Meier, Margaret (b. New York, 7 March 1936; *Who's Who*)
1987   *On the Edges of Calm* (70 minutes; libretto by composer). Performed Redlands, CA, November 1987.

Meiman, Dominic
1979   *The Ring of the Fettucines* (55 minutes; libretto by Marie King and Edward Ehringer).
1987   *A Midsummer Night's Dream.* Performed by Baroque Opera and Stage Struck, New York, 16 May 1987.
-    *Jack and the Beanstalk* (55 minutes). Listed in *OPERA America Bulletin*, 1989.

Menges, Edward (in Krohn)
- *Jacinta* (comic opera).
- *The Suicides* (1 act).

Menken, Alan
  1979 *God Bless You, Mr. Rosewater* (on Vonnegut). Performed New York, May 1979.

Menn, Joseph Henry
- *Golden Poppy Girl*. Krohn says "numerous performances."

Mennifield, Normal Lavelle (b. 1906)
- *Mystery Masquerade*.

Mennini, Louis Alfred (b. Erie, PA, 18 November 1920; brother of Peter Mennin; ASCAP; *Amerigrove*; *WhoAm*; *Who's Who*)
  1951 *The Well* (45 minutes; libretto by composer). Performed Rochester, NY, 8 May 1951.
  1955 *The Rope* (chamber opera; 1 act—45 minutes; libretto by composer after Eugene O'Neill). Performed at Berkshire Music Festival, MA, 8 August 1955.

Menotti, Gian-Carlo (b. Cadegliano, Italy, 7 July 1911; in U.S. from 1918; *Amerigrove*; *Who's Who*)
  (Menotti writes his own librettos.)
  1922 *The Death of Pierrot.*
  1936 *Amelia Goes to the Ball* (*Amelia al ballo*) (opera buffa; 1 act—60 minutes; libretto translated to English by George Mead). Performed at Curtis Institute, Philadelphia, 4 January 1937, and by Metropolitan Opera, New York, 3 March 1938 and 11 January 1939. Published by Franco Colombo.
  1939 *The Old Maid and the Thief* (musical farce; 1 act). Broadcast on NBC 22 April 1939; staged in Philadelphia, 11 February 1941 (broadcast on NBC radio). Published by Ricordi.
  1942 *The Island God* (*Ilo e Zeus*) (tragic opera; 1 act; translated by Fleming McLeish). Première by Metropolitan Opera, New York, 20 February 1942, then withdrawn by composer.
  1945 *The Medium* (tragic opera; 2 acts). Performed New York, 8 May 1946; later by Opera Ebony of New York, Virgin Islands, 11 November 1988. Published by G. Schirmer. Video of 1951 motion picture: Video Artists International VAI OP-4 and 69002 (VHS) and 29002 (Beta).
  1947 *The Telephone* (farce or opera buffa; 1 act). Performed New York, 18 February 1947; by Metropolitan Opera, New York, 31 July 1965; and more recently by Four Corners Opera, 22 June 1990. Published by G. Schirmer; recorded by Columbia.
  1949 *The Consul* (musical drama; 3 acts). Performed Philadelphia, 1 March 1950. Pulitzer Prize, 1950. Published by G. Schirmer; recorded by Decca. Video of Spoleto Festival, 1977: Music Masters.
  1951 *Amahl and the Night Visitors* (50 minutes). Composed for NBC television; first televised 24 December 1951. Staged innumerable

times from 1952. Published by G. Schirmer. Video: Video Artists International 69032 (VHS) and 29032 (Beta), 1979; Videotakes; Home Vision AMA01.

1954   *The Saint of Bleeker Street* (3 acts). Performed New York, 27 December 1954, and Philadelphia, 20 November 1989. Pulitzer Prize, 1955. Published by G. Schirmer, 1955. Recorded by RCA Victor. Video of New York City Opera, 1978: Classical Video.

1956   *The Unicorn, the Gorgon and the Manticore* (madrigal ballet or madrigal fable; 60 minutes), for chorus, 10 dancers, 9 instruments. Performed Washington, DC, 21 October 1956. Published by Franco Colombo.

1958   *Maria Golovin* (3 acts). Performed at Brussels World's Fair, Belgium, 20 August 1958, and in New York, 5 November 1958.

1963   *Labyrinth* (television opera; 1 act—40 minutes). Telecast on NBC-TV, New York, 3 March 1963.

1963   *Le Dernier Sauvage* (*L'ultimo selvaggio*) (opéra bouffe; 3 acts; American subject). Performed by Opéra-Comique, Paris, France, 21 October 1963, and, as *The Last Savage* (translated by George Mead), by Metropolitan Opera, New York, 23 January and 31 December 1964.

1964   *Martin's Lie* (children's church opera; 1 act). Performed Bristol, England, 3 June 1964. Telecast on CBS-TV, October 1964.

1968   *Help, Help the Globolinks!* (1 act—1 hour). Performed by Staatsoper, Hamburg, Germany, 21 December 1968, and at Santa Fe, NM, 1 August 1969.

1971   *The Most Important Man.* Performed New York, 3 December 1971.

1973   *Tamu-Tamu* (2 acts—70 minutes; in Indonesian and English). Commission by Eighteenth International Congress of Anthropological and Ethnological Sciences. Première at Studebaker Theatre, Chicago, 5 September 1973. Kornick.

1976   *The Hero* (comic opera; 3 acts). Commission and première by Opera Company of Philadelphia, 1 June 1976. Kornick.

1976   *The Egg* (children's church opera; 1 act—60 minutes). Première at Washington Cathedral, DC, 17 June 1976; performed at Brooklyn Academy of Music, New York, 13 November 1980. Kornick.

1978   *The Trial of the Gypsy* (children's opera), with piano. Performed New York, 24 May 1978.

1979   *Chip and His Dog* (children's opera), with piano. Performed Guelph, Canada, 5 May 1979.

1979   *Juana la loca* [or simply *La Loca*] (3 acts; about the daughter of Ferdinand and Isabella of Spain). Commission by Beverly Sills. Première by San Diego Opera, 3 June 1979; performance by New York City Opera, 16 September 1979. Kornick.

1982   *A Bride from Pluto* (a science-fiction opera for children). Commission by Kennedy Center Education Program. Performed New York, 14 April 1982.

1982   *The Boy Who Grew Too Fast* (40 minutes). Performed by Opera Delaware, Wilmington, 24 September 1982.

1986   *Goya* (3 acts; about Goya and the Duchess of Alba). Commission by Washington Opera and Paris Opera. Première by Washington Opera, DC, 15 November 1986; on PBS "Great Performances" series, 1986. Kornick.

1988　*The Wedding* (comic opera; 2 acts; about a Korean wedding).
Commission by 1988 Summer Olympic Games, Seoul, South Korea.
Performed Seoul, 16 September 1988.
(Menotti has received a commission from Spoleto Festival, USA, for
a children's opera.)

Merkin, Robby (ASCAP)
1988　*Wide-Awake Jake* (1 act; libretto after Helen Young's book; for
children). NEA grant. Performed by TADA!, New York, 15 July
1988.
-　*Games* (libretto by composer; for children). NEA grant.

Mernit, William
1985　*Surrender* (1 act; libretto by Diane Foley). Performed by Theater
for the New City, New York, 3 January 1985.

Merryman, Marjorie (b. Oakland, CA, 9 June 1951; *WhoAm*)
1986　*Antigone* (1 act). Performed at Boston University, 2 May 1986.

Metcalf, Clarence
1953　*The Town Musicians of Bremen* (90 minutes; libretto by Gilbert O.
Ward). Performed Rochester, NY, 8 May 1951.

Mettee, David (ASCAP)
1985　*Fahrenheit 451* (2 acts; libretto by Georgia Bogardus Holof after
Bradbury). Performed Waterford, CT, August 1985 and 21 August
1986; and Fort Wayne, IN, 11 November 1988.
1988　*Internal Combustion* (libretto by Georgia Bogardus Holof; about the
invention of the automobile). Performed Jersey City, NJ, 27 July
1988.

Meyer, James
1986　*Rumpelstiltskin* (40 minutes; libretto by composer after the fairy
tale). Performed St. Louis, 1986.
1989　*Laclede's Landing* (composed in collaboration with the fourth grade
of Carman Trails School). Performed St. Louis, 16 April 1989 and
6 October 1989.

Meyerowitz, Jan (b. Breslau, Germany [now Wroclaw, Poland], 13 April 1913; in
U.S. from 1946; *Amerigrove*)
1948　*Simoon* (1 act; libretto by P. Stephens after Strindberg). Performed
at Tanglewood Festival, MA, 2 August 1949 (*Baker's*: 2 August
1950). Published by Marks.
1950　*The Barrier* (or *The Mulatto*) (2 acts; libretto by Langston Hughes).
Performed New York, 18 January 1950; also by Teatro San Carlo,
Naples, Italy, 1971. Score in the New York Public Library.
1951　*Eastward in Eden* (renamed *Emily Dickinson*) (5 scenes; libretto by
D. Gardner). Performed Detroit, MI, 16 November 1951.
1953　*Bad Boys at School* (comic opera; 40 minutes; libretto by composer
after J. Nestroy). Performed at Tanglewood Festival, MA, 17
August 1953.
1955　*The Meeting* (1 act—originally the second act of *Eastward in Eden*).
Performed Falmouth, MA, 16 September 1955.

1957   *Esther* (3 acts; libretto by Langston Hughes). Performed at University of Illinois, Urbana, 17 March 1957.

1959   *Port Town* (1 act; libretto by Langston Hughes). Performed at Tanglewood Festival, MA, 4 August 1960.

1961   *Godfather Death* (3 acts; libretto by P. Stephens). Performed New York, 2 June 1961.

1965   *I rabbini* (radio opera; 2 acts). Broadcast by Radio Italiani, Italy, 5 December 1965.

1967   *Die Doppelgängerin* (after Gerhart Hauptmann's *Winterballade*, to which title the opera was later changed). Performed Hanover, Germany, 5 December (*Baker's*: 29 January) 1967.

 -     *Five Wise, Five Foolish.*

Meyers, Emerson (b. Washington, DC, 27 October 1910; Anderson; *Who's Who*)
1959   *Dolcedo* (for television; libretto by Father Dominic Rover). Performed at Catholic University, Washington, DC, April 1959.

Meyers, Nicholas
1974   *Mother Ann* (about the Shakers). NEA grant.
1974   *Apple Pie* (surrealist opera; 90 minutes; libretto by Myrna Lamb). Performed New York, 12 December 1976.

Miceli, Giuseppe
1912   *Alma Latina.* Performed Los Angeles, 1912.

Michalsky, Donal (b. Pasadena, CA, 13 July 1928; d. Newport Beach, CA, 31 December 1975 or 1 January 1976; *Amerigrove*; *Baker's*)
1975   *Der arme Heinrich* (miracle play). Performed Fullerton, CA, 1977. The score was burned in the fire that took his life.

Michelet, Michel (b. Kiev, Ukraine, 26 June 1894; to U.S. in 1941; Anderson; *Baker's*)
1972   *Hannele* (libretto after Hauptmann).

Middleton, Robert L. (b. Diamond, OH, 18 November 1920; Anderson)
1948   *Life Goes to a Party* (1 act). Performed at Tanglewood Festival, MA, 13 April 1948.
1954   *The Nightingale Is Guilty* (1 act). Performed Boston, 5 March 1954.
1961   *Command Performance* (opera-concerto; 4 acts; libretto by Harold Wendell Smith). Performed Poughkeepsie, NY, 11 November 1961.

Milano, Robert L. (b. Brooklyn, NY, 4 May 1936; Anderson)
1959   *The Hired Hand* (1 act). Performed New York, 23 March 1959.
1967   *Flight into Egypt* (chancel opera). Performed Pittsburgh, PA, 29 August 1967.
1969   *Rejoice and Be Glad* (Christmas opera).

Milburn, Ellsworth (b. Greensburg, PA, 6 February 1938; Anderson; *Baker's*)
1973   *Gesualdo.*

Mildenberg, Albert (b. Brooklyn, NY, 13 January 1878; d. there [Anderson: Raleigh, NC], 3 July 1918; Anderson; *Baker's*; Hipsher)
- 1903   *The Wood Witch* (light opera; libretto by composer). Performed New York, 25 May 1903 (Anderson: 1905; Hipsher: 1909).
- 1910   *Raffaelo* (1 act). Concert performance, Naples, Italy, 1910.
- 1911   *Michael Angelo* (*Angèle*) (grand opera; libretto by composer). Accepted for performance by Vienna Opera, but the composer withdrew it to offer it for a prize, 1911, by Metropolitan Opera, New York—but the score and libretto (in 3 languages) disappeared before reaching the judges. The composer was attempting to reconstruct it when he died.
- 1912   *Love's Locksmith* (light opera; libretto by composer). Performed New York, 1912.

Miles, Robert Whitfield (b. Roanoke, VA, 26 June 1920; *WhoAm*)
- 1984   *Good Times* (90 minutes; libretto by Chandler Warren after Barrie's *The Old Lady Shows Her Medals*). Performed by Musical Theater Works, New York, 15 May 1984.
- 1986   *Sunshine Vistas* (1 hour; about a Sun Belt retirement community).

Milford, Kim
- 1986   *All Bets Off*, with Daniel Troob (140 minutes; libretto by composers, Jamie Donnelly, and John Maccabee, about a present-day Pygmalion). Performed by National Music Theater Network, New York, 10 March 1986, and Minneapolis, 15 March 1986.

Millard, Harrison (b. Boston, 27 November 1830; d. there, 10 September 1895; *Amerigrove*; Hipsher)
- 1873   *Deborah*. Performed New York, 1873 (Hipsher: never performed).
- 1883   *Uncle Tom's Cabin*. Performed Toronto, Canada, 1883.

Miller, Alma Grace (Cohen)
- 1953   *The Whirlwind* (1 act). Performed Arlington, VA, 24 September 1953.

Miller, Daniel
- 1985   *Whatever Happened to the Girl Next Door?* (libretto by Eliza Miller). Performed by American Theater of Actors, New York, March 1985.

Miller, David
- 1981   *Ben* (1 hour; libretto by composer; in English and French—about mistranslation). Performed Brussels, Belgium, and Riverdale, MD, both on 24 January 1981.

Miller, Edward J. (b. Miami, FL, 4 August 1930; Anderson)
- 1969   *The Young God* ("a vaudeville"; 30 minutes). Performed Hartford, CT, 30 April 1969.

Miller, Frank
- 1953   *Thespis* (2 acts). Performed New York, 16 January 1953.

Miller, Gertrude (b. 1906?)
1963   *The Cherokee and the Deacon's Daughter.*

Miller, Lewis M. (b. New Rochelle, NY, 27 December 1947; Anderson)
1970   *The Imaginary Invalid* (3 acts; libretto after Molière). Performed Fort Hays, KS, February 1970.
1978   *Letters from Spain* (after Beaumarchais). Performed Fort Hays, KS, 20 January 1978.

Miller, Michael R. (b. Lisbon, Portugal, 24 July 1932; Anderson)
1963   *A Sunny Morning* (1 act; libretto after Quintero). Performed at New York University, New York, September 1963.

Miller, Newton
1969   *The Flying Machine* (1 act). Performed at University of Redlands, CA, 23 January 1969.

Milner, Richard P.
1980   *Super Soap* (2 acts; libretto by composer). Performed at Courtyard Theatre, New York, 1987, and Symphony Space, New York, 1987.

Minetti, Carlo (b. Intra, Lago Maggiore, Italy, 4 December 1868; d. Pittsburgh, 31 July 1923; Hipsher)
-    *Edane the Fair.*

Minshull, John
1801   *Rural Felicity.* Performed New York, 1801.
1831   *New Year's Morning.* Performed New York, 1831.

Misterly, Eugene William (b. Los Angeles, 25 September 1926; Anderson; WhoAm)
1950   *The Cask of Amontillado.* Later revised.
1962   *Bettina.* Performed by Highland Park Symphony, 1964.
1964   *Henry V* (3 acts). Performed by Highland Park Symphony, 1969.
1968   *The Tell-Tale Heart.*

Mitchell, Robert (ASCAP)
1980   *Examination* (1 act). Performed New York, 25 January 1980.
1985   *Rappaccini's Daughter* (libretto by Tom Toce after Hawthorne). Performed New York, 16 September 1985.

Mohaupt, Richard (b. Breslau, Germany [now Wroclaw, Poland], 14 September 1904; d. Reichenau, Austria, 3 July 1957; to U.S. in 1939; Amerigrove)
1949   *The Legend of the Charlatan* (pantomime, "mimodrama").
1954   *Double Trouble* (*Zwillingskomödie*) (65 minutes; libretto after Plautus). Performed Louisville, KY, 4 December 1954. Recorded by Louisville. Published by Associated Music.

Mokrejs, John (b. Cedar Rapids, IA, 10 February 1875; d. there, 22 November 1968; Anderson; Hipsher)
1917   *Sohrab and Rustrum* (grand opera; 1 act; libretto by composer after poem by Matthew Arnold).

- *The Mayflower* (operetta).
- *When Washington Was Young* (children's opera).

Mollenhauer, Edward (or Eduard) (b. Erfurt, Germany, 12 April 1827; d.
Owatoma, MN, 7 May 1914; *Amerigrove* [same as the following?])
1863 *The Corsican Bride* (light opera).
1878 *Manhattan Beach, or Love Among the Breakers* (light opera).

Mollenhauer, Friedrich (1818-85; b. in Germany; in U.S. from 1853)
1861 *The Corsican Bride.* Performed New York, 1861.
1881 *The Breakers.* Performed New York, 1881.

Mollicone, Henry (b. Providence, RI, 20 March 1946; Anderson; *WhoAm*)
1970 *Young Goodman Brown* (50 minutes; libretto after Hawthorne).
Performed Glens Falls, NY, summer 1970. Published by Belwin-
Mills.
1978 *The Face on the Bar-Room Floor* (melodrama [or opera]; 1 act—25
minutes; libretto by John S. Bowman). Commission and première
by Central City Opera, CO, 22 July 1978; performances at Lake
George, NY, 8 August 1980; by Houston Opera Studio, April
1981; Chamber Opera Theatre of New York, 17 December 1982;
San Diego State University Opera, 24 April 1986; Central City
Opera, CO, 5 August 1989; and Four Corners Opera, 22 June
1990. Kornick. Recorded by CRI, 1981.
1979 *Starbird* (1 act—50 minutes; libretto by Catherine Pogue; for
children). Commission and première by Houston Grand Opera
Studio, TX, 17 May 1979, also 30 April 1981; and San Jose, CA,
winter 1989. Kornick. Published by Belwin-Mills, 1980.
1981 *Emperor Norton* (formerly *The Intruder: In Search of Emperor
Norton*; 1 act—55 minutes; libretto by Catherine Pogue).
Commission by San Francisco Opera. Performed San Francisco, 14
May 1981.
1982 *The Mask of Evil* (formerly *A Vampire Tale*; 1 act; libretto by Kate
Pogue). Performed Minneapolis, 30 April 1982. Published by
Belwin-Mills.
1982 *Carmilla*; libretto after LeFanu). NEA grant, 1982.
1985 *Lilith* (1 act; libretto by composer). Performed Houston, TX, 6
June 1985.
1985 *Hotel Eden* (3 acts; libretto by Judith Fein, on parts of the Book of
Genesis). OPERA America grant, 1987. Commission by Hidden
Valley Opera, Carmel Valley, CA. Performed Carmel Valley,
1987; and San Jose, CA, 25 November 1989.
1990 *The Tumbler of Notre Dame* (in collaboration with Carolyn
Silberman). Performed Santa Clara, CA, 20 April 1990.
- *La Baunderie* (*The Laundry*) (libretto by Howard Richardson after
Guerdon, about the Minotaur). *COS*-2.
- *Feather and the Heart.* Commission by Shreveport Opera, Southern
Opera, and North Carolina Opera.
(Mollicone also has a commission from the Opera Theatre of Saint
Louis, MO.)

Monk, Meredith (b. Lima, Peru, 20 November 1943, of American parents;
 Amerigrove; Cohen; *Who's Who*)
 1971 *Vessel* (opera epic), for 20 and 70 voices, electric organ, 7
  dulcimers.
 1973 *Education of the Girlchild.*
 1976 *Quarry*, for 40 voices, 2 organs, piano, flute.
 1979 *Dolmen Music* (1 act—6 sections; libretto by composer, about
  archaeology). Performed by LaMama Annex, New York, 1979.
 1980 *Recent Ruins.* Performed Nanterre, France, 26 February 1980.
 1981 *Specimen Days* (libretto by composer). Performed at New York
  Shakespeare Festival, New York, 2 December 1981.
 1983 *The Games: Days of Wrath* (multimedia; 90 minutes; libretto by
  composer and Ping Chong, on the future in space; in several
  languages). Performed West Berlin, Germany, 28 November 1983;
  and at Next Wave Festival, Brooklyn, NY, 9 October 1984.
 1986 *Acts from Under and Above*, with Lanny Harrison (90 minutes;
  libretto by composers; the second part uses rags by Albright,
  Ashwander, and Tenney). Performed by LaMama E.T.C., New
  York, 3 April 1986.
 1986 *Turtle Dreams.* German Critics' Prize. Performed by LaMama
  E.T.C., New York, 22 April 1986. Recorded by ECM/Polygram.
 1988 *Do You Be?.* Performed Vancouver, Canada, 5 April 1988.
 1988 *Book of Days* (30 minutes; libretto by composer; an operatic version
  of her own film). Performed St. Paul, MN, May 1988.
 1991 *Atlas* (libretto by composer). Commission by Houston Grand
  Opera, with the American Music Theater Festival and the Walker
  Art Center. Première by Houston Grand Opera, Houston, TX, 22
  February 1991. See profile in *New York Times Magazine*, 30 June
  1991.

Monroe, B.
 1989 *The Insanity of Mary Girard* (libretto by composer). Performed
  Seattle, WA, 13 March 1989.

Montgomery, Bruce (b. Philadelphia, 20 June 1927; Anderson; *Who's Who*)
 1974 *The Amorous Flea* (after Molière's *School for Wives*). Performed
  Delaware, OH, 30 October 1974.
 - *John Barleycorn.* Published by Novello.

Moore, Carman Leroy (b. Lorain, OH, 8 October 1936; ASCAP; *Amerigrove*;
 Baker's; Southern; *WhoAm*; *Who's Who*)
 1981 *The Masque of Saxophone's Voice.*
 1982 *Combinations.* Performed Lenox, MA, 7 July 1982.
 1983 *The Wild Gardens of the Loup Garou* (music theater; on 25 poems
  by Ishmael Reed and Colleen McElroy). Performed at Judson
  Memorial Church, New York, May 1983.
 1983 *Distraugher: or, The Great Panda Scandal* (music theater).
 1987 *Paradise Relost* (music theater; libretto by Oyamo). Performed by
  New Dramatists Workshop, New York, 1 April 1987.
 1989 *Franklin and Eleanor* (musical).

Moore, Charles (b. Vinita, OK, 23 May 1938; Anderson)

1988   *I Can Sing That Better* (1 act; libretto by composer). Performed at DePaul University, Chicago, 21 April 1988.

Moore, David A. (b. Stillwater, OK, 23 February 1948; Anderson)

1973   *Jephtha* (2 acts; libretto by composer).

Moore, Dorothy Rudd (also Dorothy Rudd-Moore; b. New Castle, DE, 4 June 1940; ACA; *Amerigrove*; Southern)

1977   *The Harlequin Twins.*

1985   *Frederick Douglass* (3 hours; libretto by composer). Performed by Opera Ebony, New York, 17 or 28 June 1985.

Moore, Douglas (b. Cutchogue, NY, 10 August 1893; d. Greenport, NY, 25 July 1969; *Amerigrove*)

1928   *Jesse James* (libretto by J. M. Brown), incomplete, unpublished.

1935   *White Wings* (2 acts; libretto by Philip Barry). Performed Hartford, CT, 9 February 1949. Published by Liebling Wood.

1936   *The Headless Horseman* (high-school opera; 1 act—1 hour; libretto by Stephen Vincent Benét after Washington Irving's *The Legend of Sleepy Hollow*). Performed Bronxville, NY, 4 March 1937. Published by E. C. Schirmer.

1938   *The Devil and Daniel Webster* (folk opera; 1 act—1 hour; libretto by Stephen Vincent Benét). Performed New York, 18 May 1929. Bispham Medal, 1944. Published by Boosey & Hawkes, 1943. Johnson labels this as "the most frequently performed opera on an American subject by an American."

1948   *The Emperor's New Clothes* (children's opera; 1 act—15 minutes; libretto by R. Abrashkin after Hans Christian Andersen). Performed New York, 19 February 1949. Published by Carl Fischer.

1949   *Puss in Boots* (children's operetta; 15 minutes; libretto by R. Abrashkin after C. Perrault). Performed New York, 18 November 1950. Published by Carl Fischer.

1949   *Giants in the Earth* (3 acts; libretto by A. Sundgaard after O. E. Rölvaag). Performed New York, 28 March 1951. Pulitzer Prize. Revised 1963. Published by Carl Fischer.

1956   *The Ballad of Baby Doe* (folk opera; 2 acts; libretto by John Latouche about Baby Doe Tabor). Performed by Central City Opera, CO, 7 July 1956; New York Center Opera, 3 April 1958 and 2 October 1988; Michigan Opera Theatre, 7 October 1988; Dayton Opera, 21 October 1988; and Fargo-Moorehead Civic Opera, 19 January 1990. Published by Chappell, 1958, or Tams-Whitmark. Video of New York City Opera, 1976 by Lincoln Center for the Performing Arts.

1957   *Gallantry* ("soap opera"; 35 minutes; libretto by Sundgaard). Performed New York, 19 March 1958. Published by G. Schirmer.

1961   *The Wings of the Dove* (2 acts; libretto by E. Ayer after H. James). Performed New York, 12 October 1961. Published by G. Schirmer.

1962   *The Greenfield Christmas Tree* (Christmas entertainment; 45 minutes; libretto by Sundgaard). Performed Baltimore, MD, 8 December 1962. Published by G. Schirmer.

1966   *Carry Nation* (2 acts; libretto by William North Jayme).
Commission by University of Kansas for its centennial and
premièred there, 28 April 1966. Published by Galaxy; recorded
by Desto.

1969   *Bliss Apocalypse*. Performed San Francisco, May 1969.

Moore, Frank L.
1982   *Wagadougou*. Performed at Hartwick College, Oneonta, NY, 4
March 1982.

Moore, Homer (b. Chautauqua County, NY, 29 April 1863; Hipsher)
(Moore wrote his own librettos.)
c 1888   *The Fall of Rome.*
        American Trilogy:
1903   *Columbus; or, The New World*. Performed St. Louis, 1903.
-      *The Pilgrims.*
1902   *The Puritans*. Concert performance, St. Louis, 1902.
1917   *Louis XIV*. Performed at Odeon, St. Louis, MO, 16 February 1917.
-      *The Elf Wife.*
-      *Joan Edvign.*

Moore, Mary Carr (b. Memphis, TN, 6 August 1873; d. Inglewood, CA, 9
January 1957; *Amerigrove*; Cohen; Hipsher)
1894   *The Oracle* (3 acts; libretto by composer). Performed San Francisco,
the composer singing the lead, 29 March 1894; also given 3 times
in Seattle, 1902.

1911   *Narcissa: or, The Cost of Empire* (grand opera; 4 acts; libretto by
Sarah Pratt Carr, concerns the American northwest). Performed at
Moore Theater, Seattle, WA, 22 April 1912, the composer
conducting; for California's Diamond Jubilee Celebration, San
Francisco, week of 7 September 1925 for 9 performances,
composer conducting; and Los Angeles, 1945. Hipsher: "the first
grand opera to be written, staged and directed by an American
woman." Bispham Medal, 1930. Published by Witmark, 1912.

1912   *The Leper*, op. 74 (tragedy; 1 act; libretto by Dudley Burrows).
Never performed, according to Hipsher.

1914   *Memories* (1 act; libretto by C. E. Banks). Performed at the
Orpheum, Seattle, WA, 31 October 1914, composer conducting.

1917   *Harmony* (1 act; libretto by various students). Performed San
Francisco, 25 May 1917.

1920   *The Flaming Arrow: or, The Shaft of Ku'pish-ta-ya*, op. 83, no. 1
(1 act; libretto by Sarah Pratt Moore after an Indian legend),
revised 1927. Première at Century Club, San Francisco, 27 March
1922, composer conducting; also performed for Los Angeles Opera
and Fine Arts Club, 25 November 1927.

1928   *David Rizzio*, op. 89 (or *Rizzio*; grand opera; 2 acts; libretto by
Emanual Mapleson Browne; in Italian). Première at Shrine
Auditorium, Los Angeles, 26 May 1932. Published by Wesley
Webster, 1937; reprint, New York: Da Capo, 1981.

1931   *Los rubios*, op. 93 (romantic opera; 3 acts; libretto by Neeta
Marquis). Commissioned by Recreation Department, Los Angeles,
for 150th anniversary of Pueblo de Los Angeles; performed there
at the Greek Theater, 10 September 1931.

1933   *Flutes of Jade Happiness* (3 acts; libretto by L. S. Moore).
Performed Los Angeles, 2 March 1934.

1935   *Legende provençale*, op. 90 (grand opera; 3 acts; libretto by Eleanore
Flaig).

Moore, Richard
1976   *Yu widi* (1 act). Performed by Omaha Opera on tour, spring 1976.

Moore, Undine Smith (b. Jarratt, VA, 25 August 1902; d. Petersburg, VA, 6 February 1989; *Amerigrove*; Cohen; Southern)
1984   *Scenes from the Life of a Martyr* (dramatic cantata, about Martin
Luther King, Jr.). Performed Ann Arbor, MI, 1985 and 1989.

Moorefield, Virgil
1987   *Defenders of the Code* (puppet pageant; 2 acts; libretto by Andrea
Balis and Theodoa Skipitares, about heredity). Performed by
Skysaver Productions, New York, 20 February 1987.

Mopper, Irving (b. Savannah, GA, 1 December 1914; Anderson)
1954   *The Door*, or *The Sire de Maledroit's Door* (50 minutes). Performed
Newark, NJ, 5 December 1954 and 2 December 1956. (Dated
1955 by Anderson.)

-    *George* (45 minutes). Published by Boosey & Hawkes.

-    *Nero's Mother.*

Moran, John
1988   *Jack Benny* (multimedia; based on the Jack Benny show).
Performed by Performance Space 122, New York, 1988, LaMama
E.T.C., New York, 28 September 1989, and in Baltimore, MD,
September 1989.

1989   *Rules of Nakedness.* Performed by LaMama E.T.C., New York,
February 1989.

1990   *The Manson Family: Helter Five-O* (multimedia opera; 75 minutes;
libretto by composer, on the Manson murders and TV series
Hawaii Five-O). Performed by Serious Fun, New York, 17 July
1990.

Moran, Robert Leonard (b. Denver, CO, 8 January 1937; *Amerigrove*)
1969   *Let's Build a Nut House* (chamber opera), in memory of Paul
Hindemith. Performed San Jose, CA, 19 April 1969.

1971   *Divertissement No. 3: A Lunchbag Opera*, with paper bags and
instruments. Telecast London, England, BBC-TV, 1971.

1974   *Metamenagerie* (department store window opera).

1975   *Durch Wüsten und Wolken*, with shadow puppets and instruments.
NEA grant.

1981   *Hitler: Geschichten aus der Zukunft.*

1982   *Erlösung dem Erlöser* (music drama), with tape loops.

1985   *The Juniper Tree*, with Philip Glass and Arthur Yorkinks (115
minutes; libretto by Yorinks after Grimm). Commission by
American Repertory Theater, Cambridge, MA. Performed New
York, March 1985, and Cambridge, MA, 6 December 1985.

1986   *Leipziger Kerzenspiel* (*Leipzig Candle Play*) ("contemporary
singspiel"; for the bicentennials of Handel, Bach, and Scarlatti).

Commission by Massachusetts Council on the Arts. Performed at Mount Holyoke College, South Hadley, MA, 1986.

Morgan, Brian
1987   *s.* Performed New Orleans, April 1987.

Morgan, Geoffrey
-    *Sunbonnet Girl* (105 minutes). Published by Willis Music.

Morgenstern, Sam (d. New York, 22 December 1989)
1984   *The Big Black Box* (1 act; libretto by Francis Steegmuller). Performed by After Dinner Opera, New York, 10 December 1984.

Moross, Jerome (b. Brooklyn, NY, 1 August 1913; d. Miami, FL, 25 July 1983; *Amerigrove*)
1941   *Susanna and the Elders* (ballet-opera; 1 act; libretto by John Latouche). Performed Augusta, GA, 21 January 1940.
1945   *Willie the Weeper* (ballet-opera; 1 act; libretto by John Latouche).
1945   *The Eccentricities of Davy Crockett* (ballet-opera; 1 act; libretto by John Latouche). Performed Wilkes-Barre, PA, 16 April 1971.
1946   *Riding Hood Revisited* (ballet-opera; 1 act; libretto by John Latouche).
1950   *The Golden Apple* (2 acts; libretto by John Latouche).
1956   *Gentlemen, Be Seated!* (libretto by Edward Eager). Ford Foundation grant. Performed by New York Center, 10 October 1963. Published by Chappell.
1980   *Sorry, Wrong Number!* (libretto after L. Fletcher). Performed Lake George, NY, 7 August 1980.

Morrill, Dexter G. (b. North Adams, MA, 17 June 1938; Anderson; *Who's Who*)
1976   *Main Travelled Roads.*

Morrill, Kam
1989   *Perlimplin* (1 hour; libretto by composer after Federico García Lorca). Performed at Curtis Institute of Music, Philadelphia, 18 February 1989.

Morris, Franklin E. (b. Phoenixville, PA, 1920; Anderson)
1959   *The Postponement* (1 act; libretto by composer). Performed Syracuse, NY, 7 May 1959.

Morris, Hayward
1981   *A View from the Bridge* (150 minutes; libretto by Stone Widney after Miller). Performed by OPERA America Showcase, January 1981.
-    *In Paradise* (3 acts). Performed by Manhattan School of Music, New York.

Morrison, Julia Maria (b. Minneapolis, MN, 26 April [year missing in Anderson and Cohen])
1966   *Smile Right Down to the Bone.*
1978?   *Equal Day and Night.*

1979   *Rübezahl* (libretto by composer).
-       *Countdown in the Cave Zone* (150 minutes; libretto by the composer after German legends, but set in the present, with flashbacks).

Morrow, Charlie (b. Newark, NJ, 9 February 1942; *Amerigrove*)
1983   *The Light Opera* (libretto by composer, using texts from ancient cultures). Performed by Western Wind and Mai Juku, LaMama E.T.C., New York, 6 June 1983.

Morse, Paul
1980   *Lexington Green: The Shot Heard around the World* (1 hour; libretto by composer). Performed Los Angeles, 11 May 1980.

Morse, Woolson (1858-97; b. in Massachusetts)
1891   *Wang* (comic opera; 2 acts).

Morton, Lawrence (b. New York, 4 October 1942; Anderson)
-       *Women* (1 act).

Moses, Abram
1939   *Melody in "I"* (1 act). Performed Baltimore, MD.

Moss, Lawrence K. (b. Los Angeles, 18 November 1927; *Amerigrove*)
1960   *The Brute* (comic opera; 20 minutes; libretto after Chekhov). Performed Norfolk, CT, 15 or 16 July 1961.
1962   *The Queen and the Rebels* (3 acts; libretto by Ugo Betti). Performed New York, 1 November 1962; by Central City Opera, CO, 1972; in Riverdale, MD, 1981-82; and College Park, MD, 7 December 1989.
1975   *Unseen Leaves* (theater piece; Walt Whitman text), for soprano, oboe, tapes, slides, lights.
1978   *Nightscape* (theater piece; libretto by J. G. Brown), for soprano, flute, clarinet, violin, percussion, dancer, tape, slides.
1980   *Dreamscape* (formerly *Nightscape*; 1 act; libretto by A. Lusby-Pinchot), for dancer, tape, lights. Performed Cheverly, MD, 18 January 1981.

Moulds, R. A.
-       *Jasmine* ("mystical opera"; 75 minutes; libretto by composer). *COS*-4.

Mueller, Grace
1976   *Women of the World Unite*. Performed Bismarck, ND, October 1976.

Mueller, Larry R. (AMC)
1973   *Little Red Riding Hood* (2 acts; after Grimm).

Mueter, John A.
1984   *Amor* (dramatic comedy; 50 minutes; libretto by composer, about Psyche and Eros in the U.S. today). Performed by After Dinner Opera, New York, 6 February 1984.

Mukherjee, Tim
1979　*Sweeney Agonistes* (on Eliot).　Performed Cambridge, MA, 8 March 1979.
1979　*You Haven't Changed* (1 act; libretto by Alain Rekke-Grillet). Performed Cambridge, MA, 28 October 1979.

Muldoon, George
1959　*Illusion for Three* (2 acts).　Performed San Francisco.

Muldowney, (Mitchell?)
1989　*The Pied Piper*.　Performed Albany, NY, 27 April 1989.

Mulhare, Mirta T.
1986　*O.T.* (libretto by composer, on Shakespeare's *Othello* in the U.S. today).　Performed Old Westbury, NY, 13 March 1986.

Muller, Gerald F. (b. Clifton, NJ, 25 July 1932; *WhoAm*)
1976　*Joshua* (bicentennial folk opera; about the War of 1812).　Performed at Montgomery College, Rockville, MD, 4 April 1976.
1978　*Chronicles*.　Performed by Montgomery Light Opera Assocation, 1978.
1981　*Mary Surratt*.　Performed at Montgomery College, 1981.

Mullins, Hugh E. (b. Danville, IL, 25 June 1922; Anderson; *WhoAm*)
1962　*The Jade Goddess* (1 act).　Performed Los Angeles, February 1962.
1963　*The Stone of Heaven* (1 act).　Performed Los Angeles, April 1963.
1963　*The Kiss* (1 act).　Performed Los Angeles, November 1963.
-　*Romeo and Juliet*.
-　*The Scarlett Letter*.

Mullins, (Hugh?)
1990　*Increase* (an all-female cast; libretto by Goldbeck).　Performed by LaMama, New York, 15 February 1990.

Mumma, Gordon (b. Framingham, MA, 30 March 1935; *Amerigrove*; *Who's Who*)
1980　*Fwynnghn*, with Pauline Oliveros and Christian Sinding ("a funky fairy tale").　Performed Valencia, CA, 5 March 1980.

Murray, Bain (b. Evanston, IL, 26 December 1926; *WhoAm*)
1987　*The Legend* (1 act; libretto by Janet Lewis after an American Indian story).　Performed Cleveland, 8 May 1987.

Murray, Jeremiah
1973　*Marriage Proposal* (1 act; libretto after Chekhov).　Performed New York, 1 February 1973.
1974　*The Beauty and the Beast* (1 act; libretto after Beaumont). Performed New York, 8 May 1974.

Murray, Lyn (b. London, England, 6 December 1909; U.S. citizen, 1929; d. Los Angeles, 20 May 1989; Anderson)
-　*Esther*.

Musgrave, Thea (b. Barnton, Midlothian, Scotland, 27 May 1928; in U.S. from 1970; *Amerigrove*; *WhoAm*; *Who's Who*)

1976   *Mary, Queen of Scots* (3 acts—129 minutes; libretto by composer after Amalia Elguera's play *Moray*). Commission by Scottish Opera. Première at Edinburgh Festival, September 1977; performances by Virginia Opera, 29 March 1978; San Francisco Spring Opera, 1979; Hinsdale Opera Theatre, IL, 20 June 1980. Kornick.

1981   *Occurrence at Owl Creek Bridge*.

1979   *A Christmas Carol* (2 acts—105 minutes; libretto by composer after the Dickins tale). Commission and première by Virginia Opera Association, 7 December 1979. Kornick.

1984   *Harriet, the Woman Called Moses* (2 acts; libretto by composer based on the life of Harriet Tubman). Commission by the Royal Opera House, Covent Garden, London, and the Virginia Opera Association. Première by Virginia Opera, Norfolk, 1 March 1985. Kornick. See Georgia A. Ryder, "Thea Musgrave and the Production of Her Opera *Harriet, the Woman Called Moses*: An Interview with the Composer," in *New Perspectives on Music*, ed. Josephine Wright with Samuel A. Floyd, Jr., Detroit Monographs in Musicology/Studies in Music, 11 (this publisher, 1992).

Myers, Amina Claudine

1987   *When the Berries Fell* (2 hours; libretto by composer). Performed at Composers Forum, New York, 20 February 1987.

Nabokov, Nicolas (b. Lyubcha, Novogrudok, near Minsk, Belorussia, 17 April 1903; d. New York, 6 April 1978; in U.S. from 1933; *Amerigrove*)

1958   *The Holy Devil* (2 acts—70 minutes; libretto by Spender about Rasputin). Performed Louisville, KY, 16 or 18 April 1958; and (as *Der Tod des Grigorij Rasputin*; 3 acts) Cologne, Germany, 27 November 1959.

1973   *Love's Labours Lost* (*Verlor'ne Liebesmuh*) (comedy; 3 acts—120 minutes; libretto by W. H. Auden and Chester Kallman after Shakespeare; German by Claus H. Henneberg). Première by Deutsche Oper at Theatre de la Monnaie, Brussels, Belgium, 7 February 1973. Kornick.

Nahay, Paul Lawrence (b. Camden, NJ, 31 May 1958; *WhoAm*; *Who's Who*)

1983   *Minute Opera/Minute Soap Opera* (two works: the second is an afterpiece; each is 1 minute long; libretto by the composer). Performed New York, 4 November 1983.

1984   *Kyag* (3 acts—10 minutes; libretto by composer). Performed College Park, MD, April 1984.

1987   *SeXeS* (minimalist opera; 1 act—30 minutes; libretto by Matthew Westbrook; the work is generated by a mathematical pattern). Performed at Charles Cowles Annex Gallery, New York, 3 October 1987.

1988   *Beauty and the Beast* (90 minutes; libretto by composer and Bob Beverage; for children). Commission by Cedar Crest Stage Co., Allentown, PA; performed there, 19 February 1988.

Najera, Edmund L. (b. in Arizona, 13 April 1936; Anderson)
 1968 *The Freeway Opera* (1 act). Performed Los Angeles, 17 November 1968.
 1977 *To Wait, To Mourn* (1 act). Performed New York, 17 March 1977.
 - *Carlotta.*
 - *Freeway Opera.*
 - *The Scarlet Letter* (2 acts; libretto after Hawthorne). *COS*-3.
 - *Secundum Lucam, Grenadilla* (opera-oratorio setting of Luke 2; in Latin and English).

Namanworth, Philip
 1979 *Alice through the Looking Glass*, with Susan Dias and Meridee Stein. Performed New York, 21 October 1979.
 - *Clap Your Hands* (1 act; libretto by Benjamin Goldstein; for children).

Nauman, Joel E.
 1981 *Aria da capo* (libretto by composer after Edna St. Vincent Millay). NEA grant, 1981.

Negri, Guido (b. Trento, Italy, 13 November 1886; Hipsher)
 - *Cleopatra* (serious opera; 3 acts; libretto by Iginio Squassoni after Shakespeare). Excerpt, "Intermezzo sinfonico," played by Atlanta Philharmonic, 5 June 1932.

Nehls, David
 1986 *Starting Another Day* (for high school students to perform; 2 acts; libretto by composer and Clive Cholerton). Commission by Shenandoah College and Conservatory, Winchester, VA; performed there, 1986-87 season.

Neikrug, Marc (b. New York, 24 September 1946; *Amerigrove*; *Who's Who*)
 1980 *Through Roses* (monodrama/theater piece; 50 minutes; libretto by composer, about life in a concentration camp), for actor and 8 instruments. International Film & TV Festival winner, 1982. Performed at Kaufman Auditorium, New York, 14 April 1981.
 1988 *Los Alamos* (150 minutes; libretto by composer and Joe Cacaci, about nuclear war). Commission by Deutsche Oper, Berlin, Germany. Performed Berlin (in a German translation by Paul Esterhazy), 1 October 1981.

Neil, William (b. 1957 [Kornick: b. 1954]; composer-in-residence, Chicago Lyric Opera beginning in 1983)
 1984 *The Devil's Stocking* (libretto by composer after Algren). One scene of this work was completed; performed Chicago, 14 June 1984.
 1985 *The Guilt of Lillian Sloan* (2 acts—90 minutes; libretto by Frank Galati, on a British murder trial of 1922). Commission by and performance by Chicago Lyric Opera, 22 June 1985, and Evanston, IL, 6 June 1986. Kornick.

Nelhybel, Vaclav (b. Polanka nad Odrou, Czechoslovakia, 24 September 1919; to
U.S. in 1957; citizen, 1962; *Amerigrove*)
1954   *A Legend.*
1974   *Everyman* (on a medieval morality play). Performed Memphis, TN,
39 October 1974.
1978   *The Station.*

Nelson, ?
1988   *In the Shadows* (video opera). Performed at Composers Forum,
Minneapolis, 9 January 1988.

Nelson, Ken
1981   *A Country Christmas Carol*, with Jack Dyville (libretto by the
composers after Dickens). Performed North Richland Hills, TX,
December 1981. Published by I. E. Clark.

Nelson, Mark
1987   *Walking through Walls*, with Bill Farber and John J. Sheehan
(multimedia; libretto by Terry Megan and Jo Ann Schmidman).
Performed by Omaha Magic Theatre, NE, 20 November 1987.
1989   *Headlights*, with Frank Fong, Rex Gray, Rich Hiatt, Lori Loree,
and Luigi Waites. Performed Omaha, NE, 28 April 1989.

Nelson, Robert (AMC; Schoep)
1985   *Tickets, Please* (25 minutes; libretto by Sidney L. Berger after D. H.
Lawrence). Performed Houston, TX, 6 June 1985, and Des
Moines, IA, 1986.
-       *The Commission* (3 acts—90-100 minutes; libretto by Stan Peters).
COS-3. Studio performance at Cockpit Theatre, London,
England.
-       *The Man Who Corrupted Hadleyville* (90 minutes; libretto by Kate
Pogue after Twain).

Nelson, Roger L.
1985   *Trio con brio* (1 or 3 acts; libretto by composer). The 1-act version
performed Evanston, IL, 12 November 1985.
-       *John Brown* (2 acts; libretto by John Driver).
(Nelson also composed the musicals *Lisa and David*, 1984, and *Mary
S.*, 1987.)

Nelson, Ron (b. Joliet, IL, 14 December 1929; ASCAP; *Amerigrove*; Schoep; *Who's
Who*)
1956   *The Birthday of the Infanta* (1 act—50 minutes; libretto by composer
after the short story by Oscar Wilde). Performed by Eastman
School of Music Opera, Rochester, NY, 14 May 1956; also on
Metropolitan Opera Studio tour, 1970. Published by Eastman
Publications, Carl Fischer.
1981   *Hamaguchi* (libretto by M. Miller).

Nembern, Kenneth
-       *The Armour of Life* (40 minutes).

Neston, Larry
- *Stone Soup* (35 minutes; libretto by composer and Gary Peterson; for children).
- *A Tale of Two Cities* (2 acts; libretto by composer and Gary Peterson after Dickens).

Neuendorff, Adolf (b. Hamburg, Germany, 13 June 1843; d. New York, 4 December 1897; in U.S. from 1854; *Baker's*)
1880 *Der Rattenfänger von Hameln.*
1882 *Don Quixote, der Ritter von der traurigen Gestalt* (prologue and 3 acts). Performed New York.
1887 *Prince Waldmeister.*
1892 *Der Minstrel* (*The Minstrel*) (3 acts). Performed New York.

Neumann, Alfred
1963 *An Opera for Easter* (1 act). Performed Silver Springs, MD, April 1963.
1963 *An Opera for Everyone* (1 act). Performed Silver Springs, MD, November 1963.
1969 *The Rites of Man.* Performed Silver Spring, MD, 18 May 1969.
- *An Opera for Christmas* (1 act; libretto by composer). Published by Belwin-Mills.

Nevin, Arthur Finley (b. Edgeworth, PA, 27 April 1871; d. Sewickley, PA, 10 July 1943; brother of Ethelbert Nevin; AMC; *Amerigrove*; Hipsher)
1900 *A Night in Yaddo Land* (masque; libretto by E. Stebbins and W. Chance). Performed New York, 1900.
1906 *Poia* (3 acts; libretto by Randolph Hartley). Performed Pittsburgh, PA, 1906, and Berlin, Germany, 23 April 1910. Published by Furstner, 1909.
1917 *A Daughter of the Forest* (originally titled *Twilight*; 1 act; libretto by Randolph Hartley). Performed by Chicago Opera Association at the Auditorium, Chicago, 5 January 1918.

Nevin, Ethelbert (b. Edgeworth, PA, 25 November 1862; d. New Haven, CT, 17 February 1901; brother of Arthur Finley Nevin; *Amerigrove*)
1898 *Lady Floriane's Dream* (pantomime; libretto by V. Thompson). Performed New York, 24 March 1898.

Newbern, Kenneth
1957 *The Armor of Life* (40 minutes). Performed New York, 26 February 1957.

Newlin, Dika (b. Portland, OR, 22 November 1923; ACA; *Amerigrove*; *Baker's*; Cohen; *Who's Who*)
- *Feather Top: An American Folk Tale* (1 act).
- *Smile Right to the Bone* (3 acts; libretto by Julia Morrison; about a country village after World War II).
(*Amerigrove*, *Baker's*, and *Who's Who* indicate she wrote three operas.)

Newton, Rhoda
- *Man in the Moon.* Published by Carl Fischer.

Nichols, Ted
   1986 *Esther, the Queen* (3 acts; libretto by composer, based on the Old
             Testament). Performed at Southern Baptist Theological Seminary,
             Louisville, KY, 22 April 1986.

Niebel, Mildred (AMC)
   –   *Friendship on Parade* (1 act). *COS*-1. Published by Flammer.

Nin-Culmell, Joaquín Maria (b. Berlin, Germany, 5 September 1908; to U.S. in
             1938; *Amerigrove*; *Who's Who*)
   1980 *La Celestina* (3 acts; libretto by composer after 16th-century
             Spanish story).

Nixon, Roger A. (b. Tulare, CA, 8 August 1921; *Amerigrove*; Schoep)
   1967 *The Bride Comes to Yellow Sky* (1 act—45 minutes; libretto by Ray
             B. West, Jr. based on the short story). Performed by Eastern
             Illinois University Opera Workshop, 20 February 1969, by San
             Francisco State University Opera Workshop, March 1969, and by
             University of California, Los Angeles, Opera Workshop, 1971.

Noda, Ken (b. New York, 5 October 1962; AMC; Anderson; *Baker's*; *Who's Who*)
   1973 *The Canary* (1 act). Performed, with piano accompaniment, at
             Brevard, NC, Music Festival, 18 August 1973. First prize in the
             National Young Composers' Contest of the National Federation of
             Music Clubs.
   1974 *The Swing* (1 act).
   1976 *The Rivalry* (45 minutes; libretto by composer; about Andrew
             Jackson). NEA grant, 1976.
   1979 *The Highwayman.*
   1980 *The Magic Turtle.*

Norden, Norris Lindsay (b. Philadelphia, 24 April 1887; d. there, 3 November
             1956; Anderson)
   1953 *Nebrahm* (or *Nebrahma*; 90 minutes. Performed Philadelphia, 1953.
   1954 *Through a Glass Darkly* (110 minutes). Performed by Ethic Society
             of Pennsylvania, May 1954.
   –   *Cinderella* (75 minutes).
   –   *The Little Match Girl* (60 minutes).

Nordoff, Paul (b. Philadelphia, 4 June 1909; d. Herdecke, Germany, 18 January
             1977; ASCAP; *Amerigrove*)
   1937 *Mr. Fortune* (libretto after S. T. Warner), revised 1957.
   1940 *The Masterpiece* (operetta; 1 act—45 minutes; libretto by F. Brewer).
             Performed Philadelphia, 24 January 1941.
   1951 *The Sea-Change* (105 minutes; libretto by S. T. Warner).
   –   *The Frog Prince* (20 minutes; libretto by composer and Hans Pusch).
             COS-4.

North, Alex (b. Chester, PA, 4 December 1910; d. 8 September 1991; AMC;
             Amerigrove; *Baker's*; *Who's Who*)
   1941 *The Hither and Thither of Danny Dither* (children's opera; 150
             minutes). Published by Marks.
       (North has also composed a substantial amount of incidental and
       film music.)

Nowak, Alison (b. Syracuse, NY, 7 April 1948; Cohen)
    1973   *Diversions and Diversion* (chamber opera; 1 act).

Nowak (or Novak), **Lionel Augustus** (b. Cleveland, OH, 25 September 1911;
          Amerigrove; *Who's Who*)
    1959   *The Clarkstown Witch* (2 acts). Performed Piermont, NY, 11 July
          1959.
    1962   *Katydid* (or *Katydiss*; 2 acts). Performed Piermont, NY, 26 July
          1962.

Noyes (or Noyes-Greene), **Edith Rowena** (b. Cambridge, MA, 26 March 1875;
          Cohen; Hipsher)
    1896   *Last Summer* (operetta). Performed Lowell, MA, 1986, and
          Quincy, MA, 1898.
    1917   *Osseo* (romantic grand opera; 3 acts; libretto by Lillie Fuller
          Mirriam based on Indian episodes). Performed at Maud Freshel's
          Theater, Brookline, MA, 1917; at Copley-Plaza Theater, Boston,
          1920; at Jordan Hall, Boston, 9 May 1922.
    1917   *Washakum* (pageant opera).

Nye, Stephen
    1981   *Miracles* (2 hours; libretto by composer, about Atlanta in 1939).
          Performed Denver, CO, June 1981 and August 1982.
    1988   *Favorite Night* (Christmas opera). Performed at New York
          University, 17 December 1988.

Oberndorfer, Marx E. (b. Milwaukee, WI, 7 November 1876; Hipsher)
    1928   *The Magic Mirror* (libretto by Grace Hofman White after Hans
          Christian Andersen). This and the following written at the
          MacDowell Colony, summers of 1927-28.
    1928   *Roseanne* (libretto by Nan Bagby Stevens after a play by David
          Belasco). Concert performance for American Opera Society,
          Chicago, 25 October 1931. Bispham Medal, 1932.

Odenz, Leon (ASCAP)
    1985   *Savings: A Musical Fable* (libretto by Dolores Prida). Performed by
          INTAR Hispanic-American Music Theatre Lab, New York, 15
          May 1985.

Ogdon, Will (Wilbur L.) (b. Redlands, CA, 19 April 1921; *Amerigrove*; *Who's
          Who*)
    1980   *The Awakening of Sappho* (chamber opera; libretto by composer
          after Lawrence Durrell). NEA grant 1975. Performed at
          University of California, San Diego, 21 October 1981.

O'Hara, Geoffrey (b. Chatham, Ontario, Canada, 2 February 1882; d. St.
          Petersburg, FL, 31 January 1967; in U.S. from 1904, citizen in
          1919; Anderson; *Baker's*)
          (These are all operettas.)

1927	*Peggy and the Pirate.*
1928	*Riding down the Sky.*
1929	*The Count and the Co-ed.*
1930	*The Smiling Sixpence.*
1931	*Lantern Land.*
1933	*Harmony Hall.*
1934	*The Princess Runs Away.*
1934	*Our America.*
1936	*Puddinhead the First.*
1943	*The Christmas Thieves.*

Olds, William Benjamin (b. Clinton, OH, 26 February 1933; Anderson)
- *The Feathered Serpent.*

Olenick, Elmer
1984 *The Diet* (opera buffa; 30 minutes; libretto by composer and Carl Gersuny). Performed by Golden Fleece, New York, 22 March 1984.

Oler, Kim
1988 *A Secret Garden* (libretto by Linda Kline and Alison Hubbard after Bernett). Performed by Theatreworks/USA, New York, 22 October 1988.

Oliver, Harold (b. Easton, MD, 15 September 1942; Anderson)
1976 *King of the Cats* (chamber opera).

Oliver, Joseph
1975 *Mar-ri-ia-a* (23 minutes; libretto by Joan Olive). Performed New York, 7 April 1975.

Oliveros, Pauline (b. Houston, TX, 30 May 1932; *Amerigrove*; Cohen; *Who's Who*)
1974 *Crow Two: A Ceremonial Opera.*
1975 *Theatre of Substitution.*
1977 *Theatre of Substitutions: Blind/Dumb/Director.*
1980 *Fwynnghn*, with Christian Sinding and Gordon Mumma ("a funky fairy tale"). Performed Valencia, CA, 5 March 1980.
1984 *Shopper's Opera* (libretto by Anthony Martin). NEA production grant to Haleakala/The Kitchen, 1984-85 season.

Olsen, David John (ASCAP)
1986 *The Black Rose of Forest Perilous* (libretto by Leslie Brody). Performed by Pennsylvania Opera Theater, Philadelphia, March 1986.
1986 *Great Departures* (improvisation piece, conceived by Lovice Weller). Performed by Minnesota Opera, St. Paul, 11 April 1986.
(NEA grant for development of a new work, 1988.)

Olsen, Richard
1986 *Tobit* (2 acts; libretto by André Ross, based on the Apochrypha). Performed Stone Ridge, NY, 31 October 1986.

O'Neal, Barry (b. New York, 9 June 1942; AMC; Anderson)
- *Dr. Jekyll and Mr. Hyde* (1 act; libretto by Robin Jones after Stevenson).

Orland, Henry (b. Saarbrücken, Germany, 23 April 1918; U.S. citizen, 1944; Anderson)
- *Man Under Glass* (music drama).

Ortiz, William (b. Salinas, Puerto Rico, 30 March 1947; *Who's Who*)
1989 *Rican* (bilingual opera, about Puerto Ricans in New York). Performed by American Opera Projects, New York, 8 November 1989 and 23 May 1990.

Osborne, William
1985 *Alice* (after Carroll). Performed Jerusalem, Israel, 19 March 1985.

Osiier (or Osier, or Ozier), **Julius**
1928 *The Bride of Baghdad.* Performed Kansas City, MO. Bispham Medal, 1932.

Ostransky, Leroy
1974 *The Melting of Molly* (comic opera). Performed by University Players, January 1974.

Overton, Hall (b. Bangor, MI, 23 February 1920; d. New York, 24 November 1972; ACA; *Amerigrove*)
1950 *The Enchanted Pear Tree* (4 scenes—45 minutes; libretto by J. Thompson after Boccaccio's *Decameron*). Performed New York, 7 February 1950.
1963 *Pietro's Petard* (1 act; libretto by R. DeMaria). Performed New York, June 1963.
1971 *Huckleberry Finn* (2 acts; libretto by composer and J. Stampfer after Twain). Performed at Juilliard School of Music, New York, 20 May 1971. Kornick.

Owen, Richard (b. New York, 11 December 1922; AMC; Anderson; *Baker's*)
1956 *Dismissed with Prejudice.*
1958 *A Moment of War* (libretto by composer). Performed Buenos Aires, Argentina, November 1964, and Houston, TX, 6 June 1985.
1965 *A Fisherman Called Peter* (50 minutes; libretto by composer). Performed Carmel, NY, 14 March 1965. Published by General Music.
1975 *Mary Dyer* (3 acts; libretto by composer from trial manuscripts, diaries, letters; about a woman Quaker hanged in Boston on 1 June 1600). Première by Eastern Opera Co. and Hudson Valley Philharmonic, Suffern, NY, 12 June 1976, the composer's wife singing the title role. Published by General Music. Kornick.
1981 *The Death of the Virgin* (1 act—50 minutes; libretto by Michael Straight, after a Caravaggio painting). Performed by OPERA America Showcase, New York, January 1981, and New York Lyric Opera, New York, 31 March 1983. Kornick.
1987 *Abigail Adams* (2 acts and epilogue—75 minutes; libretto by composer after Adams papers). Première by New York Lyric

Opera, New York, 18 March 1987 (in honor of the Bicentennial of the U.S. Constitution). Kornick.

1989   *Tom Sawyer* (children's opera; 1 hour; libretto by composer after Mark Twain). Performed at Manhattan School of Music, New York, 9 April (*Baker's*: 2 April) 1989.

Oxfordshire, T. Snyder (Schoep)
-   *St. George* (1 act—25 minutes; libretto from an anonymous play).

Ozier, Julius. *See* Osiier, Julius

Padron, Enido (ASCAP)
1987   *Tango Bar* (libretto by Suarez). Performed by INTAR Hispanic-American Music Theatre Lab, New York, 12 January 1987.

Padwa, Vladimir (b. Krivyakino, Russia, 8 February 1900; U.S. citizen, 1949; AMC; Anderson)
-   *Compartment No. 7* (1 act; libretto by composer and Lorrie Wechsler, about a trip on the Orient Express in 1936).

Page, Nathaniel Clifford (b. San Francisco, 26 October 1866; d. Philadelphia, 12 May 1956; *Baker's*, 5th ed.)
(All works listed in Freer, 1924.)
1889   *The First Lieutenant.* Performed San Francisco, 1889.
-   *Carlotta.*
-   *Villiers.*
-   *Zadis.*

Page, Nick (William R.)
1979   *Olly Olly End Free* (45 minutes; libretto by composer; for children). Performed at First Parish Church, Lexington, MA, 1979.
1983   *Attack on the Windmills* (80 minutes; libretto by composer; for children). Commission by Rivers School, Weston, MA; performed there, 1983.

Paine, John Knowles (b. Portland, ME, 9 January 1839; d. Cambridge, MA, 25 April 1906; *Amerigrove*; Hipsher)
1862   *Il pesceballo* (comic opera; libretto by F. J. Child and J. R. Lowell), music mostly arranged from Mozart, Rossini, Bellini, Donizetti. Lost.
1898   *Azara* (grand opera; 3 acts; libretto by composer after the medieval trouvère story "Aucassin et Nicolette"). Concert performance with piano at Chickering Hall, Boston, 7 May 1903; concert performance with orchestra by the Cecilia Society, 9 April 1907; never staged. Piano-vocal score, Leipzig: Breitkopf & Härtel, 1901; full score, 1908.

Palmer, Carleton
1979   *Calhoun's Christmas* (puppet opera; libretto by Blanche Thebom after McGimsey). Performed Little Rock, AR, December 1979.

Paltridge, James Gilbert, Jr. (b. Albany, CA, 28 June 1942; Anderson)
1980   *Timon Afinskin* (2 acts; libretto after C. Kinbote).

Pannell, Raymond
1973   *Exiles* (libretto by Beverly Pannell). Performed at Stratford Festival, Ontario, August 1973.

Papale, Henry
1958   *The Master Thief* (libretto by Dan Pocienicki). Performed at Duquesne University, Pittsburgh, PA, 6 November 1958.
1964   *The Shovel-Toothed Witch* (35 minutes). First prize, Penn Radio Show.
1965   *The Only Green Planet* (1 act).
-    *The Balloon* (abstract tragedy; 1 act). *COS*-1.

Pape, Andrew
1989   *Houdini the Great* (75 minutes; libretto by Erik Clausen). Performed Copenhagen, Denmark, 18 March 1989.

Para, Donald
1979   *The Cask of Amontillado* (after Poe). Performed Kalamazoo, MI, May 1979. Videotaped.

Parelli, Attilio (b. Monteleone d'Orvieto, near Perugia, Italy, 31 May 1874; d. there, 26 December 1944; in U.S. in 1906-25; *Baker's*)
1912   *I dispettosi amanti* (1 act). Performed in Philadelphia, 6 March 1912.
1921   *Fanfulla.* Performed Trieste, Italy, 11 February 1921.

Parelli, Natale
1850   *Belshazzar* (4 acts). Performed Philadelphia, 1850.
1858   *Clarissa Harlow.* Performed (in Italian) Vienna, Austria, 1858; and (in English) Philadelphia, 1866, the composer conducting.

Park, Stephen F. (b. Austin, MN, 23 September 1911; ASCAP; Anderson)
1959   *Sally Back and Forth* (1 act). Performed Tampa, FL, 6 October 1959.
1959   *Storm Gathering* (5 scenes). Performed Tampa, FL, 6 October 1959.

Parker, Alice (b. Boston, 16 December 1925; AMC; Anderson; Cohen; *Who's Who*)
1971   *The Martyr's Mirror* (sacred opera; 2 acts—100 minutes; libretto by John L. Ruth after a 17th-century book). Commission by Mennonite Church. Performed Lansdale, PA, 10 October 1971. Published by E. C. Schirmer.
1982   *The Ponder Heart* (libretto by composer after Eudora Welty). Performed Jackson, MS, 10 September 1982.
1975   *The Family Reunion* ("backyard opera"; 1 act—1 hour). NEA grant, 1974. Published by Carl Fischer.

1977   *Singer's Glen.*

Parker, Horatio (b. Auburndale, MA, 15 September 1863; d. Cedarhurst, NY, 18 December 1919; *Amerigrove*; Hipsher)
1910   *Mona*, op. 71 (3 acts; libretto by Brian Hooker). Première by Metropolitan Opera, New York, 14 March 1912. Metropolitan Opera $10,000 prize, 1911, for the best opera in English by a native-born American composer. Vocal score published by G. Schirmer, 1911. At AMRC.
1914   *Fairyland*, op. 77 (3 acts; libretto by Brian Hooker). Performed 6 times, Los Angeles, beginning 1 July 1915, for the National Federation of Music Clubs, which awarded a prize of $10,000, and the city of Los Angeles for its biennial, 1914. Vocal score published by G. Schirmer, 1914.
1916   *Cupid and Psyche*, op. 80 (masque; 3 acts; libretto by J. J. Chapman). Performed New Haven, CT, 16 June 1916.

Parmentier, Francis Gordon (b. Green Bay, WI, 24 April 1923; *WhoAm*)
1959   *The Little Prince* (1 act). Performed San Francisco, 1959.

Parris, Robert (b. Philadelphia, 21 May 1924; ACA; *Amerigrove*)
1960   *Mad Scene. COS*-1.

Partch, Harry (b. Oakland, CA, 24 June 1901; d. San Diego, 3 September 1974; *Amerigrove*)
1951   *Oedipus* (music drama), for 10 solo voices, original instruments; revised 1952-54. Performed at Mills College, Oakland, CA, 14 March 1952.
1960   *Revelation in the Courthouse Park* (musical tragedy; 1 act—85 minutes; libretto by composer after Euripides's *The Bacchae*), for 16 solo voices, 4 speakers, dancers, large instrumental ensemble. Performed Urbana, IL, 11 April 1961, and Philadelphia, 6 October 1987.
1961   *Water! Water!* (farcical "intermission"; libretto by composer on an American Indian ritual). Performed Urbana, IL, 9 March 1962.
1966   *Delusion of the Fury: A Ritual of Dream and Delusion* (dramatic work; 2 acts; libretto by composer). Performed at University of California, Los Angeles, 9 January 1969.

Pasatieri, Thomas (b. New York, 20 October 1945; *Amerigrove*)
1965   *The Women* (1 act—14 minutes; libretto by composer). Performed Aspen, CO, 20 August 1965.
1966   *La Divina* (1 act—25 minutes; libretto by composer). Performed New York, 16 March 1966. Published by Presser.
1967   *Padrevia* (1 act—55 minutes; libretto by composer after Boccaccio). Performed Brooklyn, NY, 18 November 1967.
1971   *Calvary* (1 act; libretto by W. B. Yeats). Performed Belleview, WA, 7 April 1971. Published by Belwin-Mills.
1972   *The Trial of Mary Lincoln* (TV opera; libretto by A. H. Bailey). Commission by National Educational Television, broadcast 14 February 1972; stage version performed 1980.
1972   *Black Widow* (3 acts and epilogue; libretto by composer after M. de Unamuno's *Dos madres*). Performed Seattle, WA, 2 March 1972.

1974   *The Seagull* (3 acts; libretto by Kenward Elmslie after the play by Anton Chekhov). Commission and première by Houston Grand Opera, TX, 5 March 1974; also performed Lake George, NY, 8 August 1980. Kornick.

1974   *Signor Deluso* (opera buffa; 1 act—30 minutes; libretto by composer after Molière's *Sganarelle*). Première by Wolf Trap Co., Greenway, VA, 17 July 1974 (*Amerigrove*: 27 July, Vienna, VA). Published by Belwin-Mills. Kornick.

1974   *The Penitentes* (3 acts; 3 acts; libretto by A. H. Bailey). Performed Aspen, CO, 3 August 1974.

1976   *Inez de Castro* (3 acts; libretto by B. Stambler). Commission and première by Baltimore Opera, 1 April 1976.

1976   *Washington Square* (tragedy; 3 acts and epilogue—110 minutes; libretto by Kenward Elmslie after the novel by Henry James). Commission and première by Michigan Opera Theatre, Detroit, MI, 1 October 1976; also performed by New York Lyric Opera Co., 13 October 1977, and by Augusta Opera Co., March 1979. Published by Belwin-Mills. Kornick.

1979   *Three Sisters* (1 act, 2 scenes—105 minutes; libretto by Kenward Elmslie after the play by Anton Chekhov). NEA grant, 1977. Première by Opera/Columbus, OH, 13 March, 1983; also performed Moscow, Russia, summer 1988. Published by G. Schirmer. Recording by Battery Records PS1333. Kornick.

1980   *Before Breakfast* (dramatic monologue; 1 act; libretto by Frank Corsaro after the play by Eugene O'Neill). Première by New York City Opera, 9 October 1980. Kornick.

1981   *The Goose Girl* (children's opera; 1 act—35 minutes; libretto by composer after the Brothers Grimm). Performed Fort Worth, TX, 15 February 1981. Published by G. Schirmer.

1983   *Maria Elena* (1 act—70 minutes; libretto by composer after a Mexican story). Commission and première by University of Arizona, Tucson, 6 April 1983. Published by G. Schirmer. Kornick.

-   *Elmer Gantry* (libretto after Lewis). Commission by Kennedy Center, Washington, DC. Published by Belwin-Mills.

Pasmore, Henry Bickford (b. Jackson, WI, 27 June 1857; d. San Francisco, 23 February 1944; *Baker's*)

-   *Amor y oro* (libretto by James Gaily; about California history).

-   *Lo-ko-rah* ("exotic opera" on a Tibetan theme).

Patacchi, Val

1958   *The Bandit* (1 act; libretto by William Ashbrook). Performed at Stephens College, Columbia, MO, 17 April 1958.

1959   *The Foundling*. Performed at Stephens College, December 1959.

-   *The Secret* (15 minutes). Performed at Stephens College.

Patterson, Franklin Peale (b. Philadelphia, 5 January 1871; d. New Rochelle, NY, 6 July 1966; Anderson; *Baker's*; Hipsher)

1915   *Mountain Blood* (150 minutes).

1918   *A Little Girl at Play (A Tragedy of the Slums)* (1 act). Several performances in Los Angeles and San Diego. Rejected by performance by Metropolitan Opera, New York, due to its gruesome story.

1918   *The Echo* (1 act—75 minutes; libretto by composer). Performed for National Federation of Music Clubs at the Auditorium, Portland, OR, 9 June 1925. Published by G. Schirmer, 1922. Bispham Medal, 1925; National Federation of Music Clubs "accomplishment award" medal.

1920   *Beggar's Love (A Little Girl at Play)* (40 minutes). Performed New York Chamber Opera, New York, 1925.

-   *Caprice* (grand opera; 3 acts).

-   *The Forest Dwellers* (1 act).

-   *Through the Narrow Gate* (grand opera; 3 acts).

Patton, Willard (b. Milford, ME, 26 May 1853; d. Minneapolis, MN, 12 December 1924; *Baker's*, 5th ed.; Hipsher)

1882   *The Gallant Garroter.*

1889   *La Fianza.*

1911   *Pocahontas* (grand opera). Performed Minneapolis, 4 January 1911.

Paul, Robert

-   *King Solomon. COS*-4.

Paull, Barberi P. (b. New York, 27 July 1946 [*Who's Who*: 1948]; she produces her works at the Barberi Paull Musical Theatre, New York, which she founded; Anderson; *Baker's*; Cohen; *Who's Who*)

1971   *Earth Pulse* (choreographic cantata; includes *musique concrète*). Performed 1971.

1975   *A Land Called the Infinity of Love* (multimedia).

Paulsen, J. Marius

1937   *The Cimbrians.* Bispham Medal.

Paulus, Stephen (b. Summit, NJ, 24 August 1949; *Amerigrove*; *Baker's*; *Who's Who*)

1979   *The Village Singer* (1 act, 5 scenes—60 minutes; libretto by Michael Dennis Browne after a story by Mary Wilkins Freeman). Commission by New Music Circle of St. Louis; première by Opera Theatre of Saint Louis, 9 June 1979. Published by European American Music Distributors. Kornick.

1982   *The Postman Always Rings Twice* (2 acts—120 minutes; libretto by Colin Graham after the novel by James M. Cain). Commission and première by Opera Theatre of Saint Louis, 17 June 1982; also performed by Fort Worth Opera, TX, 1 March 1985, by Minnesota Opera, 31 October 1987, by Greater Miami Opera, 14 March 1988, and in Washington, DC, 21 January 1989. Kornick.

1984   *The Woodlanders* (3 acts; libretto by Colin Graham after the novel by Thomas Hardy). Première by Opera Theatre of Saint Louis, 13 June 1985. Kornick. Piano-vocal score published by European American Music Corp.

1991   *Harmoonia* (children's opera; 1 act—45 minutes; libretto by Michael Dennis Browne), accompaniment by piano and synthesizer. Commission by Des Moines Metro Opera.

Pavlakis, Christopher (b. Haverhill, MA, 26 March 1928; information from composer)

1954　*How Do You Do, Sir?* (chamber opera for soprano, baritone, and 9 instruments; Noh comedy; libretto is the play by Alfred Kreymborg). Performed by After Dinner Opera, Lincoln Center, New York, 3 October 1983, and at Queensborough Community College, Bayside, NY.

Payne, John (b. New York, 23 May 1941; Anderson)

1968　*Ode to Gravity* (live electronic theater event), with Carol Law and Charles Amirkhanian. Performed San Francisco, 21 September 1968.

Pearce, Stephen Austen (b. Brompton, Kent, England, 7 November 1836; d. Jersey City, NJ, 9 April 1900; in U.S. from 1872; *Baker's*)

-　　*La Belle Américaine.*

Peaslee, Richard Cutts (b. New York, 11 June 1930; Anderson; *Who's Who*)

1984　*Animal Farm* (150 minutes; libretto by Adrian Mitchell and Peter Hall after Orwell). Performed London, England, 1984, and Baltimore, MD, 17 June 1986.

1984　*Tanglewood Tales* (1 hour; libretto by Kenneth Cavander after Hawthorne). Performed by First All Children's Theatre, New York, 23 December 1984.

1986　*Vienna: Lusthaus* (*Vienna: Pleasure-House*) (1 act—65 minutes; libretto by Charles Mee, Jr., about Vienna at the turn of the century; conceived by Martha Clarke). Performed by Music Theatre Group/Lenox Arts Center, New York, 8 April 1986.

1986　*The Green Knight* (50 minutes; libretto by Kenneth Cavander after *Sir Gawain and the Green Knight*; for children). Commission Lincoln Center Institute, New York, 1986. Performed in New York schools.

1986　*We* (2 hours; libretto by Adrian Mitchell after Zamyatin). Commission by Minnesota Opera, St. Paul, 1986.

1987　*The Hunger Artist* (libretto by Richard Greenberg after Kafka; in English, Czech, Yiddish, and German; conceived by Martha Clarke). Performed by Music-Theatre Group, New York, 6 February 1987.

1989　*Miracolo d'amore* (*Miracle of Love*) (55 minutes; on a variety of authors and painters; elements of chance). Commission by New York Shakespeare and Spoleto USA Festivals. Performed Charleston, SC, 20 May 1989.

1989　*The Snow Queen* (105 minutes; libretto by Adrian Mitchell after Andersen). Commission by Empire State Institute for the Performing Arts. Performed Albany, NY, 1889-90 season.

1990　*Ubu Lear* (20 minutes; libretto by Christopher Durang after Jarry's *Ubu Roi* and Shakespeare's *King Lear*). Commission by New York Shakespeare Festival. Ten Minute Musicals Project winner. Performed San Francisco, 15 February 1990.

1990　*Endangered Species* (libretto by Charles Mee; conceived by Martha Clarke). Performed at Next Wave Festival, Brooklyn, NY, fall 1990.

Peel, John
    1979   *The Pythia* (monodrama; 22 minutes; libretto after Valery). Commission by Collage, Boston; performed there, 1979.

Pelissier, Victor (b. ?Paris, France, ca. 1740-50; d. ?New Jersey, ca. 1820; in Philadelphia in 1792 and 1811-14; in New York in 1793-1811; *Amerigrove*; Porter)
    1793   *The Death of Captain Cook* (pantomime).
    1794   *Danaides: or, Vice Punished* (pantomime; 3 acts). Première at Southwark Theatre, Philadelphia, 8 October 1794.
    1794   *Sophia of Brabant* (pantomime). Performed Philadelphia, 1 November 1794.
    1794   *Harlequin Pastry Cook* (pantomime). "As performed in Paris"; performed Philadelphia, 21 November 1974.
    1795   *La Forêt noire* (pantomime). Performed New York, 30 March 1795.
    1796   *The Archers: or, Mountaineers of Switzerland* (opera; 3 acts). Additions to the opera by Benjamin Carr. Première, New York, 18 April 1796.
    1796   *Gil Blas* (serio-comic pantomime). Première, Philadelphia, 16 May 1796; also performed New York, 1802.
    1796   *Robinson Crusoe* (pantomime). Performed New York, 15 June 1796.
    1796   *Edwin and Angelina: or, The Banditti* (comic opera; 3 acts; libretto by Elihu H. Smith after Oliver Goldsmith). Première, New York, 19 December 1796.
    1797   *Ariadne Abandoned by Theseus on the Isle of Naxos* (melodrama). Performed New York, 26 April 1797. (*Amerigrove*: "one of the earliest and most influential melodramas composed in America.")
    1799   *Sterne's Maria: or, The Vintage* (opera; 2 acts; libretto by William Dunlap). Performed New York, 14 January 1899.
    1799   *The Fourth of July: or, Temple of American Independence* ("allegorical musical drama"). Performed New York, 4 July 1799.
    1800   *Virgin of the Sun* (grand operatic drama; 3 acts; libretto by Anton von Kotzebue, translated by William Dunlap). Première, New York, 12 March 1800.
    1800   *Castle of Otranto* (comic opera; libretto after Horace Walpole's *The Castle of Otranto*). Première, New York, 7 November 1800.
    1801   *Obi: or, Three-Fingered Jack* ("grand panomimical drama" with songs; 3 acts; libretto by John Fawcett). Première, Boston, 31 March 1801; also performed New York, 1802.
    1802   *The Merry Gardener: or, The Night of Adventures* (comic opera; 2 acts; libretto by William Dunlap from the French). Première, New York, 3 February 1802.
    1802   *Raymond and Agnes: or, The Bleeding Nun* (pantomime; 2 acts; libretto after M. G. Lewis's novel *The Monk*). Performed Boston, 7 May 1802; also New York, 1804.
    1803   *A Tale of Mystery*, with James Hewitt (melodrama; 3 acts; libretto by T. Holcroft). Performed New York, 16 March 1803.
    1803   *The Good Neighbor*. Performed New York.
    1804   *The Wife of Two Husbands*. Performed New York.
    1805   *Valentine and Orso: or, The Downfall of Agramant* (melodrama; 2 acts; libretto by Thomas Dibdin). Performed New York, 1805.
    1805   *The Bridal Ring* (melodrama). Performed New York, 1805.

1807   *Thesis and Ariadne* ("serious pantomimical melodrame"; 1 act).
        First performed in Paris; U.S. première, Philadelphia, 16 March
        1807.
1810   *Mother Goose* (pantomime). Performed Philadelphia, 1810.
1813   *La Fille Hussar* (*The Female Hussar*) (pantomime; libretto by James
        Sanderson). Performed New York, 13 June 1813.
1814   *Ella Rosenberg* (melodrama; 2 acts; libretto by James Kenney).
        Première, Boston, 20 April 1814.
-       *The Lady of the Lake* (melodrama; libretto by Charles Dibdin).
1794   *The Milleners: or, The Wooden Block* (afterpiece with singing and
        dancing; 2 acts). Première, Charleston, 6 May 1794.
        (Pelissier also composed incidental music for at least eighteen plays.
        Some of the music for the above was published in *Pelissier's
        Columbian Melodies* [Philadelphia, 1811-12], ed. Karl Kroeger,
        Recent Researches in American Music, 13-14 [A-R Editions,
        1984].)

Peltoniemi, Eric (ASCAP)
1987   *Ten November* (libretto by Steven Dietz). Performed by Actors
        Theatre of St. Paul, MN, 30 October 1987.

Pemberton, Charles E.
1934   *The Painter of Dreams* (prologue and 1 act—15 minutes). Performed
        Los Angeles, May 1934.

Pen, Polly (ASCAP)
1985   *Goblin Market* (libretto by Peggy Harmon after Christina Rossetti).
        Performed at Vineyard Theater, New York, 17 October 1985.
        (Pen also composed a musical, *Songs on a Shipwrecked Sofa*, 1987.)

Penn, Arthur A. (b. London, England, 13 February 1875; d. New London, CN, 6
        February 1941; in U.S. from 1903; ASCAP; *Amerigrove*)
        (Penn wrote his own librettos.)
-       *Captain Crossbones* (comic opera).
-       *The China Shop* (comic opera).
-       *Ladies' Aid* (comic opera; 1 act—50 minutes). Performed
        Milwaukee, WI, 1955.
-       *Mam'zelle Taps* (comic opera).
-       *Yokahama Maid* (comic opera).
-       *Your Royal Highness*.

Pentland, Barbara Lally (b. Winnipeg, Canada, 2 January 1912; Canadian, but
        studied at Juilliard and Tanglewood; *Baker's*; *Who's Who*)
1940   *Beauty and the Beast* (ballet-pantomime), for two pianos.
1952   *The Lake* (1 act; libretto by Dorothy Livesay). Performed
        Vancouver, 3 March 1954.

Perera, Ronald (b. Boston, 25 December 1941; *Amerigrove*)
1982   *The White Whale* (monodrama; 29 minutes; libretto by the
        composer). Performed Amherst, MA, 20 April 1982.
1988   *The Yellow Wallpaper* (100 minutes; libretto by Constance Congdon
        after Gilman; conceived by Mark Harrison). NEA grant, 1988.
        Performed at Smith College, Northampton, MA, 17 May 1989.

Peretti, Hugo (d. 1985; ASCAP)
　　1986　*Jokers*, completed by Luigi Creatore and George David Weiss after
　　　　　Peretti's death (libretto by composer after Coburn's *The Gin
　　　　　Game*). Performed by Goodspeed Opera, Chester, CT, 14 October
　　　　　1986.

Perkins, John MacIvor (b. St. Louis, 2 August 1935; *Amerigrove*)
　　1958　*Divertimento* (chamber opera; libretto by Wayne D. Shirley).
　　　　　Performed at Lowell Opera House, MA, spring 1958; and Chicago,
　　　　　1960?.
　　1980　*Andrea del Sarto* (operatic monologue; 1 act; libretto after
　　　　　Browning). Performed at Washington University, St. Louis, 27
　　　　　September 1981.

Perlroth, Gil
　　1984　*Good Friends*. Performed Waterford, CT, 3 June 1984.
　　-　　*Christmas Is for Children* (50 minutes; libretto by composer).

Perry, Julia Amanda (b. Lexington, KY, 25 March 1924; d. Akron, OH, 24 April
　　　　　1979; AMC; *Amerigrove*; Cohen; Southern)
　　1953　*The Cask of Amontillado* (1 act—30 minutes; libretto after Poe).
　　　　　Performed New York, 20 November 1954. Published by Southern.
　　1964　*The Selfish Giant* (opera-ballet; 3 acts; libretto by composer after
　　　　　Oscar Wilde). Prize, American Academy of Arts and Letters.
　　-　　*The Bottle* (1 act; libretto by composer). Published by Southern
　　　　　Music, 1955.
　　-　　*Three Warnings*.

Persichetti, Vincent (b. Philadelphia, 6 June 1915; d. there, 14 August 1987
　　　　　[according to *Notes*, June 1988; *Baker's* has August 13];
　　　　　Amerigrove)
　　1976　*The Sibyl: A Parable of Chicken Little*, op. 135 (3 scenes—75
　　　　　minutes; libretto by composer). Performed by Pennsylvania Opera
　　　　　Theatre, Philadelphia, 13 April 1985. Published by Presser.

Peter, Darrell
　　1953　*The Parrot* (television opera; 1 act). Telecast on NBC-TV, New
　　　　　York, 24 March 1953.

Peters, William Frederick (b. Sandusky, OH, 9 August 1876; d. Englewood, NJ, 1
　　　　　December 1938; Anderson)
　　-　　*Iole* (operetta).
　　-　　*The Purple Road*.

Petersen, Marian F. (b. Salt Lake City, UT, 4 July 1926; Anderson; *WhoAm*)
　　-　　*The Wife of Usher's Well* (mini-opera).

Peterson, Charles
　　1987　*Night! Youth! Paris! and the Moon!* (libretto after Collier).
　　　　　Performed Milwaukee, WI, 8 July 1987.

Peterson, Liz
 1985   *The Wind in the Willows* (1 act—75 minutes; libretto by the composer
        after Grahame). Performed Wichita, KS, 1985. Published by
        Coach House Press.

Peterson, Thomas (b. Northfield, MN, 20 May 1959; ASCAP; *Who's Who*)
 1989   *Sakajawea: The Woman with Many Names* (2 acts; libretto by Bill
        Borden—best libretto, Opera Now! Competition, Minneapolis—on
        the Indian guide of the Lewis & Clark Expedition). Performed
        Grand Forks, ND, 15 September 1989.

Petrauskas, Mikas (b. Kaunas, Lithuania, 19 October 1873; d. there, 23 March
        1937; in U.S. in 1907-30; *Baker's*)
 1917? *The King of the Forest.* Published in 1918.
 1919   *Vestures* (*The Wedding*). Performed Boston.
 1920   *Velnias Isradejas* (*The Devil Inventor*). Performed South Boston,
        MA, 20 May 1920, the composer singing the leading role.
 1924   *Egle, Zalciu Karaliene* (*Egle, Queen of the Snakes*). Performed
        South Boston, MA, 30 May 1924, the composer singing the part of
        the King of the Snakes.

Phelps, Ellsworth C. (b. Middletown, CN, 11 August 1827; d. Brooklyn, NY, 29
        November 1913; *Baker's*, 5th ed.)
  -     *The Last of the Mohicans* (libretto undoubtedly after James
        Fenimore Cooper).

Philipp, Adolf (b. Hamburg, Germany, 29 January 1864; d. New York, 30 July
        1936; in U.S. from 1890; *Amerigrove*)
        (Most of Philipp's musicals and operettas were written in German,
        and many of them were translated to English for the Broadway
        stage—titles below in parentheses. This list, from *Amerigrove*, is of
        musicals with libretto by the composer, unless indicated otherwise,
        and is selective. All were performed in New York.)
 1893   *Arme Maedchen* (*Poor Girls*, 1894).
 1893   *Der Corner Grocer aus der Avenue A* (*About Town*, 1894).
 1894   *Ein New Yorker Brauer* (*From Across the Pond*, 1907). Performed
        more than 700 times, to 1909; and, revised as *Über'n grossen
        Teich*, was performed more than 1300 times at the Deutsch-
        Amerikanischer Theater in Berlin, Hamburg, and elsewhere.
 1897   *Klein Deutschland.*
 1897   *New York bei Nacht.*
 1901   *Im Lande der Freiheit.*
 1909   *Alma, wo wohnst du?* (operetta; *Alma, Where Do You Live?*, by G.
        Hobart, 1910).
 1910   *Theresa sei nicht böse* (operetta; *Teresa Be Mine*, 1910).
 1912   *Auction Pinochle / Une Partie de cartes* (operetta; *Auction Pinochle*,
        by E. Paulton, 1914).
 1913   *Adele* (operetta; libretto by E. Paulton).
 1913? *Das Mitternachtsmädel* (operetta; *The Midnight Girl*, by E. Paulton,
        1914).
 1913   *Two Lots in the Bronx.*
 1914   *My Shadow and I.*

1915   *The Girl Who Smiles* (operetta; libretto by E. Paulton).
1915   *Sadie from Riverside Drive.*
1915   *Two Is Company* (operetta; libretto by E. Paulton).
1920   *Mimi* (libretto by E. Paulton).

Phillips, Burrill (b. Omaha, NE, 9 November 1907; d. Berkeley, CA, 22 June
             1988; ASCAP; *Amerigrove*)
1947   *Don't We All?* (opera buffa; 1 act—30 minutes; libretto by A.
             Phillips). Performed Rochester, NY, 9 April or 9 May 1949.
1981   *The Unforgiven* (3 acts; libretto by A. Phillips).
  -     *A Lion by the Tail.*

Phillips, H(arry) Garrett (b. Columbus, GA, 4 November 1941; *WhoAm*)
1970   *The Princess and the Frog Prince* (after Hans Christian Andersen).
             Performed at University of Alabama, Tuscaloosa, March 1970.

Phillips, Peter
1969   *Mantra* (jazz-rock opera). Performed Seattle, WA, 18 May 1969.

Phillipus, Christian L. (b. Gronigen, Netherlands, 13 July 1887; Hipsher)
1924   *Notre Dame* (after Victor Hugo).
1926   *Richelieu* (after the play by Lord Lytton).

Piastro, Josef (Borissoff) (b. Kerch, Crimea, 1 March 1889; d. Monrovia, CA, 14
             May 1964; in U.S. from 1920; Anderson; *Baker's*)
  -     *Cigarette.*
  -     *Corn Popper.*
  -     *Lolita.*

Pickhardt, Ione (b. Hempstead, Long Island, NY, 27 May 1900; Hipsher)
1930   *Moira* (grand opera; 3 acts; libretto by George Gibbs, Jr.).

Piket, Frederick (b. Constantinople/Istanbul, Turkey, 6 January 1903, of
             Austrian parents; d. Bayside, NY, 28 February 1974; U.S. citizen,
             1946; ASCAP; Anderson; *Baker's*)
1920   *Satan's Trap* (libretto by Charles S. Levy). Performed New York,
             26 November 1960 or 1961.
1955   *Isaac Levi* (1 act). Performed White Plains, NY, 11 December 1955.
1967   *Trilby* (1 act). Performed New York, 15 May 1967.
1972   *No Stars Tonight.* Performed at Lincoln Center, New York, 1972.

Pimsleur, Solomon (b. Paris, France, 19 September 1900; d. New York, 22 April
             1962; in U.S. from 1903; ACA; *Amerigrove*)
  -     *Diary of Anne Frank* (only 2 acts completed).
  -     *Reign of Terror* (4 acts; libretto after Odets's *Till the Day I Die*).

Pine, Margaret
1988   *The Master and Margarita* (libretto by Sherry Kramer after
             Bulgakov). Performed by New Dramatists, New York, 1988-89
             season.

Pinkham, Daniel (b. Lynn, MA, 5 June 1923; ACA; *Amerigrove*; *Who's Who*)
1979   *The Passion of Judas*. Performed Montréal, Canada, 25 March 1979.
1982   *The Dreadful Dining Car* (libretto by composer after Mark Twain), for mezzo, actors, soloists, chorus, small ensemble.
1985   *The Left-Behind Beasts* (on Farber). Commission by Children's Opera Program and James Otis School, Boston. Performed Boston, summer 1985.
\-   *The Garden of Artemis* (25 minutes).

Pirani, Eugenio (b. Bologna, Italy, 8 September 1852; d. Berlin, Germany, 12 January 1939; in U.S. for a time from 1905; *Baker's*, 5th-8th eds.)
1902   *The Witch's Song*. This work had been performed in Prague, 1902, as *Das Hexenlied*. Performed Brooklyn, NY, 1909.
1906   *Black Blood*. Performed New York, 1906.

Pisarsky, Cathryn
\-   *Robin Hood* (1 hour; libretto by composer). Performed at Main Street Theatre, Houston, TX. Published by I. E. Clark. *COS*-4.

Pisk, Paul Amadeus (b. Vienna, Austria, 16 May 1893; d. Hollywood, CA, 12 January 1990; to U.S. in 1936; AMC; *Amerigrove*; *Baker's*; *WhoAm*)
1931   *Schattenseite* (monodrama).

Pittman, Evelyn LaRue (b. McAlester, OK, 6 January 1910; Cohen; *Who's Who*)
1948   *Again the River* (libretto by Helen Schuyler).
1954   *Cousin Esther* (folk opera; 4 acts; libretto by composer), revised 1956. Performed Paris, France, 1956, and 8 May 1957, and at Carnegie Hall, New York, 26 September 1962. Broadcast on WNYC radio, New York, during the American Music Festival of 1963.
1970   *Freedom Child* (about Martin Luther King Jr.). Performed 1971-72 season, on tour in the United States, Norway, Sweden, and Denmark, and 1978 in central Europe. Video, 1986.
1978   *Jim Noble*. Performed Oklahoma City, OK, during Black History Week, 1979.

Pitton, Robert
\-   *The Monk and the Hangman's Daughter* (210 minutes; libretto by composer after Bierce). *COS*-4.

Platthy, Jeno (b. Dunapataj, Hungary, 13 August 1920; *WhoAm*)
1976   *Bamboo* (bicentennial opera; 2 acts; libretto by Rosemarie Steeg after a 10th-century Japanese story). Performed by Prince George Civic Opera Co., Largo, MD, 23 June 1976.

Pliska, Greg
1986   *Finding Your Way* (libretto by Eduardo Machado). Performed by New Dramatists, New York, December 1986.
1987   *The Secret Garden* (libretto by David Ives after Burnett). Performed by Pennsylvania Opera Theater (where Pliska had a residency), Philadelphia, 16 December 1988; by New Dramatists, New York, 15 December 1988; and Philadelphia, 8 March 1991.

Polifrone, Jon J. (b. Durand, MI, 10 January 1937; Anderson)
    1966   *The Kentucky Story* (madrigal opera; 1 act). Performed
            Barbourville, KY, February 1966.
    1966   *The Wicked Sam and the Devil* (madrigal opera; 1 act). Performed
            Evanston, IL, February 1966.
    1978   *The Legend of Ruth's House* (1 act; about the Pacific northwest).
            Performed Omaha, NE, 21 October 1978.

Pollock, Robert Emil (b. New York, 8 July 1946; Anderson; *WhoAm*)
    -     *The Nose* (chamber opera; libretto after Gogol).

Pommer, William H.
        (This list of works is from Krohn.)
    1877   *The Mummy.*
    -     *The Daughter of Socrates.*
    -     *The Fountain of Youth.*
    -     *The Legend of Etheldethe/wethelberga.*
    -     *Marion'w Men.*
    -     *Naldino.*
    -     *The Queen of the Buccaneers* (romantic comic opera; 3 acts).
    -     *The Student's Ruse.*

Pope, Anne
    1988   *Hotel Martinique*, with Frank Jump (libretto by Frank Jump and
            Kevin Malony, about the infamous welfare hotel). Performed at
            Irish Arts Center, New York, 15 December 1988.

Poples, Henry
    1958   *The Master Thief* (1 act). Performed Pittsburgh, PA, 5 November
            1958.

Portas, Lynn
    1986   *Father Father* (libretto by Daniel Clancy). Performed by TRG
            Repertory, New York, November 1986 and May 1987.

Portnoy, Gary
    1983   *Preppies*, with Judy Hart Angelo. Performed at Promenade
            Theatre, New York, 9 August 1983.

Pos, Michael
    1984   *Voices of Mira* (25 minutes; libretto by composer). Performed at
            Peabody Conservatory of Music, Baltimore, MD, 22 February
            1984.

Post, Douglas
    1989   *The Real Life Story of Johnny de Facto* (libretto by composer).
            Performed Waterford, CT, summer 1989.

Pote, Allen
    1989   *The Seaplane*. Performed Pensacola, FL, 28 October 1989.

Potter, Edward C. (b. Chicago, 5 January 1860; Hipsher)
-      *Ishtar* (grand opera; 3 acts; libretto after novel *Ishtar of Babylon* by the composer's sister Margaret Horton Potter).

Pouhe, Joseph Frank
1969   *Pantomime* (1 act). Performed by Metropolitan Opera Studio, New York, 7 January 1969, and 10 May 1971.

Pound, Ezra (b. Hailey, ID, 30 October 1885; d. Venice, Italy, 1 November 1972; *Amerigrove*)
1923   *Le Testament de Villon* (libretto by composer after the works of François Villon). Performed Paris, France, 1924; broadcast on BBC radio, London, England, 1931.
1932   *Cavalcanti* (a selection from the works of 13th-century poet Guido Cavalcanti). Performed by Arch Ensemble for Experimental Music, San Francisco, 28 March 1983.

Powell, Felix Loren (b. Centralia, WA, 16 September 1933; *WhoAm*)
1974   *The Magician* (television opera). NEA grant, 1974.

Powell, Jarrad. *See* Dresher, Paul

Powell, John (b. Richmond, VA, 6 September 1882; d. there, 15 August 1963; *Amerigrove*)
-      *Juth and Holofernes.* On Freer's list.

Pozdro, John Walter (b. Chicago, 14 August 1923; ASCAP; *Baker's*)
1961   *Hello, Kansas!* (libretto by Allen Crafton on the occasion of the centennial of the state). Performed at University of Kansas, Lawrence, 12 June 1961.
1976   *Malooley and the Fear Monster* ("family opera"; 1 hour). Performed 6 and 13 February 1977, Lawrence, KS; and on tour in Kansas (Salina, Concordia, Hoxie, Colby, Manhattan, and Sterling), 1978.

Pratt, Silas Gamaliel (b. Addison, VT, 4 August 1846; d. Pittsburgh, PA, 30 October 1916; *Amerigrove*; Hipsher)
1871   *Antonio* (revised as *Lucille*; see below). Selections performed at Farwell Hall, Chicago, 1874.
1882   *Zenobia, Queen of Palmyra* (4 acts; libretto by composer). Concert performance at Central Music Hall, Chicago, 15–16 June 1882; staged at McVicker's Theater, 26 March 1883, and Twenty-Third Street Theater, New York, 21 August 1883. Vocal score published Boston, 1882.
1887   *Lucille* (revision of *Antonio*). Performed at Columbia Theater, Chicago, 14 March 1887.
1892   *The Triumph of Columbus.* Performed New York, 12 October 1892.
-      *Ollanta* (libretto by composer).

Presser, William Henry (b. Saginaw, MI, 19 April 1916; Anderson; *WhoAm*)
1959   *The Whistler* (chamber opera; 1 act), for soprano, baritone, string quartet, piano. Performed Hattiesburg, MS, 14 February 1959.

1962   *The Belgian Doll*. Performed Tallahassee, FL, 1962.

Previn, André (b. Berlin, Germany, 6 April 1929; *Amerigrove*; *Who's Who*)
    1978   *Every Good Boy Deserves Favour* (1 act—58 minutes; libretto by Tom Stoppard), for actors and orchestra. Performed at Temple University, Philadelphia, 18 August 1978. Published by Faber Music.
    1984   *Rough Crossing* (2 acts; libretto by Tom Stoppard after Molnar's *The Play's the Thing*). Performed London, England, 30 October 1984; and Montgomery, AL, 15 February 1987.

Price, ?
    1982   *Adventures of Tom Sawyer* (1 act; libretto by Mason). Performed by Children's Theater, Minneapolis, 1982–83 season.

Prochazka, David
    1988   *Gilgamesh* (1 act; libretto by David Sanchez after the ancient legend). Performed by Chicago Opera Theater, November 1988.

Procter, Leland (b. Newton, MA, 24 March 1914; ACA; Anderson; *Baker's*)
    1958   *Eve of Crossing* (1 act—75 minutes).

Proulx, Richard (b. St. Paul, MN, 3 April 1937; Anderson)
    1986   *The Beggar's Christmas* (libretto by Brother Augustine Towey after Aurelio). NEA grant, 1985–86; commission by Opera Sacra, Buffalo, NY. Performed Buffalo, July 1987 and December 1988.

Provenzano, Aldo (b. Philadelphia, 3 May 1930; Anderson)
    1968   *The Cask of Amontillado* (1 act; libretto obviously after Poe). Performed Rochester, NY, 26 April 1968.

Prunty, William
    1960   *The Lotus Tree* (or *The Lotus*). Performed Morgantown, WV, 13 May 1960.

Ptaszyńska, Marta (b. Warsaw, Poland, 29 July 1943; in U.S. from 1972; *Amerigrove*; Cohen; *Who's Who*)
    1972   *Oscar from Alva* (television opera; libretto by composer after Byron). Received Polish radio and television award.

Puerner, Charles
    1892? *The Trumpeter of New Amsterdam*.

Pugh, Ann
    1979   *Heidi*, with Betty Utter (on Spyri). Performed New York, November 1979.

Pullano, Frank L. (b. Niagara Falls, NY, 4 July 1934; *WhoAm*)
    1990   *Sarah's Gift*. Performed Fredonia, NY, 8 December 1990.

Pullis (or Polis), Steven?
    -    *The Woodlanders* (on Hardy). Commission by Saint Louis Opera.

Putsche, Thomas Reese (b. Scarsdale, NY, 29 June 1929; *WhoAm*)
  1958   *The Cat and the Moon* (30 minutes; libretto after Yeats). Performed
         Hartford, CT, 22 May 1960. Published by Seesaw, 1958.

Quincy, George (ASCAP)
  1987   *Passionate Extremes* (90 minutes; libretto by Thayer Q. Burch).
         Performed by Musical Theatre Works, New York, 9 November
         1987, 2 May 1988 and 28 September 1988.
         (Quincy also composed the musical *A Visit*, 1981.)

Rabinoff, Sylvia (Mrs. Benno; b. New York, 10 October [no year given];
         Anderson; Cohen)
  -      *Hamlet, the Flea* (operetta; for children).

Raboy, Asher
  1984? *The Ill-Fated Princess*. Performed Binghamton, NY.

Raffman, Relly (b. New Bedford, MA, 4 September 1921; Anderson)
  1964   *Midas*.

Raigorodsky, Natalia (or Natalie; Leda Natalia Heimsath; Mrs. Harter; b. Tulsa,
         OK, 1929; Cohen; *WhoAm*)
  1969   *The Promise of Peace* (dramatic sacred oratorio; 40 minutes; libretto
         based on the New Testament). Performed by Opera Theatre of
         Washington, DC, 18 October 1981.
  1982   *The White Cliffs of Dover*. Performed by Opera Theatre of
         Washington, DC, 1982-83 season.

Raines, Vernon McCaffery
  1955   *The Happy Prince* (40 minutes; libretto after Wilde). Performed
         Emporia, KS, December 1955.

Ramsier, Paul (b. Louisville, KY, 23 September 1927; Anderson)
  -      *The Man on the Bearskin Rug* (1 act—25 minutes; libretto by James
         Edward). Published by Boosey & Hawkes.

Ran, Shulamit (b. Tel-Aviv, Israel, 21 October 1949; *Amerigrove*; Cohen)
  1967   *The Laughing Man* (television pantomime).

Randegger, Giuseppe Aldo (b. Naples, Italy, 17 February 1874; d. New York, 30
         November 1946; in U.S. from 1893 [Anderson: from 1900];
         Hipsher)
  -      *The Promise of Medea* (1 act; libretto by composer's wife Henriette
         Brinker-Randegger).

Rapchak, Lawrence
>   1990   *The Life Work of Juan Diaz* (84 minutes; libretto by Carl Ratner after Bradbury). Performed by Chamber Opera Chicago, 21 April 1990.

Raphling, Samuel (b. Fort Worth, TX, 19 March 1910; d. New York, 8 January 1988; ASCAP/AMC; Anderson; *Baker's*)
>   1956   *Dr. Heidegger's Experiment* (1 act). Performed New York, 18 February 1956.
>   1979   *Nathan the Wise* (prologue and 4 scenes; libretto after Lessing). Performed New York, 9 February 1979.
>   1980   *Mrs. Bullfrog* (1 act; libretto by composer after Hawthorne). Performed New York, 8 July 1980.
>   1980   *La Diva* (80 minutes; libretto by James V. Hatch).
>   1985   *The Cowboy and the Fiddler* (1 act; libretto by composer). Performed Houston, TX, 6 June 1985.
>   -   *Liar-Liar* (children's opera).
>   -   *Tin Pan Alley* (1 act).
>   1-act operas on four Hawthorne stories:
>   -   *President Lincoln* (2 acts).
>   -   *Prince Hamlet.*
>   -   *Johnny Pye and the Fool-Killer.*
>   -   *Peter Bees.*

Rapoport, Eda Ferdinand (b. Dvinsk, Latvia, 1886 [Anderson: 1900]; d. New York, 9 May 1968; Anderson; Cohen)
>   1945   *G. I. Joe* (1 act—60 minutes).
>   -   *The Fisherman and His Wife* (opera-fantasy; 1 act—60 minutes; libretto after Grimm).

Rasbach, Oscar (b. Dayton, KY, 2 August 1888; d. Pasadena, CA, 24 March 1975; *Amerigrove*)
>   1933   *Dawn Boy* (American Indian subject; 1 act; libretto by Cecily Allen). Published by G. Schirmer.
>   -   *Open House.*

Raskin, John (ASCAP)
>   1988   *Poison Hotel*, with Bob Davis (libretto by Allan Finneran; requires audience participation). Performed by Soon 3, San Francisco, October 1988.

Ratcliff, Cary
>   1985   *The Legend of Ellis Island* (or *The Ellis Island Opera*; 1 act; libretto by Robert Koch). Performed Penfield, NY, 7 December 1985.

Ratner, Leonard Gilbert (b. Minneapolis, MN, 30 July 1916; Anderson; *Baker's*; *Who's Who*)
>   -   *The Necklace* (40 minutes; libretto after Guy de Maupassant). Published by Mercury/Presser.

Rauscher, Henry. *See* Humphreys-Rauscher, Henry S.

Ravosa, Carl C.
-     *Johnny Appleseed* (35 minutes). *COS*-1. Published by G. Schirmer.

Rea, Alan (b. Rochester, NY, 22 February 1933; Anderson; Schoep)
1976   *The Fête at Coqueville* (1 act—52 minutes; libretto by Betty Iacovetti based on story by Zola). Performed by Fresno Opera Association, CA, 9-11 April 1976.
1980   *Old Pipes and the Dryad* (24 minutes; libretto after Stockton). Performed Fresno, CA, 20 February 1980.
1981   *The Magic Knapsack* (30 minutes; libretto by William Monson). Performed Fresno, CA, 1981.
1984   *The Prince of Patches* (for children). Performed Fresno, CA, October 1984.
1986   *The Owl's Secret* (libretto by William Monson). Performed Fresno, CA, 31 October 1986.
1988   *As the Opera World Turns* (45 minutes; libretto by William Monson, teaching children about opera and featuring music from well-known operas). Performed Fresno, CA, 18 May 1988.

Read, Gardner (b. Evanston, IL, 2 January 1913; BMI; *Amerigrove*; *Who's Who*)
1967   *Villon*, op. 122 (3 acts; libretto by James Forsyth). Performed at OPERA America Showcase, New York, 7 January 1981.

Reale, Paul V. (b. New Brunswick, NJ, 2 March 1943; AMC; Anderson; *Baker's*)
1976   *The Waltz King* (20 minutes; libretto after Andrew Marvel). Performed at University of California, Los Angeles, 8 May 1976.
1980   *The Ballad of the Sleazy Cafe* (music drama, 1 act). Performed at University of California, Los Angeles, 20 February 1980.

Ream, Marc
1985   *RareArea* (70 minutes; libretto by George Coates). Performed Berkeley, CA, 22 June 1985.
1987   *Actual Sho* (85 minutes; libretto by George Coates, about a spiritual journey). Commission by Theater der Welt, Stuttgart, Germany; performed there, June 1987, and at New Performance Festival, San Francisco, 8 July 1987.
1989   *Right Mind* (formerly *Nowhere Now Here*; libretto by George Coates, about the life of Lewis Carroll). SMARTS Corporation grant. Performed Los Angeles, 2 October 1989.

Redding, Joseph Deighn (b. Sacramento, CA, 13 September 1859; Hipsher)
1917   *The Land of Happiness* (libretto by Charles Templeton Crocker). A "grove play" for the Bohemian club, in which David Bispham performed the leading role. Rewritten as:
1925   *Fay-Yen-Fan* (grand opera; 3 acts; in French). Première at Monte Carlo Opera House, Monaco, 26 February 1925; American première by San Francisco Grand Opera Co. at Columbia Theater, 11 January 1926.

Reed, H. Owen (b. Odessa, MO, 17 June 1910; AMC; *Amerigrove*; *Who's Who*)
1936   *The Masque of the Read Death* (ballet-pantomime).
1955   *Peter Homan's Dream* (2 acts—2 hours; libretto by J. Jennings). Performed East Lansing, MI, 13 May 1955. Published by Mills

Music. Arranged as a musical, 1971. (Also titled *Michigan Dream*.)

1960   *Earth Trapped* (chamber dance-opera; 18 minutes; libretto by Hartley B. Alexander). Performed East Lansing, MI, 24 February 1962.

1974   *Living Solid Face* ("chamber dance opera"; 27 minutes; libretto by Hartley B. Alexander and F. W. Coggan). Performed at University of South Dakota, 28 November 1976 and 10 February 1977.

1980   *Butterfly Girl and Mirage Boy* (chamber dance-opera; 24 minutes; libretto by composer and Hartley B. Alexander on an American Indian legend). Performed East Lansing, MI, 13 May 1980.

Reeves-Phillips, Sandra

1983   *Opening Night*, with Corliss Taylor-Dunn (2 acts; libretto by the composers). Performed by AMAS Repertory Theatre, New York, 21 April 1983.

Rehrer, William

1980   *The Tell-Tale Heart* (1 act). Performed Seattle, WA, March 1980.

Reichert, James A. (b. Toledo, OH, 12 May 1932; Anderson)

-    *Other Voices, Other Rooms* (after Truman Capote). New York State Bicentennial Commission.

Reid, Catherine

1988   *Pitcher Perfect* (3 acts; libretto by David Ives after Kleist's *Der zerbrochene Krug* switched to nineteenth-century Indiana). Commission by Indianapolis Opera, IN; performed there June 1988, January 1989, and 1991.

Reif, Paul (b. Prague, Bohemia, 23 March 1910; d. New York, 7 July 1978; U.S. citizen, 1943; Anderson; *Baker's*)

1965   *Mad Hamlet* (3 acts; libretto by Robert Corcoran). Published by Leslie Productions.

1965   *Portrait in Brownstone* (2 acts; libretto by Henry Butler after Auchincloss). Performed New York, 15 May 1966. Published by Leslie Productions.

1972   *The Artist* (multimedia, with artist Larry Rivers). Performed New York 17 April 1972. Published by Seesaw Music.

1974   *The Curse of Mauvais-Air* (chamber opera buffa; 40 minutes). Performed New York, 9 May 1974. Recorded by Gregg Smith Singers, 1978.

-    *Campaign* (1 act). *COS*-2. Published by Seesaw Music.

Reinagle, Alexander (b. Portsmouth, England, 1747, baptized 23 April 1756; d. Baltimore, 21 September 1809; in U.S. from 1786; *Amerigrove*; Porter)

(Unless indicated otherwise, all of these were performed in Philadelphia, and the music is now mostly lost. Reinagle "was the first in America to replace the harpsichord with the piano in the orchestra pit"—*Amerigrove*. Detailed information below from Porter, and Robert Hopkins's preface to *Alexander Reinagle: The*

Philadelphia Sonatas, Recent Researches in American Music, 5 [Madison: A-R Editions, 1978].)

1792   *Don Juan: or, The Libertine Destroyed* ("tragical pantomimical entertainment"; 2 acts; libretto by Carlo Delpini). Première, 16 April 1792.

1793   *The Grateful Lion: or, Harlequin Shipwrecked* (comic pantomime), compiled, with overture, by Reinagle. First U.S. performance, New York, 6 July 1793. See also *Harlequin Shipwreck'd*, below.

1794   *Sailor's Landlady: or, Jack in Distress* (pantomime). Première, 3 March 1794.

1794   *Robin Hood: or, Sherwood Forest* (comic opera), "additional airs" by Reinagle to the light opera by William Shield. Performed 10 March 1794.

1794   *St. Patrick's Day: or, The Scheming Lieutenant*, "Occasional Overture" to Richard Sheridan's farce. Performed 17 March 1794.

1794   *La Forêt noire*, "serious pantomime" with the "overture etc., entirely new, composed by Mr. Reinagle." Performed 26 April 1794.

1794   *The Spanish Barber: or, The Fruitless Precaution*, "additional airs by Messrs. Reinagle and [Benjamin] Carr" for Samuel Arnold's light opera. Performed 7 July 1794.

1795   *Harlequin Shipwreck'd: or, The Grateful Lion* (afterpiece), "new pantomime . . . music compiled from Pleyel, Gretri [*sic*], Giornowicki [*sic*], Reeves [*sic*], Moorehead, etc. The new music by Mr. Reinagle." Performed 2 January 1795.

1795   *The Purse: or, Benevolent Tar* (afterpiece or musical drama; 1 act), "accompaniments and new airs" by Reinagle to the light opera by William Reeve. Performed 7 January 1795.

1795   *The Volunteers*, "musical entertainment . . . in two acts . . . the overture and music entirely new, composed by Mr. Reinagle" (comic opera; libretto by Susannah Rowson). Performed 21 January 1795. Fourteen items published Philadelphia: for the author, 1795; reprinted in Scheifer, 5:5-22.

1795   *Auld Robin Gray: or, Jamie's Return from America*, "the new music, with a Scotish [*sic*] medley overture, by Mr. Reinagle" for the light opera by Samuel Arnold (2 acts). Performed 4 May 1795.

1795   *The Sicilian Romance: or, The Apparition of the Cliffs* (afterpiece), "musical dramatic tale in 2 acts . . . the music composed by Mr. Reinagle" (2 acts; libretto by Henry Siddons). Performed 6 May 1795.

1795   *Harlequin's Invasion*, "speaking pantomime . . . by . . . David Garrick . . . with an entirely new medley overture by Mr. Reinagle" (3 acts; libretto by David Garrick). Performed 12 June 1795.

1796   *The Warrior's Welcome Home* (pantomime or divertisement). Première, 10 February 1796.

1796   *The Witches of the Rocks: or, Harlequin Everywhere* (afterpiece; pantomime), "with an entire new overture, songs, chorusses [*sic*] and recitatives, composed by Mr. Reinagle." Performed 26 February 1796.

1796   *The Lucky Escape: or, The Ploughman Turned Sailor* (afterpiece), "new pantomime dance . . . founded on [Charles] Dibdin's celebrated ballad of that name. The music selected from his most admired songs, and adapted with new accompaniments and an overture, by Mr. Reinagle." Performed 14 March 1796.

1796   *Shamrock: or, St. Patrick's Day* (speaking pantomime). Première, 18 March 1796.

1797   *Columbus: or, The Discovery of America* (melodrama, or incidental music; 5 acts; libretto by Thomas Morton). Performed 30 October 1797 (Porter: 30 January 1797). *The Music in the Historical Play of Columbus, Composed and adapted for the Piano Forte, Flute or Violin* (Philadelphia: for the author, [n.d.]).

1797   *The Savoyard: or, The Repentant Seducer*, "musical farce in two acts, . . . the music composed by Mr. Reinagle." Première, 12 July 1797.

1798   *The Italian Monk*, after Samuel Arnold?, "music and accompaniments by Mr. Reinagle" for the play by James Boaden (3 acts). Performed 11 April 1798.

1798   *Gentle Shepherd* (pantomime). Première, 16 April 1798.

1799   *The Arabs of the Desert: or, Harlequin's Flight from Egypt* (afterpiece), "entire new pantomime olio . . . with a new overture and music composed by Mr. Reinagle." Performed 13 April 1799.

1800   *The Double Disguise* (musical farce/light opera; 2 acts; libretto by Mrs. Harriet Horncastle Hook). Performed 18 April 1800.

1800   *Harlequin Freemason*, "Masonic Overture" for Charles Dibdin's pantomime (2 acts?; libretto by J. Messink). Performed 21 April 1800.

1803   *Harlequin Restored: or, The Gift of the Seasons* (pantomime). Première, 26 December 1803.

c 1804   *Raymond and Agnes: or, The Bleeding Nun* (pantomime; 2 acts; libretto based on Matthew Gregory Lewis's novel *The Monk*). Performed ca. 1803-04.

1805   *The Wife of Two Husbands*, with Benjamin Carr and Rayner Taylor, overture (melodrama; 5 acts; libretto by James Cobb after Guilbert Pixérécourt's *La Femme à deux maris*). Performed 1 March 1805.

1807   *The Black Castle: or, Spectre of the Forest*, with James Hewitt (melodrama; 2 acts). Première, 20 March 1807.

-   *The Stranger*. One item from this work is in AMRC.

(Reinagle also composed incidental music to Susannah Rowson's play *Slaves in Algiers: or, A Struggle for Freedom*, 1794; *The Constellation: or, A Wreath for American Tars*, 1799; *The Secret*, 1799; *Pizzaro: or, The Spaniards in Peru*, with Rayner Taylor, 1800; *Edwy and Elgiva*, 1801; *The Sailor's Daughter*, 1804; and *Mary, Queen of Scots*, 1806.)

Reiners, Anne

1964   *Cindy* (1 act). Performed Eureka Springs, AR, 27 July 1964.

Reise, Jay (b. New York, 9 February 1950; Anderson; *WhoAm*)

1978   *Alice at the End* ("operatic tableau"), for soprano, actress, 6 players. Performed Hamilton, NY, 1 August 1978.

1988   *Rasputin* (2 hours; libretto by composer and Frank Corsaro). Commission by New York City Opera. Performed at Guggenheim

Museum, New York, 13 March 1988, and by New York City Opera, 17 September 1988. Kornick.

Reiser, Alois (b. Prague, Bohemia, 4 April 1887; d. Los Angeles, 4 April 1977; in U.S. from 1914?; Anderson; *Baker's*)
- 1923   *Gobi* (prelude and 3 scenes—4 hours). First and last performance, New York, 29 July 1923.
-     *Daphne* (150 minutes).

Repper, Charles (b. Alliance, OH, 3 January 1886; d. Boston, 24 October 1974; Anderson)
-     *The Dragon of Wu Foo* (operetta).
-     *Penny Buns and Roses* (operetta).

Rescia, Richard R. (b. Aqawam, MA, 12 February 1930; *Who's Who*)
- 1964   *Portrait* (1 act). Performed Amherst, MA, 25 April 1964.
-     *Ashes of Roses.*

Reti, Rudolph (b. Užice, Serbia, 27 November 1885; d. Montclair, NJ, 7 February 1957; to U.S. in 1938; *Amerigrove*; Anderson)
- 1935   *David and Goliath* (ballet-opera).
-     *Ivan and the Drum.*

Reuter, Florizel von (b. Davenport, IA, 21 January 1890; d. Waukesha, WI, 10 May 1985; *Baker's*)
- 1947   *Postmaster Wynn* (after Pushkin). Performed Berlin, Germany, 1947.

Reynolds, I. E.
-     *Ruth* (biblical opera). Performed Southwestern Baptist Seminary, Forth Worth, TX?

Reynolds, Roger (b. Detroit, MI, 18 July 1934; AMC; *Amerigrove*; *Who's Who*)
- 1962   *The Emperor of Ice Cream* (theater piece; libretto by Wallace Stevens), for 8 soloists, percussion, piano, double bass; revised 1974. Performed New York, 19 March 1965, and at University of Wisconsin-Milwaukee (conducted by this compiler), 17 November 1965. Published by C. F. Peters in 1964.
- 1970   *I/O: A Ritual for 23 Performers* (after a concept by Buckminster Fuller), including 9 female vocalists, 9 male mimes, 2 performers, 2 flutes, 2 clarinets, electronics, slides. ("I/O" = "in/out.") Performed Pasadena, CA, 24 January 1971. Published by Peters.

Rhea, Raymond (b. Littleton, CO, 28 December 1910; d. in Texas; Anderson)
-     *Courtweek* (folk opera). Performed Corpus Christi, TX?

Rhoads, Mary Ruth (b. Philadelphia, 28 January 1920; Cohen; *WhoAm*)
- 1981   *Horyuji* (multimedia, for chorus, dancers, and chamber orchestra; 1 act). Performed Greeley, CO, 4 May 1984.

Rhodes, Phillip (b. Forest City, NC, 6 June 1940; AMC; *Amerigrove*)
- 1975   *Odysseus* (12 minutes). NEA grant, 1975.

1980 *Gentle Boy* (1 act—45 minutes; libretto by composer and Jane Rhodes after Hawthorne), revised 1987. Minnesota State Arts Board grant. Performed Northfield, MN, 2 April 1982, and Tallahassee, FL, 12 June 1987.

1983 *The Magic Pipe* (comic opera; 45 minutes; libretto by the composer, Jackson Bryce, and Jane Rhodes after Hawthorne's "Feathertop"). Commission by Minnesota Composers' Forum and McKnight Foundation. (*Baker's* date: 1989.)

Rice, Edward Everett (b. Brighton, MA, 21 December 1848; d. New York, 16 November 1924; *Amerigrove*)

1874 *Evangeline* (libretto by J. C. Goodwin). Performed New York, 27 July 1874. Published 1877. *Amerigrove*: "the most popular American musical stage work of its decade, one of the first works to be called a 'musical comedy,' and perhaps the first of its genre in the USA to have a fully original score without adapted or interpolated songs."

1880 *Hiawatha* (libretto by N. L. Childs). Performed New York, 21 February 1880.

1880 *Revels* (libretto by J. J. McNally). Performed New York, 25 October 1880.

1884 *Adonis* (libretto by W. Gill). Performed New York, 4 September 1884.

1887 *The Corsair* (libretto by J. Braham after G. Byron). Performed New York, 18 October 1887.

1893 *1492* (libretto by R. A. Barnet). Performed New York, 15 May 1893.

1895 *Excelsior, Jr.* (libretto by R. A. Barnet). Performed New York, 29 November 1895.

  (Rice's songs also appeared in works by others; i.e., the actor John Brougham's burlesque *Po-ca-hon-tas: or, The Gentle Savage*, 1855.)

Rice, Michael

- *The Good Woman of Setzuan* (libretto by composer and Eric Bentley after Brecht). *COS*-4.

Rice, Richard

1989 *The Ransom of Red Chief* (70 minutes; libretto by composer after O. Henry).

Richard, Mae

1990 *Space for Two* (libretto by Nancy Ford). Performed San Francisco, 15 February 1990.

Richardson, Claibe

1989 *From the Bodoni County Songbook Anthology* (libretto by Frank Gagliano). Performed New York, September 1989.

Richardson, Howard

1978 *A Thread of Scarlet* (libretto by E. G. Kosakoff). Performed New York, 30 November 1978.

Richmond, Gordon
1962   *The Wild Beasts* (2 acts). Performed at Juilliard School, New York, 17 May 1962.

Richter, Francis William (b. Minneapolis, MN, 1888; Hipsher, 430)
-    *The Grand Nazar.*

Richter, Marion Morrey (b. Columbus, OH, 2 October 1900; Anderson; Cohen)
1950   *This Is Our Camp* (operetta for children). Published Boston: C. C. Birchard, 1955.
1956   *Distant Drums* (3 acts).

Rickard, Gene P.
1978   *Butler's Lives of the St.s* (1 hour; many authors, including Goethe, Shakespeare, and Melville). Performed New York, 13 January 1978.
1980   *Headshots* (1 act). Performed New York, 20 June 1908.
-    *Van Gogh/Gaugin.* Performed New York. *COS*-3.

Ridgway, Charles Arthur (b. New York, 1878)
1933?   *Jack of Hearts.* Cited in Rodríguez.

Riesenfeld, Hugo (b. Vienna, Austria, 26 January 1879; d. Hollywood, CA, 10 September 1939; to U.S. in 1907; Anderson)
-    *Merry Martyr* (operetta). Cited in Rodriguez.

Rieti, Vittorio (b. Alexandria, Egypt, 28 January 1898 of Italian descent; in U.S. from 1940, citizen in 1944; *Amerigrove*)
1949   *Don Perlimplin* (prologue and 3 scenes; libretto by Federico García Lorca; in Spanish). Performed Urbana, IL, 30 March 1952. Published by Associated Music.
1954   *Viaggio d'Europa* (radio opera; libretto by P. Masino). Performed Rome, Italy, 1955.
1957   *The Pet Shop* (1 act—40 minutes; libretto by C. White). Performed New York, 14 April 1958. Published by General Music.
1960   *The Clock* (2 acts; libretto by C. White). Published by General Music.
1966   *Maryam the Harlot* (1 act; libretto by composer and C. Nicolas [*Amerigrove*: by C. White]). Published by Associated Music.

Riggio, Donald Joseph (b. Cleveland, OH, 13 June 1926; *WhoAm*)
1990   *Rotunda, Rotunda, Let Your Hair Down* (libretto by Suzanne Riggio). Performed 1 April 1990.

Rigoni, Robert
1976   *The Red Death* (1 act). Performed Alton, IL, 16 July 1976.
1977   *A Cup of Coffee* (1 act). Performed Alton, IL, 24 June 1977.

Riley, Dennis Daniel (b. Los Angeles, 28 May 1943; *Amerigrove*; *Who's Who*)
1984   *Rappaccini's Daughter* (90 minutes—10 scenes; libretto by composer and Joseph Pazillo after Hawthorne). NEA grant.
1983   *Cats' Concert* (children's opera; libretto by Joseph Pazillo).

Rivas, Fernando (ASCAP)

> 1987   *Carmelita's Boiler Time Machine* (libretto by Troiano). Performed by INTAR Hispanic-American Music Theatre Lab, New York, 13 January 1987.
>
> 1988   *When Galaxy 6 and the Bronx Collide* (1 act; libretto by Migdalia Cruz). Commission by DUO Theater/Teatro DUO, New York. Performed there, 12 February 1988.
>
>   *Triple Decker*, a trilogy commissioned by INTAR Hispanic-American Arts Center:
>
> 1988   *Alma* (1 act; libretto by Ana Maria Simo after de Quevedo). Performed at First New York International Festival of the Arts, New York, 15 June 1988.
>
> 1988   *Welcome Back to Salamanca* (1 act; libretto by Migdalia Cruz after Cervantes). Performed at First New York International Festival of the Arts, New York, 15 June 1988.
>
>   -   The third opera of the trilogy is planned as a 1-act work after Lope de Rueda, with libretto by Manuel Pereiras.
>
>   (Rivas was also awarded an NEA grant, 1988, for a "musical documentary," to a libretto by Max Ferra. He composed a musical with Tito Puente, *Lovers and Keepers*, 1986.)

Rivers, Samuel Carhorne "Sam" (b. El Reno, OK, 25 September 1930; Southern)

> 1973   *Solomon and Sheba* (Afro-American jazz opera). Performed by Harlem Opera Society, New York, June 1973.
>
> 1975   *Black Cowboys* (jazz opera; libretto by Emory Taylor). Performed by Harlem Opera Society, New York, 30 May 1978.
>
> 1978   *Hodges & Co.* (2 acts; about black cowboys). Performed by Harlem Opera Society, June 1978.

Rizzo, Phil

> 1980   *Christ, the Man from Galilee* (4 acts—130 minutes; libretto by composer after the Gospels). NEA fellowship.

Roach, Max (b. New Land [*Baker's*: Elizabeth City], NC, 10 January 1924; AMC; *Amerigrove*)

> 1987   *Midsummer Night's Dream* (jazz work; libretto by George Ferencz after Shakespeare). Performed by San Diego Repertory Theatre, CA, September 1987.
>
>   -   Meet the Composer/Reader's Digest commission, with performances projected for Berkeley and San Diego, CA.

Robb, John Donald (b. Minneapolis, MN, 12 June 1892; ASCAP; *Amerigrove*)

> 1949   *Little Jo* (1 act). Performed Albuquerque, NM, 8 January 1950.
>
>   -   *Come Along with Me.*
>
>   -   *Dontaro* (1 act; Japanese subject).
>
>   -   *Joy Comes to Dead Horse* (musical play).

Robb, Willard

> 1961   *The Twilight Saint* (1 act). Performed Norfolk, VA, March 1961.

Roberts, Arthur (b. New York, 6 July 1912; ASCAP/AMC; *Who's Who*)

> 1957   *A Lunar Requiem* (1 act—65 minutes; libretto by composer after Heinlein's *Requiem*). Revised 1978.

-      *Muckle-Mouthed Meg* (1 act—1 hour, libretto after an old Irish legend). *COS*-4.

Robertson, Edwin C. (b. Richmond, VA, 26 November 1938; Anderson)
1988   *The Well* (libretto by Grace Hawthorne after the New Testament account of Jesus and the woman at Jacob's well). Performed Birmingham, AL, 17 November 1988. The libretto was also set by K. Lee Scott.

Robertson, Hugh Sterling, II (b. New York, 19 January 1940; d. Bedford, NY, 15 November 1973; Anderson)
-      *The Atheist*. *COS*-2.

Robinson, Ben
1989   *Out of Order*. Performed by Music Theatre Group, New York, 6 July 1989.

Robinson, Earl (b. Seattle, WA, 2 July 1910; d. there, 20 July 1991; *Amerigrove*; *Baker's*)
1938   *Processional* (musical).
1939   *Sing for Your Supper* (musical).
1954   *Sandhog* (folk opera; libretto by W. Salt after Dreiser).
1962   *One Foot in America* (musical).
1976   *Earl Robinson's America* (musical).
1978   *David of Sassoon* (folk opera; libretto by composer). Performed Fresno, CA, 1978.
1981   *Listen for the Dolphin* (children's musical; 2 acts; libretto by composer). Performed Santa Barbara, CA, 1981.
1983   *Song of Atlantis* (music drama; 2 acts; libretto by composer).

Robinson, McNeil (b. Birmingham, AL, 16 March 1943; *WhoAm*)
1979   *Medea* (libretto by Imogene Howe). Published by Presser.

Robinson, Scott (b. Syracuse, NY, 1964)
1989   *The Volunteer* (15 minutes; libretto by composer). Performed Binghamton, NY, 24 March 1990.

Robinson, Walter
1988   *Look What a Wonder Jesus has Done* (folk opera, about Denmark Vesey). See *Time*, 12 September 1988, 12f.

Robjohn, William James (1843-1920). *See* Florio, Caryl

Robledo, Ed
1985   *Steeltown*, with Bruce Barthol (libretto by composers). Performed by San Francisco Mime Troupe, 13 November 1985.

Robyn, Alfred George (b. St. Louis, 29 April 1860; d. New York, 18 October 1935; *Amerigrove*)
       (Most, but not all, of Robyn's stage works are comic operas. Many are in the Boston Public Library.)
1883   *Manette*. Performed St. Louis, August 1893.

1888   *Beans and Buttons.* Krohn says this work was "the most successful
        of all."
1893   *Jacinta, The Maid of Manzanillo* (Mexican comic opera; libretto by
        William H. Lepere). Performed 22 May 1893.
1903   *The Yankee Consul.*
1905   *The Gypsy Girl.*
1907   *Fortune Land.*
1907   *The Yankee Tourist.*
1912   *All for the Ladies.*
-       *The Boys from Home.*
-       *The Court Martial.*
-       *The Duchess d'Aze.*
-       *The Girl from Frisco.*
-       *Merlin* (grand opera).
-       *Padishah.*
-       *Princess Beggar.*
-       *A Slim Legacy.*
-       *A Soldier in Petticoats.*
-       *A Stray King.*
-       *Will o' the Wisp* (grand opera).

Rochberg, George (b. Paterson, NJ, 5 July 1918; AMC; *Amerigrove*; *Who's Who*)
1975   *Phaedra* (monodrama; libretto by Gene Rochberg after R. Lowell).
        NEA grant. Performed Syracuse, NY, 9 January 1976. Published
        by Presser.
1982   *The Confidence Man* (2 acts and epilogue—2 hours; libretto by Gene
        Rochberg after the novel by Herman Melville). Commission and
        première by Santa Fe Opera, NM, 31 July 1982. Kornick.

Rockwell, Jeffrey
1989   *Rip Van Winkle* (libretto by J. Sherwood Montgomery; performed
        by children). Commission by San Diego Opera. Performed San
        Diego, CA, 18 October 1989.

Roder, Milan (b. Osijek, Slavonia, 5 December 1878; d. Hollywood, CA, 23
        January 1956; U.S. citizen, 1920; Anderson)
-       *Around the World* (comic opera).
-       *Jelka.*

Rodgers, Lou
1977   *Antigone.* Performed New York, 29 October 1977.
1978   *The Specialist* (1 act). Performed New York, 1 April 1978.
1980   *Thursday's Child* (70 minutes; libretto by composer; for
        children—includes children in the cast). Performed by Golden
        Fleece, New York, 31 October 1980.
1982   *Miyako* (1 hour; libretto by composer after a Japanese Noh play).
        Performed by Golden Fleece, New York, 7 May 1982.
1986   *Places Everyone* (1 act; libretto by William Cotter). Performed by
        Golden Fleece, New York, 8 June 1986.
1987   *The Wishing Tree* (on poems by William Cotter). Performed by
        Golden Fleece, New York, 26 March 1987.

1988 *The Warrior Saint* (27 minutes; libretto by composer, about Joan of Arc). Performed by Golden Fleece, New York, 13 December 1988.

- *The Acquitaine Dialogues.* In progress, *COS*-4.

Rodgers, Mary (b. New York, 11 January 1931; daughter of Richard Rodgers; ASCAP; Anderson; Cohen)

1988 *The Griffin and the Minor Canon* (libretto by Ellen Fitzhugh and Wendy Kesselman, or Marshall Barer, after Stockton). Performed by Music-Theatre Group, Stockbridge, MA, 10 August 1988; and New York, 6 July 1989 (fifteen performances).

Rodgers, Richard (b. Hammels Station, Long Island, NY, 28 June 1902; d. New York, 30 December 1979; *Amerigrove*)

(Of Rodgers's thirty-two musicals, two have been produced as operas, both of them with libretto by Oscar Hammerstein II:)

1943 *Oklahoma!* (2 acts). Première at St. James Theatre, New York, 31 March 1943. Performed by Minnesota Opera, 8 July 1989 (thirty-four performances); by Knoxville Opera, 15 July 1989, Los Angeles Music Center Opera, 22 June 1990, and Augusta Opera, 6 September 1990. Recordings: Random House (1943), RCA (1979). Kornick.

1945 *Carousel* (prelude and 2 acts). Première at Majestic Theatre, New York, 19 April 1945; performed by Music Theatre of Lincoln Center, New York, by Chicago Lyric Opera, 9 June 1990, and by Houston Grand Opera, 15 June 1990. Kornick.

(Also in Kornick: *The Boys from Syracuse*, 1938, *South Pacific*, 1949, *The King and I*, 1951, *Flower Drum Song*, 1958, and *The Sound of Music*, 1959.)

Rodriguez, Robert Xavier (b. San Antonio, TX, 28 June 1946; ASCAP/AMC; *Amerigrove*; *WhoAm*)

1978 *Le Diable amoureux* (*Les Visiteurs du soir*; *The Devil in Love*) (55 minutes; libretto by composer and Frans Boerlage after Cazotte). NEA fellowship. Telecast by KERA-TV, Dallas, TX, 11 April 1979; performed Wichita Falls, TX, 1982.

1982 *Suor Isabella* (*Sister Isabella*) (comic opera; 1 act—1 hour; libretto by Daniel Dibbern after Giovanni Boccaccio's *Decameron*). Commission by National Endowment for the Arts. Première at University of Texas, Dallas (with piano), 7 July 1982; performed at Boston University (with orchestra), 3 May 1984. Kornick.

1985 *Tango* (comic chamber opera; 1 act—22 minutes; libretto by composer after texts from 1913 and 1914). Commission by NEA, for Voices of Change, Dallas, TX, Chicago Ensemble, Chicago, and Twentieth-Century Consort, Washington, DC. Première in Dallas, 29 January 1986. Kornick.

1986 *The Ransom of Red Chief* (1 act—55 minutes; libretto by Daniel Dibbern after a story by O. Henry). Sesquicentennial commission, Mesquite, TX. Première by Lyric Opera of Dallas, Mesquite, 10 October 1986. Kornick.

1987 *Monkey See, Monkey Do* (25 minutes; libretto by Mary Duren after a folk legend; in Spanish and English). A puppet opera also available for live performance. Commission by Dallas Opera and Puppet Opera Theater, TX. Performed Dallas, 26 January 1987.

1988   *The Old Majestic* (formerly *Backstage at the Majestic*; 2 acts—90 minutes; libretto by Mary Duren). Commission by San Antonio Festival. Première at University of Texas, San Antonio, 28 May 1988. Kornick.

Rodríguez, Thomas

1987   *Remote Control*, with Jaime Acosta and José García (libretto by Rosalba Rolan, in English and Spanish). Performed by Pregones Puerto Rican Theater Collective, New York, 30 December 1987.

Rogers, Bernard (b. New York, 4 February 1893; d. Rochester, NY, 24 May 1968; ASCAP; *Amerigrove*; Hipsher)

1922   *Deirdre.*

1930   *The Marriage of Aude* (lyric drama; 1 act; libretto by Charles Rodda). Performed at Festival of American Music, Eastman School, Rochester, NY, 22 May 1931; also performed Chicago, 1937. Bispham Medal, 1932.

1944   *The Warrior* (tragic opera; 1 act; libretto by Norman Corwin; about Samson and Delilah). Alice M. Ditson Award for opera. Première by Metropolitan Opera, New York, 11 January 1947.

1950   *The Veil* (1 act; libretto by R. Lawrence). Performed at Indiana University, Bloomington, 18 May 1950. Published by Southern Music.

1954   *The Nightingale* (1 act—65 minutes; libretto by composer after Hans Christian Andersen). Performed Rochester, NY, or New York, 10 May 1955.

1957   *The Musicians of Bremen.* Performed Rochester, NY, July 1957.

Rogers, Eddy (b. Norfolk, VA, 23 September 1907; d. Denver, CO, 8 October 1964; Anderson)

-   *Nella.*

Rogers, Lou

1978   *The Specialist* (1 act; libretto by Stuart Michaels). Première by Golden Fleece, New York, 1978. Kornick.

Roma, Caro (b. East Oakland, CA, 10 September 1869; d. there, 23 September 1937; *Amerigrove*)

-   *God of the Sea.*

Romani, Romano (b. 1887 in Livarno)

(Romani composed operas before emigrating to the U.S. But these works are listed in Rodriguez as composed in the U.S.:)

-   *Fedra.*

-   *Lunina.*

-   *Rosana.*

Romberg, Sigmund (b. Nagykanizsa, Hungary, 29 July 1887; d. New York, 9 November 1951; in U.S. from 1909; *Amerigrove*; kindly doublechecked by William A. Everett, whose dissertation is on Romberg)

1917   *Maytime* ("a play with music"; 4 acts; libretto by Rida Johnson Young and Cyrus Wood). First performed at Shubert Theatre, New York, 16 August 1917.

1921   *Blossom Time* (operetta; libretto by Dorothy Donnelly). First performed at Ambassador Theatre, New York, 29 September 1921.

1924   *The Student Prince* (operetta; 4 acts; libretto by Dorothy Donnelly). First performed at Jolson Theatre, New York, 22 December 1924; revised 1943; Marin Opera Company, 7 October 1988; and New York Opera, 7 May 1989 (on tour).

1926   *The Desert Song* ("musical play"; 2 acts; libretto by Otto Harbach and Oscar Hammerstein II). First performed at Casino Theatre, New York, 30 November 1926; London, 1927; by Chautauqua Opera, NY, 15 July 1989, and Central City Opera, CO, 1 August 1989.

1927   *My Maryland* (operetta; 3 acts; libretto by Dorothy Donnelly; about Barbara Frietchie). First performed at Jolson Theatre, New York, 12 September 1927.

1928   *The New Moon* (libretto by Oscar Hammerstein II). First performed at Imperial Theatre, New York, 19 September 1928; recently by Gold Coast Opera, 2 April 1988; at Wolf Trap, 25 June 1989; New York Opera, 19 July 1989; and by Tri-Cities Opera, Binghamton, NY, 1990.

1945   *Up in Central Park* (operetta; lyrics by Herbert and Dorothy Fields). First performed at Century Theatre, New York, 27 January 1945.

1948   *My Romance* (operetta; libretto by Rowland Leigh). First performed at Shubert Theatre, New York, 19 October 1948. The last traditional operetta produced by the Shubert Co.

(Romberg composed 30 operettas, of which this is a selection.)

Roosevelt, Joseph Willard (b. Madrid, Spain, 16 January 1918, of American parents; AMC; Anderson; *Baker's*; *Who's Who*)

1974   *And the Walls Came Tumbling Down* (1 act—55 minutes; libretto by Lofton Mitchell, about blacks in New Amsterdam in 1664), with chamber orchestra. NEA grant. Première at Harlem School of the Arts, New York, 16 March 1976. Kornick.

Root, George Frederick (b. Sheffield, MA, 30 August 1820; d. Bailey Island, ME, 6 August 1895; *Amerigrove*)

1852   *The Flower Queen: or, The Coronation of the Rose* (operatic cantata; libretto by Fannie J. Crosby). Performed New York, 1852.

1853   *Daniel: or, The Captivity and Restoration* (operatic cantata; libretto by C. M. Cady and Fannie J. Crosby).

1854   *The Pilgrim Fathers* (operatic cantata; libretto by Fannie J. Crosby).

1857   *The Haymakers* (operatic cantata). Piano-vocal score published in New York by Mason Bros., 1857. Ed. Dennis R. Martin in Recent Researches in American Music, 9-10 (Madison: A-R Editions, 1984).

1860   *Belshazzar's Feast* (operatic cantata; libretto by B. F. Edmands).

Rorem, Ned (b. Richmond, IN, 23 October 1923; ASCAP/AMC; *Amerigrove*; Anderson; *Who's Who*)

1952   *A Childhood Miracle* (40 minutes; libretto by E. Stein after Hawthorne's *Snow Image*). Performed by Punch Opera, New York, 10 May 1955. Published by Southern Music.

1956   *The Robbers* (1 scene—28 minutes; libretto by composer after Chaucer's "The Pardoner's Tale"). Performed at Mannes College, New York, 14 April 1958. Published by Boosey & Hawkes.

1965   *Miss Julie* (2 acts; libretto by Kenward Elmslie after Strindberg). Performed by New York City Opera, 4 November 1965. Published by Boosey & Hawkes.

1967   *The Last Day* (1 act; libretto by Jay S. Harrison). Performed New York, 22 May 1967.

1968   *Three Sisters Who Are Not Sisters* (3 acts; libretto by Gertrude Stein). Performed at Temple University, Philadelphia, 24 July 1971. Published by Boosey & Hawkes.

1968   *Bertha* (1 act—25 minutes; libretto by K. Koch). Performed New York, 26 November 1973. Published by Boosey & Hawkes.

1970   *Fables* (5 short operas; libretto by J. de la Fontaine, translated by M. Moore). Performed at University of Tennessee at Martin, 21 May 1971. Published by Boosey & Hawkes.

1976   *Hearing* (chamber opera; 5 scenes—50 minutes; libretto by James Holmes after poems by Kenneth Koch). Première by Gregg Smith Singers, St. Stephen's Church, New York (unstaged), 15 March 1977. Published by Boosey & Hawkes. Kornick.

–   *The Anniversary* (1 act). *COS*-1.

Rosen, Jerome William (b. Boston, 23 July 1921; Anderson; *Baker's*; *WhoAm*)

1979   *Calisto and Melibea* (3 acts—80 minutes; libretto by composer and Edwin Honig after a 15th-century romance). Performed at University of California, Davis, 31 May 1979.

Rosen, Lewis (AMC)

–   *Hester* (after Hawthorne's *The Scarlet Letter*). *COS*-2.

Rosner, Arnold (b. New York, 8 November 1945; *Amerigrove*)

1984   *The Chronicle of Nine*, op. 81 (libretto by F. Stevenson).

Ross, Pamela

1989   *Carreno!* (libretto by Gene Frankel, about Teresa Carreño). Performed at Gene Frankel Theater, New York, 12 October 1989.

Ross, Walter Beghtol (b. Lincoln, NE, 3 October 1936; Anderson; *Baker's*; *WhoAm*; *Who's Who*)

1972   *In the Penal Colony* (chamber opera; 1 act). Performed at University of Virginia?

Roth, Michael S.

1983   *Hopi Prophecies* (3 acts—100 minutes; libretto by composer and Daniel Schreier after three Hopi legends). Performed by New York Theatre Workshop, 1983.

(Roth also composed a musical, *The Nain Rouge*, 1985.)

Roy, Jeffrey (ASCAP)
>   1988   *Penguins* (1 act; libretto by Ana Maria Simo). Commission by DUO
>   Theater/Teatro DUO, New York. Performed there, 12 February
>   1988.
>   1988   *Ted & Edna* (libretto by Ana Maria Simo). Performed by New
>   Dramatists, New York, 29 September 1988 and 25 April 1989.

Roy, Klaus George (b. Vienna, Austria, 24 January 1924; to U.S. in 1940, citizen
>   1944; *Amerigrove*; *WhoAm*; *Who's Who*)
>   1957   *Sterlingmann: or, Generosity Rewarded* (45 minutes). Telecast on
>   WGBH-TV, Boston, 18 April 1957. Published by Presser.

Rubin, ?
>   1986   *The Girl Who Stole His Heart* (libretto by Brody). Performed San
>   Francisco, 22 June 1986.

Rubin, Amy
>   1977   *Viva Reviva.* Performed Stockbridge, MA, 11 August 1977.

Rubino, Pasquale
>   1932   *Il filo d'Arianna* (3 acts). Performed New York, 1938.

Rubinstein, Arthur
>   1983   *Booth Is Back in Town* (libretto by Gretchen Cryer and Austin
>   Pendleton). Performed at PepsiCo Summerfare, Purchase, NY, 7
>   July 1983.

Rubinstein, Beryl (b. Athens, CA, 26 October 1898; d. Cleveland, OH, 29
>   December 1952; *Amerigrove*)
>   1938   *The Sleeping Beauty* (or *The Sleeping Princess*; 150 minutes; libretto
>   by John Erskine). Performed at Juilliard School, New York, 19
>   January 1938. Bispham Medal, 1940.

Rudenstein, Roger
>   1984   *Metamorphosis* (1 hour; libretto by composer after Kafka).
>   Performed 1985.
>   1986   *Faustus* (2 hours; libretto by composer after Marlowe and Goethe).
>   Performed by Center for Contemporary Opera, New York, 10
>   January 1986.
>   1988   *Jesus of Nazareth* (3 acts—138 minutes; libretto by composer, on the
>   life of the historical Jesus). Performed by New Camerata Opera,
>   New York, 21 October 1988.

Rudin, Andrew (b. Newgulf, TX, 10 April 1939; Anderson; *WhoAm*)
>   1972   *The Innocent.* Performed Philadelphia, 19-21 May 1972.
>   1981   *Three Sisters* (3 acts—140 minutes; libretto by William Ashbrook
>   after Chekhov). Performed by PRISM, New York, 2 March 1981.

Rudin, Richard (AMC)
>   -   *An Ordinary Man.* *COS*-3.

Rue, Gary
<blockquote>
1989   *Mensing* (libretto by Michael Robins). Performed at Illusion Theater, Minneapolis, 19 May 1989.
</blockquote>

Ruger, Morris Hutchins (b. Superior, WI, 2 December 1902; Anderson)
<blockquote>
1936   *Gettysburg* (1 act). Performed at Hollywood Bowl, Los Angeles, 23 September 1938.

1953   *The Fall of the House of Usher* (1 act). Performed Los Angeles, 15 April 1953.
</blockquote>

Ruggles, Carl (b. East Marion, MA, 11 March 1876; d. Bennington, VT, 24 October 1971; *Amerigrove*; Hipsher)
<blockquote>
1923   *The Sunken Bell* (libretto by Charles Henry Maltzer after Garhart Hauptmann's *Die versunkene Glocke*). Destroyed, except for sketches, by the composer after the New York Metropolitan Opera suggested that the bell could be made of papier-maché instead of metal.
</blockquote>

Runcie, Constance Faunt le Roy (Mrs. James; b. Indianapolis, IN, 15 January 1836; d. Winnetka, IL, 17 May 1911; Cohen; Hipsher)
<blockquote>
-   *The Prince of Asturias*. Perhaps the first romantic opera by an American woman.
</blockquote>

Rundgren, Todd (b. Upper Darby, PA, 22 June 1948; *Amerigrove*)
<blockquote>
1988   *Up Against It* (libretto by Tom Ross after Orton). NEA grant, 1988. Performed at New York Shakespeare Festival, New York, August or December 1989.
</blockquote>

Rusche, Marjorie Maxine (b. Sturgeon Bay, WI, 18 November 1949; ASCAP; Anderson; Cohen)
<blockquote>
1095   *Dance of Death* (2 acts; libretto by Dan Pinkerton). Performed Milwaukee, WI, 2 February 1985.
</blockquote>

Russell, Robert (AMC)
<blockquote>
-   *End of Day*.

-   *So How Does Your Garden Grow?* (1 act). *COS*-1.
</blockquote>

Russo, William Joseph (b. Chicago, 25 June 1928; ASCAP/AMC; *Amerigrove*; Anderson)
<blockquote>
1961   *John Hooton* (jazz opera; 1 act; libretto by composer). Performed in Chicago schools, 1966-67 season.

1963   *The Island* (libretto by A. Mitchell). Commission from BBC, London.

1964   *The Land of Milk and Honey* (1 act; libretto by S. Douglass).

1967   *Antigone* (libretto by A. A. Hoge).

1970   *A Cabaret Opera* (chamber opera; libretto by Cummings, Stein, Auden, Pound, and others). Restaged as *Paris Lights* (performed New York, 24 January 1980), *Boulevard*, *The Alice B. Toklas Hashish Fudge Review* (New York, 8 December 1977), *The Shepherds' Christmas* (Chicago, December 1979), *Americans in Paris*.

1970   *Joan of Arc* (chamber opera).
</blockquote>

1971   *Aesop's Fables* (rock opera; libretto by Jon Swan), revised 1972. Performed New York, 17 August 1972

1971   *The Shepherds' Christmas* (chamber opera; libretto by Jon Swan after the medieval *Second Shepherd's Play*). Performed Columbia College, Chicago, December 1980.

1974   *Isabella's Fortune* (comic opera; 1 act; libretto by A. Williams based on commedia dell'arte). Performed Chicago, 11 September 1974.

1974   *Pedrolino's Revenge* (comic opera; 1 act; libretto by J. Abarbanel). Performed New York, 11 September 1974.

1976   *A General Opera* (chamber opera; 1 act; libretto by Arnold Weinstein).

1984   *The Payoff* (cabaret opera; libretto by D. Declue).

1988   *Dubrovsky*.

1989   *Talking to the Sun* (multimedia; libretto from several poets). Performed Columbia College, Chicago, 6 March 1989. Published by Southern Music.

Ruthman, ?

1987   *Aladdin* (libretto by Buck after *Arabian Nights*). Performed Albany, NY, 15 May 1987.

Rydberg, Steven

1983   *Adventures of Babar* (1 act). Performed by Children's Theatre, Minneapolis, 21 October 1983.

1984   *Frankenstein.* Performed by Children's Theatre, Minneapolis, 10 February 1984.

Ryterband, Roman (b. Lodz, Poland, 2 August 1914; U.S. citizen, 1964; Anderson)

-   *Fantômes rebelles* (opera grotesque).

Rzewski, Frederic Anthony (b. Westfield, MA, 13 April 1938; *Amerigrove*; *WhoAm*; *Who's Who*)

1967   *Impersonation* ("audiodrama").

1980   *The Price of Oil* (35 minutes; libretto by composer). Commission by Hoketus Ensemble, Amsterdam, Netherlands, 1980. Performed Banff, Canada, 30 October 1981.

1985   *The Persians* (libretto by composer after Aeschylus). Performed Montpellier, France, 23 July 1985.

-   *The Island.* Commission from BBC, London, England. *COS*-1.

Sabin, Wallace Arthur (b. Culworth, Northamptonshire, England, 15 December 1869; d. St. Louis, 23 November 1937; *Amerigrove*)

1906   *St. Patrick at Tara.* Revived 1934.

1918   *The Twilight of the Kings.*

     (Freer indicates the first was an opera; *Amerigrove*, about both: "scores to two of the Bohemian Club's Grove Plays.")

Sable, Daniel
    1955   *The Informer* (1 act). Performed Columbus, OH, 11 March 1955.

Sacco, P. Peter (b. Albion, NY, 23 October 1928; *Amerigrove*; *Who's Who*)
    1967   *Mr. Vinegar* (chamber opera for children; 1 act; libretto by M. Alessi and composer). Performed Redding, CA, 12 May 1967.

Sachs, Norman (AMC)
    -    *Gambler's Paradise*, with Mel Mandel. *COS*-3.

Sahl, Michael (b. Boston, 2 September 1934; ASCAP; *Amerigrove*; *Who's Who*)
    1974   *Biograffiti* (1 act; libretto by composer). Performed New York, 14 December 1974.
    1975   *The Conjurer*, with Eric Salzman ("pop opera"; 1 act [*Amerigrove*: 2 acts]; libretto by composers). Performed at Public Theater, New York, 1 June 1975, produced by Joseph Papp.
    1976   *Stauf*, with Eric Salzman (2 acts—100 minutes; libretto by composers after the Faust legend). Première by Cubiculo (Quog Music Theatre), New York, 25 May 1976; performed at American Music Theatre Festival, Philadelphia, 1 October 1986 and 19 September 1987 (Kornick: September 20).

    1977   *Civilization and Its Discontents*, with Eric Salzman ("a bedroom opera"; 1 act—45 minutes; libretto by composers). Première by American Musical and Dramatic Academy, New York, 19 May 1977. Revived as radio opera, 1978-79; on National Public Radio, 1980. Recording: Nonesuch N-78009. Kornick. Prix Italia, 1980.
    1977   *An Old-Fashioned Girl* (libretto by composer after Dreiser's *Sister Carrie*). Performed New York, 19 May 1977.
    1978   *Noah*, with Eric Salzman (2 acts—105 minutes; libretto by composers). Première at Pratt Institute, Brooklyn, NY, 10 February 1978; also performed at Washington Square Methodist Church, New York, 1978. Kornick.
    1979   *The Passion of Simple Simon*, with Eric Salzman (3 acts—90 minutes; libretto by composer). Première by Theatre for the New City, New York, 24 January 1979; also performed on National Public Radio, 1979-80. Kornick.
    1988   *Dream Beach* (3 acts; libretto by Howard Pflanzer). Performed by Jewish Association for Services for the Aged, New York, 20 March 1988.
    1982   *Boxes* ("music theater work for radio"; 75 minutes; libretto by composer and Eric Salzman). Seagram Award. Performed and published by National Music Theater Network, New York, 11 October 1988.
    1985   *Big Jim & the Small-Time Investors* (libretto by Ned Johnson), with Eric Salzman. NEA grant, 1985-86.

St. Germain, Mark
    1990   *Johnny Pye and the Fool Killer* (libretto by Randy Courts). Performed New Brunswick, NJ, 7 February 1990; and New York, March 1990.
    -    *The Gift of the Magi* (libretto by Randy Courts after O. Henry).

Salzman, Eric (b. New York, 8 September 1933; *Amerigrove*; Anderson; *Who's Who*)

1967   *Foxes and Hedgehogs* (libretto by John Ashbery). Première New York, 30 November 1967; performed London, England, by BBC Symphony Orchestra, conducted by Pierre Boulez, 1972.

1968   *The Peloponnesian War* (libretto by D. Nagrin).

1969   *The Nude Paper Sermon* (50 minutes; libretto by John Ashbery and W. Stephenson), for actor, Renaissance consort, chorus, and electronics. Performed New York, 21 March 1969. Recorded by Nonesuch.

1971   *Voices* (a cappella radio opera on biblical texts). Performed on WBAI, December 1971.

1973   *Lazarus* (libretto from 12th- and 20th-century texts). Performed New York, 16 February 1974.

1975   *The Conjurer. See* Sahl, Michael.

1976   *Stauf. See* Sahl, Michael.

1977   *Civilization & Its Discontents. See* Sahl, Michael.

1985   *Big Jim and the Small Time Investors. See* Sahl, Michael.

1985   *Towards a New American Opera* (mixed-media).

Saminsky, Lazare (b. Vale-Hotzulovo, near Odessa, Ukraine, 8 November 1882; d. Port Chester, NY, 39 June 1959; in U.S. from 1920; ASCAP; *Amerigrove*)

1916   *The Vision of Ariel* (1 act). Performed Chicago, 9 May 1954.

1924   *The Gagliarda of a Merry Plague* (or *The Plague's Galliard*; opera-ballet; 1 act; after Edgar Allan Poe's *The Masque of the Red Death*). Performed at Times Square Theater, New York, 22 February 1925. Hipsher, 430.

1928   *The Daughter of Jephta* (or *Jephta's Daughter*; opera-ballet; 3 scenes).

1938   *Julian, the Apostate Caesar* (3 acts; or two operas: *Julian* and *The Apostate Caesar*).

Sampson, David George (b. Charlottesville, VA, 26 January 1951; Anderson)

-   *The War Prayer* (30 minutes; libretto by composer and Johanna Keller after Twain). NEA fellowship.

Sams, Carol

1977   *Salome, Daughter of Herodias* (libretto by Ivan Janer). Performed Seattle, WA, 19 January 1977.

1982   *Benjamin Ballou* (libretto by Ralph Rosenblum). Performed by University of Washington Opera Theatre at NOA convention, Portland, OR, 11 November 1982.

1983   *The Beauty and the Beast* (1 act; libretto by composer after the fairy tale). Performed at University of Southern California, Los Angeles, 16 December 1983.

Samuel, Gerhard (b. Bonn, Germany, 20 April 1924; *Amerigrove*; *Who's Who*)

1976   *Johnny* (libretto by Jack Larsen after Jonah and the whale). Performed Valencia, CA, spring 1976.

1981   *The Blood of the Walsungs* (libretto by Roger Brunyate after Mann). Performed Cincinnati, 1981-82 season.

Sanders, Robert L. (b. Chicago, 2 July 1906; d. Delray Beach, FL, 26 December
1974; *Amerigrove*)
  1943 *L'Ag'ya* ("choreographic drama"; choreography by Katherine
     Dunham). Performed at Hollywood Bowl, 1944.

Sandow, Gregory (b. New York, 3 June 1943; AMC; *WhoAm*)
  1975 *The Fall of the House of Usher* (1 act; libretto by Thomas N. Disch
     after Poe). Performed New York, 1975 and 3 February 1979.
  1975 *The Richest Girl in the World Finds Happiness* (1 act—20-25
     minutes; libretto by Robert Patrick). Commissioned by Michael
     Feinjold. Première by Theatre at Noon, New York, 1 December
     1975. Kornick.
  1977 *A Christmas Carol* (1 act—90 minutes; libretto by composer after
     Dickens). Première by Eastern Opera Theatre, Stratford, CT, 21
     December 1977 (Kornick: February 21).
  1980 *Frankenstein* (3 acts; libretto by Thomas N. Disch after Mary
     Shelley's novel). Performed Glens Falls, NY, 7 August 1980, and
     Brookville, NY, June 1981 and 25 June 1982. Kornick.

Sapp, Gary J. (b. Abilene, TX, 11 May 1944; Anderson)
  - *Uto* (chamber opera based on a Japanese Noh drama), for 4 soloists,
    chorus, dancer, chamber ensemble.

Sargon, Simon A. (b. Bombay, India, 6 April 1938; ASCAP; *Who's Who*)
  1984 *Thirst* (1 act; libretto by composer after O'Neill). Performed at
     Southern Methodist University, Dallas, TX, 10 October 1984.
  - *King Saul* (libretto by composer after the Old Testament). *COS*-4.

Savage, James
  1976 *Sanderson's Other World* (1 act). Performed Willoughby, OH, 10
     March 1976.
  1976 *The Proposal* (1 act; libretto by Timothy Ryan after Chekhov).
     Performed Willoughby, OH, 1976.

Savine, Alexander (b. Belgrade, Serbia, 26 April 1881; d. Chicago, 19 January
1949; to Winnipeg in 1908, and in U.S. from 1922; Anderson)
  1919 *Xenia* (1 act). Performed Zurich, Switzerland (in Serbian), 29 May
     1919; and New York (in English), 21 March 1925.
  1943 *The Girl from Sanjak* (4 acts). Performed Chicago, 3 October 1943.

Saylor, Bruce (b. Philadelphia, 24 April 1946; AMC; *Amerigrove*)
  1976 *My Kinsman, Major Molineux* (1 act—50 minutes; libretto by Cary
     Plotkin after Nathaniel Hawthorne). Première by Opera
     Workshop, Pittsburgh, PA, 28 August 1976. Kornick.

Saylor, Maurice
  1984 *Express: A Bus Ride in 1 Act* (libretto by composer). Performed at
     George Washington University, Washington, DC, March 1984 and
     August 1984.

Scarborough, Jan
  1982 *The Majestic Kid* (libretto by Mark Medoff). Performed at Oregon
     Shakespeare Festival, Eugene, 1982.

Scarim, Nicholas (ASCAP)
  1979 *Sumidagawa* (30 minutes; libretto by composer after a Japanese Noh
        play). Performed New London, CT, 27 July 1979. Published by
        Belwin-Mills.
  1980 *Don't Park in Our Park* (4 acts; libretto by Paul Levin; disco rock
        opera). Performed New York, 16 February 1980.
  1980 *The Father* (3 acts without intermission; libretto by composer after
        Strindberg). Performed New York, 29 May 1980.
  1981 *We're Gonna Drive Them Crazy* (rock opera; 30 minutes; libretto by
        composer after Aristophanes *Lysistrata*; to be performed by high-
        school students). Performed by Office of Youth Employment,
        New York, July 1981.
  1986 *The Owl and the Pussycat* (libretto after Lear). Performed by
        Downtown Music Productions, New York, 9 November 1986.
  1988 *My Shadow* ("children's masque"; 5 minutes; libretto after
        Stevenson). Commission by Downtown Music Productions, New
        York; performed there, March 1988.
  1988 *It's Tough to Make a Nickel* (30 minutes; libretto by the composer,
        for grades 1-6). Performed by New York Tenement Museum on
        tour, 1988.
  -     *We Want a Place* (on urban life; for grades 1-6). *COS*-4.

Scarmolin, A. Louis (b. Schio, Italy, 30 July 1890; d. Wyckoff, NJ, 13 July 1969;
        to U.S. at age 10; ASCAP/AMC; Anderson; *Baker's*)
  1950 *The Interrupted Serenade* (35 minutes). Performed Lindenhurst,
        NY, 19 May 1950; Union City, NJ, 26 May 1974. Published by
        Franco Colombo.
  -     *The Caliph* (1 hour).
  -     *The Magic Dream* (1 act). Published by Carl Fischer. *COS*-1.
  -     *The Oath* (115 minutes).

Schaaf, Edward Oswald (b. Brooklyn, NY, 7 August 1869; d. Newark, NJ, 25
        June 1939; *Baker's*, 5th ed.)
        (*Baker's* says Schaaf composed 1 grand opera and "8 smaller
        operas.")

Schad, Walter Charles (b. Brooklyn, NY, 24 August 1889; d. New York, 16
        February 1966; ASCAP; Anderson)
  1938 *Plango* (3 acts). Performed Islip, NY, 1938.

Schaefer, Conrad Bryant (Hipsher)
  -     *Bridges of Stars: or, The Impressment* (3 acts; "research opera").

Schaeffer, William
  -     *The Nightingale and the Rose* (60 minutes; libretto by the composer
        after Wilde).

Scharfman, Nitra
  1975 *The Lieutenant*, with Gene Curty and Chuck Strand (rock opera).
        Performed New York, 11 March 1975.

Schelle, George Michael (b. Philadelphia, 22 January 1950; Anderson; *Who's Who*)
1989   *Soap Opera* (or *Le scelte d'amore*; *The Choices of Love*) (chamber opera; 5 scenes—5 commercials—90 minutes; libretto by the composer; parody of opera and television soap operas). Performed at Butler University, Indianapolis, IN, 8 June 1989.

Schemmer, Tony
1980   *Phaust* (libretto by composer, about Faust in modern times). Performed Cambridge, MA, 4 April 1980.

Schermerhorn, Kenneth (b. Schenectady, NY, 20 November 1929; *Amerigrove*; *Who's Who*)
1981   *The Scarlet Letter* (after Hawthorne). Performed by Florentine Opera, Milwaukee, WI, 1981-82 season.

Schickele, Peter (= P. D. Q. Bach; b. Ames, IA, 17 July 1935; *Amerigrove*; *Who's Who*)
1974   *The Knight of the Burning Pestle* (libretto by F. Beaumont and J. Fletcher, adapted by B. Jones). The only one on this list not attributed to P. D. Q. Bach.
1975   *The Stoned Guest (S.86 proof)* (a "half-act opera"—35 minutes; libretto by composer), for off-coloratura soprano, mezzanine soprano, bargain-countertenor, basso blotto, houndentenor-dog, instruments. Première at Weber State College, Ogden, UT, November 1975. Published by Elkan Vogel; recorded on Vanguard VSD 6536. Kornick.
1982   *A Little Nightmare Music*, music arranged from Mozart's *Eine kleine Nachtmusik* (1 act—20 minutes; libretto by composer). Première at Carnegie Hall, New York, 27 December 1982. Kornick.
1984   *The Abduction of Figaro* (parody opera; 3 acts—150 minutes; libretto by composer). NEA grant. Première by Minnesota Opera, Minneapolis, 24 April 1984; also performed in Stockholm, Sweden, July 1989. Published by Presser. Kornick.
1988   *Oedipus Tex* (spoof; 1 act—30 minutes; libretto by composer). Première as oratorio at Jessie Jones Hall, Houston, TX, 1 April 1986; as opera on Plymouth Music Series, Minneapolis, 15 March 1988. Kornick.
-       *Hansel & Gretel & Ted & Alice* (1 act); for bargain-countertenor, harpsichord beriberitone/calliope, piano.

Schiff, David (b. Bronx, NY, 30 August 1945; *Amerigrove*)
1976   *Gimpel the Fool* (Yiddish libretto by Isaac Bashevis Singer). First written with piano accompaniment; expanded in 1979-80 for instruments suggesting a klezmer band. Performed New York, 16 May 1979 and 6 March 1980.
1982   *Dubliners* (libretto by Joyce).

Schifrin, Lalo (b. Buenos Aires, Argentina, 21 June 1932; in U.S. from 1958; *Amerigrove*)
1989   *Frida* (libretto by Hilary Beecher or Migdalia Cruz after the life of the Mexican artist). OPERA America grant, 1989. Performed Philadelphia, 1991.

Schimmel, William Michael (b. Philadelphia, 22 September 1946; Anderson; *WhoAm*; *Who's Who*)

1979   *The Old Man* (30 minutes; libretto by Wallace Shawn). Performed Stockbridge, MA, summer 1979.

1980   *Jane Avril* (90 minutes; libretto by Jane Maria Robbins, about the Paris dancer). Performed Westport, CT, 21 August 1980; and at Provincetown Playhouse, New York, August 1983.

1983   *Dreams of Dirty Women* (30 minutes; libretto by composer after St. Augustine). Performed at Merry Enterprise Theatre One Act Play Festival, New York, August 1980.

1981   *Il fornicatione* (satire; 20 minutes; libretto by Charles Green). Performed by Manhattan Punch Line, New York, fall 1981.

1982   *Four Tantrick Pieces* (1 act; libretto by composer and Micki Goodman). Performed by Studio-Muse, New York, spring 1982.

1982   *The Juniper Tree: A Tragic Household Tale*, with Wendy Kesselman (70 minutes; libretto by Wendy Kesselman after Grimm). NEA grant. Performed Stockbridge, MA, 7 July 1982.

1982   *Spanish Suite* (20 minutes; libretto by composer and Micki Goodman after Unamuno). Performed at Carnegie Recital Hall, New York, 1982.

1982   *A Little Wine with Lunch* (90 minutes; libretto by John Hartz). Performed at Merry Enterprise Theatre, New York, summer 1982.

1983   *Dick Deterred* (75 minutes; libretto by composer and David Edgar, about the Watergate scandal as a parody of Shakespeare's *Richard III*). Performed at William Redfield Theater, New York, January 1983.

1983   *People II—The Species Strikes Back* (90 minutes; libretto by Scott Burris). Performed at New Broadway Theatre, Chicago, spring 1983.

1983   *Anthology for a Spacial Buenos Aires* (10 minutes; libretto by the composer and Micki Goodman, about Borges and Le Corbusier). Performed by Studio-Muse, New York, fall 1983.

1984   *In Praise of Capital Punishment* (70 minutes; libretto by the composer and Scott Burris). Performed at William Redfield Theatre, New York, 11 November 1984.

-   *David and Bathsheba* (1 act).

Schirmer, William Louis (b. Cleveland, OH, 25 February 1941; Anderson; *WhoAm*)

1969   *The Glass Menagerie.*

1983   *Our Town.* Performed Jacksonville, FL, 1983-84 season.

Schlein, Irving (b. New York, 18 August 1905; ASCAP/AMC; Anderson)

-   *Stackalee* (1 act). *COS-1.*

Schmidt, Harvey (b. Dallas, TX, 12 September 1929; *Amerigrove*)

1960   *The Fantasticks* (musical; 2 acts; libretto by Tom Jones after Edmund Rostand's *Les Romanesques*). Première at Sullivan Street Playhouse, New York, 3 May 1960; performed as an opera by Skylight Comic Opera, Milwaukee, WI, 1988. Recorded by Polygram (1964). Kornick.

1963   *110 in the Shade* (musical theater; 2 acts; lyrics by Tom Jones, based on N. Richard Nash's *Rainmakers*). Première at Broadhurst

Theatre, New York, 24 October 1963; performed by New York City Opera in a run beginning 21 July 1992. Recorded by RCA. Kornick.

Schmidt, Karl (b. Schwerin, Mecklenburg, Germany, 24 September 1864; d. 1950; citizen, 1906; Hipsher)

1930   *Lady of the Lake* (grand opera; 3 acts; libretto by Wallace Taylor Hughes after Sir Walter Scott). Performed by American Opera Society of Chicago, 6 December 1931. Bispham Medal, 1930.

Schmitz, Alan

1978   *Julius Caesar* (4 acts; libretto after Shakespeare). Performed New Brunswick, NJ, 7 April 1978.

Schneider, Joshua

1989   *Ladies* (libretto by Eve Ensler, about women's shelters in New York). Performed by Music-Theatre Group, New York, 4 April 1989.

Schoen, ?

1986   *Traveling in My Chair* (libretto by Shearer). Performed by Music Theatre Festival, San Francisco, 1 July 1986.

Schoenefeld, Henry (b. Milwaukee, WI, 4 October 1857; d. Los Angeles, 4 August 1936; to U.S. 1879; *Amerigrove*; Hipsher)

-   *Atala: or, The Love of Two Savages* (3 acts; libretto by Bernard McConville after René Chateaubriand's work of the same name; about Indians in Florida).

-   *Wachicanta* (Indian pantomime-ballet).

Schoenhard, Carol

1976   *The Dollmaker* (American folk opera). Performed New Wilmington, PA, January 1976.

Schonthal-Seckel, Ruth (b. Hamburg, Germany, 27 June 1924; U.S. citizen, 1956; Anderson)

1980   *The Courtship of Camilla* (1 act; after Milne's *Ugly Duckling*).

1989   *Princess Maleen* (70 minutes; libretto by composer and Wallis Wood after Grimm; for children). Commission by Westchester Conservatory, White Plains, NY; performed there, 20 May 1989.

Schoop, Paul (b. Zürich, Switzerland, 31 July 1909; d. Los Angeles, 1 January 1976; to U.S. early; Anderson; *Baker's*)

-   *The Enchanted Trumpet* (comic opera).

Schramm, Harold (b. Chicago, 3 July 1935; AMC; Anderson)

1966   *Shilappadikaram* (*The Ankle Bracelet*) (40 minutes; libretto by Alain Danielou after a story in 2nd-century Tamil). Performed New York, 13 April 1966. Published by Music Corporation of America.

Schreier, Daniel
1983   *Hopi Prophecies*, with Michael S. Roth (100 minutes; libretto by
        composers after three Hopi legends). Performed New York
        Theatre Workshop, New York, 1983.

Schreiner, Elissa
-       *Sneakers* (55 minutes; libretto by Sunnie Miller, Judith Weinstein,
        and Arnold Somers). Published Dramatic Publishing Co.

Schroeder, William A. (b. Brooklyn, NY, 10 November 1888; d. Wilton, CN, 20
        April 1960; Anderson; Hipsher—not to be confused with William A.
        Schroeder, b. Brooklyn, NY, 24 April 1921)
-       *Atala* (libretto by Rida Johnson Young).

Schryock, Buren (b. Sheldon, IA, 13 December 1881; d. San Diego, CA, 20
        January 1974; Anderson; *Baker's*; Hipsher)
        (Schryock wrote his own librettos.)
1930   *Flavia* (4 acts). Performed 1946? *Baker's* dates it 1930-46.
1948   *Mary and John.*
1951   *Nancy and Arthur.*
1954   *Malena and Nordico.*
1955   *Tanshu and Sanchi.*

Schubert, Peter (b. New York, 1 April 1946; *WhoAm*)
1983   *Perpetual* (multimedia; after Ellen Terry). Performed by Opera
        Uptown, New York, 8 May 1983.
1986   *The Bus to Stockport and Other Stories*, with John Cage and Eric
        Valinsky. Performed by Opera Uptown, New York, 20 February
        1986.

Schuller, Gunther (b. New York, 22 November 1925; BMI; *Amerigrove*; *Baker's*;
        Who's Who)
1966   *The Visitation* (3 acts; after Kafka's *The Trial*). Performed
        Hamburg, Germany, 12 October 1966; New York, 28 June 1967;
        and San Francisco, 28 October 1967. Published by Associated
        Music.
1970   *The Fisherman and His Wife* (children's opera; 1 hour—13 scenes;
        libretto by John Updike after Grimm). Performed Boston, 8 May
        1970.
1982   *Der gelbe Klang*, put together by Schuller from piano sketches by
        Thomas de Hartmann, a Russian composer—including editing and
        orchestration (surrealist multimedia work; 45 minutes; libretto by
        Vassily Kandinsky). Performed by Speculum Musicae, New York,
        9 February 1982.
-       *Der Besuch alten Dame* (libretto after Dürrenmatt).

Schuman, William (b. New York, 4 August 1910; d. there, 2 February 1992;
        Amerigrove; *Who's Who*)
1952   *The Mighty Casey* (1 act; libretto by Jeremy Gury after E. L.
        Thayer). Performed Hartford, CT, 4 May 1953, at Museum of
        Modern Art, New York, 11 May 1961, and by Glimmerglass
        Opera, Cooperstown, NY, 1987, and 24 June 1990. Revised as the

cantata *Casey at the Bat*, performed Washington, DC, 6 April 1976.

1988　*A Question of Taste* (1 act—50 minutes; libretto by J. D. McClatchy after Roald Dahl's "Taste"). Commission for Glimmerglass Opera, Cooperstown, NY, by a grant from the Eugene V. and Clare Thaw Charitable Trust. Performed there, August 1988, by Juilliard School, New York, 1 September 1988 and January 1989, and Glimmerglass Opera, Cooperstown, 24 June 1989 (Kornick has this last performance as première). Published by Presser. (*Baker's* puts this opera as being composed by Gunther Schuller!)

Schumann, Walter (b. New York, 8 October 1913; d. Minneapolis, MN, 21 August 1958; BMI; Anderson; *Baker's*)

1953　*John Brown's Body.* Performed Los Angeles, 21 September 1953.

Schwartz, Francis (b. Altoona, PA, 10 March 1940; ASCAP; *Amerigrove*; Anderson; *Baker's*)

1968　*Auschwitz*, for tape, lights, odors, movement. Performed San Juan, Puerto Rico, 15 May 1968.

1970　*My Name's Caligula, What's Yours?*, for 3 actor-instrumentalists. Performed New York, 2 March 1975.

1974　*Yo protesto.* Performed San Juan, Puerto Rico, 23 March 1974.

1975　*Caligula.* Performed New York, 3 March 1975.

1975　*Time, Sound, and the Hooded Man.* Performed Buenos Aires, Argentina, 16 July 1975.

1976　*Is There Sex in Heaven?* (chamber opera).

1988　*Los 10,000 ojos* (libretto by Roberto Ramos Perea). Performed San Juan, Puerto Rico, July 1987 and July 1988.

Schwartz, Herman

-　*Negro Opera* (1 act).

Schwartz, Marvin (b. Bronx, NY, 4 February 1937; Anderson)

1971　*Look and Long* (2 acts; libretto after Gertrude Stein). Performed Lake Placid, NY, 27 July 1971 (Anderson: commission and première by the After Dinner Opera Company, 1972).

Schwartz, Paul (b. Vienna, Austria, 27 July 1907; in U.S. from 1938; ACA; Anderson)

1956　*The Experiment* (40 minutes; libretto by composer's wife Kathryn Schwartz after Hawthorne). Performed Gambier, OH, 27 January 1956.

Schwarz, Ira Paul (b. Sheldon, IA, 24 February 1922; Anderson; *WhoAm*)

1965　*All in Black My Love Went Riding* (1 act; libretto by Gary Luckert). Performed Minot, ND, 11 November 1965.

1968　*The Wedding.*

1989　*Martin Luther and Beloved Community.* Performed Brockport, NY, 1989.

Scott, ?

1986　*Size 12* (libretto by Glover). Performed by San Francisco School of Dramatic Arts, 8 July 1986.

Scott, K. Lee (b. Langdale, AL, 19 April 1950; ASCAP)
1985   *The Woman at the Well* (chancel opera; libretto by Grace Hawthorne after the New Testament story of Jesus and the woman at Jacob's well). Commission by Samford University, Birmingham, AL; performed there, 10 April 1985. The libretto was also set by Edwin C. Robertson.

Scott, Robert Owens
1987   *A Charles Dickens Christmas* (libretto by Douglas Cohen and Thomas Tuce). Performed by Theatreworks/USA, New York, 1987-88 season.

Scott, Tom (b. Campbellsburg, KY, 28 May 1912; d. New York, 12 August 1961; Anderson; *Baker's*)
1956   *The Fisherman* (70 minutes; after Wilde). (Anderson: 1936.)

Seager, Gerald
1971   *The Marriage of the Grocer of Seville* (1 act). Performed Columbus, OH, February 1971.

Seagrave, Malcolm
1977   *Birthday of the Infanta* (1 act; libretto by Janet Winters after Wilde). Performed by Hidden Valley Opera, Carmel Valley, CA, 2 April 1977.
1987   *The Fall of Freddy the Leaf*. Performed by Hidden Valley Opera, Carmel Valley, CA, June 1987.

Seale, Stan
1985   *Singing School* (libretto by Lurrine Burgess; for children). Performed at Southern California Conservatory, Sun Valley, CA, 23 December 1985.

Secunda, Sholom (b. Alexandria, Russia, 23 August 1894; d. New York, 13 June 1974; citizen, 1918; associated with Yiddish Theater, New York, 1916-73, for which he wrote over 40 operettas; Anderson; *Baker's*)
1925   *Sulamith.*
1933   *I Would if I Could* (operetta; originally in Yiddish), including song "Bei mir bist du schön."

Selden, Margery Stomne (b. Chicago; *Who's Who*)
1977   *The New Dress* (20 minutes). Performed at College of Saint Elizabeth, NJ, 20 October 1977.

Seletsky, Harold
1987   *Song of Insanity: A Schizophrenic Journey* (1 act). Performed by Golden Fleece, New York, 16 June 1987.

Selig, Robert Leigh (b. Evanston, IL, 29 January 1939; Anderson; *Baker's*)
1972   *Chocorua* (1 act; libretto by Richard Moore), for voice, chorus, chamber orchestra. Performed Tanglewood, MA, 6 August 1972 (Anderson: August 2).

Sellars, James (b. Fort Smith, AR, 8 October 1943; *Amerigrove*)
1960 *The Family* (1 act; libretto by W. Giorda).
1979 *Chanson dada* (monodrama; after three poems by Tristan Tzara), for mezzosoprano and small orchestra. Performed by Brooklyn Philharmonic Orchestra, Meet the Moderns Series, New York, 26 April 1985.
1984 *The Turing Opera* (21 scenes; libretto by T. Meyer).

Selley, Harry Rowe
- *Leila* (3 acts).
- *Lotus Sun.*
- *Romeo and Juliet.*

Selmer, Kathryn Lande (b. Staten Island, NY, 6 November 1930; Anderson; Cohen)
- *The Shoemaker and the Elf* (children's opera).
- *The Princess and the Pea* (children's opera).
- *The Princess Who Couldn't Laugh* (children's opera).

Sendrey, Albert Richard (b. Chicago, 26 December 1911; Anderson; *Baker's*)
1971 *Bohème-a-Go-Go* (rock opera).

Serlin, Jerome
1988 *1000 Airplanes on the Roof*, with Philip Glass and David Henry Hwang. Performed at American Music Theater Festival, New York?, 21 September 1988; and London, England, October 1989.

Serulnikoff, Jack
1960 *This Evening* (1 act). Performed Bennington, VT, 20 June 1960.

Sessions, Roger (b. Brooklyn, NY, 28 December 1896; d. Princeton, NJ, 16 March 1985; *Amerigrove*)
1910 *Lancelot and Elaine* (libretto after Tennyson).
1947 *The Trial of Lucullus* (1 act; libretto after Bertold Brecht). Performed Berkeley, CA, 18 April 1947, composer conducting.
1963 *Montezuma* (3 acts; libretto after G. A. Borghese). Performed West Berlin, Germany, 19 April 1964; Ann Arbor, MI, 3 November 1971; Boston, 31 May 1976 (this last listed as American première by Anderson). Published by Edward B. Marks.

Seymour, John Laurence (b. Los Angeles, 18 January 1893; d. 2 February 1986; ASCAP; *Amerigrove*; *Baker's*; Hipsher)
(*The Affected Maids*, *The Devil and Tom Walker*, and *A Protégé of the Mistress* are mentioned in *Hollywood Daily Citizen*, 31 October 1921.)
1920 *Les Précieuses ridicules* (*The Affected Maids*) (1 act; libretto after Molière's work of the same title).
1921 *The Devil and Tom Walker* (operetta; 3 acts; libretto by H. C. Tracy after Washington Irving). Performed 1926 or 1942. (*Baker's* date: 1942; Hipsher: 1926.)
1921 *The Protégé of the Mistress* (1 act; Hipsher: 4 acts).
1922 *Bachelor Belles* (operetta; libretto by R. Seymour).

1934   *In the Pasha's Garden* (tragic opera; 1 act; libretto by Henry Chester Tracy after Harrison Griswold Dwight). Première by Metropolitan Opera, New York, 24 January 1935. Bispham Medal, 1945.

1936   *Golden Days* (operetta; libretto by composer).

1936   *Hollywood Madness* (operetta; libretto by composer).

1937   *Two Gentlemen of Verona* (operetta).

1942   *The Three Brothers* (operetta).

1949   *Ming Toy* (musical).

1960   *The Lure and the Promise* (musical).

1970   *Ramona* (libretto by H. C. Tracy). Performed Provo, UT, 11 November 1970.

1977   *Ollanta, el Jefe Kolla* (in Spanish; libretto by F. Diaz de Medina).

-     *Antigone* (*The Snake Woman*) (5 acts).

-     *The Closed Gate* (pantomime).

-     *The Maid, the Demon, and the Samurai* (pantomime).

Shackelford, Rudy (b. Newport News, VA, 18 April 1944; *Amerigrove*)
1975   *The Wound-Dresser* (monodrama; text by Walt Whitman).

Shadle, Charles
1989   *Friends and Dinosaurs* (35 minutes; libretto by Helen O'Keefe; for children, with audience participation). Commission and première by Longwood Opera, Needham, MA, 20 May 1989.

Shaffer, Jeanne Ellison (b. Knoxville, TN, 25 May 1925; ASCAP; Anderson; Cohen; *WhoAm*)
1977   *The Ghost of Susan B. Anthony* (chamber opera; 1 act). Performed at Huntingdon College, Montgomery, AL, 12 November 1977.

1980   *The Heart of Dixie* (libretto by Robert S. Barmettler). Performed at Huntingdon College, 20 November 1980.

1986   *The End of the Line* (1 act; libretto by Robert S. Barmettler). Performed at Huntingdon College, 2 November 1986.
     (Shaffer also composed a musical, *Balls!*, 1985.)

Shaffer, Sherwood (b. Beeville, TX, 15 November 1934; AMC; Anderson; *WhoAm*)
1981   *A Winter's Tale* (40 minutes; libretto by Walter Freimanis). Performed by OPERA America Showcase, January 1981.

Shahan, Paul W. (b. Grafton, WV, 2 January 1923; Anderson)
1963   *The Stubblefield Story.*

Shapiro, Michael Jeffery (b. Brooklyn, NY, 1 February 1951; *Who's Who*)
-     *The Love of Don Perlimplin and Belissa in the Garden* (1 hour; libretto after Federico García Lorca). *COS*-3.

Shapleigh, Bertram (b. Boston, 15 January 1871; d. Washington, DC, 2 July 1940; *Amerigrove*; *Baker's*)
     (*Amerigrove*: he wrote 2 grand operas and five 1-act operas.)

Sharkey, Jack
- *And on the Sixth Day* (libretto by composer and Dave Reiser; Christmas opera, covering the whole period from creation to Christmas). Published by Samuel French.
(Sharkey also composed three musicals, all listed in *COS*-4.)

Sharpley, John
1988 *The Twelve Months Brothers.*

Shatin, Judith (b. Brookline, MA, 21 November 1949; ACA; Anderson; Cohen; *WhoAm*)
1981 *Follies and Fancies* (55 minutes; libretto by composer and Gloria Russo after Molière's *Les Précieux Ridicules*). Performed Charlottesville, VA, 14 August 1981.
1983 *Job* (opera-oratorio), for 10 singers and piano.
1990 *Carreño* (1 act; about Teresa Carreño). Performed by Golden Fleece, New York, June 1990.

Shaw, James R. (b. Philadelphia, 27 August 1930; Anderson; *WhoAm*)
1982 *Beanstalk!* (libretto by Joseph Robinette). Performed by New York Children's Theatre, Pleasantville, NY, 1982. Published by I. E. Clark.
1984 *The Wedding of the Widow Wade* (1 act). Performed at Glassboro State College, NJ, 12 April 1984.
1987 *The Minion and the Three Riddles* (50 minutes; libretto by Joseph Robinette, for performance by adults or children). Commission by National Federation of Music Clubs; performed at their convention, Miami, FL, 26 April 1987. Published by MMB Music.
- *Ashes, Ashes, All Fall Down* (1 act; libretto by Joseph Robinette; for children). Published by Dramatic Publishing Co.
- *The Legend of the Sun Child* (50 minutes; libretto by Joseph Robinette; for children). Published by Dramatic Publishing Co.
- *Penny and the Magic Medallion* (1 hour; libretto by composer and Joseph Robinette; for children). Performed Glassboro, NJ. Published by I. E. Clark.

Shawn, Allen E. (b. New York, 27 August 1948; *Who's Who*)
1983 *The Music Teacher* (105 minutes; libretto by Wallace Shawn).

Sheehan, John J.
1981 *Objective Love* (libretto by Terry Megan). Performed by Omaha Magic Theatre, NE, July 1981.
1983 *Aliens under Glass II.* Performed by Omaha Magic Theatre, NE, 1983.
1984 *Aliens Alive.* Performed by Omaha Magic Theatre, NE, January 1984.
1984 *Astro*Bride*, with Joe Budenholzer and Jerry Kazakevicius (1 act; science fiction libretto by Jo Ann Schmidman). Performed by Omaha Magic Theatre, NE, 21 December 1984.
1985 *The Rip-it-Up Hate Aggregate Rape Tapes*, with Joe Budenholzer (libretto by James Larson). Performed by Omaha Magic Theatre, NE, 22 February 1985.

1987   *Walking through Walls*, with Bill Farber and Mark Nelson (multimedia; libretto by Megan Terry and Jo Ann Schmidman). Performed by Omaha Magic Theatre, NE, 20 November 1987. (Sheehan also composed three musicals, all listed in *COS*-4.)

Sheffer, Jonathan Bard
1980   *Camera Obscura* (curtain-raiser; 10 minutes; libretto by Robert Patrick). Performed Waterford, CT, 18 July, 1980.

1981   *The Mistake* (35 minutes; libretto by Stephen Wadsworth, about a soprano during the intermission of a concert). Performed by Central City Opera, Denver, CO, 16 August 1981.

Sheffer, Paul
1961   *A Fifth for Bridge* (1 act). Performed San Francisco, 3 December 1961.

(Sheffer also composed a musical, *The Rise of David Levinsky*, 1983.)

Shelley, Harry Rowe (b. New Haven, CT, 2 June 1858; d. Short Beach, CT, 12 September 1947; *Amerigrove*; Hipsher)
1910   *Romeo and Juliet* (3 acts).

1911   *Old Black Joe* (1 acts; libretto by C. M. Greene).

-   *Leila* (3 acts).

-   *Lotus San.*

Sheng, Bright
(1989-90 composer-in-residence, Chicago Lyric Opera.)

Shephard, Thomas Z. (AMC)
1979   *The Last of the Just* (1 act; libretto by Gerald Walker after Schwarzbart). Performed Aspen, CO, August 1979.

-   *That Pig of a Molette* (libretto by Sheldon Harnick).

Shere, Charles Everett (b. Berkeley, CA, 20 August 1935; AMC; *Amerigrove*; *Baker's*; WhoAm)
1978   *The Bride Stripped Bare by Her Bachelors, Even* (3 hours—3 acts; libretto by composer, about the painter Marcel Duchamp after Duchamp's account of his work). This opera incorporates the composer's *The Box of 1914*. Performed at Mills College, Oakland, CA, 1 December 1984.

1981   *The Box of 1914* (2 acts—20 minutes; libretto by Marcel Duchamp based on his work of the same name, related to his *The Bride Stripped Bare by Her Bachelors, Even*). NEA fellowship. Première by New Music Ensemble, San Francisco Conservatory, 30 January 1981. Kornick.

1987   *Ladies Voices* (5 acts—7 minutes; libretto after Gertrude Stein). Commission by Noh Oratorio Society. Performed at Berkeley Art Center, CA, 30 October 1987.

1989   *I Like It to Be a Play* (11 minutes; libretto after Gertrude Stein), for tenor, baritone, bass, string quartet. Commission by Noh Oratorio Society. Performed San Francisco, 6 February 1989.

Sherman, Kim Daryl (b. Elgin, IL, 6 August 1954; ASCAP; Cohen)
1979   *Claire.*
1983   *Lenny and the Heartbreakers*, with Scott Killiam (libretto by the
           composers and Kenneth Robins). Performed at New York
           Shakespeare Festival, New York, 22 December 1983.
1986   *Femme fatale* (libretto by Laura Farabough, about Mata Hari and
           Greta Garbo). Performed by Minnesota Opera, Minneapolis, 11
           April 1986.
1987   *A Long Island Dreamer* (libretto by Paul Selig). Performed by
           Minnesota Opera, St. Paul, 9 April 1987.
1989   *Red Tide* (30 minutes; libretto by Paul Selig). OPERA America
           grant. Performed by Minnesota Opera, Minneapolis, 23 March
           1987.

Shields, Alice Feree (b. New York, 18 February 1943; ACA; Anderson; Cohen;
           WhoAm)
1975   *Odyssey* (1 act), for 2 soloists, male chorus, chamber orchestra.
           NEA grant. *COS*-2.
1978   *Shaman* ("full length"), for singers, amplified chamber orchestra,
           and tape. Performed by American Chamber Opera, New York, 8
           May 1987.
1989   *Wraecca* (15 minutes; libretto by composer after Anglo-Saxon
           poems). Performed by Golden Fleece, New York, 27 June 1989.

Shiflett, Melissa
1989   *Without Colors* (20 minutes; libretto by Mac Wellman after Calvino).
           Performed by Minnesota Opera, Minneapolis, 23 March 1989.

Shinn, Randall (b. Clinton, OK, 28 September 1944; ASCAP; Anderson)
1986   *Wilbur!* Performed Tempe, AZ, 25 April 1986.
    -     *Claire* (libretto by Levin Dawson). Arizona State University grant.

Shore, William
1964   *Wharf's Edge* (30 minutes; libretto by Kenneth Janes). Performed
           New York, 28 February 1964.

Short, Ron
1986   *Pretty Polly* (libretto by composer and Don Baker; for children).
           Performed Whitesburg, KY, 6 October 1986.

Siegal, Donald
1979   *A Long Way to Boston*, with Michael Lohman and Susan
           Birkenhead. Performed East Haddam, CT, 11 September 1979.
1986   *212* (libretto by Victor Joseph; about the House Un-American
           Activities Committee in the 1950s). Performed by Musical
           Theatre Works, New York, 10 November 1986.

Siegel, Norman
1970   *Who Stole the Crown Jewels* (libretto by Jean Reavey). Performed
           New York, December 1970.

Siegmeister, Elie (b. New York, 15 January 1909; d. Manhasset, Long Island, NY, 10 March 1991; BMI/AMC; *Amerigrove*; *Baker's*)

1942   *Doodle Dandy of the USA* (play with music; 2 hours; libretto by Saul Lancourt). Performed New York, 26 December 1942. Published by Musette.

1944   *Sing Out, Sweet Land* (musical; 150 minutes; libretto by Walter Kerr). Performed Hartford, CT, 10 November 1944. Published by Northern Music.

1945   *A Tooth for Paul Revere.* (In neither *Amerigrove* nor *Baker's*.)

1952   *Darling Corie* (1 act; libretto by Lewis Allen). Performed at Hofstra University, Hempstead, NY, 18 February 1954. Published by Chappell.

1955   *Miranda and the Dark Young Man* (60 minutes; libretto by Edward Eager). Performed Hartford, CT, 9 May 1956. Published by Shawnee Press.

1958   *The Mermaid in Lock No. 7* (50 minutes; libretto by Edward Mabley). Performed Pittsburgh, PA, 20 July 1958. Published by Peters.

1963   *Dublin Song* (3 acts; libretto by Edward Mabley after O'Casey's *The Plough and the Stars*). Performed St. Louis, 15 May 1963. Revised as:

1969   *The Plough and the Stars.* Performed Baton Rouge, LA, 16 March 1969.

1976   *Night of the Moonspell* (comedy; 3 acts; libretto by Edward Mabley after Shakespeare's *Midsummer Night's Dream*). Commission and première by Shreveport Symphony Society, LA, 14 November 1976. Kornick.

1982   *The Marquesa of O* (2 hours; libretto by Norman Rosten after von Kleist). NEA fellowship.

1985   *Angel Levine* (1 act; libretto by Edward Mabley after Bernard Malamud). Performed by Jewish Opera at the Y, New York, 5 October 1985.

1985   *The Lady of the Lake* (1 act; libretto by Edward Mabley after Malamud). Performed by Jewish Opera at the Y, New York, 5 October 1985.

Sierra, Roberto (b. Vega Baja, Puerto Rico, 9 October 1953; ASCAP; *Baker's*; *WhoAm*; *Who's Who*)

1984   *El mensajero de plata* (*The Silver Messenger*) (chamber opera; 2 acts; libretto by Myrna Casas, about life in Puerto Rico). NEA and OPERA America grants. Commission by Opera de Camera and Continuum, San Juan. Performed there, 12 April 1986 and 9 October 1986.

1985   *Estrella de Mar* (libretto by Myrna Casas, about life in Puerto Rico). Performed San Juan, summer 1985.

Sierra, Ruben

1988   *Voices of Christmas.* Performed Seattle, WA, 13 April 1984.

Sifler, Paul John (b. Ljubljana, Slovenia, 31 December 1911; U.S. citizen, 1936; Anderson; *WhoAm*)

1972   *The Nine Suitors* (operetta). Published by Fredonia Press.

Silsbee, Ann Loomis (b. Cambridge, MA, 21 August 1930; Anderson; Cohen; *WhoAm*)

1984   *The Nightingale's Apprentice* (45 minutes; libretto by Margaret Weaver; for children). Commission by TROIKA Association, Ithaca, NY; performed there, 13 April 1984.

1989   *The People Tree* (1 hour; libretto by composer). Commission by First Street Playhouse, New York; performed there, May 1989 and 1989-90 season.

Silver, Sheila Jane (b. Seattle, WA, 3 October 1946; Anderson; Cohen; *WhoAm*; *Who's Who*)

1985   *The Thief of Love* (130 minutes; libretto by composer after a Bengali story). Performed by National Music Theater Network, New York, June 1985.

Silverman, Faye-Ellen (b. New York, 2 October 1947; Anderson; Cohen; *WhoAm*; *Who's Who*)

1974   *The Miracle of Nemirov* (chamber opera; 1 act; libretto by composer). Published by Seesaw Music. *COS*-2.

Silverman, Stanley Joel (b. New York, 5 July 1938; *Amerigrove*; *WhoAm*)

1968   *Elephant Steps* (2 acts; libretto by Richard Foreman). Performed Tanglewood, MA, 7 August 1968.

1969   *The Satyricon* (libretto by Peter Raby). Performed Stratford, Ontario, Canada, 4 July 1969.

1971   *Dream Tantras for Western Massachusetts* ("A Musical Strategy"; libretto by Richard Foreman). Performed Stockbridge, MA, 12 August 1971.

1972   *Doctor Selavey's Magic Theatre* ("absurdist opera"; libretto by T. Hendry and Richard Foreman). Performed Stockbridge, MA, 12 August 1972.

1972   *Oedipus the King* (after Anthony Burgess). Performed Minneapolis, MN, November 1972.

1973   *Stage Leers and Love Songs*. Performed Stockbridge, MA, 15 August 1973.

1974   *Hotel for Criminals* (satire; 2 acts—90 minutes; libretto by Richard Foreman after Louis Feulliade's silent films). Commission by National Opera Institute. Première at Lenox Arts Center, Stockbridge, MA, 14 August 1974; also performed by Music-Theatre Performing Group, Exchange Theatre, Wesbeth, NY, 30 December 1974. Kornick.

1974   *Up from Paradise* (musical play; after Arthur Miller's *The Creation of the World and Other Business*). Performed Ann Arbor, MI, summer 1974; at Kennedy Center, Washington, DC, 1977; Whitney Museum, New York, 1982; and by Jewish Repertory Theatre, New York, 1983.

1978   *The American Imagination* (libretto by Richard Foreman). Performed New York, 18 February 1978.

1980   *Madame Adare* (satire; 1 act—60 minutes; libretto by Richard Foreman). Commission and première by New York City Opera, 9 October 1980. Published by International Creative Management. Kornick.

1981   *The Columbine String Quartet Tonight* (90 minutes; libretto by Tina Howe). Performed Stockbridge, MA, 2 July 1981.

1984   *The Golem* (musical play).

1984   *Africanis instructus* (musical play; 100 minutes; libretto by Richard Foreman). Commission by Massachusetts Council on the Arts and Humanities. Performed Stockbridge, 8 August 1984, and at Lenox Arts Center, NY, 14 January 1986. Published by International Creative Management.

1986   *A Good Life* (75 minutes; libretto by Jeff Moss after the Russian story used by Stravinsky in *L'Histoire du soldat*; for children). Performed at Kennedy Center, Washington, DC, April 1986. Published by International Creative Management. Video tape available.

1986   *Black Sea Follies* (formerly called *Shostakovich*; 2 hours; libretto by Paul Schmidt, about Shostakovich and Stalin, incorporating music by Shostakovich). Performed Stockbridge, MA, 6 August 1986. Published by International Creative Management. Video tape available.

1989   *Paradise for the Worried* (libretto by Holly Anderson after early 20th-century sources; conceived by Kinematic). Performed Stockbridge, MA, 5 July 1989. Published by International Creative Management.

1990   *Love and Science* (libretto by Richard Foreman). OPERA America grant. Performed Stockbridge, MA, 5 July 1990.

Simeone, Harry (b. Newark, NJ, 11 May 1911; Anderson)
1956   *The Emperor's New Clothes* (2 acts). Televised on CBS-TV, New York, 1956. Published by Shawnee Press.

Simmons, Homer (b. Evansville, IN, 6 August 1900; Anderson)
-    *Red Riding Hood*.

Simon, Stephen (b. New York, 3 May 1937; *Amerigrove*)
1976   *Casey at the Bat*. Performed White Plains, NY, 15 May 1976.

Simons, Netty (b. New York, 26 October 1913; ACA; Anderson; *WhoAm*)
1958   *The Bell Witch of Tennessee* (1 act—60 minutes; libretto by Joan Simons).

Sinding, Christian
1980   *Fulynnghn*, with Gordon Mumma and Pauline Oliveros ("a funky fairy tale").

Singer, André (b. in Hungary, 1 November 1907; U.S. citizen, 1944; Anderson)
-    *Alcottiang* (3 scenes). *COS*-1.

Singleton, Alvin (b. Brooklyn, NY, 28 December 1940; *Amerigrove*)
1976   *Dream Sequence, '76* (2 acts; libretto by composer). Performed Graz, Austria.

1981   *Necessity is a Mother* (wordless drama).

Siposs, George
1986   *Modesta Avila* (110 minutes; based on an incident in California history). Performed Westminster, CA, 10 October 1986.

Sirota, Robert (Benson) (b. New York, 13 October 1949; *WhoAm*)
1982   *Bontshe the Silent* (chamber opera; 1 hour; libretto by Robert B. Shaw after Peretz). NOA New Opera Competition finalist. Performed at Harvard University, 8 May 1982.
1987   *The Tailor of Gloucester* (for children; 1 act; libretto after Beatrix Potter). Performed at Boston University, 7 February 1987.

Sirotta, Michael
1985   *Mythos Oedipus*, with Elizabeth Swados, Connie Alexander, Genji Ito, and David Sawyer (90 minutes; libretto by Ellen Stewart after Sophocles; in Greek). Performed Delphi, Greece, summer 1985, and by LaMama, New York, 6 February 1988.

Sistarelli, Umberto (he played in the Los Angeles Symphony in 1920)
-    *La perla di donges.*
-    *Ponce de Leon.*

Six, Herbert
1966   *Without Memorial Banners* (jazz opera; 2 acts; libretto by Dan Jaffe). Performed at University of Missouri-Kansas City, 24 March 1966.
1971   *All Cats Turn Gray When the Sun Goes Down* (jazz opera; libretto by Dan Jaffe). Performed New York, 21 May 1971.

Skilton, Charles Sanford (b. Northampton, MA, 16 August 1868; d. Lawrence, KS, 12 March 1941; ASCAP; *Amerigrove*; *Baker's*; Hipsher; additional help from James Anthony Smith, whose M.A. thesis is on Skilton)
1927   *Kalopin* (3 acts; libretto by Virginia Nelson Palmer after an Indian legend). Bispham medal, 1930. Unperformed.
1930   *The Sun Bride* (1 act; libretto by Lillian White Spencer after an Indian legend). Broadcast on NBC radio, New York, 17 April 1930. Also entitled *Bluefeather*.
1936   *The Day of Gayomair* (or *The Day of Gayoman*; prologue, 2 scenes; libretto by Allen Crafton after Friedrich Gerstäcker). Unperformed.

Skinner, Doug
1985   *The Courtroom* (libretto by Bill Irwin). Performed Stockbridge, MA, 23 April 1985.

Skloff, Michael
1990   *Jekyll and Hyde* (1 hour; libretto by Marta Kaufman and David Crane after Stevenson's story transposed to a Cleveland high school). Performed by Theatreworks/USA, New York, June 1990.

Slater, Neil
1972   *Again D. J.* (libretto by Nick Rossi after the Don Juan legend). Performed Bridgeport, CT, 5 May 1972.

Slater, Walter (b. Chicago, 12 October 1880; Hipsher)
1916　*Jael* (1 act; biblical story). Written for the Hinshaw competition.

Slates, Philip M. (b. Canton, OH, 24 September 1924; d. Indianapolis, IN, 1966;
　　Anderson)
　　　Double Bill (librettos by composer):
1956　*The Bargain* (1 act). Performed Athens, OH, 26 July 1956.
1956　*The Candle* (1 act). Performed Athens, OH, 26 July 1956.
　-　　*Pierrot of the Minute* (1 act).

Small, Richard J.
1989　*The Tournament*. BMI College Musical Competition winner.
　　　Performed Danbury, CT, 1989.

Smart, Gary L. (b. Cuba, IL, 19 December 1932; Anderson; *WhoAm*)
1974　*The Tempest*. NEA grant.

Smit, Leo (b. Philadelphia, 12 January 1921; *Amerigrove*)
1969　*The Alchemy of Love* (2 acts; libretto by Fred Hoyle). Published by
　　　Presser. (Date in Anderson: 1967.)
1975　*A Mountain Eulogy* (melodrama after Peter Ibsen's *Peer Gynt*), for
　　　speaker and piano.
1978　*Magic Water* (chamber opera; libretto by composer after
　　　Hawthorne), for 10 performers.

Smith, David Stanley (b. Toledo, OH, 6 July 1877; d. New Haven, CT, 17
　　　December 1949; *Amerigrove*; Hipsher)
1911　*Merry Mount*, op. 36 (libretto by Lee Wilson Dodd after
　　　Hawthorne). Score at the Yale School of Music, New Haven, CT.
　　　Amerigrove date: 1914; Hipsher: 1912-13.

Smith, Gregg (b. Chicago, 21 August 1931; *Amerigrove*)
1985　*Aesop Fables* (for children). Performed DeKalb, IL, 11 April 1985.
1990　*Rip Van Winkle* (children's opera; 1 act). Performed Syracuse, NY,
　　　3 May 1991.

Smith, Hale (b. Cleveland, OH, 29 June 1925; *Amerigrove*; Southern)
1953　*Blood Wedding* (chamber opera; 3 acts; after Federico García
　　　Lorca). Performed Cleveland, 1953.

Smith, Julia Frances (b. Denton, TX, 25 January 1911; d. New York, 8 April
　　　1989 [*Baker's*: April 27]; *Amerigrove*; Cohen)
1939　*Cynthia Parker* (3 acts—90 minutes; libretto by composer and Isabel
　　　Fortune after a Texas legend). Performed Denton, TX, 16
　　　February 1940. Revision of 1977 commissioned by University of
　　　Texas, Austin; performed there, 5 December 1985.
1943　*The Stranger of Manzano* (prologue and 1 act; libretto by J. W.
　　　Rogers). Performed Dallas, TX, 6 May 1947.
1946　*The Gooseherd and the Goblin* (1 act—50 minutes; libretto by
　　　Josephine F. Roule after C. D. Mackay). Performed New York,
　　　22 February 1947 (broadcast on WNYC radio), New London, CT,
　　　10 November 1949, and Amarillo, TX, 7 or 8 December 1977.
　　　Published by Presser, 1949.

1954   *Cockcrow* (1 act—25 minutes; libretto by C. D. Mackay after Grimm). Performed Austin, TX, 22 April 1954. Published by Presser, 1954.

1966   *The Shepherdess and the Chimney Sweep* (Christmas opera; 1 act—30 minutes; libretto by C. D. Mackay). Performed Fort Worth, TX, 28 December 1967. Published by Presser.

1973   *Daisy* (2 acts—90 minutes; libretto by Bertita Harding about Juliette Gordon Lowe, founder of the Girl Scouts). Commission by Opera Guild of Greater Miami and Girl Scout Council of Tropical Florida. Première by Greater Miami Opera Association, FL, 3 November 1973; also performed 29 April 1977 (on tour spring of 1978). Published by Presser, 1973. Recorded on Orion ORS 76248. Kornick.

Smith, Larry Alan (b. Canton, OH, 4 October 1955; *WhoAm*)
1980   *Aria da capo* (1 act; libretto after Millay). Commission by Chamber Opera Theatre, Chicago; performed there, 11 June 1980.

Smith, Leland Clayton (b. Oakland, CA, 6 August 1925; *Amerigrove*)
1955   *Santa Claus* (1 act—5 scenes; libretto after e. e. cummings). Performed Chicago, 9 December 1955. Published by Presser.

Smith, Leo
1985   *The Seventh Prayer* ("Rastagarian Opera"; libretto by the composer). Performed Hartford, CT, 27 April 1985.

Smith, Russell (b. Tuscaloosa, AL, 23 April 1927; *Amerigrove*)
1955   *The Unicorn in the Garden* (comic opera; 1 act; libretto by James Thurber). Performed Hartford, CT, 2 May 1957. Published by G. Schirmer.
1974   *The Tempest* (after Shakespeare). NEA grant.
1976   *King Lear* (after Shakespeare). NEA grant.

Smith, Stuart Saunders (b. Portland, ME, 16 March 1948; Anderson; *WhoAm*)
1990   *Tunnels* (1 act; libretto by composer). Performed by Golden Fleece, New York, June 1990.

Smolanoff, Michael Louis (b. New York, 11 May 1942; *WhoAm*)
-     *Vercingetorix* (*Vercintegorix* in *COS*-2; 1 act; libretto by Frank Quilkin). Published by Seesaw Music.

Snell, Gordon
1959   *Gentlemen's Island* (1 act). Performed Westport, CT, 9 August 1959.

Snopek, Sigmund, III (b. Milwaukee, WI, 25 October 1950; Anderson; *WhoAm*)
1976   *Return of the Spirit*, with rock group, actors, and dancers.
1977   *One Room Life*, with rock group, actors, and dancers.

Snow, David Jason (b. Providence, RI, 8 October 1954; Anderson; *WhoAm*)
1989   *Spa Lady from Hell* (*Heilbaddame aus Holle*) (5 minutes; libretto by composer).

Snyder, Leo (b. Boston, 1 January 1918; Anderson)
  1979   *The Princess Marries the Page.* Performed Boston, 25 May 1979.

Sobolewski, Eduard (b. Königsberg, Germany [now Kaliningrad], 1 October 1804
      [Hipsher: 1808]; d. St. Louis, 17 May 1872; in U.S. from 1859;
      Amerigrove; *Baker's*; Hipsher)
  1859   *Mohega, die Blume des Waldes* (3 acts; libretto, in German, by
      composer, about an American Indian girl saved by Pulaski).
      Performed Milwaukee, WI, 11 October 1859. See *Sentinel*, 17
      October 1959.
  1859   *An die Freude* (melodrama). Performed Milwaukee, 1859.

Sokolov, Elliot (b. New York, 16 September 1953; Anderson; *WhoAm*)
  1987   *The Nightingale* (for children). Performed by Open Eye, New
      York, 19 October 1987.
  1987   *The Odyssey* (libretto by Amie Brockway after the Greek).
      Performed by Open Eye, New York, 7 November 1987.

Sokolov, Noel
  1961   *The Franklin's Tale* (80 minutes after Chaucer). Performed Baton
      Rouge, LA, 10 November 1961. Published by Presser.
  -      *The Pardoner's Tale* (50 minutes; libretto after Chaucer). Published
      by Presser.

Solly, Bill (ASCAP)
  1980   *Mrs. Moses* (libretto by composer and Donald Ward). Performed
      New York, April 1980.
      (Solly also composed *The All-American Backstage Musical*, 1983.)

Solomon, Joyce Elaine (b. Tuskegee, AL, 11 May 1946; ASCAP; Cohen; *WhoAm*)
  1988   *A Tribute to Winnie Mandela.* Part of a projected trilogy, *Elegies
      for the Fallen.* Performed by After Dinner Opera, New York, 28
      February 1988.

Somers, Harry Stewart (b. Toronto, Canada, 11 September 1925—he is Canadian;
      Baker's)
  1975   *Louis Riel.* Commission for the Bicentennial. Performed at
      Kennedy Center, 23 October 1975.

Sondheim, Stephen (b. New York, 22 March 1930; *Amerigrove*; *Who's Who*)
  1966   *A Funny Thing Happened on the Way to the Forum* (libretto by B.
      Shevelove and L. Gelbart after Plautus). Première, New York, 8
      May 1962.
  1964   *Anyone Can Whistle* (libretto by A. Laurents). Première, New York,
      4 April 1964.
  1970   *Company* (2 acts; lyrics by composer, book by George Furth).
      Première at Alvin Theatre, New York, 26 April 1970. Recorded
      on Columbia OS-3550. Kornick.
  1971   *Follies* (1 or 2 acts; lyrics by composer, book by James Goldman).
      Première at Winter Garden Theatre, New York, 4 April 1971.
      Recorded on Capitol SO-761. Kornick.
  1973   *A Little Night Music* (2 acts; lyrics by composer, book by Hugh
      Wheeler after Ingmar Bergman's film *Smiles of a Summer Night*).

Première at Shubert Theatre, New York, 25 February 1973 [*Amerigrove*: February 23]; performances by Madison Opera, 5 April 1989, New York Opera, November 1990, and telecast on PBS, 7 November 1990. Recorded on Columbia JS 32265. Kornick.

1974   *The Frogs* (libretto by Shevelove after Aristophanes). Première, New Haven, CN, 20 May 1974.

1976   *Pacific Overtures* (kabuki/musical theater; 2 acts; lyrics by composer, book by John Weidman with additional material by Hugh Wheeler). Première at Winter Garden, NY, 11 January 1976; performed as an opera in London. Recording by RCA (1977). Kornick.

1979   *Sweeney Todd, the Demon Barber of Fleet Street* (musical theater/opera; lyrics by composer, book by Hugh Wheeler after C. Bond). Première at Uris Theatre, New York, 1 March 1979; Performed by New York City Opera, 1984; Houston Opera, 1984; Arkansas Opera Theater, 2 June 1989. Recorded on RCA Red Seal CBL 2-3379. Kornick.

1981   *Merrily We Roll Along* (libretto by George Furth after George S. Kaufman and Moss Hart). Première, New York, 16 November 1981.

1983   *Sunday in the Park with George* (2 acts; libretto by the composer, book by James Lapine, about Georges Seurat and his painting *A Sunday Afternoon on the Island of La Grand Jatte*). Performed by Playwrights Horizons, New York, summer 1983 before its opening as a musical in New York, 23 April 1984 (Kornick: première at Booth Theatre, New York, 2 May 1984). Pulitzer Prize, 1985. Published by Music Theatre International. Recorded by RCA.

1985   *Into the Woods* (2 acts; libretto by composer and James Lapine after Grimm). Performed by Playwrights Horizons, New York, fall 1985 and 1986, and at Old Globe Theater, San Diego, CA, 4 December 1986. Published by Music Theatre International.

1986   *Anyone Can Whistle* (3 acts; libretto by composer and Arthur Laurents). Performed by Dupree Studio Theater, Los Angeles, 12 December 1986. Published by Music Theatre International. Recorded by Columbia.

1989   *Assassins* (1 act; libretto by composer and John Weidman; surrealistic; about nine would-be presidential assassins).

Sorrentino, Charles (b. Sicily, Italy, 13 August 1906; at CBS, New York, 1931-60)

\-   *The Candelabra* (1 act—60 minutes).

Sosin, Donald Paul (AMC)

1977   *Esther* (biblical; 50 minutes). Performed Huntington, NY, 6 March 1977.

\-   *Evangeline* (150 minutes; after Longfellow). Performance at Staten Island, NY, projected but date not yet set.

Sousa, John Philip (b. Washington, DC, 6 November 1854; d. Reading, PA, 6 March 1932; *Amerigrove*)

1879   *Katherine* (operetta; 3 acts; libretto by W. J. Vance).

1881   *Florine* (operetta; libretto by M. A. Denison). Unfinished.

1882   *The Smugglers* (operetta; 2 acts; libretto by Vance after F. C. Burnand's *The Contrabandista*). Performed Washington, DC, 25 March 1882.

1884   *Désirée* (operetta; 2 acts; libretto by E. M. Taber after J. M. Morton's *Our Wife*). Performed Washington, DC, 1 May 1884.

1886   *The Queen of Hearts* (operetta; 1 act; libretto by E. M. Taber). Performed Washington, DC, 12 April 1886.

1888   *The Wolf* (operetta; 3 acts; libretto by composer).

1893   *The Devil's Deputy* (operetta; libretto by J. C. Goodwin). Unfinished.

1895   *El Capitan* (operetta; 3 acts; libretto by Charles Klein). Performed New York, 1895; Boston, 13 April 1896 (ran for four years); London, England, 1899 (ran for 140 performances); by Mississippi Opera, 14 November 1989, and Skylight Opera, Milwaukee, WI, 2 August 1990.

1897   *The Bride Elect* (operetta; 3 acts; libretto by composer). Performed New Haven, CT, 28 December 1897.

1898   *The Charlatan* (operetta; 3 acts; libretto by Charles Klein). Performed Montréal, Canada, 29 August 1898.

1899   *Chris and the Wonderful Lamp* (operetta; 3 acts; libretto by G. MacDonough). Performed New Haven, CT, 23 October 1899.

1905   *The Free Lance* (operetta; 2 acts; libretto by H. B. Smith). Performed Springfield, MA, 26 March 1906.

1911   *The Glass Blowers* (operetta).

1913   *The American Maid* (operetta; 3 acts; libretto by L. Liebling). Performed Rochester, NY, 27 January 1913.

1915   *The Irish Dragoon* (operetta; 3 acts; libretto by J. Herbert after C. Lever's *Charles O'Malley*).

1915   *The Victory* (operetta; libretto by E. W. Wilcox). A musical based on Sousa's *Teddy and Alice* (about Theodore Roosevelt), was put together by Richard Kapp in 1985.

Southard, Lucien H. (b. Sharon, VT, 4 February 1827; d. Augusta, GA, 10 January 1881; *Baker's*, 5th ed.)

1855   *The Scarlet Letter*. Performed Boston, summer 1855.

1858   *Omano* (4 acts; about American Indians; libretto in Italian). Concert performance Boston, 1858. Score in the Boston Public Library.

Spangenberg, Saul

1989   *Chinese Charade* (*El chino de la charada*), with Sergio García Marruz (Spanish libretto by Emilia Conde and Anita Velez; English libretto by Manuel Pereiras). Performed by Puerto Rican Traveling Theater, New York, 9 August 1989.

Spektor, Mira J. (b. in Europe; AMC; Cohen; *WhoAm*)

1973   *The Housewives' Cantata* ("feminist music theater work"; libretto by June Siegel and Willy Holtzman). Performed at Theater at Noon, New York (as a revue), September 1973, Lincoln Center, New York (as a short opera), April 1979, and Theatre Four, New York (as a full-length opera), 17 February 1980.

1982   *Lady of the Castle* (1 hour; libretto by composer and Andrea Balis after Lea Goldberg). Performed at Theatre for the New City,

New York, 4 February 1982; and New York Singing Teachers
Association, 8 May 1982.

1985 *The Passion of Lizzie Borden* (15 minutes; after a Ruth Whitman
poem). Conceived by the Aviva Players, Marymount College, New
York. Performed at State University of New York, Buffalo, 13
July 1986.

Spelman, Timothy Mather (b. Brooklyn, NY, 21 January 1891; d. Florence, Italy,
21 August 1970; *Amerigrove*; Hipsher)

1909 *How Fair, How Fresh Were the Roses* (melodrama; poem by
Turgeniev). Performed Brooklyn, NY, 1909.

1911 *Snowdrop* (pantomime; 4 acts). Performed Brooklyn, NY.

1913 *The Romance of the Rose* ("wordless fantasy"). Performed Boston,
October 1913, and (revised) St. Paul, MN, 4 December 1915,
conducted by composer.

1920 *La magnifica* (*The Magnificent One*; music drama; 1 act; libretto by
his wife Leolyn Louise Everett-Spelman, on an American subject).
Published by Chester.

1928 *The Sea Rovers* (libretto by composer).

1930 *The Sunken City* (grand opera; 3 acts; libretto by composer).

1935 *Babakan* (fantastic comedy; 1 act; libretto by composer).

1943 *The Courtship of Miles Standish* (libretto after Longfellow).

Spencer, David

1990 *Pulp* (libretto by Bruce Peyton). Ten Minute Musicals Project
winner. Performed San Francisco, 15 February 1990.

Spencer, James Houston (b. Malone, NY, 28 July 1895; d. Adrian, MI, 3
September 1967; Anderson)

1937 *Song of Solomon.*

Spencer, Judy

1989 *The Snow Queen* (children's opera; libretto by Ranfolf Pearson).
Performed by On Stage Productions, New York, 4 February 1989.

1989 *The Emperor's New Clothes* (children's opera; libretto by Owen
Robertson). Performed by On Stage Productions, New York, 7
October 1989.

Spenser, William (1852-1933; b. in Pennsylvania)

1886 *The Little Tycoon* (comic opera; 2 acts). Performed Philadelphia.
Over 500 performances in its first run; over 7,000 since.

1894 *The Princess Bonnie.* Performed in Philadelphia. 1,039
performances.

Spivack, Larry (ASCAP)

1986 *Cathedral* (comic opera; 2 acts; libretto by Paul David White; about
the Thirty Years' War). Performed by Center for Contemporary
Opera, New York, 15 May 1986.

Spratlan, Lewis (b. Miami, FL, 5 September 1940; *Amerigrove*; *WhoAm*)

1977 *Life Is a Dream* (3 acts—2 hours; libretto by P. Calderón). NEA
grant, 1976. Performed by New Haven Opera Theatre, February

1978. Rockefeller Foundation and New England Conservatory second prize, 1979.

Stahl, Jule
- *The Bat Poet* (1 hour; libretto by Betty Britto after Jarrell; for children). Performed Columbus, GA. *COS*-4.

Stahl, Richard
1884 *Puritan Days*, with Earl Marble (same subject as Hanson's *Merry Mount*).

Stair, Patty (b. Cleveland, OH, 12 November 1869; d. there, 26 April 1926; *Amerigrove*; *Baker's*; Cohen)
- *The Fair Brigade* (light opera; 3 acts).
- *An Interrupted Serenade.*
- *Sweet Simplicity* (light opera).

Stalvey, Dorrance (b. Georgetown, SC, 21 August 1930; Anderson; *Baker's*; *WhoAm*)
1975 *Allegory of the Cave.* NEA grant.

Stambaugh, J. Mark (AMC)
1980 *The Death of Anton Webern* (1 act).
1987 *The Phoenix* (75 minutes; libretto by composer). Performed Baltimore, MD, 30 January 1987.

Stametz, Lee
- *Lurking on the Railroad*, with Raymond Hannisian (2 acts; libretto by Dutton Foster). Published by Dramatic Publishing Co. *COS*-4.

Stamos, Spyros
1946 *Marco Bozzaris* (3 acts). The original, by Paul Carreri, a Verdi student, was performed in Athens, Greece, in 1860; Stamos added act 2, plus parts of acts 1 and 3. Performed at Civic Opera House, Chicago, 9 June 1946 (in Greek). See *Chicago Sun*, 9 June 1946, part 6, p. 4.

Stapleton, James
1983 *Prodigal Son.* Performed by Opera Uptown, New York, 8 May 1983.

Starer, Robert (b. Vienna, Austria, 8 January 1924; left Austria 1938; in U.S. from 1947; *Amerigrove*; *Who's Who*)
1956 *The Intruder* (1 act—55 minutes; libretto by M. A. Pryor). Performed New York, 4 December 1956. Published by Mercury.
1967 *Pantagleize* (3 acts; libretto by composer after M. de Ghelerode). Performed New York, 7 April 1973, and Brooklyn, NY, 1974.
1974 *The Last Lover* (1 act—40 minutes; libretto by Gail Godwin after legends about a woman called Pelagia in Antioch, 4th century). Première at Caramoor Festival, Katonah, NY, 2 August 1975. Published by Music Corporation of America. Kornick.
1978 *Apollonia* (melodrama [*Amerigrove*: opera]; 2 acts—90 minutes; libretto by Gail Godwin). NEA grant. Première by Minnesota

Opera, St. Paul, 22 May 1979 [*Amerigrove*: 1978]; performed at Brooklyn College, NY, 3 May 1990. Published by Music Corporation of America. Kornick.

1981   *Anna Margarita's Will* (monodrama; 15 minutes; libretto by Gail Godwin). Performed by New York Workshop Theatre, New York, 6 February 1981.

1983   *Mystic Trumpeter* (1 act; libretto after Walt Whitman). Performed at Brooklyn College, NY, 4 February 1983.

Stearn, A. E.
1913   *The Mojave Maid*, with Emily McCord.

Stearns, Theodore (b. Berea, OH, 10 June 1880 [Hipsher: 1875]; d. Los Angeles, 1 November 1935; Anderson; Hipsher)
1895   *Endymion* (libretto by composer after the poem by Keats).
1919   *Snowbird* (opera-ballet; 1 act; libretto by composer). Première by Chicago Civic Opera at the Auditorium, 13 January 1923; repeated 15 December 1923; also performed at Staatsoper, Dresden, Germany, 7 November 1928, with 16 subsequent performances. Bispham Medal, 1925.
1926   *Atlantis* (*Co-o-za*) (lyric drama; prologue, 2 acts, and epilogue; libretto by composer). Freer, 1930, noted "the first performance to be in Dresden or Frankfurt in 1931."
-    *Hiawatha*. Unfinished.

Steding, Walter
1988   *Maraya—Acts of Nature in Geological Time*, with Carl Stone (1 hour; libretto by Ping Chong). Performed by Fiji Co., New York, January 1988.

Steele, ?
1986   *Lila-Bye* (libretto by Marcus). Performed at San Francisco School of Dramatic Arts, 7 July 1986.

Steele, (Catherine) Lynn (b. Beaumont, TX, 27 May 1951; Cohen; *WhoAm*)
1969   *Flea Circus* (operetta).
1982   *Dominique* (3 acts). Published by American University, Washington, DC.

Steely, Yvonne
1987   *'Tite Rouge* (1 act; about Haiti). Performed at Houston Baptist University, TX, 11 December 1987.

Stein, Alan (b. Chicago, 22 January 1949; Anderson)
1973   *A Dove in the Rainbow* (based on the story of Noah). Performed Urbana, IL, 13 December 1973.

Stein, Leon (b. Chicago, 18 September 1910; ACA; *Amerigrove*; Schoep; *WhoAm*; *Who's Who*)
1954   *The Fisherman's Wife* (1 act—70 minutes; libretto by Roslyn Rosen based on Grimm Brothers story). Performed St. Joseph, MI, 10 January 1955.

1955   *Deirdre* (1 act—90 minutes; libretto after William Butler Yeats), accompanied by piano. Performed by University of Chicago Quadrangle Club, 18 May 1957.

Stein, Meridee
1979   *Alice through the Looking Glass*, with Susan Dias and Philip Namanworth. Performed New York, 21 October 1979.

Steiner, Emma Roberts (b. in Alaska, 1850 [Cohen: b. Baltimore, 1852]; d. New York, 27 February 1929; she conducted over 6,000 opera performances of 50 operas, and composed nine operas; *Baker's*)
1889   *Fleurette* (comic opera; 2 acts). Performed San Francisco, 1889; New York, 1891.
1894   *Day Dreams* (operetta).
1900   *The Man from Paris* (operetta).
-    *The Alchemist* (operetta).
-    *La Belle Marguerite* (operetta).
-    *Brigands* (operetta).
-    *Burra Pundit* (operetta).
-    *The Little Hussar* (operetta).

Steininger, Frank K. W. (b. Vienna, Austria, 12 June 1906; to U.S. in 1935; Anderson)
-    *Song Without Words* (operetta).
-    *Centennial Spectacle*. Written for Topeka, KS.

Steinke, Greg A. (b. Fremont, MI, 2 September 1942; Anderson; *WhoAm*; *Who's Who*)
1977   *Twelfth Night* (a mini-drama). Performed Olympia, WA, 17 April 1977.

Stenberg, Jordan (b. Fresno, CA, 31 May 1947; Anderson)
1969   *Mind over Matter* (film opera).
1970   *The Clock Struck One* ("opera-play for voices, instruments, and dervish dancers").

Stepleton, James Irvin (b. Muncie, IN, 28 April 1941; Anderson)
1969   *For Those Who Will Say Yes* (chamber opera).

Stern, Arthur
-    *A Rare Bird: or, Love Wins Out* (1 act; libretto by composer). *COS-1*.

Stern, Max (b. Valley Stream, NY, 31 March 1947; Anderson)
1968   *The Philosophy Lesson* (libretto after Molière).

Sterna, Curtis L.
1933   *Land of Wonders*.

Stevens, Glenn (b. Chesaning, MI, 26 July 1899; Anderson)
-    *The Legend of Tucumcari*.

Stevens, Noel Scott
>   1961   *The Enchanted Canary* (1 act). Performed Bemidji, MN, 18 March
>   1961.

Stewart, Frank Graham (b. La Junta, CO, 12 December 1920; Anderson; *WhoAm*)
>   1974   *To Let the Captive Go* (chamber opera; 1 act; libretto by John
>   Hubsky). Première at Mannes College, New York, 5 March 1974.
>   Published by Seesaw Music. Kornick.

Stewart, Humphrey John (b. London, England, 22 May 1856; d. San Diego, 28
>   December 1932; in U.S. from 1886; *Amerigrove*; Hipsher)
>   1889   *Bluff King Hal* (romantic opera; 3 acts; libretto by Daniel
>   O'Connell, revised by Allan Dunn). Première, San Francisco,
>   1911. Published in 1911 as *King Hal*.
>   1890   *His Majesty* (comic opera; libretto by Peter Robertson). Performed
>   San Francisco, 1900. Manuscript lost in the Great Fire in San
>   Francisco, 1906.
>   1900   *The Conspirators* (comic opera; libretto by Clay M. Greene).
>   Performed San Francisco, 1900. Lost in same fire.
>   1903   *Montezuma.* Performed San Francisco. Bispham Medal, 1929.
>   1910   *The Oracle.* Performed San Francisco.
>   1924   *The Hound of Heaven* (sacred music drama; libretto by Francis
>   Thompson). Performed San Francisco, 24-26 April 1924;
>   presented as an oratorio at Spreckels Theater, San Diego, 9 March
>   1925. Bispham medal, 1925.

Stewart, Robert (b. Buffalo, NY, 6 March 1918; Anderson; *WhoAm*)
>   1965   *The Curl* (1 act). Performed Lexington, VA, 27 April 1965.

Still, William Grant (b. Woodville, MS, 11 May 1985; d. Los Angeles, 3
>   December 1978; ASCAP; *Amerigrove*; Southern)
>   1935   *Blue Steel* (3 acts; libretto by Carlton Moss and Bruce Forsythe;
>   about a voodoo cult in southern U.S.). Guggenheim Foundation
>   grant.
>   1936   *From the Furnace of the Sun* (libretto by Sherwood Trask, based on
>   an African subject). Unfinished; the manuscript is housed at Yale
>   University.
>   1941   *Troubled Island* (3 acts; libretto by Langston Hughes and Verna
>   Arvey, about the Dessalines revolt in Haiti). Performed by City
>   Center Opera, New York, 31 March, 10 April, and 1 May 1949;
>   broadcasts on WOR radio, New York, 21 February and 23 April
>   1943, and WNYC radio, New York, 14 February 1949.
>   1941   *A Bayou Legend* (melodrama; 3 acts—120 minutes; libretto by Verna
>   Arvey after a 19th-century Mississippi legend). Première by
>   Opera/South, Jackson State University, MS, 15 November 1974;
>   televised by Opera/South for PBS-TV, October 1979 (broadcast 15
>   June 1981); performed at East Los Angeles City College, CA, 13
>   February 1976. Kornick.
>   1943   *A Southern Interlude* (60 minutes; libretto by Verna Arvey).
>   Reworked as *Highway 1, U.S.A..*.
>   1950   *Costaso* (3 acts; libretto by Verna Arvey, about Spanish-American
>   settlers in the U.S.). Performed Jackson, MS, 10 April 1981, and
>   Flagstaff, AZ, April 1989.

1951   *Mota* (3 acts—105 minutes; libretto by Verna Arvey based on an African subject).

1956   *The Pillar* (3 acts—2 hours; libretto by Verna Arvey based on an American Indian subject).

1958   *Minette Fontaine* (melodrama; 3 acts—2 hours; libretto by Verna Arvey, on the subject of voodoo in New Orleans). Première by Baton Rouge Opera, LA, 22 October 1958; also performed there 24 October 1984. Kornick.

1962   *The Peaceful Land* (1 act). Performed at University of Miami, FL, May 1962.

1962   *Highway 1, U.S.A.* (melodrama; 1 act—60 minutes; libretto by Verna Arvey). Première at Festival of Contemporary International Music, University of Miami, FL, 11 May 1963; performed at West Virginia State College, 30 April 1967, Citrus College, Los Angeles, 15 March 1970, and by Opera/South, Jackson State University, MS, 19 November 1972. Kornick.

Stiller, Andrew Philip (b. Washington, DC, 6 December 1946; Anderson; *Who's Who*)

1978   *Lavender* (chamber opera).

Stocker, Stella Prince (b. Jacksonville, IL, 3 April 1858; d. 1925; Cohen)

1893   *Gannymede*. Performed at the Chicago World's Fair, 1893.

-    *Beulah*.

-    *The Marvels of Manabush* (Indian pantomime; 3 acts).

-    *Queen of Hearts*.

-    *Raoul*.

Stoddard, Martha

1986   *Hansel and Gretel* (30 minutes; libretto by composer). Commission by Humboldt State University, Arcata, CA, February 1986.

Stoessel, Albert (b. St. Louis, 11 October 1894; d. New York, 12 May 1943; ASCAP; *Amerigrove*)

1937   *Garrick* (3 acts; libretto by Robert Simon). Performed at Juilliard School, New York, 24 February 1937. Bispham Medal, 1937-38. Published by J. Fischer.

Stoeving, (Carl Heinrich) Paul (b. Leipzig, Germany, 7 May 1861; d. New York, 24 December 1948; left Germany 1896, mostly touring; in U.S. from 1914; *Baker's*)

-    *Gaston and Jolivette*. Performed New Haven, CT?

Stokes, Eric (b. Haddon Heights, NJ, 14 July 1930; AMC; *Amerigrove*; *Baker's*; Schoep)

1969   *Horspfal* (2 acts—115 minutes; libretto by Alvin Greenberg; "concerns the misadventures of American Indians since the coming of white men"—*Amerigrove*). Performed by Center Opera Co. (now Minnesota Opera), Minneapolis, 15 February 1969; at Hunter College, 1971.

1974   *Minnesota Coloring Book No. I and No. II*. NEA grant.

1977   *Happ: or, Orpheus in Clover* (libretto by composer). Performed Minneapolis, MN, 1 October 1977.

1978   *The Jealous Cellist and Other Acts of Misconduct* (150 minutes; libretto by A. Greenberg). Performed by Minnesota Opera, Minneapolis, 2 February 1979.

1982   *Itaru the Stonecutter* (libretto by composer).

1984   *The Further Voyages of the Santa Maria* (libretto by A. Greenberg).

1984   *Apollonia's Circus*.

1988   *We're Not Robots, You Know* (for children; libretto by Keith Gunderson; versions for both stage and television), for vocal quintet and optional marching vocal quintet and instrumental ensemble. Performed by New Opera of Chicago, 15 May 1988.

Stone, Carl (b. Los Angeles, 10 February 1953; *Amerigrove*)

1988   *Maraya—Acts of Nature in Geological Time*, with Walter Steding (1 hour; libretto by Ping Chong). Performed by Fiji Co., Mew York City, January 1988.

Stonerook, ?

1987   *A Christmas Peril* (libretto by Seale after Dickens). Performed Moorpark, CA, 4 December 1987.

Stornaiuolo, Vincenzo

1984   *Anonymous* (libretto by Giancarlo de Matteis). Performed by AMAS Repertory Theatre, New York, 25 October 1984.

Stothart, Herbert (b. Milwaukee, WI, 11 September 1885; d. Los Angeles, 1 February 1949; *Amerigrove*)

1925   *Song of the Flame*, with George Gershwin (musical [except Gershwin called it an opera]; 2 acts and epilogue; libretto by Oscar Hammerstein II and Otto Harbach). Performed New York, 30 December 1925.

Stover, Franklin Howard (b. Sacramento, CA, 5 November 1953; Anderson; *WhoAm*)

1983   *Ketchup* (80 minutes; libretto by Russell Edson). *COS*-4.

Straight, Willard (b. Ft. Wayne, IN, 18 July 1930; ASCAP; Anderson)

1967   *Toyon of Alaska* (3 acts; libretto by Frank Brink). Performed Anchorage, AL, 7 July 1967.

Strakosch, Maurice (b. Gross-Seelowitz [now Židlochovice], near Brünn [now Brno], Moravia, 15 January 1825; d. Paris, France, 9 October 1887; in U.S. in 1848-61; *Amerigrove*; *Baker's*)

1851   *Giovanna prima di Napoli* (3 acts). Performed New York.

Stramiello, Ernest

1940   *Maggio Fiorentino* (2 acts; in Italian). Performed at Brooklyn Academy of Music, 1940.

Strand, Chuck

1975   *The Lieutenant*, with Gene Curty and Nitra Scharfman (rock opera). Performed New York, 11 March 1975.

Strassburg, Robert (b. New York, 30 August 1915; ASCAP; Anderson; *Baker's*; *WhoAm*)

1955 *Chelm* (comic folk opera; Hassidic Gothem; 1 act). Performed White Plains, NY, 11 February 1955.

Strauss, John L. (b. New York, 28 April 1920; ASCAP; Anderson)

1961 *The Accused* (monodrama; 1 act; libretto by Shepherd Kerman). Performed New York 7 May 1961; telecast on CBS-TV, 30 September 1961.

Strickland, Lily Teresa (b. Anderson, SC, 28 January 1887; d. Hendersonville, NC, 6 June 1958; *Amerigrove*; *Baker's*; Cohen)

1933 *Jewel of the Desert* (operetta).
1946 *Laughing Star of Zuni* (operetta).
- *Joseph.*
- *Woods of Pan.*

Strilko, Anthony (b. 1931; Anderson)

- *The Last Puppet* ("tragedy in 1 act"—60 minutes; libretto by Harry Duncan). Published by Presser. *COS*-1.

Stringer, Alan W. (b. El Paso, TX, 15 January 1938; Anderson; *WhoAm*)

- *Young Goodman Brown.*

Stringfield, Lamar (b. near Raleigh, NC, 10 October 1897; d. Asheville, NC, 21 January 1959; *Amerigrove*)

1929 *The Mountain Song* (3 scenes).
1953 *Carolina Charcoal* (musical folk comedy; 2 acts).

Strouse, Charles (b. New York, 7 June 1928; ASCAP; *Amerigrove*)

1977 *Annie* (musical; libretto by T. Meehan). Performed New York, 21 April 1977.
1980 *The Emperor's Nightingale* (1 act). Performed New York, March 1980.
1980 *Singers* (1 act; libretto by Herbert Grossman). Performed by Eastman Opera, Rochester, NY, 1 February 1980.
1980 *Nightingale* (1 act—132 minutes [Kornick: 70 minutes]; libretto by composer after the Hans Christian Andersen story). Première at First All Children's Theater, New York, March 1980; performed by Central City Opera, CO, summer 1981; First All Children's Theatre, New York, June 1981 and March 1982; and at Wolf Trap, VA, 16 April 1982. Kornick.
1987 *Martin Luther King, Jr.* (libretto by Leslie Lee). Performed by Theatreworks/USA, New York, 10 January 1987.
1988 *Lyle, the Crocodile* (for children). Performed Albany, NY, 19 February 1988.
1988 *Charlotte's Web* (2 acts; libretto by composer and Joseph Robinette after White). Performed Wilmington, DE, March 1988 and 17 February 1989.
1989 *Annie 2* (musical; libretto by Martin Charmin and Thomas Meehan after the comic strip *Little Orphan Annie*; sequel to *Annie*, 1976). Performed at Kennedy Center, Washington, DC, 22 December 1989, and by Goodspeed Opera, Chester, CT, 17 May 1990.

- *Charles & Algernon* (2 acts; libretto by David Rogers after Keynes's *Flowers for Algernon*).
- *What Is There to Sing About?* (for children; 30 minutes; libretto after Hofmannsthal's *Everyman*).

Strube, Gustav (b. Ballenstedt, Germany, 3 March 1867; d. Baltimore, MD, 2 February 1953; in Baltimore from 1891; *Amerigrove*)
1916 *Ramona* (3 acts). Performed Baltimore, MD, 28 February 1938. Revised as:
1938 *The Captive* (75 minutes; about Jamaica). Performed Baltimore, MD, 28 February 1938. Score at the Peabody Conservatory, Baltimore.

Stucken, Frank Van der. *See* Van der Stucken, Frank

Stuessy, Joseph (b. Houston, TX, 14 December 1943; Anderson; *WhoAm*)
1972 *Does the Pale Flag Advance?* (2 acts).

Sublette, Ned (b. Lubbock, TX, 8 July 1951; *Amerigrove*)
1976 *Stanzas* (radio opera; 1 act; libretto by D. Antin).
1977 *Symmetrical Performance* (radio opera; libretto by composer).
1980 *Supernatural Love* (radio opera; "performer improvising on his diary").
1986 *Fire Works*, with R. I. P. Hayman ("country and western Chinese opera"; libretto by Valeria Vasilevski and Ruth Maleczech). Performed Waterford, CT, 1986, and by Seattle Repertory Theatre, WA, September 1988.

Subotnick, Morton (b. Los Angeles, 14 April 1933; *Amerigrove*; *Who's Who*)
1982 *The Double Life of Amphibians* (70 minutes). Commission by Mme. Pierre Schlumberger. Performed at IRCAM, Paris, France, January 1982.
1987 *Hungers* (70 minutes; libretto by Ed Emshwiller). Commission by Los Angeles Fringe and Austrian Arts Festivals. Performed at Los Angeles Fringe Festival, CA, 26 September 1987.
1987 *Jacob's Room* (libretto after Woolf's *Jacob's Room*, Wiesel's *Night*, and Gage's *Eleni*; first 1 act, later 3 acts). OPERA America grant, 1987. Performed St. Paul, MN, 2 November 1987, 5 May 1988, 20 September 1988, and May 1989.

Sully, Francis T.
1883 *Fortunio and His Seven Gifted Sons* (3 acts). Performed Philadelphia, 1883.

Summer, David
(Summer writes his own librettos.)
1981 *The Tenor's Suite* (55 minutes; libretto after Wedekind's *Der Kammersanger*). Performed Philadelphia, 12 September 1981.
1983 *Hippolytus* (2 hours; libretto after Euripides). Performed Pittsburgh, PA, 18 August 1983.
1989 *Courting Disaster* (4 acts; 200 minutes; libretto after Boccaccio's *Decameron*).

—   *And the Dead Shall Walk the Earth* (comic opera; libretto after Boccaccio's *Decameron*).

Summer, Joseph Steven (b. Pittsburgh, PA, 16 February 1956; Anderson)
—   *Hippolytus* (2 acts).

Sur, Donald (b. Honolulu, HI, 1935; Anderson)
1976   *The Hunt for the Unicorn*. NEA grant.

Surette, Thomas Whitney (b. Concord, MA, 7 September 1861; d. there, 19 May 1941; *Amerigrove*)
1889   *Priscilla: or, The Pilgrim's Proxy* (operetta; libretto after Longfellow). Performed Concord, MA, 6 March 1888—more than 1,000 performances. Published by Boston Music, 1889.
1897   *The Eve of Saint Agnes* (operetta). Also published.
1899   *Cascabel: or, The Broken Tryst*. Performed Pittsburgh, PA.

Susa, Conrad (b. Springdale, PA, 26 April 1935; Anderson; *Baker's*; *WhoAm*)
1973   *Transformations* (120 minutes; libretto after Anne Sexton's book of the same name). Commission and première by Minnesota Opera, Minneapolis, 5 May 1973; also performed by Manhattan Theatre Club, May 1976; Amsterdam, 2 April 1977; by Wolf Trap Opera, 1985. Kornick. Published by E. C. Schirmer.
1974   *Painted Bird* (2 acts; libretto after Kosinski). NEA grant.
1975   *Black River* (3 hours; libretto by composer and Richard Street after Michael Vesy's *Wisconsin Death Trap*). Performed by Minnesota Opera, 1 November 1975 (*COS-2*: May 1975) and 21 February 1981.
1983   *The Love of Don Perlimplín* (chamber opera; 1 act; libretto by composer and Richard Street after Federico García Lorca). Performed at New Performance Gallery, San Francisco, July 1984; Purchase, NY, 2 August 1984; by Florida State Opera at Florida State University, Tallahassee, 7-9 March 1985; and College Park, MD, 2 December 1989.
—   *The Lives and Loves of Lola Montez* (libretto by Richard Street). Commission by Houston Grand Opera, TX. *COS-3*.

Swados, Elizabeth (b. Buffalo, NY, 5 February 1951; *Amerigrove*)
1980   *The Haggadah* (after Wiesel and the Book of Exodus). Performed New York, 1 April 1980.
1981   *Alice in Concert* (libretto by composer after Carroll). Performed New York Public Theater, January 1981.
1984   *The Beautiful Lady* (libretto by composer). Performed by City Stage, New York, October 1984.
1985   *Mythos Oedipus*, with Connie Alexander, Sheila Dabney, Genji Ito, David Sawyer, and Michael Sirotta. Performed Delphi, Greece, summer 1985; and by LaMama, New York, 6 February 1988.
1987   *Fragments of a Greek Trilogy* (4 hours; libretto by Andrei Serban after Euripides's *Medea* and *The Trojan Women* and Sophocles's *Electra*; in Greek, Latin, and other languages). Performed by LaMama, New York, 14 January 1987.

1988   *Esther: A Vaudeville Megillah* (libretto by composer after the Bible and Weisel's lecture "Beauty and Commitment"). Performed at 92nd Street Y, New York, 28 February 1988.

1989   *The Pied Piper* (2 acts; for children). Commission by Orlando Opera, FL. Performed there, January 1989 and April 1991.

1989   *The Red Sneaks* (libretto by composer; about drug addiction, after the movie *The Red Shoes*; company-developed). Performed by Theater for a New Audience, New York, 28 June 1988.

(Swados has also composed 9 musicals.)

Sweet, Reginald (b. Yonkers, NY, 14 October 1885; d. 1950; Anderson)

-    *Riders to the Sea* (1 act).

Swenson, Warren Arthur (b. Okanogan, WA, 27 April 1937; Anderson)

1963   *The Legend of Pecos Bill* (folk opera).

1985   *A Slice of Life* (libretto by Stephen Sechrist). Performed at St. Michael's Hall, New York, 7 June 1985.

Swift, Richard (b. Middlepoint, OH, 24 September 1927; *Amerigrove*; *Who's Who*; *WhoAm*)

1964   *The Trial of Tender O'Shea* (1 scene; libretto by D. Swift). Performed at University of California, Davis, 12 August 1964.

Swisher, Gloria Agnes Wilson (b. Seattle, WA, 12 March 1935; AMC; Anderson; Cohen; *WhoAm*; *Who's Who*)

1963   *The Happy Hypocrite* (chamber opera; 3 acts; libretto by High Frank after Beerbohm). (Cohen date: 1965.)

1982   *The Artist and the Other* (chamber opera; 35 minutes; libretto by Willy Clark). Performed Seattle, WA, 11 June 1982.

Sydeman, William (b. New York, 8 May 1928; *Amerigrove*)

1970   *Malediction* (2 acts; libretto by composer after Tristram Shandy). Performed New York, 1970. Published by Seesaw Music.

1971   *Full Circle* ("mini-music-drama for three singers and electrified performers"). Performed New York, 1971. Published by Seesaw Music.

1982   *Aria da capo* (libretto after Edna St. Vincent Millay).

Taffs, Anthony (b. London, England, 15 January 1916; U.S. citizen, 1954; Anderson)

1960   *The Ten Virgins* (1 act). Performed Albion, MI, May 1960.

1963   *Noah* (1 act; libretto by composer). Performed Albion, MI, 10 February 1963.

1964   *The Summons* (libretto by James Brock). Performed Albion, MI, 7 June 1964.

1967   *Lilith* (1 act; libretto after McDonald). Performed Albion, MI, 6 February 1967.

Talley, Ted
>   1988   *Coming Attractions* (libretto by Jack Feldman). Performed Santa
>   Maria, CA, January 1989.

Talma, Louise (b. Arcachon, France, 31 October 1906; to U.S. 1922;
>   ASCAP/AMC; *Amerigrove*; Cohen)
>   1958   *The Alcestiad* (3 acts; libretto by Thornton Wilder). Senior
>   Fulbright Research grant. Performed, in German (transl. H.
>   Herlitschka), Frankfurt am Main, Germany, 1 March 1962—the
>   first by an American woman produced by a major European opera
>   house.
>   1976   *Have You Heard, Do You Know?* (37 minutes; libretto by the
>   composer). NEA grant, 1975. Performed at Whitney Museum,
>   New York, 18 January 1981.

Tamkin, David (b. Chernigov, Russia, 28 August 1906; d. Los Angeles, 21 June
>   1975; in U.S. as an infant; Anderson; *Baker's*)
>   1931   *The Dybbuk* (libretto by composer's brother Alex Tamkin after
>   Ansky). Performed by New York City Opera, 4 October 1951.
>   1962   *The Blue Plum Tree of Esau* (libretto by Alex Tamkin).

Tandler, Adolf (in Los Angeles from about 1910)
>   1926   *Fluff* (comic opera). Los Angeles Opera and Fine Arts Club prize,
>   1926.
>   -   *Johanna* (or *Joanna*; serious subject).
>   (Rodríguez credits Tandler with two comic operas.)

Tanenbaum, Elias (b. Brooklyn, NY, 20 August 1924; ACA; Anderson; *WhoAm*)
>   1983   *Last Letters from Stalingrad* (35 minutes; based on letters from
>   German soldiers in Russia in 1942). Performed Valencia, CA,
>   March 1983.
>   1988   *Keep Going by George* (or *By George*; monodrama; 1 act).
>   Performed by Golden Fleece, New York, 7 April 1988.

Tanner, Frieda (Mrs. F. G.; b. in St. Louis)
>   -   *Watouska: or, The White Lily* (American Indian subject). In Krohn.

Tanner, Jerre Eugene (b. Lock Haven, PA, 5 January 1939; Anderson; *WhoAm*)
>   1974   *The Naupaka Floret*.
>   1977   *Ka lei no kane* (*A Lei for Kane*) (1 act; libretto by Harvey Hess
>   after a Hawaiian legend). Performed by Opera Players of Hawaii,
>   Honolulu, 6 May 1977, and on a statewide tour.
>   1980   *Pupu-Kani-Oe*.
>   1985   *The Kona Coffee Cantata* ("Hawaiian-Baroque chamber opera";
>   companion-piece to J. S. Bach's *Coffee Cantata*). Performed by
>   Uptown Opera, Spokane, WA, 13 November 1986.

Taranto, Vernon Anthony, Jr. (b. New Orleans, 16 November 1946; Anderson;
>   *WhoAm*)
>   1986   *The Cistern* (1 act; libretto by composer after Bradbury).
>   Performed at Louisiana State University, Baton Rouge, 20
>   February 1986.

Tate, Toby
    1985   *The Stone Angel* (1 hour; libretto by composer after a Japanese Noh drama). Performed College Park, MD, 30 March 1985.

Taub, Bruce Jeffrey H. (b. New York, 6 February 1948; AMC; Anderson)
    1975   *Passion, Poison, and Petrification: or, The Fatal Gazogene* (chamber opera; 1 act—23 minutes; libretto by composer after the play by George Bernard Shaw). NEA grant, 1975. Premiere by Composers Ensemble, New York, 1 April 1976. Kornick. Published by C. F. Peters.
    1979   *Waltz on a Merry-Go-Round* (3 acts).

Taylor, Clifford (b. Avalon, PA, 20 October 1923 in Pennsylvania; d. Abington, PA, 19 September 1987; Anderson; *Baker's*)
    1973   *The Freak Show* (*The Man of Stone*) (1 hour; libretto by Edward Lind). NEA grant. (*Baker's* date: 1975.)
        (In addition, Taylor was commissioned to compose "a patriotic opera" for the U.S. Bicentennial by the Pennsylvania Council on the Arts.)

Taylor, Deems (b. New York, 22 December 1885; d. there, 3 July 1966; *Amerigrove*; Hipsher)
    1908   *The Echo* (musical play; 2 acts).
    1916   *The Breath of Scandal* (also *The Mistress of the Seas*; operetta; 2 acts; libretto by J. M. Flagg).
    1926   *The King's Henchman*, op. 19 (lyric drama; 3 acts; libretto by Edna St. Vincent Millay). Commission and première by Metropolitan Opera, New York, 17 February 1927, also performed 3 February 1928 and 16 February 1929 (14 performances, 1927-29); also Los Angeles, 1936—110 performances by 1929. Published by J. Fischer, 1930. Bispham medal, 1929.
    1930   *Peter Ibbetson*, op. 20 (romantic drama; 3 acts; libretto by composer and Constance Collier after George Du Maurier). Première by Metropolitan Opera, New York, 7 February 1931; a total of 16 performances in 1931-35. Juilliard Foundation award.
    1942   *Ramuntcho*, op. 23 (lyric drama; 3 acts; libretto by composer after Pierre Loti). Performed Philadelphia, 10 February 1942.
    1958   *The Dragon* (1 act; libretto by composer after Lady Gregory). Performed New York, 6 February 1958. Published by J. Fischer.
    -    *A Kiss in Xanadu* (pantomime; 3 acts). Published by J. Fischer. At AMRC.

Taylor, Emory (b. Sylvania, GA, 13 May 1934; *WhoAm*)
    1978   *Hodges & Co.*, with Roland Alexander and Sam Rivers (2 acts; about black cowboys in the American West). Performed by Harlem Opera Co., Houston, TX, June 1978.
    -    *Sheba* (jazz opera). Performed by Harlem Opera Society, New York. Later expanded as:
    -    *Solomon & Sheba*. Performed at Clark Center, New York.

Taylor, Rayner (b. London, England, 1747; d. Philadelphia, 17 August 1825; in
U.S. from 1792; *Amerigrove*; Porter)

1778   *Buxom Joan* (burletta, comedy; 1 act). Première at Little Theatre,
Haymarket, London, 25 June 1778; performed Philadelphia, 30
January 1801. Edited and realized by Gregory Sandow (published
by Presser, 1975).

1793   *Capocchio and Dorinna: or, The Happy Captive* ("mock Italian opera
. . . dressed in character . . . consisting of recitative, airs and
duets"), based on Colley Cibber's *The Temple of Dullness*, music
by Thomas Arne. Performed Annapolis, MD, 20 January 1793.
Music lost. Sonneck-Upton, 54.

1793   *The Gray Mare's the Best Horse.* Performed Annapolis, MD, 20
January 1793. Music lost. Sonneck-Upton, 169.

1793   *The Old Woman of Eighty-Three* ("comic burletta . . . dressed in
character . . . consisting of recitative, airs and duets"). Performed
Annapolis, MD, 28 February 1793. Music lost. Sonneck-Upton,
314.

1795   *The Shipwrecked Mariners Preserved: or, La Bonne Petite Fille*
(speaking pantomime, marine spectacle; libretto by Susannah
Rowson). Première, Baltimore, 26 November 1795.

1796   *The Irish Taylor: or, The Humours of the Thimble* ("burletta in one
act . . . with the new grand overture and accompaniments, the
composition of the celebrated Mr. Taylor"). Première, City
Theatre, Charleston, SC, 7 April 1796.

1800   *Pizzaro: or, The Spaniards in Peru* ("celebrated tragedy in 5 acts . .
. written by Augustus von Kotzebue, and adapted to the English
stage, by Richard Brinsley Sheridan . . . the music composed by
Mr. Reinagle and Mr. Taylor"). Performed Philadelphia, 1800.
Score lost. Sonneck-Upton, 332.

1814   *The Æthiop: or, The Child of the Desert* (incidental music; libretto
by William Diamond). Performed at Chestnut Street Theatre,
Philadelphia, 1 January 1814; also at Philadelphia Theatre, 12
March 1817. Piano-vocal score (titled *The Ethiop*) published
Philadelphia: G. E. Blake, 1814; reprint, Schleifer, 5:25-48. See
Victor Fell Yellin, "Rayner Taylor's Music for *The AEthiop*,"
American Music 4/3 (Fall 1986): 249-67, and 5/1 (Spring 1987):
20-47.

Taylor-Dunn, Corliss

1983   *Opening Night*, with Sandra Reeves-Phillips (2 acts: libretto by
composers). Performed by AMAS Repertory Theatre, New York,
21 April 1983.

Tcherepnin, Alexander (b. St. Petersburg, Russia, 21 January 1899; d. Paris,
France, 29 September 1977; U.S. citizen, 1958; *Amerigrove*;
WhoAm)

1952   *The Farmer and the Nymph*, op. 72 (or *The Farmer and the Fairy*;
40 minutes; libretto by G. Cardelli after Siao Yu). Performed
Aspen, CO, 13 August 1952. Published by Marks (*COS*-1 says
Boosey & Hawkes).

Tcherepnin, Ivan (b. Issy-les-Moulineaux, near Paris, France, 5 February 1943; U.S. citizen, 1960; *Amerigrove*)
1977 *Santur Opera*, for santur and electronics. Anderson: "not a traditional opera, but does have a dramatic plot." Performed New York, 12 January 1979.

Teitelbaum, Richard Lowe (b. New York, 19 May 1939; *Amerigrove*; *Who's Who*)
1989 *Golems* (1 hour; libretto by composer after a Jewish legend). Performed by Heritage Chamber Orchestra, New York, 14 March 1989.

Telson, Bob
1981 *Sister Suzie Cinema* (20 minutes; libretto by Lee Breuer after the "doo-wop" of the 1950s). Performed by Public Theater, New York, 1981.
1989 *The Warrior Ant* (12 hours; libretto by Lee Breuer; incorporates Afro-Caribbean and Bunraku music). NIMT grant. Performed at Composers' Showcase, New York, 16 June 1986, and at Spoleto Festival U.S.A., Charleston, SC, 31 May 1988.

Temko, Peter
1985 *The Butterfly That Stamped* (1 act; libretto by Sue Spencer after Kipling's *Just So Stories*). Performed at University of Tennessee, Chattanooga, 11 November 1985.
1985 *The Elephant Child* (1 act; libretto by Sue Spencer after Kipling's *Just So Stories*). Performed at University of Tennessee, Chattanooga, 11 November 1985.
1989 *Just So Stories* (libretto after Kipling). Performed by Chattanooga Symphony and Opera Association, TN, 1 March 1989.

Tenney, David
- *The Appropriation* (satire; 1 hour; libretto by Steven Tenney, about American politics).

Terhune, Anice Potter (pseud.: Morris Stockton; b. Hampden, MA, 27 October 1873; d. Pompton Lakes, NY, 9 November 1964; Anderson; *Baker's*; Cohen)
1904 *Hero Nero.*
1911 *The Woodland Princess* (operetta).

Terry, Megan
1990 *Body Leaks*, with Marianne de Pury and Luigi Waites (multimedia). Performed Omaha, NE, 27 April 1990.

Tgettis, Nicholas Chris (b. Salem, MA, 1 September 1933; Anderson; *WhoAm*)
1978 *Sappho* (chamber opera). Performed Peabody, MA, 19 June 1978.

Thayer, Fred M., Jr. (b. Ithaca, NY, 19 December 1941; Anderson)
- *The Tinker's Wedding* (chamber opera; 1 act).

Themmen, Ivana Marburger (b. New York, 7 April 1935; Cohen; *WhoAm*)
1977 *Lucian* (2 acts; libretto by Norman Simon). Performed New York 6 June 1977.

Thomas, Augusta Reed (ASCAP)
> 1987   *Psychies* (1 act; libretto by Andrew Barron). Performed by Chicago
> Opera Theater, 2 May 1987.

Thomas, Edward (b. in Minnesota, 1924; ASCAP)
> 1978   *Desire under the Elms* (3 acts—2 hours; libretto by Joe Masteroff
> after the play by Eugene O'Neill). Performed New London, CT,
> 10 August 1978; by OPERA America Showcase, New York, 13
> January 1986, and New York Opera Repertory Theater, New
> York, 10 January 1986 and 11 January 1989 (Kornick: première
> by New York Opera Repertory Theatre, City Center, NY, 13
> January 1989). Published by National Music Theater Network.
> 1986   *Six Wives* (libretto by Joe Masteroff, about Henry VII). Performed
> Waterford, CT, 14 August 1986.

Thomas, Gertrude Auld
> 1936   *Hazila.* Performed Los Angeles, 1936.

Thomas, John Rogers (b. Newport, Wales, 26 March 1830; d. New York, 5 April
>   1896; in U.S. from 1849; *Amerigrove*)
> 1876   *Diamond Cut Diamond* (operetta).

Thomas, Judie
> 1979   *Clever Jack and the Magic Beanstalk* (1 act; libretto by John
> Forster). Performed New York, 31 October 1979.

Thomas, Karen P. (b. Seattle, WA, 17 September 1957; Cohen; *WhoAm*)
> 1987   *There Must Be a Lone Ranger* (20 minutes; libretto by composer).
> Commission by Soundwork. Performed by Performa '87, Seattle,
> WA, 6 November 1987.

Thomas, Richard Pearson
> 1984   *Cafe Vienna, 1907* (libretto by composer). Performed Waterford,
> CT, 3 June 1984.

Thompson, Randall (b. New York, 21 April 1899; d. Boston, 9 July 1984;
>   *Amerigrove*)
> 1942   *Solomon and Balkis* (1 act—43 minutes; libretto after Kipling's *The
> Butterfly That Stamped*). Broadcast on CBS radio, New York, 29
> March 1942; staged, Cambridge, MA, 14 April 1942. Published
> by G. Schirmer.
> 1961   *The Nativity According to St. Luke* (7 scenes; libretto after St. Luke
> by R. Rowlands). Performed Cambridge, MA, 13 December 1961.
> Published by E. C. Schirmer.
> (Thompson also composed incidental music for *Torches*, 1920, *The
> Grand Street Follies*, 1926, *The Straw Hat*, 1926, and *The Battle
> of Dunster Street*, 1953.)

Thompson, Waddy
> 1980   *All Are Not Frogs Who Gape for Flies* (1 act; libretto by the
> composer). Performed Encompass Music Theater, New York, 22
> June 1980.

1981   *The Girl on the Via Flaminia* (1 act—135 minutes; libretto by Elsa Rael after Alfred Hays). Performed by Encompass Music Theatre, New York, 21 June 1981.

1989   *Eyeless Tears in a Universe of Ether* ("dance/music theatre work"; 1 act—1 hour; libretto by Robert Epstein). Performed by Dia Art Foundation, New York, 27 April 1989.

Thoms, Hollis (AMC)

1979   *Socrates and Criton* (1 act).

1981   *Fables* (1 act—45 minutes; libretto by composer after Aesop; for children). Performed Winchester-Thurston School, Pittsburgh, PA, fall 1981.

Thomson, Virgil (b. Kansas City, MO, 25 November 1896; d. New York, 30 September 1989; *Amerigrove*; Hipsher)

1933   *Four Saints in Three Acts* (libretto by Gertrude Stein). Performed Ann Arbor, MI, 20 May 1933; Hartford, CT, 8 February 1934 (cited as world première); by Metropolitan Opera at 44th Street Theater, New York, 20 February 1973; and New York, 1986. Bispham Medal, 1932. Published by Music Press, 1948. In AMRC.

1947   *The Mother of Us All* (libretto by Gertrude Stein). Commission by Alice M. Ditson Fund. Performed at Columbia University, New York, 7 May 1947, and New York, 1986. Published by Music Press, 1947. In AMRC.

1968   *Lord Byron* (3 acts—99 minutes; libretto by Jack Larson). Commission by Metropolitan Opera, New York. Première at Juilliard School, 20 April 1972. Published by Southern Music. Kornick.

       (See *New Yorker*, 15 December 1986, which indicates three productions of *Four Saints in Three Acts* and four of *The Mother of Us All*.)

Thorne, Francis (Burritt), **Jr.** (b. Bay Shore, NY, 23 June 1922; *Amerigrove*; WhoAm)

1961   *Fortuna* (operetta; 2 acts; libretto by A. Weinstein). Performed New York, 20 December 1961.

1965   *Opera Buffa for Opera Buffs* (1 act; after Mozart).

1977   *Diamond Dozen.* NEA grant.

Threadgill, Henry (ASCAP)

1985   *The Green Step* (libretto by Donald Sanders after Kenneth Koch's poetry). NEA New American Works grant, 1985-86 season. Performed at New York Art Theatre Institute, New York, 1985-86 season.

-     *Nola Blue* (libretto by Thulani Davis). "In progress," *COS*-4.

Tierney, Thomas

1985   *Narnia* (150 minutes; libretto by composer, Ted Drachman, and Jules Tasca after Lewis's *The Lion, the Witch and the Wardrobe*). Performed London, England, 1985, and by Pace Productions, New York, 29 September 1986. Published by Dramatic Publishing.

1987   *Three and a Half Husbands* (libretto by Ted Drachman and Vincent Dowling after Dorothy Fuldheim). Performed by Cleveland Opera, OH, April and November 1987.

1988   *Susan B!* (1 act; libretto by Ted Drachman and Jules Tasca; about Susan B. Anthony). Performed by Theatreworks/USA, New York, 19 November 1988.

Tietjens, Paul (b. St. Louis, MO, 22 May 1877; d. there, 25 November 1943; ASCAP; Anderson)

1902   *The Wizard of Oz* ("musical extravaganza"). Performed at Chicago Grand Opera House, June 1902. In Krohn.

1935   *The Tents of the Arabs* (2 acts). Performed at Columbia University, New York, 7 August 1935.

-    *The Hangman's Daughter.*

(Tietjens also composed incidental music for James M. Barrie's *A Kiss for Cinderella.*)

Tilles, Nurit

1989   *The Fourth Part of a Trilogy: Broken Cups*, with Brooks Williams ("inter-art work"; libretto by Beatrice Roth). Performed Minneapolis; at Yellow Springs Institute, PA; Staten Island, NY; by Hangar Studio, NH; by Performing Garage, New York; Minneapolis, MN; by St. Mark's Danspace, New York; and by Performing Garage, New York, 20 May 1989.

Tinsley, Sterling

1985   *A Flight of Eagles* (1 act; libretto by Kate Pogue). Performed Houston, TX, 6 June 1958.

Tipton, Clyde (b. Richmond, VA, 17 August 1934; Anderson)

-    *Medea* (aleatoric opera scenes).

-    *The Forced Marriage* (aleatoric opera scenes; libretto after Molière).

Tipton, Julius R., III (b. Memphis, TN, 4 March 1942; Anderson)

-    *Judas.*

Tipton, Lewis Campbell

1895   *Powhatan*, with John A. West (3 acts; libretto by William A. Baker). Performed Evanston, IL, 1895.

Tirindelli, Pier Adolfo (b. Conegliano, Italy, 5 May 1858; d. Rome, Italy, 6 February 1937; in Cincinnati, 1896-1920; *Baker's*)

1897   *Blanc et noir* (in French). Performed Cincinnati, 15 December 1897.

Tittle, Stephen

1978   *Butler's Lives of the St.s*, with Richard Gibson and Gene Rickard (1 hour; libretto by Ann Wilson). Performed New York, 13 January 1978. Videotaped.

Titus, Hiram (b. Minneapolis, MN, 28 January 1947; ASCAP; *Baker's*)

1980 *Rosina* (2 acts; libretto by Barbara Field after Beaumarchais). Première by Minnesota Opera, Minneapolis, 26 April 1980. Kornick.

1980 *The Virgin Unmasked* (2 acts; libretto by Sharon Holland after Fielding, and including portions of Fielding's ballad opera). Performed by Children's Theatre, Minneapolis, 1980-81 season.

1983 *The Secret Garden* (on Burnett). Performed by Children's Theatre, Minneapolis, 16 September 1983.

1987 *The Sand Hills* (1 act; libretto by David Parrish after an American Indian legend). Performed Los Angeles, 28 March 1987.

1990 *Mother Goose* (libretto by Constance Congdon). Performed Minneapolis, 12 January 1990.

\- *Lucky Lady* (1 act; libretto by Kate Pogue; for children). NEA grant. *COS-4.*

Toch, Ernst (b. Vienna, Austria, 7 December 1887; d. Los Angeles, 1 October 1964; in U.S. from 1934; *Amerigrove*)

1927 *The Princess and the Pea.* Performed as *Die Prinzessen auf der Erbse*, Baden-Baden, Germany, 17 July 1927. Performed New York, 1940?

1962 *The Last Tale*, op. 88 (90 minutes; libretto by Melchior Lengyel after *The Arabian Nights*). Published by Mills Music.

Tonning, Gerard (b. Stavanger, Norway, 25 May 1860; d. New York, 10 June 1940; in U.S. from 1887; *Baker's*; Hipsher)

1910 *Leif Erikson* (3 acts; in Norwegian; libretto by C. M. Thuland after the Icelandic sagas). Sponsored by Leif Erikson Lodge of Sons of Norway. Première at Moore Theater, Seattle, WA, 10 December 1910, repeated with same cast Tacoma, WA, 12 March 1911; 3rd act performed at Brooklyn Academy of Music, NY, 4 October 1924.

1913 *All in a Garden Fair* (libretto by Mrs. H. W. Powell). Performed at Moore Theater, Seattle, WA, 1 November 1913, conducted by composer. On the same evening was presented:

1913 *In Old New England* (dramatic sketch; libretto by Sarah Pratt Carr; about life in Colonial America and including "authentic Colonial songs"—Johnson).

1917 *Blue Wing* (3 acts). Performed Seattle, WA, 1917.

\- *Woman's Wiles: or, Love Triumphant* (pantomime; text by composer).

Torke, Michael (b. Milwaukee, WI, 22 September 1961; *Who's Who*)

1986 *The Directions* (11 minutes; libretto by composer based on the telephone yellow pages). Performed Heraklion, Crete, 22 August 1986, and at Boston University, 1 May 1987.

Townsend, Douglas (b. New York, 8 November 1921; *Amerigrove*; *WhoAm*; *Who's Who*)

1947 *3 4-Minute Operas* (libretto by composer).

1947 *3 Folk Operettas* (libretto by O. Brand).

1954 *Lima Beans* (chamber opera; 25 minutes; libretto by Kreymborg). Performed by Twilight Concerts at Carnegie Recital Hall, New York, 7 January 1956. Published by Mercury.

Track, Gerhard (b. Vienna, Austria, 17 September 1934; to U.S. in 1958; Anderson; *WhoAm*; *Who's Who*)

1976   *Minnequa* (libretto by R. P. Dickey, based on an incident in Pueblo in 1896). Performed Pueblo, CO, January 1976.

1976   *The Reindeer's Surprise.*

Traetta, Philip (b. Filippo Trajetta in Venice, Italy, 8 January 1777; d. Philadelphia, 9 January 1854; in U.S. from 1799; *Amerigrove*; Porter)

1810   *Harlequin's Triumph in War and Peace* (musical farce; 2 acts; libretto by composer). Performed at City Tavern, New York, 22 January 1810.

\-   *The Venetian Maskers.*

Travis, Roy (b. New York, 24 June 1922; AMC; *Amerigrove*; *WhoAm*)

1965   *The Passion of Oedipus* (2 acts; libretto by composer after Sophocles). Première at University of California, Los Angeles, 8 November 1968.

1982   *The Black Bacchants* (2 acts; libretto by composer after Euripides). Based on West African rhythms.

Trefousse, Roger Philip (*WhoAm*)

1980   *Hoosick Falls* (1 act; libretto by Jane DeLynn). Performed New York, 20 June 1980.

1981   *The Monkey Opera* (40 minutes; libretto by Jane DeLynn, based on the statement that if a monkey typed forever it would eventually type out "Hamlet"). Performed by Encompass, at the Music Theater, New York, 1981, and at Brooklyn Academy of Music, NY, 17 April 1982.

1986   *The Composing of the Heliotrope Bouquet* (libretto by Eric Overmyer). Commission by New York Opera Repertory Theatre, New York; performed there, 1 October 1986 and September 1989.

\-   *The Emergence and Disappearance of the Giant Reptiles* (1 act; libretto by Jane DeLynn).

Tregillus, H. G. (AMC)

\-   *Gasparilla* (2 acts). *COS*-1.

\-   *Good Queen Bess* (2 acts). *COS*-1.

Treharne, Bryceson (b. Merthyr Tydfil, Wales, 30 May 1879; d. New York, 4 February 1948; to U.S. in 1927; Anderson; *Baker's*)

\-   *Abe Lincoln* (operetta).

\-   *A Christmas Carol* (operetta).

\-   *The Toymaker* (operetta).

Trimble, Lester Albert (b. Bangor, WI, 29 August 1923; d. New York, 31 December 1986; BMI; *Amerigrove*; *WhoAm*)

1962   *Boccaccio's Nightingale* (2 acts; libretto by George M. Ross after Boccaccio), revised 1983.

Trinkhaus, George J. (b. Bridgeport, CN, 13 April 1878; d. Ridgewood, NJ, 19 May 1960; Anderson)
- *Wizard of Avon.*

Trogan, Roland Bernard (b. Saginaw, MI, 6 August 1933; Anderson; *WhoAm*)
1953   *The Hat Man* (1 act). Performed Interlochen, MI, 1 August 1953.

Trogan, Stanley
1973   *The Wandering Scholar* (30 minutes; libretto after Hans Sachs, 1550). Performed Portland, OR, 4 December 1973.
- *Andrew Jackson, Old Hickory.* Commission in Portland, OR, for the U.S. Bicentennial. *COS-2.*

Troob, Daniel
1985   *Lost Illusions* (150 minutes; libretto by David Morgan after Balzac). Performed by National Music Theater Network, New York, 25 November 1985 and 20 March 1989.
1986   *All Bets Off*, with Kim Milford (140 minutes; libretto by the composers, Jamie Donnelly and John Maccabee; about a present-day Pygmalion). Performed by National Music Theater Network, New York, 10 March 1986, and Minneapolis, 15 March 1986. Published by National Music Theater Network.

Trow, George W. S.
1978   *The Tennis Game.* Performed New York, 18 February 1978.

Truesdale, Tad
1977   *Godsong*, with Hamilton Grandison (libretto by composers after James Weldon Johnson poems). Performed by LaMama, New York, 1977.
1980   *Daddy, Daddy* ("blues drama"; 2 acts). Performed by LaMama, New York, 3 December 1980.

Trythall, Gil(bert) (b. Knoxville, TN, 28 October 1930; AMC; *Amerigrove*; *Who's Who*)
1960   *The Music Lesson*, op. 4 (opera buffa; 1 act). *COS-1.*
1982   *The Terminal Opera* (multimedia; 26 minutes; libretto by Sheryl Evans). Performed Knoxville, TN, 23 October 1982. Revised 1987.

Tsontakis, George
1982   *Erotokritos* (opera-oratorio; 11 scenes; libretto by the composer and Loukas Skipitaris after Kornaros's 17th-century poem; in Greek with English narration). Performed by Metropolitan Greek Chorale, New York, 15 May 1982.

Tunick, Jonathan (b. New York, 19 April 1938; *Amerigrove*)
1985   *Days of Wine and Roses* (libretto by J. P. Miller after his TV play). Performed Waterford, CT, 18 August 1985.

Turner, Thomas
1969   *Four Thousand Dollars* (80 minutes; libretto by Vance Bourjaily). Performed Iowa City, IA, 6 March 1969.

Turok, Paul Harris (b. New York, 3 December 1929; *Amerigrove*; *Baker's*;
WhoAm; *Who's Who*)
1955   *Scene: Domestic* (chamber opera; libretto by composer). Performed
Aspen, CO, 2 August 1973.
1975   *Richard III* (4 acts; libretto by composer after Shakespeare).
Performed Philadelphia, 28 April 1980.
1979   *A Secular Masque* (1 act; libretto after Dryden). *COS-3*.

Turrin, Joseph Egido (b. Clifton, NJ, 4 January 1947; Anderson; *WhoAm*; *Who's
Who*)
1976   *Feathertop* (chamber opera; 2 acts).

Twombly, Mary Lynn (b. New York, 8 January 1935; Anderson; Cohen)
1964   *The Little Match Girl* (operetta for young voices. *COS-1*.
1969   *Who Are the Blind?* (operetta).

Tyler, Edwina Lee
1988   *Song of Lawino*, with Tiye Gireaud (70 minutes; libretto by Valeria
Vasilevski after Okot p'Bitek). NEA interarts grant. Performed
by Dance Theatre Workshop, Los Angeles, December 1988.

Underwood, Lucas (b. Salzburg, Austria, 22 November 1902; U.S. citizen, 1945;
Anderson)
1951   *The Holy Night* (Christmas opera; 1 act). Performed Stockton, CA,
1951.

Underwood, Pierson (AMC)
-        *Sourwood Mountain* (1 act). *COS-1*.

Underwood, William L. (b. Greenwood, MS, 9 March 1940; Anderson; *WhoAm*)
1974   *A Medicine for Melancholy* (1 act; libretto after story by Ray
Bradbury). Performed at Henderson State College, AR, 30 April
1974.
1977   *Jorinda and Joringel* (1 act). Commission by Arkansas Opera
Theatre, Little Rock. Tour, 1977-78 season.

Ussachevsky, Vladimir (b. Hailar, Manchuria, 21 October 1911; d. New York, 2
January 1990; in U.S. from 1931; *Amerigrove*)
1967   *Mourning Becomes Electra*. *See* Levy, Marvin David

Utter, Betty (Cohen)
1979   *Heidi*, with Ann Pugh (musical; libretto by composers after Spyri).
Performed New York, November 1979.

Valenti, R.
1971   *The Pledge.* Performed New York, 25 March 1971.

Valinsky, Eric (ASCAP)
1984   *Freshwater* (1 act; on Woolf); developed in rehearsal with Rhonda Rubinson and Peter Schubert. Performed by Opera Uptown, New York, 19 October 1984.
1986   *The Bus to Stockport and Other Stories,* with John Cage and Peter Schubert. Performed by Opera Uptown, 20 February 1986.
1986   *Skit Night on Mount Fuji* (libretto by Peter Schubert). Performed by Opera Uptown, New York, 2 November 1986.

Valkenburg, Warner Van
1936   *The Gay Grenadiers.* Performed Los Angeles.

Van Ausdal, Caroline
1988   *In Spider's Garden* (30 minutes; libretto by composer, about the effect of divorce on children; for children). Commission by Friends Music Camp, Barnesville, OH. Performed there, summer 1988.

Van Broekhoven, John (b. Beek, Holland, 23 March 1856; d. 1930; Hipsher)
1905   *A Colonial Wedding* (1 act; about the Puritans). Performed Cincinnati.
-    *Camaralzaman* (3 acts).

Van der Stucken, Frank (b. Fredericksburg, TX, 15 October 1858; d. Hamburg, Germany, 16 August 1929; *Amerigrove*)
-    *Vlasda.* Not produced.

Vandervelde, Jan
1986   *Seven Sevens* (7 parts; libretto by Judy MacGuire). Performed Minneapolis, MN, 11 April 1986, and by Minnesota Opera, St. Paul, November 1987, January 1988, fall 1988, and 1989-90 season.

Van de Vate, Nancy Hayes (b. Plainfield, NJ, 39 December 1930; Anderson; *Baker's*; Cohen; *WhoAm*; *Who's Who*)
1960   *In the Shadow of the Glen* (chamber opera; libretto after Synge), for soprano, 2 tenors, baritone, piano.
1960   *The Death of the Hired Man* (chamber opera; libretto after Robert Frost).
1983   *A Night in the Royal Ontario Museum* (theater piece), for soprano and tape. Performed Washington, DC, 13 April 1984.
1986   *The Saga of Cocaine Lil* (theater piece), for mezzo-soprano, 4 singers, percussion. Performed Frankfurt am Main, Germany, 20 April 1988.

Van Etten, Jane (Mrs. Alfred Burritt Andrews; b. St. Paul, MN; Hipsher)
1914   *Guido Ferranti* (1 act; libretto by Elsie M. Wilbor from Oscar Wilde's play *The Duchess of Padua*). Première by Century Opera Co. at the Auditorium, Chicago, 29 December 1914. Bispham

Medal, 1926. Hipsher: ". . . first opera written by an American woman and presented by an organization with the standing of the Century Opera Company."

Van Grove, Isaac (b. Philadelphia, 5 September 1892; d. 1979; Hipsher)
1925   *The Music Robber* (opéra comique; 2 acts; libretto by Richard L. Stokes, concerning Mozart's last 4 months). Act 1 performed at American Theater of Musical Productions, 14 June 1925, when he received the Bispham Medal. Act 2 completed May 1926; the whole performed by Zoological Gardens Opera Co., Cincinnati, 4 July 1926.
1959   *The Other Wise Man* (60 minutes). Performed Bentonville, AR, 14 July 1959.
1964   *The Shining Chalice* (1 act; libretto by Janice Lovoos). Performed Eureka Springs, AR, 30 July 1964.
1966   *Ruth* (Biblical opera; 27 minutes; libretto by Janice Lovoos). Performed Eureka Springs, AR, 22 July 1966.
1976   *The Prodigal—His Wandering Years* (1 act; libretto by Janice Lovoos, set in the 1st century B.C. in Egypt). Performed Eureka Springs, AR, 18 July 1976.

Van Tieghem, David
1990   *Urchin 1* (55 minutes; libretto by composer and Tina Dudek; science fiction subject). Performed by Performance Space 122, New York, 5 January 1990.
  –   *The Vendler Television Playhouse* (libretto by Susan Rice, about early television).

Veazie, George Augustus (b. Boston, 18 December 1835; d. Chelsea, MA, 20 November 1915; *Baker's*, 5th ed.)
(*Baker's* states that Veazie composed several light operas.)

Vecchione, Glen
1988   *The Tunisia Lunch and Fountain.* Performed by Musical Theatre Works, New York, 21 June 1988.

Venanzi, Henry
1984   *Three Days to Perfection* (45 minutes; libretto by several authors, on Manes's *Be a Perfect Person in Just Three Days*, developed by Cincinnati Opera ECCO/Robert E. Lewis Intermediate School). Performed Sharonville, OH, 16 February 1984.

Venth, Carl (Karl) (b. Cologne, Germany, 16 [Hipsher: 18] February 1860; d. San Antonio, TX, 29 January 1938; to U.S. in 1880, citizen 1885; *Baker's*, 5th ed.; Hipsher)
1923   *Pan in America* ("lyric dance drama"; 1 act). National Federation of Music Clubs prize; performed at its convention in Asheville, NC, 13 June 1923.
1926   *The Rebel* ("fairy opera" with dance; 5 scenes; libretto by composer). Performed Fort Worth, TX, 29 May 1926.
1935   *La vida de la mision* (about an Indian uprising in San Antonio). Performed San Antonio, TX, through a gift specified in his widow's will, 28 October 1959 (*Baker's* says 1958).

- *Alexander's Horse* ("musical play"; text by Lord Barry).
- *Cathal* ("short music drama"; 1 act; text by Fiona MacLoyd).
- *Dolls* ("musical extravaganza"; libretto by composer).
- *Jack* ("music drama"; 1 act; text by Earl Hard adapted by composer).
- *The Juggler* (libretto by composer), for soprano, alto, baritone.
- *Lima Beans* ("short opera"; adapted from a "scherzo play" by Kreymborg).
- *The Sun God* ("oriental opera"; 1 act; libretto by composer). (*Baker's*: "etc.")

Venuto, Rocco
1896 *The Three Enemies* (grand opera). Performed Kansas City, MO, 11 April 1896, and at the St. Louis Fair, 1904.
1924 *The Disciple* (1 act).

Vernon, Ashley (b. Kurt Manschinger in Zeil-Wieselburg, Austria, 25 July 1902; d. New York, 23 February 1968; in U.S. from 1940, when he adopted his new name; *Baker's*)
1953 *The Barber of New York* (70 minutes; libretto by Greta Hartwig, after 18th-century poems). Performed New York, 26 May 1953. Published by Mercury.
1955 *Grand Slam* (25 minutes). Performed Stamford, CT, 25 June 1955. Published by Mercury.
1956 *Cupid and Psyche* (1 hour; libretto by Greta Hartwig). Performed Woodstock, NY, 27 July 1956. Published by Mercury.
1969 *The Triumph of Punch* ("opera buffa"; 70 minutes). Performed Brooklyn, NY, 25 January 1969. Published by Mercury.

Verrall, John (b. Britt, IA, 17 June 1908; ACA; *Amerigrove*)
1951 *The Cowherd and the Sky Maiden* (2 acts—90 minutes; libretto by E. Ehephard after a Chinese legend). Performed Seattle, WA, 17 January 1952.
1952 *The Wedding Knell* (chamber opera; 1 act; libretto after Hawthorne). Performed Seattle, WA, 5 December 1952.
1955 *Three Blind Mice* (chamber opera; 1 act; libretto by G. Hughes). Performed Seattle, WA, 22 May 1955.

Villa-Lobos, Heitor (b. Rio de Janeiro, Brazil, 5 March 1887; d. there, 17 November 1959; *Baker's*)
1948 *Magdalena* (2 acts). Première, Los Angeles, 26 July 1948.
1956 *Yerma* (libretto after Lorca). Première, Santa Fe, NM, 12 August 1971.

Vinatieri, Felix (b. 1834? in Turin, Italy; in U.S. from 1859)
1889? *The American Volunteer* (libretto by composer). Performed Yankton, SD, 4 March 1961. See *New York Times*, 2 April 1961.
- *The Barber of the Regiment.*
- *Heart and Love.*
- *One Summer in Texas.*

Vincent, Henry Bethuel (b. Denver, CO, 28 December 1872; d. Erie, PA, 7 January 1872; Anderson)
1906   *Esperanza.* Performed Washington, DC.
-     *Indian Days* (operetta).

Vincent, John (b. Birmingham, AL, 17 May 1902; d. Santa Monica, CA, 21 January 1977; *Amerigrove*)
1969   *Primeval Void* (opera buffa; 1 act; libretto by composer and H. Reese). Performed Vienna, Austria, 14 May 1973.

Viola, Albert T.
-     *Head over Heels* (libretto by composer and William S. Kilborne, Jr., after Hecht/Goodman's *The Wonder Hat*, done as *commedia dell'arte*). Published by Samuel French.

Virsi, Salvatore
1928   *Vanna.* Performed New York.
1945   *Il cancelleto d'oro* (1 act). Performed New York, 18 May 1945, and Brooklyn, NY, 26 April 1947.
1948   *Sulamita* (1 act). Broadcast on WNYC radio, New York, 19 December 1948.
1955   *The Princess and the Spindle* (3 acts). Performed Bronx, NY, 6 May 1955.
-     *The Sleeping Beauty.*

Vodery, Will (b. Philadelphia, 8 October 1885; d. New York, 18 November 1951; *Amerigrove*; Vodery enjoyed a distinguished career on Broadway, including *Ziegfeld's Follies*, 1913-32.)
1922   *Blue Monday.*

Vogrich, Max (b. Hermannstadt, Transylvania, 24 January 1852; d. New York, 10 June 1916; in U.S. 1886-1902 and 1914-16, plus visits; *Baker's*)
1893   *King Arthur.* Performed Leipzig, Germany, 26 November 1893. (*Baker's* states that he composed "several operas to his own librettos" during his years in the U.S.)

Vollinger, William Francis (b. Hackensack, NJ, 28 June 1945; AMC; Anderson; *WhoAm*)
1980   *The Witnesses* (1 act—24 minutes; libretto by composer, about modern China).
-     *Psychic Phenomena* (chamber opera).

Vollrath, Carl Paul (b. New York, 26 March 1931; AMC; Anderson; *WhoAm*; *Who's Who*)
1964   *The Quest* (prologue and 2 acts; libretto by composer, about a medieval crusade). Performed by Florida State University Workshop, Tallahassee, 10 June 1966.

Von Tilzer, Harry (b. Detroit, MI, 8 July 1872; d. New York, 10 January 1946; *Amerigrove*)
1905   *The Fisher Maiden* (comic opera; libretto by A. J. Lamb). Performed New York, 5 October 1903.

1909 *The Kissing Girl* (comic opera; libretto by S. Stange and lyrics by V. P. Bryan). Performed Chicago, 25 October 1909.

Vooss, Vladimir A. (b. Harbin, China, 27 August 1944; U.S. citizen, 1963; AMC; Anderson)
1975 *Sophia Prunikos* (multimedia opera).
1977– *City of Light* (electronic opera; 1 act). NEA grant.

Wad, Emmanuel
1933 *Swing Low* (1 act). Performed Baltimore, MD, 13 December 1933.

Wade, James (b. Granite City, IL, 5 January 1930; Anderson)
1948 *Old Christmas* (10 minutes).
1976 *The Martyred* (libretto after novel by Richard E. Kim). Performed Seoul, Korea, 18 April 1970. See *SAI Panpipes*, May 1978, 29.
1978 *A Wicked Voice.*

Wagenaar, Bernard (b. Arnhem, Netherlands, 18 July 1894; d. York, ME, 19 May 1971; in U.S. from 1920; ASCAP; *Amerigrove*)
1943 *Pieces of Eight* (chamber opera; 2 acts; libretto by E. Eager). Performed at Columbia University, New York, 10 May 1944.

Wagner, Joseph Frederick (b. Springfield, MA, 9 January 1900; d. Los Angeles, 12 October 1974; ASCAP; *Amerigrove*)
1964 *New England Sampler* (1 act; libretto by J. Karsavina after Chekhov's *The Marriage Proposal*). Performed Los Angeles, 26 February 1965.

Wagner, Thomas (b. Brackenridge, PA, 24 February 1931; ASCAP; Anderson)
1963 *The Crocodile* (1 act; libretto after Dostoevsky). Performed at New York University, September 1963.
- *The Beggar. COS*-1.
- *The Wheat Remains.*

Waites, Luigi
1989 *Headlights*, with Frank Fong, Rex Gray, Rich Hiatt, Lori Loree, and Mark Nelson (about literacy). Performed by Omaha Magic Theatre, NE, 28 April 1989.
1990 *Body Leaks*, with Marianne de Pury (multimedia; libretto by Megan Terry, Sora Kim, and Jo Ann Schmidman). Performed by Omaha Magic Theatre, NE, 27 April 1990.

Wald, Max (b. Litchfield, IL, 14 July 1889; d. Dowagiac, MI, 14 August 1954; Anderson; *Baker's*; Hipsher)
1936 *Mirandolina* (grand opera; 3 acts; libretto by composer after Carlo Goldoni's *La locandiera*).
1942 *Gay Little World* (comic opera).
1951 *A Provincial Episode* (1 act—45 minutes; American subject). Performed Athens, OH, 17 July 1952.

Walden, Russell (ASCAP)
    1985   *Agnes* (libretto by Wendy Lamb and Michael John La Chiusa).
            Richard Rodgers grant, 1986. Performed by Playwrights
            Horizons, New York, 1985-86 season.
    1985   *Eulogy for Mister Hamm* (libretto by Wendy Lamb). Richard
            Rodgers grant, 1986. Performed by Playwrights Horizons, 1985-
            86 season.
            (Walden also composed the musical *Break*, 1986.)

Walden, William
    1983   *This Week I'm Famous* (libretto by composer). Charles River
            Creative Arts Program contest winner, 1983. Performed Dover,
            MA, July 1983.

Waldman, Robert (ASCAP)
    1974   *Saturday Matinee.* NEA grant.
    1989   *The Play's the Thing* (formerly *Shakespeare: or, What You Will*;
            libretto by Edward West; for children). Performed by
            Theatreworks/USA, New York, January 1989.
            (Waldman also composed a jazz musical, *America's Sweetheart*,
            performed in Hartford, CT, 8 March 1985.)

Wales, Evelyn
    1955   *Little Gypsy Gay* (1 act—50 minutes). Performed Milwaukee, WI,
            1955.

Walker, Donald Burke (b. Ventura, CA, 18 December 1941; Anderson)
    1976   *Fortitude* (9 scenes). Performed at University of South Florida,
            Tampa, 1977.

Wallace, Stewart
    1985   *Soapopera* (rock opera; 1 act; libretto by Jim Morgan). Performed
            by Texas Opera Theater, Houston, 6 June 1985.
    1987   *Where's Dick* (3 acts; libretto by Michael Korie). OPERA America
            grant, 1986; ASCAP Young Composers' grant, 1987. Commission
            by Opera/Omaha, NE. Performed by Playwrights Horizons, New
            York, 22 June 1987, Opera/Omaha, 24 September 1987, and Texas
            Opera Theater, Houston, 24 May 1989 (Kornick gives the last as
            the première, on 1 June 1989).
    1989   *Kabbalah*, with Michael Korie. Performed Brooklyn, NY (*COS*-4
            says by New Music America, New York), 16 November 1989.
            (Wallace also composed *Three Complaints*, a musical, 1985; and
            Madonna, "a musical comedy on the New Testament," 1985.)

Wallach, Joelle (b. New York, 29 June [no year given]; Cohen; *WhoAm*)
    1988   *The King's Twelve Moons* (40 minutes; libretto after Grimm's "The
            Twelve Dancing Princesses").

Walth, Gary
    1989   *The Star and the Sceptre.* Performed at Minot State University,
            ND, January 1989.

Ward, Dale
 1980 *Dialog/Curious George*, with Christopher Knowles and Robert
    Wilson. Performed New York, 24 June 1980.

Ward, Diane (Corajane Diane Bunce; b. Jackson, MI, 19 January 1919; Anderson;
   Cohen)
 - *Visiting the Bancrofts*.
 - *The Little Dipper* (operetta).

Ward, Michael (ASCAP)
 1982 *Personals* (1 act). Performed by Golden Fleece, New York, 26
    February 1982.
 1982 *Photograph* (1 act; libretto after Gertrude Stein). Performed by
    Golden Fleece, New York, 26 February 1982.
 1982 *Songs for a City* (1 act; libretto after Brecht). Performed by
    Golden Fleece, New York, 26 February 1982.

Ward, Robert (Eugene) (b. Cleveland, OH, 13 September 1917; *Amerigrove*; *Who's
   Who*)
 1955 *He Who Gets Slapped* (*Pantaloon*) (3 acts; libretto by Bernard
    Stambler after Andreyev's play *He Who Gets Slapped*), revised
    1973. Performed by Juilliard School, New York, 17 May 1956.
    Published by Galaxy.
 1960 *The Crucible* (4 acts; libretto by Bernard Stambler after Arthur
    Miller). Performed by New York Opera, 26 October 1961, by
    Pennsylvania Opera Theater, 27 October 1988, and in Des Moines,
    IA, 1 July 1989. Published by Galaxy. New York Critics Circle
    award and Pulitzer Prize, 1960.
 1964 *The Lady from Colorado* (light opera; 2 acts; libretto by Bernard
    Stambler after H. Croy). Première by Central City Opera, CO, 3
    July 1964 (Kornick: July 17). Pulitzer Prize.
 1973 *Claudia Legare* (tragedy; 4 acts—160 minutes [Kornick: 3 acts—120
    minutes]; libretto by Bernard Stambler after Henrik Ibsen's *Hedda
    Gabler*). Première, Minneapolis, 14 April 1978. Published by
    Galaxy. Kornick.
 1981 *Abelard and Heloise* (prelude and 3 acts; libretto by Jan Hartman).
    NEA grant. Première by Charlotte Opera, NC, 19 February 1982.
    Kornick.
 1982 *Minutes till Midnight* (product of an NEA grant for *The Secret
    Weapon*; 3 acts; libretto by composer and Daniel Lang; takes place
    in the future). Commission and première by Greater Miami
    Opera, FL, 4 June 1982 (Kornick: June 5).

Ward-Steinman, David (b. Alexandria, LA, 6 November 1936; AMC; *Amerigrove*;
   Who's Who)
 1968 *The Tale of Issoumbochi* (20 minutes; libretto by Susan Lucas after
    a Japanese story). Performed San Diego, CA, 18 April 1968.
    Published by Marks.
 1976 *Tamar* (mixed-media music-drama; 3 acts; libretto by William
    Adams after Robinson Jeffers). *COS*-2.

Ware, Harriet (Mrs. Hugh M. Krumhaar; b. Waupun, WI, 26 August 1877; d.
New York, 9 February 1962; Anderson; *Baker's*; Cohen; Hipsher)
- *Priscilla.* Bispham medal, 1923. (Hipsher, 1934: composer at work
on this opera.)
- *Sinner's Saint.*
- *Undine* ("lyric tone poem"; 1 act; libretto by Edward Markham),
for women's chorus, piano solo, orchestra. Première by Eurydice
Chorus, Philadelphia; also by New York Symphony Orchestra; and
by Washington, Los Angeles and Marine Band orchestras.
Performed Baltimore, MD, as a ballet. Bispham medal, 1923.
Published by Presser.
- *Waltz for Three* (operetta).

Wargo, Richard (b. 1957; ASCAP)
(Wargo writes his own librettos.)
1979 *The Crystal Mirror* (3 acts—100 minutes; libretto after Hawthorne's
Dr. Heidegger's Experiment). Performed Rochester, NY, 28 April
1979. Published by Belwin-Mills.
A Chekhov Trilogy:
1984 *The Seduction of a Lady* (comic chamber opera; 1 act—42 minutes;
libretto after Neil Simon's *The Good Doctor* from Anton Chekhov's
story). Performed by National Institute for Music Theater, New
York, 11 May 1984; at Florida State University, Tallahassee, 7-9
March 1985; and at Lake George Opera Festival, Glens Falls, NY,
10 August 1985. Kornick.
1984 *The Music Shop* (farce; 1 act—1 hour; libretto after Anton Chekhov's
short story "Forgot"). Performed Minneapolis, 26 December 1984,
16 May 1985, and 25 September 1985. The entire trilogy
performed Chautauqua, NY, July 1990. Kornick.
1987 *A Visit to the Country* (1 act). Commission and première by Greater
Miami Opera, FL, winter 1987.

Warhol, Mark
1986 *Sam* (2 acts—100 minutes; libretto by James Swindell). Performed at
Rice University, Houston, TX, 2 November 1986.

Waring, Kate (Katherine Finlay; b. Alexandria, LA, 22 April 1953; Cohen; *Who's
Who*)
1988 *Rapunzel* (chamber opera; libretto by Rudiger Gollnick after
Grimm; in German). Performed Bonn, Germany, 7 November
1989.

Warner, Russell
1988 *Reefer Madness* (libretto by John Mangano; a parody of the movie).
Performed by Theatre for the New City, New York, 14 April
1988.
(Warner also composed a musical, *Opera Line*, 1986.)

Warren, Betsy Frost (Warren-Davis; b. Boston; Cohen; *WhoAm*)
1987 *The Gift of the Magi* (18 minutes; libretto by David McCord after
O. Henry). Performed New Orleans, 1985, and 6 December 1987.

Warren, Richard Henry (b. Albany, NY, 17 September 1859; d. South Chatham, MA, 3 December 1933; *Amerigrove*; Hipsher)
1880   *Igala.*
1882   *All on a Summer's Day.*
1886   *Magnolia.*
1889   *The Rightful Heir* ("romantic opera").
1897   *Phyllis* ("romantic opera"). Performed at Waldorf-Astoria Theater, New York, 7-21 May 1900.

Warwick, Mary Carol (b. Lumberton, NC, 28 October 1939; Cohen; *WhoAm*) (Warwick writes her own librettos.)
1985   *The Twelve Months Brothers.* Commission by Margo Mattison.
1985   *Lealista* (2 acts—90 minutes; after Hemingway's *The Fifth Column*). Performed at Southwest Texas State University, San Marcos, 29 March 1985.
1985   *Sisters of Faith* (50 minutes; about Texas in the 1880s). Commission for the Texas sesquicentennial festival by Texas Composers and Southwest Texas University. Performed at Southwest Texas State University, San Marcos, 27 April 1986, and New Branfels, TX, spring 1986.
1988   *The Last Leaf* (35 minutes; after O. Henry). Performed at University of Houston, TX, 27 April, 1988, and Lumberton, NC, 10 September 1989.
1989   *Twins* (1 act—1 hour; about a touring sideshow in the American South). Performed at University of Houston, TX, 28 April 1989. Scheduled for performance in Houston, spring 1992.
1990   *Drycop's Dilemma* (25 minutes; set in a forest; for children). Performed Houston, TX, spring 1991.

Washburn, Gary Scott (b. Tulsa, OK, 14 January 1946; AMC; Anderson)
-    *Hanbleceya.* NEA grant.

Waters, J. Kevin, S.J. (b. Seattle, WA, 24 June 1933; Anderson; *WhoAm*)
1971   *The Mask of Hiroshima.* Performed at Santa Clara University, CA.
1972   *Job* ("musico-drama"). Performed Frascati, Italy.
1978   *Dear Ignatius, Dear Isabel* (1 acts). Commissioned for 125th anniversary of and performed at Loyola College, Baltimore, 4 May 1978.

Wathall, Alfred G. (1880-1938; in U.S. from 1890; taught at Northwestern University)
1898   *The Belles of Stamboul.*
1903   *The Sultan of Sulu* ("a musical satire"; 2 acts).

Watson, Walter Robert (b. Canton, OH, 13 October 1933; Anderson; *WhoAm*)
1981   *Deborah Sampson* (1 act; libretto by composer, about a woman fighting in the Revolutionary War). Performed at University of Georgia, Athens, 9 April 1981.

Watts, Wintter (b. Cincinnati, OH, 14 March 1884; d. Brooklyn, NY, 1 November 1962; Anderson; *Baker's*)
-    *Pied Piper.*

Wayditch, Gabriel (birth name Baron Gabriel Wajditsch Verbovac von Dönhoff; b. Budapest, Hungary, 28 December 1888; d. New York, 28 July 1969; in U.S. from 1907; Anderson; *Baker's*)
(Wayditch wrote his own librettos, in Hungarian.)

1939   *Horus*. Performed, at composer's expense, Philadelphia, 5 January 1939.
-    *Anthony of Padua*.
-    *Buddha*.
-    *The Caliph's Magician* (1 act—2 hours; his shortest opera).
-    *The Catacombs*.
-    *The Heretics* (8 hours—his longest).
-    *Jesus before Herod*. Performed in concert form by San Diego Symphony, 5 April 1979.
-    *Maria Magdalena*.
-    *Maria Tesztver*.
-    *Neptune's Daughter*.
-    *Nereida*.
-    *Opium Dreams*.
-    *Sahara*.
-    *The Venus Dwellers*.

Wayne, Hayden (b. Bronx, NY, 2 March 1949; *WhoAm*)

1987   *Neon, A Street Opera* ("theatre noir"). Performed by Nola Studios, New York, November 1987.

Weaver, Brent

1990   *Silence*. Performed at Clayton State College, Morrow, GA, 1990.

Webber, John C. (b. Croydon, Surrey, England, 4 May 1949; AMC; *WhoAm*; *Who's Who*)

1981   *The Nativity* (30 minutes; libretto by Rembert Herbert after a Chester miracle play with addition text; includes congregational hymn singing). Commission by St. James Church, Washington, DC; performed there, 24 December 1981.
-    *A Full Moon in March* (libretto after the play by W. B. Yeats).

Weber, Bertha

1932   *The Mysterious Characters of Mr. Fu*. Performed Oakland, CA, 1932.

Weber, Joseph (b. Antioch, CA, 31 July 1937; Anderson)

1986   *Sor Maria* (1 act—50 minutes; libretto by composer and Michele Larsson, about a 17th-century abbess; in Spanish). Performed Santa Fe, NM, 4 April 1986. Published by Larsson/Weber.

Webster, William Byron

1987   *The Little Match Girl* ("grand chamber opera"; 150 minutes; libretto by composer). Published by W. B. Webster.

Wehner, George (b. 1890)
(Wehner wrote his own librettos.)

1959   *Frisco Mame* (1 act). Performed at Central Park Mall, New York, 12 February 1959, and Church of the Neighbor, New York, 1961.

1961   *The Mark of Kings* (1 act). Performed at Central Park Mall, New York, 24 June 1961.

1961   *So Sings the Bell* (or *So Sing the Bells*; 1 act). Performed at Central Park Mall, New York, 24 June 1961.

1961   *The Amiable Best* (1 act). Performed at Central Park Mall, New York, 25 July 1961.

1961   *Two Tales of Ancient China*. Performed at Central Park Mall, New York, 11 July 1961.

1961   *The Wild Swan* (3 scenes). Performed at Central Park Mall, New York, 18 July 1961.

1961   *The Star in the Night* (2 acts). Performed at Central Park Mall, New York, 8 and/or 22 August 1961.

1964   *Into a Silence* (3 acts; about an atomic war). Performed at Central Park Mall, New York, 18 July 1964.

1965   *Three Days After* (or *Road to Emmaus*; 1 act). Performed by Amato Opera, New York, 18 June 1965.

-     *The Heavenly Party* (1 act).

-     *Prairie Peace Day* (1 act).

Weidberg, Ron

1984   *Dracula* (3 acts—105 minutes; libretto by Irwin Donald Nier after Stoker). Performed by American-Israeli Opera, New York, 11 March 1984.

1986   *Waiting for Godot* (2 acts; libretto after Beckett). Performed Bloomington, IN, April 1986.

1986   *The Muse of Eloquence* (libretto by Irwin Donald Nier). Performed by Opera Uptown, New York, 2 November 1986.

Weigel, Eugene (b. Cleveland, OH, 11 October 1910; *Amerigrove*; *Baker's*)

1953   *The Lion Makers* (libretto after Hindu folktales).

1958   *The Mountain Child* (1 act; libretto by R. O. Bowen). Performed Missoula, MT, 27 July 1958.

Weigl, Karl (b. Vienna, Austria, 6 February 1881; d. New York, 11 August 1949; in U.S. from 1938; *Amerigrove*)

1975   *The Pied Piper of Hamelin* (1 act). Performed New York, May 1975. Published by General Music.

Weil, Oscar (1840-1921)

-     *In Mexico*.

Weill, Kurt (b. Dessau, Germany, 2 March 1900; d. New York, 3 April 1950; in U.S. from 1935; *Amerigrove*)

1933   *The Threepenny Opera* (American libretto by Marc Blitzstein). The opera had been performed, as *Die Dreigroschenoper*, in Baden-Baden, 1927. Performances in U.S.: Waltham, MA, 14 June 1952; Philadelphia, 16 December 1946; by Arkansas Opera Theatre, 1989; Opera/Omaha, 1989; Skylight Comic Opera, Milwaukee, WI, 1989; and in Los Angeles, 10 September 1989.

1935   *My Kingdom for a Cow*.

1936   *The Eternal Road* (revision of *Der Weg der Verheissung*, 1935; biblical drama; prologue and 3 acts; libretto by Franz Werfel, revision by L. Lewisohn). Performed at Manhattan Opera House, New York, 7 January 1937.

1938　*Knickerbocker Holiday* (operetta; libretto by Maxwell Anderson). Performed Hartford, CT, 26 September 1938, and at Ethel Barrymore Theatre, New York, 19 October 1938.

1939　*The Ballad of Magna Carta* (scenic cantata; libretto by Maxwell Anderson). Broadcast on CBS radio, 4 February 1940.

1940　*Lady in the Dark* (musical play; libretto by Moss Hart and Ira Gershwin). Performed at Alvin Theatre, New York, 23 January 1941.

1944　*The Firebrand of Florence* (operetta; libretto by E. J. Mayer and Ira Gershwin). Performed at Alvin Theatre, New York, 22 March 1945.

1946　*Street Scene* (tragedy—"Broadway opera"; 2 acts; lyrics by Langston Hughes, book by Elmer Rice). Performed at Adelphi Theatre, New York, 9 January 1947; Dusseldorf, Germany, 1948; Philadelphia, 16 December 1946; and by New York Opera, 1959 and 6 October 1989. Published by Chappell, 1948. Kornick.

1948　*Down in the Valley* (college opera; 1 act; libretto by A. Sundgaard; incorporates Kentucky songs). Performed at Indiana University, Bloomington, 15 July 1948. Many performances. Published by G. Schirmer.

1948　*Love Life*, reworked by Alan Jay Lerner as *Praise House*. Performed by American Music Theater Festival, spring 1990.

1949　*Lost in the Stars* (musical tragedy; libretto by Maxwell Anderson after Alan Paton's *Cry, the Beloved Country*). Première at Music Box Theatre, New York, 30 October 1949; also performed by New York City Opera, 1958, and on Broadway, New York, 1974. Film, 1974; recorded by MCA, 1976. Kornick.

-　*The Boy Who Said Yes* (30 minutes). Published by Associated Music.

-　*Royal Palace*, op. 17 (1 act).

-　*The Seven Deadly Sins.*

-　*The Shah Has His Photograph Taken* (30 minutes).

Weinberg, Jacob (b. Odessa, Ukraine, 7 July 1879; d. New York, 2 November 1956; in U.S. from 1926, citizen 1934; *Amerigrove*)

1934　*The Pioneers of Israel* (translation of *Hechalutz*). Performed Jerusalem, 1925, in Hebrew.

Weinberger, Jaromir (b. Prague, Bohemia, 8 January 1896; d. St. Petersburg, FL, 8 August 1967; in U.S. off-and-on from 1922, permanently from 1939, citizen 1948; *Amerigrove*; Anderson; *Baker's*; David Z. Kushner, "Jaromir Weinberger (1896-1967): From Bohemia to America," *American Music* 6/3 [Fall 1988]: 293-313)

c　1926　*Kocourkov.*

1926　*Schwanda, the Bagpiper* (*Švanda dudák*; *Schwanda, der Dudelsackpfeifer*; singspiel; 2 acts; libretto by Milos Kareš). Première at National Theater, Prague, 27 April 1927; also performed Breslau (translated by Max Brod), 16 December 1928, and by Metropolitan Opera, New York, 7 November 1931. Performed 2,000 times, in various languages, 1927-31. Published by Universal Edition.

1931   *The Beloved Voice* (*Die geliebte Stimme*). Performed Munich, Germany, 28 February 1931.

1932   *The Outcasts of Poker Flat* (*Lidé z Pokerflatu*) (based on the story by Bret Harte). Performed Brno, Czechoslovakia, 19 November 1932.

1932   *Na ruzich ustlano* (*Bed of Roses*) (operetta). Performed Prague, 1934.

1933   *Frühlingssturme* (operetta). Performed Berlin, Germany, 1933.

1937   *Wallenstein* (*Valdstejn*) (after the tragedy by Schiller). Performed Vienna, Austria, 18 November 1937 and February 1938.

-   *Apropo co dela Andula* (operetta).

-   *Cisar pan na tresnich* (operetta).

Weiner, Lawrence (b. Cleveland, OH, 22 June 1932; Anderson; *WhoAm*)
1982   *Chipita Rodríguez* (2 acts—2 hours; libretto by Leo Carillo and John Wilson, about the hanging of a woman in Texas; in English). Première by Corpus Christi Symphony, TX, 3 April 1982. Kornick.

Weiner, Lazar (b. Kiev, Ukraine, 24 October 1897; d. New York, 10 January 1982; in U.S. from 1914; *Amerigrove*)
1956   *The Golem* (prologue, 2 scenes, and epilogue; libretto by R. Smolover). Performed White Plains, NY, 13 January 1957, and at 92nd Street Y, New York, 1981.

Weisberg, Steve
1989   *A Guest of Honor: Scott Joplin* (2 acts; libretto by Howard Pflanzer; includes some Joplin music). Performed by Jewish Association for Services to the Aged, New York, 26 February 1989.

Weisgall, Hugo (b. Ivançice [Eibenschütz], Moravia, 13 October 1912; in U.S. from 1920, citizen 1926; ASCAP; *Amerigrove*; *Who's Who*)
1932   *Night* (1 act; libretto after S. Asch).

1934   *Lillith* (1 act; libretto after L. Elman).

1950   *The Tenor* (1 act—70 minutes; libretto by K. Shapiro and E. Lert after Wedekind's *Der Kammersänger*). Performed Baltimore, MD, 1 February 1952. Published by Presser; recorded by CRI.

1952   *The Stronger* (1 act—25 minutes; libretto by R. Hart after Strindberg). Performed Westport, CT, with piano, 9 August 1952, and New York, with orchestra, January 1955; by Encompass Theater, New York, 1980, and Opera Ensemble of New York, 5 October 1988. Published by Presser. Recorded by CRI.

1956   *Six Characters in Search of an Author* (3 acts; libretto by Dennis Johnston after Pirandello). Performed New York, 26 April 1959, and Chicago, 1990. Published by Presser.

1958   *Purgatory* (1 act—35 minutes; libretto after Yeats). Performed Washington, DC, 17 February 1961. Published by Presser.

1959   *The Gardens of Adonis* (prologue and 2 scenes; libretto by John Olon-Scrymgeour after Shakespeare and A. Obey's *Venus and Adonis*), revised 1977-81. NEA grant.

1963   *Athalia* (2 acts—105 minutes; libretto by R. F. Goldman after Racine). Performed New York, 17 February 1964. Published by Presser.

1968   *Nine Rivers from Jordan* (prologue and 3 acts; libretto by Denis Johnston after his novel). Première by New York City Opera, 9 October 1968. Kornick.

1976   *Jenny: or, The Hundred Nights* (1 act—80 minutes; libretto by John Hollander after Yukio Mishima's translation of a Noh play, *Sotoba Komache*). NEA grant. Première by Juilliard American Opera Center, New York, 22 April 1976. Published by Presser. Tape at AMC.

1988   *Will You Marry Me?* (1 act—23 minutes; libretto by Charles Kondek after Alfred Sutro's play *A Marriage Has Been Arranged*). Commission and performance by Opera Ensemble of New York, New York, 5 October 1988 and 8 March 1989 (Kornick has the last as the première).

1990   *Queen Esther* (or *Esther*; libretto by Charles Kondek after the Old Testament). Commission by San Francisco Opera.

\-   *Henry IV* (libretto after Pirandello).

Weiss, Adolph (b. Baltimore, MD, 12 September 1891; d. Van Nuys, CA, 12 February 1971; ACA; *Amerigrove*)

1930   *The Libation Bearers* (choreographic cantata; 2 acts—90 minutes; libretto after Aeschylus).

\-   *David* (libretto by D. H. Lawrence), with speakers and orchestra. Incomplete.

Weiss, Elliot

1981   *Cocktails at Five* ("a musical look at middleclass malaise"; libretto by Michael Champagne). Performed by Encompass Theater, New York, 12 May 1981.

Weiss, George David

1986   *Jokers*; begun by Hugo Peretti, and completed after Peretti's death by Weiss and David Creatore. Performed Chester, CT, 14 October 1986.

Welch, David

1988   *Studio: A Dance Opera* (libretto by Michael Alasa, about the Ballets Russes). Performed by DUO Theatre/Teatro DUO, New York, 14 April 1988.

1989   *Peggy and Jackson* (libretto by Michael Alasa, about Peggy Guggenheim and Jackson Pollock). Performed by DUO Theatre/Teatro DUO, New York, 8 May 1989.

Welcher, Dan Edward (b. Rochester, NY, 2 March 1948; Anderson; *WhoAm*)

1987   *Della's Gift* (drama; 2 acts—69 minutes; libretto by Paul Woodruff after O. Henry's "The Gift of the Magi"). Première by University of Texas Opera Theatre, Austin, 26 February 1987. Tape available from Theodore Presser. Kornick.

Weller, Beverly

\-   *Santa's Christmas Tree* (2 acts; libretto by composer). *COS*-4.

Welsh, Wilmer Hayden (b. Cincinnati, OH, 17 July 1932; Anderson; *WhoAm*; *Who's Who*)
    1985   *Waiting for Lila Sinclair* (30 minutes; libretto by composer after Odets's *Waiting for Lefty*). Commission by Davidson College, NC; performed there, 1985.

Wentz, Earl
    1987   *A Minuet* (on Louis Parker). Performed at Metropolitan-Duane United Methodist Church, New York, 1 November 1987.

Wernick, Richard (b. Boston, 19 January 1934; *Amerigrove*; *WhoAm*)
    1959   *Maggie* (libretto after H. Crane). Incomplete.

Wess, Jill
    1985   *Jack* ("surreal musical fantasy"; libretto by composer and Chris Mellie, about coming of age). Performed at Henry Street Settlement, New York, June 1985.

West, John A.
    1895   *Powhatan*, with Lewis Campbell Tipton. Performed Evanston, IL, 1895.

Westergaard, Peter (b. Champaign, IL, 28 May 1931; *Amerigrove*; *Who's Who*)
    1953   *Charivari* (chamber opera; 9 movements). Performed Cambridge, MA, 13 May 1953.
    1966   *Mr. and Mrs. Discobbolus* (chamber opera; 17 minutes; after E. Lear). Performed at Columbia University, New York, 21 March 1966, and by American Chamber Opera, New York, 1987.
    1984   *The Tempest* (3 acts—160 minutes; libretto by composer after Shakespeare). New Jersey State Council on the Arts and American Music Center grants. Performed Princeton, NJ, 29 June 1984 and March 1987, and Lawrenceville, NJ, June 1991.

Wetzler, Hermann Hans (b. Frankfurt am Main, Germany, 8 September 1870; d. New York, 29 May 1943; born of American parents and spent his childhood in U.S. but returned to Frankfurt for his musical education; *Amerigrove*; *Baker's*)
    1928   *Die baskische Venus*, op. 14 (libretto after Mérimée). Performed Leipzig, 18 November 1928.

Wheeler, (William) Scott (b. Washington, DC, 24 February 1952; Anderson; *WhoAm*)
    1989   *The Construction of Boston* (1 act—50 minutes; libretto by Kenneth Koch). Guggenheim Foundation grant. Performed Boston, 27 January 1989.

White, Clarence Cameron (b. Clarksville, TN, 10 August 1880; d. New York, 30 June 1960; *Amerigrove*; Hipsher; Southern)
    1932   *Ouanga* (libretto by John F. Matheus, on Haitian history). Concert performance by Three Arts Club, Chicago, 13 November 1932; stage performance New York, 18 June 1941; by National Negro Opera Co. at Metropolitan Opera House, New York, May 1956; at

Carnegie Hall, New York, September 1956; and by Harry T. Burleigh Music Association, South Bend, IN, June 1949. Bispham medal, 1932.

1952 *Carnival Romance* (libretto perhaps by composer).
(White also composed incidental music to the play *Tambour* by John F. Matheus, 1929.)

White, Claude (b. 1949)
1988 *The Last Page* (1 act; libretto by Linda Brovsky; for children). Performed by Opera Theatre of Saint Louis, MO, 10 January 1988.
1988 *Love, Death, and High Notes* (comedy; libretto by Linda Brovsky; an introduction to opera for children). Commission and première by Opera Theatre of Saint Louis at Parkway Central Senior High School, St. Louis, 1 October 1988. Kornick.

White, Frances (ASCAP)
1984 *The Letter* (libretto by composer). Performed at Brooklyn College, NY, 3 February 1984.

White, John D. (b. Rochester, MN, 28 November 1931; *WhoAm*; *Who's Who*)
1962 *The Legend of Sleepy Hollow* (3 acts; libretto by Martin Nurmi after Irving). Commission by Kent State University, OH; performed there, 28 February 1962.

White, Louie L. (b. Spartanburg, SC, 1 August 1921; Anderson)
- *Jephthah* (chancel opera).

White, Michael (b. Chicago, 6 March 1931; Anderson; *WhoAm*)
1962 *The Dybbuk*. Commission for the Seattle World's Fair, 1962.
1965 *Through the Looking Glass* (libretto after Carroll).
1968 *The Metamorphosis* (libretto by Milton Goldberg after Kafka). Performed Philadelphia, 3 May 1968.
1971 *The Passion According to a Cynic*.
1973 *The Ancient Vespers*.
1974 *The Prophet*.
1981 *Diary of a Madman* (1 hour; libretto by composer after Gogol). Performed by OPERA America, New York, January 1981.

White, Raymond W.
1965 *The Selfish Giant* (2 acts; libretto after Wilde). Performed Cleveland, 30 November 1965.

White, Richard
1987 *Antonelli's Nose* (libretto by composer). Performed by Brooklyn Opera Theater, New York, 5 December 1987.

Whitely, Bessie W. (Cohen: Bessie Marshall Whitely; b. St. Louis, 1871; AMC)
1913 *Hiawatha's Childhood* (libretto by composer). National Federation of Music Clubs prize, 1913.
- *Pandora* (libretto after Longfellow's "Masque of Pandora").
- *Sarita* (libretto by composer, on a Mexican subject).

Whithorne, Emerson (b. Cleveland, OH, 6 September 1884; d. Lyme, CT, 25 March 1958; *Amerigrove*)
(Whithorne supposedly composed operas. He also composed incidental music for O'Neill's *Marco Millions*, 1928.)

Whiting, George Elbridge (b. Holliston, MA, 14 September 1840; d. Cambridge, MA, 14 October 1923; *Amerigrove*; Hipsher)
1893   *Lenora* (in Italian; 1 act).

Whitmer, Thomas Carl (b. Altoona, PA, 24 June 1873; d. Poughkeepsie, NY, 30 May 1959; *Amerigrove*; Hipsher)
1951   *Oh, Isabel* (1 act—55 minutes).
     Six Spiritual Music-Dramas, all completed before 1924, when Freer cited them; they were awarded the Bispham Medal within the period 1933-36:
     The Creation (2 acts).
     The Covenant (prologue, ballet, and 3 acts).
     Nativity (prologue and 2 acts).
     Temptation (2 connected acts).
     Mary Magdalene (2 acts).
     The Passion (5 acts).

Whiton, Peter
1958   *The Bottle Imp* (3 acts). Performed Wilton, CT, 10 April 1958.

Wick, Otto (b. Krefeld, Germany, 8 July 1885; d. Austin, TX, 9 November 1957; to U.S. in 1905; Anderson)
-    *For Art's Sake* (operetta).
-    *The Lone Star*.
-    *Matasuntha* (music drama).
-    *Moon Maid* (light opera).

Wickham, Florence (b. Beaver, PA, 1880; d. New York, 20 October 1962; Anderson; *Baker's*; Cohen)
1938   *Rosalind* (or *Rosalynd*) (operetta; prologue and 2 acts; libretto after Shakespeare's *As You Like It*). Performed Dresden, Germany, November 1938, and Carmel, NY, 1989.
1957   *The Legend of Hex Mountain* (operetta).
-    *Ancestor Maker*.

Wienhorst, Richard William (b. Seymour, IN, 21 April 1920; Anderson; *WhoAm*)
1989   *The Runaway Cowboy* (3 scenes—30 minutes; libretto by Sylvia Pick). Performed Victoria, TX, 1990-91 season.

Wiggin, Charles
1976   *The Doctor's Duty*. Performed Fredonia, NY, 24 April 1976.

Wiggins, Phil
1989   *Chewin' the Blues with Bowling Green John and Harmonica Phil*, with John Cephas (libretto by Jeff Church). Performed at Ethnic Diversity Festival, Washington, DC, 17 February 1989.

Wigglesworth, Frank (b. Boston, 3 March 1918; *Amerigrove*; *WhoAm*)

1959   *Between the Atoms and the Stars* (play with music; libretto by J. Timmons).

1969   *The Willowdale Handcar: or, The Return of the Black Doll* (1 act; libretto by Edward Gorey). Performed New York, 28 May 1969.

Wilder, Alec (b. Rochester, NY, 16 February 1907; d. Gainesville, FL, 24 December 1980; *Amerigrove*; *Baker's*)

1951   *The Lowland Sea* (1 act—55 minutes; libretto by Arnold Sundgaard; American subject). Performed Montclair, NJ, 8 May 1952.

1952   *Sunday Excursion* (25 minutes; libretto by Arnold Sundgaard). Performed New York, 17 April 1953, Chicago, May 1953, and Interlochen, MI, 1953.

1953   *Cumberland Fair* (1 act; libretto by Arnold Sundgaard). Performed Montclair, NJ, 22 May 1953.

1953   *Miss Chicken Little* (musical fable; 1 act; libretto by W. Engvick). Televised by CBS-TV, New York, 27 December 1953; stage production, Piermont, NY, 29 August 1958.

1954   *Kittiwake Island* (2 acts; libretto by Arnold Sundgaard). Performed Interlochen, MI, 7 August 1954.

1955   *Ellen* (libretto by W. Engvick).

1955   *The Long Way* (2 parts; libretto by Arnold Sundgaard). Performed Nyack, NY, 3 June 1955.

1958   *The Impossible Forest* (1 act—60 minutes; libretto by Arnold Sundgaard). Performed Westport, CT, 13 July 1958.

1975   *The Opening* (comic opera; 28 minutes; libretto by Arnold Sundgaard).

1973   *The Truth About Windmills* (chamber opera; 1 act; libretto by Arnold Sundgaard). Performed Rochester, NY, 14 October 1973.

1974   *The Tattooed Countess* (chamber opera). NEA grant, 1974.

-    *The Churkendoose* (children's opera).

-    *Herman Ermine in Rabbit Town* (children's opera).

-    *Rachetty Pachetty House* (children's opera).

    (Wilder also composed the musicals *Clues to a Life*, with Marty Palitz, performed at Vineyard Theatre, New York, 3 February 1982; and *Jack in the Country*, libretto by Sundgaard after Oscar Wilde's *The Importance of Being Earnest*.)

Wilder, Bonnie

-    *The Music Dreaming Man* (about the composer Lowell Mason; performed by children). *COS*-4.

Wilding-White, Raymond (b. Caterham, Surrey, England, 9 October 1922; in U.S. from 1947; AMC; *Amerigrove*; *Baker's*; *WhoAm*)

1952   *The Tub* (chamber opera; 3 acts; libretto after Boccaccio's *Decameron*), for SATB and piano.

1952   *The Selfish Giant: A Fable for Television* (2 acts—30 minutes; libretto by composer after Oscar Wilde). Performed Cleveland, 1965.

1962   *Yerma* (3 acts; libretto after Federico García Lorca.

1968   *Monday Morning at the Gargoyle Works* ("action piece"), for 5 performers.

Wiley, Bob
-     *A Bone of Contention* (1 act—75 minutes). Published by Boosey & Hawkes.

Wilkinson, Paul
    1979   *Epi-Psychidion, A Place for the Soul* (15 minutes; libretto by composer). Performed at University of Minnesota, Minneapolis, 1 June 1979.

Willey, James Henry (b. Lynn, MA, 1 October 1939; Anderson; *WhoAm*; *Who's Who*)
    1975   *Commentary VI: or, The Death of Mozart* (theater piece for soprano and narrator). NEA grant. Performed by the University of Massachusetts Group for New Music, 1976.

William, Scott (ASCAP)
    1983   *Lenny and the Heartbreakers*, with Kim Sherman (libretto by the composers and Kenneth Robins). Performed at New York Shakespeare Festival, New York, 22 December 1983.

Williams, Brooks
    1989   *The Fourth Part of a Trilogy: Broken Cups*, with Nurit Tilles (interart work; libretto by Beatrice Roth). Performed at Playwrights Center, Minneapolis; Yellow Springs Institute, PA; Staten Island, NY; Hangar Studio, NH; Walker Art Center, Minneapolis; St. Mark's Danspace, New York; and Performing Garage, New York, 20 May 1989.

Williams, David H. (b. Kansas City, MO, 27 July 1946; Anderson)
-     *The Witch of Worcestershire* (operetta).

Williams, David McK. (b. Caernarvonshire, Wales, 20 February 1887; d. Oakland, CA, 13 March 1978; to U.S. as a child; *Amerigrove*; Anderson)
    1943   *Florence Nightingale* (3 acts). Performed at St. Bartholomew's Church, New York, 4 May 1943.
-     *Enchanted Waters* (operetta).

Williams, Guy Bevier (native of Detroit, MI; Hipsher)
    1933   *The Master Thief* (3 acts; libretto by Frances Tipton). Performed Pasadena, CA, 28 November 1963.
    (Rodríguez says Williams also composed "three one-act operas.")

Williams, Jack Eric (b. Odessa, TX, 28 March 1944; ASCAP; Anderson)
    1964   *The Hinge Tune* (1 act). Performed Interlochen, MI, 13 May 1965.
    1970   *We Gave Him Piano Lessons*. Performed Myrtle Beach, SC, 8 August 1971.
    1971   *Alexander the Great*. Performed Columbia, SC, 8 August 1971.
    1973   *Eyes at Treblinka* (musical drama).
    1983   *Mrs. Farmer's Daughter*. Première at Pepsico Summerfare, Purchase, NY, July 1983; revised for performance at American Music Theatre Festival, 1984. Kornick.
    (Williams also composed the musical *Swamp Gas and Shallow Feelings*, 1988.)

Williams, Julius Penson (b. Bronx, NY, 22 June 1954; *WhoAm*; *Who's Who*)
   1985   *Guinevere* (libretto by Anita Rosenau). Performed Aspen, CO, 3
         August 1985.

Williams, Ron
   1984   *Charley and the Pirates* (for children; libretto by Jody Smith).
         Performed Richmond, VA, 17 October 1984.

Williams, Ronald Ray (b. Muhlenberg County, KY, 12 April 1929; *WhoAm*; *Who's
         Who*)
   1951   *The Introduction* (15 minutes). Performed Greencastle, IN, 13 April
         1951.
   1953   *Oleander Red* ("dramatic scene"; 1 act). Performed Cincinnati, 1
         April 1953.

Willson, Meredith (b. Mason City, IA, 18 May 1902; d. Santa Monica, CA, 15
         June 1984; *Amerigrove*)
   1957   *The Music Man* (romantic comedy; 2 acts; lyrics and book by
         composer). Première at Majestic Theatre, New York, 19
         December 1957. Recording: Capital W-990, SW-990. Kornick.
         (Willson also composed 3 more musicals.)

Wilson, Irving M.
   -   *King Zim of Zniba*.

Wilson, John
   -   *Baker's Dozen*.

Wilson, Lynn
   1990   *Dead Seal at McClure Beach* (after Bly). Performed by Downtown
         Music Productions, New York, 28 April 1990.

Wilson, Paul
   1986   *Hear I Stand* (2 acts). Performed by Black Music Association, New
         York, 3 November 1986.

Wilson, Robert (b. Waco, TX, 4 October 1941; *Amerigrove*)
   1979   *Death, Destruction, and Detroit*, with Alan Lloyd (2 acts).
         Performed Berlin, Germany, 13 February 1979.
   1980   *Dialog/Curious George*, with Dale Ward and Christopher Knowles.
         Performed New York, 24 June 1980.
         (Wilson also contributed to *The CIVIL warS*, 1983, by Philip Glass
         and others.)

Winkler, David (b. Chicago, 11 October 1948; ASCAP; Anderson)
   1987   *All's Well That Ends Well* (2 acts; libretto by composer and David
         Pfeiffer after Shakespeare). Performed by Dell'Arte Players, New
         York, 30 January 1987.
   1987   *The Bacchae* (2 acts; libretto after Euripides). Performed by
         Dell'Arte Players, New York, September 1987.
   1988   *Arms Akimbo* (1 act; libretto by composer, on the Webster definition
         of "akimbo"). Performed Aspen, CO, 12 July 1988.

Winokur, Roselyn M. (b. Trenton, NJ; Cohen; *WhoAm*)
(Winokur writes her own librettos.)

1981   *Rip Van Winkle* (1 act; libretto after Irving). Performed Chappaqua, NY, 25 October 1981.

1981   *The Nutcracker and the Mouse King.* Performed White Plains, NY, 1981.

1982   *The Birthday Party* (monodrama; 1 act; for children). Performed Chappaqua, NY, March 1982.

1983   *Byline Nellie Bly* (musical; 1 act). Alliance Theatre Company/Atlanta Children's Theatre Contest winner, 1983 (Cohen: 1982).

Winslow, Richard Kenelm (b. Indianapolis, IN, 15 March 1918; Anderson)

1952   *Sweeny Agonistes* (1 act; libretto after Eliot). Performed New York, 20 May 1953.

1955   *Adelaide* ("a fantasy"; 1 act). Performed Middletown, CT, 1957-58 season.

1960   *Ikon.*

1960   *Theater Song.*

1964   *Alice* (1 act; libretto by Susan McAllester after Carroll). Performed Hartford, CT, January 1964.

1974   *Endgame* (libretto after Beckett). Performed Kingston, RI, 6 November 1974.

Winter, N.

1976   *Papa B on the D Train.* Performed by Harlem Opera Company, New York, 15 July 1976.

Wister, Owen (1860-1938)

1883   *La Serenade* (1 act). Performed Boston, 1883.

c 1883 *Montezuma.*

c 1890 *Charlemagne.*

1924   *Watch Your Thirst: A Dry Opera in Three Acts* (libretto by the composer). Performed Boston, 1924, 1927, and 1933. Libretto published by Macmillan, 1923.

-    *Villon.*

Witni, M. (AMC)

-    *The Dark of Summer* (1 act—45 minutes).

Wodnansky, Wilhelm

-    *The Wish Machine* (science fiction; 3 acts; libretto by M. Trace Johnson). *COS*-3.

Wolf, Anton

1976   *Madame Jumel* (3 acts—2 hours; libretto by Roger Squire, about the second wife of Aaron Burr). Performed at State University of New York, Buffalo, 3 December 1976.

1984   *François Villon: L'Enfant sans souce* (*François Villon: The Carefree Child*) (1 act; libretto by Paul V. Hale, on the poet's life). Performed at Buffalo State College, NY, 17 May 1984.

Wolf, Sally (ASCAP)
>   1978   *The Emperor's Nightingale* (38 minutes; libretto by Lurrine Burgess
>   after Andersen). Performed Sun Valley, CA, 27 June 1978.
>   1978   *A Christmas Fable* (25 minutes; libretto by Lurrine Burgess after
>   Dickens's *A Christmas Carol*). Performed Sun Valley, CA, 19
>   December 1978.
>   1979   *The Three Feathers* (35 minutes; libretto by Lurrine Burgess after
>   Grimm). Performed Sun Valley, CA, 26 June 1979.
>   1980   *Snow-White and the Seven Dwarfs* (libretto by Lurrine Burgess after
>   Grimm). Performed Sun Valley, CA, 24 March 1980.
>   1986   *Robin Hood* (libretto by Lurrine Burgess; for children). Performed
>   Sun Valley, CA, 23 June 1986.

Wolf, Winifred
>   -   *The Happy Ending.*

Wolfe, George
>   1981   *The Rewards of Ambition* (2 acts; libretto by composer after
>   Garnet). Performed Harrisonburg, VA, 30 April 1981.

Wolfe, Jacques (b. Botoshan, Romania, 29 April 1896; d. Bradenton, FL, 22 June
>   1973; to U.S. in 1898; ASCAP; *Amerigrove*)
>   1939   *John Henry* (musical play).
>   1951   *Mississippi Legend* (2 acts). Performed New York, 24 April 1951.
>   1957   *The Trysting Place* (1 act). Performed Coral Gables, FL, 6
>   November 1957.

Wolpe, Stefan (b. Berlin, Germany, 25 August 1902; d. New York, 4 April 1972;
>   in U.S. from 1938; *Amerigrove*; *Baker's*)
>   1938   *Israel and His Land.*
>   1952   *Cantata about Sport.*
>   1968   *Street Music*, for baritone, speaker, 5 instruments,
>   1968   *Cantata* (texts by Hölderin, Herodotus, and Robert Creeley).
>   -   *Unnamed Lands.*

Wood, Joseph (Roberts) (b. Pittsburgh, PA, 12 May 1915; ACA; Anderson;
>   *Baker's*; *WhoAm*; *Who's Who*)
>   1942   *The Mother* (35 minutes; libretto by Hurd Hatfield after Andersen).
>   Performed at Juilliard School, New York, 9 February 1942, and in
>   New York, 1945.

Wood, Kevin Joseph (b. Bronx, NY, 19 June 1947; Anderson; *WhoAm*; *Who's Who*)
>   1977   *Peter.*

Wood, Russell
>   1972   *The Emperor's New Clothes* (1 act; libretto after Andersen).
>   Performed Chicago, 12 February 1972.

Woodard, James Philips (b. Rocky Mount, NC, 21 November 1929; Anderson;
>   *WhoAm*; *Who's Who*)
>   -   *The Three Strangers* (2 acts—100 minutes; libretto by Paul Gaston
>   after Hardy). Published by MMB Music.

Woodbury, Arthur Neum (b. Kimball, NE, 20 June 1930; Anderson; *Baker's*;
    WhoAm)
   1969   *Recall.*

Wood-Hill, Mabel (b. Brooklyn, NY, 12 March 1870; d. Stamford, CN, 1 March
    1954; Anderson; Cohen)
   1931   *The Adventures of Pinocchio* (pantomime). Performed New York,
        13 April 1931.
   -     *The Jolly Beggars.*

Wooding, Russell
   1921   *Halcyon Days in Dixie*, with Wooding's Jubilee Quintet and violinist
        Joseph Douglass. Performed Washington, DC, 1921. An "attempt
        at music drama based on themes of Negro life and music"—*Negro
        Musician* 1/2 (February 1921): 18, quoted in Mark Tucker, "The
        Renaissance Education of Duke Ellington," *Black Music in the
        Harlem Renaissance*, ed. Samuel A. Floyd, Jr. (Westport:
        Greenwood, 1990), 118.

Woodward, S.
   1822   *The Deed of Gift.*

Woolf, Benjamin Edward (b. London, England, 16 February 1836; d. Boston, 7
    February 1901; in U.S. from ca. 1840; *Amerigrove*; *Baker's*)
   1880   *Lawn Tennis: or, Djakh and Djill* ("operatic comedietta").
        Performed Boston, 1880.
   1883   *Pounce & Co.* (comic opera or operetta; libretto by composer).
        Performed Boston, 1883.
   1894   *Westward Ho!* (libretto by Richard Ware). Performed Boston, 31
        December 1894.
        (Woolf also collaborated with Julius Eichberg, who composed *The
        Doctor of Alcantara*, 1862.)

Woollen, Russell (b. Hartford, CT, 7 January 1923; ACA; *Amerigrove*)
   1959   *The Decorator* (1 act; libretto by F. and D. Getlein). Performed at
        Catholic University, Washington, DC, April 1959. Broadcast on
        NBC, New York, 24 May 1959.

Woolsey, Mary Hale (b. Spanish Fork, UT, 21 March 1899; d. 1969; Anderson;
    Cohen)
   -     *The Enchanted Attic* (operetta).
   -     *The Giant Garden* (operetta).
   -     *The Happy Hearts* (operetta).
   -     *Neighbors in the House* (operetta).
   -     *Starflower* (operetta).

Wright, Kenneth W. (b. Hastings, NE, 1913; Anderson)
   1965   *Wing of Expectation* (3 acts; libretto by composer, about Lincoln).
        Performed Lexington, KY, 7 April 1965.
   -     *Call it Square* (chamber opera).

Wright, Maurice Willis (b. Front Royal, VA, 17 October 1949; *Amerigrove*;
    WhoAm)
    1980   *The Fifth String* (1 act—1 hour; libretto by composer after Sousa).

Wright, Michael (ASCAP)
    1987   *Whores of Heaven* (2 acts; libretto by composer, David Wells, and
              Luisa Newton). Performed by I Comici Confidanti, New York,
              February 1987.

Wright, Morris
    1965   *The Legend* (1 act; about the Aga Aga Indians). Performed Muncie,
              IN, 28 January 1965.

Wright, Robert (b. 1914 in Florida)
    1953   *Kismet*, musical based on the music of Borodin. Performed by Tri-
              Cities Opera, Binghamton, NY, 29 October 1988.

Wrightson, Herbert James (1869-1949; b. in England; in U.S. from 1897)
              (Wrightson composed two melodramas.)

Wuorinen, Charles (b. New York, 9 June 1938; *Amerigrove*; *Baker's*; *Who's Who*)
    1967   *The Politics of Harmony* (masque).
    1974   *Profile of a Composer*. Performed Wheatleigh, MA, 26 July 1974.
    1975   *The W. of Babylon: or, The Triumph of Love over Moral Depravity*
              ("Baroque burlesque" opera; 2 acts—2 hours; libretto by Renaud
              Charles Bruce). New York State Council on the Arts and National
              Opera Institute grants. Partially performed by Light Fantastic
              Players, Manhattan School of Music, New York, 15 December
              1975; complete performance, San Francisco, 20 January 1989.
              Kornick.

Wykes, Robert A. (b. Aliquippa, PA, 19 May 1926; ASCAP; *Baker's*)
    1952   *The Prankster* (chamber opera; 30 minutes). Performed Bowling
              Green, OH, 12 January 1952.

Wyton, Alec (b. London, England, 3 August 1921; in U.S. from 1950; *Amerigrove*;
            WhoAm)
    1977   *The Journey with Jonah* (90 minutes; libretto after L'Engle).
              Performed, All Souls Parish, Ashville, NC, 1977, and Hartford,
              CT, 9 June 1978.

Yang, Daniel S. P.
    1972   *Black Dragon Residence* (libretto by composer after a 16th-century
              Peking opera). Performed Honolulu, HI, 17 February 1972.

Yannatos, James D. (b. New York, 13 March 1929; ACA; Anderson; *Baker's*;
            WhoAm)
    1971   *The Rocket's Red Blare*. Performed Cambridge, MA, 6 May 1971.

1974   *Silence Bottle* (children's opera).

Yannay, Yehuda (b. Timisoara, Romania, 26 May 1937; U.S. citizen, 1977;
        Anderson; *Baker's*)
1981   *All Our Women* (musical theater/chamber opera; 1 act; libretto by
        composer). Commission by Wisconsin Arts Board. Performed at
        University of Wisconsin, Milwaukee, 22 October 1981.

Yarden, Elie (b. Philadelphia, 7 June 1923; Anderson; *WhoAm*)
1970   *Eros and Psyche* (chamber opera).

Yarmolinsky, Ben
1989   *Blanche* (libretto after Balzac's *Le Pêche venial*). Performed by
        American Opera Projects, New York, 15 November 1989.

Yavelow, Christopher Fowler Johnson (b. Cambridge, MA, 15 June 1950;
        Anderson; *WhoAm*)
1983   *The Passion of Vincent Van Gogh* (3 acts—3 hours; libretto by
        Monique Yavelow based on official documents and texts by
        Gaugin). NEA, Camargo Foundation, and International Research
        and Exchanges Board grants. *COS*-4.
1987   *Countdown* (1 act; libretto by Laura Harrington). Southwest
        Virginia Opera Society competition winner. Performed by Boston
        Lyric Opera, MA, February 1987, and Southwest Virginia Opera,
        Roanoke, 2 November 1988.

Yelton, Art
-       *Pecos Bill Rides Again* (2 acts; libretto by Michael Bigelow Dixon
        and Valerie Smith). Published by Dramatic Publishing. *COS*-4.

Yeston, Maury (b. Jersey City, NJ, 23 October 1945; *Baker's*)
1979   *Nine* (1 act, or full length; libretto by composer and Mario Fratti,
        or by the composer and Arthur Kopit, after Fellini's *8*).
        Performed by Opera Company of Philadelphia, New London, CT,
        or Waterford, CT, 27 July 1979 (the two sets of data come from
        COS-3 and *COS*-4—at least they agree on the dates); and at 46th
        Street Theatre, New York, 9 May 1982.
1987   *One Two Three Four Five* (libretto by composer and Larry Gelbart,
        based on the Pentateuch). Performed by Manhattan Theatre Club,
        New York, 10 November 1987 and 9 December 1988.
1990   *Goya* (on the artist's life). Performed New York, 1990-91 season.
        (These three were designated as musicals, but their subjects and
        places of performance suggest another category.)

York, Francis L. (1861-1955)
-       *The Inca* (comic opera). In Johnson.

York, Walter Wynn (b. Claremont, CA, 6 August 1914; Anderson)
1974   *The Bostonians*.
1977   *The Perennial Philosophy*. Performed at Kennedy Center,
        Washington, DC, 5 May 1977.

Young, Mrs. Bicknell (Eliza Mazzucato)
-   *The Maid and the Reaper* (1 act). Performed Chicago.
    (Also a comic opera by her performed in Salt Lake City, UT.)

Young, Victor (b. Bristol, TN, 9 April 1889; d. Ossining, NY, 2 September 1968;
    Anderson; *Baker's*)
-   *A Happy Week* (operetta).

Young, Willie Fong
1982   *American Passion* (libretto by Fred Burch). Performed Cambridge,
    MA, 10 November 1982.

Yuan, Sung Fu
1983   *Tao Yuan* (2 acts; libretto by composer after a 4th-century Chinese
    story). Performed by Bel Canto Opera, New York, 24 June 1983.

Zador, Eugene (b. Bátaszék, Hungary, 5 November 1894; d. Hollywood, CA, 4
    April 1977; in U.S. from 1939; ASCAP; *Amerigrove*; Schoep)
1939   *Christopher Columbus* (libretto by J. Mohácsi). Performed New
    York, 8 October 1939.
1964   *The Virgin and the Fawn* (libretto by L. Zilahy). Performed Los
    Angeles, 24 October 1964.
1966   *The Magic Chair* (libretto by George Jellinek after F. Karinthy).
    Performed Baton Rouge, LA, 14 May 1966.
1968   *The Scarlet Mill* (2 acts; libretto by George Jellinek after F.
    Molnár). Performed Brooklyn, NY, 26 October 1968.
1971   *The Inspector General* (3 acts; libretto by composer after N. Gogol).
    Revised and performed Los Angeles, 11 June 1971.
1974   *Yehu, a Christmas Legend* (1 act—30 minutes; libretto by Anna
    Együd). Première by Los Angeles Bureau of Music, 21 December
    1974. Kornick. Published by Carl Fischer.
-   *Forever Rembrandt* (1 act).

Zahab, Roger
1982   *Hawk Run* (17 minutes; libretto by Thomas Piechowski, about a coal
    mining town). Brooklyn College Chamber Opera competition
    winner, 1983. Performed New York, 9 May 1982, and at
    Brooklyn College, NY, 4 February 1983.
1985   *Zone 3: The Watchman* (22 minutes; libretto by William Boswell).
    Commission by Brooklyn College, NY; performed there, February
    1985.
1986   *Hegemony* (1 act—100 minutes; libretto by Thomas Piechowski).
    Scoring not yet completed.

Zahler, Noel Barry (b. New York, 10 May 1951; Anderson; *WhoAm*)
-   *Automata* (1 act—50 minutes; libretto by Robert Ornstein). *COS*-4.

332

Zaimont, Judith Lang (b. Memphis, TN, 8 November 1945; *Amerigrove*; Cohen; *WhoAm*; *Who's Who*)
- 1983   *The Thirteen Clocks* (chamber opera).
- 1985   *Goldilocks and the Three Bears* (1 act—50 minutes; libretto by Doris Lang Kosloff). Commission by Connecticut Opera, Opera Express, Chappaqua, NY. Performed there, 5 January 1986.

Zampini, Francesco
- 1982   *Maria Rappaccini* (libretto after Hawthorne). Performed by Florida Lyric Opera, Clearwater, 9 November 1982.

Zaninelli, Luigi (b. Raritan, NJ, 30 March 1932; Anderson; *WhoAm*)
-   -   *Vicksburg 1863* (chamber opera).

Zawadsky, Pat
- 1982   *The Secret in the Toyroom* (1 hour; libretto by composer, about child abuse). Commission by Portage County Council on Human Sexuality, WI. Performed by Cooperative Educational Services Agency No. 7 (a tour of schools), 1982. Published by I. E. Clark.
- 1985   *The Dragon in the Closet* (50 minutes; libretto by composer; for children). Performed Stevens Point, WI, November 1985. Published by National Music Theater Network.
- 1987   *Milady* (2 hours; libretto by composer, on the princess to become Elizabeth I of England, but set in the 20th century). Performed by National Music Theater Network, New York, NY, 9 March 1987. Published by National Music Theater Network.

Zech, Frederick, Jr. (b. Philadelphia, 10 May 1858; d. San Francisco, 25 October 1926; *Amerigrove*; *Baker's*' Hipsher)
- 1896   *La Paloma: or, The Cruise of the Excelsior* (3 acts; libretto by Mrs. M. Fairweather-Widemann; on an American subject). Performed San Francisco, 1896.
- 1914   *Wa-Kin-Yon: or, The Passing of the Red Man* (3 acts; libretto by Mrs. M. Fairweather-Widemann). Performed San Francisco, 1914.

Zechwer, Camille (b. Philadelphia, 26 June 1875; d. Southampton, NY, 7 August 1924; *Amerigrove*)
-   -   *Jane and Janetta*, op. 20 (3 acts). Never performed.

Zeisl, Eric (b. Vienna, Austria, 18 May 1905; d. Los Angeles, 18 February 1959; in U.S. from 1939; *Amerigrove*)
- 1937   *Leonce und Lena*. Performed Los Angeles, 1952.
- 1959   *Job* (libretto by J. Kafka after J. Roth), 1939-41, 1957-59, incomplete.

Zilevicius, Juozas (b. Plunge, Lithuania, 16 March 1891; to U.S. in 1929; Anderson)
-   -   *Lietuvaite* (operetta).

Zimbalist, Efrem (b. Rostov-na-Donu, Russia, 5 May 1889; d. Reno, NV, 22 February 1985; in U.S. from 1911; *Amerigrove*; *Baker's*)
- 1920   *Honeydew* (musical comedy; 2 acts). Performed Stamford, CT, and New York, 1920.

1956   *Landara.* Performed Philadelphia, 6 April 1956.

Ziskin, Victor (b. New York, 18 March 1937; Anderson)
1971   *Young Abe Lincoln*, with Joan Javits, Richard Bernstein, and John Allan (1 act). Performed New York, February 1971.

Zito, Vincent
1972   *Sgagnarelle* (libretto after Molière). Performed at New York University, New York, 20 December 1972.

Zoch, Steven
1979   *The Quester Experiment* (science fiction; 2 acts). Performed at University of Arkansas, Little Rock, 19 April 1979.

Zöllner, Heinrich (b. Leipzig, Germany, 4 July 1854; d. Freiburg im Breisgau, Germany, 4 May 1941; in New York, 1890-98; *Baker's*)
1893   *Matteo Falcone* (1 act). Performed New York, 1894.
1895   *Bei Sedan.* Performed Munich, Germany, 1895, and New York, 1896.

Zupko, Ramon (b. Pittsburgh, PA, 14 November 1932; *Amerigrove*; *WhoAm*)
1970   *Third Planet from the Sun*, for dancers, tape, musicians, film, and slides. Performed Chicago, 1970.
1976   *Proud Music of the Storm* (multimedia musical theater; libretto by Whitman), for orchestra, two bands, chorus, dancers, films, slides, and tape, with costumes and sets. Bicentennial work. Performed at Western Michigan University, Kalamazoo, 4 December 1976.

Zur, Menachem (b. Tel Aviv, Israel, 6 March 1942; U.S. citizen, 1976; AMC; Anderson; *Who's Who*)
1970   *The Affairs* (1 act; libretto by composer). Performed Mannes College of Music, New York, 1970. Published by Seesaw Music Corporation.
1983   *Pygmalion* (chamber opera; 12 minutes; libretto by composer). Brooklyn Center for the Performing Arts Chamber Opera competition, 1983, second prize. Performed at Brooklyn College, NY, 18 February 1983.
-    *Neighbors* (3 acts—150 minutes; libretto by Harold Mason).

Zytowski, Carl (b. St. Louis, 17 July 1921; AMC; *WhoAm*; *Who's Who*)
1976   *The Town Musicians of Bremen* (incorporates some music of Schubert; 40 minutes). Performed at University of California, Santa Barbara, November 1976, and Des Moines, IA, 1982.
1979   *Pinocchio* (incorporates some music of Rossini; 50 minutes). Performed at University of California, Santa Barbara, 20 January 1979.
1981   *Thomas of Canterbury* (1 act—8 scenes; libretto by composer, about Thomas à Becket; uses some medieval texts). Performed at University of California, Santa Barbara, 6 June 1981.
1982   *The Play of the Three Shepherds* ("music drama for church performance"; 1 act; libretto by composer after the medieval mystery play). Performed at University of California, Santa Barbara, November 1982.

1984   *The Play of the Three Maries at the Tomb* ("music drama for church performance"; 1 act; libretto by composer after medieval mystery plays). Performed at University of California, Santa Barbara, 22 April 1984.

About the Author

EDITH BORROFF *is a composer and historian. She earned the B.Mus. and M.Mus in composition from the American Conservatory and the Ph.D. in the history of music from the University of Michigan.*

As a composer she has worked in a variety of musical types (including opera) and mediums; she has received over thirty-five commissions in the past fifteen years.

As a scholar she has produced nine books and over a hundred and fifty articles, scholarly papers, and lectures. Her writings include Music in Europe and the United States, *a general history. Her interests include American music, the sciences and the arts, French eighteenth-century music (the area of her doctoral dissertation), and the arts in prehistory.*

She has taught at the American Conservatory, Eastern Michigan University, and the State University of New York at Binghamton, the last for nineteen years. She retired in 1992, after forty-nine years.